AF743867

Luxemburger Juristische Studien –
Luxembourg Legal Studies

edited by

Faculty of Law, Economics and Finance
University of Luxembourg

Volume 16

Eleftheria Neframi/Mauro Gatti (eds.)

Constitutional Issues of EU External Relations Law

Nomos

The Deutsche Nationalbibliothek lists this publication in the Deutsche Nationalbibliografie; detailed bibliographic data are available on the Internet at http://dnb.d-nb.de

ISBN 978-3-8487-3399-6 (Print)
978-3-8452-7713-4 (ePDF)

British Library Cataloguing-in-Publication Data
A catalogue record for this book is available from the British Library.

ISBN 978-3-8487-3399-6 (Print)
978-3-8452-7713-4 (ePDF)

Library of Congress Cataloging-in-Publication Data
Neframi, Eleftheria / Gatti, Mauro
Constitutional Issues of EU External Relations Law
Eleftheria Neframi / Mauro Gatti (eds.)
452 p.
Includes bibliographic references and index.

ISBN 978-3-8487-3399-6 (Print)
978-3-8452-7713-4 (ePDF)

1st Edition 2018
© Nomos Verlagsgesellschaft, Baden-Baden, Germany 2018. Printed and bound in Germany.

This work is subject to copyright. All rights reserved. No part of this publication may be reproduced or transmitted in any form or by any means, electronic or mechanical, including photocopying, recording, or any information storage or retrieval system, without prior permission in writing from the publishers. Under § 54 of the German Copyright Law where copies are made for other than private use a fee is payable to "Verwertungsgesellschaft Wort", Munich.

No responsibility for loss caused to any individual or organization acting on or refraining from action as a result of the material in this publication can be accepted by Nomos or the editors.

Preface

It is with abundant pleasure that I introduce the volume before you, *Constitutional Issues of EU External Relations Law*, edited by my colleagues Professor Eleftheria Neframi and Dr Mauro Gatti.

As Dean of the Faculty of Law, Economics and Finance (FDEF), it is always a source of great satisfaction to behold the end product of original research conducted at the University of Luxembourg. The EUGIA project (the European Union as Global International Actor and the Question of Competence), coordinated by Professor Neframi and from which the majority of the contributions in this volume have emerged, provides a sparkling example of our Faculty's dynamic, international scientific orientation.

The quality of the chapters herein, hinted at by the presence of eminent academics as well as esteemed practitioners in the field of EU external action, speaks for itself. The volume is sure to prove a rich addition to the ongoing debates in said field and beyond, at a time when the very identity of the European Union – both internally and in the wider world – remains in a state of flux.

Indeed, the theme of the EU's identity is present throughout this volume. Much has changed in the Union, and around the Union, since the seminal *ERTA* case: the Union's external relations now address a number of issues, ranging from trade to anti-terrorism policy and international cooperation in criminal matters. The enlargement of the EU's sphere of action raises novel issues in terms of the core principles on which the Union is founded, including the attribution of competences and respect for European values. By focusing on recent developments in EU external relations, the contributions to this volume offer precious insight into the main constitutional challenges faced by the Union.

Lastly, as Dean of the FDEF I wish to express my pride that it is Luxembourg which has provided the forum for this important contribution to the Union's external action debate, whilst extending my warmest congratulations to my dear colleagues Professor Neframi and Dr Gatti for their success in bringing together the voices which fill the pages that follow.

Professor Katalin Ligeti
Dean of the Faculty of Law, Economics and Finance,
University of Luxembourg
July 2018

Contents

Introduction

Eleftheria Neframi and Mauro Gatti

The legal regime for the external relations of the European Union (EU) is commonly acknowledged, in EU law literature, to be highly specific. External relations are studied as a distinct field of action, in which the fundamental principles structuring the EU legal order find particular expression.[1] Moreover, external relations and action have their own place in the Treaties: the Treaty on European Union (TEU), for example, defines the status of the Common Foreign and Security Policy (CFSP)[2] and establishes external action as a proper mission of the Union,[3] with external action objectives subject to a global approach,[4] while the Treaty on the Functioning of the European Union (TFEU) devotes an entire part to external action covering external policies.[5] Furthermore, according to the case law of the Court of Justice of the European Union (CJEU), specific requirements in the field of the Union's external action give a specific content to fundamental EU law principles, such as the principle of loyal cooperation.[6]

1 In addition to the abundant literature devoted to EU external relations, important writings deal with the application of EU law principles in the field of the external action of the Union. See, for example: M. Cremona (ed), *Structural Principles in EU External Relations Law* (Oxford: Hart Publishing, 2018); R. Schütze, T. Tridimas (eds), *Oxford Principles of European Union Law* (Oxford: Oxford University Press, 2018).

2 Title V of the TEU.

3 Article 3, paragraph 5, TEU.

4 Article 21 TEU.

5 Part Five of the TFEU concerns "the Union's External Action".

6 Unity in external representation, especially in the context of mixed agreements, requires a reinforced duty of loyal cooperation between the Union and its Member States. According to the Court of Justice, "it is essential to ensure close cooperation between the Member States and the (Union) institutions, both in the process of negotiation and conclusion and in the fulfilment of the commitments entered into. That obligation to cooperate flows from the requirement of unity in the international representation of the (Union)". Ruling of 14 November 1978, 1/78, *Draft Convention of the International Atomic Energy Agency on the Physical Protection of Nuclear Materials, Facilities and Transports*, EU:C:1978:202, paras 34-38; Opinion of 19 March 1993, 2/91, Convention no. 170 of the International Labour Orga-

The Union's ability to undertake external action is part of its identity. "In its relations with the wider world", the Union pursues an objective of being a global actor[7] beyond the specific policy objectives.[8] Nevertheless, at the same time, "the Union's action on the international scene shall be guided by the principles which have inspired its own creation, development and enlargement".[9] Besides, the Union "shall ensure consistency between the different areas of its external action and between these and its other policies".[10]

It follows that, in addition to the demand for substantive consistency, which is an expression of the unity of the EU legal order in both its internal and external dimensions, the specific status of the external relations of the Union must accommodate and be aligned with the fundamental principles of the EU legal order. Significant literature has already been dedicated to the balance between the specific features of the Union's external action and the need to respect the constitutional and institutional framework

nization concerning safety in the use of chemicals at work, EU:C:1993:106, para 36; Opinion of 15 November 1994, 1/94, *Competence of the Community to Conclude International Agreements Concerning Services and the Protection of Intellectual Property*, EU:C:1994:384, para 108.

7 M. Cremona, "The Union as Global Actor: Roles, Models and Identity", *Common Market Law Review* 41, n°2 (2004), 553; R. Holdgaard, *External Relations Law of the European Community : Legal Reasoning and Legal Discources* (Alphen aan den Rijn: Kluwer Law International, 2008), 377. D. Kochenov, F. Amtenbrick, "Introduction: The Active Paradigm of the Study of the EU's Place in the World", in D. Kochenov, F. Amtenbrick (eds), *The European Union's Shaping of the International Legal Order* (Cambridge: Cambridge University Press, 2013), 1; J. Larik, "Shaping the International Legal Order as an EU Objective, in D. Kochenov, F. Amtenbrick (eds), *supra*, 62.

8 According to Article 3, paragraph 5, TEU, "In its relations with the wider world, the Union shall uphold and promote its values and interests and contribute to the protection of its citizens. It shall contribute to peace, security, the sustainable development of the Earth, solidarity and mutual respect among peoples, free and fair trade, eradication of poverty and the protection of human rights, in particular the rights of the child, as well as to the strict observance and the development of international law, including respect for the principles of the United Nations Charter".

9 Article 21, paragraph 1, TEU.

10 Article 21, paragraph 3, 2nd sub-paragraph, TEU.

of the EU legal order.[11] It is indeed on that basis that the CJEU established the autonomy of the EU legal order with regard to international law.[12]

The present book invites the reader to rethink some questions raised in EU external relations law in the light of recent developments in the case law of the Court of Justice, from the perspective of the constitutional foundations of the Union. It does not, however, aim to exhaustively address the Lisbon Treaty's important contributions to EU external relations and all of the recent developments in EU external relations law. Rather, the various chapters invite the reader to take a second look at the balance between the specific legal regime for EU external action and the constitutional fundamentals of the EU legal order, such as: the principles of conferral, loyalty, institutional balance, as well as the rule of law, democracy, and fundamental rights protection. The accommodation between specificity and fundamental principles is, thus, a transversal constitutional issue.

It should be noted that the specific place of EU external action in the EU legal order has been established progressively. Although policies with external dimension (such as the common commercial policy) fell under the European Community's competences, it was only in the *ERTA* judgment that the Court acknowledged the international personality of the European Community and the importance of external action tools to the attainment of its internal objectives.[13] Moreover, the Member States progressively entrusted the European Union with foreign affairs competence – the CFSP, constituting as such a specific feature –, and with a common approach to external action policies and objectives. External action has progressively become more than a tool to attain policy objectives (internal- or even external-oriented); it is the expression of the proper identity

---

11 *Supra* note 1. See also : M. Cremona, A. Thies (eds), *The European Court of Justice and External Relations : Constitutional Challenges* (Oxford : Hart Publishing, 2016); G. De Baere, *Constitutional Principles of EU External Relations* (Oxford : Oxford University Press, 2008).

12 C. Eckes, "International Rulings and the EU Legal Order: Autonomy as Legitimacy?", in M. Cremona, A. Thies (eds), *The European Union and International Dispute Settlement* (Oxford: Hart Publishing, 2017), 161.

13 The Court of Justice held that the former Article 201 CE, concerning legal personality of the former European Community, « means that in its external relations the Community enjoys the capacity to establish contractual links with third countries over the whole field of objectives defined in part one of the treaty". Judgment of 31 March 1971, *Commission* v *Council (European Agreement on Road Transport–ERTA)*, 22/70, EU:C:1971:32, para 14.

of the Union. This move, however, is situated in the legal order of the European Union: it stems from the Treaties, it is aligned to the overall integration objective and, thus, must accommodate the fundamentals of EU law. The move from policy-oriented external action objectives to a general objective of being an actor in the international scene is indeed enshrined in the EU constitutional order as part of the identification of the Union. The identity that the Member States want the Union to affirm in the international scene is a projection of its internal evolution in terms of values and principles.

The chapters of the book provide different perspectives on classic EU constitutional issues, having regard for the external relations' specific features. They encourage reconsideration of the inherent specificity of the Union's external action in its unique constitutional framework and in the light of recent developments, which express both a reinforcement of the external action potentialities and the external projection of its internal evolution. The underlying assumption is the endogenous specifity stemming from the assigned objectives, which impacts the scope and role of fundamental principles operating in the EU constitutional framework. It implies, in turn, a unique scope and functioning of the principle of conferral itself, as well as an accommodation of the need to preserve and promote the EU identity with the demand for efficiency, the latter opening the Union's balancing between external objectives and internal limits to exogenous influence.

***

Defining EU External Action Objectives and Competences

The first part of the book discusses the endogenous specificity of EU external action, stemming from the particular relationship between competences and objectives. Following the principle of conferral,[14] the exercise of a competence depends on the determination of the legal basis related to the corresponding objective. The relationship between competences and objectives is expressed in two different respects. On the one hand, this re-

14 Article 5, paragraph 2, TEU: "Under the principle of conferral, the Union shall act only within the limits of the competences conferred upon it by the Member States in the Treaties to attain the objectives set out therein. Competences not conferred upon the Union in the Treaties remain with the Member States".

lationship determines the choice of legal basis for the Union's action: what competence pursues a specific objective? And, in view of the conclusion of an international agreement, what competence corresponds to the objective pursued by the external measure? On the other hand, this relationship affects the nature of the competence on which depends the kind of the action to be conducted: may the Union act alone or must it act alongside its Member States?

Concerning the choice of legal basis, the specificity of the relationship between competences and objectives lies in a less-strict correspondence in comparison with the internal field of action. To be sure, each external competence has its specific policy objectives. However, contrary to the internal field, external action is characterised by the global approach of objectives, under the general objective of being an international actor.[15] The coexistence of specific policy objectives and the global approach means that, to determine the proper legal basis of an external action, a link between competence and objective is to be established, but, at the same time, the scope of an external competence may be broadly conceived. Moreover, an external competence does not necessarily pursue an external policy objective, but external action of the Union may serve internal objectives. Finally, the objective guiding the choice of legal basis is not necessarily that which is determined by the intention of the parties in the conclusion of the agreement, but may be mostly determined by the fragmented perspective of EU law.

These issues are elucidated by *Cremona,* who studies the scope and the boundaries of the express external competences. She underscores that the approach of the Court of Justice is based on the overall framework of action for EU foreign affairs: Article 21 TEU allows a legal basis to cover objectives corresponding to different competences and, therefore, invites a rethinking of the absorption doctrine,[16] as well as the distinction between essential and ancillary elements of external action. *Cremona* illustrates the

---

15 Article 21, paragraph 2, TEU states especially in a) and h): "The Union shall define and pursue common policies and actions, and shall work for a high degree of cooperation in all fields of international relations, in order to: (a) safeguard its values, fundamental interests, security, independence and integrity; (…) (h) promote an international system based on stronger multilateral cooperation and good global governance". *Supra* note 7.

16 "According to settled case-law, the choice of the legal basis for a European Union measure, including the measure adopted for the purpose of concluding an international agreement, must rest on objective factors amenable to judicial review, which

global assessment of an international agreement, taking as a starting point the Union's objective in the field of the common commercial policy (CCP). *Neframi* highlights the Union's perspective and the influence of the general objective of being an international actor with regard to the scope of the CCP, which goes beyond an instrumental approach and covers provisions that, seen individually, may be linked to other fields of competence. Moreover, *Neframi* focuses on the broad concept of the CCP with regard to sustainable development objectives resulting from Opinion 2/15,[17] which gives an EU-perspective of the absorption doctrine. As she points out, it is the broadly defined scope of an EU competence and of the corresponding objective that allows the absorption of provisions of an international agreement, which could give rise to the centre of gravity test.

The global approach to external action objectives raises further difficulties, as far as a specific competence is conferred to the Union without specific objectives corresponding to the policy field. *Cremona* analyses the integration of the CFSP in the general framework of the Union's external action and its relationship to the other competences. She argues that, in practice, express external competences, such as the CFSP, tend to prevail over implied external competences, which pursue an internal objective. The broad scope of external policies is the expression of the prevalence of the finalist approach over the instrumental approach. Even if the objective of an external action measure is an internal one that could allow the exercise of an implied external competence, and even if, in the implementation of the international agreement, an internal policy instrument is needed, the broad scope of the external action objectives in their global approach allows the Court of Justice to favour the express legal basis beyond a strict correspondence between objectives and competences. The exercise of an

include the aim and content of that measure. If examination of a European Union measure reveals that it pursues a twofold purpose or that it has a twofold component and if one of those is identifiable as the main or predominant purpose or component, whereas the other is merely incidental, the measure must be founded on a single legal basis, namely, that required by the main or predominant purpose or component". Judgment of the Court of 11 June 2014, *Commission* v *Council*, C-377/12, EU:C:2014:1903, para 34. See S. Adam, "The Legal Basis of International Agreements of the European Union in the Post-Lisbon Era", in I. Govaere and others (eds), *The European Union in the World; Essays in Honor of Marc Maresceau* (Leiden: Martinus Nijhoff, 2014), 78.

17 Opinion of 16 May 2017, 2/15, *EU Singapore Free Trade Agreement*, EU:C:2017:376.

express external competence, instead of an implied one, presents an interest where the express external competence is exclusive (as is the CCP), but also as a confirmation of the importance of external action objectives, which allows the Union to use, as *Cremona* points out, a wide variety of instruments (even borrowed from internal policy fields) and explains the adaptation of constitutional principles to the requirement of efficiency, as is seen in the second part of the book.

The acceptance of a broad scope for the CFSP, however, is not necessarily without shortcomings. By adopting the perspective of the transversal objective of security, *Gatti* suggests that the Court of Justice has privileged the preservation of a space of action for the CFSP, thereby restraining the scope of the Area of Freedom, Security and Justice (AFSJ). There might be, therefore, the risk that a broad interpretation of the CFSP's scope might entail the absorption of acts from AFSJ and other policies, notably development cooperation, thereby expanding the latitude of the intergovernmental method in external relations.

Concerning the nature of the external competence on which depends the form of the Union's action – whether the Union concludes an EU-only or a mixed agreement – it is certainly closely related to the identified objective of the action. Although this is also the case in the internal field, as the principle of subsidiarity governs the use of EU competences with regard to the necessity to attain the corresponding objective, some specific issues are raised in the external relations field.[18]

Bosse Platière studies the functioning of the subsidiarity principle in the external action of the Union. While there is no formal opposition to the use of the principle directly in the external action field, she notes that subsidiarity operates mainly in the exercise of the internal competences, which leads to the exclusive nature of the implied external competence through the criterion of affecting the common rules or altering their scope, known as *ERTA* effect,[19] codified in Article 3, paragraph 2, TFEU.[20] How-

18 F. Castillo de la Torre, "The Court of Justice and External Competences After Lisbon: Some Reflections on the Latest Case Law", in P. Eeckhout, M. Lopez Escudero (eds), *The European Union's External Action in Times of Crisis* (Oxford, Hart Publishing, 2016), 129.

19 *Supra* note 13.

20 "The Union shall also have exclusive competence for the conclusion of an international agreement when its conclusion is provided for in a legislative act of the Union or is necessary to enable the Union to exercise its internal competence, or in so far as its conclusion may affect common rules or alter their scope".

ever, in such a case, implied external competence is exclusive, not because of the need to realise the corresponding internal objective, but because of the loyalty obligation to preserve the common rules, as underlined by *Delgado Casteleiro.*

The question is whether the principle of subsidiarity can operate directly in the external field. *Bosse Platière* does not exclude the exercise of external competence according to that principle. However, a distinction should still be made between express and implied external competences. In the case of express external competences of shared nature (as the environmental competence), the use of the subsidiarity criterion should not be excluded. However, Article 216, paragraph 1, TFEU provides that the Union may conclude an international agreement where the Treaties so provide. The question, thus, is whether subsidiarity operates with regard to the specific objective or whether the assignment of an external action objective implies that the Union may act regardless of a necessity test. *Neframi* notes that the subsidiarity test in the internal field has an impact on the nature of the implied external competence and, thus, does not need to be done in view of the conclusion of an international agreement, as it determines the scope of the *ERTA* effect. Indeed, in the field of harmonisation, common rules do not completely coincide with the provisions of an international agreement if a margin of discretion is left to the Member States. Nevertheless, the exercise of internal competence through the adoption of common rules may lead to a broader preemption in the external field, to the extent international provisions are deemed to fall under a field that is largely covered by common rules and where the subsidiarity test is already completed.

Despite the broad scope of the *ERTA* effect, it does not always confer exclusivity on the external competence. In such a case, the action of the Union in the external field depends on the necessity to achieve the corresponding objective or even the objective linked to an international agreement, when globally assessed.

Chamon revisits the conditions of the exercise of shared implied external competence and sheds light on the question of facultative or compulsory mixity from the perspective of Article 216, paragraph 1, TFEU, which provides that the Union may conclude an international agreement where it "is necessary in order to achieve, within the framework of the Union's policies, one of the objectives referred to in the Treaties". Following the position of the Court of Justice in its *Germany* v *Council* ruling,[21] the lack of *ERTA* exclusivity does not necessarily lead to the conclusion of a mixed agreement. Compulsory mixity is limited to the absence of EU external competence for part of an international agreement while the lack of exclusivity gives rise to facultative mixity. That means that an implied shared external competence can be directly exercised in the external field if it is considered necessary with regard to the attainment of the corresponding objective. The difference with regard to the necessity criterion for the principle of subsidiarity seems to be that necessity is assessed, not with regard to qualitative or quantitative criteria in reference to the Member States action, but with regard to the opportunity to act in the external field. It is, thus, more a question of political will than the consequence of a loyalty obligation with regard to the attainement of the relevant objective.

Such an evolution allows the Union to overcome the limits of the *ERTA* effect that were clarified in Opinion 2/15. *Pigeon* analyses the basis and limits of the *ERTA* effect with regard to the potential to affect the Treaties. Because portfolio investments do not fall under the scope of the CCP, the question has been whether the implied external competence of the Union could be considered exclusive on the basis of the affectation of Article 63 TFEU related to the freedom of movement of capital. His chapter explains the reasons for the Court of Justice's negative response thereto and clarifies the scope of the *ERTA* doctrine. Even if the *ERTA* effect implies a limitation on Member States' action through the establishment of exclusivity, the limitation of its scope is balanced through the recognition of the ability to exercise shared implied external competence.

***

Balancing EU Values with External Action Objectives

The Union's overarching objective of being an effective international actor impacts not only the relationship between objectives and competences and, thus, the principle of conferral, but also other principles and values of the Union. To be truly effective on the international scene, the Union must

21 Judgment of 5 December 2017, *Germany* v *Council, (Amendment of the Convention concerning International Carriage by Rail – COTIF)*, C-600/14, EU:C:2017:935.

adapt its action to the specificities of the international environment. Democratic values, fundamental rights, and the rule of law – the values on which the Union is founded and is supposed to promote in its relations with the rest of the world – may have to be subtly adjusted to accommodate the objective of being an effective international actor.

In the first place, although the conduct of the international relations should not affect the Union's commitment to representative democracy (at least in principle), the Union may have to restrain parliamentary prerogatives in order to effectively conduct external action. As noted by *Flavier*, the full involvement of parliaments in foreign affairs could jeopardise the secrecy of international negotiations. Accordingly, the Treaties restrain the European Parliament's powers in external relations. While the European Parliament generally plays the role of co-legislator, it merely holds the power to approve most international agreements and is simply consulted in respect of some treaties, notably those regarding the CFSP. *Kuijper* argues, however, that the restrictions on the European Parliament's powers may be less prominent than they appear at first sight. Recent judgments leave to the European Parliament powers of general scrutiny of CFSP treaty-making, through a forceful recognition of its right to be fully informed by the Council at all stages of the treaty-making process.[22] Such a right of the Parliament is, indeed, quintessential to the EU's institutional balance.

Secondly, like representative democracy, transparency must also sometimes be sacrificed for the sake of effectiveness in foreign policy. Access to information is an essential condition for the realisation of democracy, but, according to *Flavier*, this should not lead one to overlook the need for effective external action. If the Union's foreign policy were entirely transparent, its negotiating strategy would become known to its counterparties, thereby hindering the attainment of the Union's objectives. Cognizant of this difficulty, the European Union courts often balance the concern for transparency against that for the effectiveness of the EU's external action,

22 Judgment of 14 June 2016, *Parliament* v *Council (Tanzania)*, C-263/14, EU:C:2016:435, para 43; Opinion of 6 December 2001, 2/00, *Cartagena Protocol*, EU:C:2001:664; Judgment of 24 June 2014, *Parliament* v *Council (Mauritius)*, C-658/11, EU:C:2014:2025.

notably by denying members of the European Parliament generalised access to directives regarding negotiation.[23]

Third, the Court of Justice itself takes the concern for effectiveness into account. It is true that the Treaties generally give broad powers to the Court in the field of external relations, broader, in fact, than the powers exercised by most of the highest courts in sovereign States, as noted by *Kuijper*. It is also true that the Court of Justice has often exercised its jurisdiction on foreign policy and declared several acts incompatible with fundamental rights. The *Kadi* saga is a case in point.[24] However, as the courts of sovereign States routinely balance judicial control and foreign policy effectiveness,[25] judicial restraint is also embraced by the Court of Justice, in order to enable better conduct of external relations.

For instance, judicial protection of rights conferred directly through international agreements is very limited. Although the Treaties expressly stipulate that international agreements are binding on both the Union and its Members States[26] – which may seem to imply that the Union and third States can agree upon rules that directly bind individuals in the Union – individuals cannot always invoke rights provided by international agreements. As shown by *Prek* and *Lefèvre*, a "subjective" element is indispensable to the direct application of an agreement: the parties must have intended to confer rights to individuals. If, on the other hand, the parties intended the agreement to be applied on the condition of reciprocity, direct application is impossible. The Union's negotiation of reciprocal benefits would indeed be ineffective if the rights conferred by international agreements were justiciable in the Union, but not in the legal orders of the other parties. Interestingly, the "subjective" element necessary for judicial protection was found to be absent from many agreements concluded by the Union. Further, the case law of the Court of Justice suggests that, frequently, rights conferred by multilateral agreements, such as those of the

23 Judgement of 4 May 2012, *Sophie In't Veld*, T-529/09, EU:T:2012:215, para. 24; Judgement of 3 July 2014, *Sophie In't Veld*, C-350/12 P, EU:C:2014:2039; Judgement of 19 March 2013, *Sophie In't Veld*, T-301/10, EU:T:2013:135.

24 Judgment of 3 September 2008, *Yassin Abdullah Kadi and Al Barakaat International Foundation* v *Council and Commission*, C-402/05 P & C-415/05 P EU:C:2008:461.

25 Domestic courts have indeed acknowledged that they should not make fundamental decisions of foreign policy, see e.g. US Supreme Court, *Goldwater* v *Carter*, 444 U.S. 996 (1979).

26 See Articles 3, paragraph 5, 21, paragraph 1, TEU and 216, paragraph 2, TFEU.

World Trade Organisation (WTO), cannot be invoked by individuals. Bilateral treaties have, in the past, been given direct effect, but recent bilateral agreements might constitute exceptions. The trend, therefore, seems to go more in the direction of the effectiveness of EU external relations and, perhaps, less in the direction of increased judicial protection in foreign affairs.

Beyond the question of direct effect of international agreements, the Court of Justice's concern for effectiveness is expressed in its limited review of restrictive measures in the field of the CFSP. As noted by *Poli*, restrictive measures that adversely affect individuals, but are not addressed to them, may escape the Court's review. More generally, the Court seems to exercise some restraint in the CFSP area. As *Fines* demonstrates, the Court leaves ample political discretion to the Council: its case law justifies the adoption of sanctions against subjects that are somehow linked to foreign governments, even if they are not involved in illegal activities or crises. Furthermore, the Court of Justice has also accepted limited transparency in this area. *Flavier* notes that the strictness of the obligation to justify denial of access to documents is variable: transparency may be limited when overriding considerations relating to the Union's security come into play, since they may preclude the communication of certain elements to otherwise interested parties.

Nevertheless, it should be noted that the exercise of the Court's jurisdiction over restrictive measures, even though limited, might demonstrate less a differentiation of, and more a unified approach to, the scope of fundamental principles in the internal and external field.

Despite the specific regime of the CFSP and its acknowledgment that judicial activism might be dangerous for the effectiveness of the Union's action, the Court of Justice restrictively interpreted the restraint on its jurisdiction. On the one hand, the Court found that it does have jurisdiction on budget and staff management acts in the area of the CFSP: in these cases, as *Kuijper* argues, the administrative character of the acts prevails over their foreign policy nature.[27] On the other hand, the Court held that it can reply to preliminary questions concerning restrictive measures targeting

27 Judgment of 12 December 2015, *Elitaliana* v *Eulex Kosovo*, C-439/13 P, EU:C:2015:753; Judgment of 19 July 2016, *H.* v *Council of the European Union*, C-455/14 P, EU:C:2016:569.

individuals, thus filling a lacuna in primary law, as noted by *Fines*.[28] Therefore, the restriction of the Court's jurisdiction does not extend to the CFSP as such, but only to the adoption of "political" foreign policy acts and, then, only insofar as those acts do not directly target an individual.

Moreover, the Court of Justice has exercised its jurisdiction on the CFSP in practice and found that the Council cannot adopt restrictive measures at will; rather, it must justify them. The Council must provide the Court, in particular, with a set of indicia sufficiently specific, precise, and consistent to establish that there is a link between the target individual and the regime being questioned, as shown by *Poli*. To strike a better balance between policy effectiveness and judicial protection, the General Court and the Court of Justice, in 2014, prepared new procedural rules, the adoption and content of which are analysed by *Rosas*. These new procedures apply to actions for annulment, where a main party wishes to base his claims on information the communication of which to the other main party would harm the security of the Union. The judges must then balance the concerns for security against the rights of the defence and specify the procedures to be adopted, such as the production of a non-confidential version or a non-confidential summary of the information or material. The hope is that this new system will contribute to an appropriate balance between legitimate security concerns and the requirements of the rule of law.

The balancing of policy effectiveness and the rule of law may, in some cases, be linked to another problem specific to external relations: the preservation of the autonomy of the EU system. Through the conduct of external relations, the Union enters into contact with the international legal order and the legal systems of third countries. This relationship is problematic, insofar as it may threaten the separation of the EU from other legal orders, a *fil rouge* that links numerous decisions of the Court since *Van Gend en Loos*.[29]

---

28 Judgment of 28 March 2017, *The Queen (PJSC Rosneft Oil Company)*, C-72/15, ECLI:EU:C:2017:236.

29 According to the Court of Justice (Judgment of 5 February 1963, *NV Algemene Transport- en Expeditie Onderneming van Gend & Loos* v *Netherlands Inland Revenue Administration*, 26/62, EU:C:1963:1), the EU legal order constitutes a new legal order of international law. However, international agreements concluded by the Union should not impact the autonomy of the EU legal order. The Court of Justice highlighted this requirement namely in Opinions 1/91, 1/09 and 2/13. See, Opinion of 14 December 1991, 1/91, *Draft agreement between the Community, on the one hand, and the countries of the European Free Trade Association, on the*

The autonomy of EU law has proved problematic, in particular, in the area of data protection. The Union's institutions have entered into arrangements on data exchange with several countries over the last decades. Though the exchange of personal data, according to EU institutions, is indispensable to fight against criminals and terrorists, the Court of Justice has repeatedly held that the right to data protection cannot be sacrificed. *Potvin-Solis* shows that the Court ensures strict control over the protection of the right to data protection, by repeatedly holding that EU authorities must make sure that, whenever personal data are transferred outside the European Union, they are subject to "adequate" protection. Interestingly, the Court seems to interpret the concepts of "adequacy" extensively, by aligning the "adequate" protection provided abroad with the protection ensured within the EU. In other words, the Union must make sure that its internal – autonomous – data protection rules are applied abroad; foreign standards, though loosely equivalent, are not acceptable. If cooperation cannot ensure an "adequate" level of protection, it must be avoided, no matter the practical consequences in terms of policy effectiveness.

The autonomy claim is, therefore, an important element in the balancing exercise between effective international action and constitutional EU law principles. As noted by *Delgado Casteleiro,* autonomy is inextricably linked to the principle of loyalty. These principles inspire the fundamental rules of EU external relations, such as the consistent interpretation with regard to international law. To be loyal to the Union and to preserve the autonomy of its legal order, the Member States must interpret provisions binding both themselves and the Union in accordance with the case law of the Court of Justice. By ensuring consistency in the interpretation of international law, the principle of loyalty thus preserves both the autonomy of the Union's legal order and its unity on the international scene, and thereby fosters the Union's effectiveness.

The relationship between autonomy and effectiveness is more problematic when it comes to the conclusion of agreements that contain dispute settlement mechanisms. Such agreements might enable international bodies to rule upon the interpretation of EU law and, particularly, on the scope

---

other, relating to the creation of the European Economic Area, EU:C:1991:490; Opinion of 8 March 2011, 1/09, *Creation of a unified patent litigation system*, EU:C:2011:123; Opinion of 18 December 2014, 2/13, *Accession of the European Union to the European Convention for the Protection of Human Rights and Fundamental Freedoms*, EU:C:2014:2454.

of EU competences, thereby impinging on the exclusive jurisdiction of the Court of Justice and the EU's autonomy. The case law of the Court suggests that even indirect threats to the Union's autonomous interpretation of its competences must be prevented. An international tribunal's decision on the allocation of international responsibility between the Union and its Member States – such as, potentially, a judgment of the European Court of Human Rights – might be especially problematic.[30] This explains, in part, why the Court of Justice ruled in Opinion 2/13 that the agreement on the EU's accession to the European Convention on Human Rights is incompatible with EU law.

Contartese and *Pantaleo* suggest solutions to resolve problems relating to the allocation of international responsibility between and among the Union and its Members States. They argue that, in light of the Court of Justice's case law, the allocation of such responsibility should never be performed by international bodies. The Union and its Member States, rather, should have the ability to internally identify the respondent party. The Union's accession agreement to the European Convention on Human Rights fell short of this requirement. The investment agreements recently concluded by the Union might be more likely to pass the autonomy test, although such an outcome cannot be taken for granted.[31]

***

The analysis of the relationship between the EU's autonomy and its objective to be effective on the international scene does not permit, *per se*, one to reach definitive conclusions as to the "special" character of EU external relations. While many elements point towards the constitutional "specialty" of external action (e.g., external competences or the special institutional balance of EU external relations), others suggest a certain degree of "normalcy" (for instance, the application of "normal" data protection standards or the expansive scope of the Court's jurisdiction). The contributions

30 P. Eeckhout, "Opinion 2/13 on EU Accession to the ECHR and Judicial Dialogue – Autonomy or Autarky?", *Fordham International Law Journal* 38 (2015), 955, at 982.

31 Possible issues may be raised in the context of the request for an Opinion submitted by the Kingdom of Belgium on 13 October 2017 regarding the Canada-EU Comprehensive Economic and Trade Agreement (CETA), Opinion proceeding 1/17, OJ 2017 C 369/2.

contained in this book nonetheless permit one to formulate two considerations.

On the one hand, it seems clear that, if there is a "specialty" of EU external relations law, it belongs to external action, broadly intended, and not specifically to the CFSP. It is true that the CFSP constitutes the core of the EU's foreign policy, which is often associated with the peculiar features of this area (e.g., judicial restraint). It is also true, however, that the CFSP is not the only part of EU external action that is affected by endogenous and exogenous peculiarities: trade policy, or treaty-making at large, are also "special" in many respects. It is also increasingly arguable whether, and to what extent, the CFSP should be seen as categorically separate from the rest of external action. While it is true that the CFSP is characterised by special actors and procedures, it seems increasingly close to other EU policies, at least in terms of judicial supervision and parliamentary control. One should also acknowledge that, in the area of foreign policy *stricto sensu,* judicial supervision and parliamentary control can hardly be complete, even at the Member State level.

On the other hand, one may note that the Union operates in the same international environment as any other international actor and is adapting in a similar manner. Like (democratic) states, the Union seeks to strike a balance between its values and the effectiveness of its external action. To be sure, the EU is perhaps more keen on protecting transparency than third states: while the EU publishes part of its negotiating documents, its partners tend to adhere to traditional diplomatic secrecy.[32] When hard interests are at stake, at any rate, the EU is capable, like any other international subject, of striking "creative" constitutional balances, as evidenced by the Court's restraint on the need to justify restrictive measures or its reluctance to give direct application to international agreements founded on reciprocity. The case might be that, while EU external relations law becomes increasingly "exceptional" in order to ensure the Union's effectiveness, it might evolve into something rather "normal", when compared to the foreign policy law of traditional international actors (i.e., the States).

---

32 For instance, it would seem that the EU has published many more documents than the US government during the negotiation of the Transatlantic Trade and Investment Partnership, cf. the website of the European Commission: http://ec.europa.eu/trade/policy/in-focus/ttip/index_en.htm, and the website of the US government: https://ustr.gov/ttip.

Part 1:
Defining EU External Action Objectives and Competences

The Principle of Conferral and Express and Implied External Competences

Marise Cremona

I. Introduction[1]

The aim of this contribution is to offer some reflections on the relationship between the Union's express and implied external competences by examining them in the light of the principle of conferral of powers. According to the principle of conferral, which is one of the most fundamental of the principles which structure the EU's external relations,[2] "the Union shall act only within the limits of the competences conferred on it by the Member States in the Treaties to attain the objectives set out therein".[3] Competences not conferred on the Union remain with the Member States.[4] This expression of the principle thus emphasises that the source of EU powers is the Member States and that those powers are to be found in the Treaties.

---

1 This is a shortened and updated version of a chapter that will appear in T. Tridimas, R. Schütze (eds), Oxford Principles of European Union Law (Oxford: Oxford University Press, 2018).

2 In Opinion 2/13 on the proposed accession of the EU to the European Convention of Human Rights, the Court of Justice refers to the "specific characteristics" of the EU and EU law, including "those relating to the constitutional structure of the EU, which is seen in the principle of conferral of powers referred to in Articles 4, paragraph 1, of the Treaty on the European Union (TEU) and 5, paragraph 1, and paragraph 2, TEU, and in the institutional framework established in Articles 13 TEU to 19 TEU". These "essential characteristics" of EU law "have given rise to a structured network of principles, rules and mutually interdependent legal relations linking the EU and its Member States, and its Member States with each other". Opinion of 18 December 2014, 2/13, *Accession of the European Union to the ECHR*, EU:C:2014:2454, paras 165-167. On the EU's structural principles in external relations law, see M. Cremona, "Structural Principles and their Role in EU External Relations Law", in M. Cremona (ed), *Structural Principles in EU External Relations Law,* (Oxford: Hart Publishing 2018).

3 Article 5, paragraph 2, TEU.

4 Articles 4, paragraph 1 and 5, paragraph 2, TEU.

Conferral is a principle applicable to both internal and external action, and to both express and implied powers. As expressed in one *locus classicus*,

> [The] principle of conferred powers must be respected in both the internal action and the international action of the Community. The Community acts ordinarily on the basis of specific powers which, as the Court has held, are not necessarily the express consequence of specific provisions of the Treaty but may also be implied from them.[5]

Both express and implied powers are here referred to as "specific powers": that is, derived from a specific provision of the Treaty, as distinct from the unspecific or residual power contained in what is now Article 352 of the Treaty on the Functioning of the European Union (TFEU).[6] Since the landmark decision in *Commission* v *Council* (*ERTA*),[7] the evolution of implied powers has been one of the defining features of EU external relations law, scholarship focusing on the basis and scope of implied external powers, their relation to internal powers and the conditions under which an implied external power may be declared exclusive.[8] Whereas debates as to the choice of legal basis have rarely explicitly turned on the relation between express and implied powers, there are signs that a shift in that relationship is taking place, which invites us to take stock. The consolidation

---

5 Opinion of 28 March 1996, 2/94, *Accession by the Community to the European Convention for the Protection of Human Rights and Fundamental Freedoms*, EU:C:1996:140, paras 24-25.

6 In Opinion 2/94, *supra* note 5, the Court described this provision, sometimes called the "flexibility clause", as "designed to fill the gap where no specific provisions of the Treaty confer on the Community institutions express or implied powers to act, if such powers appear none the less to be necessary to enable the Community to carry out its functions with a view to attaining one of the objectives laid down by the Treaty" (para 29) and was careful to make clear that it could not be used to undermine the principle of conferral (para 30).

7 Judgment of 31 March 1971, *Commission* v *Council,* 22/70, EU:C:1971:32.

8 See e.g. R. Schütze, *European Constitutional Law* (Cambridge and New York: Cambridge University Press, 2012), 187–222; P. Eeckhout, *EU External Relations Law*, 2nd ed (Oxford and New York: Oxford University Press, 2011), 70–164; G. De Baere, *Constitutional Principles of EU External Relations* (Oxford and New York: Oxford University Press, 2008), 9–32; M. Cremona, "Defining Competence In EU External Relations: Lessons from the Treaty Reform Process", in A. Dashwood, M. Maresceau (eds.), *Law and Practice of EU External Relations: Salient Features of a Changing Landscape* (Cambridge and New York: Cambridge University Press, 2008), 34; M. Cremona, "EU External Relations: Unity and Conferral of Powers", in L. Azoulai (ed), *The Question of Competence in the European Union* (Oxford: Oxford University Press, 2014), 65-85.

of the *ERTA* line of case law in the Treaty of Lisbon, in particular in Articles 3, paragraph 2 and 216, paragraph 1, TFEU, as well as the development of practice and law since the Treaty of Lisbon came into force in 2009, invite us to rethink the relationship between these two types of "specific power".

The prevailing impression is that – and despite some collecting together of the provisions on external action in dedicated Titles of the TEU and TFEU as a result of the Lisbon Treaty – external competence is still highly fragmented. Certainly there are many different potential legal bases in the Treaties, both express and implied, and disagreements about the appropriate legal basis for international action have not diminished. But if we examine the reality of practice over the last few years we can identify a different trend, towards a consolidation of EU external action and international treaty-making practice on the basis of a number of key express external competences of broad scope.

Two factors have certainly contributed to this trend. The first is the distinct preference on the part of the Court for choosing where possible a single legal basis for a Union act, whether an autonomous measure or the decision concluding an international agreement, based on its "main or predominant purpose". The Court refers to the possibility of using two or more legal bases as "by way of exception" and subject to there being no incompatibility between them.[9] The second factor is the wide scope given to the EU's express external competences, and in particular to certain cen-

9 For a recent example of what has become a standard form of words, see Judgment of the Court of 11 June 2014, *Commission* v *Council*, C-377/12, EU:C:2014:1903, para 34: "According to settled case-law, the choice of the legal basis for a European Union measure, including the measure adopted for the purpose of concluding an international agreement, must rest on objective factors amenable to judicial review, which include the aim and content of that measure. If examination of a European Union measure reveals that it pursues a twofold purpose or that it has a twofold component and if one of those is identifiable as the main or predominant purpose or component, whereas the other is merely incidental, the measure must be founded on a single legal basis, namely, that required by the main or predominant purpose or component. By way of exception, if it is established that the measure pursues several objectives which are inseparably linked without one being secondary and indirect in relation to the other, the measure must be founded on the various corresponding legal bases. However, no dual legal basis is possible where the procedures required by each legal basis are incompatible with each other (see, *inter alia,* Judgment of 19 July 2012, *Parliament* v *Council,* C-130/10, EU:C:2012:472, paras 42 to 45 and the case-law cited)".

tral external policy fields: the Common Foreign and Security Policy (CFSP), the Common Commercial Policy (CCP), development cooperation policy, and Association Agreements. These policies are very different in kind but have in common their breadth and their ability, when used as the basis for international action, to encompass a wide range of commitments and activities.

This trend invites us to reconsider the rationale for implied powers in the light of the principle of conferral. In fact, despite their codification in the Lisbon Treaty, implied external powers are of less importance than in the past, and this is not only because new express competences have been added over the years, both general and sectoral. External powers that are implied from internal competence-conferring provisions are certainly not redundant; they are still used in particular where the EU concludes a sectoral agreement such as a convention on private international law or a bilateral fisheries agreement, where the internal sectoral competence may be the most appropriate basis for external action. But their function is less central than we might think, especially when we read a provision such as Article 216, paragraph 1, TFEU.[10]

II. The Principle of Conferral and Express External Competence

The relationship between the principle of conferral and an external competence, which has been expressly conferred, might seem simple, but the nature of these competences can help us to understand the principle of conferral as a structural principle. We will here consider three important fields of express external competence: the CCP, the CFSP, and development cooperation, and we will focus on how the Court of Justice determines the scope of these competences and their relation to other, more specifically sectoral, implied external powers. Despite the obvious differences between these policy fields, as legal bases for conferred competences they have common features which are characteristic of EU external relations. The Treaties establish a set of general external objectives applicable to all external relations activity[11] and, in the case of the CCP and development cooperation, additional policy-specific objectives (liberalization of inter-

10 See below for the text of Article 216, paragraph 1, TFEU.

11 Articles 3, paragraph 5, and 21 TEU.

national trade in the case of the CCP and the reduction and eventual elimination of poverty in the case of development cooperation). The CFSP, in contrast, relies on the general external objectives turned into more specific policy objectives by the political institutions.[12] The Treaties mandate the EU to engage in external policy-making and provide instruments to enable it to do so (including different types of international agreement), and as long as the instruments used are designed to operate within the respective policy field they are open-ended as to the specific objectives of that policy-making. This has allowed the Court, in considering the boundaries of express external competences, to adopt an approach based on the overall framework of the action and, where this context is external, to give preference to broadly-conceived express external policy competences such as the common commercial policy or the common foreign and security policy.

A. The Common Commercial Policy

From Opinion 1/75 onwards it was clear that the CCP was not limited to dealing with tariffs and trade barriers but rather was a "concept having the same content whether it is applied in the context of the international action of a state or to that of the Community".[13] And CCP powers can be used to achieve purposes which go beyond those of trade policy, to include development,[14] environmental protection,[15] the expression of political disapproval,[16] and the promotion of human rights.[17] In the post-Lisbon period,

---

12 According to Article 24, paragraph 1, TEU the CFSP is to be "defined and implemented" by the European Council and Council.

13 Opinion of 11 November 1975, 1/75, EU:C:1975:145.

14 Judgment of 26 March 1987, *Commission* v *Council,* 45/86, EU:C:1987:163.

15 Judgment of 29 March 1990, *Greece* v *Council,* C–62/88, EU:C:1990:153.

16 In 1982 it was agreed for the first time to use the CCP competence, Article 113 EEC (now Article 207 TFEU) as the legal basis for a Community instrument imposing economic sanctions – by reducing quotas – against the Soviet Union as a reaction to the imposition of martial law in Poland: Council Regulation (EEC) No 596/82 of 15 March 1982 amending the import arrangements for certain products originating in the USS, OJ 1982 L 72/15. See also Judgment of 14 January 1997, *The Queen, ex parte Centro-Com Srl* v *HM Treasury and Bank of England,* C-124/95, EU:C:1997:8.

17 For example, the positive and negative human rights-related conditionality introduced into the EU's Generalised System of Preferences.

following the expansion of CCP exclusive competence to cover trade in services, the commercial aspects of intellectual property and foreign direct investment,[18] attention has been focused on the relationship between CCP competence and powers which may be derived from the EU's internal competence. The Court has adopted an approach which emphasises the external dimension (trade with third countries) over the existence of internal sectoral legislation.

In *Daiichi Sankyo* the Court was not faced with a legal basis question, but rather with the question of its jurisdiction to interpret the Agreement on Trade-Related Aspects of Intellectual Property Rights (TRIPS), the World Trade Organisation (WTO) agreement on trade-related intellectual property rights (IPR).[19] The action concerned patents for pharmaceuticals and the national court submitted a number of questions on the interpretation to be given to Articles 27 and 70 of the TRIPS. The Court's previous case law on TRIPS[20] and on mixed agreements more generally[21] would suggest that its jurisdiction to interpret the agreement depends on the degree to which the Union had exercised its competence (i.e. legislated) in the field covered by the agreement. The Member States submitting observations in the case took the view that this approach was still valid and that intellectual property should be seen as a shared competence within the framework of the internal market. The Commission, however, took a different approach. It argued that since the Lisbon Treaty revised and expanded the scope of the CCP in Article 207 TFEU, the whole of the TRIPS now falls within the CCP as being concerned with "the commercial aspects of intellectual property", and must therefore be subject as a whole to the EU's exclusive competence and the interpretational jurisdiction of the Court. Thus the scope of the CCP in relation to TRIPS was at issue.

The Court's approach to interpreting the phrase "the commercial aspects of intellectual property" in Article 207 TFEU is striking. Instead of

---

18 Article 207 TFEU.

19 Judgment of 18 July 2013, *Daiichi Sankyo Co. Ltd, Sanofi-Aventis Deutschland GmbH* v *DEMO Anonimos Viomikhaniki kai Emporiki Etairia Farmakon*, C-414/11, EU:C:2013:520.

20 Judgment of 14 December 2000, *Parfums Christian Dior SA* v *TUK Consultancy BV and others*, C-300/98 & C-392/98, EU:C:2000:688, and Judgment of 11 September 2007, *Merck Genéricos – Produtos Farmacêuticos,* C-431/05, EU:C:2007:496.

21 Judgment of 8 March 2011, *Lesoochranárske zoskupenie*, C-240/09, EU:C:2011:125.

starting from the nature of IPR, seeking to distinguish aspects which may be classified as "commercial aspects" from others, the Court starts with the nature of the EU's trade policy, the CCP. In other words, it first defines the scope of the CCP and then moves from that to see which aspects of TRIPS (not IPR in general) fall within that scope. And the CCP, the Court says, is first of all concerned with trade with non-member countries, and not trade within the internal market. In this way it deflects a criticism that an over-broad interpretation of "the commercial aspects of intellectual property" would empty of real meaning the concept of IPR as part of internal market law. Then the Court turns to its tried-and-tested formula for the scope of the CCP:

> "[A] European Union act falls within the common commercial policy if it relates specifically to international trade in that it is essentially intended to promote, facilitate or govern trade and has direct and immediate effects on trade".[22]

Only those IPR rules "with a specific link to international trade" would fall within the scope of the CCP.[23] The next step is to focus on the TRIPS. The Court takes the view that the whole of TRIPS has a "specific link to international trade": it is an integral part of the WTO system and is linked to the other WTO agreements inter alia through the possibility of cross-retaliation. The Court rejects the argument that those parts of TRIPS which deal with the *substance* of rights fall rather within the scope of the internal market. The objective of those rules in TRIPS, it says, is the liberalisation of international trade and not the harmonisation of Member State laws. Importantly, this finding does not prevent the adoption of future internal EU legislation on the harmonisation of IPR based on internal competences, albeit this should be carried out in conformity with the EU's obligations under TRIPS. Thus the Court does not define "commercial aspects" of intellectual property by reference either to TRIPS or to a systematic categorization of intellectual property law rules. The phrase is defined in terms of the Court's own previous definition of the CCP: measures which are intended to promote, facilitate or govern trade. The rules in TRIPS which define the scope of IPR – which may have other purposes in other contexts – could here be seen as linked to international trade.

---

22 Judgment of 18 July 2013, *Daiichi Sankyo Co. Ltd*, *supra* note 19, para 51.
23 *Id.*, para 52.

The approach adopted in *Daiichi Sankyo* was affirmed in Opinion 2/15,[24] where the Court held that the provisions on IPR in the EU-Singapore free trade agreement (EUSFTA) fell within the scope of the CCP. The purpose of the provisions, the Court held, was to guarantee entrepreneurs from both the EU and Singapore an adequate level of protection of their IPR so as to "increase the benefits from trade and investment" and liberalization of trade.[25] The fact that the agreement referred to other international conventions that go beyond the "commercial aspects" of IPR (including, for example, provisions on moral rights) did not take these provisions outside the scope of the CCP: such references were not sufficient for moral rights "to be regarded, in its own right, as a component of that agreement".[26]

We have used these cases to illustrate the Court's approach to interpreting the scope of the CCP, but we should not assume that every international agreement in the field of IPR will likewise fall under the CCP. In Opinion 3/15, for example, the Court refused to accept an argument of the Commission that all rules relating to IPR except those concerned with moral rights fall within the CCP, on the ground that this "would lead to an excessive extension of the field covered by the common commercial policy by bringing within that policy rules that have no specific link with international trade".[27]

---

24 Opinion of 16 May 2017, 2/15, *EU Singapore Free Trade Agreement*, EU:C:2017:376.

25 *Id.*, paras 122-126.

26 *Id.*, para 129.

27 Opinion of 14 February 2017, 3/15, *Marrakesh Treaty to Facilitate Access to Published Works for Persons who are Blind, Visually Impaired or Otherwise Print Disabled,* EU:C:2017:114, para 85. In Opinion 3/15 the Court was asked whether the EU had exclusive competence to conclude the Marrakesh Treaty to facilitate access to published works for persons who are blind or visually impaired. Its first conclusion was that exclusive competence could not be based on CCP powers: its main purpose was not commercial, nor "to promote, facilitate or govern international trade" but to improve access to published works for blind and visually impaired people. The Court then went on to consider competence to conclude the treaty under implied powers based on the existence of secondary legislation dealing with copyright, finding that on this basis EU competence was indeed exclusive.

We can see a similar logic at play in the context of trade in services in *Commission* v *Council* (conditional access services),[28] in which the Court was asked to determine the appropriate legal basis for the conclusion of a Convention on the legal protection of those offering audio-visual and information society services on a conditional basis. The Council's view was that the Convention should be concluded as a mixed agreement on the basis of implied external competence relating to the internal market (Article 114 TFEU), whereas the Commission argued that the Convention fell within the scope of the CCP and thus exclusive competence. Internal legislation, coinciding in part with the scope of the Convention, had been adopted under Article 114, and the Convention effectively extends this internal market harmonisation to third country parties, as well as providing for additional measures on sanctions and remedies for unlawful activity, which go beyond the current internal EU legislation.

The Court held that this link to internal legislation based on Article 114 TFEU did not entail that an external agreement covering the same ground should necessarily also be based on implied external powers deriving from Article 114. It followed the line of reasoning it used in *Daiichi Sankyo*, defining the scope of the CCP and then analyzing the Convention to see whether it is concerned with international trade. The Convention was concerned, the Court found, not with trade in services between Member States but with trade in services between Member States and third countries. The predominant purpose of external trade is confirmed for the Court by the presence of a disconnection clause: in their mutual relations (i.e. within the internal market), the EU Member States are to apply EU rules where they exist, rather than the rules established by the Convention:

> "Article 11(4) of the Convention confirms that, since the approximation of the legislation of Member States in the field concerned has already been largely achieved by Directive 98/84, the primary objective of the Convention is not to improve the functioning of the internal market, but to extend legal protection of the relevant services beyond the territory of the European Union and thereby to promote international trade in those services".[29]

Although aspects of the Convention go beyond the existing EU legislation, and thus can be seen as aimed at improving the functioning of the internal market, the Court held that these were "incidental" effects and not

28 Judgement of 22 October 2013, *Commission* v *Council*, C-137/12, EU:C:2013:675.

29 *Id.*, para 67.

their main purpose. Thus here the presence of existing internal market legislation, instead of indicating that an internal market legal basis should be used for an international agreement covering the same ground, has the opposite effect: it demonstrates that the purpose of the Convention was not internal harmonisation but external markets (and imports from third countries into the EU market).

Thus in deciding whether a measure falls within the CCP the focus of the Court has been on identifying a link to external trade rather than on categorizing different aspects of IPR, services regulation or foreign investment.[30] This approach to defining the scope of the CCP allows it to cover a broad spectrum of rules operating at the international level without however displacing the operation of the (shared) internal market competence where rules are adopted within the EU. It thus reflects Article 207, paragraph 6, TFEU, which can be sensed in the background to these judgments: CCP powers should not be used to encroach on the internal legal bases for regulation.[31] It is an approach which follows the same logic as that applied by the Court in relation to the SPS and TBT agreements in Opinion 1/94.[32]

Opinion 2/15 on the EU-Singapore free trade agreement, while following the logic just described, brings another dimension to this picture and the potential use of CCP competence. The Court was at pains to draw attention to the altered external policy context of the CCP: the fact that as a result of the Lisbon Treaty the CCP must be "conducted in the context of the principles and objectives of the Union's external action".[33] An examination of those principles and objectives allowed the Court to conclude that "the objective of sustainable development henceforth forms an inte-

30 On defining the scope of foreign direct investment so as to include investment protection as well as market access, see Opinion 2/15 (*supra* note 24), paras 94-96. It should be noted that the Court relied on the use of the phrase foreign direct investment in Article 207 TFEU as the basis for excluding from the scope of the CCP all investment that is not direct; however it also made it clear that direct investment fulfils the test of having a direct and immediate effect on international trade, whereas indirect investment (such as portfolio investment) does not: see paras 83-84.

31 Opinion of 16 May 2017, 2/15, *supra* note 24, para 164.

32 Opinion of 15 November 1994, 1/94, *Competence of the Community to Conclude International Agreements Concerning Services and the Protection of Intellectual Property*, EU:C:1994:384, paras 30-33.

33 Article 207, paragraph 1, TFEU.

gral part of the common commercial policy",[34] and that the whole of the agreement's chapter on sustainable development could be brought within the scope of the CCP. The possibility for trade instruments to be linked to non-trade objectives is not new,[35] but here we see for the first time an explicit recognition that the policy objectives of the CCP itself extend beyond trade liberalization.

B. The Common Foreign and Security Policy

Although the Lisbon Treaty preserved a degree of specificity for the CFSP,[36] it changed the relationship between the CFSP and other external competences, integrating the CFSP into the general framework of EU external action, including its general objectives and procedures for treaty-making. The requirement that non-CFSP powers must be used where possible, which was based on the Court's interpretation of Article 47 EU,[37] no longer applies. The current Article 40 TEU provides that the different procedures and institutional powers granted by the CFSP provisions on the one hand and other EU competences on the other should not be affected by the implementation of either the CFSP or other competences respectively. The "non-affect" requirement operates in both directions. It is thus necessary to determine the boundary between the CFSP and other EU competences in order to allocate the appropriate legal basis and corresponding procedures and powers of the institutions, and this falls within the Court's jurisdiction under Article 275 TFEU. Three cases decided since the coming into force of the Lisbon Treaty throw light on the nature of CFSP competence and its relation to other competences, as well as on the role of the Court in upholding the principle of conferral.

---

34 Opinion 2/15, *supra* note 24, para 147.

35 See references in notes 14, 15, 16 and 17.

36 See Article 24, paragraph 1, TEU, which refers to "specific rules and procedures", including a limited role for the Court of Justice.

37 Judgment of 29 May 2008, *Commission* v *Council*, C-91/05, EU:C:2008:288. As expressed by Advocate General Mengozzi in that case at para 116 of his Opinion, "Article 47 EU aims to keep watertight, so to speak, the primacy of Community action under the EC Treaty over actions undertaken on the basis of Title V and/or Title VI of the EU Treaty, so that if an action *could* be undertaken on the basis of the EC Treaty, it must be undertaken by virtue of that Treaty". Opinion of AG Mengozzi of 19 September 2007, EU:C:2007:528.

The first case concerns counter-terrorism measures, and the choice between two legal bases, one falling within the Treaties" provisions on external action, the other within the Area of Freedom, Security and Justice (AFSJ).[38] The Council and Parliament disagreed over the appropriate legal basis for Regulation 1286/2009/EU, which amended Regulation 881/2002/EC, the main Regulation implementing UNSCR 1390 (2002) and imposing restrictive measures against persons and entities associated with Al Qaeda and the Taliban. The contested Regulation was designed to amend the procedures in the 2002 Regulation so as to comply with the Court judgments in (inter alia) the *Kadi* case.[39] Regulation 881/2002 was based on Articles 60, 301 and 308 of the Treaty establishing the European Community (EC), legal bases which were found in *Kadi I* to be appropriate.[40] Under Articles 60 and 301 EC, which concerned restrictive measures directed at third states, the 2002 Regulation had been preceded by a CFSP measure, in this case Common Position 2002/402/CFSP. The amending Regulation was adopted shortly after the coming into force of the Lisbon Treaty on the basis of Article 215 TFEU which is the equivalent of former Article 301 EC, again linked to the 2002 Common Position.[41]

Article 215 TFEU might therefore appear the logical legal basis for this amended Regulation. But the Treaty of Lisbon also introduced a new provision, Article 75 TFEU in the Title on the Area of Freedom, Security and Justice (AFSJ), which envisages the adoption of regulations for the purpose of combating terrorism which would define a "framework for administrative measures with regard to capital movements and payments, such as the freezing of funds, financial assets or economic gains belonging to, or owned or held by, natural or legal persons, groups or non-State enti-

---

38 Judgment of 19 July 2012, *European Parliament* v *Council*, C-130/10, EU:C:2012:472. See also, in this volume, the chapter by Mauro Gatti.

39 Judgment of 3 September 2008, *Yassin Abdullah Kadi and Al Barakaat International Foundation* v *Council and Commission*, C-402/05 P & C-415/05 P EU:C:2008:461.

40 M. Cremona, "EC Competence, "Smart Sanctions" and the Kadi Case", *Yearbook of European Law*, 28 (2009), 559.

41 Articles 60 and 308 EC were no longer needed since Article 215 TFEU, while following closely the wording of former Article 301 EC, has been amended to include financial as well as economic restrictions, and also to cover measures directed at natural or legal persons, groups and other non-State entities, as well as third States.

ties". The delimitation between these two provisions was not (and still is not) clear,[42] and yet it matters because measures based on Article 75 TFEU are adopted by way of the ordinary legislative procedure with the European Parliament as co-legislator, whereas under Article 215 TFEU the Regulation is adopted by the Council, and the Parliament must simply be "informed". The Court decided in favour of Article 215 TFEU in three steps.

First, as in the cases on the CCP we have already discussed, the Court starts by defining the scope of the relevant alternative legal bases. Article 215 TFEU specifically relates to external action, whereas Article 75 TFEU does not. Article 215 TFEU refers to third countries, it is placed within the Title on external action, and it requires the prior adoption of a CFSP decision. Article 75 TFEU, on the other hand, makes no reference to external activities, countries or policies, and expressly refers to achieving the objectives set out in Article 67 TFEU, that is, the creation of the AFSJ, an internal objective. This analysis implies that where a measure is essentially external, preference should be given to an express external legal basis over an internal legal basis.

Second, the Court held that the Regulation was essentially external since it relates to global activities, it responds to a threat of international scope (international terrorism), it is intended to give effect to a United Nations Security Council resolution, and is linked to a CFSP Decision (the procedural prerequisite mentioned above). The Court does not seek to make a distinction between "internal" and "external" terrorism (any more than it sought to distinguish between "commercial" and other aspects of IPR), simply saying that combating terrorism may be an objective of external action.

Third, although combating terrorism is referred to expressly in Article 75 TFEU, Article 215 TFEU can also be used for this purpose (and its precursors had been so used); thus the Court held that Article 75 TFEU is not a *lex specialis* on counter-terrorism which should take precedence. Indeed, the Court says, combating international terrorism and its financing in order to preserve international peace and security are explicit objectives of the

42 See M. Cremona, "EU External Action in the JHA Domain: A Legal Perspective", in M. Cremona, J. Monar, S. Poli (eds), *The External Dimension of the Area of Freedom, Security and Justice* (Brussels: Peter Lang-P.I.E., 2011), 99-100.

Union's external action.[43] Thus the Court prefers an explicitly external competence (Article 215 TFEU) over an express reference to counter-terrorism (Article 75 TFEU). Even where the substance of a measure (counter-terrorism) seems to fall within the scope of an AFSJ provision the latter was not preferred over an explicitly external legal basis where the measure is regarded as external in nature. As the Court put it, "Articles 75 TFEU and 215 TFEU relate to different European Union policies that pursue objectives which, although complementary, do not have the same scope".[44]

In this case, therefore, the choice was between a CFSP-linked external legal basis and an internal legal basis. Our second case[45] concerned the correct procedural legal basis under Article 218 TFEU for the conclusion of an international agreement, the issue being whether the agreement should be regarded as "exclusively" relating to the CFSP. The Council had concluded an agreement with Mauritius against the background of the EU's military mission "Atalanta", a CSDP mission designed to contribute to the deterrence, prevention and repression of piracy off the coast of Somalia.[46] The UN Security Council resolution to which the EU's mission is a response calls for cooperation between States "in the investigation and prosecution of persons responsible for acts of piracy and armed robbery off the coast of Somalia, consistent with applicable international law including international human rights law",[47] and the EU's Joint Action provides that persons detained who are suspected of piracy may be transferred to another State for prosecution, if that State consents and provided that "the conditions for the transfer have been agreed with that third State in a

43 Judgement of 22 October 2013, *Commission* v *Council*, *supra* note 28, para 61. Note that the Court simply points out that the preservation of international peace and security is an external objective – as it is, under Article 21, paragraph 2, c, TEU; unlike Advocate General Bot, the Court does not link this objective directly to the CFSP: see in comparison the opinion of AG Bot, of 31 January 2012, C-130/10, EU:C:2012:50, paras 62-64.

44 *Id.*, para 66.

45 Judgment of 24 June 2014, *European Parliament* v *Council*, C-658/11, EU:C:2014:2025. See also, in this volume, the chapter by Pieter Jan Kuijper.

46 EU NAVFOR Somalia – Operation Atalanta, Council Joint Action 2008/851/CFSP, OJ 2008 L 301/33. In March 2012 the operating mandate was extended until December 2014. Piracy is defined by Art. 101 of the United Nations Convention on the Law of the Sea.

47 United Nations Security Council Resolution of 2 June 2008, S/RES/1816 (2008).

manner consistent with relevant international law, notably international law on human rights, in order to guarantee in particular that no one shall be subjected to the death penalty, to torture or to any cruel, inhuman or degrading treatment".[48] As a result the EU has entered into agreements with some States in the region who are prepared to accept suspected pirates detained for prosecution, and the agreement with Mauritius was one of these.[49] The dispute between the Parliament and the Council was over the procedure for concluding the agreement. The Council concluded the agreement as a CFSP agreement, based on Article 37 TEU and following the procedure set out in Article 218, paragraphs 5 and 6, TFEU; as an agreement relating (in the Council's view) exclusively to the CFSP it was negotiated by the High Representative, who also proposed the signing and conclusion of the agreement, and there was no requirement to obtain the consent of, or even to consult, the European Parliament. The Parliament however argued that, as well as its CFSP dimension, the agreement contained elements that fell within the AFSJ (judicial cooperation in criminal matters and police cooperation) as well as development cooperation, and did not therefore "relate exclusively" to the CFSP within the meaning of Article 218, paragraph 6, TFEU.

The Court relied in this case on the fact that the Parliament apparently accepted that a substantive CFSP legal basis was appropriate.[50] Following the Advocate General, it first of all linked the choice of procedural legal basis to the choice of substantive legal basis. In other words, an agreement would "exclusively relate" to the CFSP for the purposes of the procedure to be applied if the agreement could be based solely on a substantive CFSP legal basis, no other non-CFSP substantive legal basis being required. This is an important step, given the Court's preference for a single

48 Council Joint Action 2008/851/CFSP, *supra* note 46, Art 12(3).

49 Council Decision 2011/640/CFSP OJ 2011 L 254/1. Agreements have also been concluded with Kenya (which subsequently ended the agreement), Tanzania (also challenged by the European Parliament: see further below) and Seychelles. See further I. Bosse-Platière, "Le volet judiciaire de la lutte contre la piraterie maritime en Somalie: les accords de transferts conclus par l'"Union européenne avec les États tiers", in *Les différentes facettes du concept juridique de sécurité. Mélanges en l'honneur de Pierre-André Lecocq* (Lille : Imprimerie centrale du Nord, 2011), 91-112.

50 The European Parliament challenged the substantive legal basis in a parallel case concerning a similar agreement with Tanzania: Judgment of 14 June 2016, *European Parliament* v *Council*, C-263/14, EU:C:2016:435, see further below.

substantive legal basis representing the "predominant purpose" or centre of gravity of an agreement; incidental or subsidiary purposes need not be reflected in additional legal bases.[51] It is certainly rational to link together procedural and substantive legal basis; as Advocate General Bot said, to decide otherwise would entail engaging in two separate enquiries over substance and procedure, which seems redundant (although given that they are dealt with in separate provisions, perhaps not completely so[52]). However, by treating the term "exclusively relates" as referring to the appropriate legal basis, and then applying standard legal basis reasoning which where possible identifies a single legal basis reflecting its predominant purpose, this approach results in a departure from the literal meaning of "exclusively", reading it in effect as "predominantly".[53] We will return to the predominant purpose approach to legal basis, and its link to the principle of conferral.

What then was the appropriate legal basis? The Court spends very little time on this point.[54] It simply refers to the fact that the Parliament itself

51 For a recent statement of this principle see *supra* note 9.

52 Although the original EEC Treaty had a tendency to combine them, the separation of substantive treaty-making powers from procedural provisions has been almost universalized by the Lisbon treaty, Art 218 TFEU now covering even CFSP agreements in terms of procedure (Art 207 TFEU contains some "Special provisions" which operate alongside Art 218 TFEU for the negotiation and conclusion of trade agreements).

53 The Advocate General justifies this by arguing correctly that otherwise there would be no, or virtually no, agreement relating "exclusively" to the CFSP since the requirement of policy coherence entails that an agreement whose centre of gravity is the CFSP will generally also relate to other EU policies, such as development cooperation: "For instance, the well-recognised interrelationship between security, development and human rights means that it would very often be possible to argue that measures taken in one of these three areas will also have some effect on the other two areas and, in that sense, also relate to those areas for the purposes of the application of Article 218, paragraph 6, TFEU. Clearly, that is not what the treaties envisage". Opinion of AG Bot of 30 January 2014, *European Parliament* v *Council*, C-658/11 EU:C:2014:41, para 23.

54 The Court's judgment does not take up the invitation in the Advocate General's opinion to establish a fundamental position on the relationship between the CFSP and (implied) external powers under the AFSJ, the "most significant constitutional challenge" according to Van Elsuwege: P. Van Elsuwege, "Securing the Institutional Balance in the Procedure for Concluding International Agreements: *European Parliament* v *Council (Pirate Transfer Agreement with Mauritius)*", *Common Market Law Review* 52, no. 5 (2015), 1379 at 1388.

had accepted during the hearing that the CFSP competence (on its own) could be used as the correct substantive legal basis for the agreement. The Parliament's main argument in the case was instead that since the agreement also served secondary or incidental aims falling within other policy fields it could not be regarded as relating "exclusively" to the CFSP for procedural purposes, even if a CFSP legal basis were all that was substantively required. Since the Court rejected that argument, linking the procedural to the substantive legal basis, it concluded that the correct procedure had been followed. It followed its frequent practice of not going further than was required to give a judgment in the particular case. The Court did not, therefore, address the question of whether the agreement indeed served secondary aims, and if so whether these were merely incidental or were substantial enough to require a separate legal basis. We should remember the Court's approach to legal basis: when it is faced with a legal basis question, it does not start by asking what legal basis it would itself have chosen for the measure; rather, it asks whether the legal basis in fact chosen is legally justifiable. The Court's willingness in this case to accept without question the institutions" own characterization of the agreement as in substance a CFSP agreement, simply because there was no institutional disagreement on the matter, is significant because the Court's jurisdiction to determine the boundary between the CFSP and other competences so as to give effect to Article 40 TEU is an important part of its jurisdiction in relation to the CFSP. It is a telling demonstration that the Court sees the distinction (and Article 40 TEU) as essentially concerned with the balance of institutional power rather than an expression of a fundamental constitutional division between types of Union competence. This is also borne out by its approach to the Parliament's right to be informed under Article 218, paragraph 10, TFEU, which stresses the role (limited but important) that the Parliament can play in the conclusion of CFSP agreements.[55]

Our third case is a second challenge by the Parliament to a very similar agreement concluded with Tanzania.[56] Here the European Parliament did contest the substantive legal basis of the agreement, arguing that in addition to the CFSP, Articles 82 and 87 TFEU should have been used since

55 The Court held that the Parliament's right to be kept informed of the negotiation of a CFSP agreement (although it has no right of consent or even formal consultation) is an essential procedural requirement: Judgment of 24 June 2014, *European Parliament* v *Council*, *supra* note 45, paras 80-86.

56 Judgment of 14 June 2016, *European Parliament* v *Council*, *supra* note 50.

the agreement also concerned judicial cooperation in criminal matters and police cooperation. Had these legal bases been included, then the Parliament's consent would have been required under Article 218, paragraph 6, a, v, TFEU. The Court's starting point is important; it referred to Articles 275 TFEU and 40 TEU as the basis for its jurisdiction but then immediately reiterated its standard approach to legal basis.[57] So it is clear that in applying Article 40 TEU the choice between a CFSP and a non-CFSP legal basis is no different from any other legal basis choice. The Court then established that the agreement has a clear link to the CFSP, since it is envisaged by, and designed to facilitate, the EU's Operation Atalanta, which is itself designed to give effect to the UN Security Council's mandate. Indeed, the agreement is "merely ancillary" to the CFSP mission and once the mission ceases it will be "devoid of purpose". Finally, the Court decided that although some of the activities envisaged by the agreement appear to relate to judicial or police cooperation (the transfer and trial of suspected pirates, together with due process safeguards), these activities are inseparably linked to the CFSP mission; they are "an instrument whereby the European Union pursues the objectives of Operation Atalanta, namely to preserve international peace and security, in particular by making it possible to ensure that the perpetrators of acts of piracy do not go unpunished".[58] It concluded that the agreement fell predominantly within the scope of the CFSP and not police or judicial cooperation. Again we find a preference not only for a single legal basis but also for an explicit external legal basis (CFSP) over an implied external dimension to an internal (AFSJ) legal basis, where the context for the act is essentially external (here, a UN Security Council Resolution and a CFSP military mission).

The key to the Court's decision was the close link between the agreement and the CFSP mission giving effect to a UN Security Council Resolution, just as the key to its decision in the counter-terrorism case was the link to a CFSP decision implementing a UN Security Council Resolution. What the Court conspicuously does not do in either case is to attempt a categorization of "security", as it appears in the Area of Freedom, Security and Justice and in the Common Foreign and Security Policy. Such a categorization had been suggested by Advocate General Bot in the Mauritius agreement case,[59] and was accepted by Advocate General Kokott in the

57 *Id.*, paras 42-44. For the standard approach, see citation *supra* note 9.

58 *Id.*, para 54.

59 Opinion of AG Bot, *supra* note 53, para 112.

Tanzania case.[60] According to this argument, "a Union action must be connected with the CFSP where the objective of that action is, first and foremost, peace, stability and democratic development in a region outside the Union". In contrast, action under the AFSJ must contribute to building freedom, security and justice within the EU. This building of the AFSJ may require external action, but in order for external action to be based on an AFSJ legal basis (such as police cooperation) it must relate back to the security of the EU itself. The argument coheres with the rationale for implied powers in that external AFSJ powers should be exercised in order to attain AFSJ Treaty objectives, which are predominantly internal.[61] Thus an international agreement on police cooperation may use an AFSJ legal basis and implied external powers as long as the agreement is directed at furthering the security of the Union, albeit it may also have a strong dimension directed at strengthening international security – the PNR agreements with the USA and Australia would be an example here,[62] as would the "SWIFT" agreement with the USA on the transfer of financial messaging data.[63] As the Advocate General recognises, however, it is often difficult to separate internal and external security in practice and security threats the other side of the world may also threaten Europe. The security of the Union cannot be confined to threats of purely domestic origin.

The Court's approach, wisely, is not to try to categorise different aspects of security but rather to focus on the international context. This is in line with the approach it has adopted, as we have seen, in deciding whether a measure falls within the CCP, where the focus has been on identifying a link to external trade rather than on categorizing different aspects of IPR, services regulation or foreign direct investment. Just as the use of services regulation instruments does not necessarily entail the use of an internal market legal basis, so the fact that police cooperation or training is involved does not *per se* bring the measure within the AFSJ.

---

60 Opinion of AG Kokott of 28 October 2015, *European Parliament* v *Council*, C-263/14, EU:C:2015:729, paras 63-70.

61 On the rationale for implied external powers, see further below.

62 Council Decision 2012/381/EU OJ 2012 L 186/3; Council Decision 2012/472/EU OJ 2012 L 215/4, both based on Articles Article 82, paragraph 1, d and Article 87, paragraph 2, a, TFEU in conjunction with Article 218, paragraph 6, a, TFEU.

63 Council Decision 2010/412/EU on the conclusion of the Agreement between the European Union and the United States of America on the processing and transfer of Financial Messaging Data from the European Union to the United States for the purposes of the Terrorist Finance Tracking Program, OJ 2010 L 195/3.

C. Development Cooperation

The third type of express external competence we shall discuss here concerns the ability of the Union to conclude development cooperation agreements of broad scope.[64] In the early years of the Community, international agreements with strong development objectives such as the Yaoundé and Lomé Conventions were concluded as association agreements, but the Maastricht Treaty introduced a specific development cooperation competence, including the possibility of concluding agreements with developing countries.[65] The scope and limits of such agreements have been contested; development after all has potentially very broad economic, social and cultural dimensions. In a case decided in 1996 the Court of Justice held that a development cooperation agreement should be characterized according to its "essential object" and could legitimately contain clauses covering many different spheres of cooperation "provided that those clauses do not impose such extensive obligations concerning the specific matters referred to that those obligations in fact constitute objectives distinct from those of development cooperation" and are "limited to determining the areas for cooperation and to specifying certain of its aspects and various actions to which special importance is attached".[66]

The conditions under which a separate legal basis would be needed for specific sectoral clauses in a development agreement have recently been addressed again by the Court and the result has been an affirmation of this earlier ruling. The case involved the signing of a framework agreement on partnership and cooperation between the EU (and its Member States) and the Philippines.[67] The Commission proposed two substantive legal bases: the common commercial policy (Article 207 TFEU) and development cooperation (Article 209 TFEU). The Council adopted its decision on the signature of the agreement adding several more legal bases: Articles 91 and 100 TFEU (transport), Article 79, paragraph 3, TFEU (readmission of illegal migrants) and Article 191, paragraph 4, TFEU (environment). The Commission challenged the addition of these legal bases, putting forward

64 Article 209 TFEU. Note that Articles 212 and 217 TFEU also provide the basis for wide-ranging cooperation and association agreements.

65 Now Articles 208-211 TFEU.

66 Judgment of 3 December 1996, *Portuguese Republic* v *Council*, C-268/94, EU:C:1996:461, paras 39 and 45.

67 Judgment of the Court of 11 June 2014, *Commission* v *Council*, *supra* note 9.

three arguments. First, that all three sectors in question fall within the scope of development cooperation as evidenced by the European Consensus on Development and the EU's financial instrument on development cooperation.[68] Second, that none of the relevant provisions in the agreement contain obligations substantial enough to require a separate legal basis, and to the extent that they establish specific objectives these are „incidental" to the main development objective. And third, that the inclusion of Article 79, paragraph 3, TFEU as a legal basis for the clause on readmission would create uncertainty since Protocols 21 and 22 would hence apply (these are the AFSJ opt-outs applicable to the UK, Ireland and Denmark) and this "variable geometry" in the application of the agreement would be "difficult for the contracting third country to follow".[69]

The Court of Justice essentially supported the Commission's arguments. It refers to the "broad notion of development cooperation", as reflected in the (non-binding) European Consensus on Development. Although development is not in the title of the agreement and appears simply to form one of its several objectives, in analyzing the agreement's provisions the Court finds that sustainable development, the Millennium Development Goals and the reduction of poverty (this last being the "primary objective" of development policy under Article 208, paragraph 1, TFEU) are among its general principles and are linked to many other provisions in the agreement. The question for the Court was whether the provisions on transport, environment and readmission contribute to the aim of development and if so, whether they contain obligations which "constitute distinct objectives that are neither secondary nor indirect in relation to the objectives of development cooperation".[70]

As far as the first question is concerned, the Court had no difficulty in finding a link between these substantive fields of cooperation and the development objectives of the EU's policy frameworks, in particular the European Consensus on Development and the EU's financial instrument

68 The European Consensus on Development, adopted as a joint statement by the Council, the representatives of the Member States meeting in Council, the Commission and the European Parliament, OJ 2006 C 46/1; The financial instrument relevant at the time was Regulation 1905/2006/EC, OJ 2006 L 378/41.

69 Opinion of AG Mengozzi of 23 January 2014, *Commission* v *Council*, EU:C:2014:29, C-377/12, para 16.

70 Judgment of the Court of 11 June 2014, *Commission* v *Council, supra* note 9, para 48.

for development cooperation. That being said, the readmission clause merits further consideration. It is hard not to conclude that its main purpose is "the implementation of another policy" – that is, the EU's policy on irregular migration.[71] The fact that it is included in a provision headed "migration and development" should not in itself be decisive. As Advocate General Mengozzi pointed out in his opinion (albeit coming finally to the same conclusion as the Court), the clauses on readmission "depart from the [agreement's] first concern – steady progress in development in the Philippines – to fulfil one of the European Union's own objectives and to serve its interests: the commitment by the contracting third country to take back its own nationals who are illegally resident in European Union territory". The "vision" is a "defensive one which places European Union interests first".[72] The Advocate General nevertheless accepted the link to development on the basis that development assistance is part of the *quid pro quo* which has induced the Philippines to accept the readmission clause. The point illustrates the difficulty of pinning down the objectives of international agreements for the purposes of identifying legal basis where the objectives of the different parties are likely to be different.

The second question was also tricky when applied to the readmission clause, since unlike the provisions on transport and environment it contains specific obligations, not merely general commitments to cooperate. The Council argued that although the obligation on a State to readmit its own nationals is derived directly from international law, the inclusion of these provisions in the agreement created additional legal effects (meaning by this, the possibility of specific enforcement measures). The Court however held that the agreement does not itself contain concrete provisions on the implementation of this obligation; instead it refers to the future conclusion of a readmission agreement. Its conclusion therefore was that the readmission clause did not contain obligations going beyond development cooperation and an additional legal basis was not necessary.

Thus we may conclude that development cooperation agreements, like the CFSP, are capable of covering a broad range of issues and, like the CCP, may accommodate a variety of different objectives. The express development cooperation competence can be used as long as the provisions of the agreement may be said to contribute – even somewhat indirectly –

---

71 *Id.*, para 44.
72 Opinion of AG Mengozzi, *supra* note 69, paras 70-71.

to the agreement's overall development aims, and as long as they do not contain substantive obligations which are sufficiently distinct to require their own separate legal basis. Again, this suggests that insofar as sectoral policies such as transport or environment are included in such broad agreements, separate sectoral legal bases using implied external powers may not in general be required. This approach of the Court of Justice forces the decision-maker to identify a predominant purpose – generally an expressly external one – and the complexity of an agreement may not be reflected in the resulting choice of a single legal basis: the ancillary or secondary objectives are less visible than if they carried their own legal basis. But we need to bear in mind the following points.

First, the Court's approach accurately reflects the reason for establishing legal basis, which is the principle of conferral. Legal basis is necessary to ground competence to act. It is not intended to be a description of the content of a measure. So only those legal bases should be included which are necessary and sufficient to ground competence. Hence the emphasis on whether the substantive obligations in an international agreement are such as to require a separate legal basis – a separate ground of competence.

Second, although the broad express legal bases discussed here may be used to subsume sectoral elements of an agreement, we are here talking about the conclusion, not the implementation of the agreement. The implementation of specific obligations in an agreement may require a different, sectoral, legal basis. This was clear in our discussion of the CCP cases, where the external and internal dimensions are kept distinct by the Court. In its discussion of the Philippines partnership and cooperation agreement, the Court – in support of its argument that an additional legal basis was not necessary – refers to the need to implement the readmission clause in the cooperation agreement through the conclusion of a specific readmission agreement.[73] In an earlier judgment on the scope of development cooperation the Court pointed out that " [t]he mere inclusion of provisions for cooperation in a specific field does not … predetermine … the legal basis of Community acts for implementing cooperation in such a field".[74] Thus it is in the context of implementation that the more specific sectoral legal bases might come into the picture: the inclusion in a development

73 Judgment of the Court of 11 June 2014, *Commission* v *Council*, *supra* note 9, para 58.

74 Judgment of 3 December 1996, *Portuguese Republic* v *Council*, *supra* note 66, para 47.

cooperation agreement of a provision on matters falling within the scope of the AFSJ, transport or other sectoral policy fields does not pre-judge the question of whether a distinct legal basis will be needed for implementing measures, whether by way of a further agreement or by way of an autonomous act.

Three recent cases involving the updating of sectoral annexes to association agreements illustrate this point. Each case concerned the appropriate legal basis for a Council decision regarding the position to be taken by the EU within the decision-making body established by an association agreement in order to take account of the EU's revision of its regulation on social security for migrant workers.[75] In each case there was a dispute as to the appropriate legal basis for the decision, with the UK disagreeing with the Council's ultimate choice. For present purposes, it is of interest that in all three cases the Court found that an internal, sectoral legal basis was necessary, confirming that the Council had been correct to use Article 48 TFEU (the basis for internal social security measures). In two of the cases – those involving the European Economic Area and the agreement with Switzerland on the free movement of persons – Article 48 TFEU was sufficient on its own, given that the agreement envisaged extending the EU's own freedom of movement legislation to the third countries in question.[76] It is only in the third case, which concerned the association agreement with Turkey, that the Court held that a combination of an internal legal basis (Article 48 TFEU) with Article 217 TFEU (the basis for association agreements) would be appropriate, since the measure was "adopted in the framework of an association agreement and is aimed at the adoption of measures coordinating social security systems".[77]

According to the principle of conferral, then, the EU may use its express treaty-making powers in these policy fields (whether CCP, CFSP or development cooperation) to conclude agreements which include provisions relating to policy fields where specific internal powers, or specific internal legislation, exist. But where particular obligations in these agreements are implemented, or the institutions they establish take decisions de-

---

75 Judgment of 26 September 2013, *UK* v *Council*, C-431/11, EU:C:2013:589; Judgment of 27 February 2014, *UK* v *Council*, C-656/11, EU:C:2014:97; Judgment of 18 December 2014, *UK* v *Council*, C-81/13, EU:C:2014:2449.

76 Judgment of 26 September 2013, *UK* v *Council*, and Judgment of 27 February 2014, *UK* v *Council*, *supra* note 75.

77 Judgment of 18 December 2014, *UK* v *Council*, *supra* note 75, para 63.

signed to further their objectives in specific fields, then the powers relative to those policy fields should be used, either alone or in conjunction with the external competence.

III. The Rationale *for Implied Powers*

Against this background, what then is the rationale for, and scope of, implied external powers? The original Treaty of Rome contained only two express external fields of action, the common commercial policy and the power to conclude association agreements and as we have seen these provisions were – and are – interpreted broadly. Nonetheless these competences clearly could not cover everything and it was quite common for Article 235 EEC (now Article 352 TFEU) to be used as an additional legal basis for non-association agreements which included provisions on cooperation in addition to trade.[78] Against this background, the Court made its decisive move in the *ERTA* decision, using the fact that the Community had legal personality as a basis for reasoning that "in its external relations the Community enjoys the capacity to establish contractual links with third countries over the whole field of objectives defined in Part One of the Treaty".[79] Whether this capacity translates into a power in a specific case depends on an examination not only of the expressly-stated external competences but also "other Treaty provisions" and measures adopted on the basis of those provisions by the Community's institutions.

The line of case law since *ERTA* establishes two basic rationales for implying external powers.[80] The first, derived from *ERTA* itself, is based on the existence of internal legislation, whether or not adopted within the framework of a common policy,[81] and is founded on pre-emption, the oc-

78 See for example Council Regulation 2300/76/EEC of 20 September 1976 concluding the Framework Agreement for commercial and economic cooperation between the European Communities and Canada, OJ 1976 L 260/1, which was based on Articles 113 and 235 EEC (now as amended Article 207 and 352 TFEU).

79 Judgment of 31 March 1971, *Commission* v *Council, supra* note 7, para 14.

80 A. Dashwood, J. Heliskoski, "The Classic Authorities Revisited", in A. Dashwood, C. Hillion (eds), *The General Law of EC External Relations* (London: Sweet & Maxwell, 2000), 11.

81 Judgment of 31 March 1971, *Commission* v *Council, supra* note 7; Opinion of 19 March 1993, 2/91, *Convention no. 170 of the International Labour Organization concerning safety in the use of chemicals at work,* EU:C:1993:106.

cupation of the field by existing Community or Union law (hence the equation in *ERTA* between the existence of the competence and its exclusive nature[82]). The second relies on the existence of an objective established by the Treaty, for the attainment of which Treaty-based internal powers may be complemented by external powers; this rationale is based on the principle of *effet utile*, the implication of powers necessary to achieve an expressly-defined objective. As recently expressed by the Court,

> "[W]henever EU law creates for those institutions powers within its internal system for the purpose of attaining a specific objective, the EU has authority to undertake international commitments necessary for the attainment of that objective even in the absence of an express provision to that effect".[83]

We can also see the *effet utile* rationale in operation in Opinion 2/15, where it provides the basis for implied (non-exclusive) external competence in the field of non-direct investment protection.[84]

> "[I]n the light of the fact that the free movement of capital and payments between Member States and third States, laid down in Article 63 TFEU, is not formally binding on third States, the conclusion of international agreements which contribute to the establishment of such free movement on a reciprocal basis may be classified as necessary in order to achieve fully such free movement, which is one of the objectives of … the FEU Treaty".[85]

Both these rationales – which we may call the *ERTA* rationale and the *effet utile* rationale – suggest an underlying distinction between the competence granted by the Treaty to act within a particular policy field (e.g. movement of capital), and the power to exercise that competence through internal

---

82 In a famous passage the Court says, "each time the Community, with a view to implementing a common policy envisaged by the Treaty, adopts provisions laying down common rules, whatever form these may take, the member states no longer have the right, acting individually or even collectively, to undertake obligations with third countries which affect those rules". Judgment of 31 March 1971, *Commission* v *Council, supra* note 7, para 17.

83 Opinion of 14 October 2014, 1/13, *Convention on the Civil Aspects of International Child Abduction*, EU:C:2014:2303, para 67, citing also Opinion of 7 February 2006, 1/03, *Competence of the Community to conclude the new Lugano Convention on Jurisdiction and the Recognition and Enforcement of Judgments in Civil and Commercial Matters,* EU:C:2006:81, para 114.

84 Opinion of 16 May 2017, 2/15, *supra* note 24, paras 239-242.

85 *Id.*, para 240.

and/or external instruments.[86] This distinction is useful conceptually to understand the rationale for implied external powers and is consistent with the use made of the term "competence" in Articles 2-6 TFEU, but it must be said at once that as far as terminology is concerned it is impossible to find a consistent distinction between "competence" and "power" in the judgments of the Court. In any event both the *ERTA* rationale and the *effet utile* rationale suggest an organic link and a complementarity between the internal competence-conferring provision and the implied external power, in the first case through the exercise of that competence at the internal level and in the second through the necessity to enter into international commitments to attain the (internal) objective. The *effet utile* rationale emphasises the Treaty objectives: it is based on external powers being required to complement internal powers so as to achieve the objectives of a Treaty-based competence, and it is this rationale that has been called the "principle of complementarity" by Dashwood and Heliskoski.[87] In contrast, in the case of the *ERTA* rationale the link between the exercise of internal competence and the existence of the external power can appear somewhat perfunctory in the reasoning of the Court of Justice, especially in cases where the site of disagreement is over the possible exclusive nature – rather than the existence – of that external power. In Opinion 1/13, for example, the reasoning takes the form of a simple assertion of an internal competence which has been exercised:

> "In the matter in issue, the 1980 Hague Convention concerns civil cooperation where children are moved across borders. The Convention thus falls within the area of family law with cross-border implications in which the EU has internal competence under Article 81, paragraph 3, TFEU. Moreover, the EU has exercised that competence by adopting Regulation 2201/2003. In those circumstances, the EU has external competence in the area which forms the subject-matter of the Convention".[88]

No attention – at this stage of identifying the existence of external powers – seems to be paid to the objectives of the internal competence; in con-

86 T Tridimas, P Eeckhout, "The External Competence of the Community and the Case Law of the Court of Justice – Principle versus Pragmatism", *Yearbook of European Law* 14, (1994), 143; R Schütze, *Foreign Affairs and the EU Constitution*, (Cambridge: Cambridge University Press, 2014), 250.

87 A Dashwood, J Heliskoski, "The Classic Authorities Revisited", *supra* note 80, at 12, preferring the term to the commonly-used "principle of parallelism".

88 Opinion of 14 October 2014, 1/13, *supra* note 83, para 68. See also Opinion of 7 February 2006, 1/03, *supra* note 83, para 134.

trast, they are extensively discussed in the context of determining whether or not the external competence is exclusive. But the objectives of the internal competence are there in the background, since they are reflected in the internal legislation on which the existence of external powers is based. Thus the priority given to protecting or facilitating internal objectives and the associated competence is common to both rationales, and both are clearly distinguishable from the argument (unsuccessfully) put forward by the Commission in Opinion 1/94 which simply claims an external competence in every policy field for which an internal competence exists.[89] On the contrary, implied external powers are inherently limited and cannot provide the basis for developing an external policy independent of the needs and functioning of the internal regime. For that, explicit external competences (such as those we were examining in the previous section) are needed. This is coherent in terms of the balance between the necessary flexibility provided by an implied powers doctrine and the need to ensure compliance with the principle of conferred powers.

These rationales for implied external powers are now visible in the Treaty provisions on external competences, which aim to reflect existing case law. According to Article 216, paragraph 1, TFEU

> "The Union may conclude an agreement with one or more third countries or international organisations where the Treaties so provide or where the conclusion of an agreement is necessary in order to achieve, within the framework of the Union's policies, one of the objectives referred to in the Treaties, or is provided for in a legally binding Union act or is likely to affect common rules or alter their scope".

We find here a reference to express external powers ("where the Treaties so provide"), to the *effet utile* rationale ("where the conclusion of an agreement is necessary in order to achieve, within the framework of the Union's policies, one of the objectives referred to in the Treaties"), and the *ERTA* rationale ("where the conclusion of an agreement … is provided for in a legally binding Union act or is likely to affect common rules or alter their scope").

What, if anything, does this provision add to the pre-existing case law? While seeking to reflect the case law on implied external powers, Article 216, paragraph 1, TFEU does not create a new substantive legal basis for

89 The argument was rejected by the Court in Opinion 1/94, the Court insisting on the need to link the external power to the specific objective established in the Treaty: Opinion of 15 November 1994, 1/94, *supra* note 32, paras 74-75.

the conclusion of international agreements. As Advocate General Kokott rightly says, "Article 216, paragraph 1, TFEU must not be confused with a general conferral of powers on the Union institutions for external action. On the contrary, an external competence can only ever be inferred from that rule in conjunction with the provisions of the Treaties, objectives of the Union, legal acts and rules of Union law mentioned in it".[90] So a substantive provision in the Treaties is still required as a legal basis for an international agreement based on implied powers, in addition to a reference to Article 218 TFEU which is the procedural legal basis for concluding international agreements. In fact although Advocate General Kokott has proposed that, where implied external powers are relied on, Article 216, paragraph 1, TFEU should be included as a legal basis alongside the substantive legal basis (the specific competence-conferring provision) to demonstrate clearly the link between the internal competence and the implied external power, neither the practice of the institutions nor the judgments of the Court have (so far) followed this approach.[91] Thus, for example, when discussing Article 63 TFEU as the basis for external competence in the field of non-direct investment protection, the Court referred to Article 216, paragraph 1, TFEU, but there was no suggestion that the latter was required as a legal basis.[92] And agreements in the field of environmental policy have been concluded on the basis of Article 192 TFEU (the internal environmental policy competence); the concluding decision may mention that the agreement "contributes to the achievement of the objectives of the environmental policy of the Union", reflecting the words of Article 216, paragraph 1, TFEU, but that provision is not included among its legal bases.[93]

---

90 Opinion of AG Kokott of 17 July 2014, *UK* v *Council*, C-81/13, EU:C:2014:2114, para 102.

91 For the Advocate General's views on this point, which this author finds convincing, see Opinion of AG Kokott of 17 July 2014, *supra* note 90, para 104; Opinion of AG Kokott of 21 March 2013, *United Kingdom* v *Council*, C-431/11, EU:C:2013:187, paras 64-70; Opinion of AG Kokott of 28 October 2015, *supra* note 60, EU:C:2015:729, para 58.

92 See *supra* note 84.

93 See for example Council Decision 2013/86/EU of 12 February 2013 on the conclusion on behalf of the European Union of the Nagoya-Kuala Lumpur Supplementary Protocol on Liability and Redress to the Cartagena Protocol on Biosafety, OJ 2013 L46/1. See also Council Decision 2013/5/EU of 17 December 2012 on the accession of the European Union to the Protocol for the Protection of the

As these examples illustrate, there is certainly still some room for implied external powers, especially for the conclusion of international agreements dealing with action in a specific sector. Agreements concerning transport,[94] agriculture[95] or fisheries[96] – when not simply forming part of a wider agreement which may be based on an express competence[97] – will be concluded under implied powers. In such cases, although there may be disputes over the precise purpose of a measure,[98] the sectoral objectives of EU policy are relatively clear. In contrast, the AFSJ and its relationship with the EU's CFSP competence, as we have already seen, raise complex questions about the nature of the AFSJ and its objectives. It has rightly been pointed out that although external action is necessary if the EU is to achieve its objective of offering its citizens an area of freedom, security and justice,[99] "the main rationale of the AFSJ as a political project is clearly an internal one", and its external dimension is instrumental to that rationale and objective, and thus "cannot be considered as an external policy in its own right, like the CCP or the CFSP, but only as an instrumental ancillary dimension of the essentially internal political project of the AFSJ".[100] The Treaty of Lisbon has not changed this essential orientation: interna-

Mediterranean Sea against pollution resulting from exploration and exploitation of the continental shelf and the seabed and its subsoil, OJ 2013 L4/13.

94 Article 207, paragraph 5, TFEU.

95 Judgment of 7 October 2014, *Germany* v *Council*, C-399/12, EU:C:2014:2258.

96 Judgment of 26 November 2014, *European Parliament* v *Council*, *European Commission v Council*, C-103/12 & C-165/12, EU:C:2014:2400.

97 Opinion of 15 November 1994, 1/94, *supra* note 32; Opinion of 30 November 2009, 1/08, *General Agreement on Trade in Services (GATS) – Schedules of Specific Commitments Concerning Market Access and Granting of National Treatment*, EU:C:2009:739; Opinion of 16 May 2017, 2/15, *supra* note 24.

98 As Opinion 2/00 illustrates, the boundary between the trade and environmental competences may not be easy to draw. See Opinion of 6 December 2001, 2/00, *Cartagena Protocol*, EU:C:2001:664; see also Judgment of 12 December 2002, *Commission* v *Council*, C-281/01, EU:C:2002:761; Judgment of 10 January 2006, *Commission* v *Parliament and Council,* C-178/03, EU:C:2006:4; Judgment of 10 January 2006, *Commission* v *Council,* C-94/03, EU:C:2006:2.

99 "The Union shall offer its citizens an area of freedom, security and justice without internal frontiers, in which the free movement of persons is ensured in conjunction with appropriate measures with respect to external border controls, asylum, immigration and the prevention and combating of crime". Article 3, paragraph 2, TEU.

100 J Monar, "The External Dimension of the EU's Area of Freedom, Security and Justice: Progress, potential and limitations after the Treaty of Lisbon", *SIEPS Re-*

tional agreements will need to show that they fall within either the *effet utile* or the *ERTA* rationale in the context of the EU's internal objectives. For an example of the former in the AFSJ field we may look to a number of agreements providing for cooperation between law enforcement agencies that have been concluded on the basis of implied external powers founded upon the AFSJ.[101] For an example of the latter, the EU is becoming increasingly active in the field of private international law, both in the adoption of internal legislation and in the conclusion of international agreements which take as their legal basis the internal legislative competence-conferring provisions on civil justice.[102] The specialised, highly sectoral nature of this legislation when used as a rationale for implied external powers has resulted in a number of rulings of exclusive external competence.[103]

IV. Conclusion

In a series of cases arising since the Lisbon Treaty it has been argued that internal Treaty powers, either one of the AFSJ powers or the internal market, should provide the – or one of the – legal bases for an external mea-

---

port 2012/1, 13. Along the same lines, see Opinion of AG Kokott of 28 October 2015, *supra* note 60, para 63.

101 See for example the PNR agreements with the USA and Australia, Council Decision 2012/381/EU, OJ 2012 L 186/3; Council Decision 2012/472/EU, OJ 2012 L 215/4, both based on Articles Article 82, paragraph 1, d, and Article 87, paragraph 2, a, TFEU in conjunction with Article 218, paragraph 6, a, TFEU.

102 See for example Council Decision on the approval, on behalf of the European Union, of the Hague Convention of 23 November 2007 on the International Recovery of Child Support and Other Forms of Family Maintenance, OJ 2011 L 192/39.

103 E.g. Opinion of 7 February 2006, 1/03, *supra* note 83; Opinion of 14 October 2014, 1/13, *supra* note 83. We do not have the space here for a full discussion of this question; see for example P. Franzina (ed), *The External Dimension of EU Private International Law after Opinion 1/13,* (Cambridge: Intersentia, 2016); A. Rosas, "Exclusive, Shared and National Competence in the Context of EU External Relations: Do such Distinctions Matter?", in I. Govaere, P. Van Elsuwege, S. Adam, E. Lannon (eds.), *The EU in the World: Essays in Honour of Marc Maresceau*, (Leiden: Martinus Nijhoff, 2013), 17; I. Govaere, "'Setting the International Scene': EU External Competence and Procedures Post-Lisbon Revisited in the Light of ECJ Opinion 1/13", *Common Market Law Review*, 52, no. 5 (2015), 1277, at 1286-1295.

sure. In only two of these cases has the argument been even partially successful.[104] The express competences (the CCP, the CFSP, development cooperation) have prevailed. This, it seems to me, is no coincidence. These external policies may seek to extend beyond the EU's borders the regulatory approach developed by the EU in building the internal market, or may use AFSJ instruments such as police cooperation to achieve their objectives; but this does not necessarily require the use of internal market or AFSJ powers. The Court has avoided categorizing as "internal" or "external" different aspects of IPR, services regulation, investment protection or security. The touchstone is not the specific instruments used but rather the context in, and the purposes for which, they are used. And as we have seen, even where a specific express external power exists (such as for readmission agreements) or specific provisions are included that will improve the functioning of the internal market, alternative legal bases may still be preferred by the Court of Justice on the ground that the centre of gravity (predominant purpose) of the measure in question lies elsewhere.

This certainly does not mean that there is no scope for an external dimension, based on implied powers, to the internal market, the AFSJ or other primarily "internal" policy fields, but such instruments will need to contribute to the attainment of the objectives for which the internal competences have been granted and to demonstrate either the *ERTA* or the *effet utile* rationale, as now expressed in Article 216, paragraph 1, TFEU, and will tend to be sectoral in nature. Agreements on visa facilitation and readmission[105] are concluded with third countries, likewise agreements on specific private international law domains; all these have a clear link to Union territory and the Union's own legal systems at domestic and European level. Agreements on law enforcement and counter-terrorism cooperation may also be concluded, and autonomous measures adopted, as long as there appears to be a link with the Union's security, and (perhaps) as long as their centre of gravity does not lie in the Union's contribution to international cooperation in the context of the United Nations. As far as the in-

104 The only exceptions are the rejection of the CCP as a legal basis for an IPR agreement (Opinion of 14 February 2017, 3/15, *supra* note 27), and the application of the exclusion of transport services and non-direct investment from the CCP (Opinion of 16 May 2017, 2/15, *supra* note 24).

105 Since the Lisbon Treaty readmission agreements have their own express legal basis in Article 79, paragraph 3, TFEU; previously they were based on implied powers.

ternal market is concerned, external measures, including regulatory agreements, are likely to fall within the expanded CCP. An internal market legal basis may be appropriate where the measure is essentially designed to improve the operation of the internal market, the external dimension serving that internal purpose. In the field of intellectual property, an agreement may be designed to harmonise IPR and improve IPR protection without being concerned with promoting international trade, and in such a case an internal market rather than a CCP legal basis would be appropriate.[106]

Given the breadth of express external policy fields and their legal bases, including the CFSP, and given the approach taken by the Court to multiple legal bases (they are exceptional), if one of the broadly-framed express legal bases is chosen by the legislature it is difficult to challenge the choice. As far as the CFSP was concerned, before the Lisbon Treaty revision this was balanced by the precedence given to the EC Treaty; now, the CFSP has equal value. In the *conditional access services* case although the legal basis chosen by the Council and challenged by the Commission was the implied internal market legal basis, the Court (as with *Daiichi Sankyo*) chose to start its reasoning with an analysis of the possible express competence – the CCP – and duly found that the agreement could be fitted within the scope of that provision. In Opinion 2/15, too, the Court starts by examining how much of the agreement can be brought within the scope of the CCP, before considering other implied external powers. In each of the cases we have discussed, then, the express legal basis was the starting point; a case needed to be made (and was not often successfully made) for turning to an implied power.

This of course is perfectly logical, and it is consistent with the principle of conferral to prefer an express over an implied power. But it also has implications for the principle of conferral. Although implied powers might seem to put some strain on that principle, in fact their connection with the Treaty's internal competences and legislation adopted in furtherance of those objectives provides an identifiable Treaty-based rationale for external action. Express external competences, on the other hand are in themselves a conferral of powers. Their open-ended nature is designed to allow the Union to develop as an external actor, using a wide variety of instruments (including those "borrowed" from internal policy fields), and evolv-

106 See e.g. Judgment of 4 September 2014, *Commission* v *Council*, C-114/12, EU:C:2014: 2151; Opinion of 14 February 2017, 3/15, *supra* note 27.

ing its objectives and priorities in line with the Treaty-based objectives and principles governing all external action, but with considerable scope for institutionally-defined policy choice. The principles governing the process whereby such policy choice is made are therefore all the more important.[107]

107 M. Cremona, "Structural Principles and their Role in EU External Relations Law", *supra*, note 2.

The Dynamic of the EU Objectives in the Analysis of the External Competence

Eleftheria Neframi

I. Introduction

The link between objectives and competences, inherent in the principle of conferral,[1] is expressed through the choice of legal basis for the conclusion of an international agreement. The legal basis determines the vertical allocation of competences between the European Union (EU) and its Member States. It is identified according to objective factors, amenable to judicial review, such as the aim and content of the international agreement and of the decision of the Council approving it.[2] In choosing the legal basis, ancillary objectives of the international agreement are absorbed by the dominant ones.[3]

However, the nature of the EU competence is not necessarily determined by the identified legal basis. Indeed, if the legal basis is an express external competence, the nature of the Union's competence stems from the Treaties. In contrast, if the legal basis is an internal competence, the nature of the EU external competence is dependent on the exclusivity criteria of

1 See Article 5, paragraph 1, of the Treaty on the European Union (TEU) : "Under the principle of conferral, the Union s hall act only within the limits of the competences conferred upon it by the Member States in the Treaties to attain the objectives set out therein".

2 Among the abundant literature: S. Adam, "The Legal Basis of International Agreements of the European Union in the Post-Lisbon Era", in I. Govaere and others (eds), *The European Union in the World; Essays in Honor of Marc Maresceau* (Leiden: Martinus Nijhoff, 2014), 78; M. Klamert, "Conflicts of Legal Basis: no Legality and no Basis but a Bright Future under the Lisbon Treaty", *European Law Review* 35, no. 4 (2010), 497; P. Koutrakos, "Legal Basis and Delimitation of Competence in EU External Relations", in M. Cremona, B. De Witte (eds), *EU Foreign Relations Law: Constitutional Fundamentals* (Oxford: Hart Publishing, 2008), 171; K. Lenaerts, "EU Federalism in 3D", in E. Cloots, G. De Baere, S. Sottiaux (eds), *Federalism in the European Union* (Oxford: Hart Publishing, 2012), 23. See also, in this volume, the chapter by Mauro Gatti.

3 See also the chapter by Merijn Chamon in this volume.

Article 3, paragraph 2, of the Treaty on the Functioning of the European Union (TFEU),[4] which are not necessarily relevant to the legal basis: the legal basis of the internal measures has no importance for the exclusivity of EU external competence according to the criterion of affecting the common rules or altering their scope or according to the condition of a provision in a legislative act.

Given that the determination of the nature of the EU external competence is decisive for the conclusion of an international agreement by the Union alone, or jointly by the Union and its Member States,[5] the choice of the legal basis according to objective criteria related to the provisions of an international agreement is not sufficient. While in the internal field the definition of the legal basis of the EU competence implies either its unconditional exercise (exclusive competence) or its exercise according to the principle of subsidiarity (non-exclusive competence), in the external field the definition of the legal basis does not answer the questions as to whether the exclusivity criteria of Article 3, paragraph 2, TFEU are met, or as to whether the conclusion of an agreement by the Union alone is possible in case of shared external competence, following Article 216, paragraph 1, TFEU.[6] From a vertical division of competences perspective and

---

4 "The Union shall also have exclusive competence for the conclusion of an international agreement when its conclusion is provided for in a legislative act of the Union or is necessary to enable the Union to exercise its internal competence, or in so far as its conclusion may affect common rules or alter their scope".

5 Undoubtedly, an international agreement falling under the EU's exclusive competence is to be approved by the Union alone. However, an agreement falling under the Union's shared competence is not necessarily a mixed agreement. See: A. Dashwood, "Mixity in the Era of the Treaty of Lisbon", in C. Hillion, P. Koutrakos (eds), *Mixed Agreements Revisited* (Oxford: Hart Publishing, 2010), 356; E. Neframi, "Vertical Division of Competences and the Objectives of the European Union's External Action", in M. Cremona, A. Thies (eds), *The Court of Justice of the European Union and External Relations Law – Constitutional Challenges* (Oxford: Oxford University Press, 2014), 73; A. Rosas, "Exclusive, Shared and National Competence in the Context of EU External Relations: Do such Distinctions Matter?", in I. Govaere and others (eds), *The European Union in the World; Essays in Honor of Marc Maresceau* (Leiden: Martinus Nijhoff, 2014) 17. See also, in this volume, the chapter by M. Chamon.

6 "The Union may conclude an agreement with one or more third countries or international organisations where the Treaties so provide or where the conclusion of an agreement is necessary in order to achieve, within the framework of the Union's policies, one of the objectives referred to in the Treaties, or is provided for in a legally binding Union act or is likely to affect common rules or alter their scope".

because of the requirement of effectiveness and the need to define whether the Union may conclude an international agreement alone or together with its Member States, the question "does the Union have exclusive competence to conclude an international agreement" prevails over the question "what is the legal basis for the conclusion of an international agreement".

Taking the nature of the EU competence as the decisive criterion for the vertical division of the external competences implies an EU-objectives-oriented analysis.

The external competence of the Union is exclusive if the international agreement falls under the common commercial policy (CCP).[7] Consequently, provided that the international agreement has a link to international trade, the starting point for the competence question analysis is the CCP's scope, which is defined according to the Union's objectives and which may lead to a broader conception of the trade objective when compared to a situation in which the starting point is an analysis of the objective of the international agreement (II).

If an agreement does not fall under the scope of the CCP, the next step is to assess the exclusive nature of the Union's implied external competence. The Court of Justice first examines the criteria of Article 3, paragraph 2, TFEU,[8] especially whether the conclusion of the agreement affects common rules or alters their scope according to the *ERTA* doctrine.[9] In this context, as is well known, the exclusive external competence of the Union stems not only from the objective comparison of EU internal rules with the provisions of the international agreement, but also from an analysis of the scope, nature and content thereof, "bearing in mind that account must be taken not only of (EU) law as it now stands in the area in question but also of its future development".[10] Besides, it is considered essential to "ensure a uniform, consistent application of the (EU) rules and the proper functioning of the system they establish in order for the full effectiveness of (EU) law to be preserved".[11] As a consequence, the EU-objectives ana-

---

7 Pursuant to Article 3, paragraph 1, TFEU, "(t)he Union shall have exclusive competence in the following areas: (…) (e) common commercial policy".

8 *Supra* note 4.

9 Judgment of 31 March 1971, *Commission* v *Council (European Agreement on Road Transport -ERTA),* 22/70, EU:C:1971:32.

10 Opinion of 7 February 2006, 1/03, *Competence of the Community to conclude the new Lugano Convention on Jurisdiction and the Recognition and Enforcement of Judgments in Civil and Commercial Matters,* EU:C:2006:81, para 126.

11 *Id.,* para 128.

lysis prevails over a neutral comparison of the EU's and the international agreement's provisions. Moreover, the definition of the legal basis has no importance for the vertical division of competences, once the criterion of Article 3, paragraph 2, TFEU is met (III).

If a Union's external implied competence turns out not to be exclusive, the Court's next step is to answer the question as to whether the conclusion of a mixed agreement is mandatory.[12] The ability of the Union to exercise its competence directly in external fields depends, however, on the objective pursued. Article 216, paragraph 1, TFEU is also based on an EU-objectives approach, entailing a particular dynamic in the exercise of the EU external competence (IV).

However, the EU-objectives-oriented analysis of the question of the competence to conclude an international agreement is not without ambiguity. It may impact the classic distinction between substantive and ancillary provisions of the international agreement, which is not necessarily in line with effectiveness (V).

II. The Scope of the Common Commercial Policy

The definition of the scope of the CCP in order to establish the exclusivity of the Union's external competence follows a methodology close to that of the choice of legal basis, according to which certain objective factors, such as the content and the purpose of the international agreement, are evaluated.[13] However, as the Court of Justice's starting point, from an effectiveness-oriented EU approach, is to define the scope of any exclusive EU competence, the initial objective examination of the content and the purpose of the international agreement is highly influenced by the EU objectives expressed in Article 207, paragraph 1, TFEU,[14] which leads to a

---

12 *Supra,* note 5.

13 B. Van Vooren, R. Wessel, *EU External Relations Law* (Cambridge : Cambridge University Press, 2014), 158.

14 "The common commercial policy shall be based on uniform principles, particularly with regard to changes in tariff rates, the conclusion of tariff and trade agreements relating to trade in goods and services, and the commercial aspects of intellectual property, foreign direct investment, the achievement of uniformity in measures of liberalisation, export policy and measures to protect trade such as those to be taken in the event of dumping or subsidies. The common commercial policy

global approach to the provisions of the international agreement (A) and to a global approach to the EU objectives (B).

A. The Global Approach to the International Agreement

In order to determine whether an international agreement falls under the scope of the CCP, the Court of Justice, following well-settled jurisprudence, examines the link between the agreement and international trade and its effects thereon.[15] The objective-factors-based approach is followed as far as the link between the agreement and international trade and its effects thereon are not evident. The Court of Justice applies, thus, the absorption doctrine, in order to distinguish between the main and the ancillary objectives of the international agreement. For instance, in Opinion 3/15, the Court of Justice held that the non-commercial objective of the Marrakesh Treaty to Facilitate Access to Published Works for Persons Who are Blind, Visually Impaired, or Otherwise Print Disabled, prevailed and, without naming a legal basis for the conclusion of that agreement, excluded it from the scope of the CCP.[16] Following an objective examination of the purpose and the content of the Lisbon Agreement on Appellations of Origin and Geographical Indications, and after examining its specific link to international trade and its effects thereon, the Court of Justice held that its commercial purpose prevailed, such that the agreement fell under the scope of the CCP.[17]

The delimitation of the scope of the CCP is more complex where the commercial purpose of the agreement as a whole is not contested, but where some of its provisions are not classic CCP instruments. In other

---

shall be conducted in the context of the principles and objectives of the Union's external action".

15 M. Cremona, "Balancing Union and Member State Interests: Opinion 1/2008, Choice of Legal Base and the Common Commercial Policy under the Treaty of Lisbon", *European Law Review* 35 (2010), 678; C. Kaddous, " The Transformation of the EU Common Commercial Policy ", in P. Eeckhout, M. Lopez Escudero (eds), *The European Union's External Action in Times of Crisis*, (Oxford: Hart Publishing, 2016), 429.

16 Opinion of 14 February 2017, 3/15, *Marrakesh Treaty to Facilitate Access to Published Works for Persons who are Blind, Visually Impaired or Otherwise Print Disabled,* EU:C:2017:114.

17 Judgment of 27 October 2017, *Commission* v *Council,* C-389/15, EU:C:2017:798.

words, the question as to whether provisions of a trade agreement, which lead to the harmonisation of internal provisions, still fall under the scope of the CCP remains. In its recent case law, the Court of Justice, starting from the Treaty drafters' objective as expressed in Article 207 TFEU, adopted a global approach to international trade agreements, thereby abandoning a fragmented instrumental approach that distinguished the content of specific provisions from the content of the agreement as a whole.

More precisely, the Court's interpretation was based on the objective of reforming the CCP to reinforce the role of the Union as a global commercial actor, especially in the framework of the World Trade Organisation (WTO). As is well known, the scope of the CCP, in view of the conclusion of the WTO agreements, had been limited by the Court's instrumental approach, which led the Court of Justice to find that those provisions of the General Agreement on Trade in Services (GATS) and Agreement on Trade-Related Aspects of Intellectual Property Rights (TRIPS) that had harmonizing effect and affected the internal market could not be considered as instruments of the CCP, despite the obvious link between the agreements and international trade.[18] The fragmented interpretation of the GATS and the TRIPS agreements has since been abandoned in subsequent case law following the entry into force of the Lisbon Treaty. As was already pointed out,[19] the Court of Justice interpreted the scope of the CCP with regard to the WTO agreements from the perspective of the objective expressed in Article 207 TFEU.

In *Daiichi Sankyo and Sanofi-Aventis Deutschland*,[20] the Court highlighted that only rules that have a specific link to international trade may be covered by the concept of "commercial aspects of intellectual property" as referred to in Article 207 TFEU.[21] However, instead of examining Article 27 of the TRIPS agreement – a provision setting out the framework for

---

18 Opinion of 15 November 1994, 1/94, *Competence of the Community to Conclude International Agreements Concerning Services and the Protection of Intellectual Property*, EU:C:1994:384.

19 See, in this volume, the chapter by Marise Cremona.

20 Judgment of 18 July 2013, *Daiichi Sankyo and Sanofi-Aventis Deutschland*, C-414/11, EU:C:2013:520.

21 For a comment, see L. Ankersmit, "The Scope of the Common Commercial Policy after Lisbon: The *Daiichi Sankyo* and *Conditional Access Services* Grand Chamber Judgments", *Legal Issues of Economic Integration*, 41 (2014), 193; A. Dimopoulos, P. Vantsiouri, "Of TRIPS and Traps: the Interpretative Jurisdiction of the Court of Justice of the EU over Patent Law", *European Law Review* 39, no. 2

patent protection – for links to international trade in order to classify its "commercial aspect", the Court took the scope of the CCP as its starting point. It observed that the scope of Article 207 TFEU was intended to cover the TRIPS agreement, which makes the whole agreement a CCP instrument. In other words, the objective of the reform of Article 207 TFEU was to cover agreements having a specific link to international trade. As Advocate General Villalon pointed out, the connection between the wording of Article 207, paragraph 1, TFEU and the wording of the TRIPS agreement is very powerful as an idea. "That peculiar expression 'commercial aspects' would not have entered primary law had an international agreement entitled the 'TRIPs' Agreement not existed for over a decade".[22] Even if he does not arrive at the same conclusion as the Court of Justice, Advocate General Villalon observed that the effectiveness of Article 207 TFEU, which introduced a real reform to the scope of the CCP, is to be taken into consideration by excluding a strict interpretation of the term "commercial aspects". Contrary to the opinion held by Advocate General Villalon, who opined that the commercial aspects of intellectual property rights do not cover harmonization instruments, such as Article 27 of the TRIPS Agreement, the Court of Justice held that the harmonizing effect of Article 27 is absorbed by the connection between the TRIPS Agreement and international trade. To put it differently, starting from the EU objective to incorporate WTO agreements in the scope of the CCP, the scope of the Union's exclusive competence is now determined by the functionality of the agreement as a whole, which makes it a CCP instrument in its entirety, despite the harmonizing effect of some of its provisions.

The Court has taken the same position in other cases beyond WTO agreements: measures having a specific link to international trade, due to their objectives, fall under the scope of the CCP and not under the external aspect of the internal market competence, even though the adoption of those measures may lead to the harmonisation of internal provisions. The *Commission* v *Council* case related to the legal basis for the Council's decision to conclude the European Convention on the legal protection of ser-

---

(2014), 210; J. Larik, "No Mixed Feelings: The post-Lisbon Common Commercial Policy in *Daiichi Sankyo* and *Commission* v *Council (Conditionnal Access Convention)", Common Market Law Review* 52, no. 3 (2015), 779.

22 Opinion of AG Villalon of 31 January 2013, *Daiichi Sankyo and Sanofi-Aventis Deutschland*, C-414/11, EU:C:2013:49, para 64.

vices based on, or consisting of, conditional access.[23] The Court found that the principal objective of the convention was to promote international trade and, thus, presented the obligatory specific link to international trade that made it a CCP instrument. Despite the existence of EU internal market rules covering the same subject and, thus, liable to support an implied external competence, the Court held that internal-market oriented measures, even stemming from the convention, were not incompatible with the CCP's scope. As Advocate General Kokott pointed out,[24] a CCP measure may lead to harmonisation of national legislation, while harmonisation of national legislation may no longer give rise to an external competence, as long as the international agreement is intended to promote trade.

With the enlargement of the scope of the CCP the Court abandons the strict parallelism between external and internal competence. The dynamic of the Union's external competence in the field of international trade is expressed through a functionalist approach that dissociates the CCP from the external aspect of the internal market: as far as a link between an agreement and international trade is established, the agreement is deemed to be a CCP instrument, despite the existence of provisions affecting the internal market, even if the concrete implementation thereof requires recourse to an internal-competence legal basis. While the WTO agreements are considered CCP instruments because of the objective underlying the reform of Article 207 TFEU, coherence implies that the effect of such an approach be generalized to all agreements with trade objective, which is thus globally assessed. The decisive element in the establishment of the link between the CCP and any potential agreement is, therefore, the identification of its international trade objective, which, beyond the WTO agreements, may stem from a classic balancing between its predominant and incidental purposes.

B. The Global Approach of the EU's Objectives

The so-called new generation of free trade agreements (NGFTAs) contain provisions falling under the CCP scope, as enlarged by the Lisbon Treaty and the Court of Justice's interpretation, such as foreign direct investment

---

23 Judgment of 22 October 2013, *Commission* v *Council*, C-137/12, EU:C:2013:675.

24 Opinion of AG Kokott of 27 June 2013, *Commission* v *Council*, C-137/12, EU:C:2013:441, para 66.

and intellectual property. However, the CCP scope does not cover the NGFTAs in their entirety. Because of their comprehensive approach, which incorporates various trade-related objectives, such as non-direct investment, public procurement, competition, and sustainable development, the NGFTAs need a detailed analysis as to the nature of the EU external competence, despite their undoubted trade objective.[25]

In Opinion 2/15, addressing the competence of the Union to conclude the free trade agreement with the Republic of Singapore (EUSFTA),[26] the Court of Justice was asked to clarify the link between the common commercial policy and the sustainable development provisions of the agreement. The EUSFTA contains, in its Chapter 13 entitled "Trade and Sustainable Development", provisions related to labour and environmental protection. Those provisions impose obligations on the parties to promote their bilateral trade and economic relationship in such a way as to contribute to sustainable development, to establish environmental and labour protection, and to adopt or modify their relevant laws and policies in a manner consistent with the agreements to which they are a party. The inclusion of sustainable development provisions in the EUSFTA aims at balancing free trade with social and environmental protection, by avoiding a reduction in the second in favor of the first and by avoiding to apply the standards of protection in a protectionist manner. According to the horizontal dimension of the absorption doctrine, the question is which of the objectives – trade, social, and/or environmental protection – are ancillary and, consequently, absorbed by the main objective.

However, in Opinion 2/15, the Court of Justice did not apply the center of gravity test. Rather, it found that the sustainable development provisions did not express a proper objective and that the trade objective was

---

25 As AG Sharpston pointed out in her opinion concerning the conclusion of the EU-Singapore free trade agreement: "The EUSFTA is a very heterogeneous agreement. That means that, of necessity, the analysis to establish competence and its (exclusive or shared) nature will need (depending on the context) to focus on an individual chapter or groups of chapters of the EUSFTA, on a part or parts of that agreement or, occasionally, on an individual provision". Opinion of AG Sharpston of 21 December 2016, Opinion 2/15, *Free Trade Agreement between the European Union and the Republic of Singapore*, EU:C:2016:992, para 82.

26 Opinion of 16 May 2017, 2/15, *Free Trade Agreement between the European Union and the Republic of Singapore*, EU:C:2017:376. See: M. Dony, "L'avis 2/15 de la Cour de justice: un 'jugement de Salomon?'", *Revue trimestrielle de droit européen* 53, no. 3 (2017), 525.

broad enough to cover social and environmental protection purposes. As a consequence, sustainable development provisions were found not to be ancillary objectives, but part of the CCP, instead.[27]

The reasoning of the Court of Justice was based on the global approach to the external action objectives pursuant to Article 21 TEU,[28] which finds a specific expression in Article 207, paragraph 1, TFEU: "(t)he common commercial policy shall be conducted in the context of the principles and objectives of the Union's external action". It, thus, held that the sustainable development provisions of the EUSFTA were an integral part of the CCP and were not to be examined as autonomous objectives, giving rise to a different competence than that of Article 207 TFEU.

The Court's perspective on the global approach of external action objectives differs from its usual center of gravity test in the examination of the different objectives of an international agreement and leads to a broad conception of the CCP objective. This was not the position of Advocate General Sharpston, who examined the sustainable development provisions of the EUSFTA as the expression of autonomous objectives giving rise to a proper competence question. Advocate General Sharpston did not apply the center of gravity test either, because the choice of the legal basis was not necessary, but instead directly considered the sustainable development objectives as distinctive and stand-alone objective, which led to the recognition, in her opinion, of a shared competence in environmental and social protection fields.[29]

---

27 S. Schacherer, *The EU as a Global Actor in Reforming the International Investment Law Regime in Light of Sustainable Development,* (Geneva Jean Monnet Working Paper, 1/2017).

28 Article 21 TEU states especially in paras 2 and 3: "2. The Union shall define and pursue common policies and actions, and shall work for a high degree of cooperation in all fields of international relations, in order to:(a) safeguard its values, fundamental interests, security, independence and integrity; (…) (d) foster the sustainable economic, social and environmental development of developing countries, with the primary aim of eradicating poverty; (…) (h) promote an international system based on stronger multilateral cooperation and good global governance. 3. The Union shall respect the principles and pursue the objectives set out in paragraphs 1 and 2 in the development and implementation of the different areas of the Union's external action covered by this Title and by Part Five of the Treaty on the Functioning of the European Union, and of the external aspects of its other policies".

29 Opinion of 21 December 2016, *supra* note 25, paras 489-503.

The position of the Court of Justice, which held that the CCP objective covers environmental and social protection, distinguished the CCP from implied external competences. Indeed, the Court of Justice could have reached the same result – that is, recognising the broad scope of the CCP and the exclusive competence of the Union – if it had found that sustainable development provisions did not occupy an important place in the agreement and were, thus, absorbed by the CCP provisions. Indeed, the Court of Justice, in the same Opinion 2/15, took that very position with regard to some of the transport policy provisions (see *infra).* By recognizing the broad scope of the CCP, through its global approach to external action objectives, the Court of Justice gave a specific – broad – dimension to the trade objective. Such a broad conception of the CCP objective implies a broad conception of the CCP competence: the CCP competence, consequently, may cover sustainable development objectives, absorbed by the trade objective as conceived in the global approach of Articles 21 TEU and 207 TFEU, without passing the center of gravity test or an assessment of the importance of the provisions under question in the specific context. The Union's global approach to external action objectives may, in that sense, be considered as prevailing over a determination of the Union's competence according to objective factors in relation to any particular agreement.

However, the Court of Justice also justified its position with regard to objective factors by highlighting that the sustainable development provisions of the EUSFTA could be considered a basis for an EU competence because of their non-prescriptive nature. The Court specifically held that "it is not the Parties' intention to harmonise the labour or environment standards of the Parties" and that the provisions under question "are intended not to regulate the levels of social and environmental protection in the Parties' respective territory but to govern trade between the European Union and the Republic of Singapore by making liberalisation of that trade subject to the condition that the Parties comply with their international obligations concerning social protection of workers and environmental protection".[30] Sustainable development provisions were, thus, assimilated to ancillary provisions, which do not create new substantive obligations and, as a consequence, did not raise the question of the Union's competence with regard thereto.

---

30 Opinion of 16 May 2017, 2/15, *supra* note 26, paras 165, 166.

It should nevertheless be noted that the reasoning of the Court of Justice is not without ambiguity. The Court justified the integration of the sustainable development provisions in the scope of the CCP also because of their effects on trade. The provisions of Chapter 13 of the EUSFTA do indeed affect trade in different ways: by balancing the standards of social and environmental protection against liberalization of trade; by eliminating disparities between the costs of producing goods and supplying services in the European Union and Singapore; and by suspending the liberalization of trade in case of breach of the provisions concerning social protection of workers and environmental protection.[31] The emphasis on the effects on trade of the sustainable development provisions is not justified if the latter are considered non-prescriptive – and thus as absorbed by the CCP objective. The effects on trade are usually examined in order to determine whether or not substantive provisions of an international agreement – which pursue their own objective – fall under the scope of the CCP. However, if the Court of Justice found the sustainable development provisions substantive, they could not fall under the scope of the CCP, because the first condition, especially intended to promote and regulate trade, would not have been met. The global approach perspective of the Union's external action objectives, instead of that of the qualification of the sustainable development provisions as CCP provisions because of their content, allowed the Court of Justice to accommodate the broad scope of the CCP with the principle of conferral: the CCP objective covers sustainable development as far as the corresponding provisions do not pursue an autonomous objective and are integral part of the CCP, which is justified through their effects on trade.

III. EU Objectives and the EU's Exclusive Implied External Competence

Despite the Court's broad conception of the CCP scope, some provisions of an international trade agreement, especially of the NGFTAs, may still not fall under Article 207 TFEU. The next step in the reasoning of the Court of Justice is to establish exclusivity according to the criteria of Article 3, paragraph 2, TFEU, concerning implied external competences.[32] In

31 *Id.*, paras 157-161.

32 F. Castillo de la Torre, "The Court of Justice and External Competences After Lisbon: Some Reflections on the Latest Case Law", in P. Eeckhout, M. Lopez Escud-

that case too, the EU-objectives approach prevails over the objective-factors-based examination of the international agreement.

In examining Article 3, paragraph 2, TFEU's exclusivity criterion of affecting common rules or altering their scope, it is established case law that, insofar as the area addressed by an international agreement is not fully covered by internal rules and, thus, there is no *ERTA*-exclusivity based on field-preemption, and insofar as there is no conflict-preemption, in the sense of antinomy between the agreement and the common rules, exclusivity of the Union's competence may stem from the cross-examination of EU and international rules.[33] According to the Court of Justice, the exclusive implied competence of the Union "must have its basis in conclusions drawn from a comprehensive and detailed analysis of the relationship between the international agreement envisaged and the EU law in force. That analysis must take into account the areas covered, respectively, by the rules of EU law and by the provisions of the agreement envisaged, their foreseeable future development and the nature and content of those rules and those provisions, in order to determine whether the agreement is capable of undermining the uniform and consistent application of the EU rules and the proper functioning of the system which they establish".[34]

It is inherent in the rationale of implied external competences that their dynamic is driven by the scope of the corresponding EU objectives, which may be broader than the scope of the internal rules that the exclusivity of the external competence aims to preserve. Indeed, exclusivity stems not only from conflict and overlap between EU and international rules, but

---

ero (eds), *The European Union's External Action in Times of Crisis* (Oxford: Hart Publishing, 2016), 129.

33 A. Arena, "Exercise of EU Competences and Pre-emption of Member States' Powers in the Internal and the External Sphere: Towards 'Grand Unification'?", *Yearbook of European Law,* 35, no. 1 (2016), 28, at 64. M. Cremona, "EU External Relations: Unity and Conferral of Powers", in L. Azoulai (ed), *The Question of Competence in the European Union* (Oxford: Oxford University Press, 2014), 69; R. Schütze, "The *ERTA* Doctrine and Cooperative Federalism", in R. Schütze, *Foreign Affairs and the EU Constitution Selected Essays* (Cambridge: Cambridge University Press, 2014), 287.

34 Opinion of 14 October 2014, 1/13, *Convention on the Civil Aspects of International Child Abduction*, EU:C:2014:2303, para 71; Judgment of 26 November 2014, *Green Network*, C-66/13, EU:C:2014:2399, para 29; Opinion of 14 February 2017, 3/15, *supra* note 16, para 108. See I. Govaere, "Setting the International Scene: EU External Competence and Procedures Post-Lisbon Revisited in the Light of ECJ Opinion 1/13", *Common Market Law Review* 53, no. 5 (2015), 1277.

also from the overlap between those objectives pursued by the EU internal rules and those pursued by the rules of the international agreement. The objectives-based-approach marks an expansion of the scope of the alteration criterion as a basis for *ERTA*-exclusivity,[35] even in case common rules are not properly affected by the provisions of an international agreement. If the provisions of the international agreement do not cover the same issues as the internal EU rules, but are an expression of the pursuit of the same objective, implied external competence of the Union is exclusive in order to ensure the proper functioning of the system and to preserve the future development of the EU internal rules. The expression "to a large extent covered by common rules" with regard to the field addressed by the exclusive implied external competence of the Union is to be understood in the light of the Union's objectives that determine the extent of the exercise of the corresponding competence. Such an approach justifies not only the proper meaning of the altering the scope of the common rules criterion, but also justifies the exclusive implied external competence of the Union with regard to the principle of conferral.

More precisely, the exercise of the internal shared competence of the Union implies a vertical balancing under the principle of subsidiarity, in order to assess the necessity of its exercise with regard to the Member States' action and with regard to their corresponding objective(s). The material scope of the adopted rules depends on the EU's choice in the exercise of the competence that the pursuit of the objective(s) justified. The material scope of the internal rules determines the scope of the internal, but not the scope of the external, preemption.[36] To the extent provisions of

35 A. Arena, *supra* note 33, at 82.

36 In *Commission* v *Council,* the *Neighbouring Rights of Broadcasting Organisations* case, the Court of Justice held that, Protocol (No 25) on the exercise of shared competence, the sole article of which states that, "when the Union has taken action in a certain area, the scope of this exercise of competence only covers those elements governed by the Union act in question and therefore does not cover the whole area", concerns, as is evident from its wording, only Article 2, paragraph 2, TFEU and not Article 3, paragraph 2, TFEU. It therefore seeks to define the scope of the exercise by the European Union of a shared competence with the Member States which was conferred on it by the Treaties, and not to limit the scope of the exclusive external competence of the European Union in the cases referred to in Article 3, paragraph 2, TFEU. Judgment of 4 September 2014, *Commission* v *Council,* C-114/12, EU:C:2014:2151, para 73. See, F. Castillo de la Torre, *supra* note 32, at 157.

an international agreement deal with issues that could have been covered by the internal rules if the institutions had made a different choice, their conclusion does not need a new assessment of the need to exercise Union competence with regard to that of the Member States: the implied external competence of the Union is exclusive, despite the absence of internal field-preemption, because the international commitments pursue the same objective as the internal rules and, thus, they alter the scope of the common rules, by completing them. Consequently, the *ERTA*-exclusivity is to be assessed with regard to the scope of the Union's objective at the basis of the internal rules.

In the *Neighbouring Rights of Broadcasting Organisations* case, the Court of Justice acknowledged the exclusive nature of the implied external competence of the Union to conclude the Council of Europe's convention despite the fact that the scope of that convention and that of the relevant EU directives did not coincide completely.[37] Starting from the objective of protecting the broadcasting organisation's neighbouring rights, which were common to both the EU directives and the convention, the Court determined that the convention's extension of the protection to pre-broadcasting signals and to retransmission by wire, which issues were not covered by the EU rules, still fell under exclusive EU external competence. While Advocate General Sharspston adopted a different position, based on the absence of affectation of the common rules,[38] the position of the Court can be justified, in view of the principle of conferral, if one assumes that the international convention enlarged the scope of the common rules without requiring a new assessment of the necessity to exercise its competence.

The differentiation between the scope of the rules and the scope of the objectives is clearer when there is complete harmonisation, where Member States have discretion to derogate from the common rules. Indeed, in the case of complete harmonisation, the provisions of an international agreement on an issue falling within the Member States' discretion still fall under exclusive implied EU external competence, as any discretion to derogate from EU law is entirely controlled by the harmonising measures

37 *Supra* note 36.

38 Opinion of AG Sharpston of 3 April 2014, *Commission* v *Council,* C-114/12, EU:C:2014:224, paras 144-166.

themselves.[39] In contrast, in the case of minimum harmonisation of the Member States' legislation, the Member States' competence to adopt stricter rules remains untouched, but exclusivity stems from exhaustive harmonisation.[40] An international rule entering in the Member States' sphere goes beyond the objective of the exercised competence of the Union and, as such, does not fall under exclusive EU competence, unless the international rule overlaps and is at odds with the EU rule (conflict preemption).

More problematic has been the establishment of the Article 3, paragraph 2, TFEU exclusivity in Opinion 3/15, concerning the competence of the Union to approve the Marrakesh Treaty to Facilitate Access to Published Works for Persons Who are Blind, Visually Impaired, or Otherwise Print Disabled.[41] At the moment of the request of the Opinion,[42] Directive 2001/29[43] did not harmonise the exceptions and limitations to the protected copyright and related rights, while the Marrakesh Treaty renders such exceptions and limitations mandatory, for the benefit of persons with disabilities. The Court of Justice found that the Member States' discretion in implementing their option to provide for an exception or limitation for the benefit of persons with disabilities "derives from the decision of the EU legislature to grant the Member States that option, within the harmonised legal framework which Directive 2001/29 establishes".[44] The Court held

39 The Court of Justice held that "the fact that [a] Directive provides for certain derogations or refers in certain cases to national law does not mean that in regard to the matters which it regulates harmonisation is not complete". Judgment of 25 April 2002, *Commission* v *France*, C-52/00, EU:C:2002:252, para 19.

40 Opinion of 19 March 1993, 2/91, *Convention no. 170 of the International Labour Organization concerning safety in the use of chemicals at work,* EU:C:1993:106. See R. Schütze, "Supremacy without Pre-emption? The Very Slowly Emergent Doctrine of Community Pre-emption", *Common Market Law Review*, 43, no. 4 (2006), 1023.

41 Opinion of 14 February 2017, 3/15, *supra* note 16. See A. Arena, "The *ERTA* Pre-emption Effects of Minimum and Partial Harmonisation Directives: Insights from Opinion 3/15 on the Competence to Conclude the Marrakesh Treaty", *European Law Review* no. 5 (2018), forthcoming.

42 Since the delivery of Opinion 3/15, the EU legislature has carried out a full harmonisation of copyright exceptions and limitations for the benefit of persons with visual disabilities. See Regulation (EU) 2017/1563, OJ 2017 L242/1; Directive (EU) 2017/1564, OJ 2017 L242/6.

43 OJ 2001 L167/10.

44 Opinion of 14 February 2017, 3/15, *supra* note 16, para 119.

that the Member States' discretion is not the expression of a shared power and, consequently, the Marrakesh Treaty falls under the exclusive implied EU external competence.

It is interesting to note that, in Opinion 3/15, exclusivity does not stem from complete harmonization. That would have been the case if the Union had harmonised limitations on copyright and related rights protection, as it did after the delivery of Opinion 3/15.[45] In that case, the Member States discretion would have been a derogation from harmonized rules. However, as the European Parliament pointed out,[46] a distinction must be drawn between exceptions relating to the scope of an EU act and exceptions relating to the rights laid down in such an act. Exceptions to the scope of an EU act, on the one hand, are the consequence of minimum harmonization, where Member States preserve their competence and the intensity of the exercise of the EU competence is limited. Exceptions to the rights laid down in an EU act, on the other hand, are the consequence of partial harmonization. It is the Union's choice not to harmonise them, because such exceptions are not related to the harmonisation's objective to preserve the functioning of the internal market. It is thus about a situation between complete harmonization, leading to an exclusive external competence, and minimum harmonization, leading to shared external competence. This intermediate state of preemption means that the Member States' discretion to introduce exceptions to protected intellectual property rights is irrelevant to the internal market objectives, which explains the absence of complete harmonization, but the Member States must still remain within the limits designed by the EU rules, which, in turn, defines the difference with regard to minimum harmonization.

The EU-perspective with regard to exclusivity of the Union's implied external competence is clearly illustrated by the Court's acknowledgment of exclusive EU competence with regard to the Marrakesh Treaty. What distinguishes that case from the *Neighbouring Rights of Broadcasting Organisations* case, while simultaneously confirming the EU-objectives perspective, is that the internal rules' objective, which is related to the internal market, does not coincide with the international agreement's objective, which concerns protection of disabled persons and non-discrimination. In the *Neighbouring Rights of Broadcasting Organisations* case, the objec-

45 *Supra,* note 43.
46 Opinion of 14 February 2017, 3/15, *supra* note 16, para 58.

tive of the international convention was protecting broadcasting rights, the same as the internal rules' objective and, as a consequence, the conclusion of the convention by the Union expanded the scope of the internal rules in a field where the EU competence had already been exercised. In the Marrakesh Treaty Opinion, the Union had exercised its internal competence to harmonise intellectual property rights protection, while leaving intact the Member States' discretion to introduce exceptions. However, in the internal field, the extent of the harmonization was to be enlarged if the Member States' exceptions affected the objectives of the internal rules. That should have been done through the conclusion of the Marrakesh Treaty by the Union, as the obligation stemming from that Treaty to introduce exceptions to the protected rights met the objective of the internal EU rules and fell not under a Member States' reserved competence, but under the Member States' discretion, the exercise of which fell under the common rules' scope. By concluding the Marrakesh Treaty, the Union would not need to reassess the necessity of the exercise of its competence. Its external competence was exclusive because the Marrakesh Treaty could affect the internal balance between EU objectives and the Member States' interests and, thus, could undermine the proper functioning of the common rules system.

It follows that, in the implied external competences field, preemption in the external field is broader than in the internal field. The criterion of external preemption is the previously described assessment of the necessity to exercise the Union's competence, regardless of the scope of the internal rules. In contrast, according to the *ERTA* criterion of affecting common rules or altering their scope, an assessment of the necessity to exercise the shared Union's competence is not to be done directly in the external field. Rather, where common rules do not cover a field with regard to which an assessment of the necessity to exercise a shared competence has not already been done and that field is covered by the provisions of an international agreement, then the conclusion of the agreement cannot be considered as altering the scope of the common rules. The conclusion of the agreement is an exercise of a shared competence that cannot be done directly in the external field on the basis of the preemption stemming from the *ERTA* criterion: the external implied competence of the Union is not exclusive according to Article 3, paragraph 2, TFEU.

This limit on the application of the *ERTA*-exclusivity explains the position of Advocate General Sharpston in Opinion 2/15 with regard to the competence of the Union to approve the transport policy provisions of the

EUSFTA. The Advocate General advanced the argument that the Union's internal rules did not cover establishment issues in maritime transports and did not cover internal waterway transport. As a consequence, Advocate General Sharpston suggested that those provisions should be considered as falling under shared external competence. However, the Court of Justice, with an obvious eye on reconciling a broad external preemption with the principle of conferral, examined the place of the provisions at issue in the Singapore agreement. The Court held that those provisions did not occupy an important place in the agreement and their scope was rather limited.[47] Thus, the Union would not exercise its competence by approving them. In other words, the relevant provisions in the agreement were found to be ancillary and absorbed due to their limited scope and, thus, they did not need to be taken into account in order to determine the Union's competence.

This position of the Court expresses an absorbing preemption in the external field, but such preemption is not possible in the internal field.[48] Moreover, said position raises further questions: if the Union concludes an agreement on the basis of an exclusive external competence and if that agreement contains ancillary provisions, is the Union deemed to have adopted common rules in the field covered by those provisions? It is difficult to argue the contrary, as the argument of the Court is a systemic interpretation based on the place of the provisions in the specific agreement. It could be argued that it would be more compatible with legal certainty to strictly apply the preemption criterion and to find that those provisions fall under shared EU competence that can, however, be exercised directly in the external field pursuant to the necessity criterion of Article 216, paragraph 1, TFEU. Indeed, as will be discussed below, Article 216, paragraph 1, TFEU offers the possibility to exercise a shared competence directly in the external field if the *ERTA* conditions are not met.

IV. The EU-Objectives' Perspective in the Exercise of a Shared Implied External Competence

The EU-perspective may intervene in a different way than impacting the qualification of the provisions of the international agreement. As men-

47 Opinion of 16 May 2017, 2/15, *supra* note 26, paras 215-218.
48 *Supra* note 36.

tioned above, in Opinion 2/15, the Court of Justice analyzed as ancillary some transport policy-related provisions of the international agreement, which by nature were normative and could require the exercise of a Union competence, because of their role in the specific agreement. Thus, they were absorbed by the transport policy provisions that the Union intended to adopt and implement in its relations with Singapore. In the same Opinion, in the portion concerning the agreement's non-direct investment provisions, the Court of Justice recognized a shared external competence of the Union based on the capital movement provision of the Treaty.[49] It acknowledged that those provisions could not be approved by the Union alone.[50] Rather, the preemption-through-absorption doctrine did not apply to the provisions related to non-direct investment and, according to the Court the absence of exclusivity would require the conclusion of a mixed agreement.

Such a different conclusion as to the transport policy and the non-direct investment provisions of the EUSFTA can be explained through an EU-objectives-based analysis. In both cases, the relevant provisions were not covered by the exclusivity criterion of Article 3, paragraph 2, TFEU, as they are not liable to affect or alter the scope of common rules.[51] In both cases, as the relevant provisions were liable to introduce rights and obligations, they correspond to a Union policy objective and require the exercise of the corresponding competence. And, in both cases, despite the absence of exclusivity, the Union could exercise its competence covering those provisions according to Article 216, paragraph 1, TFEU.

More precisely, in *Germany* v *Council* (*COTIF*)[52] the Court of Justice clarified the meaning of Article 216, paragraph 1, TFEU and its relationship with Article 3, paragraph 2, TFEU, concerning the question of the exercise of a Union's external competence. While an implied exclusive competence using the criteria of Article 3 TFEU leads to the conclusion of an international agreement by the Union alone and the question of mixity does not even comes under consideration,[53] Article 216, paragraph 1,

49 Opinion of 16 May 2017, 2/15, *supra* note 26, paras 225-241.

50 *Id.*, para 244.

51 See, in this volume, the chapter by Nicolas Pigeon.

52 Judgment of 5 December 2017, *Germany* v *Council, (Amendment of the Convention concerning International Carriage by Rail – COTIF),* C-600/14, EU:C:2017:935.

53 *Supra,* note 5.

TFEU provides that the Union may conclude an international agreement if it is necessary in order to achieve, within the framework of the Union's policies, one of the objectives referred to by the Treaties. On the one hand, this provision distinguishes the Union's express from its implied external competence[54] and confirms that the existence of an implied external competence is to be distinguished from its exclusive character. On the other hand, Article 216, paragraph 1, TFEU is related to the vertical dimension of the absorption doctrine,[55] as it appears to suggest that the Union may conclude an EU-only agreement if it is necessary to attain one of its objectives, even if the agreement contains provisions falling under shared competence. In such a way, provisions falling under shared competence are absorbed by those falling under exclusive EU competence.

However, in order to acknowledge that Article 216, paragraph 1, TFEU allows a vertical effect of the absorption doctrine, it is also necessary to acknowledge that the exercise of the shared EU competence is not only driven by the corresponding objective (which requires its definition and, thus, the legal basis choice), but is also subject to a global assessment of the objectives expressed in the different provisions of the agreement and the general EU objective of being an international actor. In this way, an agreement can be approved by the Union alone, even if it contains provisions falling under shared competence and even if the Union does not intend to exercise its competence with regard to those provisions. The Union may exercise its competence to conclude the international agreement as a whole, which implies that the objectives related to its exclusive competence absorb those related to shared competence.

Such a global approach has the merit of avoiding the qualification of some provisions of an agreement as ancillary, not because of objective elements, but because of the Union's objectives. With respect to the EUSFTA, that approach could have allowed the Union to exercise its external competence with regard to the whole agreement and, on the basis of Arti-

54 "The Union may conclude an agreement with one or more third countries or international organisations where the Treaties so provide or (...)".

55 It could be qualified as vertical dimension of the absorption doctrine the absorption of provisions falling under shared competence by those falling under exclusive competence. Such a dimension determines the vertical division of competences, while the horizontal dimension relates to the choice of legal basis according to the center of gravity test. See, in this volume, the chapter by Merijn Chamon.

cle 216, paragraph 1, TFEU, to attain the main objective expressed for the agreement – that of commercial policy – in combination with the general objective of acting as a global international actor. Such an approach, still guided by the Union's objectives, would not need to distinguish between the non-direct investment provisions, which are not absorbed and need the exercise of the Union's competence, and the transport-related provisions that were found, in Opinion 2/15, to be absorbed because of their ancillary nature in the specific context. Such an approach would thus have the merit of legal certainty.

Nevertheless, it seems that the interpretation of Article 216, paragraph 1, TFEU, in *Germany* v *Council,* precludes a global assessment of the Union's objectives when faces with the conclusion of an international agreement. On the contrary, the decision confirms the strict interpretation of the principle of conferral. The Court of Justice explicitly referred to Opinion 2/15 in *Germany* v *Council*:

> "Admittedly, the Court found, in paragraph 244 of that Opinion, that the relevant provisions of the agreement concerned, relating to non-direct foreign investment, which fall within the shared competence of the European Union and its Member States, could not be approved by the Union alone. However, in making that finding, the Court did no more than acknowledge the fact that, as stated by the Council in the course of the proceedings relating to that Opinion, there was no possibility of the required majority being obtained within the Council for the Union to be able to exercise alone the external competence that it shares with the Member States in this area".[56]

It follows from this statement that the exercise of a shared implied external competence directly in the external field (without passing from the criterion of affecting the common rules or altering their scope), although possible, is subject to an assessment of the necessity thereof in order to attain the specific corresponding objective. Consequently, at that stage, the mere definition of the nature of the EU external competence is not sufficient, rather the exact legal basis therefor must be determined.

Besides, the Court of Justice acknowledged that the Union, in light of the ability granted by Article 216, paragraph 1, TFEU, could approve – alone – only the non-direct investment provisions of the EU-Singapore agreement and not all of the provisions falling outside the exclusive competence of the Union (such as the investor-State dispute settlement (ISDS) provisions), although that could have been possible if the global approach

56 Judgment of 5 December 2017, *Germany* v *Council, supra* note 52, para 68.

had prevailed. As a consequence, the transport-related provisions outside the exclusive EU competence could not be deemed to be covered by the exercise of the shared competence, because the Union did not have the intention to exercise its competence with regard to those provisions.

Despite the rejection of the global approach with regard to Article 216 paragraph 1, TFEU, the policy-objective approach still entails a proper dynamic allowing the exercise of the Union's shared implied external competence. It should be noted that the rejection of such a global approach is indeed justified with regard to the principle of conferral: first, it does not contravene the correspondence between competences and objectives; second, a specific legal basis is required for the exercise of the EU competence which cannot be based merely on Article 216, paragraph 1, TFEU.

V. Concluding Remarks: Dynamic of EU-Objective-Based Analysis of the External Competence versus Content-Based Analysis of the International Agreement

As shown in the previous paragraphs, the analysis of the vertical division of external competences following an EU-objectives-based perspective allows a broad conception of the CCP objective, a broad interpretation of the *ERTA*-exclusivity and the exercise of the EU shared implied external competence.

However, the question as to what provisions of an international agreement the EU and Member States competence has to be determined depends, not on an analysis of EU objectives, but on an assessment of the content of the agreement as such. Indeed, it is settled case law that the non-substantive provisions of an international agreement – those that aim to ensure the effective implementation of the substantive provisions – do not raise a competence question, but are considered ancillary. They therefore "fall within the same competence as the substantive provisions which they accompany".[57]

Non-substantive provisions typically create a specific institutional framework for the implementation of the substantive provisions of the agreement and establish procedures, mechanisms and obligations (such as exchange of information). Such institutional provisions include the dispute

57 Opinion of 16 May 2017, 2/15, *supra* note 26, para 276.

settlement regime set out in the agreement. As the Court of Justice reiterated in its Opinion 2/15, "the competence of the European Union in the field of international relations and its capacity to conclude international agreements necessarily entail the power to submit to the decisions of a court which is created or designated by such agreements as regards the interpretation and application of their provisions".[58] In Opinion 2/15, the Court of Justice held that the dispute settlement regime between the contracting parties did not raise a proper question of competence, as it formed part of the institutional framework for the substantive provisions of the agreement.[59]

Beyond such institutional provisions, and because they are intended to ensure the effectiveness of the substantive provisions, provisions imposing respect for general principles and fundamental rights (such as transparency, good administration, and effective judicial protection in the implementation of the agreement), are also considered ancillary.[60] However, despite their procedural nature and their aim to ensure the effectiveness of substantive provisions, they are not considered ancillary provisions that impose precise procedural obligations on the parties. For instance, the EU and the Member States have jointly concluded the so-called Aarhus Convention on Access to Information, Public Participation in Decision-making and Access to Justice in Environmental Information. To determine the sphere of competence with regard to the provisions of the Aarhus convention, the Court of Justice did not examine the substantive EU law in the environmental field; rather, it looked to the procedural directives adopted by the Union.[61] Provisions of the Aarhus convention, therefore, cannot be considered ancillary with regard to substantive environmental legislation.

It follows that the distinction-between-substantive-and-ancillary criterion for provisions of an international agreement, which establishes if the competence question is raised, lies in the establishment of prescriptive and precise obligations for the parties that impact the exercise of their compe-

---

58 *Id.*, para 298. Opinion of 14 December 1991, 1/91, *First Opinion on the EEA Agreement*, EU:C:1991:490, paras 40 and 70; Opinion of 8 March 2011, 1/09, *Agreement creating a Unified Patent Litigation System*, EU:C:2011:123, para 74; Opinion of 18 December 2014, 2/13, *Accession of the European Union to the ECHR*, EU:C:2014:2454, para 182.

59 *Id.*, para 303.

60 *Id.*, paras 281-284.

61 Judgment of 8 March 2011, *Lesoochranárske zoskupenie VLK,* C-240/09, EU:C:2011:125.

tence and involve specific commitments relating to their administrative or judicial organisation. Ancillary provisions are thus identified according to an objective assessment of the content of the international agreement.

However, in Opinion 2/15, the EU-objectives-based analysis affected the content-based identification of the competence-related provisions of the EUSFTA.

First, the sustainable development provisions of the EUSFTA were not qualified as ancillary, even though the Court held that they did not raise a competence question. They were instead considered absorbed by the CCP objective. In that context, the agreement's sustainable development provisions did not introduce new commitments and they could have been considered non-substantive. The Court of Justice's reasoning is not clear in that regard: the provisions at issue could have been absorbed by the CCP, even if the Court of Justice had not underlined their non-prescriptive nature, merely because of their effects on international trade. By raising the question of their non-prescriptive character, the Court of Justice intended to justify – with regard to the principle of conferral – a broad conception of the CCP objective, but introduced uncertainty as to the qualification of a provision as ancillary.

Second, the ISDS provisions of the EUSFTA, while by definition institutional (and, therefore, ancillary) were found to raise a competence question. Despite the fact that the ISDS regime could apply to situations falling under both EU and Member States' competence (given that the Court of Justice held that non-direct investment provisions fall under shared competence), the competence to approve provisions introducing that regime should have been assessed separately. The Court of Justice held that "such a regime, which removes disputes from the jurisdiction of the courts of the Member States, cannot be of a purely ancillary nature ... and cannot, therefore, be established without the Member States' consent.[62] As a consequence, the Court held that approval of the ISDS provisions "falls not within the exclusive competence of the European Union, but within a competence shared between the European Union and the Member States".[63]

62 Opinion of 16 May 2017, 2/15, *supra* note 26, para 292. See C. Contartese, "The Autonomy of the EU Legal Order in the ECJ's External Relations Case Law: From the "Essential" to the "Specific Characteristics" of the Union and Back Again", *Common Market Law Review,* 54, no. 5 (2017), 1625, 1667.

63 *Id.,* para 293.

It is interesting to note that, while in the sustainable development provisions analysis the EU-objectives dynamic prevailed over legal certainty, in the ISDS provisions analysis of the competence question the EU-objectives dynamic seems to regress. As well-known, the ISDS regime also raised an important question regarding compatibility with the autonomy of the EU legal order.[64] In Opinion 2/15, this question was transformed into a question of competence.[65] Consequently, the ISDS provisions require the conclusion of a mixed agreement, as they affect the Member States' obligation, even when the dispute would have concerned direct investment and otherwise would have fallen under EU exclusive competence. Moreover, the provisions do not correspond to a policy objective and are not covered by the Union's ability to exercise its shared competence pursuant to Article 216, paragraph 1, TFEU. However, despite the apparent regression of the EU-objectives dynamic, by transforming a question of compatibility into a question of competence, the Court of Justice revealed a new potential of the EU-objectives-approach, that of conciliating autonomy with effectiveness, which it should finally be up to the Union and its Member States.

---

64 On 13 October 2017, Belgium submitted a request for an Opinion regarding the ISDS mechanism in the Canada-EU Comprehensive Economic and Trade Agreement (CETA). Opinion proceeding 1/17, OJ 2017 C 369/2.

65 Opinion 2/15 addresses only the question of competence with regard to that mechanism. Concerning the question of compatibility with the autonomy of the EU legal order see C. Eckes, "International Rulings and the EU Legal Order: Autonomy as Legitimacy?", in M. Cremona, A. Thies, R. Wessel (eds), *The European Union and International Dispute Settlement,* (Oxford: Oxford Hart Publishing, 2017), 161; A. Rosas, "The EU and International Dispute Settlement" *Europe and the World, A Law Review* 7, no. 1 (2017), 23.

Conflict of Legal Bases and the Internal-External Security Nexus: AFSJ versus CFSP

Mauro Gatti

I. Introduction

Since the Union has conferred powers only, it must tie its measures to Treaty provisions – the so-called "legal bases" – which empower it to act. [1] To determine the correct basis of a measure, one should apply the "centre of gravity" doctrine, whereby the choice of the legal basis must rest on objective factors amenable to judicial review, which include the aim and content of that measure. [2] However, given the functional overlap between EU policies, it is sometimes difficult to identify the appropriate legal basis of a Union act.

The choice of legal bases may seem a question of technical detail, but has significant constitutional implications. [3] The correct allocation of legal bases ensures the appropriate delimitation of EU policies and competences. It also makes sure that the correct procedures are followed, that each institution exercises the powers conferred on it, and that, consequently, the EU's institutional balance is respected. Therefore, to proceed on an incorrect legal basis is liable to render an act invalid, particularly where the appropriate legal basis lays down a procedure for adopting acts that is different from that which has in fact been followed. [4]

Identifying the correct legal basis is particularly problematic in the field of security management. Security is among the main objectives of the

1 Opinion of 6 December 2001, 2/00, *Cartagena Protocol*, EU:C:2001:664, para 5.
2 See, *inter alia*, Judgment of 26 March 1987, *Commission* v *Council*, 45/86, EU:C:1987:163, para 11; Judgment of 11 June 1991, *Commission* v *Council* (*Titanium dioxide*), C-300/89, EU:C:1991:244, para 10.
3 Opinion of AG Kokott of 28 October 2015, *Parliament* v *Council* (*Tanzania*), C-263/14, EU:C:2015:729, para 4.
4 Judgment of 14 June 2016, *Parliament* v *Council* (*Tanzania*), C-263/14, EU:C:2016:435, para 43; Opinion of 6 December 2001, 2/00, *supra* note 1, para 5.

Union,[5] and is promoted, in particular, through two policy frameworks: (*i*) The Area of Freedom Security and Justice (AFSJ), dealing *inter alia* with anti-terrorism measures, external border management, judicial cooperation in criminal matters, and police cooperation; (*ii*) The Common Foreign and Security Policy (CFSP), covering all areas of foreign policy and all questions relating to the Union's security, including the Common Security and Defence Policy (CSDP).

A security-related measure may potentially find its legal basis in either of these policy areas. The selection of either an AFSJ or CFSP legal basis may raise constitutional issues, in terms of the principles of access to justice, democratic principles, and institutional balance. [6] The AFSJ, like most Union policies, is managed through procedures that generally reflect the archetypal "Community method". [7] The CFSP, by contrast, is a predominantly intergovernmental decision-making framework, characterised by the limited role played by the Court of Justice,[8] the Commission, and the Parliament. [9] To protect, and circumscribe, the specificities of the CFSP, Article 40 of the Treaty on the European Union (TEU) affirms that this policy must not affect the application of non-CFSP procedures and the extent of the powers of the institutions laid down by the Treaties for the exercise of non-CFSP competences (and *vice-versa*).

---

5 See the preamble of the TEU, pursuant to which the Union should promote "security and progress in Europe and in the world".

6 See Opinion of AG Bot of 30 January 2014, *Parliament* v *Council* (*Mauritius*), C-658/11, EU:C:2014:41, para 4.

7 The Commission has the (almost) exclusive power of initiative, as well as the power of policy implementation (which it shares with the Member States). The Parliament and the Council, generally acting by qualified majority, share the legislative power. In addition, legal acts fall under the jurisdiction of the Court of Justice.

8 See Articles 24, paragraph 1, TEU and 275 TFEU. In any event, the Court seems to have given a narrow interpretation of restrictions on its jurisdiction in the area of CFSP: see Judgment of 19 July 2016, *H* v *Council, Commission and EUPM,* C-455/14 P, EU:C:2016:569; Judgment of 28 March 2016, *Rosneft,* C-72/15, EU:C:2017:236, paras 58-81. See further the chapters by Pieter Jan Kuijper, Sara Poli, Hugo Flavier and Francette Fines in this volume.

9 Opinion of AG Bot of 30 January 2014, *Parliament* v *Council* (*Mauritius*), *supra* note 6, para 5.

Although several scholars have investigated the "centre of gravity" doctrine and the CFSP/AFSJ divide, [10] the issue remains unclear. Three post-Lisbon judgments – *Smart sanctions* (2012) [11] and the two so-called *Pirates* cases: *Mauritius* (2014) [12] and *Tanzania* (2016) [13] – may potentially shed some light on this topic. The present contribution analyses the case law, distilling the elements that, according to the Court, may allow EU institutions to properly identify the legal bases of security-related acts. The analysis also elucidates the shortcomings in the reasoning of the Court and suggests alternative solutions that might increase legal clarity.

It is worth noting that the present analysis concerns solely the conflict of AFSJ and CFSP legal bases, and does not address the delimitation of the AFSJ and other EU policies, such as the protection of personal data. [14] Moreover, the analysis does not focus on the cumulating of legal bases. This problem is potentially relevant, [15] but was not essential for solving the aforementioned cases. [16]

---

10 See e.g. A. Engel, "Delimiting Competences in the EU: CFSP versus AFSJ Legal Bases", *European Public Law* 47, no. 1 (2015), 47; G. de Baere, T. Van den Sanden, "Interinstitutional Gravity and Pirates of the Parliament on Stranger Tides: The Continued Constitutional Significance of the Choice of Legal Basis in Post-Lisbon External Action", *European Constitutional Law Review* 12, no. 1 (2016), 85-113; I. Govaere, V. Demedts, "Quelle définition de l'"externe" en matière d'ELSJ? Le cadre et les enjeux", in C. Flaesch-Mougin and L. S. Rossi (eds), *La dimension extérieure de l'espace de liberté, de sécurité et de justice de l'Union européenne après le traité de Lisbonne* (Bruxelles: Bruylant 2013), 489.

11 Judgment of 19 July 2012, *Parliament* v *Council* (*Smart sanctions*), C-130/10, EU:C:2012:472.

12 Judgment of 24 June 2014, *Parliament* v *Council* (*Mauritius*), C-658/11, EU:C:2014:2025.

13 Judgment of 14 June 2016, *Parliament* v *Council* (*Tanzania*), *supra* note 4.

14 See Opinion of the Court of 26 July 2017, 1/15, *Draft agreement between Canada and the European Union (PNR)*, EU:C:2016:656.

15 See, in particular, Judgment of 19 July 2012, *Parliament* v *Council* (*Smart sanctions*), *supra* note 11, para 47.

16 It is worth noting that *Mauritius* and *Tanzania* cases concern international agreements, which may arguably be founded on both CFSP and non-CFSP legal bases: see F. Naert, "The Use of the CFSP Legal Basis for EU International Agreements in Combination with Other Legal Bases", in J. Czuczai, F. Naert (eds), *The EU as a Global Actor – Bridging Legal Theory and Practice: Liber Amicorum in Honour of Ricardo Gosalbo Bono* (Leiden: Brill | Nijhoff, 2017), 394-423, at 403-409; S. Adam, "The Legal Basis of International Agreements of the European Union in the Post-Lisbon Era", in I. Govaere and others (eds), *The European Union in the World: Essays in Honour of Marc Maresceau* (Leiden: Martinus Nijhoff, 2014),

The study begins, in section II, by exploring the cause of the difficulties in this sector, namely the potential overlap of AFSJ and CFSP initiatives. Then the paper investigates the recent case law, highlighting the techniques that the Court used to solve the conflict of legal bases between the AFSJ and the CFSP. Section III shows that the Court has primarily adopted a teleological approach, based on the distinction between "internal" and "international" security. Section IV demonstrates that the Court has complemented the teleological approach with a contextual reading of the contested measures. The conclusion elucidates the limits of the case law and suggests alternative solutions (section V).

II. Legal Bases of Security-Related Acts: The AFSJ/CFSP Conundrum

The objectives of the Area of Freedom, Security and Justice and of the Common Foreign and Security Policy are interrelated. Both policy areas are connected, in particular, with the need for security. [17] The CFSP pursues the general objectives of the EU's external action, as set out in Article 21 TEU, including safeguarding the EU's security and preserving peace and international security. [18] The CSDP has slightly more specific objectives, since it is intended to pursue peace-keeping and conflict prevention and to strengthen "international security".[19]

The AFSJ, on the other hand, should generally ensure "a high level of security", as well as the absence of internal border controls and a common policy on asylum, immigration and external border control (Article 67 TFEU). The EU's external action in the AFSJ should arguably contribute to pursuing the general objectives of the EU's policy on foreign affairs (Article 21 TEU), including safeguarding the EU's security and preserving peace and international security.

65, at 78-81; M. Gatti, P. Manzini, "External Representation of the European Union in the Conclusion of International Agreements" *Common Market Law Review* 49, no. 5 (2012), 1703, at 1720-1723.

17 Opinion of AG Bot of 30 January 2014, *Parliament* v *Council* (*Mauritius*), *supra* note 6, para 107. See also E. Neframi, "L'aspect externe de l'espace de liberté, de sécurité et de justice: quel respect des principes et objectifs de l'action extérieure de l'Union?", in C. Flaesch-Mougin and L. S. Rossi (eds), *supra* note 10 at 521.

18 Article 21, paragraph 2, letters (a) and (c) TEU.

19 Article 42, paragraph 1, TEU.

Since the aims of the CFSP and the AFSJ seem to overlap, the application of the "centre of gravity" doctrine to security-related acts may be complicated. This is the case, in particular, for anti-terrorism measures. Such measures may pertain to the area of CFSP, because they may pursue foreign policy objectives, given the transnational nature of certain terrorist groups. Indeed, the EU has adopted numerous CFSP anti-terrorism measures over the years. These measures are implemented through a two-stage procedure: first, the Council adopts a CFSP decision providing for restrictive measures against natural or legal persons; then the Council adopts a decision, based on Article 215 TFEU, through which it implements the previous CFSP instrument. The Lisbon reform has complicated the framework by introducing another legal basis for anti-terrorism measures. According to Article 75 TFEU (an AFSJ provision), the Union may define administrative measures with respect to capital movements and payments, "as regards preventing and combating terrorism and related activities". In light of Article 75 TFEU, one may wonder whether recourse to Article 215 TFEU for anti-terrorism measures is still warranted.[20]

The Court of Justice addressed this question in the *Smart sanctions* case. The dispute concerned a Council Decision based on Article 215 TFEU, which provided, *inter alia*, for the freezing of the funds of certain persons allegedly linked to terrorist organisations. The European Parliament submitted that Article 215 TFEU did not constitute a valid legal basis: the decision should have been adopted on the basis of Article 75 TFEU. The Court ruled in favour of the Council, stating that Article 215 TFEU may constitute the legal basis of restrictive measures, including those designed to combat terrorism. *Smart sanctions* seems therefore to resolve, to a large extent, the conflict between Articles 75 and 215 TFEU; however, the solution proposed by the Court is not entirely satisfactory, since it appears to rely on an artificial distinction between internal and international security (see section III below).

A second area of CFSP/AFSJ conflict relates to judicial and police cooperation with third States. Cooperation between judicial authorities is essential in the fight against cross-border threats to security, including terrorism, financial crime and human trafficking. The EU has conducted numerous activities in this sector, including, in particular, the conclusion of two

20 See. A. Ott, "Case C-130/10 European Parliament v. Council of the European Union, Judgment of 19 July 2012, not yet reported", *Maastricht Journal of European and Comparative Law,* no. 4 (2012), 589, at 593.

agreements on the processing of Passenger Name Record (PNR) with Australia and the US. [21] These agreements are founded on Articles 82 and 87 TFEU, [22] which concern judicial and police cooperation (AFSJ). [23] The Union has concluded two other important agreements linked to judicial cooperation, regarding the transfer of suspected pirates apprehended by the CSDP mission EUNAVFOR Somalia (Operation Atalanta) [24] to Tanzania and Mauritius. [25] Unlike the PNR agreements, these agreements were not concluded on the basis of Articles 82 and 87 TFEU, but are founded on Article 37 TEU, the basis for international agreements in the area of CFSP. It is possible to speculate as to whether the Union may validly conclude an agreement on the transfer of prisoners on a CFSP legal basis, even if this matter "undoubtedly has a certain affinity" with the AFSJ. [26]

In fact, the Parliament brought actions contesting the agreements with Mauritius and Tanzania, alleging their incompatibility with the Treaties on several grounds. The position of the Parliament in the *Mauritius* case was not entirely clear: at the hearing, it argued that the agreement with Mauri-

---

21 See Council Decision 2012/381/EU, OJ 2012 L 186/3; Council Decision 2012/472/EU, OJ 2012 L 215, p. 4. The Union is also seeking to conclude a PNR agreement with Canada. See Proposal for a Council Decision on the conclusion of the EU-Canada PNR Agreement, COM(2013) 528 final. However, the proposed agreement has been found incompatible with primary law in Opinion of 26 July 2017, 1/15, *supra* note 14.

22 It is worth noting that the international agreements concluded by the EU are generally based on at least two legal bases: a substantive legal basis (such as a CFSP or AFSJ provision) and a procedural legal basis (Article 218 TFEU). Since the procedural aspects are not relevant for the present analysis, this paper does not take Article 218 TFEU into account, and refers only to substantive legal bases.

23 In Opinion of 26 July 2017, 1/15, *supra* note 14, the Court held that the agreement with Canada must be based jointly on Article 16, paragraph 2, TFEU and Article 87, paragraph 2, letter a, TFEU; the issue is immaterial for the purpose of the present analysis, which does not deal with data protection (Article 16, paragraph 2, TFEU).

24 Council Joint Action 2008/851/CFSP, OJ 2008 L 301, p. 33, last amended by Council Decision 2016/713/CFSP, OJ 2016 L 125/12.

25 Council Decision 2014/198/CFSP, OJ 2014 L 108, p. 1; Council Decision 2011/640/CFSP, OJ 2011 L 254, p. 1. The EU also concluded agreements with the Seychelles and Kenya, but before the Lisbon reform: see Council Decision 2009/293/CFSP, OJ 2009 L 79, p. 47 and Council Decision 2009/877/CFSP, OJ 2009 L 315, p. 35.

26 Opinion of AG Kokott of 28 October 2015, *Parliament* v *Council* (*Tanzania*), *supra* note 3, para 61.

tius should have been based on both CFSP and AFSJ provisions, [27] yet it was not maintaining by its plea that the agreement should have been founded on a substantive legal basis other than Article 37 TEU. [28] Because of this uncertainty in the applicant's position, the Court did not take a definitive view on the correct substantive legal basis, but concentrated on procedural issues, based on another complaint raised by the applicant. In *Tanzania,* by contrast, the Parliament claimed that the Court should have annulled the decision concluding the agreement with Tanzania, because *inter alia* that agreement should have been based on Article 37 TEU and Articles 82 and 87 TFEU. The Court rejected the Parliament's plea, arguing that the agreement with Tanzania falls predominantly within the scope of the CFSP, and not within the scope of judicial cooperation in criminal matters or police cooperation, and, consequently, the contested decision could legitimately be based on Article 37 TEU alone. [29] To determine the legal basis of the agreement with Tanzania, the Court complemented the teleological approach (see section III) with a contextual interpretation of the contested measure, thereby raising some concerns (see section IV).

III. The Problematic Distinction between Internal and External Security

In order to identify the legal basis of an EU measure, the Court of Justice often tends to put the emphasis on its objectives, rather than focusing on its content. [30] Such a teleological approach is problematic in post-Lisbon external relations, since Article 21 TEU provides for a list of objectives that are common to all EU external actions. In principle, this issue might

---

27 Opinion of AG Bot of 30 January 2014, *Parliament* v *Council* (*Mauritius*), *supra* note 6, para 40.

28 Judgment of 24 June 2014, *Parliament* v *Council* (*Mauritius*), *supra* note 12, para 44. See further H. Merket, *The EU and the Security-Development Nexus: Bridging the Legal Divide,* Studies in EU External Relations 12 (Brill | Nijhoff, 2016), 289-290.

29 Judgment of 14 June 2016, *Parliament* v *Council* (*Tanzania*), *supra* note 4, para 55.

30 M. Klamert, "Conflicts of Legal Basis: No Legality and No Basis but a Bright Future under the Lisbon Treaty?", *European Law Review* 35, no. 4 (2010), 497, at 505. There are, of course, exceptions, see e.g. S. Poli, "The Legal Basis of Internal Market Measures with a Security Dimension. Comment on Case C-301/06 of 10/02/2009", *European Constitutional Law Review* 6, no. 1 (2010), 137, at 150-151.

be partially resolved by examining the specific objectives of each policy, as listed in the TFEU (e.g. the AFSJ aims at ensuring a high level of security, *ex* Article 67 TFEU).[31] However, such a solution is not available in the case of the CFSP, since, after the Lisbon reform, this policy does not have any objective of its own.

The argument has been made that, since the Lisbon reform has eliminated the CFSP-specific objectives, one should pay less attention to the objectives of a measure when applying the "centre of gravity" doctrine. [32] According to some authors, the teleological indeterminacy of the CFSP may even raise the question of what ultimately remains of this policy after Lisbon. [33] The presumption that "normal" (non-CFSP) EU law should predominate is (allegedly) deeply ingrained in the judicial psyche. [34] Hence, there is a risk that non-CFSP competences might "encroach upon CFSP powers which would endanger the latter's special character". [35] Interestingly, the case law discussed in this paper allays these fears, and actually raises the opposite concern, as this section and the next one will show.

To preserve the specific character of the CFSP, Advocate General Bot proposed a radical solution in *Smart sanctions* and *Mauritius*: identifying "CFSP-specific" objectives. He started from the assumption that certain objectives set out in Article 21 TEU (including safeguarding the EU's security and strengthening international security) are among those "traditionally assigned" to that policy under pre-Lisbon Article 11, paragraph 1,

---

31 See further E. Neframi, "Commentaire de l'article 21 TUE'", in O. Dubos, S. Platon (eds), *Commentaire du Traité sur l'Union européenne* (Berlin: Springer, forthcoming). See also Opinion of AG Bot of 30 January 2014, *Parliament* v *Council* (*Mauritius*), *supra* note 6, para 88.

32 M. Klamert, *supra* note 30, 505. See also A. Engel, *supra* note 10, 54; P. van Elsuwege, "On the Boundaries between the European Union's First Pillar and Second Pillar: A Comment on the ECOWAS Judgment of the European Court of Justice", *Columbia Journal of European Law* 15, no. 3 (2009), 531, at 545-546. Cf. Opinion of AG Bot of 30 January 2014, *Parliament* v *Council* (*Mauritius*), *supra* note 6, para 85.

33 C. Hillion, "A Powerless Court? The European Court of Justice and the Common Foreign and Security Policy", in M. Cremona, A. Thies (eds), *The European Court of Justice and External Relations Law* (Oxford: Hart 2014), 47.

34 P. Craig, *The Lisbon Treaty: Law, Politics and Treaty Reform* (Oxford: Oxford University Press, 2010), 415-416; see also P. J. Cardwell, "On 'Ring-fencing' the Common Foreign and Security Policy in the Legal Order of the European Union", *Northern Ireland Law Quarterly* 64, no. 4 (2013), 443, at 451.

35 A. Engel, *supra* note 10, 54.

TEU. [36] EU actions that pursue the objective of preserving peace and strengthening international security should consequently be regarded as falling within the sphere of the CFSP. [37] Advocate General Bot's approach has been criticised in the literature, because it seems to contradict the spirit of the Lisbon reform. [38] Had the Member States wanted to insert CFSP-specific objectives, they would have placed them in the CFSP chapter of the TEU.[39] Instead, they set up a list of objectives common to the entire external action – including the CFSP. [40] In any event, Advocate General Bot's theory on the traditional objectives of the CFSP seems not to have fallen on fertile ground, since the Court of Justice did not discuss it in either *Smart sanctions* or one of the subsequent cases.

A second theory introduced by Advocate General Bot – the distinction between internal and international security – has proved more successful. As is well known, "internal and external security are inseparable". [41] The EU's Global Strategy, for instance, expressly affirms that "our security at home depends on peace beyond our borders". [42] Advocate General Bot has acknowledged the interdependence of internal and international security, at least in principle. For instance, in *Smart sanctions* he refused to subscribe to the Council's view that the delimitation of the respective spheres of application of Articles 75 and 215 TFEU should have been based on a distinction between "internal" and "international" terrorists. [43] Furthermore, in *Mauritius* he noted that the distinction between internal and international security "is not always clear", because crime in a certain

---

36 Opinion of AG Bot of 31 January 2012, *Parliament* v *Council* (*Smart sanctions*), C-130/10, EU:C:2012:50, para 63. See also, to that effect, J. Larik, *Foreign Policy Objectives in European Constitutional Law* (Oxford University Press, 2016), 215.

37 Opinion of AG Bot of 31 January 2012, *Parliament* v *Council* (*Smart sanctions*), *supra* note 36, paras. 63-64. See also Opinion of AG Bot of 30 January 2014, *Parliament* v *Council* (*Mauritius*), *supra* note 6, para 87.

38 See further G. De Baere, T. Van den Sanden, *supra* note 10, 106; H. Merket, *supra* note 28, 292.

39 C. Hillion, *supra* note 33, 22.

40 G. De Baere, T. Van den Sanden, *supra* note 10, 106; C. Hillion, *supra* note 33, 22.

41 The Stockholm Programme — An open and secure Europe serving and protecting citizens, OJ 2010 C 115, p. 1, para 7.

42 Shared Vision, Common Action: A Stronger Europe: A Global Strategy for the European Union's Foreign and Security Policy, http://eeas.europa.eu/archives/docs/top_stories/pdf/eugs_review_web.pdf, 7.

43 Opinion of AG Bot of 31 January 2012, *Parliament* v *Council* (*Smart sanctions*), *supra* note 36, para 75.

region may pose a threat to both the internal security of the Union and the stability of the region concerned. [44]

On closer inspection, however, it appears that Advocate General Bot did draw a distinction between internal and international security, and argued that the delimitation of the respective spheres of application of the AFSJ and the CFSP should be based on that distinction. In *Smart sanctions,* he took the view that the contested measure was correctly adopted on the basis of Article 215 TFEU on account of its "CFSP" dimension. That dimension derived from the principal objective of the measure: combating "international" terrorism in order to maintain "international" peace and security. [45]

Advocate General Bot rendered the distinction between internal and international security more explicit in *Mauritius.* He noted that measures concerning the AFSJ, whether of a purely internal nature or having an external dimension, must be taken with the aim of furthering freedom, security and justice "inside the Union". [46] Indeed, "Article 67(1) TFEU provides that 'the Union shall constitute an [AFSJ]'". [47] According to Advocate General Bot, this implies that an international agreement on police or judicial cooperation may be based on an AFSJ provision only if such cooperation has a direct link with the aim of the "internal security" of the Union. [48] Advocate General Kokott followed the same approach in *Tanzania,* arguing that the contested measure could be founded on a CFSP provision, since it was intended to promote "international security outside the territory of the Union" and lacked "a specific connection *with security within the European Union*". [49]

Unlike its Advocates General, the Court did not expressly draw a distinction between internal and international security in either *Smart sanctions* or *Tanzania.* Nonetheless, it seemed to implicitly accept the existence of such a distinction, and referred to it in order to justify the use of

44 Opinion of AG Bot of 30 January 2014, *Parliament* v *Council* (*Mauritius*), *supra* note 6, para 113.
45 Opinion of AG Bot of 31 January 2012, *Parliament* v *Council* (*Smart sanctions*), *supra* note 36, para 72.
46 Opinion of AG Bot of 30 January 2014, *Parliament* v *Council* (*Mauritius*), *supra* note 6, para 109.
47 *Ibid.*
48 *Id.,* para 112.
49 Opinion of AG Kokott of 28 October 2015, *Parliament* v *Council* (*Tanzania*), *supra* note 3, paras 67-67 (emphasis in the original).

CFSP legal bases in both cases. In *Smart sanctions,* the Court held that the AFSJ and the CFSP "pursue objectives which, although complementary, do not have the same scope". [50] While the combating of "terrorism" may well be among the objectives of the AFSJ, the objective of combating "international terrorism" in order to preserve "international peace and security" nevertheless corresponds to the objectives of the external action. [51] In other words, while AFSJ legal bases may be used to fight against terrorism in general (presumably, domestic terrorism), international terrorism is to be fought through external relations instruments.

The CFSP, in particular, can be used to fight against international terrorism, which indeed constitutes a threat to "international security". [52] Therefore, Article 215, paragraph 2, TFEU (a legal basis used to implement CFSP decisions) constitutes the appropriate legal basis for measures directed against suspected terrorists who, "having regard to their activities globally" and to the "international dimension" of the threat they pose, affect fundamentally the Union's external activity. [53] In other words, the "international" dimension of terrorism and the threat it poses to "international" security seem to justify the use of a foreign policy (CFSP) tool in this area. This seems to suggest, *a contrario,* that, when terrorism constitutes a threat for "internal" security, an AFSJ legal basis might be necessary.

In *Tanzania,* the Court seemed more cautious about the distinction between internal and international security, but nonetheless appeared to uphold it. The Court based its analysis mostly on a contextual interpretation of the agreement with Tanzania, arguing that it constitutes an instrument whereby the European Union pursues the objectives of Joint Action 2008/851/CFSP, setting up Operation Atalanta. [54] The peculiarities and shortcomings of this contextual approach are discussed in the next section. It is already important to note, in any event, that the Court accepted that the objective of Operation Atalanta, and consequently the objective of the agreement with Tanzania, is to preserve "international peace and security". Since the agreement with Tanzania promotes "international" security, it

50 Judgment of 19 July 2012, *Parliament* v *Council* (*Smart sanctions*), *supra* note 11, para 66.

51 *Id.,* para 61.

52 *Id.,* para 63.

53 *Id.*, para 78.

54 Judgment of 14 June 2016, *Parliament* v *Council* (*Tanzania*), *supra* note 4, para 54.

falls predominantly within the scope of the CFSP, and does not require an AFSJ legal basis. [55] The Court thus seems again to accept, albeit implicitly, that the CFSP pursues objectives of international security, while the AFSJ is meant to promote security within the Union.

The distinction between internal and international security, expressly endorsed by the Advocates General and implicitly accepted by the Court, seems to be problematic. In the first place, such a distinction finds only limited support in primary law. The Treaties use the expression "internal security" only to affirm that Union law does not impinge on the Member States' capacity to maintain their "internal security" (Articles 72 and 276 TFEU), and to describe a Committee set up within the Council (Article 71 TFEU). The objectives of the AFSJ encompass, more generally, the maintenance of a high level of "security" (Article 67 TFEU), which is not qualified as "internal". Strengthening "international" security, on the other hand, is explicitly mentioned as a transversal objective of the entire Union's action on the international scene (Article 21 TEU), which therefore includes the external dimension of the AFSJ. Such an objective cannot, therefore, be ascribed solely to the CFSP framework. Strengthening "international security" is, to be sure, an objective of the CSDP, as recognised by Article 42, paragraph 1, TEU, but it does not belong exclusively to the CSDP. In fact, restrictive measures aimed at individuals allegedly involved in terrorist activities might well strengthen international security, as noted by the Court in *Smart sanctions,* but do not have a CSDP legal basis.

In the second place, it may be very difficult to distinguish between threats to internal and international security in practice. Advocate General Bot acknowledged this problem in *Smart sanctions,* by noting that one cannot distinguish between internal and international terrorists, since "terrorism does not recognise borders". [56] Even a terrorist organisation whose targets are limited to a specific geographical area may have international off-shoots, in particular for the purpose of financing its activities. [57] The attacks in Paris and Brussels (2015 and 2016, respectively) confirm that an international terrorist group, such as the so-called Islamic State, may threaten security within the EU. In fact, terrorism has not always been re-

55 *Id.*, para 55.
56 Opinion of AG Bot of 31 January 2012, *Parliament* v *Council* (*Smart sanctions*), *supra* note 36, paras 75-76.
57 *Id.*, para 76.

garded as a threat to "international security" in the case law of the Court of Justice. In the *PNR* judgment and, more recently, in Opinion 1/15, the Court held that the international agreements on the transfer of Passenger Name Record data contribute to the fight against terrorism and, consequently, safeguard "public security". [58] Since they pursue such an objective, these agreements should have an AFSJ legal basis (Article 87, paragraph 2, (a), TFEU), as recognised in Opinion 1/15. [59] Considering that terrorism should be fought through an AFSJ measure, one might assume that terrorism constitutes a threat to "internal" security (even if the Court speaks of "public" security).

It may be argued that the targets of the PNR agreements are not different from those of the restrictive measures at issue in *Smart sanctions*. Such targets may include, in particular, the same physical persons, such as members of *Al Qaeda* or the Islamic State. It seems paradoxical that such persons may be considered, in one case, a threat to internal security (*PNR*) and, in another case, a threat to "international" security (*Smart sanctions*). How may two EU measures targeting the same terrorists pursue different objectives, to the point of being based on different Treaty provisions?

A possible solution to this paradox appears, *prima facie*, to lie in the geographical location of the effects of the EU's activities, as suggested by Advocate General Kokott in *Tanzania.* In her view, the agreement with Tanzania does not have a specific connection to security within the EU, because "the cooperation with Tanzania does not seek to combat and prosecute piracy off European coasts, but in the much more distant Horn of Africa". [60] Even this solution, however, appears unsatisfactory on closer inspection. If the agreement with Tanzania had to be concluded on a CFSP basis because the Horn of Africa is "distant", would an identical agreement with a closer country, such as Morocco, have to be based on an AFSJ

58 Opinion of 26 July 2017, 1/15, *supra* note 14, para 81; Judgment of 30 May 2006, *Parliament* v *Council* (*PNR*), C-317/04 and C-318/04, EU:C:2006:346, para 55. See also Opinion of AG Mengozzi of 8 September 2016 in Opinion procedure 1/15, EU:C:2016:656, para 2.

59 The PNR agreement with Canada should also be based on Article 16 TFEU (data protection), see Opinion of 26 July 2017, 1/15, *supra* note 14; however, that provision is not directly related to security and is consequently not relevant for the purpose of the present analysis.

60 Opinion of AG Kokott of 28 October 2015, *Parliament* v *Council* (*Tanzania*), *supra* note 3 , para 67.

provision? [61] Advocate General Bot asked as similar question in *Smart sanctions*: if a terrorist group which usually operates within the EU decides to collaborate with other terrorist groups located outside the EU, do the persons associated with the first group lose their status as "internal" terrorists and become "international" terrorists? [62]

The above considerations suggest that the distinction between internal and international security is, to a large extent, arbitrary. Consequently, it seems to be hardly conducive to transparency and predictability in applying the "centre of gravity" doctrine.

A purely teleological approach is insufficient to solve the conundrum of the legal bases of security-related acts. A more viable solution is offered by the letter of the "centre of gravity" doctrine: the case law requires the interpreter of a measure to examine both its aim and its content. [63] Paying greater attention to the content of the contested measures might have led to quite different outcomes in the recent cases. The content of the agreements at issue in *Mauritius* and *Tanzania* is very close to the AFSJ: as acknowledged by Advocate General Kokott, these agreements contain "a number of provisions that are typical of cross-border judicial cooperation in criminal matters and cross-border police cooperation". [64] Hence, their legal bases should arguably have included Articles 82 and 87 TFEU, as requested by the Parliament. [65] Similar considerations are applicable to *Smart sanctions*. The contested measure concerned the freezing of terrorists' funds, an issue that falls squarely within the scope of Article 75

61 It is true that, in principle, the legal basis which has been used for the adoption of other EU measures which might, in certain cases, display similar characteristics is irrelevant in terms of identifying the legal basis of a measure, see Judgment of 27 February 2014, *United Kingdom* v *Council*, C-656/11, EU:C:2014:97, para 48. However, it would be bizarre if the Union used completely different procedures to conclude virtually identical instruments, for the sole reason that those instruments concern activities which are presumed to take place in different areas.

62 Opinion of AG Bot of 31 January 2012, *Parliament* v *Council* (*Smart sanctions*), *supra* note 36, para 76.

63 See Opinion of AG Wahl of 8 September 2016 in Opinion procedure 3/15, EU:C:2016:657, footnote 43.

64 Opinion of AG Kokott of 28 October 2015, *Parliament* v *Council* (*Tanzania*), *supra* note 3, para 60; see also Judgment of 14 June 2016, *Tanzania, supra* note 4, para 47.

65 Regarding the cumulating of CFSP and AFSJ legal bases in the case of international agreements, see *supra* note 16.

TFEU, an AFSJ provision which deals specifically with the "freezing of funds" of terrorists.

Interestingly, the Court of Justice chose another solution: instead of complementing the teleological approach with an analysis of the content, it focused on the *context* of the contested measures in order to determine their legal bases.

IV. Contextual Interpretation: The Dangers of the "Super-Absorption" of Legal Bases

If teleological interpretation does not permit an easy identification of the legal bases of security-related acts, contextual reading might perhaps be better suited to fulfil the promise of objective review.[66] As Advocate General Kokott noted in *Tanzania,* when applying the "centre of gravity" doctrine, regard must be had to objective factors amenable to judicial review, which include not only the aim and content of the contested decision, "but also the context of that decision". [67] Similarly, Advocate General Bot argued in *Mauritius* that the assessment of the centre of gravity of the measure concerned must also take account of the context of that measure. [68]

Advocate General Bot analysed in detail the context of the agreement with Mauritius, describing its close links with Operation Atalanta. He noted that the agreement organises the modalities for the transfer of suspected pirates and associated seized property from EUNAVFOR to the Republic of Mauritius and frames the conditions for the treatment and prosecution of those persons. [69] The agreement is allegedly essential to the proper implementation of Operation Atalanta, whose mission is to contribute to the deterrence, prevention and repression of acts of piracy. It would be difficult to achieve the objective of the mission "if persons who have committed acts of piracy were not subject to prosecution and could therefore re-

---

66 M. Klamert, *supra* note 30, 505.

67 Opinion of AG Kokott of 28 October 2015, *Parliament* v *Council* (*Tanzania*), *supra* note 3, para 59. See also Judgment of 27 February 2014, *UK* v *Council*, *supra* note 61, para 50. See also Judgment of 26 September 2013, *UK* v *Council,* C-431/11, EU:C:2013:589, para 48; Judgment of 18 October 2014, *UK* v *Council*, C-81/13, EU:C:2014:2449, para 38.

68 Opinion of AG Bot of 30 January 2014, *Parliament* v *Council* (*Mauritius*), *supra* note 6, para 37.

69 *Id.*, para 59.

sume their criminal activities immediately". [70] The agreement with Mauritius is therefore intrinsically linked to the conduct of the Atalanta military operation, [71] and may even be regarded as an "implementing measure for the Joint Action [2008/851/CFSP], of which it forms an integral part". [72]

The Court of Justice followed a similar approach in *Tanzania.* Unlike its Advocates General, the Court did not expressly affirm that context must be taken into account in the assessment of the centre of gravity. Nonetheless, it did analyse the context of the agreement with Tanzania. According to the Court, the EU-Tanzania agreement is an essential element in the effective realisation of the objectives of Operation Atalanta, since it helps to ensure that pirates do not go unpunished. [73] At the same time, Operation Atalanta is an essential logical precondition for the agreement: "were there to be no such operation, that agreement would be devoid of purpose". [74] This suggests that the aim of the agreement is provide for an instrument – the transfer of pirates – whereby the EU pursues the objectives of Operation Atalanta, namely to preserve international peace and security. [75] Since the Agreement is "merely ancillary to the EUNAVFOR action", the Court concluded that it falls predominantly within the scope of the CFSP. [76]

The contextual interpretation of the agreements with Mauritius and Tanzania embraced by Advocate General Bot and the Court has four main shortcomings. In the first place, the Court and its Advocate General seem to pay too much attention to the context (and the objectives) of the contested measures, and seem to ignore their content, which is no less important, as noted in the previous section.

Second, their contextual interpretation of the contested measures is based on the assumption that promoting "international" security is an objective of the CFSP. As argued in the previous section, however, the distinction between internal and international security is far from straightforward. Even if the contested measures pursued the objectives of Operation

70 *Id.*, paras 71-73.
71 *Id.*, para 78.
72 *Id.*, para 70.
73 Judgment of 14 June 2016, *Parliament* v *Council* (*Tanzania*), *supra* note 4, para 49.
74 *Id.*, para 51.
75 *Id.*, para 54.
76 *Id.*, paras 51 and 55.

Atalanta, as the Court affirms, they would not necessarily pursue CFSP aims, since the CFSP shares its objectives with the rest of the external action (Article 21 TEU).

Third, the Court and Advocate General Bot appear to overemphasise the connection between the agreements and Operation Atalanta. Contrary to their assertions, the agreements with Mauritius and Tanzania do not seem to be essential to the proper implementation of Operation Atalanta. The persons apprehended by EUNAVFOR can be transferred, not only to third States, but also to the competent authorities of the flag Member States which took them captive. [77] In fact, it is only when the flag Member State cannot, or does not wish to exercise its jurisdiction, that a captive may be transferred to a third State, such as Mauritius or Tanzania. [78] The agreements with third States are indispensable for this purpose, since EUNAVFOR cannot transfer any person to a third State "unless the conditions for the transfer have been agreed with that third State in a manner consistent with relevant international law". [79] It would seem, therefore, that the agreements with Mauritius and Tanzania are not simply a corollary of Operation Atalanta, but constitute an expression of the Member States' policy in criminal matters. Instead of prosecuting the pirates themselves, the Member States decided to outsource such prosecution to third States, via agreements concluded by the European Union and third States. Since the purpose of such agreements is related to criminal justice, it would not have been unreasonable to include at least Article 82 TFEU among the legal bases of those agreements.

Fourth and most importantly, the Court and Advocate General Bot might have paid insufficient attention to the aim and content of the contested measure *per se*. In accordance with settled case law, the choice of the legal basis of an EU act must rest on objective factors, including the aim and content of "that measure". In other words, as noted by the Court, the legal basis for a measure must be determined having regard to "its own" aim and content. [80] In *Tanzania* and *Mauritius,* the Court and its Ad-

77 See Joint Action 2008/851/CFSP, *supra* note 24, Article 12, paragraph 1, first indent. See also the arguments of the Parliament, summarised in para 30 of Judgment of 14 June 2016, *Parliament* v *Council* (*Tanzania*), *supra* note 4.

78 See Joint Action 2008/851/CFSP, *supra* note 24, Article 12, paragraph 1, first indent.

79 *Id.*, Article 12, paragraph 1, last subparagraph.

80 Judgment of 27 February 2014, *UK* v *Council*, *supra* note 61, para 48.

vocate General defined the legal basis of the contested agreement, not in light of the aim and content of "that measure", but in light of the aim of another measure: Joint Action 2008/851. *Tanzania* would thus seem to introduce an exception to the general test on the centre of gravity: the choice of the legal basis of an "ancillary" EU act does not rest on its own aim and content, but depends on the legal basis of another, predominant, act.

This approach is reminiscent of the well-established doctrine of "absorption" of legal bases, whereby the leading objective of a measure absorbs its other components. [81] Pursuant to this doctrine, if an EU act has two components, one of which is predominant and the other ancillary, only the legal basis of the predominant component is used. The recent case law seems to envisage a sort of "super-absorption" of legal bases: if one act is ancillary to another, it should be founded on the latter's legal basis. The external aspect of the AFSJ is thus "absorbed by the exercise of the Union's foreign policy competence to serve the objectives of the CFSP". [82] Such an outcome is allegedly in line with the Treaties (according to Advocate General Bot), since "the requirement of consistency encourages the Council to integrate aspects relating to other Union policies into the CFSP measures which it adopts". [83]

At first sight, it might seem that the principle of external action consistency, set out in Article 21, paragraph 3, TEU, justifies the "super-absorption" of legal bases. [84] Pursuant to the requirement of consistency, the Union should mobilise its different external action competences through a "global approach", [85] in order to pursue its goals and, eventually, to rein-

81 M. Maresceau, *Bilateral Agreements Concluded by the European Community*, Collected Courses of the Hague Academy of International Law (Leiden: Brill | Nijhoff, 2004), 157.

82 Opinion of AG Bot of 30 January 2014, *Parliament* v *Council* (*Mauritius*), *supra* note 6, para 118.

83 *Id.*, para 24.

84 The word "coherence" arguably describes the content of Articles 21, paragraph 3, TEU and 7 TFEU better than the word "consistency". For the sake of simplicity, the word "consistency" is used here, since it is also used in the English version of the Treaties. See M. Gatti, *European External Action Service: Promoting Coherence through Autonomy and Coordination,* Studies in EU External Relations (Leiden: Brill | Nijhoff, 2016), 30-32.

85 The expression is borrowed from E. Neframi, "Le rapport entre objectifs et compétences : de la structuration et de l'identité de l'Union européenne", in E. Neframi (ed), *Objectifs et compétences dans l'Union européenne* (Bruxelles : Bruylant 2013), 5.

force the European identity and its independence on the international scene. [86] One of the main obstacles to consistency in EU external relations derives from the fragmentation of decision-making procedures and, in particular, from the *summa divisio* between the CFSP and the rest of the external action. It might be argued, therefore, that the concern for consistency might justify, on some occasions, a certain degree of interference between EU external policies. [87] Consequently, it seems theoretically possible that the Union might occasionally have to integrate aspects relating to other Union policies into the CFSP.

However, it does not seem that such integration was necessary in the *Mauritius* and *Tanzania* cases. The use of CFSP legal bases does not seem to have increased the Union's consistency on the international scene. The EU's external action would have been equally consistent and effective if the Union had chosen to conclude the agreements with Mauritius and Tanzania on the basis of AFSJ provisions (or by using both CFSP and AFSJ legal bases). In fact, the use of AFSJ legal bases would hardly have affected the EU's ability to speak with one voice or to effectively transfer the pirates apprehended by Atalanta. As the integration of AFSJ elements into CFSP acts was not conducive to increased consistency, it does not seem possible to argue that the requirement of consistency justified an expansive interpretation of the scope of the CFSP in these cases.

A proper interpretation of external action consistency actually confirms that AFSJ legal bases were necessary in *Mauritius* and *Tanzania*. The structure of the Treaties suggests that the Union should ensure consistency in its external relations, while maintaining separate external actions. The already-cited Article 40 TEU expressly stipulates that the CFSP should not affect other policies (and *vice versa*). Moreover, Article 21, paragraph 3, TEU stipulates that the Union must ensure consistency between the "different areas" of its external action. Article 7 TFEU similarly affirms

86 See I. Bosse-Platière, *L'article 3 du traité UE: recherche sur une exigence de cohérence de l'action extérieure de l'Union européenne* (Bruxelles: Bruylant 2009), 524; E. Neframi, *L'action extérieure de l'Union européenne: Fondements, moyens, principes* (Paris: Librairie générale de droit et de jurisprudence, 2010), 141; I. Bosse-Platière, "L'objectif d'affirmation de l'Union Européenne sur la scène internationale", in E. Neframi (ed), *Objectifs et compétences dans l'Union Européenne* (Bruxelles: Bruylant 2013), 268.

87 See M. Gatti, *supra* note 84, 49-58; R. Wessel, "The Inside Looking Out: Consistency and Delimitation in EU External Relations", *Common Market Law Review* 37, no. 5 (2000), 1135.

that the Union must ensure consistency between its "policies" (in the plural). The combination of Articles 21 and 40 TEU and Article 7 TFEU arguably suggests that the Union should ensure synergy among its different policies to better attain its objectives.

In light of these provisions, a Union action for the repression of acts of piracy (Operation Atalanta) may come under the CFSP, while the more detailed definition of the modalities for the transfer and the treatment of the persons concerned (the agreements with Mauritius and Tanzania) falls outside the scope of the CFSP.[88] It seems indeed reasonable that the Union may enter into agreements on police and judicial cooperation, based on AFSJ legal bases, to support military missions, founded on CFSP provisions. All these activities pursue the same goal, that is, fostering the EU's security, but have different content. They should consequently be conducted separately, on different legal bases, but also consistently.

V. Conclusion

The assessment of the legal bases of EU acts is often problematic, and is particularly complicated in the field of security. The EU pursues the security objective through two policy frameworks: the Common Foreign and Security Policy and the Area of Freedom, Security and Justice.

In its recent case law, the Court has defined the legal basis of security-related acts through a teleological and contextual interpretation of contested measures, shedding some light on this matter. The case law makes it clear that sanctions against "international" terrorists are to be adopted within the CFSP framework. Similarly, it would seem that instruments which are ancillary to CFSP operations may be based on CFSP provisions. The recent case law has perhaps the advantage of preserving a space of action for the CFSP, whose viability had been cast into doubt. The Court might have thus reassured the Member States that it does not seek to "communitarise" foreign policy via the back door, as some precedents might perhaps have suggested. [89]

88 See *a contrario* Opinion of AG Bot of 30 January 2014, *Parliament* v *Council* (*Mauritius*), *supra* note 6, para 57.

89 One may think, in particular, of: Judgment of 28 April 2015, *Commission* v *Council* (*Air Transport Agreement*), C-28/12, EU:C:2015:282; Judgment of 7 Novem-

However, the recent case law may be affected by some shortcomings. In the first place, the Court seems to have identified the legal bases of the contested measures solely in light of their objectives and context, disregarding their content, thereby reducing predictability and transparency in the allocation of legal bases. Second, the recent case law appears to be inspired by an artificial distinction between internal and international security, which is probably unjustified and likely to generate further uncertainty in the application of the "centre of gravity" doctrine. [90] Third, the Court seems to take contextual interpretation too far, to the point of accepting the "absorption" of AFSJ measures by CFSP instruments, thereby contradicting the principle of consistency and blurring the delimitation of EU policies.

Given its shortcomings, the recent case law on security-related measures appears not to ensure a clear and sound demarcation of the CFSP and the AFSJ. Moreover, it could excessively extend the scope of the CFSP, to the detriment of the AFSJ and other policy areas. The recent case law may thus raise fresh concerns about the preservation of formerly Community policies, which had been allayed by the *ECOWAS* case. [91] In the future, the Council might argue, for instance, that certain international cooperation projects are "ancillary" to ongoing CSDP operations and that, pursuant to the *Tanzania* case law, they should be "absorbed" by the CFSP. Thus, a project on security sector reform financed by the Instrument Contributing to Peace and Stability [92] might now be considered as "ancillary" to a CSDP mission providing support for security sector reform in a third country. [93]

---

ber 2014, *Germany* v *Council* (*OIV*), C-399/12, EU:C:2014:2258; Judgment of 20 April 2010, *Commission* v *Sweden* (*PFOS*), C-246/07, EU:C:2010:203.

90 See M. Klamert, *supra* note 30, 505; N. Emiliou, "Opening Pandora's Box: The Legal Basis of Community Measures before the Court of Justice", *European Law Review* 19, no. 5 (1994), 488, 499.

91 Judgment of 20 May 2008, *Parliament* v *Council* (*ECOWAS*), C-91/05, EU:C:2008:288.

92 Parliament and Council Regulation 230/2014/EU, OJ 2014 L 77, p. 1.

93 This might have been the case, for instance, for the project "Support to MoD organization and administration capacity with a view to enable civilian oversight of the defence sector in Central African Republic", which was operative between June 2015 and December 2016, see www.insightonconflict.org/maps/icsp. This project might potentially be seen as ancillary to the CSDP Military Advisory Mission in the Central African Republic, see Council Decision 2015/78/CFSP, OJ 2015 L 13, p. 8 (in particular, Article 1 thereof).

Such a reinforcement of the gravitational attraction of the CFSP is arguably unwarranted and would hardly represent a positive constitutional development in the framework of EU external relations. As the CFSP remains predominantly intergovernmental and is subject to limited judicial overview, its overextension might have a negative impact on access to justice, the EU's democratic principles, and institutional balance.

L'application du principe de subsidiarité dans le cadre de l'action extérieure de l'Union européenne / The Principle of Subsidiarity within the External Action of the European Union

Isabelle Bosse-Platière

Abstract

Prescribed in Article 5 TEU, the principle of subsidiarity is one of the constitutional principles of the EU regarding the exercise of non-exclusive powers of the European Union. Its function in the EU system is to determine the pertinent level of action considering the criteria of insufficiency of Member States action and added value of the one conducted by the EU (Article 5, paragraph 3, TEU).

The question addressed in this chapter is whether and to what extent the principle of subsidiarity is applicable in the external action of the EU. This is a very sensitive question considering the symbolic dimension of subsidiarity as a federal principle. Considering the general nature of the principle, there is no doubt it is applicable in the field of external action of the EU, although it rarely motivates the decisions to conclude international agreements. Nevertheless, the application of the subsidiarity principle may raise important issues regarding the visibility of the EU on the international stage. The first issue concerns the scope of the principle in the context of a complex distribution of external powers between the EU and Member States. As is well known, it is not easy to determine the exact nature of the external competences of the EU and the principle shall not apply when the conditions provided in Article 3, paragraph 2, TFEU are fulfilled. The first two conditions are quite simple to assess, as they require the previous adoption of an internal act. One can assume that the subsidiarity test was carried out when internal acts were adopted, long before international agreements were adopted. The third condition – the criterion of necessity – is much more interesting regarding the implementation of subsidiarity. In this context, subsidiarity and necessity derive from the same logic: the realisation of the objectives set out in the Treaties. The implementation of subsidiarity in case of non-exclusive powers can concern a large range of situations in which this principle plays a more or less important role:

shared competences (Article 4, paragraph 2, TFEU), parallel competences (Article 4, paragraphs 3 and 4, TFEU) and the competence in the CSFP area. The second question regarding the implementation of subsidiarity in the external action concerns its consequences for the Member States and for the EU institutions. For the Member States, the principle requires that the complementarity of both national and European actions shall be respected. As for the institutions, a better involvement of national parliaments during the negotiation process could be a solution ensuring an efficient ratification of mixed agreements as well as respect of subsidiarity.

***

« Principe d'essence politique »[1], le principe de subsidiarité avait fait une apparition remarquée en droit primaire lors de l'Acte unique européen[2], mais ce n'est qu'avec le traité de Maastricht qu'il a acquis la portée de principe du droit de l'Union européenne qu'on lui connaît aujourd'hui[3]. Désormais inscrit à l'article 5 du Traité sur l'Union européenne (TUE), il est, avec le principe de proportionnalité, l'un des deux principes qui « régissent l'exercice des compétences [de l'Union] ». S'appliquant aux compétences non exclusives attribuées à l'Union, il a essentiellement pour fonction de permettre la détermination du niveau pertinent de l'action, celui auquel devront s'exercer les compétences au regard de l'objectif poursuivi, en fonction des critères posés à l'article 5, paragraphe 3, TUE d'insuffisance de l'action des Etats membres d'une part, et de la valeur ajoutée de l'action de l'Union d'autre part. Considéré à la fois comme un frein au développement excessif de la réglementation de l'Union dans les domaines où la compétence de principe reste entre les

1 Commission européenne, *Le principe de subsidiarité*, SEC (1992) 1990 final, 27 octobre 1992, reproduit in *Revue trimestrielle de droit européen,* vol. 28, n°4/1992, p. 728.

2 Lors de l'attribution à la Communauté européenne d'une nouvelle compétence en matière d'environnement.

3 V. K. Lenaerts, P. Van Ypersele, « Le principe de subsidiarité et son contexte : étude de l'article 3B du traité CE », *Cahiers de droit européen,* vol. 10, n°1-2/1994, p. 3; H. Bribosia, « Subsidiarité et répartition des compétences entre la Communauté et les Etats membres. Commentaire sur l'article 3B du traité de Maastricht », *Revue du marché unique européen*, n°4/1992, p. 165.

mains des Etats[4] et comme un « principe instrumental »[5] favorisant l'action de l'Union dans ces domaines, le principe de subsidiarité est frappé d'une incontestable ambiguïté[6]. Il joue en tout cas un rôle ambivalent dans la construction européenne, compte tenu de l'appréciation très politique sur laquelle repose sa mise en œuvre et de la difficulté de son contrôle juridictionnel[7].

Si le principe de subsidiarité a fait l'objet de nombreuses analyses en droit de l'Union européenne[8], son application en droit des relations extérieures a assez peu mobilisé la doctrine[9]. Sans doute cette relative indifférence peut-elle s'expliquer par le fait que ce principe est très rarement évoqué au titre de la motivation des actes en matière externe. Tout au plus le trouve-t-on abordé, de manière souvent lapidaire, voire elliptique, dans les éléments juridiques présidant à la présentation des propositions d'actes élaborées par la Commission européenne[10]. La Cour de justice, quant à elle, n'a jamais été appelée à trancher un litige dans lequel était en cause l'application du principe de subsidiarité en matière externe.

---

4 V. D. Gadbin, « Organisation des compétences et stratégies d'intégration communautaire après le traité de Maastricht », *Revue du droit public*, n°5/1995, p. 1293.

5 G. Strozzi, « Le principe de subsidiarité dans la perspective de l'intégration européenne : une énigme et beaucoup d'attentes », *Revue trimestrielle de droit européen,* vol. 30, n°3/1994, p. 375.

6 M. Blanquet, « Compétences de l'Union européenne. Exercice – Régulation », *JurisClasseur Europe Traité,* Fasc. 175, septembre 2014, point 16.

7 C. Blumann, « Le contrôle juridictionnel des principes de subsidiarité et de proportionnalité en droit de l'Union européenne », in *La Constitution, l'Europe et le droit. Mélanges en l'honneur de Jean-Claude Masclet*, Publications de la Sorbonne, 2013, p. 439; B. Bertrand, « Un principe politique saisi par le droit. La justiciabilité du principe de subsidiarité en droit de l'Union européenne », *Revue trimestrielle de droit européen*, vol. 48, n°2/2012, p. 329.

8 Pour une analyse récente, v. T. van den Brink, « The Substance of Subsidiarity : the Interpretation and Meaning of the Principle after Lisbon », in M. Trybus, L. Rubini (dir.), *The Treaty of Lisbon and the Future of European Law and Policy*, Birmingham, Edward Elgar Publishing, 2012, p. 160.

9 Une référence est toutefois à signaler : A. Martinache, « Une application de la subsidiarité : la Cour de justice et les compétences externes », *Revue des affaires européennes/ Law & European Affairs,* vol. 8, n°1-2/1998, p. 63.

10 Par exemple, voir la proposition de décision concernant la conclusion du protocole modifiant l'accord de transport aérien entre la Communauté européenne et ses Etats membres d'une part et les Etats-Unis d'Amérique, d'autre part, COM(2010) 208 final/2, 4 mai 2010, 10 p.

Il est vrai que l'affirmation de l'Union en tant qu'acteur sur la scène internationale est toujours une question sensible pour les Etats membres qui restent des sujets de droit international. Et la dimension symbolique du principe de subsidiarité en tant que principe d'essence fédéral n'est pas un facteur encourageant. L'application de la subsidiarité « à l'externe » est donc susceptible de revêtir des enjeux importants en termes de visibilité de l'Union sur la scène internationale, parfois au détriment de celle des Etats membres. Faut-il pour en autant en déduire que ce principe ne serait pas opposable à l'action extérieure ou, plus largement, que celle-ci serait rétive à son application? A l'évidence, non. Tout d'abord, il découle d'une jurisprudence bien établie de la Cour que l'absence d'une référence explicite au principe de subsidiarité dans la motivation d'un acte ne fait pas obstacle à ce qu'il ait effectivement présidé à son adoption[11] et donc à son contrôle. Ensuite, inséré au sein du titre I du TUE consacré aux « Dispositions communes », l'article 5 TUE est formulé en termes généraux : le paragraphe 1er établit les rapports entre les principes d'attribution, de subsidiarité et de proportionnalité pour l'ensemble des compétences de l'Union[12] et le paragraphe 3 TUE définit les conditions de mise en œuvre du principe de manière générale, sous réserve de son application aux compétences non exclusives de l'Union. D'ailleurs, dans son avis 2/94, la Cour de justice a pris soin de préciser que le respect du principe d'attribution des compétences « s'impose tant pour l'action interne que pour l'action internationale de la Communauté »[13]. Il en découle que la même constatation doit être également faite pour les principes qui régissent l'exercice des compétences.

Certes, une telle interprétation pourrait éventuellement être contredite par une interprétation de l'article 5, paragraphe 3, TUE en liaison avec le protocole n° 2 sur l'application des principes de subsidiarité et de proportionnalité, qui se réfère uniquement aux « actes législatifs », c'est-à-dire, en vertu de l'article 289, paragraphe 3, du Traité sur le fonctionnement de

11 Arrêt de la Cour du 13 mai 1997, *Allemagne / Parlement européen et Conseil*, C-233/94, EU:C:1997:231, point 28.

12 « Le principe d'attribution régit la délimitation des compétences de l'Union. Les principes de subsidiarité et de proportionnalité régissent l'exercice de ces compétences ».

13 Avis de la Cour du 28 mars 1996, 2/94, *Adhésion de la Communauté européenne à la Convention européenne de sauvegarde des droits de l'homme et des libertés fondamentales,* EU:C:1996:140, point 24.

l'Union européenne (TFUE), aux « actes juridiques adoptés par procédure législative ». Or, on sait que la qualification de la procédure de conclusion des accords externes prescrite à l'article 218 TFUE en tant que procédure législative peut prêter à discussion[14]. Toutefois, si une interprétation restrictive devait être retenue, faisant de la procédure de l'article 218 TFUE une procédure innommée, non législative, cela aurait peu d'incidence sur l'application du principe de subsidiarité à l'action extérieure de l'Union européenne. En effet, le protocole n° 2 n'a pas pour fonction de définir la portée du principe; il a seulement pour objet d'en préciser les modalités de mise en œuvre et de contrôle s'agissant des actes législatifs. Il n'exclut donc pas que le principe, rédigé en termes très généraux à l'article 5 TUE, puisse être applicable à l'ensemble de l'activité de l'Union, y compris son action extérieure.

L'application du principe de subsidiarité en matière d'action extérieure pose de redoutables questions, compte tenu de la complexité du mode de répartition des compétences externes de l'Union et de ses Etats membres et de leur exercice. En effet, l'application du principe de subsidiarité suppose qu'aient été préalablement résolues les questions liées à l'existence et surtout à la nature de la compétence. Or, la détermination de la nature de la compétence externe est souvent une question délicate qui nécessite un effort interprétatif dont les rouages ne sont parfois pas seulement juridiques et ne sont d'ailleurs pas nécessairement étrangers à une certaine logique de subsidiarité (I). Parallèlement, l'application de la subsidiarité est également sous-tendue par des enjeux politiques internationaux toujours sensibles en termes d'affirmation de l'Union et de préservation de la liberté d'action des Etats membres. Elle revêt donc une dimension plus institutionnelle : à ce titre, elle constitue un principe fondamental de l'Union

---

14 V. arrêt de la Cour du 21 décembre 2015, *Conseil / Front Polisario,* C-104/16 P, EU:C:2016:973. Dans ses conclusions présentées le 13 septembre 2016, l'Avocat général Wathelet, confirmant en cela la position retenue précédemment par le Tribunal (v. arrêt du Tribunal du 10 décembre 2015, *Front Polisario / Conseil*, T-512/12, EU:T:2015:953), considère que la procédure de conclusion des accords externes doit être considérée comme une procédure législative (v. conclusions présentées le 13 septembre 2016, EU:C:2016:677, points 151 à 161) mais dans son arrêt, la Cour ne se prononce pas sur cette question. En revanche, dans l'arrêt du 6 septembre 2017, *Slovaquie et Hongrie / Conseil* (C-643/15 et C-647/15, EU:C:2017:631) la Cour semble infirmer la thèse défendue par l'Avocat général Wathelet. Sur les incidences de cette question sur le contrôle de la subsidiarité en matière externe, voir *infra.*

en liaison avec le principe d'ouverture et l'objectif de « création d'une union sans cesse plus étroite entre les peuples de l'Europe dans lesquelles les décisions sont prises le plus près possible des citoyens, conformément au principe de subsidiarité »[15]. Dès lors, dans un contexte actuel marqué par une crispation des Etats membres sur la question des compétences externes et par des tensions vives entre l'Union et les Etats membres autour de la négociation et de la ratification de certains accords[16], notamment mixtes, la question se pose de savoir si la subsidiarité ne pourrait pas apparaître comme un facteur de rationalisation de ces relations au service d'une meilleure articulation des niveaux de pouvoirs européens et étatiques en matière externe (II).

I. Le champ d'application du principe de subsidiarité confronté à la complexité du mode d'organisation des compétences externes

Le champ d'application du principe de subsidiarité est défini à l'article 5, paragraphe 3, TUE par défaut : il s'applique « dans les domaines qui ne relèvent pas de [la] compétence exclusive » de l'Union. Dès lors, la règle posée par le traité est *a priori* fort simple : à partir du moment où une mesure est envisagée par l'Union européenne dans un domaine qui ne relève pas de sa compétence exclusive, l'adoption de cette mesure est soumise au respect du principe de subsidiarité et ne peut donc se justifier que si elle satisfait aux conditions, fixées à l'article 5, paragraphe 3, TUE. Or, envisagée à l'aune des compétences externes, cette règle se heurte en pratique à la difficulté de déterminer avec certitude la nature des compétences externes, et ce malgré les clarifications apportées par le traité

15 C'est également en ce sens que l'ex-article 2 TUE, dans sa version antérieure au traité de Lisbonne, prévoyait que « les objectifs de l'Union sont atteints conformément aux dispositions du présent traité, dans les conditions et selon rythmes qui y sont prévus, dans le respect du principe de subsidiarité ». C'est ce qui d'ailleurs avait pu justifier que l'on considère alors que la subsidiarité était applicable à l'ensemble de l'UE, y inclus les 2ème et 3ème piliers. A ce sujet, v. H. Bribosia, « Subsidiarité et répartition des compétences entre la Communauté et ses Etats membres », *supra* note 3, spéc. p. 178.

16 Tensions dont se font l'écho les nombreux contentieux portés devant la Cour de justice depuis l'entrée en vigueur du traité de Lisbonne et dans lesquels sont en cause l'articulation des compétences et des pouvoirs en matière externe.

de Lisbonne[17]. Il en découle que le principe ne saurait s'appliquer lorsque l'Union dispose d'une compétence exclusive pour conclure un accord externe (A). Parallèlement, le régime des compétences partagées étant moins monolithique que ne le laissent penser les dispositions des traités, derrière le caractère englobant de la formule des « compétences non exclusives » se dessine une mosaïque de situations au sein de laquelle le principe de subsidiarité s'appliquera de manière variable (B).

A. La non-application du principe de subsidiarité aux compétences externes exclusives

La détermination des compétences exclusives conditionne le champ d'application du principe de subsidiarité. Les traités envisagent deux hypothèses de compétences exclusives pour lesquelles l'exclusion du principe de subsidiarité se pose de manière différente : l'exclusivité par nature et l'exclusivité par exercice.

Les compétences exclusives par nature sont définies de manière exhaustive par le TFUE à l'article 3, paragraphe 1er. Elles ne soulèvent pas de problème particulier au regard de principe de subsidiarité dans la mesure où, par définition, il ne trouve pas à s'appliquer. En effet, les domaines concernés ont fait l'objet d'un transfert de compétences des Etats à l'Union, les privant ainsi du droit d'agir conformément à l'article 2, paragraphe 1, TFUE[18]. Outre la politique commerciale commune qui est, en tant que telle une politique externe[19], l'article 3, paragraphe 1, TFUE en-

---

17 I. Bosse-Platière, « Le traité de Lisbonne et la clarification des compétences », *Revue du marché commun et de l'Union européenne*, n° 520, juillet-août 2008, p. 441; C. Flaesch-Mougin, « Les compétences externes de l'Union européenne », in *Commentaire Mégret, Relations extérieures*, Bruxelles, Editions de l'Université Libre de Bruxelles, à paraître, 112 p.; E. Neframi, « La compétence de l'Union européenne pour conclure un accord international », in *Revue de droit public*, n° 6/2016, p. 1639.

18 « Lorsque les traités attribuent à l'Union une compétence exclusive dans un domaine déterminé, seule l'Union peut légiférer et adopter des actes juridiquement contraignants, les Etats membres ne pouvant le faire par eux-mêmes que 'sils sont habilités par l'Union, ou pour mettre en œuvre les actes de l'Union ».

19 Ainsi que la Cour l'a affirmé dans son avis 1/75 s'agissant de la politique commerciale commune, « on ne saurait, dès lors, admettre que, dans un domaine tel que celui [de l'arrangement OCDE faisant l'objet de la demande d'avis] et qui relève de la politique d'exportation et plus généralement de la politique commerciale

visage quatre autres domaines de compétences exclusives de l'Union[20] mais dont la dimension externe est variable[21], voire inexistante[22].

L'autre hypothèse d'exclusivité envisagée à l'article 3, paragraphe 2, TFUE est plus intéressante à évoquer au regard du principe de subsidiarité, dans la mesure où la nature de ces compétences ne s'impose pas d'emblée. L'exclusion du principe de subsidiarité ne se présume donc pas mais dépend de l'exercice de la compétence. Il s'agit de la codification par le traité de Lisbonne de la jurisprudence de la Cour de justice relative aux compétences implicites et qui reprend les conditions d'exclusivité de la compétence externe découlant de cette jurisprudence, initialement fixées dans l'arrêt *AETR*[23] et précisées par la suite notamment dans l'avis 1/94[24], les arrêts dits « Ciels ouverts »[25] ou encore l'avis 1/03[26]. L'article 3, paragraphe 2, TFUE prévoit que « L'Union dispose également d'une compétence exclusive pour la conclusion d'un accord international lorsque cette conclusion est prévue dans un acte législatif de l'Union, ou est nécessaire pour lui permettre d'exercer sa compétence interne, ou dans la mesure où elle est susceptible d'affecter des règles communes ou d'en altérer la portée ». Le champ d'application de cette disposition est néan-

---

commune, il y ait une compétence des Etats membres parallèle à celle de la Communauté, dans l'ordre communautaire aussi bien que dans l'ordre international ». V. avis de la Cour du 11 novembre 1975, 1/75, *Arrangement OCDE concernant une norme pour les dépenses locales*, EU:C:1975:145.

20 Il s'agit de l'union douanière, de l'établissement de règles de concurrence nécessaire au fonctionnement du marché intérieur, de la politique monétaire des Etats membres dont la monnaie est l'euro et de la conservation des ressources biologiques de la mer dans le cadre de la politique commune de la pêche.

21 C'est le cas de la politique monétaire pour les Etats membres qui ont l'euro qui donne lieu à relativement peu d'accords externes et à la conservation des ressources biologiques de la mer.

22 Ainsi, l'union douanière n'a pas d'autre volet externe que la politique commerciale commune et, en matière de concurrence, l'exclusivité de la compétence est circonscrite à l'établissement des règles « nécessaires au bon fonctionnement du marché intérieur ».

23 Arrêt de la Cour du 31 mars 1971, *Commission / Conseil (AETR)*, 22/70, EU:C:1971:32.

24 Avis de la Cour du 15 novembre 1994, 1/94, *Compétence de la Communauté pour conclure les accords issus du cycle d'Uruguay*, EU:C:1994:384.

25 Parmi les 7 arrêts, v. par exemple, arrêt de la Cour du 5 novembre 2002, *Commission / Allemagne*, C-476/98, EU:C:2002:631.

26 Avis de la Cour du 7 février 2006, 1/03, *Compétence de la Communauté pour conclure la nouvelle Convention de Lugano,* EU:C:2006:81.

moins plus large que la seule théorie des compétences implicites dans la mesure où elle est également susceptible de s'appliquer dans le cadre de l'exercice d'une compétence externe expressément prévue par le traité. En principe, il ne devrait pas y avoir application du principe de subsidiarité dans cette hypothèse mais, en réalité, la situation est plus complexe qu'il n'y parait : il s'agit, en effet, de compétences partagées entre les Etats membres et l'Union, telles qu'elles sont énoncées à l'article 4, paragraphe 1, TFUE, et qui acquièrent le statut de compétences exclusives car elles ont été exercées préalablement au plan interne ou simultanément au plan externe par l'Union. Dès lors, il n'est pas exclu que le principe de subsidiarité ait un rôle à jouer dans l'exercice préalable de la compétence. Il convient, à cet égard, de distinguer les différentes situations envisagées par l'article 3, paragraphe 2, TFUE.

Les deux premières supposent l'adoption préalable par l'Union d'un acte interne qui conduit à l'exclusivité de la compétence externe, soit parce que cet acte prévoit la conclusion d'un accord, soit parce qu'il fixe des règles communes susceptibles d'être affectées par la conclusion d'un accord. On peut alors penser que c'est au stade de l'adoption de l'acte interne que le principe de subsidiarité a été amené à s'appliquer. Par exemple, dans l'avis 1/13, la Cour était interrogée sur le point de savoir si l'acceptation de l'adhésion d'un pays tiers à la Convention de La Haye de 1980 sur les aspects civils de l'enlèvement international d'enfant relevait de la compétence exclusive de l'Union[27]. Au terme d'une « analyse globale et concrète de la relation existant entre l'accord international envisagé et le droit de l'Union en vigueur [...] afin de vérifier si l'accord en question est susceptible de porter atteinte à l'application uniforme et cohérente des règles de l'Union »[28] – en l'occurrence le règlement (CE) n° 2201/2003[29] – la Cour conclut à l'exclusivité de la compétence de l'Union. Dans ce cas, le principe de subsidiarité a bien trouvé à s'appliquer à l'externe, mais de manière indirecte, le « test de subsidiarité » ayant été réalisé en amont, au stade de l'adoption de l'acte interne, ce que vien-

---

27 Avis de la Cour du 14 octobre 2014, 1/13, *Adhésion d'États tiers à la convention de La Haye*, EU:C:2014:2303.

28 *Id.,* point 74.

29 Règlement (CE) n° 2201/2003 du Conseil du 27 novembre 2003 relatif à la compétence, la reconnaissance et l'exécution des décisions en matière matrimoniale et en matière de responsabilité parentale abrogeant le règlement (CE) n° 1347/2000, *JO* L 338, du 23 décembre 2003, p. 1.

nent d'ailleurs confirmer les dispositions du règlement (CE) n° 2201/2003[30]. Au stade de la procédure de conclusion de l'accord, il n'est donc plus besoin de s'interroger sur la pertinence ou la valeur ajoutée d'une action européenne. Les Etats membres ont, lors de l'adoption de l'acte interne, entériné l'idée que cette valeur ajoutée serait susceptible de se prolonger au plan externe : soit ils l'ont explicitement prévu dans l'acte – c'est l'hypothèse de la clause habilitante – soit cette valeur ajoutée est implicite dans le cas où la conclusion d'un accord est susceptible d'affecter les conditions de l'application de l'acte.

Mais qu'en est-il lorsque l'examen du droit interne ne permet pas de conclure à l'exclusivité de la compétence? Autrement dit qu'en est-il lorsque le critère de l'affectation des règles internes ne peut s'appliquer par insuffisance du taux de couverture[31] et que l'effet préemptif de l'exercice préalable de la compétence interne n'est pas suffisant pour se prolonger à l'externe? Cet aspect mérite d'autant plus d'être souligné que le Protocole n° 25 restreint l'effet préemptif de l'exercice de la compétence aux seuls « éléments régis par l'acte » et non à la totalité du domaine[32]. Ce fut le cas, par exemple, en matière sociale, lors de l'avis 2/91 relatif à la Convention n° 170 de l'OIT[33] ou encore, en matière environnementale pour la conclusion du Protocole de Cartagena ayant donné lieu à l'avis 2/00[34]. Dans ce cas, et également lorsque la compétence interne de

30 V. le considérant n° 32 du règlement précité qui motive l'adoption de l'acte au regard des critères de la subsidiarité fixés à l'ex-article 5 CE.

31 Selon la Cour, le critère de l'affectation des règles internes doit être interprété en ce sens que « la portée des règles communautaires est susceptible d'être affectée ou altérée par de tels engagements internationaux lorsque ces derniers relèvent d'un domaine déjà couvert en grande partie par de telles règles ». Pour une application concrète, v. arrêt de la Cour du 26 novembre 2014, *Green Network SpA*, C-66/13, EU:C:2014:2399, point 31.

32 En vertu du Protocole n° 25, « En ce qui concerne l'article 2, paragraphe 2, TFUE relatif aux compétences partagées, lorsque l'Union mène une action dans un certain domaine, le champ d'application de cet exercice de compétence ne couvre que les éléments régis par l'acte de l'Union en question et ne couvre donc pas tout le domaine ».

33 Avis de la Cour du 19 mars 1993, *Convention n° 170 de l'Organisation internationale du Travail concernant la sécurité dans l'utilisation des produits chimiques au travail*, 2/91, EU:C:1993:106.

34 Avis de la Cour du 6 décembre 2001, *Protocole de Cartagena*, 2/00, EU:C:2001:664.

l'Union ne donne pas lieu à l'adoption de règles communes[35], la compétence entre l'Union et les Etats membres est partagée et, en principe, potentiellement aussi bien les Etats membres que l'Union sont en droit d'agir, dans le respect du principe de subsidiarité. De fait, on peut penser que même si le test de subsidiarité a été fait lors de l'adoption de l'acte interne, il devrait être à nouveau fait si l'Union a l'intention d'exercer sa compétence au plan externe. En réalité, on peut se demander si, dans une telle situation, le principe de subsidiarité trouve réellement à s'appliquer dans la mesure où, en matière externe et sauf cas particuliers[36], une compétence partagée conduit en principe à la conclusion d'un accord mixte.[37] Dès lors, la mixité – c'est-à-dire la participation conjointe de l'Union et des Etats membres à la conclusion de l'accord – pourrait rendre sans objet la question du choix du niveau pertinent de l'action, sauf si l'on considère que l'Union peut exercer une compétence implicite partagée sur le plan externe[38].

Une question reste cependant en suspens : lorsque l'Union « choisi[t] d'exercer [sa compétence] partagée en devenant partie à [une] convention », selon la formule de la Cour dans l'arrêt dit de l'Usine MOX[39], à quelles considérations obéit ce choix? Il y a en effet nécessairement un moment où l'Union décide d'exercer sa compétence, même conjointement avec les Etats membres. On peut penser qu'elle le fait parce qu'elle considère – et les Etats membres avec elle – que cela représente un intérêt pour la réalisation de ses objectifs et une valeur ajoutée par rapport à l'action des Etats membres. Certes, la conclusion ou l'adhésion de l'Union à une convention internationale a une dimension globalisante et il n'est pas toujours aisé de répartir les causes juridiques, en termes de compétences, présidant à une telle décision. Les déclarations de compétences qui accom-

35 Avis de la Cour du 16 mai 2017, *Accord de libre échange avec la République de Singapour,* 2/15, EU:C:2017:376, points 227 et s. V. la contribution de Nicolas Pigeon dans cet ouvrage.

36 Ce sont les cas visés à l'article 4, paragraphes 3 et 4, TFUE. Voir *infra* B.

37 E. Neframi, *L'action extérieure de l'Union européenne. Fondements, moyens, principes*, Paris, Systèmes Droit, LGDJ, 2010, p. 76.

38 V. dans ce volume, les contributions de Merijn Chamon et de Eleftheria Neframi. V. aussi arrêt de la Cour du 5 décembre 2017, *Allemagne /Conseil,* C-600/14, EU:C:2017:935.

39 Arrêt de la Cour du 30 juin 2006, *Commission / Irlande,* C-459/03, EU:C:2006:345, point 120.

pagnent les décisions de conclusion d'une convention internationale[40], adoptées par le Conseil, rendent parfaitement compte de cette étroite imbrication de compétences nationales, de compétences exclusives de l'Union et enfin de compétences partagées, la frontière entre les deux dernières étant d'ailleurs susceptible d'évoluer en fonction des règles internes adoptées. Quoiqu'il en soit, si le principe de subsidiarité n'est pas expressément visé dans les motivations des décisions de conclusion adoptées par le Conseil, il n'est pas exclu que, s'agissant des domaines de compétences couverts par une convention, une « certaine logique de subsidiarité »[41] ait présidé à leur adoption. Par exemple, dans la décision de conclusion de l'Accord de Paris sur le climat adoptée en octobre 2016[42], le Conseil indique que cet accord est conforme aux objectifs de la politique environnementale de l'Union et que la mise en œuvre de l'accord requiert une action conjointe avec ses Etats membres. La déclaration de compétence qui accompagne la décision, quant à elle, confirme la compétence de l'Union en matière d'environnement, conformément à l'article 191 TFUE, sans autre précision quant au partage de cette compétence avec les Etats membres dans le champ couvert par l'Accord de Paris.

Il convient enfin d'évoquer la dernière hypothèse d'exclusivité par exercice des compétences externes prévue par l'article 3, paragraphe 2, TFUE, relative au critère dit de nécessité. Dans l'avis 1/76 concernant l'institution d'un Fonds européen d'immobilisation de la navigation sur le Rhin et la Moselle, la Cour a en effet considéré que « la compétence pour engager la Communauté vis-à-vis des tiers découle néanmoins de manière implicite des dispositions du traité établissant la compétence interne, pour autant que la participation de la Communauté à l'accord international, comme en l'occurrence, est nécessaire à la réalisation des objectifs de la Communauté »[43]. Par la suite, la Cour a retenu des conditions très strictes

---

40 C. Flaesch-Mougin, « Déclaration de compétences et affirmation de l'identité de l'Union européenne sur la scène internationale », in *Mélanges en l'honneur du Professeur Joël Molinier*, Paris, LGDJ, 2012, p. 233.

41 A. Martinache, « Une application de la subsidiarité : la Cour de justice et les compétences externes », *supra* note 9, p. 63.

42 Décision (UE) 2016/1841 du Conseil du 5 octobre 2016 relative à la conclusion, au nom de l'Union européenne, de l'accord de Paris adopté au titre de la convention-cadre des Nations unies sur les changements climatiques, *JO* L 282, du 19 octobre 2016, p. 1.

43 Avis de la Cour du 26 avril 1977, *Fonds européen d'immobilisation de la navigation intérieure*, 1/76, EU:C:1977:63, point 4.

d'application du critère de nécessité qui rendent difficile sa mise en œuvre pratique[44]. On peut néanmoins se demander si l'application du critère de nécessité n'entretient pas des liens étroits avec celle du principe de subsidiarité. En effet, les deux procèdent de la même logique : la réalisation des objectifs des traités commande l'action de l'Union. Dès lors, on peut considérer que l'exercice directement à l'externe par l'Union de sa compétence partagée, en application du critère de nécessité, conformément à l'article 3, paragraphe 2, TFUE, se confond avec l'application du principe de subsidiarité dans ce contexte. Ainsi, s'agissant par exemple des accords concernant la libéralisation des visas ou des accords de réadmission, il n'est pas toujours évident, sur la base des propositions ou des décisions de conclusion, de déterminer si leur adoption obéit au principe de subsidiarité ou à un critère de nécessité au sens de l'avis 1/76. Pour autant, si le résultat est le même, critère de nécessité et principe de subsidiarité ne doivent pas être confondus, dans la mesure où leur régime et leurs conséquences pour les Etats sont très différentes. Dans le cas du critère de nécessité visé à l'article 3, paragraphe 2, TFUE, l'exercice par l'Union de sa compétence conduit à un dessaisissement des Etats membres. La compétence change donc en quelque sorte de nature pour devenir exclusive. En revanche, dans le cadre de l'application du principe de subsidiarité, la compétence demeure partagée et pourrait donc être récupérée par les Etats membres si l'Union cessait de l'exercer.

B. L'application du principe de subsidiarité à une mosaïque de compétences externes non exclusives

Les traités envisagent plusieurs catégories de compétences non exclusives qui ne peuvent en aucun cas devenir exclusives par exercice. Ces catégories sont celles qui sont le plus directement concernées par l'application du principe de subsidiarité. Il s'agit des compétences partagées dites parallèles, des compétences d'appui, de coordination et de complément et enfin de la compétence de l'Union en matière de politique étrangère et de sécurité commune (PESC).

S'agissant tout d'abord des compétences dites parallèles, il s'agit des domaines de compétences partagées prévus à l'article 4, paragraphes 3 et

44 Voir l'interprétation donnée du critère de nécessité dans l'avis 1/94, *supra* note 24.

4, TFUE : la recherche, le développement technologique et l'espace d'une part et la coopération au développement et l'aide humanitaire d'autre part. Est aussi vraisemblablement concernée par cette catégorie, bien qu'elle ne soit pas mentionnée à l'article 4 TFUE, la compétence de l'Union en matière de coopération économique, financière et technique[45]. Pour ces domaines et par dérogation à l'article 2, paragraphe 2, TFUE, la préemption ne joue pas et l'exercice par l'Union de sa compétence ne saurait donc « avoir pour effet d'empêcher les Etats membres d'exercer la leur ». Le caractère parallèle de la compétence de l'ancienne Communauté en matière de développement et d'aide humanitaire a été reconnu par la Cour de longue date, avant même son inscription dans le traité[46]. Il découle des dispositions du TFUE que, dans les domaines de compétences partagées parallèles, l'Union peut conclure des accords avec des tiers ou des organisations internationales. Disposant d'une compétence, l'Union peut l'exercer seule, sans le concours des Etats membre. La pratique confirme d'ailleurs cette règle : ainsi l'Union conclut seule les accords de coopération scientifique et technique avec les Etats tiers et, même si la pratique a évolué depuis[47], la Communauté a conclu seule les premiers accords de coopération avec les pays tiers d'Amérique latine et d'Asie[48]. Cette situation s'impose pour des motifs liés à l'application du principe de subsidiarité.

Dans le cadre de la recherche et de développement technologique, les accords ont pour objet d'étendre aux Etats tiers concernés les bénéfices et le régime du programme-cadre pluriannuel de l'Union[49]. Fondée notamment sur l'article 182 TFUE[50], l'adoption de ce programme a été motivée

45 Sur ce point, voir C. Flaesch-Mougin, « Les compétences externes de l'Union européenne », *supra* note 17, p. 96-97.

46 Arrêt de la Cour du 30 juin 1993, *Parlement européen / Conseil et Commission*, C-181/91 & C-248/91, EU:C:1993:271 et arrêt de la Cour du 2 mars 1994, *Parlement européen / Conseil*, C-316/91, EU:C:1993:271.

47 Voir C. Flaesch-Mougin, « Les compétences externes de l'Union européenne », *supra* note 17.

48 C. Flaesch-Mougin, J. Kasmi, J. Lebullenger « Les relations de la Communauté européenne avec les pays d'Asie et d'Amérique latine (ALA) », *JurisClasseur Europe*, Fasc. 2230, septembre 2005.

49 Règlement (UE) n° 1291/2013 du Parlement européen et du Conseil du 11 décembre 2013 portant établissement du programme-cadre de recherche et d'innovation « Horizon 2020 » (2014-2020), *JO* L 347 du 20 décembre 2013, p. 104.

50 L'autre base juridique est l'article 173 TFUE relatif à la compétence de l'UE en matière d'industrie.

au regard du principe de subsidiarité[51] et prévoit explicitement la possibilité d'y associer les pays tiers[52]. Toutefois, ainsi que le souligne Catherine Flaesch-Mougin, cette clause habilitante « acquiert dans ce cas une fonction différente de celle qu'elle joue dans les domaines de compétences partagées ordinaires : alors qu'elle entraine, dans cette hypothèse, l'exclusivité de la compétence externe de l'Union, la clause habilitante, dans un domaine interne relevant d'une compétence partagée de type parallèle, fonde sa compétence externe et permet de justifier son intervention au plan externe »[53]. S'agissant de la coopération au développement et de l'aide humanitaire, le principe de subsidiarité est implicitement inscrit au sein des dispositions même du traité dans la mesure où les articles 209, paragraphe 2, TFUE et 214, paragraphe 4, TFUE donnent compétence à l'Union pour conclure « tout accord utile » à la réalisation des objectifs dans ces domaines. Cela implique que l'utilité d'un accord doit faire l'objet d'une évaluation dont les critères peuvent être ceux de la subsidiarité : insuffisance de l'action des Etats membres et valeur ajoutée de l'accord au regard des objectifs poursuivis. Certes, le principe, en lui-même, n'est pas systématiquement évoqué dans la motivation des décisions de conclusion des accords externes. Néanmoins, on le retrouve parfois dans les motivations juridiques présentées par la Commission dans sa proposition de décision de signature ou de conclusion des accords fondés, au moins partiellement, sur l'article 209 TFUE[54]. Il est en revanche systématiquement présent dans les instruments unilatéraux : c'est le cas, par exemple, pour les sept règlements fixant les instruments de l'Union européenne pour le financement de l'action extérieure de l'Union. Fondés sur les articles 209

51 Voir le considérant 48 du règlement (UE) n° 1291/2013 *supra* note 49.

52 *Id.*, article 7.

53 C. Flaesch-Mougin, « Les compétences externes de l'UE », *supra* note 17 p. 98.

54 V. par exemple la proposition de décision du Conseil relative à la signature, au nom de l'Union et à l'application provisoire de l'accord-cadre entre l'Union européenne et ses Etats membres d'une part et l'Australie d'autre part, JOIN (2016) 8 final, 14 avril 2016, 6 p. spéc. p. 2-3.

TFUE et 212 TFUE[55], ces règlements sont tous motivés au regard du principe de subsidiarité[56].

Dans les domaines énoncés à l'article 6 TFUE, l'Union « dispose d'une compétence pour mener des actions pour appuyer, coordonner ou compléter l'action des Etats membres ». Cette compétence peut également se prolonger au plan externe afin de « favoris[er] la coopération avec les pays tiers et les organisations internationales » [57]. Même si la possibilité de conclure un accord n'est pas expressément prévue, la pratique témoigne notamment d'accords sectoriels conclus par l'Union dans les domaines concernés, y compris historiquement, sur le fondement de la compétence subsidiaire de la Communauté. La compétence de l'Union s'exerce conformément à l'article 2, paragraphe 5, TFUE dans le respect du principe de subsidiarité, envisagé de manière ascendante et justifiant l'action au niveau de l'Union. Les dispositions propres à chaque domaine sont fortement marquées par l'idée que les actions de l'Union « dans leur finalité européenne » doivent apporter une valeur ajoutée aux politiques nationales, sans remettre en cause leurs compétences. On notera d'ailleurs une certaine « indistinction du titulaire »[58] dans la dimension externe de ces compétences, les dispositions du TFUE se référant indifféremment à « L'Union et les Etats membres »[59]. Cela n'a toutefois pas empêché l'Union de conclure seule des accords dans les domaines relevant de ces compétences. Ce fut par exemple le cas pour les accords avec le Canada ou les Etats-Unis établissant un cadre de coopération en matière d'en-

---

55 A l'exception de l'instrument d'aide à la préadhésion qui est uniquement fondé sur l'article 212 TFUE (coopération financière et technique) et l'instrument de partenariat et de coopération qui, en sus des articles 209 et 2012 TFUE est également fondé sur l'article 207 TFUE.

56 V., par exemple, le considérant 21 du règlement (UE) n° 236/2014 du Parlement européen et du Conseil énonçant les règles et modalités communes pour la mise en œuvre des instruments de l'Union européenne pour le financement de l'action extérieure, *JO* L 77 du 15 mars 2014, p. 95.

57 C'est le cas en matière d'éducation et de formation professionnelle (articles 165, paragraphe 3 et 166, paragraphe 3, TFUE), de culture (article 167, paragraphe 3, TFUE), de santé (article 168, paragraphe 3, TFUE) et de réseaux transeuropéens (article 171, paragraphe 3, TFUE).

58 M. Blanquet, *Compétences de l'Union européenne. Architecture générale – Délimitation*, JurisClasseur Europe, Fasc. 170, janvier 2012, point 170.

59 V. par exemple, l'article 165, paragraphe 3, TFUE s'agissant de l'éducation, la formation professionnelle, jeunesse et sport.

seignement supérieur, de formation et de recherche[60] ou pour des accords avec la Bosnie-Herzégovine, la Serbie-Monténégro ou la Croatie concernant leur participation à certains programmes européens[61]. Toutefois, dans ces hypothèses, comme précédemment pour la recherche et le développement technologique, le « test de subsidiarité » a été réalisé antérieurement, lors de l'adoption des programmes de l'Union que ces accords ont vocation à étendre à des Etats tiers.

Enfin, la question de l'application du principe de subsidiarité à la PESC est un peu plus problématique. Sans entrer dans les débats relatifs à la nature de la compétence de l'Union en matière de PESC qui n'est pas qualifiée par les traités[62], il peut être soutenu de manière certaine qu'elle n'est pas une compétence exclusive[63]. Le principe de subsidiarité étant formulé en termes généraux à l'article 5, paragraphes 1er et 3, TUE, il est d'application générale et devrait donc être applicable dans le cadre de la PESC[64], même si évidemment il ne saurait faire l'objet d'un contrôle juridictionnel compte tenu de l'incompétence de la Cour. On notera néanmoins que dans un arrêt de 2006, le Tribunal a considéré qu'il n'était pas possible pour un requérant d'invoquer une violation du principe de subsidiarité lorsque la Communauté adopte, dans le cadre communautaire, des mesures restrictives prévues par une position commune PESC[65].

60 Pour l'accord avec le Canada : *JO* L 397 du 30 décembre 2006, p. 15. Pour l'accord avec les Etats-Unis : *JO* L 346 du 9 décembre 2006, p. 34.

61 V. *JO* L 192 du 22 juillet 2005, p. 9 (accord avec la Bosnie-Herzégovine), p. 16 (accord avec la Croatie) et 29 (accord avec la Serbie-Monténégro).

62 Le traité se borne à établir l'existence d'une compétence de l'Union pour « définir et mettre en œuvre une politique étrangère et de sécurité commune, y compris la définition progressive d'une politique de défense commune » (article 2, paragraphe 4, TFUE; v. également l'article 24 TUE). Mais la PESC n'est identifiée dans aucune des catégories de compétences visées aux articles 3, 4 et 6 TFUE.

63 Les Déclarations 13 et 14 insistent sur le fait que la PESC ne porte pas atteinte aux compétences de chaque Etat membre pour l'élaboration et la conduite de sa propre politique étrangère.

64 Déjà avant le traité de Lisbonne, le principe de subsidiarité était visé à l'ex-article 2 TUE en vertu duquel « les objectifs de l'Union sont atteints conformément aux dispositions du présent traité, dans les conditions et selon les rythmes qui y sont prévus, dans le respect du principe de subsidiarité, tel qu'il est défini à l'article 5 du TCE ». Cette disposition permettait de considérer qu'il était applicable aux deuxième et troisième piliers.

65 Arrêt du Tribunal du 12 juillet 2006, *Ayadi / Conseil*, T-253/02, EU:T:2006:200.

Même si le traité de Lisbonne a fait disparaître la référence à un critère de nécessité pour la conclusion des accords externes en matière de PESC[66], les dispositions du TUE confirment l'importance du principe de subsidiarité dans ce cadre : notamment l'article 28, paragraphe 1, TUE prévoit que « lorsqu'une situation internationale exige une action opérationnelle de l'Union, le Conseil adopte les décisions nécessaires ». Le traité de Lisbonne renforce d'ailleurs l'emprise de la subsidiarité dans la mesure où l'ex-article 14 TUE envisageait « certaines situations où une action opérationnelle est jugée nécessaire ». Même si les deux expressions véhiculent la même idée de « besoin impérieux »[67], l'emploi du singulier nous semble plus propice à l'application de la subsidiarité : en effet, c'est l'examen d'une situation internationale particulière – et non « certaines situations » envisagées de manière vague et au pluriel – qui justifiera que l'Union agisse. Elle le fera donc nécessairement par référence à la valeur ajoutée que représentera une telle action par rapport à celles des Etats membres pris isolément. Inversement, les Etats pourront considérer que la situation en cause ne justifie pas l'intervention de l'Union. En pratique, tous les accords dans le domaine de la PESC et fondés sur le seul article 37 TUE[68] ont été conclus par l'Union seule. Même si le principe de subsidiarité n'est pas évoqué dans la motivation des actes, on ne voit pas quelle autre considération pourrait justifier l'exercice par l'Union de sa compétence. En réalité, la plupart des accords PESC déjà conclus visent à permettre la participation des Etats tiers aux opérations de gestion des crises menées par l'Union européenne[69] et sont prévus par les décisions portant création de ces missions. Pour autant, la compétence de l'Union reste partagée dans la mesure où l'article 3, paragraphe 2, TFUE réserve l'exclusivité par exercice aux cas où la conclusion de l'accord est « prévue

66 L'ex-article 24 TUE prévoyait que « Lorsqu'il est nécessaire de conclure un accord avec un ou plusieurs Etats ou organisations internationales en application du présent titre… » alors que l'article 37 TUE se borne à établir la compétence de l'UE pour conclure des accords dans le domaine de la PESC.

67 E. Daniel, *La politique opérationnelle de l'Union européenne dans le cadre de la PESC : singularités et cohérences*, Thèse, Université de Paris I, juillet 2016, 687 p., spéc. p. 173.

68 La situation est différente pour les accords d'association post-Lisbonne qui sont fondés sur la double base juridique de l'article 217 TFUE et de l'article 37 TUE.

69 V. C. Schneider, « La participation des Etats tiers aux opérations de gestion des crises », in I. Bosse-Platière, C. Rapoport (dir.), *L'Etat tiers en droit de l'Union européenne*, Bruxelles, Bruylant, 2013, p. 255.

dans un acte législatif de l'Union ». Or, conformément à l'article 24 TUE, l'adoption d'acte législatif est exclue dans le domaine de la PESC.

II. La mise en œuvre du principe de subsidiarité au service d'une meilleure articulation des niveaux de pouvoirs dans le cadre de l'action extérieure

Dans le cadre de l'action extérieure de l'Union, la mise en œuvre matérielle du principe de subsidiarité requiert principalement la satisfaction des objectifs fixés par les traités en étroite complémentarité avec les actions nationales (A). D'un point de vue institutionnel, cette mise en œuvre requiert une clarification du rôle des différents acteurs, voire la promotion de celui des parlements nationaux, s'agissant plus particulièrement du contrôle de la subsidiarité (B).

A. La complémentarité des politiques et actions nationales et de l'Union sous le sceau de la subsidiarité

L'appréciation de la valeur ajoutée de l'action de l'Union se fait à l'aune de plusieurs éléments qui tiennent à la satisfaction des objectifs dc l'action extérieure de l'Union européenne et qui doivent, s'agissant des principales compétences externes non exclusives de l'Union que sont la PESC et la coopération avec les tiers, s'apprécier au regard d'une exigence de complémentarité des actions nationales et européennes. En tant que « concept dynamique qui doit être appliqué à la lumière des objectifs énoncés dans le traité »[70], la subsidiarité de l'action de l'Union doit être mise en œuvre à la lumière du système d'objectifs de l'action extérieure tel que mis en place par le traité de Lisbonne.

Certes, l'article 5, paragraphe 3, TUE se réfère aux objectifs de « l'action envisagée », au singulier. Mais le traité de Lisbonne enchâsse chaque action externe – conclusion d'un accord ou acte unilatéral – dans un réseau d'objectifs à la fois sectoriels et généraux. Par exemple, chaque acte adopté dans le cadre de la coopération au développement poursuit non seulement l'objectif qui lui est propre, mais doit également conduire à la

70 Conclusions du Conseil européen d'Edimbourg, 12 décembre 1992, p. 19.

réalisation de l'objectif spécifique de cette politique, de « réduction, et à terme, d'éradication de la pauvreté »[71] et *in fine* doit s'inscrire, à l'instar de toute l'action extérieure de l'Union, dans le respect des objectifs généraux formulés à l'article 21 TUE. Dès lors, ainsi que le prévoit l'article 209, paragraphe 2, TFUE, l'examen de l'utilité d'un accord externe dans ce domaine doit conduire à apprécier s'il permettra la réalisation de l'ensemble de ces objectifs, à la fois sectoriels et généraux. Ainsi que l'a énoncé la Cour, « la décision portant signature d'un accord avec un pays tiers relevant d'un domaine de compétences de l'Union [...] implique d'apprécier, dans le respect des lignes stratégiques fixées par le Conseil européen ainsi que des principes et des objectifs de l'action extérieure de l'Union énoncés à l'article 21, paragraphes 1 et 2, TUE, les intérêts de l'Union dans le cadre des relations avec le pays tiers concerné et d'opérer des arbitrages entre les intérêts divergents relevant de ces relations »[72].

Une telle opération n'est pas étrangère au « test d'efficacité comparative »[73] auquel obéit la mise en œuvre du principe de subsidiarité[74]. La réalisation des objectifs de l'article 21 TUE impose donc de s'interroger sur la valeur ajoutée de l'action de l'Union, dans les domaines ne relevant pas de sa compétence exclusive. Or, certains domaines de l'action extérieure -par exemple, les questions touchant à la sécurité de l'Union dans ses différentes dimensions – sont très empreints d'une logique de subsidiarité. A cet égard, la nouvelle stratégie globale de sécurité présentée par la haute représentante F. Mogherini en octobre 2015[75] fait du principe d'unité, en réalité défini à l'aune de la subsidiarité[76], un des principes d'action de l'UE sur la scène internationale.

---

71 Article 208, paragraphe 1, TFUE.

72 Arrêt de la Cour du 28 juillet 2016, *Conseil / Commission*, C-660/13, EU:C:2016:616, point 39.

73 Commission européenne, *Le principe de subsidiarité*, *supra* note 1, p. 729.

74 D'autant plus que l'impératif de satisfaire les objectifs de l'article 21 TUE ne concerne pas que les politiques, externes par nature mais également « les autres politiques dans leurs aspects extérieurs » (Article 21, paragraphe 3, TUE).

75 « Shared Vision, Common Action: A stronger Europe. A global Strategy for European Union's Foreign and Security Policy ». V. les conclusions du Conseil européen du 28 juin 2016 (EUCO 26/16); Page internet dédiée sur le site du SEAE : http://europa.eu/globalstrategy/].

76 « Together we will be able to achieve more than Member States acting alone or in a uncoordinated manner ». *id.*, p. 16.

L'unité de l'action est indissociable de la complémentarité des politiques nationales et européenne[77], telle qu'elle a été réaffirmée et même précisée par le traité de Lisbonne pour les compétences relevant de « la coopération avec les pays tiers et l'aide humanitaire »[78]. La complémentarité implique en effet une prise en compte réciproque – et donc une mise en cohérence – des politiques respectives de l'Union et des Etats membres, tant dans leur définition que dans leur mise en œuvre. La prise en compte par l'Union des politiques nationales s'effectue dans le cadre du principe de subsidiarité, dont la complémentarité est une déclinaison, alors que la prise en compte par les Etats membres de la politique de l'Union devrait s'effectuer en vertu du principe de loyauté. La mise en œuvre du principe de subsidiarité s'analyse donc comme permettant d'assurer la complémentarité des actions des Etats membres et celles de l'Union, au service des objectifs de l'action extérieure.

Néanmoins, en dépit de leurs liens étroits, subsidiarité et complémentarité ne se confondent pas totalement. En réalité, elles ne doivent pas être mises sur le même plan. En effet, à un moment donné, lorsqu'une action est « envisagée », la mise en œuvre du principe de subsidiarité permet que l'unité d'action de l'Union soit assurée, par substitution à l'action étatique. Dès lors qu'une action envisagée remplit les conditions d'application de la subsidiarité, la question de la complémentarité avec les actions étatiques disparaît. Toutefois, cette unité d'action, par application du principe de subsidiarité n'est que ponctuelle. L'article 5, paragraphe 3, TFUE se réfère d'ailleurs aux objectifs de « l'action envisagée » (au singulier). L'application du principe de subsidiarité peut donc entraîner une substitution de l'action de l'Union à l'action étatique mais n'empêche pas qu'il existe, au niveau global de la conception, de la définition et de la mise en œuvre des politiques nationales et de l'Union, un impératif de complémentarité. Dans le cadre de la procédure de conclusion des accords externes, la mise en œuvre de cet impératif repose conjointement sur la Commission eu-

---

77 I. Bosse-Platière, *L'article 3 du traité UE : Recherche sur une exigence de cohérence de l'action extérieure de l'Union européenne*, Bruxelles, Bruylant, 2009, p. 627.

78 Titre III de la 5ème partie du TFUE. Désormais, la politique de coopération au développement (article 209, paragraphe 1, TFUE), la coopération économique, financière et technique (article 212, paragraphe 1, TFUE) et l'aide humanitaire (article 214, paragraphe 1, TFUE) de l'Union d'une part, et les politiques et actions des Etats membres, d'autre part « se complètent et se renforcent mutuellement ».

ropéenne (ou le haut représentant pour les affaires étrangères et la politique de sécurité) et sur le Conseil[79] et vraisemblablement intervient très tôt.

En effet, à la différence de la procédure législative présidant à l'adoption des actes internes, la procédure de conclusion des accords externes prévue à l'article 218 TFUE se caractérise par le fait que son déclenchement requiert l'accord des deux institutions, le Conseil et la Commission (ou le haut représentant si l'accord porte exclusivement sur la PESC). Conformément aux paragraphes 2 et 3 de l'article 218 TFUE, c'est le Conseil qui autorise l'ouverture des négociations mais il ne peut le faire que si la Commission (ou le haut représentant) lui a présenté une recommandation à cette fin. Cette règle se justifie pour des raisons à la fois d'unité, de cohérence et de crédibilité de l'Union à l'égard des Etats tiers[80]. Dès lors, on peut penser que, si un test de subsidiarité est effectué, celui-ci a lieu très en amont de l'adoption de la décision de signature et, plus encore, de conclusion de l'accord. Il doit avoir lieu tout au début de la procédure, dès l'adoption par la Commission de la recommandation d'ouvrir des négociations et la formalisation par le Conseil de la décision autorisant la Commission à négocier l'accord. C'est à ce stade que les deux institutions décident conjointement de l'opportunité, voire de la nécessité pour l'Union de conclure cet accord au regard des objectifs envisagés. Ces actes étant très rarement publiés, il est cependant difficile d'apprécier la manière dont se déroule la discussion entre les deux institutions quant à la pertinence d'un accord éventuel et sa complémentarité avec les politiques nationales.

79 Il s'agit d'une dimension de l'exigence de cohérence de l'action extérieure de l'Union européenne qui est prescrite à l'article 21, paragraphe 3, al. 2, TUE et dont la concrétisation repose sur le Conseil et la Commission, assistés du haut représentant.

80 En effet, il serait préjudiciable que la Commission commence à négocier un accord sans avoir au moins l'assurance que le Conseil – qui adoptera la décision finale de conclusion – est d'accord sur le principe même de l'accord.

B. *Le contrôle de la subsidiarité dans le cadre de la procédure de conclusion des accords externes : vers une implication accrue des parlements nationaux?*

En ce qui concerne le contrôle de la subsidiarité, seront seulement abordés quelques aspects relatifs à sa dimension politique[81], notamment le rôle des parlements nationaux[82] tel qu'il a été renforcé par le traité de Lisbonne[83], et seront évoquées quelques pistes de réflexion dans le contexte des accords mixtes[84]. En effet, parmi les contraintes découlant de la pratique des accords mixtes, figure la nécessité de leur ratification par les Etats membres selon leurs règles constitutionnelles nationales, ce qui nécessite l'intervention de près d'une quarantaine de parlements nationaux. L'actualité récente a démontré les difficultés que cela peut générer pour l'Union et ses Etats membres. Ce fut le cas lors du referendum consultatif aux Pays-Bas du 6 avril 2016 par lequel les électeurs se sont prononcés contre la ratification de l'accord d'association entre l'Union européenne et l'Ukraine[85]. En outre, à l'automne 2016, le Parlement régional de Wallonie a exercé des pressions préalables à la signature de l'accord économique et commercial global avec le Canada, utilisant son pouvoir de veto à la ratification de l'accord par la Belgique. Ces évènements, qui sont le reflet d'une certaine défiance des citoyens à l'égard de l'action de l'Union, posent de réels

81 S'agissant du contrôle juridictionnel de la subsidiarité en matière externe, il nous semble encore plus difficile à mettre en œuvre dans le cadre de l'action extérieure de l'Union que dans le cadre de ses politiques et actions internes. Bien que la Cour ait établi des critères d'examen de la satisfaction des conditions de l'article 5, paragraphe 3, TUE et ait à de nombreuses reprises contrôlé un acte de l'UE au regard de ces critères, son examen ne l'a jamais conduite à annuler un acte pour cette raison. La large marge d'appréciation dont bénéficie le législateur de l'Union justifie pleinement le contrôle restreint du juge.

82 Plus généralement sur cette question, v. C. Rapoport, « Les parlements nationaux et l'action extérieure de l'Union européenne », *Revue des affaires européennes / Law & European Affairs,* n°1/2014, p. 55.

83 J. V. Louis, « Quelques remarques sur l'avenir du contrôle du principe de subsidiarité », in *Mélanges en hommage à Georges Vandersanden*, Bruxelles, Bruylant, 2009, p. 283.

84 Sur la problématique des accords mixtes, v. E. Neframi, *Les accords mixtes de la Communauté européenne*, Bruxelles, Bryulant, 2007, 711 p.; C. Hillion, P. Koutrakos (dir.), *Mixed Agreements Revisited*, Oxford, Hart Publishing, 2010, 418 p.

85 *JO* L 161 du 29 mai 2014, p. 3.

problèmes pour l'affirmation de l'Union en tant qu'acteur international et pour la crédibilité de son action à l'égard des tiers. En tout cas, ils invitent à réfléchir à des solutions alternatives, dans le respect à la fois de la répartition des compétences et des principes démocratiques. Une meilleure implication des parlements nationaux autorisant leur intervention sous le sceau du contrôle de la subsidiarité, pourrait être une piste de réflexion. Il paraît ainsi possible de promouvoir l'application du Protocole n° 2, et notamment la procédure de contrôle du principe de subsidiarité[86], conduisant la Commission européenne à transmettre plus systématiquement aux parlements nationaux les propositions de décision de signature des accords externes ne relevant pas des compétences exclusives de l'Union[87].

D'un point de vue juridique, cela n'irait pas sans quelques clarifications préalables. D'une part, il conviendrait que la question de la nature de la compétence pour conclure ces accords externes soit réglée plus tôt qu'elle ne l'est actuellement. En pratique, cette question est volontairement et pour des raisons politiques, laissée dans le flou dans toute la phase précédente, de l'autorisation de négocier au déroulement des négociations. Ce n'est donc qu'au moment de l'adoption de la décision de signature de l'accord que cette question – à laquelle est étroitement liée celle de la mixité de l'accord – est abordée. Or, comme le fait observer à juste titre l'Avocat général E. Sharpston, « résoudre la question de la compétence, avant le début des négociations garantit indubitablement que seules les parties compétentes prendront place à la table des négociations, [...], offre une certaine sécurité juridique et sert les intérêts de l'Union, des Etats membres et des tierces parties associées aux négociations »[88].

La seconde clarification nécessaire est relative à la qualification de la procédure de conclusion des accords externes en tant que procédure

86 Articles 6 et 7 du Protocole n° 2 sur l'application des principes de subsidiarité et de proportionnalité.

87 En pratique, il arrive que la Commission transmette ses propositions aux parlements nationaux mais il ressort d'un examen des informations disponibles sur le site de la Commission d'une part que cette transmission n'est pas systématique et, d'autre part, qu'elle ne se fait pas nécessairement au titre de l'application du Protocole n° 2. Voir le site : http://ec.europa.eu/dgs/secretariat_general/relations/relations_other/npo/index_en.htm.

88 Conclusions de l'Avocat général E. Sharpston présentées le 3 avril 2014 dans l'affaire C-114/12, *Commission / Conseil (Négociation d'une convention du Conseil de l'Europe sur la protection des droits des organismes de radiodiffusion)*, EU:C:2014:224, point 116.

législative, puisqu'en effet la procédure prévue par le Protocole n° 2 s'applique pour « les projets d'actes législatifs »[89]. Si, avant le traité de Lisbonne, on pouvait émettre des doutes quant à la nature de la procédure prévue à l'ex-article 300 CE, il semble désormais possible de considérer que celle de l'article 218 TFUE constitue une procédure législative spéciale au sens de l'article 289, paragraphes 2 et 3, TFUE[90]. Le Tribunal s'était prononcé en ce sens dans l'arrêt *Front Polisario/Conseil*[91], mais dans son arrêt rendu sur pourvoi, la Cour ne s'est pas penchée sur cette question[92]. En revanche, dans un arrêt plus récent[93], la Cour a considéré qu'un acte juridique ne peut être considéré comme législatif que s'il a été adopté surle fondement d'une disposition du traité se référant expressément à une procédure législative, ordinaire ou spéciale[94]. Bien que l'arrêt n'intervienne pas en matière de relations extérieures et ne concerne pas la procédure de l'article 218 TFUE, cette position – qui demande à être confirmée – viendrait infirmer celle retenue par le Tribunal dans l'arrêt *Front Polisario/Conseil* précité.

Il n'en demeure pas moins qu'une application plus systématique du Protocole n° 2 à la procédure de conclusion des accords externes pourrait contribuer à renforcer l'implication des parlements nationaux : cela leur permettrait non seulement de faire entendre leurs préoccupations sur le contenu futur des accords relativement tôt dans la procédure mais également d'en hypothéquer collectivement la signature, en vertu de l'article 7,

89 Article 5 du Protocole n° 2, *supra* note 87.

90 En vertu de l'article 289, paragraphe 3, TFUE est un acte législatif, un acte adopté par procédure législative. Or, l'adoption d'une décision par le Conseil avec la participation du Parlement européen constitue une procédure législative spéciale (article 289, paragraphe 2, TFUE).

91 Arrêt du Tribunal du 10 décembre 2015, *Front Polisario / Conseil, supra* note 14, points 70 à 71.

92 Arrêt de la Cour du 21 décembre 2016, *Conseil / Front Polisario, supra* note 14. En revanche, dans ses conclusions présentées le 13 septembre 2016, l'Avocat général M. Wathelet, répondant au Conseil qui considérait que le Tribunal avait commis une erreur de droit sur ce point, avait rejoint la position du Tribunal considérant que la procédure de conclusion des accords externes de l'article 218 TFUE devait être qualifiée de procédure législative spéciale au sens du traité (EU:C:2016:973, points 151-161).

93 Arrêt de la Cour du 6 septembre 2017, *Slovaquie et Hongrie / Conseil, supra* note 14.

94 *Id.,* point 62.

paragraphe 2, du Protocole[95] en contraignant la Commission à réexaminer sa proposition. Le caractère collectif du carton jaune – au moins un tiers des voix attribuées aux parlements nationaux – permettrait d'assurer le respect du principe démocratique, sans que, à lui seul, un parlement national (ou régional) ne puisse bloquer la conclusion d'un accord externe. Ce contrôle de la subsidiarité dans ce contexte pourrait même permettre d'assurer le respect des intérêts étatiques, sans pour autant conduire à la négociation d'un accord mixte, là où ce n'est pas juridiquement nécessaire. Il permettrait, en tout cas, de répondre à la tendance, regrettable mais de plus en plus importante, des Etats membres d'imposer la mixité de certains accords alors qu'elle ne se justifie pas nécessairement compte tenu des bases juridiques retenues[96]. C'est le cas notamment des accords de partenariat et de coopération[97] signés ou conclus postérieurement à l'entrée en vigueur du traité de Lisbonne ou pour les accords de partenariat stratégique[98]. Si ces revendications étatiques procèdent de considérations essentiellement politiques, plus que juridiques, visant à limiter toute action internationale de l'Union suspectée d'être trop autonome, il n'en demeure pas moins qu'elles ouvrent aussi la voie à une contestation possible de ces accords par les parlements nationaux au moment de leur ratification, minorant du même coup le rôle du Parlement européen. Une application plus systématique du principe de subsidiarité dans ce contexte devrait donc d'autant plus être promue.

---

95 En vertu de l'article 7, paragraphe 2, du Protocole n° 2, « Dans les cas où les avis motivés sur le non-respect par un projet d'acte législatif du principe de subsidiarité représentent au moins un tiers de l'ensemble des voix attribuées aux Parlements nationaux, conformément au deuxième alinéa du paragraphe 1, le projet doit être réexaminé ».

96 Il s'agit des articles 207 TFUE et 209 TFUE pour les APC et des articles 31 TUE, 37 TUE et 212 TFUE pour les APS. Sur le caractère juridiquement contestable de la mixité des APC, voir C. Flaesch-Mougin, « Les compétences externes de l'Union européenne », *supra* note 17, p. 99.

97 Voir par exemple, la Décision (UE) 2016/2117 du 29 septembre 2016 relative à la conclusion, au nom de l'Union, de l'accord-cadre global de partenariat et de coopération entre l'Union européenne et ses Etats membres d'une part et la République socialiste du Vietnam, d'autre part, *JO* L 329 du 3 décembre 2016, p. 6.

98 Par exemple, la Décision (UE) 2016/2118 du Conseil du 28 octobre 2016 relative à la signature, au nom de l'Union européenne, et à l'application provisoire de l'accord de partenariat stratégique entre l'Union européenne et ses Etats membres, d'une part, et le Canada, d'autre part, *supra* note 60.

Constitutional Limits to the Political Choice for Mixity

Merijn Chamon[*]

I. Introduction

Given that mixity is one of the most characteristic features of the European Union's external action,[1] it is fitting to explore part of the constitutional framework that governs and structures the phenomenon in this volume. All the more so because mixity is mired in controversy, generally receiving a bad press from EU external relations scholars. As Weiler, himself more sympathetic to mixity, already noted in 1983 "it has been quite common to [...] regard mixed agreements as an obstacle and impediment to the process of European integration and thus to condemn them or at best to tolerate them as a necessary evil".[2] In constitutional terms, the phenomenon of mixity finds its origin in the specific allocation of competences in the EU legal order as informed by the principle of conferred powers. From the 1990s onwards and to ensure the manageability of mixity in practice, the Court of Justice has added the constitutional principle of sincere cooperation to the equation, identifying a duty of cooperation between the Member States and the EU institutions to ensure unity in the external representation of the Union and the Member States.[3] The shift in ju-

---

* I would like to thank Gesa Kübek for remarks on an earlier draft. All errors or omissions remain mine.

1 Kadelbach and Eekhout note that the majority of the EU's agreements are mixed, while Cremona refers to the majority of important agreements. See S. Kadelbach, "Handlungsformen und Steuerungsressourcen in den EU-Außenbeziehungen", in A. Hatje, P.-C. Müller-Graf (eds), *Europäische Außenbeziehungen* (Baden-Baden: Nomos, 2014), 227; P. Eeckhout, *EU External Relations Law* (Oxford: Oxford University Press, 2011), 212; M. Cremona, "EU External Relations: Unity and Conferral of Powers", in L. Azoulai (ed), *The Question of Competence in the European Union* (Oxford: Oxford University Press, 2014), 78.

2 J. Weiler, "The External Legal Relations of Non-Unitary Actors: Mixity and the Federal Principle", in D. O'Keeffe, H. Schermers (eds), *Mixed Agreements* (Deventer: Kluwer, 1983), 37.

3 C. Hillion, "'Mixity and Coherence in EU External Relations: The Significance of the 'Duty of Cooperation'", in C. Hillion, P. Koutrakos (eds), *Mixed Agreements Re-*

risprudential focus, henceforth emphasising pragmatic solutions on the exercise of shared or concurrent EU and Member States' competences has been criticised as pushing out the more fundamental question regarding the existence of (EU) competence.[4] Although law scholars should not fool themselves into believing they hold any sway over the judges at the Court, it is interesting to note that the Court in a more recent case seems to have returned to the question of competence, this time through the principle of the autonomy of the EU legal order. The still developing framework governing (and restricting) mixity is then composed of the principles of conferral, loyalty and autonomy, with the precise rules flowing from these principles still to be determined.

II. Mixity's Constitutional Foundations

The European Union has been described as an open federation in light of the fact that both the Union and its constituent entities may engage, independently from each other, in international relations.[5] The open character of the EU's federative Union thereby stands in stark contrast to the (more typical) statal federations where the federal principle is thrown overboard in external legal relations and the state acts as a unitary actor in relation to the outside world, as if it were not a federation at all.[6] While the choice for an open federation is laudable in light of federalism's value of diversity, it evidently comes at a price of greater complexity (and the risk of undermining unity). An additional complicating factor for the EU is that the EU Treaties have conferred shared competences on the EU. As a result, the open EU federation requires constitutional mechanisms in order to determine, in specific cases, which level of government is to act externally and to what extent. Supervening exclusivity, codified by the Lisbon Treaty in Article 3, paragraph 2, of the Treaty on the Functioning of the European Union (TFEU), is one such mechanism originally worked out by the Court

---

visited: the EU and its Member States in the World (Oxford: Hart Publishing, 2010), 87-88.

4 M. Cremona, *supra* note 1, 74.

5 R. Schütze, *Foreign Affairs and the EU Constitution: Selected Essays* (Cambridge: Cambridge University Press, 2014), 173.

6 J. Weiler, *supra* note 2, 37-38.

of Justice.[7] Mixity is another, and was developed by the institutions and the Member States. While it has not been enshrined in EU primary law,[8] the Court has explicitly sanctioned the practice in its established case law.[9]

Thus, the phenomenon of mixity, that is of agreements concluded by EU and all, or some, Member States with another entity (state or international organization) under international law,[10] is typically explained by two legal considerations, which in turn are informed by the EU's principle of conferred powers.[11] First, mixity is a consequence of the limited scope of the EU's competences: when an international agreement which the EU would like to conclude deals with matters not wholly coming within the competences conferred on the EU, the involvement of the EU Member States in the agreement is legally required. Second, even if the matters dealt with in the international agreement do come under the EU's competences, the involvement of the EU Member States is only legally precluded if every single matter comes under the EU's exclusive competences.[12] If not, the EU may exercise some of its shared competences, in respect of

7 Supervening exclusivity ruling out a role of the Member States (despite the EU being an open federation) explains why Weiler praised the federalist merits of mixity.

8 Only the Euratom Treaty explicitly foresees mixity in Article 102. The Treaty of Nice added a reference to mixed agreements in Article 133, paragraph 6, EC but this was taken out of the Treaties again by the Lisbon Treaty. The latter then only hints at mixity for the conclusion of the EU's accession to the European Convention on Human Rights (in Article 218, paragraph 8, TFEU).

9 See i.a. Opinion of the Court of 26 April 1977, 1/76, *Draft Agreement establishing a European laying-up fund for inland waterway vessels,* EU:C:1977:63, para 7; Opinion of the Court of 19 March 1993, 2/91, *Convention no. 170 of the International Labour Organization concerning safety in the use of chemicals at work,* EU:C:1993:106, paras 36-39; Judgment of 2 March 1994, *Parliament* v *Council,* C-316/91, EU:C:1994:76, para 26.

10 S. Kadelbach, *supra* note 1, 227.

11 See also P. Eeckhout, *supra* note 1, 213-214.

12 Until the recent judgment of the Court in *Germany* v *Council* (see *infra* note 15) some Member States typically assumed that mixity is required whenever an agreement is not fully covered by EU exclusive competences. See also *infra* note 76. Still, this point of view was not limited to the Member States. Pre-Lisbon Neframi also remarks that agreements coming under shared EU competences cannot be concluded by the EU alone if the *ERTA* and Opinion 1/76 doctrines do not apply. See E. Neframi, *Les accords mixtes de la Communauté européenne : aspects communautaires et internationaux* (Bruxelles: Bruylant, 2007), 107-111. See also G. Garzón Clariana, "La mixité: le droit et les problèmes pratiques", in J. Bourgeois (ed), *La Communauté européenne et les accords mixtes* (Maastricht: Presses interuniversitaires européennes, 1997), 16. In addition, the Court sowed some confu-

which Article 2, paragraph 2, TFEU provides: "Member States shall exercise their competence to the extent that the Union has not exercised its competence". Thus, as long as the EU refrains from exercising such shared competences, a question which is ultimately in the hands of the EU Council, there is scope for Member State action and, hence, mixity.

III. Constraining Compulsory Mixity

It follows from the above that a distinction should at least be made between compulsory and facultative mixity.[13] Although the Court created some confusion on facultative mixity in Opinion 2/15 by finding that the EU could not conclude the Singapore Free Trade Agreement (EUSFTA) on its own given that some of its provisions came under the EU's shared competences,[14] it set the record straight in *Germany* v *Council* where Germany argued that the EU only has an external competence if it is exclusive.[15] The Court firmly rejected this suggestion,[16] and clarified its finding in Opinion 2/15 by noting that in that case it had taken into account the political context and had assumed that the required majority would not be

---

sion on this in its Opinion on the Singapore FTA but afterwards corrected itself in *Germany* v *Council*.

13 Different typologies of mixity have been proposed in the past. See H. Schermers, "A Typology of Mixed Agreements", in D. O'Keeffe, H. Schermers (eds), *Mixed Agreements*, *supra* note 2, 23-33; A. Rosas, "The European Union and Mixed Agreements", in A. Dashwood, C. Hillion (eds), *The General Law of EC External Relations* (London: Sweet & Maxwell, 2000), 203-207; M. Maresceau, "A Typology of Mixed Bilateral Agreements", in C. Hillion, P. Koutrakos (eds), *Mixed Agreements Revisited, supra* note 3, 11-29. The added value of these typologies has also been questioned, see P. Eeckhout, *supra* note 1, 213-214.

14 The Court found that some aspects of the FTA came under shared (rather than exclusive) EU competence and hence the agreement could not be concluded by the EU alone. See Opinion of 16 May 2017, 2/15, *EU- Singapore Free Trade Agreement*, EU:C:2017:376, paras 243-244, 282. This would imply that facultative mixity does not exist and that instead the EU can only conclude compulsory EU-only agreements (pursuant to exclusive EU competences) or compulsory mixed agreements.

15 See Judgment of 5 December 2017, *Germany* v *Council*, C-600/14, EU:C:2017:935, para 38.

16 *Id.*, paras 47-51.

found in the Council for the EU to exercise its shared competences on its own.[17]

In light of Weiler's statement, facultative mixity is often seen as an obstacle to European integration, while compulsory mixity is seen as a necessary evil. Going beyond mere value judgements, this contribution aims to address the question whether the constitutional principles identified earlier may in some way structure or limit the institutions' and Member States' choice for mixity in EU external action.

At first sight, there can only be a genuine choice for mixity in the case of facultative mixity. On the other hand, when part of an agreement relates to an exclusive national competence, mixity would seem inevitable (i.e. compulsory). This traditional view is captured by the "pastis metaphor"[18] which Advocate General Kokott in the *Vietnam WTO Accession* case presented in the following way: "Individual aspects of an agreement for which the Community has no competence internally 'infect' the agreement as a whole and make it dependent on the common accord of the Member States. [...] Just as a little drop of pastis can turn a glass of water milky, individual provisions, however secondary, in an international agreement based on the first subparagraph of Article 133(5) EC can make it necessary to conclude a shared agreement".[19] Such mixity, even if it is compulsory, may then in fact be a type of hidden facultative mixity, since Member States in the past have often insisted on the inclusion of such unnecessary "secondary" provisions to ensure that an envisaged agreement must (legally) be concluded as a mixed agreement.[20]

---

17 *Id.*, para 68.

18 The pastis metaphor had earlier been coined by then Trade Commissioner Pascal Lamy in a slightly different context. Arguing for a generalization of qualified majority voting in EU Trade Policy during the Convention on the future of Europe, he noted: "The Treaty of Nice has been a step in the right direction, but too many pockets of unanimity survive. And under the Pastis principle, a little drop of unanimity can taint the entire glass of QMV water". See P. Lamy, *The Convention and Trade Policy: Concrete Steps to Enhance the EU's International Profile*, Speech, Brussels, 5 February 2002, p. 3.

19 Opinion of AG Kokott of 26 March 2009, *Commission* v *Council*, C-13/07, EU:C:2009:190, para 121.

20 The example of provisions on political dialogue is often cited in this regard. G. Garzón Clariana, *supra* note 12, 22. See G. De Baere, *Constitutional Principles of EU External Relations* (Oxford: Oxford University Press, 2008), 235-236. Post-Lisbon, clauses on political dialogue may be covered by the Common Foreign and Security Policy and do not require mixity anymore. Commenting on AG Sharp-

This traditional view should be juxtaposed with the view that would apply the absorption doctrine to provisions of an ancillary nature. Typically the absorption doctrine is applied horizontally when the EU institutions have to identify the legal basis for EU action. Pursuant to the established case law of the Court of Justice,[21] the choice of legal basis is not left to the discretion of the legislature but must be based on objective factors, notably the aim and the content of the measure to be adopted. If a measure pursues different aims, one of which is the main objective while the other is merely ancillary, the main objective 'absorbs' the ancillary objective and the measure should be adopted solely pursuant to the legal basis corresponding to the main objective.[22]

Can the absorption doctrine also be applied vertically to the effect that ancillary provisions which happen to come under (exclusive) national competences are absorbed by the provisions coming under EU competence? Recently, Advocate General Wahl seemed to suggest so in his Opinion on the Marrakesh Treaty when he observed, albeit in passing, that "a mixed agreement would be required, generally, where an international agreement concerns coexistent competences: that is, it includes a part which falls under the exclusive competence of the Union and a part which falls under the exclusive competence of the Member States, without any of those parts being ancillary to the other".[23]

In support of his (implied) assertion that compulsory mixity might be avoided by applying the absorption doctrine, Advocate General Wahl relied on Opinion 1/94 and *Portugal* v *Council*. In Opinion 1/94, the Com-

ston's Opinion in 2/15 in which the termination of Member States' existing investment Treaties was qualified as an exclusive national competence, Kleimann opined that such clauses are redundant in the EU's new generation free trade agreements. Under this reasoning, their inclusion would also result in false mixity. See D. Kleimann, "Reading Opinion 2/15 : Standards of Analysis, the Court's Discretion, and the Legal View of the Advocate General", *EUI Working Papers*, no. 23 (2017), 22.

21 See *inter alia* the case law cited in Opinion of 6 December 2001, 2/00, *Cartagena Protocol*, EU:C:2001:664, para 23.

22 See A. De Walsche, "La procédure de conclusion des accords internationaux", in J-V. Louis, M. Dony (eds), *Relations Extérieures* (Bruxelles: Editions de l'Université de Bruxelles, 2005), 81-82; M. Maresceau, *Bilateral Agreements Concluded by the European Community* (Den Haag: Martinus Nijhoff, 2006), 156-157.

23 Opinion of AG Wahl of 8 September 2016, Opinion 3/15, EU:C:2016:657, para 122. In the Council, several Member States had noted that the absorption doctrine could not be applied vertically. See Council doc. 8305/14 ADD 1, p. 3.

mission had argued that the TRIPS agreement (provisions harmonising intellectual property protection) could be brought under the trade notion of Article 113 EEC since earlier agreements concluded pursuant to Article 113 EEC contained provisions on intellectual property. [24] The Court dismissed this, noting that those provisions in earlier agreements were "extremely limited in scope", while confirming that "the Community and its institutions are entitled to incorporate within external agreements otherwise falling within the ambit of Article 113 ancillary provisions for the organization of purely consultative procedures or clauses calling on the other party to raise the level of protection of intellectual property".[25]

A clearer application of the absorption doctrine could be found in *Portugal* v *Council*, where Portugal questioned the legal basis used to conclude a cooperation agreement with India. Relying on Opinion 1/94, Portugal argued that the legal bases related to trade policy and development policy could not be used to include a general provision on intellectual property protection in the agreement.[26] In this regard, the Court noted that the obligations assumed were very limited. The commitment to facilitate

---

24 Specifically, the EEC-USSR agreement on trade in textile products provided in Article 20: "As regards intellectual property, at the request of either Contracting Party, consultations shall be held [...] with a view to finding an equitable solution to problems relating to the protection of marks, designs or models of articles of apparel and textile products". The interim agreements with Bulgaria, Czechoslovakia and Hungary provided (in Articles 37, 36 and 35) that those countries "shall continue to improve the protection of intellectual, industrial and commercial property rights in order to provide [...] a level of protection similar to that provided in the Community [...], including comparable means of enforcing such rights". See the EEC-USSR agreement, OJ 1989 L 391/2; EEC-Bulgaria agreement, OJ 1993 L 323/2; EEC-Czechoslovakia agreement, OJ 1992 L 115/2; EEC-Hungary agreement, OJ 1992 L 116/2.

25 Opinion of 15 November 1994, 1/94, *Competence of the Community to Conclude International Agreements Concerning Services and the Protection of Intellectual Property*, EU:C:1994:384, paras 67-68.

26 The specific provision *in casu* was Article 10 of the Agreement, which provided that: "The Contracting Parties undertake to ensure as far as their laws, regulations and policies allow that suitable and effective protection is provided for intellectual property rights, including patents, trade or service marks, copyright and similar rights, geographical designations (including marks of origin), industrial designs and integrated circuit topographies, reinforcing this protection where desirable. They also undertake, wherever possible, to facilitate access to the data bases of intellectual property organizations". See EEC-India Cooperation Agreement, OJ 1994 L 223, p. 24.

access to databases for instance "ha[d] only a very limited scope and [was] ancillary in nature".[27] The Court therefore concluded that the scope of the resulting obligations was not as such to constitute objectives different from the general objective of development cooperation.[28] While the Court thereby undeniably applied the absorption doctrine it must be noted that, differently from what Advocate General Wahl seemed to imply, there was no exclusive national competence at issue. Instead, Portugal had argued that the EU did not have an exclusive competence pursuant to Articles 113 and 130y EEC [29] while the Council rightly noted that the lack of an exclusive EU competence did not mean that the EU lacked competence to conclude the agreement on its own.[30]

In addition to the cases mentioned by Advocate General Wahl, Rosas has referred to Opinion 1/78 to argue that "the provisions relating to possible 'coexistent' Member States competences may be of such a limited relevance that they should be seen as 'ancillary' (subsidiary) to the essential objectives of the agreement. If this is the case, Member States participation would not be necessary – or, in cases of exclusive Community competence, even legally admissible".[31] Indeed, in Opinion 1/78, the Court confirmed that the conclusion of the agreement on natural rubber came within the EU's exclusive competences on trade depending on how the

27 Judgment of 3 December 1996, *Portugal* v *Council*, C-268/94, EU:C:1996:461, para 75.

28 *Id.*, para 76.

29 See *id.*, para 69. This illustrates the typical (political) reasoning followed by the Member States to date: if an agreement does not wholly come under EU exclusive competences, mixity is presented as an automatic consequence. As Heliskoski notes, this is plainly erroneous even if AG Pergola seemed to concur with Portugal when he noted that when "the Community does not enjoy exclusive competence …, matters have to be regulated by means of mixed agreements". See Opinion of AG Pergola of 23 May 1996, *Portugal* v *Council*, C-268/94, EU:C:1996:207, para 41; J. Heliskoski, *Mixed Agreements as a Technique for Organizing the International Relations of the European Community and its Member States* (The Hague: Kluwer Law International, 2001), 42.

30 Note however that the Council only half-heartedly defended the possibility of the EU exercising shared competences on its own: "[The Council] considers that the Community had the power to conclude the Agreement without the participation of the Member States since the clause in the Agreement concerning intellectual property has only limited scope and involves substantial obligations only on the part of India". See Judgment of 3 December 1996, *Portugal* v *Council*, C-268/94, EU:C:1996:461, para 71.

31 A. Rosas, *supra* note 13, 204.

mechanism set up by the agreement would be financed (by EU or Member States' funds). The Court took care to point out that from a substantive point of view the agreement in any case was covered by the current Article 207 TFEU. Other provisions in the agreement such as those on technological assistance and labour conditions on the other hand could not "modify the description of the agreement which must be assessed having regard to its essential objective rather than in terms of individual clauses of an altogether subsidiary or ancillary nature".[32] According to Rosas, if such ancillary provisions nonetheless trigger mixity, one can speak, especially if exclusive EU competences are at issue, of false mixity.[33]

The views of Advocate General Wahl seem difficult to square with those of Advocate General Kokott but it should be noted that Advocate General Kokott used her pastis metaphor when interpreting the very complex amendments made by the Nice Treaty to Article 133 EC and especially the relationship between the fifth and sixth paragraph of that Article. According to the Advocate General, "Article 133(6) EC is not an exception to the first subparagraph of Article 133(5) EC and, as such, to be interpreted narrowly …. At the same time, [Article 133(6) EC] counteracts a main-purpose test operating to the disadvantage of the areas of competence of the Member States". [34] Thus, despite having worded her pastis metaphor in general terms, Advocate General Kokott did not as such rule out a main-purpose test (and the resulting absorption doctrine) when deciding on the vertical delimitation of competences (rather than the horizontal cases in which it is typically applied).

To sum up, while the above case law tends to support applying the absorption doctrine in order to avoid a situation of facultative mixity, two key points must be addressed before transposing this finding to instances of compulsory mixity. First, apart from *Portugal* v *Council*, these cases involved the common trade policy, an *a priori* exclusive competence of the

32 Opinion of 4 October 1979, 1/78, *International Agreement on Natural Rubber*, EU:C:1979:224, para 56.

33 A. Rosas, *supra* note 13, p. 205. See also J. Heliskoski, *supra* note 29, 68. Similarly Gilsdorf criticized the Member States' insistence on mixed agreements when certain provisions are not covered by EU competence, ignoring the often ancillary nature of these provisions. See P. Gilsdorf, "Die Außenkompetenzen der EG im Wandel – Eine kritische Auseinandersetzung mit Praxis und Rechtsprechung", *Europarecht* 31, no. 2 (1996), 161.

34 Opinion of AG Kokott of 26 March 2009, *Commission* v *Council*, C-13/07, EU:C:2009:190, para 120.

EU.[35] Second, none of the cases actually involved the absorption of provisions coming under exclusive national competence.

In addition, the correct application of the absorption doctrine in general remains rather murky, as was further illustrated in the Opinion procedure on EUSFTA.[36] Advocate General Sharpston found that the Investor State Dispute Settlement (ISDS) mechanism's function was to make the enforcement of the EUSFTA more effective and opined that in line with the Court's case law,[37] "dispute settlement and mediation mechanisms are ancillary in nature, the allocation of competences between the European Union and the Member States for such mechanisms is necessarily the same as for the substantive provisions to which they relate. In other words, those mechanisms are not in themselves capable of altering the allocation of competences between the European Union and its Member States".[38] The Court on the other hand noted that the specific arrangement for ISDS in the EUSFTA was worked out in such a way that disputes brought for arbitration are removed from the jurisdiction of the national courts. Such a regime then "cannot be of a purely ancillary nature [...] and cannot, therefore, be established without the Member States' consent".[39] The Advocate General and the Court clearly disagreed on this point but the Court, unfortunately, is not particularly forthcoming on the precise reason why the mechanism's repercussions were too significant to be qualified as ancillary.[40] In addition, lack of EU competence resulting from the non-ancillary nature of the mechanism seems a *non sequitur*: if the provisions on ISDS

35 This is why Kaniel refers to cases such as Opinion 1/78 as cases involving an 'ancillary exclusive power'. See M. Kaniel, *The Exclusive Treaty-Making Power of the European Community up to the Period of the Single European Act* (The Hague: Kluwer Law International, 1996), 55-57.

36 In this regard, Kleimann has argued that for the purpose of determining the predominant and ancillary provisions of an act the Court should, as a matter of systemic coherence, apply the same 'objective factors amenable to judicial review' which it applies for determining an act's legal basis. See D. Kleimann, *supra* note 20, 12.

37 See Opinion of 16 May 2017, 2/15, *supra* note 14, para 276.

38 Opinion of AG Sharpston of 21 December 2016, Opinion 2/15, EU:C:2016:992, para 529.

39 Opinion of 16 May 2017, 2/15, *supra* note 14, para 292.

40 It may be noted that the Court did not explicitly find that the mechanism touches on an exclusive national competence. Thus, even if it noted that it would not deal with the FTA's compatibility with the Treaties (see para 30) the Court may also have felt that the mechanism could not be qualified as ancillary because of its

were too significant to be absorbed by the provisions on trade and transport the question should have become whether there might still be EU competence pursuant to another legal basis in the Treaties.

IV. Facultative Mixity and its Critique

Leaving the area of compulsory mixity behind and focusing on the EU's shared competences brings us to a second and perhaps more pressing issue. In cases of shared competence (or generally when an agreement is not completely covered by Article 3 TFEU), the EU institutions may opt not to make use of the EU's competences, leaving the legal space open for the Member States to be involved in the process.[41] The situation in which a potential EU-only agreement is turned into a mixed agreement may be described as typical facultative mixity.[42]

Given that mixity is perceived as hampering the effectiveness of EU external action,[43] the question arises of why the Member States would insist on being involved in the conclusion of such agreements in their own capacity as subjects of international law. This question has been well documented, [44] although nothing radically new has been added to the insights formulated in this regard by Ehlermann in 1983.[45] Today, the most important reason for the Member States' insistence on mixity, when it is not legally required, is, allegedly, their wish to remain 'visible' on the international stage.[46]

---

repercussions on the preliminary ruling procedure, even if the FTA itself rules out the direct effect of its provisions.

41 See J. Heliskoski, *supra* note 29, 25.

42 See A. Rosas, *supra* note 13, 205-206. Klamert rightly remarks that facultative mixity is also at issue when a mixed agreement covers exclusive Member State and shared (EU and Member State) competences. See M. Klamert, *The Principle of Loyalty in EU Law* (Oxford: Oxford University Press, 2014), 183-184. However, such facultative mixity will not be discussed in the present contribution.

43 C. Hillion, *supra* note 3, 90.

44 A. Dashwood, "Why Continue to Have Mixed Agreements at All?", in J. Bourgeois (ed), *La Communauté européenne et les accords mixtes*, *supra* note 12, 96-97.

45 C-D. Ehlermann, "Mixed Agreements: A List of Problems", in David O'Keeffe & Henri Schermers (eds), *Mixed agreements, supra* note 2, 4-9.

46 R. Schütze, *supra* note 5, 203.

Recourse to mixity, both in cases of compulsory and facultative mixity, has been criticised in legal doctrine. Schütze for instance argues that it ought to be avoided and laments that the Court of Justice has given its judicial blessing to an uncontrolled resort to mixity.[47] Even an ardent supporter like Dashwood has conceded that the 'inconveniences' that are sometimes caused by mixed agreements should be minimised.[48] In this regard, he has proposed that where practicable, mixity should be avoided by excising dispensable elements from the agreement if these elements would trigger (compulsory) mixity and the Commission should convince the Member States (in areas of shared competence) that they do not lose anything by agreeing to conclude EU-only agreements.[49] Here Dashwood sees a role for the Commission in alleviating the Member States' fears of a "reverse *ERTA*" doctrine. Under this doctrine, the exercise by the EU of external competences would pre-empt Member States' acting in the field internally, rendering the competence an exclusive EU competence (thus reversing *ERTA*, where the exercise by the EU of an internal competence can result in the pre-emption of Member States acting externally).[50] However, even if the Commission would argue against a reverse *ERTA* doctrine,[51] it should be noted that this issue is not really in the hands of the Commission in the first place. This may explain why the Member States

47 *Id.*, 204-205 (see especially footnote 140).

48 A. Dashwood, *supra* note 44, 93.

49 *Id.*, 97. Dashwood further proposed to introduce certain rules in primary law governing mixed agreements. It is open for debate however whether a Treaty change would be legally required. While this would seem to be the case for Dashwood's proposal allowing the Council to unanimously adopt common positions in areas of exclusive Member States competence, it must be noted the Court in the *FAO* case implicitly accepted that the Council could represent and bind the Member States in their individual capacity. See P. Eeckhout, *supra* note 1, 246; C. Timmermans, "Organising Joint Participation of EC and Member States", in A. Dashwood, C. Hillion (eds), *The General Law of EC External Relations*, *supra* note 13, 243-244.

50 M. Cremona, *supra* note 1, 70.

51 In its observations in Opinion 2/92, the Commission rejected a reversal of the *ERTA* doctrine but not a reversed *ERTA* doctrine when it noted: "the fact that the Member States retain certain internal powers cannot necessarily be relied upon for the purpose of conferring external powers on them". See Opinion of 24 March 1995, 2/92, *Competence of the Community or one of its institutions to participate in the Third Revised Decision of the OECD on national treatment*, EU:C:1995:83.

introduced Article 207, paragraph 6, TFEU through the Lisbon Treaty.[52] As Klamert notes, the Court itself has never ruled on whether an international agreement, concluded under shared EU competence, might constitute a 'common rule' in itself under the *ERTA* doctrine,[53] a question which would precede the question on whether there might be a reverse *ERTA* doctrine.

In contrast to Dashwood, Eeckhout argues that, given all the disadvantages associated with mixity, it is best avoided.[54] Eeckhout also foresees a role for the Court, arguing that "the requirement of the unity in the international representation of the EU demands pure EU agreements" in cases where the agreement is wholly covered by (non-exclusive) EU competences.[55] Eeckhout does not further develop this argument himself, but it would arguably require the Court to take a qualitative step via its case law. As noted above, the Court, reasoning from the constitutional principle of sincere cooperation, has developed a duty of cooperation between Member States and the EU based on "unity in the international representation of the EU" in order to "attenuate the plurality inherent to mixity".[56] Pursuant to this case law, unity in the international representation of the EU imposes a number of obligations on the Member States so as to make mixity manageable. Eeckhout's suggestion should then be seen as rather radical since the requirement of unity would be used to preclude any recourse to mixity instead of simply managing it.

Timmermans, also critical of mixity, has observed that the focus should be on the question "whether Community competence exists and what are the advantages of exercising it? If these advantages are obvious, Member

52 Article 207, paragraph 6, TFEU provides: "The exercise of the competences conferred by this Article in the field of the common commercial policy shall not affect the delimitation of competences between the Union and the Member States, and shall not lead to harmonisation of legislative or regulatory provisions of the Member States in so far as the Treaties exclude such harmonisation". On the different ways to interpret Article 207, paragraph 6, TFEU, see J.A. Bischoff, "Just a Little Bit of "Mixity"? The EU's Role in the Field of International Investment Protection Law", *Common Market Law Review* 48, no. 6 (2011), 1541-1543.

53 M. Klamert, *supra* note 42, 186.

54 P. Eeckhout, *supra* note 1, 264-265.

55 *Id.*, 265.

56 C. Hillion, *supra* note 3, 90.

States should act through the Community".[57] Expounding on this, he notes that mixed agreements in areas coming under the EU's parallel competences (see Article 4, paragraphs 3 and 4, TFEU) do not seem objectionable while a free choice for mixity in areas coming under shared competences (Article 4, paragraph 2, TFEU) does.[58] A rather cynical example (and probably not on Timmermans' mind at the time) of a practical advantage to EU-only agreements may be found in the Association Agreement between the EU and Kosovo. Normally, the Stabilization and Association Agreements (SAAs) concluded between the EU and the ex-Yugoslav countries take the form of mixed agreements.[59] The SAA with Kosovo[60] however has been concluded as an EU-only agreement following a request from the five EU Member States that do not recognise Kosovo's independence.[61] The 'advantage' for these Member States of concluding an EU-only agreement is clear but the Council decision concluding the agreement makes it equally clear that this in no way changes the Member States' general approach of insisting on mixity.[62] Still, the other practical advantage

57 C. Timmermans, "Organising Joint Participation of EC and Member States", in A. Dashwood, C. Hillion (eds), *The General Law of EC External Relations*, *supra* note 13, 247.

58 C. Timmermans, "The Court of Justice and Mixed Agreements", in *The Court of Justice and the Construction of Europe: Analyses and Perspectives on Sixty Years of Caselaw* (The Hague: TMC Asser Press, 2013), 663.

59 See e.g. the Stabilisation and Association Agreement (SAA) with Bosnia and Herzegovina, OJ 2015 L 164, p. 2; SAA with the Republic of Serbia, OJ 2013 L 278, p. 16; SAA with the Republic of Montenegro, OJ 2010 L 108, p. 3.

60 SAA with Kosovo, OJ 2016 L 71, p. 3. Discussing this SAA and its EU-only nature, see P. Van Elsuwege, "Legal Creativity in EU External Relations: The Stabilisation and Association Agreement between the EU and Kosovo", *European Foreign Affairs Review* 22, no. 3 (2017), 393-409.

61 The report of the UK House of Commons committee on European Scrutiny reveals that the other Member States (or at least the UK) agreed to this request on the condition that the unique nature of the agreement would be stressed so as to not set a precedent for future agreements. See point 27.22 of the Documents considered by the Committee on 21 July 2015.

62 Recital 5 of the Decision's preamble provides: "This is an EU-only agreement. The commitments and cooperation to be entered into by the Union under this Agreement relate only to the areas covered by the EU acquis or existing Union policies. The signing and conclusion of this Agreement as an EU-only Agreement is without prejudice to the nature and scope of any similar agreements to be negotiated in the future. It is also without prejudice to the powers of the EU institutions conferred on them in the Treaties and the positions of EU institutions and Member States on competences". See Council Decision 2016/342, OJ 2016 L 71, p. 1.

of realising a more swift ratification process is also obvious in the case of the Kosovo SAA. Where the time between signature and entry into force of the other SAAs ranged between 3 and 8 years,[63] the Kosovo SAA entered into force six months following its signature.[64]

In short, the suggested ways of addressing the issue of facultative mixity range from the practical (focus on advantages of EU-only agreements),[65] over the political (the Commission should build trust) to the legal (the Court should step in). From a constitutional point of view, Eeckhout's suggestion, being tied to the principle of sincere cooperation, stands out as the most relevant avenue to explore.[66] Even if the practical and the political route may yield results, recourse to mixity would still be a purely political choice: Member States may be swayed by practical or political reasons to agree to make full use of the EU's shared competences (and thus to conclude an EU-only agreement) but they would not be legally prevented from insisting on mixity.

V. Constitutional Limits to Facultative Mixity

Given its non-obligatory nature, more ways ought to exist to limit facultative compared to compulsory mixity. One of the potential avenues has of course already been explored above: fully applying the absorption doctrine

63 The Serbia SAA was signed on 29/04/2008 and entered into force on 01/09/2013; the Bosnia and Herzegovina SAA was signed on 16/06/2008 and entered into force 01/06/2015; the Montenegro SAA was signed on 15/10/2007 and entered into force on 01/05/2010.

64 To be precise, the Kosovo SAA was signed on 01/10/2015 and entered into force on 01/04/2016.

65 It should be noted that Timmermans' argument could transcend the 'purely' practical and take on legal qualities. As Timmermans explains, the earlier case law of the Court (notably Opinion 1/76 and Ruling 1/78) could be read as confirming EU-only agreements as the default category of EU external action, resulting in a specific justification requirement for concluding a facultative mixed agreement. Yet, "this line of case law has not been further developed. As from Opinion 2/91, full emphasis falls on the quest for exclusivity". See C. Timmermans, *supra* note 58, 663-664. See also R. Schütze, *supra* note 5, 203-204.

66 This is not to say that it is the only relevant avenue to explore. Arguably, the role played by the Commission in the 'Community Method' also has a constitutional dimension but it is doubtful whether any clear limits or constraints could be deduced from it.

may result in ancillary provisions of an agreement that come under a shared EU competence being absorbed by the main provisions of that agreement. If the latter come under an exclusive EU competence, as with, for instance, the Free Trade Agreement with Korea,[67] the question as to the level (EU or Member State) at which competences will be exercised, does not arise and the agreement will be an EU-only one.[68]

To explore further legal routes to limit recourse to facultative mixity, the different approaches of a number of Advocate Generals may again be juxtaposed. In addition to the Court's ruling in *US Air Transport Agreement*, the Opinions of Advocates General Sharpston, Wahl and Kokott already referred to above will assist us in our quest to identify a constitutional limit to mixity.

A. *Facultative Mixity as a Political Choice*

Undoubtedly Advocate General Sharpston has put forward the most conservative or traditional understanding of the 'triggering' of mixity in her Opinion on the EUSFTA.[69] Before coming to the questions posed by the Commission in this procedure, the Advocate General sets out the Lisbon

67 The agreement with Korea was concluded at the time as a mixed agreement because of the Protocol on cultural cooperation. See the Protocol on Cultural Cooperation, OJ 2011, L 127/1418. However, the greatest part of this protocol does not impose clear obligations on either of the parties. The only such obligations may be found in Article 5(4-5) of the Protocol which entitles co-produced audiovisual works of both parties to benefit from the other party's promotion schemes. It could have been argued that these provisions do not justify recourse to a mixed agreement and should have been absorbed by the agreement's main aim. However, following Opinion 2/15 a further argument for the (compulsory) mixity of the agreement may be found in the FTA's provisions on portfolio investment. Rather questionably, the Court in Opinion 2/15 found that a Treaty provision such as Article 63 TFEU cannot be affected in the *ERTA* sense and as a result, the provisions on portfolio investments came under a shared competence and could not be approved by the EU alone. See Opinion of 16 May 2017, 2/15, *supra* note 14, paras 233-244.

68 In the 1990s, Gilsdorf indeed criticised the tendency to conclude "trade *and*" agreements to justify mixity even if the non-trade provisions could be easily absorbed by the dominant trade provisions. See P. Gilsdorf, *supra* note 33, 162.

69 The Commission's observations in Opinion 2/92 exemplify how deeply entrenched this view is, even in the most supranationally oriented circles: discussing the competence for the EU's participation in the OECD's decision, the Commis-

framework on the existence and exercise of EU external competences. Discussing the situation in which there is no *a priori* or supervening exclusivity (under Article 3, paragraphs 1 and 2, TFEU) she notes that an EU external competence will only exist (abstraction made of the EU's supporting competences) when a shared competence under Article 4 TFEU can be linked to one of the cases described in Article 216, paragraph 1, TFEU. As to the exercise of such an external competence, the Advocate General remarks that the EU has a right of pre-emption but "[i]f the European Union does not choose to exercise that right, external competence — like internal competence — will remain with the Member States and it follows that they (and not the European Union) will be competent to negotiate, sign and conclude an international agreement whose subject matter falls within that area of shared competence".[70]

Remarkably, Advocate General Sharpston then proceeded to qualify the EU legislature's discretion in exercising its competences externally, finding that the EU could not simply "assert external competence over any area of shared competence listed in Article 4 irrespective of whether it has chosen to exercise that right internally".[71] The reasoning behind this assertion by the Advocate General is unclear[72] but upholding it would impose a limit on autonomous EU external action. It is, furthermore, at odds with

---

sion advocated an application of the *ERTA* and Opinion 1/76 doctrines and further considered that "the Community legislature would have a discretion either to assume all the obligations arising within the framework of the OECD or to leave the Member States some latitude in matters not covered by Community legislation". See Opinion of 24 March 1995, 2/92, *supra* note 51, EU:C:1995:83, para 29.

70 Opinion of AG Sharpston of 21 December 2016, Opinion 2/15, *supra* note 38, para 73.

71 *Id.*, para 74.

72 Perhaps the confusion that a shared EU competence can only be exercised externally when it has already been exercised internally can be traced back to Opinion 1/94 in which the Court noted (as regards the competence to conclude the TRIPs): "The Community is certainly competent to harmonize national rules on those matters, ... But the fact remains that the Community institutions have not hitherto exercised their powers in the field of the 'enforcement of intellectual property rights' .... It follows that the Community and its Member States are jointly competent to conclude TRIPs". See Opinion of 15 November 1994, 1/94, *supra* note 25, paras 104-105. However, as was remarked by commentators at the time, the Court in that Opinion "did not explicitly answer the first question put to it by the Commission. That was to know whether the Community had, as such, the competence to conclude all parts of the WTO Agreement relating to GATS and TRIPS". See Editorial Comments, "The Aftermath of Opinion 1/94 or How to Ensure Unity of

the Council's argument that the decision on who exercises shared competences (the EU or the Member States) is a political choice, even though the Advocate General confirmed this argument in the very same paragraph.[73]

While this political choice typically falls in favour of the Member States rather than the EU, it could in principle fall either way. According to the Advocate General, the detailed procedure of Article 218 TFEU, which is dominated by the Council, contains "the legal safeguards underpinning that political choice".[74] Thus, the Advocate General concludes that, for agreements covering areas of shared competences, "the Member States together (acting in their capacity as members of the Council) have the power to agree that the European Union shall act or to insist that they will continue to exercise individual external competence".[75]

Following Advocate General Sharpston's reasoning, the Member States have an unfettered choice to make use or not of the EU's shared competences and the procedure under Article 218 TFEU is even read as a safeguard guaranteeing the political nature of that choice. Furthermore, the only limit to this political choice which can be read in Advocate General Sharpston's analysis is a limit favouring mixity, since she sees the EU barred from simply asserting its external competences if the EU has not first exercised its competences internally.

Representation for Joint Competences", *Common Market Law Review* 32, no. 2 (1995), 386. As a result, the Court concluded there was to be joint competence because it had already taken into account the fact that the Member States were not willing to let the EU exercise its competences to the fullest.

73 At face value, the AG's assertion also conflicts with the doctrine resulting from Opinion 1/76 (codified by the Lisbon Treaty in Article 216, paragraph 1, TFEU) as well as with the Court's finding in Opinion 2/91 in which it noted that the EU "enjoys an internal legislative competence in the area of social policy. Consequently, Convention No 170 … falls within the Community's area of competence". See Opinion of 19 March 1993, 2/91, *Convention no. 170 of the International Labour Organization concerning safety in the use of chemicals at work,* EU:C:1993:106, para 17.

74 Opinion of AG Sharpston of 21 December 2016, Opinion 2/15, *supra* note 3, para 74.

75 *Id.*, para 75 (emphasis in original).

B. *Limits Flowing from Article 18 of the Vienna Convention on the Law of Treaties*

The analysis of Advocate General Wahl in the Opinion procedure on the Marrakesh Treaty stands in stark contrast to that of Advocate General Sharpston. After having determined the existence of EU competence and proposing Articles 19 and 207 TFEU as the joint legal basis for the decision concluding the Marrakesh Treaty, Advocate General Wahl elaborated on the nature of the EU's competence. Apparently, the Hungarian government argued that if the agreement came under shared competences it ought to be concluded as a mixed agreement.[76] The Advocate General rightly refuted this,[77] noting that even if Article 3, paragraph 2, TFEU were not applicable, this would not inevitably call for mixity. Instead, "The choice between a mixed agreement or an EU-only agreement, when the subject matter of the agreement falls within an area of shared competence (or of parallel competence), is generally a matter for the discretion of the EU legislature".[78] Advocate General Wahl thus confirmed the political nature of this decision, following the traditional understanding of facultative mixity. The novelty in the Advocate General's reasoning resides in what follows, since he argued that the decision is only predominantly, rather than wholly, political in nature and therefore subject to, albeit limited, judicial review. Qualifying this judicial review, the Advocate General clearly proposed to apply the Court's general marginal review test: "the legality of a measure adopted in those fields can be affected only if the measure is manifestly inappropriate having regard to the objective which the competent institution is seeking to pursue".[79] Expounding on when the choice for mixity in cases of facultative mixity would be manifestly inappropriate, the Advocate General identified at least two scenario. Recourse to mixity would thus be illegal if the agreement was concluded to tackle an urgent, pressing, issue. In such a case, having to wait for 29 ratification procedures to

---

76 Opinion of AG Wahl of 8 September 2016, Opinion 3/15, *supra* note 23, para 119. See also *supra* notes 12 and 29.

77 The Court later did so as well in *Germany* v *Council*, see Judgment of 5 December 2017, *supra* note 15.

78 Opinion of AG Wahl, *supra* note 23, para 119.

79 *Id.*, para 120. On this standard of review in general, see P. Gilliaux, "L'intensité du contrôle de la légalité par les juridictions communautaires", *Journal de droit européen* 17, no. 156 (2009), 43.

be completed might take so much time that realizing the agreement's objective would be put in jeopardy. Secondly, the same length of time might in some cases result in a breach by the EU of the principle of *pacta sunt servanda*.

The fact that the Advocate General ties these two scenarios to the settled case law of the Court on marginal review may indicate that those scenarios are just two illustrations from an open-ended list. Still even these two illustrations raise a number of questions. Firstly, the reliance on the principle of *pacta sunt servanda* may appear premature, since under Article 26 of the Vienna Convention on the Law of Treaties (VCLT) the principle only applies to treaties that have entered into force.[80] However, the problem identified by the AG is precisely that the entry into force would be forthcoming because of the cumbersome ratification procedures. Instead, the Advocate General seems to have had Article 18 VCLT in mind.[81] Pursuant to Article 18(a) VCLT, a party "is obliged to refrain from acts which would defeat the object and purpose of a treaty when it has signed the treaty or has exchanged instruments constituting the treaty subject to ratification, acceptance or approval, until it shall have made its intention clear not to become a party to the treaty". The threshold required is therefore rather high, as the party's conduct should effectively defeat the object and purpose of the agreement.[82] More fundamentally, it appears that the first scenario (referring to the objective of the treaty) identified by Advocate General Wahl may therefore be subsumed under the second scenario, begging the question whether this is in fact the main (or only) scenario in which the standard for showing a manifest error of assessment would be met.

Regardless of these open questions, which the Advocate General did not elaborate upon and which the Court did not have to deal with either since it found, like the Advocate General, that the EU had exclusive competence, Advocate General Wahl undoubtedly suggested a legal check on

80 See A. Austen, "Pacta Sunt Servanda", in *Max Planck Encyclopedia of Public International Law*.

81 Confirming that Article 18 VCLT is binding on the EU, see Judgment of 22 January 1997, *Opel Austria* v *Council*, T-115/94, EU:T:1997:3, para 90.

82 See P. Palchetti, "Article 18 of the 1969 Vienna Convention: A Vague and Ineffective Obligation or a UsefulMeans for Strengthening Legal Cooperation?", in E. Cannizzaro (ed), *The Law of Treaties Beyond the Vienna Convention* (Oxford: Oxford University Press, 2011), 27-28.

the 'political choice' for facultative mixity. It should nevertheless be noted that the limit suggested by Advocate General Wahl finds its origin in international public law rather than in EU constitutional law itself. In this regard, this legal route is fundamentally different from Eeckhout's suggestion which relies on EU law.

C. Limits Flowing from the Union Interest and Unity in the EU's International Representation

Advocate General Kokott in her Opinion on Vietnam's accession to the WTO made a number of interesting observations, which could amount to another constitutional limit on mixity. The questions at issue in this case were whether the Council decision agreeing to Vietnam's accession to the WTO should have been adopted based only on Article 133, paragraphs 1 and 5, EC as proposed by the Commission and whether Article 133, paragraph 5, EC (like Article 133, paragraph 1, EC) came under the EU's exclusive competence as the Commission claimed. The Advocate General was sympathetic to the practical argument observing that "exclusive competence for the Community in the field of trade in services and the commercial aspects of intellectual property would be better suited for ensuring the effective representation of European interests at international level"[83] but ultimately found differently and noted, together with the Council, that under the Nice Treaty there was neither a priori nor supervening exclusivity for trade in services and the commercial aspects of intellectual property.

Following the traditional approach, the conclusion would be that the Member States in the Council are free to decide whether the EU or the Member States will exercise their shared powers. Here, the Advocate General disagreed, noting that "contrary to the view taken by the Council, it does not necessarily follow, from the mere fact that Article 133(5) EC does not provide for exclusive Community competence, that the Member States were automatically entitled to be involved alongside the Community in adopting the decision on Vietnam's accession to the WTO".[84] According to the Advocate General, the reason for this lay in the concurrent rather than parallel nature of the EU's trade competence and also in a prac-

83 Opinion of AG Kokott of 26 March 2009, *Commission* v *Council*, C-13/07, EU:C:2009:190, para 63.

84 *Id.*, para 66.

tical argument since mixed action would make it more difficult "to represent effectively the interests of the Community and its Member States outwardly".[85] Here, the Advocate General was careful to limit her finding to the EU's trade policy: "Agreements to which the Member States as well as the Community are parties are consequently out of place in the common commercial policy. They should be permitted only where the Community on its own has no or insufficient power and therefore has to rely on the involvement of its Member States at international level". Yet, it should be clear that the practical argument regarding the 'effective outward representation of the EU and the Member States' interests' cannot *a priori* be limited to the EU's Common Commercial Policy (CCP).[86]

A further question, which is raised by the Advocate General's proposition is whether invoking the effective representation of the EU's interests is a purely practical argument or whether it may somehow be juridified.[87] In this regard it may be noted that the Court relied on the idea of Union (Community) interest in Opinion 1/75 in order to establish an exclusive EU competence [88] and in *Hermes* and *Dior* [89] in order to establish its jurisdiction to interpret mixed agreements. According to Cremona, the legal notion of Union interest finds its basis in Article 4, paragraph 3 of the Treaty on European Union (TEU) and functions as a bridge between the principle of primacy and the duty of cooperation. Thus, primacy puts substantive limits on the Member States' competences, while the duty of co-

85 *Id.*, para 72. For further practical reasons, see *id.*, para 73.

86 Purely practically, the CCP might be a unique case, but from a legal perspective the real distinction would seem to lie in whether the EU exercises a shared or parallel competence, as also noted by AG Kokott. under parallel competences, Member States would retain a right to act.

87 According to Ortino, the meta-principle of effectiveness underlies and informs most of the EU's general principles, including the principle of sincere cooperation. See M. Ortino, "A Reading of the EU Constitutional Legal System through the Meta-Principle of Effectiveness", *Cahiers de droit européen* 52, no. 1 (2016), 94-95.

88 Opinion of 11 November 1975, 1/75, EU:C:1975:145.

89 Judgment of 16 June 1998, *Hermès*, C-53/96, EU:C:1998:292; Judgment of 14 December 2000, *Parfums Christian Dior*, Joined Cases C-300/98 & C-392/98, EU:C:2000:688. For a discussion, see P. Koutrakos, "Interpretation of Mixed Agreements", in C. Hillion, P. Koutrakos (eds), *Mixed Agreements Revisited, supra* note 3, 118-123.

operation imposes procedural requirements on the Member States.[90] As the *PFOS* case has shown,[91] these procedural requirements may amount to a duty for the Member States to remain silent in international fora. Although *PFOS* has been criticised for blurring the boundary between exclusive and shared EU competences (imposing a duty to abstain on Member States in both cases),[92] it could form a springboard for further developing the duty of cooperation. In essence, in *PFOS*, Sweden could not exercise its shared competence because of the existence of a Union position. Similarly, Advocate General Kokott proposed that Member States ought to refrain from exercising their shared competence, thereby leaving the legal space to the EU. As noted above in relation to Eeckhout's suggestion, the qualitative difference between the two scenarios would lie in the fact that *PFOS* was about exercising shared competence in the framework of a mixed agreement, whereas further pursuing AG Kokott's suggestion would result in preventing the conclusion of a mixed act in the first place.

The duty of cooperation would thus take (another) qualitative leap since its traditional function is to ensure the manageability of mixed agreements. As the Court explained in Opinion 1/08: "The requirement of unity in the international representation of the Community calls in addition for close cooperation between the Member States and the Community institutions in the process of negotiation and conclusion of [mixed] agreements".[93] A further development of the duty as sketched out above would take on a new function, since it would simply pre-empt mixity. In a reasoning that may be squared with Eeckhout's suggestion, the requirement of unity in the international representation of the Union would call for close cooperation whereby Member States are required to cooperate solely within the EU framework. Put differently, the qualitative leap would result in a (new)

90 M. Cremona, "Defending the Community Interest: the Duties of Cooperation and Compliance", in M. Cremona, B. de Witte (eds), *EU Foreign Relations Law: Constitutional Fundamentals* (Oxford: Hart, 2008), 126-127.

91 Judgment of 20 April 2010, *Commission* v *Sweden*, C-246/07, EU:C:2010:203.

92 A. Delgado Casteleiro, J. Larik, "The Duty to Remain Silent: Limitless Loyalty in EU External Relations?", *European Law Review* 36, no. 4 (2011), 539.

93 Opinion of 30 November 2009, 1/08, *General Agreement on Trade in Services (GATS) – Schedules of Specific Commitments Concerning Market Access and Granting of National Treatment*, EU:C:2009:739, para 136.

positive obligation -the obligation to act solely through the EU- rather than a simple negative obligation.[94]

Before such a positive obligation is put forward, a number of objections would have to be addressed. Firstly such a new obligation would immediately have to be qualified as it would otherwise result in a duty to resort to EU-only agreements in areas of shared (non-parallel) competences. This would be difficult to square with Article 2, paragraph 2, TFEU unless it is assumed that the latter does not apply to the EU's external relations.[95] However, Advocate General Kokott's attempt to distinguish the CCP and other EU policies shows how cumbersome it may be to show in practice how the EU interest (in a specific case) requires an EU-only agreement. Kokott herself juxtaposed the area of international trade with the area of international development cooperation. Supposedly, the effectiveness of the latter is not hampered if both the EU and its 28 Member States act concurrently. In addition, the Advocate General warned of the risk that individual Member States would (ab)use 'reinforced unanimity' in order to secure individual concessions, and that third countries might pressure individual EU Member States to acquire concessions from the EU as a whole. The latter situation may prove to be a slippery slope, since it applies in a lot of cases and cannot *a priori* be restricted to the area of the EU's CCP.[96] In any event, it would seem that, if contested before the Court, the Council's decision on whether to proceed with a mixed or an EU-only agreement can be subject to only marginal review by the Court, in line with the suggestions of Advocate General Wahl in his Opinion on the Marrakesh Treaty. A second objection would be that the Court has imposed the duty

---

94 In this regard, Neframi has noted: "the unity of external representation is an objective stemming from the obligation to assert the EU identity on the international sphere and falls under the loyalty obligation to abstain from any measure that could jeopardize its attainment. The negative obligation is indeed liable to conciliate the requirement of unity with the maintenance of national sovereignty and individual international action". See E. Neframi, " The Duty of Loyalty: Rethinking its Scope through its Application in the Field of EU External Relations", *Common Market Law Review* 47, no. 2 (2010), 355.

95 Since Article 2, paragraph 2, TFEU is formulated without any reservations it may be assumed that it applies generally. See also C. Timmermans, *supra* note 58, 661, see footnote 6.

96 A possibility here could be to introduce a presumption in favour of EU-only agreements, which the EU institutions and the Member States can rebut by demonstrating how the EU interest is not negatively affected by the conclusion of a mixed (rather than EU-only) agreement.

of cooperation to make mixity manageable, not to do away with it. Specifically, the Court has developed the duty of (close) cooperation to counter the Commission's argument that the implementation of mixed agreements would pose practical problems, finding that such problems "cannot modify the answer to the question of competence".[97] A counter-argument here would be that only the exercise, but not the existence, of Member States' competences would be affected.[98]

D. Limits Flowing from the Autonomy of the EU Legal Order and the Institutional Balance

A final constitutional check on the choice for facultative mixity may be identified in the recent *US Air Transport Agreement* case. This case could be read as confirming the idea that upholding the EU's autonomy and the institutional balance required by the Treaties constrains the EU institutions and the Member States in their recourse to 'mixed' solutions. The conditional tense is important here since the Commission *in casu* did not challenge the mixed nature of the agreement itself,[99] only the Council's decision to adopt a single hybrid act (together with the Member States) on the provisional application (by both the EU and the Member States) of a mixed agreement.

In essence, the Commission's argument boiled down to the proposition that hybrid decisions are not foreseen under the Treaties and should therefore not be tolerated. Presented in such a way, the Commission's case looked rather problematic, since the agreement to which the contested de-

---

97 Opinion of 15 November 1994, 1/94, *supra* note 25, para 107; Opinion of 6 December 2001, 2/00, *supra* note 21, para 41; Opinion of 30 November 2009, 1/08, *supra* note 93, para 127.

98 In turn, an obvious criticism here would be that the distinction between the existence (unaffected) and exercise (affected) of a competence is purely theoretical. If a competence does not come with the concomitant power it is null. See V. Constantinesco, *Compétences et pouvoirs dans les Communautés européennes: contribution à l'étude de la nature juridique des communautés* (Paris: Librairie Générale de Droit et de Jurisprudence, 1974), 82-83.

99 See Opinion of AG Mengozzi of 29 January 2015, *Commission* v *Council*, C-28/12, EU:C:2015:43, para 38; Judgment of 28 April 2015, *Commission* v *Council*, C-28/12, EU:C:2015:282, para 46.

cision related was a mixed agreement and therefore a hybrid itself.[100] Before the Court, the Council also tried to bring this point home by arguing that the use of a hybrid act co-authored by the Member States "is entirely consistent with the mixed nature of the underlying agreements and with the fact that the Member States are in certain respects exercising their own competences. It is a permissible consequence of concluding mixed agreements with which it is in legal symmetry".[101] Tying its argument to the principle of sincere cooperation the Council also argued that the use of hybrid decisions is an expression of close cooperation between the EU and the Member States and of the requirement of unity in the EU's external representation.[102]

The Council's argument was not without merit. After all, if the Court of Justice has found that the EU's constitutional charter tolerates facultative mixed agreements, why would it be opposed to the logical consequence of mixity in an internal EU act? The key to understanding the Court's ruling is provided by the Court itself in the opening statements to its findings, where it reminds us of its *Van Gend & Loos* ruling: "the founding treaties of the European Union, unlike ordinary international treaties, established a new legal order".[103] Rules from the international (or national) legal order(s) cannot simply be transposed to the new EU legal order since it is autonomous. This helps in understanding the error in the Council's argument: a mixed agreement may indeed be hybrid, but comes into being, thrives and perishes in the international legal order; the contested hybrid decision however was an act internal to the autonomous EU legal order.[104]

100 See also T. Verellen, "On Hybrid Decisions, Mixed Agreements and the Limits of the New Legal Order: *Commission v Council* ("US Air Transport Agreement")", *Common Market Law Review* 53, no. 3 (2016), 742.

101 Opinion of AG Mengozzi of 29 January 2015, *supra* note 99, para 28.

102 *Id.*, para 29.

103 Judgment of 28 April 2015, *Commission* v *Council*, *supra* note 99, para 39.

104 While the question of provisional application of international agreements is also governed by international law, notably Article 25 of the Vienna Convention on the Law of Treaties, it is in essence a question of domestic law. As Lefeber notes "Treaty limits to provisional application will often result from the limited powers of the representatives of the negotiating States to agree to the provisional application of a treaty. The powers of the competent organ, usually the government, to agree to a treaty on a provisional basis may be limited by national law". See R. Lefeber, "Treaties, Provisional Application", *Max Planck Encyclopedia of Public International Law*, May 2011, para 14.

The logic or permissibility (as referred to by the Council) of pursuing "hybridity" fails when one moves from the international to the EU legal order.

Crucially, it should be noted that the Court never expressed a view on whether hybrid decisions as such are tolerated in the EU legal order. Instead the Court referred to Article 218 TFEU and Article 13, paragraph 2, TEU, implying it is not really concerned with the hybrid nature of a decision but that it is instead simply interested in ensuring that whatever the EU institutions do, the "procedures, conditions and objectives" set out in the Treaties are respected.[105] This had not been the case since the contested decision was an act of both the Council and the Member States, while Article 218, paragraph 5, TFEU stipulates that only the Council may decide on the provisional application of an agreement. Second, a single procedure had been used to adopt, in essence, two distinct decisions, which are subject to two incompatible decision-making procedures. The Court concluded from this that Article 218, paragraph 8, TFEU had necessarily been infringed.

As noted, the mixed nature of the agreement itself was not at issue in *US Air Transport Agreement* and opinions diverge as to whether the Court's ruling will hamper the management of mixed agreements in practice.[106] If it does, the ruling might make recourse to (facultative) mixed agreements less attractive and might thereby indirectly limit mixity. More important for our present enquiry is whether a party, such as the Commission, could rely on similar reasoning in order to challenge the decision to conclude a facultative mixed agreement rather than an EU-only agreement itself. Does the choice for inter-governmental action in cases where EU action is possible undermine the autonomy of EU law, specifically by undermining the prerogatives of the EU institutions (and hence institutional balance)?[107] In a different context, the Court did not support such a rea-

105 Of course, it could be argued that hybrid decisions *per se* infringe these "procedures, conditions and objectives" but the Court did not (have to) express a view on this point.

106 Compare the evaluation by T. Verellen, *supra* note 100, and A. P. van der Mei, "EU External Relations and Internal Inter-Institutional Conflicts – The Battlefield of Article 218 TFEU", *Maastricht Journal of European and Comparative Law* 23, no. 6 (2016), 1056.

107 A further illustration may be seen in the Opinion of AG Wathelet in *Commission* v *Council*. The Council and Member States had referred to previous practice in relation to transport agreements to justify the presence of detailed procedural

soning in the *Pringle* case[108] but the argument may be revived in the light of *US Air Transport Agreement* and the general rise of inter-governmental decision-making in the (broader) EU-context.[109] Although not expressly writing in terms of the EU's autonomy or its institutional balance, in the 1990's Gilsdorf also observed that the Treaty provisions on the negotiation, conclusion and binding effect of agreements concluded by the EU are not only frustrated but also undermined by the involvement of Member States in their capacity as sovereign States.[110] Especially when bilateral agreements are at issue,[111] facultative mixity may upset the EU's institutional balance because it complicates the EU institutions' decision-making

---

obligations in the Council's negotiating directives (adopted pursuant to Article 218, paragraph 4, TFEU) for an agreement with Australia. The AG stressed that the latter was to be concluded as an EU-only agreement whereas the earlier agreements had been mixed and consequently found that prior practice to be irrelevant. See Opinion of AG Wathelet of 17 March 2015, *Commission* v *Council*, C-425/13, EU:C:2015:174, para 152. The institutional balance argument for limiting mixity is clear here: if a qualitative difference between negotiating directives for mixed and EU-only agreements is accepted whereby the Commission is more restrained when it negotiates mixed agreements, the Council could be undermining the institutional balance when it insists on negotiating an envisaged agreement as a (facultative) mixed agreement rather than as an EU-only agreement.

108 See Judgment of 27 November 2012, *Pringle*, C-370/12, EU:C:2012:756, paras 67-68.

109 In relation to this, see the rise of the so called Union method used for addressing the eurocrisis (ESM, Fiscal Compact), the banking crisis (IGA), the unitary patent package (unified patent court), the migration crisis (EU-Turkey statement), etc. See J-V. Louis, "Les réponses à la crise", *Cahiers de droit européen* 47, no. 2 (2011), 355-356; Editorial Comments, *Common Market Law Review* 51, no. 1 (2014), 9; Editorial Comments, *Common Market Law Review* 54, no. 3 (2017), 689. On the new Union method in general, see T. Eijsbouts, J-H. Reestman, "Editorial: In search of the Union Method", *European Constitutional Law Review* 11, no. 3 (2015), 425-433.

110 P. Gilsdorf, *supra* note 33, 162.

111 Gilsdorf especially takes issue with bilateral (rather) than multilateral mixed agreements. This is because, as Van der Loo and Wessel explain "In the case of bilateral agreements, the EU and its Member States are presented as one party despite the need for all of them to sign and ratify the agreement [...] In the case of multilateral mixed agreements, the EU and its Member States are more clearly parties in their own right". See G. Van der Loo, R. Wessel, "The Non-Ratification of Mixed Agreements: Legal Consequences and Solutions", *Common Market Law Review* 54, no. 3 (2017), 736.

aspired by the Treaties, exposing it in an accentuated manner to the domestic policies of every single Member State.[112]

VI. Conclusion

The traditional and among practitioners still prevailing view is that the choice for mixity (in so far as mixity is not legally required) is a purely political one: Member States may and will insist on being involved as parties to the agreement whenever the agreement is not wholly covered by EU exclusive competences. That approach significantly hampers the EU in its external action, which begs the question whether the political choice for (facultative) mixity should not somehow be legally qualified and, if so, how this could be done, without imposing EU exclusivity. A number of suggestions to this end, drawing on EU constitutional and international law, made by both academics and Advocates General have been explored in this contribution. While some appear more promising (and legally sound) than others, the Court has yet to follow up on any of them.

To limit mixity, the Court could further clarify its absorption doctrine or rely on the international law principle of good faith. It could also further develop its established case law on the duty of cooperation to include a duty for the Member States to abstain from exercising their competences as fully-fledged subjects of international law in areas of shared competences. Alternatively the Court could derive such a duty from the requirement to uphold the autonomy of the EU legal order and to safeguard institutional balance. Although this could not be discussed in the present contribution, the case for the Court to do so only seems to be strengthened by a new surge of inter-governmentalism in the guise of the Union method that has begun to take hold of EU integration in recent years.

As has also been noted however, developing these constitutional (or other) limits to mixity cannot result in a wholesale ban on facultative mixity. Developing such legal limits therefore entails both clarifying the standard against which the Court may test the choice for mixity and determining the appropriate degree of judicial review.

112 P. Gilsdorf, *supra* note 33, 163.

Droit primaire et compétences externes implicites. Réflexions à partir de l'avis 2/15 de la Cour de justice de l'Union européenne / Primary Law and the Theory of Implied External Competences: Some Thoughts after Opinion 2/15

Nicolas Pigeon

Abstract

Since the Lisbon Treaty came into force, the constitutional framework of the EU's external action received considerable attention, especially from the Court of justice of the European Union. Such attention is motivated, at least in part, by the ambiguity of EU external competences. Although the Member States agreed, with the Lisbon Treaty, to establish for the first time a catalogue of competences in primary law, which significantly extends the scope of EU's external action, the Member States regularly invoke the principle of conferral of powers, thereby stressing their position as "Masters of the Treaties".

Opinion 2/15 exemplifies the tension between the EU, which tries to exercise its newly acquired competences to the largest extent possible, and the Member States, which struggle to find legal arguments to minimise the extension of the EU's reach. In the middle of this political and legal conflict, stands the principle of conferral of powers. Although never mentioned in Opinion 2/15, the principle of conferral of powers is at the heart of the reasoning of the intervening parties and of the Court regarding the scope and nature of the EU's competences and powers.

This is true, in particular, for investment competences. Articles 206 and 207 TFEU confer exclusive competences to the EU only in respect of foreign direct investment, and consequently do not allow per se EU-only international agreements on investment protection, which normally cover non-direct investments. To fill this lacuna, the Commission invoked an implied external competence for non-direct investments. This competence should be exclusive – on the basis of the *ERTA* case law, codified in Article 3, paragraph 2, TFEU – or, at least, shared – on the basis of the necessity branch of Article 216, paragraph 1, TFEU.

Although the Court of justice rejected the exclusivity claim, arguing that primary law could not constitute "common rules" within the meaning of article 3, paragraph, 2 TFEU, it admitted the existence of an EU external implicit power of a non-exclusive nature on the basis of Article 216, paragraph 1, TFEU. This external power is, according to the Court, necessary to achieve the objective enshrined in Article 63 TFEU, that is, the geographic extension of the free movement of capital.

***

Le cadre constitutionnel de l'action extérieure de l'Union européenne est l'objet d'une attention soutenue de la part de la Cour de justice de l'Union européenne (Cour de justice) depuis l'entrée en vigueur du traité de Lisbonne. Les trois avis prononcés en formation solennelle dans la première moitié de l'année 2017 suffiraient à l'attester[1]. Les arrêts en la matière, nombreux et importants, rendus depuis le 1er décembre 2009 le confirment de manière incontestable[2]. De manière générale, comme a pu le faire remarquer le professeur Marise Cremona, la Cour de justice ne prend cependant pas, ou peu, partie sur le contenu de l'action extérieure de l'Union[3]. Elle se positionne davantage sur les principes qui structurent le cadre constitutionnel au sein duquel les institutions et les États membres doivent pouvoir définir l'action extérieure de l'Union, c'est-à-dire son identité sur la scène internationale.

Bien que n'étant pas systématiquement au cœur des débats, le principe d'attribution des compétences occupe à cet égard une place toute partic-

---

1 Avis de la Cour du 14 février 2017, 3/15, *Traité de Marrakech visant à faciliter l'accès des aveugles, des déficients visuels et des personnes ayant d'autres difficultés de lecture des textes imprimés aux œuvres publiées*, EU:C:2017:114; Avis de la Cour du 16 mai 2017, 2/15, *Accord de libre-échange entre l'Union européenne et la République de Singapour*, EU:C:2017:376; Avis de la Cour du 26 juillet 2017, 1/15, *Transfert des données des dossiers passagers aériens depuis l'Union vers le Canada*, EU:C:2017:592.

2 Pour un panorama approfondi de ces arrêts, v. not. : R. Gosalbo-Bono, F. Naert, « The Reluctant (Lisbon) Treaty and Its Implementation in the Practice of the Council », in P. Eeckhout, M. Lopez-Escudero (dir.), *The European Union's External Action in Times of Crisis*, Oxford, Hart Publishing, 2016, p. 13.

3 M. Cremona, « Structural Principles and their Role in EU External Relations Law », in M. Cremona (dir.), *Structural Principles in EU External Relations Law*, Oxford, Hart Publishing, 2018, p. 3-29.

ulière, parce que fondamentale pour l'Union européenne. Il est en effet « le premier principe structurel qui doit être posé avant de se pencher sur une possible application de tout autre principe régissant les relations extérieures »[3] de l'Union. Le caractère cardinal de ce principe, de longue date reconnu par la Cour de justice[4], a été rappelé avec insistance par les États membres au sein du traité de Lisbonne. Nombreuses sont les dispositions qui indiquent que l'Union ne peut agir que dans la limite des pouvoirs qui lui sont conférés par les traités. Ainsi, l'article 5, paragraphe 1, du traité sur l'Union européenne (TUE) dispose que « [l]e principe d'attribution régit la délimitation des compétences de l'Union » et l'article 5, paragraphe 2, TUE qu'« [e]n vertu du principe d'attribution, l'Union n'agit que dans les limites des compétences que les États membres lui ont attribuées dans les traités pour atteindre les objectifs que ces traités établissent. Toute compétence non attribuée à l'Union dans les traités appartient aux États membres »[5]. Par cette répétition et, notamment, l'établissement d'un catalogue de compétences[6], les États membres ont certainement souhaité manifester qu'ils étaient bel et bien les maitres des traités[7], donc du développement des compétences de l'Union. Toutefois, cette clarification a, au moins en partie, échoué et de nombreux éléments de complexité et d'incertitudes demeurent[8]. La politique commerciale commune, pourtant fleuron de l'action extérieure de l'Union, n'échappe pas à ce constat. Son champ d'application incertain a en effet contraint la Cour de justice à prendre position à plusieurs reprises pour mettre un terme (temporaire) à

---

3 I. Govaere, « Compétence – Attribution des compétences post-Lisbonne: entre clarté et complexité », in C. Lalumiere (dir.), *Abécédaire de droit de l'Union européenne : En l'honneur de Catherine Flaesch-Mougin*, Rennes, Presses universitaires de Rennes, 2017, p. 121.

4 Avis de la Cour du 28 mars 1996, 2/94, *Adhésion de la Communauté à la Convention de sauvegarde des droits de l'homme et des libertés fondamentales*, EU:C:1996:140, points 23-24. Pour une confirmation récente, v. arrêt de la Cour du 5 décembre 2017, *Allemagne/ Conseil*, C-600/14, EU:C:2017:935, point 44.

5 Chose que répète mot pour mot l'article 4 TUE. Voir aussi la Déclaration n° 18, concernant la délimitation des compétences, annexée à l'acte final de la conférence intergouvernementale qui a adopté le traité de Lisbonne.

6 Art. 2 à 6 TFUE.

7 Quitte même, selon le professeur Pieter Jan Kuijper, à rejeter ensuite leur propre traité. V. P. J. Kuijper, « From the Board – Litigation on External Relations Power after Lisbon: The Member States Reject Their Own Treaty », *Legal Issues of Economic Integration*, vol. 43, n° 1/2016, p. 1.

8 I. Govaere, *supra* note 4, p.136.

des divergences d'interprétation le concernant[9]. Le domaine des investissements en est un parfait exemple puisqu'il a imposé à la Cour un travail déterminant de définition de la compétence européenne qui entre en résonnance directe avec le principe des compétences d'attribution[10].

Dans le domaine des investissements, l'étendue matérielle de la compétence externe explicite et exclusive de l'Union au titre de la politique commerciale commune est limitée aux investissements étrangers directs[11], c'est-à-dire aux opérations « qui servent à créer ou à maintenir des relations durables et directes entre le bailleur de fonds et l'entreprise à qui ces fonds sont destinés en vue de l'exercice d'une activité économique »[12]. Tous les types d'investissements ne relèvent donc pas de la compétence exclusive de l'Union sur ce fondement[13], en particulier les investissements indirects, dits de portefeuille[14]. Or, des difficultés surgissent en raison de la couverture matérielle des accords internationaux relatifs aux investissements que l'Union souhaite négocier et conclure en lieu et place de ses États membres. Sans qu'il soit nécessaire d'entrer ici dans

---

9 V. not. arrêt de la Cour du 18 juillet 2013, *Daiichi Sankyo et Sanofi-Aventis Deutschland*, C-414/11, EU:C:2013:520; arrêt de la Cour du 22 octobre 2013, *Commission/Conseil*, C-137/12, EU:C:2013:675.

10 Nous n'aborderons pas dans le cadre de cette étude l'établissement, par la Cour de justice, de la compétence exclusive de l'Union en matière de protection des investissements sur la base des dispositions explicites du TFUE relatives à la politique commerciale commune.

11 Articles 206 et 207, paragraphe 1, TFUE.

12 Arrêt de la Cour du 12 décembre 2006, *Test Claimants in the FII Group Litigation*, C-446/04, EU:C:2006:774, points 180-181.

13 Article 3, paragraphe 1, e, TFUE.

14 Selon la Cour de justice, les investissements de portefeuille peuvent se définir comme « [...] l'acquisition de titres sur le marché des capitaux effectuée dans la seule intention de réaliser un placement financier sans intention d'influer sur la gestion et le contrôle de l'entreprise [...] ». V. arrêt de la Cour du 21 octobre 2010, *Idryma Typou*, C-81/09, EU:C:2010:622, point 48. Ces investissements posent des problèmes différents que les investissements directs. Ils ne donnent pas lieu à un établissement, donc les enjeux règlementaires sont autres. Il s'agit essentiellement de mouvements de capitaux et de participation des investisseurs étrangers dans le marché des capitaux. V. A. Dimopoulos, *EU Foreign Investment Law*, Oxford, Oxford University Press, 2011, spéc. p. 104-105; R. Torrent, « Pourquoi un revirement de la jurisprudence "golden share" de la Cour de justice de l'Union européenne est-il indispensable? », in H. Van Rompuy (dir.), *A Man for All Treaties : Liber Amicorum en l'Honneur de Jean-Claude Piris*, Bruxelles, Bruylant, 2012, p. 539, spéc. p. 540-541.

le détail de la définition conventionnelle de l'investissement, il est cependant tout à fait certain qu'un décalage existe entre la compétence exclusive de l'Union sur le fondement de la politique commerciale commune et la couverture matérielle du chapitre relatif à la protection des investissements des accords qu'elle souhaite conclure[15]. En d'autres termes, la compétence exclusive de l'Union au titre de l'article 207 du Traité sur le fonctionnement de l'Union européenne (TFUE) n'est pas suffisante pour couvrir l'intégralité des opérations d'investissements couvertes par ces accords. Cela n'a toutefois rien d'irrémédiable. L'insuffisance de l'article 207 TFUE ne signifie pas que l'Union ne peut pas tirer d'un autre fondement le reste de compétence nécessaire pour faire coïncider ses compétences et le champ d'application des accords internationaux qu'elle souhaite conclure. C'est à ce titre que la Commission a fait appel à la théorie des compétences implicites en tentant d'établir, de manière innovante, des relations entre cette théorie et le droit primaire[16]. Une partie de la doctrine l'a suivie sur cette voie[17]. D'autres l'ont partiellement critiquée[18]. L'Avocat général Eleanor Sharpston et l'Assemblée plénière de la Cour de justice ont ainsi été amenés à se prononcer sur la thèse défendue par la Commission européenne[19]. L'hypothèse d'une compétence exclusive par affectation de la règle posée par l'article 63 TFUE est écartée – le droit primaire ne relevant pas de la catégorie des règles communes visées par l'ar-

---

15 V. par ex. M. Bungenberg, « The Scope of Application of EU (Model) Investment Agreements », *Journal of World Investment & Trade*, vol. 15, n° 3-4/2014, p. 402.

16 Commission européenne, Communication au Parlement européen, au Conseil, au Comité économique et social européen et au Comité des régions – Vers une politique européenne globale en matière d'investissements internationaux, Bruxelles, 7 juillet 2010, COM (2010) 343 final, p. 9; Commission européenne, Proposition de règlement du Parlement européen et du Conseil établissant un cadre pour la gestion de la responsabilité financière liée aux tribunaux de règlement des différends investisseur-État mis en place par les accords internationaux auxquels l'Union européenne est partie, Bruxelles, 21 juin 2012, COM (2012) 335 final, p. 3.

17 R. Vidal Puig, « The Scope of the New Exclusive Competence of the European Union with Regard to Foreign Direct Investment » *Legal Issues of Economic Integration*, vol. 40, n° 2/2013, p. 133, spéc. p. 152-154; F. Erlbacher, *Recent Case Law on External Competences of the European Union: How Member States Can Embrace Their Own Treaty*, The Hague, CLEER, 2017, spéc. p. 27-29.

18 F. Ortino, P. Eeckhout, « Towards an EU Policy on Foreign Direct Investment », in A. Biondi, P. Eeckhout, S. Ripley (dir.), *EU Law After Lisbon*, Oxford, Oxford University Press, 2012, p. 312.

19 Conclusions de l'Avocat général Sharpston, présentées le 21 décembre 2016, Avis 2/15, EU:C:2016:992; Avis de la Cour du 16 mai 2017, 2/15, *supra* note 1.

ticle 3, paragraphe 2, TFUE (I). Toutefois, la Cour de justice admet que l'Union dispose d'une compétence externe implicite partagée sur le fondement combiné de l'article 216, paragraphe 1, TFUE et de la compétence de l'Union relative au marché intérieur (article 4, paragraphes 1 et 2, a, TFUE) en jugeant elle-même de sa nécessité au regard des objectifs fixés par le droit primaire. Si l'existence de la compétence de l'Union est ainsi directement déterminée par la Cour sur le seul fondement d'une interprétation des dispositions du droit primaire, un contrôle politique demeure néanmoins sur l'opportunité de son exercice (II).

I. La non-application du critère d'affectation des règles communes à l'égard du droit primaire

La thèse de la Commission est relativement simple dans son énoncé. En vertu de l'article 3, paragraphe 2, TFUE,

> « [l]'Union dispose également d'une compétence exclusive pour la conclusion d'un accord international lorsque cette conclusion est prévue dans un acte législatif de l'Union, ou est nécessaire pour lui permettre d'exercer sa compétence interne, ou dans la mesure où elle est susceptible d'affecter des règles communes ou d'en altérer la portée ».

Par conséquent, il serait possible d'étendre la compétence exclusive de l'Union aux investissements autres que directs, donc de portefeuille (ou indirects[20]), en ayant recours aux dispositions du TFUE relatives à la libre circulation des capitaux. Plus particulièrement, c'est la troisième branche de l'article 3, paragraphe 2, TFUE qui est mobilisée. Selon la Commission, la compétence externe implicite exclusive de l'Union en matière d'investissements de portefeuille résulte du fait que la conclusion d'un accord international en la matière est susceptible d'affecter des règles communes ou d'en altérer la portée. La règle commune en cause serait celle

20 Il n'est pas certain que l'intégralité des investissements couverts par le chapitre sur la protection des investissements puisse se résumer aux investissements directs et aux investissements de portefeuille. En particulier, les nouvelles formes de l'investissement, constituées notamment de droits de nature contractuelle, devraient vraisemblablement être distinguées. Or, la compétence externe de l'Union en la matière peut également être débattue. Compte tenu des limites de la présente contribution, nous n'aborderons pas ce sujet. V. A. Dimopoulos, *supra* note 15, p. 105; T. Fecák., *International Investment Agreements and EU Law*, Alphen aan den Rijn, Kluwer Law International, 2016, spéc. p. 191.

posée dans l'article 63, paragraphe 1, TFUE en vertu duquel « [...] toutes les restrictions aux mouvements de capitaux entre les États membres et entre les États membres et les pays tiers sont interdites ». L'originalité de cette position de la Commission tient essentiellement au fait que la règle commune susceptible d'être affectée n'est pas, comme ce fût toujours le cas dans la jurisprudence relative aux compétences externes implicites, une règle issue du droit dérivé mais relève de la catégorie du droit primaire. L'Avocat général Sharpston et l'Assemblée plénière de la Cour de justice n'ont pas suivi la Commission dans cette extension de la notion de règles communes au sens de la théorie des compétences externes implicites. Si leurs raisonnements respectifs diffèrent sur certains points, deux arguments principaux sont avancés au soutien de ce refus : la filiation entre l'article 3, paragraphe 2, TFUE et la jurisprudence issue de l'arrêt *AETR*[21], d'une part (A), et la primauté du droit primaire sur les accords internationaux de l'Union, d'autre part (B).

A. La transposition de la notion de règles communes au sens de la jurisprudence issue de l'arrêt AETR *dans le cadre de l'article 3, paragraphe 2, TFUE*

En rappelant le lien qu'elle a décidé de maintenir entre la jurisprudence issue de l'arrêt *AETR* et l'interprétation de la troisième branche de l'article 3, paragraphe 2, TFUE, la Cour de justice rappelle solennellement quelle est la signification de cette jurisprudence (1). Son avis rendu en Assemblée plénière le 16 mai 2017 a, en outre, le mérite de proposer une clarification innovante du fondement de cette jurisprudence, en insistant notamment sur l'auteur des règles communes à protéger et donc, implicitement, sur le principe de loyauté (2).

1. Une approche classique du parallélisme entre compétences internes et externes

La Cour de justice insiste, tout d'abord, sur la continuité qui doit être établie entre l'interprétation de l'article 3, paragraphe 2, TFUE et sa ju-

---

21 Arrêt de la Cour du 31 mars 1971, *Commission/Conseil (AETR)*, 22/70, EU:C:1971:32.

risprudence antérieure relative aux compétences externes implicites[22], en particulier dans le cadre de la logique dite « *AETR* »[23]. Il est vrai que, à plusieurs reprises, la Cour de justice a indiqué que la troisième branche de l'article 3, paragraphe 2, TFUE devait être interprétée conformément à l'ensemble des précédents jurisprudentiels en la matière[24] : l'exclusivité d'une compétence externe implicite dépend ainsi de l'exercice préalable d'une compétence interne se traduisant par la production de droit dérivé, lui-même constitutif de règles communes susceptibles d'être affectées ou dont la portée peut être altérée[25]. Sans ambiguïté, l'Assemblée plénière (ré)affirme donc que

> « [...] constituent des "règles communes" les dispositions de droit dérivé que la Communauté, devenue l'Union, a progressivement instaurées et que, lorsque l'Union a ainsi exercé sa compétence interne, elle doit, parallèlement, jouir d'une compétence externe exclusive pour éviter que les États membres prennent des engagements internationaux qui seraient susceptibles d'affecter ces règles communes ou d'en altérer la portée »[26].

La compétence externe exclusive implicitement acquise par l'Union lui sert ainsi de prolongement externe des règles posées, par elle, sur le plan interne. Elle constitue à ce titre une dimension bien spécifique du par-

---

22 Avis de la Cour du 16 mai 2017, 2/15, *supra* note 1, points 231-234; V. aussi, Conclusions de l'Avocat général Sharpston, *supra* note 20, point 352.

23 Arrêt de la Cour du 31 mars 1971, *Commission/Conseil (AETR), supra* note 22, point 17 : « qu'en particulier, chaque fois que, pour la mise en œuvre d'une politique commune prévue par le traité, la Communauté a pris des dispositions instaurant, sous quelque forme que ce soit, des règles communes, les États membres ne sont plus en droit, qu'ils agissent individuellement ou même collectivement, de contracter avec les États tiers des obligations affectant ces règles ».

24 V. par ex. : arrêt de la Cour du 4 septembre 2014, *Commission/Conseil*, C-114/12, EU:C:2014:2151, point 67; arrêt de la Cour du 26 novembre 2014, *Green Network*, C-66/13, EU:C:2014:2399, point 28.

25 Avis de la Cour du 15 novembre 1994, 1/94, *Compétence de la Communauté pour conclure des accords internationaux en matière de services et de protection de la propriété intellectuelle*, EU:C:1994:384, point 77; Avis de la Cour du 24 mars 1995, 2/92, *Compétence de la Communauté ou de l'une de ses institutions pour participer à la troisième décision révisée du Conseil de l'OCDE relative au traitement national,* EU:C:1995:83, points 31-33. Cette interprétation de la logique AETR est largement partagée par la doctrine : V. par ex. : V. Michel, « Les compétences externes implicites : continuité jurisprudentielle et clarification méthodologique », *Europe*, n° 10/2006; E. Neframi, *L'action extérieure de l'Union européenne : fondements, moyens, principes*, Paris, LGDJ, 2010, p. 59.

26 Avis de la Cour du 16 mai 2017, 2/15, *supra* note 1, point 233.

allélisme entre les compétences internes et externes : il s'agit d'un parallélisme fonctionnel destiné à préserver l'effectivité et l'uniformité du droit de l'Union. Cette liaison de la théorie des compétences externes implicites avec l'idée d'un parallélisme entre les compétences internes et les compétences externes est d'ailleurs confirmée par les deux autres cas de figure de l'article 3, paragraphe 2, TFUE qui prévoi que l'Union dispose aussi d'une compétence externe exclusive lorsque la conclusion d'un accord international « est prévue dans un acte législatif de l'Union, ou est nécessaire pour lui permettre d'exercer sa compétence interne ». Elle ne doit cependant pas être exagérée. Sauf à remettre en cause la répartition des compétences et, *in fine*, le principe des compétences d'attribution, la naissance d'une compétence externe implicite exclusive sur le fondement du critère de l'affectation n'a rien d'automatique dès lors qu'une compétence interne correspondante existe. Encore faut-il, d'une part, que cette compétence interne ait été exercée et, d'autre part, que les domaines des règles internes et externes concordent au point qu'il existe un risque d'affectation des premières par les secondes. Comme l'a indiqué la Cour de justice dans l'avis 1/13,

> « [...] l'Union ne disposant que de compétences d'attribution, l'existence d'une compétence, de surcroît de nature exclusive, doit trouver son fondement dans des conclusions tirées d'une analyse globale et concrète de la relation existant entre l'accord international envisagé et le droit communautaire en vigueur. Cette analyse doit prendre en considération les domaines couverts, respectivement, par les règles communautaires et par les dispositions de l'accord envisagé, leurs perspectives d'évolution prévisibles ainsi que la nature et le contenu de ces règles et dispositions, afin de vérifier si l'accord en question est susceptible de porter atteinte à l'application uniforme et cohérente des règles communautaires et au bon fonctionnement du système qu'elles instituent »[27].

---

27 Avis de la Cour du 14 octobre 2014, 1/13, *Convention sur les aspects civils de l'enlèvement international d'enfants*, EU:C:2014:2303, point 74. V. aussi : arrêt de la Cour du 4 septembre 2014, *Commission/Conseil, supra* note 25, point 74; arrêt de la Cour du 26 novembre 2014, *Green Network, supra* note 25, point 33. Pour une analyse de cette jurisprudence, v. F. Castillo de la Torre, « The Court of Justice and External Competences after Lisbon: Some Reflections on the Latest Case Law » in P. Eeckhout, M. Lopez-Escudero (dir.), *supra* note 2, p. 129; A. Rosas, « EU External Relations: Exclusive Competence Revisited », *Fordham International Law Journal*, vol. 38, n° 4/2015, p. 1073.

Dans son avis 2/15, l'Assemblée plénière ne procède pas à cette analyse dans la mesure où l'article 63 TFUE n'est pas constitutif, selon elle, d'une règle commune au sens de l'article 3, paragraphe 2, TFUE.

2. *Une clarification originale du fondement de la jurisprudence* AETR *: le rôle du principe de loyauté*

Consciente de cet écueil, la Commission avait tenté de faire valoir deux arguments principaux. En premier lieu, elle avançait que l'article 3, paragraphe 2, TFUE ne distingue pas entre le droit dérivé et le droit primaire. Ceci est parfaitement exact et, pourrait-on ajouter, le Traité sur le fonctionnement de l'Union européenne lui-même parle alternativement de règles communes pour désigner soit ses propres dispositions[28], soit des normes issues du droit dérivé[29]. Ainsi, selon l'adage *ubi lex non distinguit, nec nos distinguere debemus*, il n'y aurait pas lieu de distinguer dans le cadre de l'article 3, paragraphe 2, TFUE. En second lieu, la Commission considérait que la nécessité d'un exercice préalable de la compétence interne était en fait purement conjoncturelle. La prise en compte systématique du droit dérivé dans la jurisprudence résulterait de la particularité des dispositions du droit primaire jusqu'alors concernées. Celles-ci ne feraient que fixer des objectifs et attribueraient aux institutions les pouvoirs correspondants en vue de leur réalisation. Elles ne permettaient donc pas d'identifier directement des règles communes[30]. Or, l'article 63 TFUE présente à cet égard une double particularité. D'une part, il est applicable aussi bien aux mouvements de capitaux intra-européens qu'extra-européens. D'autre part, il se suffit à lui-même en ce sens que la règle posée n'a pas besoin d'être complétée, mise en œuvre, par du droit dérivé[31]. La Commission ajoutait que sa thèse était tout à fait compatible avec la logique profonde de la jurisprudence *AETR* selon laquelle la compétence

---

28 Le Titre VII de la Troisième partie du TFUE est intitulé : « Les règles communes sur la concurrence, la fiscalité et le rapprochement des législations ».

29 L'article 40 TFUE, relatif à l'organisation commune des marchés agricoles, évoque l'adoption de « règles communes en matière de concurrence ». De même, l'article 91 TFUE évoque l'adoption de « règles communes applicables aux transports internationaux [...] ».

30 Conclusions de l'Avocat général Sharpston, *supra* note 20, point 277.

31 Arrêt de la Cour du 14 décembre 1995, *Sanz de Lera e.a.*, C-163/94, EU:C:1995:451, point 41.

implicite exclusive de l'Union se justifie fondamentalement par la sauvegarde nécessaire de l'unité du marché intérieur et de l'application uniforme du droit de l'Union.

Pour la Cour de justice, cet argumentaire n'est pas déterminant et méconnait la « [...] motivation inhérente à la règle de compétence externe exclusive contenue dans l'arrêt [AETR] »[32]. Cette méconnaissance résulte de la volonté

> « [...] d'étendre la portée de cette règle, à présent inscrite à l'article 3, paragraphe 2, dernier membre de phrase, TFUE, à un cas de figure qui, comme en l'occurrence, concerne non pas des règles de droit dérivé instaurées par l'Union dans le cadre de l'exercice d'une compétence interne qui lui a été conférée par les traités, mais une règle de droit primaire de l'Union adoptée par les auteurs de ces traités »[33].

L'Assemblée plénière se place donc sur le terrain de l'auteur et du moment de l'adoption des normes internes susceptibles de donner naissance à une compétence externe implicite exclusive pour écarter la thèse de la Commission. Lors de la rédaction des traités, les États membres n'engagent qu'eux mêmes et ne sont soumis à d'autres règles que celles qui résultent du droit international public. En revanche, l'adoption de droit dérivé dans le cadre de l'ordre juridique de l'Union, d'une part, place les États membres dans un institution commune – le Conseil – qui fonctionne selon des règles préexistantes et, d'autre part, les fait interagir avec d'autres institutions, principalement la Commission et le Parlement européen, selon des règles et procédures elles aussi préexistantes. Surtout, les règles de droit dérivé qui découlent de l'exercice des compétences internes de l'Union ont pour auteur l'Union et non pas les États membres, comme c'est le cas pour les traités. Dans cette optique, la théorie des compétences externes implicites peut effectivement être interprétée comme une modalité de prévention de toute déloyauté des États membres envers l'Union. Appliqué au droit primaire, un tel raisonnement n'est en revanche pas tenable : l'Union ne peut pas devenir exclusivement compétente pour négocier des engagements internationaux susceptibles de porter atteinte à des règles qui lui sont étrangères, même si, paradoxalement, celles-ci sont ses règles fondatrices.

---

32 Avis de la Cour du 16 mai 2017, Avis 2/15, *supra* note 1, point 234.
33 *Ibid.*

Il ne s'agit donc pas de substituer l'Union aux États membres dans le cadre des relations extérieures à chaque fois qu'une règle issue du droit de l'Union est susceptible d'être affectée par l'action conventionnelle autonome des États membres. Il s'agit de les empêcher de porter atteinte par l'extérieur à l'application uniforme des règles à l'élaboration desquelles ils ont participé sur le plan interne, et dont ils doivent assurer l'application effective. Autrement dit, la logique *AETR* est inhérente à l'ordre juridique de l'Union : elle ne trouve à s'appliquer qu'en lien avec des règles formées selon les procédures fixées par cet ordre juridique. Elle ne peut donc pas s'appliquer au regard de règles formées en dehors de cet ordre juridique, en l'occurrence à l'occasion de la rédaction des traités. Si l'idée de l'indispensable sauvegarde de l'application uniforme du droit de l'Union n'est pas abandonnée, la Cour de justice ajoute toutefois que la logique *AETR* ne joue que dans le cadre de l'ordre juridique de l'Union; elle ne lui préexiste pas.

B. La primauté du droit primaire sur les accords internationaux de l'Union

Le second temps du raisonnement de la Cour dans l'avis 2/15 consiste à affirmer qu'il est impossible que les accords internationaux affectent ou altèrent le sens du droit primaire (1). Conformément au principe des compétences d'attribution, les traités fondateurs échappent à toute modification unilatéralement décidée par l'Union (2).

1. Une affectation impossible du droit primaire en raison de sa primauté

Le deuxième moyen qu'utilise la Cour de justice pour écarter la thèse de la Commission européenne est lié au premier dans la mesure où il a pour effet de singulariser le droit primaire du droit dérivé. La démarche est cependant différente : alors qu'il était question, dans un premier temps, de dissocier les deux normes au regard de leur auteur et de l'ordre juridique de leur formation, le raisonnement de la Cour de justice est situé ici du point de vue interne à l'ordre juridique de l'Union. En effet, l'Assemblée plénière rappelle le principe de primauté du droit directement issu des traités sur le droit dérivé, « y compris les accords conclus par l'Union avec des États tiers »[34]. Cette affirmation solennelle de la hiérarchie des normes dans l'ordre juridique de l'Union doit être saluée, même si elle était déjà largement admise[35]. Elle permet à la Cour de justice d'ajouter que

> « [...] ces actes, [...], puisent leur légitimité dans les [...] traités et ne sauraient, en revanche, exercer une influence sur le sens ou la portée des dispositions de ceux-ci. Lesdits accords ne sont, dès lors, pas susceptibles d'"affecter" des règles de droit primaire de l'Union ou d'"altérer la portée" de celles-ci, au sens de l'article 3, paragraphe 2, TFUE »[36].

Si une telle affirmation peut se comprendre, elle n'en est pas moins surprenante. Compte tenu du premier argument mis en avant pour rejeter la thèse de la Commission, celui-ci peut paraître, si ce n'est contradictoire, du moins incohérent. En effet, la Cour de justice fait application d'une doctrine dont elle vient de rejeter l'applicabilité. Autrement dit, à partir du moment où la doctrine *AETR* ne peut pas jouer à l'égard du droit primaire, était-il nécessaire de préciser que des engagements internationaux ne peuvent l'affecter ou en altérer la portée? Sans doute peut-on interpréter ce deuxième pan du raisonnement de l'Assemblée plénière comme un moyen de dire qu'en tout état de cause la thèse de la Commission doit être écartée, et ceci indépendamment du point de vue adopté. Il reste que le fondement de la décision de la Cour de justice sur ce point devient incertain : d'une part, la portée du premier argument en ressort amoindrie puisqu'en faisant application de la doctrine *AETR* à l'égard du droit primaire, même si c'est pour l'écarter, la Cour sous-entend implicitement mais nécessairement que sa non applicabilité dans cette hypothèse n'est peut-être pas indiscutable. D'autre part, l'affirmation selon laquelle des traités ne sauraient exercer une influence sur le sens ou la portée des dispositions du droit primaire n'est elle-même pas dénuée d'incertitudes.

2. *L'absorption du critère d'affectation par celui de l'incompatibilité*

La Cour de justice invite manifestement à bien distinguer entre, d'un côté, l'affectation et l'altération de la portée des règles communes et, de l'autre,

---

34 Avis de la Cour du 16 mai 2017, 2/15, *supra* note 1, point 235.

35 Arrêt de la Cour du 10 mars 1998, *Allemagne/Conseil*, C-122/95, EU:C:1998:94. V. aussi : J. Rideau, « Accords internationaux », *Répertoire de droit européen*, Paris, Dalloz, 2011, paragraphes 579-590.

36 Avis de la Cour du 16 mai 2017, 2/15, *supra* note 1, point 235.

l'incompatibilité entre des normes internes et externes. En effet, à défaut d'une telle distinction, l'affirmation de l'Assemblée plénière selon laquelle des accords internationaux ne sont « pas susceptibles d'"affecter" des règles de droit primaire de l'Union ou d'[en] "altérer la portée" » serait contredite par l'existence même de la procédure d'avis issue de l'article 218, paragraphe 11, TFUE. Celle-ci vise à prévenir les situations d'incompatibilité entre les accords internationaux de l'Union et le droit primaire en subordonnant, en cas d'incompatibilité, l'entrée en vigueur des premiers à leur modification ou à la révision des traités[37]. Cette distinction s'inscrit d'ailleurs dans la continuité de la jurisprudence antérieure dans la mesure où la notion d'affectation au sens de l'article 3, paragraphe 2, TFUE ne dépend pas de l'existence d'une incompatibilité[38]. La Cour de justice a effectivement qualifié d'exclusive une compétence externe implicite dans des affaires où les règles communes et les dispositions de l'engagement international n'étaient pas incompatibles. L'analyse à laquelle procède la Cour dans ces affaires vise à déterminer si les règles communes seront modifiées par l'accord international. C'est ce qui explique son insistance sur l'analyse comparée des dispositions d'ordre général, telles les définitions ou le champ d'application des règles[39], et la prise en compte des « perspectives d'évolution prévisibles » des règles communes[40]. La Cour de justice cherche ainsi à sauvegarder le fonctionnement et l'objet des règles communes plutôt qu'à identifier des situations d'incompatibilité entre les normes en cause[41]. La notion d'affectation est donc plus large que la notion d'incompatibilité : si toute affectation n'implique pas une incompatibilité, l'inverse est en revanche probablement vrai. Or, en raison de la primauté du droit primaire, si des accords internationaux peuvent être in-

37 Ce qui, soit dit en passant, signifie que des accords internationaux peuvent bel et bien affecter le droit primaire.

38 Avis de la Cour du 19 mars 1993, 2/91, *Convention n° 170 de l'Organisation Internationale du Travail concernant la sécurité dans l'utilisation des produits chimiques au travail,* EU:C:1993:106, points 25-26; arrêt de la Cour du 4 septembre 2014, *Commission/Conseil, supra* note 25, point 71; arrêt de la Cour du 26 novembre 2014, *Green Network, supra* note 25, point 32.

39 V. par ex. arrêt de la Cour du 4 septembre 2014, *Commission/Conseil, supra* note 25, points 87-98.

40 V. par ex. arrêt de la Cour du 26 novembre 2014, *Green Network, supra* note 25, points 61-64.

41 F. Castillo de la Torre, « The Court of Justice and External Competences after Lisbon: Some Reflections on the Latest Case Law », *supra* note 28, p. 162.

compatibles avec ses dispositions, il ne peuvent en aucun cas exercer une influence sur son sens ou sur la portée de ses dispositions.

Pourtant, il nous semble que la frontière entre ces deux catégories de rapports normatifs peut parfois être très difficile à établir. En témoignent par exemple les affaires où la Cour a eu à connaître des traités bilatéraux d'investissement de certains États membres[42]. L'incompatibilité qu'a constatée la Cour entre ces traités bilatéraux et le droit de l'Union résultait du fait qu'une de leurs dispositions était susceptible de porter atteinte à l'effectivité des pouvoirs du Conseil issus directement du chapitre du traité établissant la Communauté européenne (CE) sur les capitaux[43]. Or, il est difficile de ne pas voir dans cette situation, au-delà d'une situation d'incompatibilité hypothétique, un cas de figure dans lequel des accords internationaux affectent ou altèrent la portée du droit primaire. Si la théorie des compétences externes implicites exclusives dans sa branche issue de l'arrêt *AETR* vise notamment à sauvegarder l'effectivité et l'uniformité du droit de l'Union, il y a bien là un cas d'affectation du droit primaire par des accords internationaux. D'ailleurs, dans l'affaire *Pringle*, la Cour a semblé admettre que des accords internationaux conclus par les États membres puissent affecter les dispositions du droit primaire, en particulier lorsque celles-ci sont attributives de compétence[44]. Aussi, dire de manière générale que des accords internationaux ne peuvent pas affecter ou altérer le sens du droit primaire peut paraître excessif.

Cela étant, ces quelques exemples ne sont peut-être pas vraiment pertinents. En effet, dans tous les cas, il s'agissait d'accords conclus par les États membres. Or, ce que dit la Cour de justice dans l'avis 2/15 est que l'Union ne peut pas acquérir une compétence exclusive sur le fondement

42 Arrêt de la Cour du 3 mars 2009, *Commission/Autriche*, C-205/06, EU:C:2009:118; arrêt de la Cour du 3 mars 2009, *Commission/ Suède*, C-249/06, EU:C:2009:119; arrêt de la Cour du 19 novembre 2009, *Commission/ Finlande*, C-118/07, EU:C:2009:715.

43 Il s'agit des ex-articles 57, paragraphe 2, TCE (devenu 64, paragraphes 2-3, TFUE), 59 TCE (devenu 66 TFUE) et 60, paragraphe 1, TCE (devenu 75 et 215 TFUE). Les États membres en question avaient manqué à leurs obligations au titre de l'ex-article 307, paragraphe 2, TCE (devenu article 351, paragraphe 2, TFUE) de faire le nécessaire pour éliminer les incompatibilités entre leurs traités bilatéraux et le droit de l'Union.

44 Arrêt de la Cour du 27 novembre 2012, *Pringle*, C-370/12, EU:C:2012:756, points 64-66 et 99-107. V. aussi : Conclusions de l'Avocat général Sharpston, *supra* note 20, points 355-356.

de l'affectation du droit primaire par l'accord envisagé. Autrement dit, l'Union ne peut pas se trouver, seule, investie du pouvoir de conclure des accords internationaux qui auraient incidemment pour effet de modifier le droit primaire. Ceci pourrait en effet équivaloir à une forme déguisée de révision des traités et serait donc en parfaite contradiction avec la procédure prévue à cet effet à l'article 48 TUE. Sur ce point, l'Avocat général Sharpston s'était exprimée de manière sans doute plus limpide que l'Assemblée plénière en affirmant que

> « [l]'argument de la Commission signifierait que l'article 3, paragraphe 2, TFUE reconnaît à l'Union le droit de conclure un accord qui affecte les traités ou en altère la portée. Or, la fonction première de l'article 3, paragraphe 2, TFUE est, comme son libellé l'indique clairement, de préciser la nature de la compétence externe de l'Union. Il ne peut pas avoir pour objet d'habiliter l'Union à "affecter" des règles de droit primaire de l'Union ou à "en altérer la portée" en concluant un accord international. Le droit primaire ne peut être modifié qu'au prix d'une révision des traités conformément à l'article 48 TUE »[45].

En définitive, il nous semble que c'est bien le principe d'attribution des compétences, qui implique que l'Union n'a pas le pouvoir de modifier elle-même la répartition des compétences, qui est au centre du raisonnement de la Cour. En refusant de reconnaître la nature exclusive de la compétence de l'Union en matière d'investissements de portefeuille sur le fondement de la troisième branche de l'article 3, paragraphe 2, TFUE, la Cour de justice a peut-être voulu signifier que l'Union ne pouvait utiliser son pouvoir de s'engager conventionnellement pour modifier ses règles fondatrices. Tout comme les accords internationaux, l'Union « puise sa légitimité » dans les traités[46]. Elle ne saurait donc les affecter ou en altérer la portée sans mettre en cause le principe des compétences d'attribution.

---

45 Conclusions de l'Avocat général Sharpston, *supra* note 20, point 354.

46 Nous faisons référence ici à la formule qu'emploie la Cour au point 235 de l'avis 2/15 selon laquelle les actes adoptés sur le fondement des traités « y compris les accords conclus par l'Union avec des États tiers, puisent leur légitimité » dans lesdits traités.

II. L'existence d'une compétence externe implicite partagée au titre des objectifs fixés par le droit primaire

Toujours à l'occasion de la procédure ayant abouti à l'avis 2/15, la Commission soutenait, à titre subsidiaire, que l'Union dispose en tout état de cause d'une compétence externe implicite partagée en matière d'investissements de portefeuille sur le fondement de l'article 216, paragraphe 1, TFUE parce que cette compétence « [...] est nécessaire pour réaliser, dans le cadre des politiques de l'Union, l'un des objectifs visés par les traités [...] »[47]. Cet objectif est celui d'achever la libre circulation des capitaux entre l'Union et les États tiers. La Cour de justice donne raison à la Commission sur ce point[48] en apportant deux précisions importantes à la théorie des compétences externes implicites partagées. D'une part, le lien nécessaire avec l'existence d'une compétence interne est vraisemblablement assoupli puisque la Cour de justice fonde essentiellement son raisonnement sur l'article 63 TFUE, qui n'attribue aucune compétence normative à l'Union (A). D'autre part, l'appréciation de la nécessité n'est plus une prérogative exclusive du législateur européen et peut ressortir également de la compétence de la Cour de justice (B).

A. L'élargissement des fondements internes possibles de la compétence externe implicite partagée

Après avoir procédé à un rappel de la signification des compétences externes implicites par nécessité (1), nous montrerons que l'avis 2/15 ouvre peut-être la voie à un élargissement des fondements internes possibles des compétences externes implicites partagées (2).

1. Rappel de la signification des compétences externes implicites par nécessité

Pour que l'Union puisse revendiquer l'existence d'une compétence externe implicite non-exclusive sur le fondement de la deuxième branche de l'article 216, paragraphe 1, TFUE, il faut qu'elle dispose d'une

47 Conclusions de l'Avocat général Sharpston, *supra* note 20, point 278.
48 Avis de la Cour du 16 mai 2017, 2/15, *supra* note 1, point 239.

compétence interne correspondante. L'analyse de la jurisprudence de la Cour, aussi bien antérieure que postérieure à l'entrée en vigueur du traité de Lisbonne en atteste[49]. Dans cette logique qui tire ses origines de l'avis 1/76[50], le pouvoir implicite de conclure des accords internationaux dont dispose l'Union résulte du lien nécessaire entre l'exercice de la compétence interne et la conclusion d'un accord international : c'est parce que l'exercice de cette compétence interne nécessite que soit conclu un accord international que ce pouvoir est reconnu. Cela étant assez bien admis, il est quelque peu surprenant de voir la Commission affirmer que l'application de cette branche de l'article 216, paragraphe 1, TFUE ne dépend pas de l'existence d'une compétence interne[51]. Selon la logique de la Commission, tout objectif de l'Union inscrit dans les traités donnerait automatiquement naissance à une compétence externe implicite non exclusive. Poussé à son terme, et au vu des objectifs très généraux que poursuit l'Union[52], ce raisonnement conduirait à faire de l'article 216, paragraphe 1, TFUE une clause générale de compétence en matière d'action extérieure. Chose que, précisément, elle ne semble pas être si l'on prend en compte l'insistance avec laquelle les États membres rappellent le principe des compétences d'attribution dans les Traités.

La Commission pouvait sans doute s'appuyer sur les incertitudes qui existent en matière de compétences externes implicites non exclusives[53] et sur celles qui découlent de la rédaction de l'article 216, paragraphe 1,

---

49 Avis de la Cour du 19 mars 1993, 2/91, *supra* note 39, point 7; Avis de la Cour du 28 mars 1996, 2/94, *supra* note 5, points 26-30; Avis de la Cour du 14 octobre 2014, 1/13, *supra* note 28, point 67. V. aussi : V. Michel, « Les objectifs de la politique juridique extérieure de l'Union européenne », in M. Benlolo-Carabot, U. Candaş, E. Cujo (dir.), *Union européenne et droit international – Mélanges en l'honneur de Patrick Daillier*, Paris, Pedone, 2012, p. 35-52, spéc. p. 45; E. Neframi, *supra* note 26, p. 67.

50 Avis de la Cour du 26 avril 1977, 1/76, *Projet d'accord relatif à l'institution d'un Fonds européen d'immobilisation de la navigation intérieure,* EU:C:1977:63, points 3-4. Arrêt de la Cour du 14 juillet 1976, *Cornelis Kramer e.a.*, 3, 4 & 6/76, EU:C:1976:114, points 16-33.

51 Conclusions de l'Avocat général Sharpston, *supra* note 20, point 364.

52 Articles 3 et 21 TUE.

53 M. Klamert, N. Maydell, « Lost in Exclusivity: Implied Non-exclusive External Competences in Community Law », *European Foreign Affairs Review*, vol. 13, n° 4/2008, p. 493.

TFUE[54]. En effet, dans la logique de l'avis 1/76, l'existence de la compétence interne est nécessaire pour que soit reconnue une compétence externe implicite de nature exclusive. Or, cette nécessité doit-elle être interprétée de manière aussi stricte s'il s'agit d'une compétence externe implicite non exclusive? La jurisprudence de la Cour de justice ne permet pas de l'affirmer avec certitude. En outre, la rédaction de l'article 216, paragraphe 1, TFUE, en comparaison notamment avec celle de l'article 3, paragraphe 2, TFUE, laisse penser que le test à appliquer pour reconnaître l'existence d'une compétence externe implicite non exclusive est moins strict que lorsqu'il est question d'une compétence de nature exclusive. À cet égard, le professeur Marise Cremona a notamment souligné[55] que le lien interne / externe avait été brisé dans le cadre de l'article 216, paragraphe 1, TFUE qui, rappelons-le dispose que « [l]'Union peut conclure un accord avec un ou plusieurs pays tiers ou organisations internationales [...] lorsque la conclusion d'un accord, soit est nécessaire pour réaliser, dans le cadre des politiques de l'Union, l'un des objectifs visés par les traités [...] ». Une comparaison avec l'article 3, paragraphe 2, TFUE laisse à ce titre supposer que l'existence d'une compétence interne n'est peut-être pas aussi impérieuse dans le cadre de l'article 216, paragraphe 1, TFUE, si par compétence interne il s'agit d'un pouvoir de décision ou d'une compétence normative interne, pour reprendre la classification des compétences établie par les professeurs Vlad Constantinesco et Valérie Michel[56]. L'article 3, paragraphe 2, TFUE énonce en effet que « [l]'Union dispose également d'une compétence exclusive pour la conclusion d'un accord international lorsque cette conclusion [...] est nécessaire pour lui permettre d'exercer sa compétence interne [...] ». Cette formule indique clairement que l'exclusivité de la compétence externe ne peut advenir dans cette hypothèse que si l'exercice d'une compétence interne en dépend entièrement, c'est-à-dire que la compétence interne ne peut pas

54 M. Cremona, « Defining Competence in EU External Relations: Lessons from the Treaty Reform Process », in A. Dashwood, M. Maresceau (dir.), *Law and Practice of EU External Relations: Salient Features of a Changing Landscape*, Cambridge, Cambridge University Press, 2008, p. 34.

55 M. Cremona, « EU External Relations: Unity and Conferral of Powers », in L. Azoulai (dir.), *The Question of Competence in the European Union*, Oxford, Oxford University Press, 2014, p. 65, spéc. p. 73. V. la contribution de Marise Cremona dans cet ouvrage.

56 V. Constantinesco, V. Michel, « Compétences de l'Union européenne », *Répertoire de droit européen*, Paris, Dalloz, 2013, paragraphe 107.

être exercée faute d'une compétence externe exclusive correspondante. L'article 216, paragraphe 1, TFUE semble plus souple à cet égard parce que plus vague sur l'identification du fondement interne de la compétence externe.

2. Le champ d'application du droit de l'Union en tant que fondement de la compétence externe

La volonté de la Commission d'assouplir le lien entre les compétences internes et externes a peut-être porté ses fruits. L'existence d'une compétence interne s'entend *a priori* comme l'existence d'une compétence normative interne, c'est-à-dire d'une disposition dans les traités sur le fondement de laquelle les institutions de l'Union peuvent adopter du droit dérivé[57]. Or, cette interprétation traditionnelle de la doctrine des compétences implicites dans sa branche issue de l'avis 1/76 est aujourd'hui peut-être dépassée puisque la Cour a décidé de suivre son Avocat général[58] qui soutenait que si la nécessité de l'existence d'une compétence interne ne saurait être contestée, il convenait cependant de ne pas limiter la signification de cette compétence interne à un pouvoir de décision, à une compétence normative. Selon l'Avocat général Sharpston, la compétence interne n'est pas synonyme de base juridique pour l'adoption de droit dérivé. La compétence interne devrait plutôt s'entendre dans le cadre de l'article 216, paragraphe 1, TFUE comme étant équivalente au champ d'application du droit de l'Union. En effet,

> « […] le deuxième cas de figure visé à l'article 216, paragraphe 1, TFUE n'est pertinent que si l'Union européenne dispose d'une compétence interne. À ces fins, une matière doit relever du champ d'application du droit de

---

57 Précisons que, dans le cadre de cette deuxième branche de l'article 216, paragraphe 1, TFUE, il n'est nullement nécessaire que du droit dérivé ait été préalablement adopté. Pour une prise de position récente très nette de la Cour à cet égard, v. arrêt de la Cour du 5 décembre 2017, *Allemagne/ Conseil*, *supra* note 5, point 52 : « La compétence externe de l'Union dans ce deuxième cas de figure n'est pas, […], assortie d'une condition relative à l'adoption préalable de règles de l'Union susceptibles d'être affectées ». V. aussi, id., points 62-69.

58 Avis de la Cour du 16 mai 2017, 2/15, *supra* note 1, points 240-242.

> l'Union et, donc, de la compétence de celle-ci. Il n'est pas nécessaire que l'Union européenne soit compétente à adopter des règles de droit dérivé »[59].

La nuance est importante puisqu'il n'existe pas de concordance parfaite entre les compétences normatives de l'Union et le champ d'application du droit de l'Union, le second étant plus large que les premières comme l'ont démontré notamment les professeurs Loïc Azoulai[60] et Eleftheria Neframi[61]. En l'espèce, cela est le cas pour l'Avocat général puisque l'article 63 TFUE (auquel elle ajoute, à titre complémentaire, les articles 114 et 352 TFUE), qui n'est pas une base juridique pour l'adoption de droit dérivé, est néanmoins interprété comme une disposition octroyant une compétence à l'Union en matière de libéralisation et de protection des investissements[62]. Sur ce point, la position de la Cour de justice est cependant moins claire. Tout en parvenant au même résultat que l'Avocat général, la Cour de justice choisit de faire référence, non pas seulement à l'article 63 TFUE, mais au titre IV de la troisième partie du TFUE qui « [...] relève de la compétence partagée entre l'Union et les États membres, au titre de l'article 4, paragraphe 2, sous a), TFUE, relative au marché intérieur »[63]. Certes, l'article 63 TFUE fait partie de ce titre IV et la Cour y fait explicitement référence au point précédent de son avis. Toutefois, en liant sa décision non pas uniquement à cette dernière disposition, mais à un ensemble de dispositions dont certaines sont incontestablement attributives de compétences normatives[64], la Cour de justice est peut-être plus réticente à adopter pleinement la position exprimée par son Avocat général. À l'avenir, l'examen de la jurisprudence relative à la

---

59 Conclusions de l'Avocat général Sharpston, *supra* note 20, point 365. L'Avocat général ajoute en note de base de page que « [l]orsqu'une matière est couverte par des règles du traité, elle relève de la compétence de l'Union. L'article 4, paragraphe 2, sous a), TFUE dispose ainsi que l'Union a une "compétence partagée" dans le domaine principal du marché intérieur ».

60 L. Azoulai, « Introduction: The Question of Competence », in L. Azoulai (dir.), *supra* note 56, p. 1; L. Azoulai, « La formule des compétences retenues des États membres devant la Cour de justice de l'Union européenne », in E. Neframi (dir.), *Objectifs et compétences dans l'Union européenne*, Bruxelles, Bruylant, 2013, p. 341.

61 E. Neframi, « Within the Scope of European Union Law: Beyond the Principle of Conferral? », in J. Van der Walt, J. Ellsworth (dir.), *Constitutional Sovereignty and Social Solidarity in Europe*, Baden Baden, Nomos, 2015, p. 69-107.

62 Conclusions de l'Avocat général Sharpston, *supra* note 20, points 367-368.

63 Avis de la Cour du 16 mai 2017, 2/15, *supra* note 1, point 241.

64 En matière de mouvements de capitaux, v. article 64, paragraphes 2 et 3, TFUE.

deuxième branche de l'article 216, paragraphe 1, TFUE sera donc nécessaire pour savoir si le fondement interne de la compétence externe implicite non exclusive doit nécessairement être une compétence normative. À cet égard, l'arrêt rendu en Grande chambre le 5 décembre 2017 dans l'affaire *Allemagne / Conseil* va plutôt dans le sens d'une approche restrictive consistant à fonder la compétence externe implicite sur une compétence normative interne[65]. On ne saurait toutefois en tirer de conclusions générales dans la mesure où la possibilité d'un autre fondement interne n'était pas discutée.

B. Le critère de nécessité : entre appréciation juridictionnelle de l'existence d'une compétence externe et contrôle politique sur son exercice

Le dernier élément sur lequel il faut insister est l'appréciation de la nécessité. En effet, il ne suffit pas qu'une compétence interne existe, aussi large que soit définie la notion de compétence interne pour les besoins de l'article 216, paragraphe 1, TFUE[66]. Encore faut-il que la conclusion de l'accord international soit nécessaire à la réalisation d'un des objectifs de l'Union fixés par les traités. Sur ce point, la rédaction de l'article 216, paragraphe 1, TFUE laisse sous entendre que le lien entre la compétence interne et l'objectif visé n'a pas à être direct. Autrement dit, l'Union peut poursuivre la réalisation d'un objectif autre que l'objectif sectoriel lié à la compétence interne en cause[67]. Ainsi, les objectifs transversaux de l'Union ainsi que ses objectifs généraux d'action extérieure pourraient, semble-t-il, justifier la reconnaissance du pouvoir de conclure un accord international dès lors qu'une compétence interne a été identifiée. Le recours au champ d'application du droit de l'Union devrait d'ailleurs faciliter cette déconnexion. Dans l'avis 2/15, la déconnexion entre la compétence interne et l'objectif poursuivi n'est pas opérée. En effet, la

65 Arrêt de la Cour du 5 décembre 2017, *Allemagne/ Conseil*, *supra* note 5, points 56-60.

66 Certains auteurs soutiennent toutefois la thèse d'un parallélisme général en vertu duquel toute compétence interne donne ipso facto lieu à une compétence externe implicite non-exclusive. V. P. Eeckhout, *EU External Relations Law*, Oxford, Oxford University Press, 2011, p. 99.

67 M. Cremona, « Defining Competence in EU External Relations », *supra* note 55, p. 34.

Cour de justice considère que l'objectif qui justifie la compétence externe implicite non exclusive est celui d'assurer pleinement la libre circulation des capitaux[68]. Il s'agit donc de l'objectif qui correspond à la compétence interne de référence[69]. Le raisonnement est le suivant : pour que la libre circulation des capitaux soit achevée, il est nécessaire de conclure des accords internationaux avec des États tiers pour obtenir des engagements de leur part en la matière et établir ainsi une réciprocité avec l'engagement unilatéral consenti par l'Union en vertu de l'article 63 TFUE. Cette position de l'Assemblée plénière pose deux questions fondamentales, à savoir comment est appréciée la nécessité (1) et, surtout, qui doit l'apprécier (2).

1. Les critères de la nécessité

Dans les deux seules affaires dans lesquelles la nécessité a été reconnue, l'avis 1/76[70] et l'arrêt *Cornelis Kramer e.a.*[71], cette nécessité résultait de la nature des choses[72]. C'est d'ailleurs sans doute pourquoi la Cour de justice considéra à l'époque que la compétence externe implicite de l'Union était exclusive parce que nécessaire à l'exercice même de ses compétences internes, c'est-à-dire à l'effet utile des dispositions des traités attributives de ces compétences normatives internes (ce qui correspond à la rédaction actuelle de l'article 3, paragraphe 2, TFUE). Le caractère assez exceptionnel de la reconnaissance de cette compétence externe implicite par nécessité a été établi plus tard, notamment dans l'avis 1/94[73] et dans les arrêts dits de *ciel ouvert*[74]. Or, la Cour ne s'est jamais vraiment prononcée sur la méthode à employer pour identifier cette nécessité. Cela peut s'expliquer par la volonté de ne pas interférer avec le pouvoir du législateur eu-

68 Avis de la Cour du 16 mai 2017, 2/15, *supra* note 1, point 240.

69 Sous réserve de l'ambiguïté de la position de la Cour que nous venons d'évoquer dans le paragraphe précédent.

70 Avis de la Cour du 26 avril 1977, 1/76, *supra* note 51.

71 Arrêt de la Cour du 14 juillet 1976, *Cornelis Kramer e.a.*, *supra* note 51.

72 V. Michel, « Les compétences externes implicites : continuité jurisprudentielle et clarification méthodologique », *supra* note 26. V. aussi, avis de la Cour du 15 novembre 1994, 1/94, *supra* note 26, point 85.

73 Avis de la Cour du 15 novembre 1994, 1/94, *supra* note 26, points 85-86 et 100.

74 V. par ex. : arrêt de la Cour du 5 novembre 2002, *Commission/Danemark*, C-467/98, EU:C:2002:625, points 54-64.

ropéen[75]. La doctrine a quant à elle envisagé la création d'un test de facilitation pour que soit reconnue l'existence d'une compétence externe implicite non exclusive[76].

Sur ce point, l'examen des conclusions de certains Avocats généraux dans le cadre de quelques affaires récentes indique que la nécessité, au sens de l'article 216, paragraphe 1, TFUE, pourrait dépendre de l'existence d'un lien étroit, spécifique, direct, entre l'accord international et la politique de l'Union. Elle revêtirait, dès lors, dans cette hypothèse, un caractère moins exceptionnel. Si l'on suit cette thèse, la nécessité pourrait alors reposer sur des critères objectifs susceptibles, au moins dans une certaine mesure, d'un contrôle juridictionnel.

Ainsi, dans ses conclusions sur l'affaire relative aux services à accès conditionnel, l'Avocat général Kokott cherche d'abord à établir la finalité principale de l'accord et, ensuite, à en évaluer les répercussions sur le marché intérieur. Considérant celles-ci comme étant insuffisantes parce que l'établissement et le fonctionnement du marché intérieur ne seraient pas améliorés par l'application de l'accord international en cause et en raison de l'absence d'incidence directe de cet accord sur le marché intérieur, l'Avocat général considère que les conditions de l'application de l'article 114 TFUE lu conjointement avec l'article 216, paragraphe 1, TFUE ne sont pas réunies[77]. De même, dans ses conclusions pour l'affaire relative à la piraterie au large de la Somalie, l'Avocat général Kokott rejette une nouvelle fois l'application de l'article 216, paragraphe 1, TFUE en tant qu'il permettrait à l'Union de conclure un accord international organisant la dimension externe de l'Espace de liberté, de sécurité et de justice (ci-après « ELSJ »). Faute de « lien suffisant » avec l'ELSJ ou de « lien spécifique avec la sécurité de l'Union », l'accord en question relève bien selon elle des bases juridiques de la politique étrangère et de sécurité commune[78]. L'Avocat général Mengozzi procède à une analyse similaire dans ses conclusions présentées à l'occasion de la procédure d'avis portant sur

75 *Ibid.* V. *infra* sous 2.

76 A. Dashwood, « The Attribution of External Relations Competence », in A. Dashwood, C. Hillion (dir.), *The General Law of E.C. External Relations*, Londres, Sweet & Maxwell, 2000, p. 115; M. Klamert, N. Maydell, *supra* note 54, p. 493.

77 Conclusions de l'Avocat général Kokott présentées le 27 juin 2013, *Commission/Conseil*, C-137/12, EU:C:2013:441, points 42-46 et 58.

78 Conclusions de l'Avocat général Juliane Kokott présentées le 28 octobre 2015, *Parlement/Conseil*, C-263/14, EU:C:2015:729, points 64-65 et 67. V. aussi les chapitres de Marise Cremona et de Mauro Gatti dans cet ouvrage.

l'accord entre le Canada et l'Union européenne relatif au transfert et au traitement de données des dossiers passagers. Selon lui, « [...] si la construction de l'ELSJ peut nécessiter une action extérieure de la part de l'Union, il faut, pour qu'un accord puisse être considéré comme relevant de l'ELSJ, qu'il présente un lien étroit avec la liberté, la sécurité et la justice au sein de l'Union, c'est-à-dire un lien direct entre la finalité de sécurité intérieure de l'Union et la coopération policière et/ou judiciaire qui est développée à l'extérieur de l'Union »[79]. Aussi, il invite la Cour de justice à « consacrer quelques développements à cette question dans l'avis qu'elle est appelée à rendre »[80]. Enfin, dans ses conclusions pour l'avis 2/15, l'Avocat général Sharpston utilise à de nombreuses reprises l'article 216, paragraphe 1, TFUE lorsque les conditions d'application de l'article 3, paragraphe 2, TFUE ne sont pas réunies[81]. S'agissant, par exemple, du secteur des transports maritimes, des transports par voies et plans d'eau navigables et des transports aériens, l'Avocat général considère que l'obtention d'engagements réciproques de la part des États tiers est nécessaire pour atteindre les objectifs du titre VI de la troisième partie du TFUE concernant la politique des transports de l'Union et que, dès lors, une compétence externe implicite partagée existe[82].

Dans ses conclusions présentées le 24 avril 2017 à l'occasion d'une affaire opposant l'Allemagne au Conseil, l'Avocat général Szpunar se penche quant à lui spécifiquement sur la question des critères permettant d'identifier la nécessité d'une compétence externe de l'Union au sens de l'article 216, paragraphe 1, TFUE. Après avoir rattaché le domaine matériel des règles de droit international en cause à une politique de l'Union – en l'occurrence celle des transports et, plus largement, le marché intérieur[83] –, l'Avocat général Szpunar considère que la nécessité doit s'interpréter largement dans le cadre de l'article 216, paragraphe 1,

---

79 Conclusions de l'Avocat général Mengozzi présentées le 8 septembre 2016, avis 1/15, EU:C:2016:656, point 102. V. au point 115 des mêmes conclusions, pour un raisonnement similaire en matière de protection des données personnelles.

80 *Id.*, points 98 et s. et 115 et s.

81 Conclusions de l'Avocat général Sharpston, *supra* note 20, points 243, 246, 251, 407, 456 et 502.

82 *Id.*, points 243, 246 et 251.

83 Conclusions de l'Avocat général Szpunar présentées le 24 avril 2017, *Allemagne / Conseil*, C-600/14, EU:C:2017:296, points 98-100.

TFUE[84] et laisser ainsi un large pouvoir d'appréciation aux institutions politiques de l'Union pour décider de son existence[85]. Ainsi, « […] le critère de la nécessité constitue un critère qui sert avant tout à exclure une compétence externe de l'Union dans les cas où l'action externe de l'Union ne permet pas d'atteindre les objectifs du traité FUE »[86]. Autrement dit, la nécessité deviendrait ici une simple non inutilité. Dès lors que la politique de l'Union a une dimension externe – et l'on peut se demander comment cette dimension externe doit elle-même s'apprécier –, l'article 216, paragraphe 1, TFUE fonderait automatiquement l'existence d'une compétence externe non exclusive correspondante, créant ainsi un parallélisme presque systématique entre les compétences internes et les compétences externes. La position de l'Avocat général implique ainsi une extension significative de la portée de l'article 216, paragraphe 1, TFUE, au-delà, selon nous, de ce que le principe des compétences d'attribution est en mesure d'autoriser. Cette position audacieuse est certes soumise, au terme de son raisonnement, à la double limite constituée par l'obligation de motivation, d'une part, et par le respect du principe de subsidiarité, d'autre part[87]. Ces limites relèvent cependant du domaine de l'exercice des compétences européennes et non de celui de leur existence.

2. L'appréciation de la nécessité

La Cour de justice ne s'est pas prononcée sur la question de la nécessité dans le cadre de l'article 216, paragraphe 1, TFUE dans les affaires relatives aux services à accès conditionnel[88], à la piraterie[89] et au projet d'accord entre le Canada et l'Union relatif au transfert des données des

---

84 *Id.*, point 101. À la différence, ajoute l'Avocat général, de la nécessité au sens de l'article 3, paragraphe 2, TFUE qui devrait être interprétée de manière plus restrictive puisqu'elle traite de la nature exclusive d'une compétence.

85 *Id.*, point 101. Bien qu'il s'agisse de principes relatifs à l'exercice des compétences de l'Union et non à leur existence, l'Avocat général ajoute que « [l]e critère de la nécessité pourrait même être vu comme une simple confirmation à caractère déclaratoire des principes de subsidiarité et de proportionnalité ».

86 *Id.*, point 102.

87 *Id.*, points 116-118.

88 Arrêt de la Cour du 22 octobre 2013, *Commission/Conseil*, *supra* note 10.

89 Arrêt de la Cour du 14 juin 2016, *Parlement/Conseil*, C-263/14, EU:C:2016:435.

dossiers de passagers aériens[90]. Le fait qu'elle ait accepté de le faire dans l'avis relatif à l'accord de libre-échange avec Singapour et dans l'affaire *Allemagne/ Conseil* doit selon nous être souligné. En effet, dans les affaires relatives aux accords dits *ciel ouvert*, elle semblait s'en remettre – conformément aux conclusions de l'Avocat général Tizzano[91]– aux procédures internes de décisions, et donc au pouvoir politique[92]. Autrement dit, si les institutions du triangle institutionnel, et en particulier le Conseil, n'avaient pas jugé l'accord international nécessaire, cette décision politique s'imposait à elle. La Cour de justice y faisait alors preuve d'une certaine retenue en refusant de juger elle-même de la nécessité de l'accord international[93]. L'Avocat général Tizzano mettait en garde contre une telle affirmation de compétence de la part de l'organe judiciaire en affirmant qu'

> « [o]n pourra débattre, éventuellement même au niveau judiciaire, du point de savoir si l'appréciation de la "nécessité" d'un accord a été concrètement exercée (ou omise) de manière légale ou non; mais on ne peut certes échapper au fait que les organes habilités à y procéder et les modalités y afférentes doivent être ceux qu'indique le traité. Autrement, nous le répétons, on risque d'introduire (ou, pire, d'attribuer à la Cour l'intention d'avoir voulu introduire) des éléments d'insécurité, voire d'arbitraire, dans la répartition des

90 Avis de la Cour du 26 juillet 2017, 1/15, *supra* note 1.

91 Conclusions de l'Avocat général Tizzano présentées le 31 janvier 2002, *Commission / Royaume-Uni de Grande-Bretagne et d'Irlande du Nord e.a.*, C-466/98 e.a., EU:C:2002:63, points 46-58. Au point 52 de ses conclusions l'Avocat général affirme que « [p]our notre part, il nous semble au contraire qu'il y a lieu d'induire de cette jurisprudence, mais surtout de la logique même du système, que la constatation de la "nécessité" d'un accord ne saurait faire abstraction de l'appréciation spécifique des institutions compétentes et des procédures prescrites selon le cas, et ce n'est qu'à la suite de cette évaluation concrète et en bonne et due forme que peut émerger le caractère exclusif de la compétence communautaire. Plus précisément, nous estimons que la nécessité de l'accord doit être constatée selon la procédure prescrite pour exercer la compétence interne parallèle lorsque celle-ci est déjà prévue et, si elle ne l'est pas, selon la procédure prévue à l'article 235 du traité ».

92 Arrêt de la Cour du 5 novembre 2002, *Commission/Danemark*, *supra* note 75, points 54-64.

93 R. Post, « Constructing the European Polity: ERTA and the Open Skies Judgments », in M. Poiares Maduro, L. Azoulai (dir.), *The Past and Future of EU Law: The Classics of EU Law Revisited on the 50th Anniversary of the Rome Treaty*, Oxford, Hart Publishing, 2010, p. 234.

> compétences entre la Communauté et les États membres, ainsi que d'altérer les procédures et les équilibres interinstitutionnels établis par le traité »[94].

En acceptant de juger elle-même de la nécessité d'un accord international pour atteindre l'objectif fixé par l'article 63 TFUE et la politique commune des transports, l'Assemblée plénière fait donc preuve d'innovation. Aussi, l'on ne peut que regretter le caractère très succinct des développements consacrés à cet approfondissement de la portée des compétences externes implicites. Dans l'avis 2/15, la Cour de justice se contente d'affirmer que la pleine liberté de circulation des capitaux est un objectif fixé par le TFUE et que seule la conclusion d'accords internationaux permet de rendre opposable une telle règle aux États tiers, qui lie déjà tous les États membres en vertu de l'article 63 TFUE. Une compétence externe est donc nécessaire pour réaliser un des objectifs fixés par les traités[95]. Dans l'affaire *Allemagne/ Conseil*, la Cour se justifie davantage. Après avoir indiqué que l'établissement de règles uniformes sur le droit privé des contrats de transport ferroviaire international relevait bien d'une politique des transports de l'Union – et la Grande chambre prend soin de préciser que ceci a été admis par l'ensemble des parties[96] –, elle avance deux arguments au soutien de la nécessité de la compétence externe de l'Union. D'une part, les règles communes que l'Union peut adopter lors de la mise en œuvre de ses compétences internes en matière de transport peuvent concerner des États tiers. Il s'agit donc d'une politique européenne qui présente, presque intrinsèquement, une dimension externe[97]. D'autre part, étant donné que la décision attaquée par le recours en annulation de l'Alle-

94 Conclusions de l'Avocat général Tizzano, *supra* note 92, point 53.

95 Avis de la Cour du 16 mai 2017, 2/15, *supra* note 1, points 239-242. Cela étant, la compétence externe implicite non exclusive qu'établit la Cour porte sur la protection des investissements de portefeuille. Or, il n'eût pas été inintéressant que la Cour justifie son choix de faire du titre IV de la troisième partie du TFUE le fondement interne d'une telle compétence externe. En effet, sauf à avoir une conception très extensive de la nécessité, il n'est pas évident que des engagements de protection des investissements de portefeuille soient nécessaire pour réaliser l'objectif de libre circulation des capitaux.

96 Arrêt de la Cour du 5 décembre 2017, *Allemagne / Conseil*, *supra* note 5, point 56.

97 *Id.*, point 59. Faisant notamment référence aux points 26 et 27 de son arrêt AETR, la Cour de justice affirme que l'article 91, paragraphe 1, a, TFUE, relatif aux transports internationaux exécutés au départ ou à destination du territoire d'un État membre, ou traversant le territoire d'un ou de plusieurs États membres, « […] concerne également, pour la partie du trajet située sur le territoire de l'Union, les transports en provenance ou à destination des États tiers[,] […] suppose donc que

magne participe à l'élaboration de normes harmonisées au niveau international, normes qui peuvent avoir un impact direct sur la définition de la politique de l'Union et sur les règles applicables dans le marché intérieur[98], une prise de position de l'Union peut être considérée comme nécessaire[99]. Un double constat s'impose donc à la suite de l'évocation de ces deux exemples : d'une part, la Cour de justice est bel et bien en mesure de décider par elle-même de l'existence d'une compétence de l'Union sur la base de la seule interprétation des objectifs fixés par le droit primaire. D'autre part, le critère de la nécessité est apprécié de manière très souple par la Cour qui procède ici davantage par affirmation que par démonstration.

La détermination de l'existence d'une compétence externe implicite non exclusive est ainsi facilitée. Elle peut en outre échapper au contrôle des institutions politiques et, *in fine*, des États membres. Ce qui ne veut cependant pas dire que ceux-ci perdent toute maitrise de ces compétences externes implicites non exclusives. Une dernière remarque doit en effet être faite sur ce point. Que la Cour de justice reconnaisse l'existence d'une compétence externe implicite non exclusive en jugeant, elle-même, de la nécessité pour l'Union de conclure un accord international ne signifie pas que l'Union puisse ensuite automatiquement exercer cette compétence. Cela ne signifie *a priori* qu'une seule chose : l'Union dispose d'une compétence externe implicite non exclusive et l'accord international n'a pas à être obligatoirement conclu sous forme mixte. En revanche, le choix

---

la compétence de l'Union s'étende à des relations relevant du droit international, [et] implique, dès lors, dans le domaine visé, la nécessité d'accords avec les États tiers intéressés ».

98 Dans le cadre de ses développements consacrés à l'obligation de motivation, la Cour indique à ce sujet que « [...] le Conseil a suffisamment motivé la décision attaquée au regard du critère de nécessité prévu par le deuxième cas de figure visé à l'article 216, paragraphe 1, TFUE, eu égard également au fait que la motivation requise par ce deuxième cas de figure est différente de celle requise par l'article 3, paragraphe 2, TFUE. En effet, les première et troisième phrases du considérant 11 de la décision attaquée, lues en combinaison avec les motifs, [...], de l'énoncé des positions établies au nom de l'Union sur les points 4, 5, 7 et 12 de l'ordre du jour de la 25e session de la commission de révision de l'OTIF dans l'annexe de ladite décision mettent en évidence la nécessité de veiller à ce que soit assurée la cohérence entre les règles du droit international en matière de transport international ferroviaire et le droit de l'Union et, partant, la nécessité d'une action externe de l'Union à cette fin ». *Id.*, points 87-88.

99 *Id.*, point 60.

d'exercer une telle compétence est en définitive une décision politique que maitrise le Conseil, dans le respect toutefois de l'obligation de motivation des actes produisant des effets juridiques[100]. Cette position, pourtant assez largement admise[101], avait toutefois été remise en cause par la Cour de justice dans l'avis 2/15. En affirmant que l'Union ne peut pas approuver seule la section A du chapitre 9 de l'accord de libre-échange avec Singapour parce que sa compétence en matière d'investissements de portefeuille est partagée[102], l'Assemblée plénière de la Cour de justice imposait la mixité dès lors que l'Union n'était pas exclusivement compétente pour l'ensemble des dispositions de l'accord. Par cette affirmation, la Cour de justice alignait les effets juridiques des compétences partagées sur ceux des compétences retenues par les États membres en exigeant, dans les deux cas, la mixité des engagements internationaux de l'Union. Il est en effet frappant de constater que la Cour de justice parvient à la même conclusion au sujet des compétences de l'Union en matière de règlement des différends entre investisseurs et États alors que la compétence qui fait défaut à l'Union dans cette seconde hypothèse relève selon toute vraisemblance des compétences que retiennent les États membres[103]. Une telle confusion, regrettable dans le cadre d'un avis dont l'unique objet était de clarifier la répartition des compétences entre l'Union et les États membres, a semble-t-il été rectifiée. La Cour de justice est revenue sur sa position en s'expliquant, de manière incidente, dans son arrêt rendu en Grande cham-

---

100 Article 296 TFUE. Voir : Arrêt de la Cour du 5 décembre 2017, *Allemagne / Conseil*, *supra* note 5, points 79-80.

101 Conclusions de l'Avocat général Wahl, présentées le 8 septembre 2016, avis 3/15, EU:C:2016:657, points 119-123; Conclusions de l'Avocat général Sharpston, *supra* note 20, points 73-75. V. aussi : L. Ankersmit, « Opinion 2/15 and the Future of Mixity and ISDS », *European Law Blog*, 18 mai 2017; F. Castillo de la Torre, *supra* note 28, p. 180; F. Erlbacher, *supra* note 18, p. 35; D. Kleimann, G. Kubek, « The Singapore Opinion or the End of Mixity as We Know It », *Verfassungsblog – On Matters Constitutional*, 23 mai 2017; D. Thym, « Mixity after Opinion 2/15: Judicial Confusion over Shared Competences », Verfassungsblog – On matters Constitutional, 31 mai 2017.

102 Avis de la Cour du 16 mai 2017, 2/15, *supra* note 1, point 244.

103 *Id.*, points 292-293 : « [...] un tel régime [de règlement des différends], qui soustrait des différends à la compétence juridictionnelle des États membres, ne saurait revêtir un caractère purement auxiliaire [...] et ne saurait, dès lors, être instauré sans le consentement de ceux-ci. Il en résulte que l'approbation de la section B du chapitre 9 de l'accord envisagé relève non pas de la compétence exclusive de l'Union, mais d'une compétence partagée entre l'Union et les États membres ».

bre le 5 décembre 2017 dans l'affaire *Allemagne/ Conseil*. Elle y justifie en effet sa prise de position dans l'avis 2/15 en indiquant s'être « [...] bornée à prendre acte de l'impossibilité, mise en avant par le Conseil au cours de la procédure relative à cet avis, de recueillir en son sein la majorité requise pour que l'Union puisse exercer seule la compétence externe qu'elle partage avec les États membres en la matière »[104]. Si cette mise au point peut rassurer en ce qu'elle rétablit la distinction (doctrinale) entre mixité obligatoire et mixité facultative[105], la démarche empruntée par la Cour est en revanche plus originale.

104 Arrêt de la Cour du 5 décembre 2017, *Allemagne/ Conseil*, *supra* note 5, point 68.

105 V. le chapitre de Merijn Chamon dans cet ouvrage.

Part 2:
Balancing EU Values with External Action Objectives

Recent Tendencies in the Separation of Powers in EU Foreign Relations: An Essay

Pieter Jan Kuijper

I. The Development of the Place of Foreign Affairs in Western Democracies Outlined

When analysing the constitutional systems of nation States, it is self-evident that separation of powers is an ideal, not the reality. In many constitutional systems, the separation of powers is better described as a form of counterbalancing the powers of the legislative, the executive and the courts. We also know that the different powers sometimes overreach themselves in their balancing battle with the other powers and then a "better" balance has to be "restored" or brought about. One could argue – tongue in cheek – that a large part of politics is overreach and reaction on the battlefield of the balance of powers between the different branches of government.

Elements of this tussle between the different powers are parliaments that put their nose into everything that the executive does and try to regiment any regulatory power delegated by law in such detail that the scope for actually governing becomes very small or even non-existent.[1] However, there are also instances where the executive abuses its delegated powers of regulation and does not return to the legislative power for guiding principles, even when that is clearly provided for, or where the executive is not transparent in its government, thus hindering the general power of oversight of the legislature.[2] Obviously, all of this can only function ful-

1 A recent example in EU foreign relations law are overly detailed directives for negotiation issued by the Council under Article 218, paragraph 4, TFEU that rob the Commission of any margin of manoeuvre. See Judgment of 16 July 2015, *Commission* v *Council,* C-425/13, EU:C:2015:483. Another example in the same field is Judgment of 6 October 2015, *Council* v *Commission,* C-73/14, EU:C:2015:663, in which the Council challenged the submission of a written statement by the Commission on behalf of the European Union without prior approval of the Council.

2 An example of this in EU foreign relations law can be found in Judgment of 24 June 2014, *Parliament* v *Council,* C-658/11, EU:C:2014:2025, where the Court

ly when the legislature is democratically elected and the executive, at the political level, is either indirectly legitimised by being supported by a majority of the legislature or is directly elected, thus benefiting from independent democratic authority. In the latter case, the separation of powers is sharper than in the first.

The ideology of the separation of powers comes to the fore at its sharpest in the relationship between the two political branches of government and the judiciary. Although there are systems where judges (and public prosecutors) are also elected, they are relatively rare. Even if the executive normally appoints judges and prosecutors, the procedure is surrounded by guarantees that the appointment is on the basis of merit. The nomination of judges is in principle for life, or until the pensionable age, and can only be cut short for well-defined reasons and according to onerous procedures.[3] The courts in turn are restricted, if they have to judge government and legislative acts, to quashing the act for specific reasons; they cannot replace the act by their judgment. The legislature has the power not only to review its own acts, but also to over-rule the courts, except if these have the authority to declare laws unconstitutional. In general, in most of such national constitutional systems the courts have been more stringent in reviewing the acts of the executive than in striking down the acts of the legislature because of the latter's superior claim to direct democratic legitimacy.

Traditionally, even in modern democracies, not only the courts, but also the legislature, have shown particular deference to the executive in the field of foreign affairs. A certain role is perhaps played here by the close

---

found that the Council infringed Article 218, paragraph 10, TFEU, when it did not immediately and fully inform the Parliament at all stages of the procedure.

3 In this respect the national safeguards for the independence of judges are better than those for the Judges and Advocates General of the European Courts. For instance, compare Article 64 of the French Constitution ("Les magistrats du siège sont inamovibles") and Article 97 of the German *Grundgesetz* ("Die Gesetzgebung kann Altersgrenzen festsetzen, bei deren Erreichung auf Lebenszeit angestellte Richter in den Ruhestand treten") with Article 253 TFEU, that provides for a renewable term of 6 years. Improvements in the selection of CJEU judges have been achieved through the activities and recommendations of the so-called 255-Committee, as introduced by the Lisbon Treaty. Several contributions about the beneficial work of this Committee are to be found in M. Bobek (ed), *Selecting Europe's Judges, A Critical Review of the Appointment Procedures to the European Courts* (Oxford: OUP, 2015).

link between the exercise of the foreign affairs power and the Head of State, whether King or President. This figure is symbolic for the one and undivided State, which interacts with other States in the same way as the proverbial billiard ball.

Parliaments have usually restricted themselves to broad policy review and limited interference with the foreign affairs budget. If parliaments legislate in this context, they do so mostly in the form of semi-constitutional acts, such as laws on the procedure for concluding treaties, acts concerning the details of the relation between treaties and customary international law on the one hand and national laws and acts of decentralised authorities on the other, laws on the immunity of international organisations present in the country, or laws laying down the framework for implementing binding decisions of international organisations. The quantity and variety of legislation on foreign affairs is normally very limited, compared with legislation in other domains of government. This tendency is even stronger in the EU, since so many questions in the field of external relations are laid down in the Treaties themselves.[4]

The judiciary usually shows the utmost restraint in striking down foreign policy related acts of the government, especially if these represent political choices. In some countries, it is not unusual for courts to express the view that foreign policy choices of the government should be respected, either because the Ministry of Foreign Affairs has superior expertise in the matter, or because there are factors involved which are considered inherently not to be amenable to judicial review.[5] The ultimate danger that the national courts encounter in foreign relations cases is that their judgments in such cases will cause political conflicts with foreign nations or

---

4 See on this tendency B. de Witte, "Too Much Constitutional Law in the European Union's Foreign Relations?" in M. Cremona and B. de Witte (eds), *EU Foreign Relations Law – Constitutional Fundamentals* (Oxford: Hart, 2008), 3-15, at 10.

5 This is the so-called "political question doctrine", which was at the heart of such US Supreme Court cases as *Baker* v *Carr* 369 US 186 (1962) and *Youngstown Sheet and Tube Cy.* v *Sawyer* 343 US 579 (1952). The latter was basically a war and foreign relations case and the former was a redistricting case, but the Court was loth to accept such doctrine, even though Justice Brennan in *Baker* v *Carr* developed elaborate criteria for political questions the Court should not decide. European Supreme Courts have been equally hesitant to accept the concept in concrete cases. See e.g. P. J. Kuijper and K. C. Wellens, "Deployment of Cruise Missiles in Europe: The Legal Battles in the Netherlands, the Federal Republic of Germany and Belgium", *Netherlands Yearbook of International Law* XVIII (1987), 145 – 218.

even result in responsibility under international law for their country. The sway that the government held over the courts in matters of foreign affairs until some 25 years ago is best illustrated by the formal letters that Ministries of Foreign Affairs sent to the courts that were confronted by questions of this kind, such as the recognition of States, questions of State immunity, the so-called Act of State and even the direct effect of treaties. The Courts were normally supposed to follow these letters.[6]

Over the last two to three decades, however, this traditional restraint on the part of the courts and the legislature vis-à-vis the executive, incarnated by the Ministry of Foreign Affairs, has been subject to erosion in most States. This is the culmination of two important long-term evolutions which have affected foreign affairs in almost all States since the Second World War. First, there is the so-called democratisation of foreign policy, that is to say foreign policy has been taking an increasingly prominent place in general political discourse, especially in Western democracies, and is no longer a subject that is principally discussed amongst a small group of specially schooled experts. Discussions on foreign policy are no longer carried on primarily by "serious people" in such exclusive clubs as the Council on Foreign Relations in New York, the Royal Institute of International Affairs in London, the *Institut français des relations internationales* in Paris, or *het Nederlands Genootschap voor Internationale Zaken* in The Hague. Ministers of Foreign Affairs and Ambassadors no longer belong in important numbers to the nobility of a country, but are products of the modern meritocracy and the Ministers have reached their position through their affiliation with a political party. The number of organisations

6 In France there was a practice of this kind relating to the question of direct effect of international agreements that was reported in Judgment of 26 October 1982, *Hauptzollamt Mainz* v *Kupferberg,* 104/82, EU:C:1982:362. In the US there was the phenomenon of the so-called "Bernstein letters", which gave the view of the Department of State on whether an act of another State, mostly in cases of nationalization, qualified as an Act of State necessitating abstention by the US courts. Moreover, the Department also wrote letters on the recognition and on the immunity of foreign States and governments. Since the adoption by Congress of the Hickenlooper amendment and the Foreign Sovereign Immunities Act in the '60s and the '70s there was less need for the Department to write such letters. See R. Mok, "Expropriation claims in the US courts: The Act of State Doctrine and the FSIA – A Road Map for the Expropriated Victim", *Pace International Law Review* 8, no. 1 (1996), 199-236, at 208-209 and C. A. Bradley, *International Law in the US Legal System* (Oxford: OUP, 2013), 10-12 and 19-21.

active in the field of foreign policy and international economic relations has grown enormously in number and diversity: think tanks of many different ideological stripes, non-governmental organizations (NGOs) such as Oxfam, Greenpeace and Amnesty International, or Human Rights Watch. Foreign policy issues thus sometimes play an important role in elections and parliaments have lost their restraint vis-à-vis the Ministry of Foreign Affairs: nominations of ambassadors are taken hostage and individual budget lines in the budget of the Ministry are cut in order to show parliamentary displeasure with detailed aspects of foreign policy.[7]

The second secular trend that has transformed foreign policy – and which is closely linked to the trend of democratisation – is the specialisation in the field. It is exemplified by the enormous growth of (specialised) international organisations at the worldwide and regional level, both in number and in size, after the Second World War. The diversity in think tanks, pressure groups and NGO's, mentioned above, is also a symptom of this specialisation. At the national level, the number of departments of government that have substantial international affairs divisions or even directorates-general has grown enormously, to the point where even Ministries of Home Affairs have such departments. This has led to considerable problems of coordination between the Ministry of Foreign Affairs, the practitioners of "high foreign policy", and the specialised ministries, the "low foreign relations" people, both inside the government at home and inside embassies and delegations abroad. In practice, the most that Ministries of Foreign Affairs are able to achieve is to play the lead coordinating role. On the other hand, when foreign policy knots have to be cut between departments or for reasons of coalition politics, central coordination has been assumed more and more over the last decades by the prime minister or the president, and by the cabinet office or kitchen cabinet of these government leaders. The European Union and its summitry have been an important force in this development, which has seen the term

7 In the European context, the European Parliament obtained certain promises from the first High-Representative and Vice-President of the Commission Lady Ashton with respect to the organization of the EEAS on its foundation, by cautioning her that it would not hesitate to use its budgetary powers. See K. Raube, "The European External Action Service and the European Parliament", *The Hague Journal of Diplomacy* 7, no. 1 (2012), 65-80, and M. Bien, "How the European Parliament had its 'say' on the EEAS", *Nouvelle Europe*, http://www.nouvelle-europe.eu/node/946, (2010).

"Sherpa" descend from the Himalayas to the presumably equally risky conference rooms in New York, Brussels, Geneva and Nairobi. This concomitant phenomenon of specialisation may usefully be called the "presidentialisation" of foreign affairs.

As far as the restraint of the judiciary in respect of questions of foreign relations is concerned, there is little doubt that everywhere courts are getting more and more involved in foreign policy questions. In part, this is a consequence of the growing number of human rights conventions and other so-called legislative conventions in international law. NGO's and individuals or groups of citizens bring more cases where specific foreign policy actions of a government are measured against such international conventions before national courts. This phenomenon was already known from the US and began to grow in Europe in the 1980s with the so-called cruise-missile cases.[8]

The anti-cruise-missile movement also serves as illustration of the fact that foreign affairs is an area of government (and of EU activity) where not only the horizontal separation of powers, between the branches of government and, within these branches, between different departments, but also the vertical separation of powers plays a role. Municipalities in the Netherlands and Germany declared themselves at the time to be "nuclear-arms-free zones". These were symbolic declarations to be sure, but they do raise the question of how far municipalities, provinces, regions or *Länder* can go in (pretending to) carry(ing) on their own foreign policy. In some unitary States, the central government can take repressive measures against foreign policy decisions of lower government bodies. In modern federal States, the extent of the foreign affairs powers of the federated States is normally well regulated in the constitution – which does not mean that there are not serious problems from time to time.[9]

---

8 For further information see P J. Kuijper and K. C. Wellens, *supra* note 5. See also L. F. M. Besselink, "The Constitutional Duty to Promote the Development of the International Legal Order: the Significance and Meaning of Article 90 of the Netherlands Constitution", *Netherlands Yearbook of International Law* 34 (2003), 89-138.

9 See the tribulations of the US government in the early 2000's on the occasion of the implementation of the International Court of Justice's judgment in the *LaGrand* cases. For further information see: B. Simma, H. Carsten, "From LaGrand and Avena to Medellin – a Rocky Road Toward Implementation", *Tulane Journal of International and Comparative Law* 14, no. 1 (2005), 7-59. A more recent assessment of the situation in the US is given by M. J. Glennon and R. D. Sloane, *Foreign Affairs*

Having thus outlined with a broad brush the development of the separation of powers in the field of foreign affairs in western democracies, and the Member States of the EU in particular, it is now time to turn to the foreign affairs powers of the EU itself and their development up until the Treaty of Lisbon, and to see whether the evolution in the Member States and elsewhere in the western world is reflected in the situation at EU level and what this means for the separation of powers, both horizontal and vertical, in the field of EU foreign relations.

II. The Evolution of EU Foreign Affairs Powers Up to the Lisbon Treaty

The twin trends of specialisation and democratisation of foreign affairs, which affected the Member States, have also influenced, after a certain delay, the development of the foreign relations powers of the European Union.

Specialisation in the field of EU foreign relations became possible as a consequence of the well-known *ERTA* decision of the Court of Justice in 1970.[10] This judgment, based on the doctrine of implied powers, extended the potential treaty-making power of the (then) EEC to all domains covered by the Treaty, and made recourse to the Community treaty-making power compulsory in cases where treaty-making action by the Member States would have affected internal EEC legislation. This doctrine has led to the entry of the Community (subsequently the Union) into more and more specialised areas of external relations, such as maritime and aviation policies, international norms on health, on product safety, on the protection of species, and on other environmental norms such as the protection of the ozone layer, in step with the development of internal rules in these and other areas. In the different versions of the EEC, EC and EU Treaties since Maastricht some of these implied foreign relations powers under the *ERTA* doctrine were made explicit in different articles in Part Three of the

---

Federalism, The Myth of National Exclusivity (Oxford: OUP 2016), in particular Chapter VI.

10 Judgment of the Court of 31 March 1971, *Commission* v *Council*, Case 22-70, EU:C:1971:32. See also J. Klabbers, "22/70, *Commission* v *Council (European Road Transport Agreement),* Court of Justice of the EC, [1971] ECR 263", in C. Ryngaert et al. (eds), *Judicial Decisions on the Law of International Organizations* (Oxford: OUP, 2016), 19-28.

TFEU. The *ERTA* doctrine itself is now enshrined in Article 3, paragraph 2, TFEU, which has recently been interpreted by the Court of Justice as authority for the continuation of the development and application of the *ERTA* doctrine as laid down in its existing case law.[11] Moreover, it has been given a fairly liberal interpretation in Opinion 2/15, especially in the context of broad international trade agreements, where (alleged) Article 3, paragraph 2, TEU powers co-exist with exclusive trade policy powers under Article 207 TFEU.[12] Hence, there is nothing that stands in the way of greater specialisation in the field of EU external relations and the need for more specialised expertise in the European External Action Service (EEAS) and the Commission.

Here we come to an interesting counterpoint to this trend of specialisation in EU foreign relations and that is the creation and development of, first, foreign policy cooperation and, later, the aspiration to conduct an actual Common Foreign and Security Policy in the EU, enshrined in an intergovernmental pillar at Maastricht. The different fields of specialised low foreign policy were there first and the instruments for high foreign policy were developed a little later, in parallel and with a separate institutional basis that was set apart from the EC/Union institutions. This separate institutional basis was first created inside the Council Secretariat and with the Secretary-General of that Secretariat as High Representative: the so-called second pillar in the Treaties of Maastricht and Amsterdam. In a way, this development was contrary to the natural development of specialisation in foreign affairs that took place in the Member States. In the Member States specialisation developed organically outwards from classic foreign policy. In the EU/EC, between Maastricht and Lisbon, classic, "high", foreign policy was placed, almost as another specialisation, alongside and separate from the "low" foreign policy in areas that were the external reflection of the internal market and the different Union policies. In the Lisbon Treaty, an attempt was made to place the "high" foreign policy in a separate quasi-institution, the EEAS, to be situated between the Commission and the Council, and under a "new" High Representative, who was nominated by the Council and the President of the Commission with a view to carrying out a double function: High-Representative of the Coun-

11 See Judgment of 4 September 2014, *Commission* v *Council (Negotiation of a CoE Convention)*, C-114/12, EU:C:2014:2151.

12 See Opinion of the Court of 16 May 2017, 2/15, *EU-Singapore Free Trade Agreement*, EU:C:2017:376.

cil in Foreign Affairs and Vice-President of the Commission (HR/VP). He or she was destined, if not to sit on top of both "high" and "low" foreign policy, at least to have a power of direction over the former and a power of coordination over the latter. This institutional adaptation is a reflection of the trend mentioned earlier, according to which the national Ministries of Foreign Affairs have sought to establish centralised control over the many bits and pieces of "low", technical foreign policy conducted by many different departments of government in the Member States. It is as if the Foreign Ministries of the Member States tried to achieve at the European level what they had never fully achieved at the national level. The likelihood of actually arriving at this objective does not seem very realistic, but it represents nevertheless a first step towards presidentialisation of EU external relations.

There can be little doubt that the trend of democratisation of foreign policy that has taken hold in the Member States has been reflected step by step in the increasing powers granted to the European Parliament (EP) in the successive treaty amendments beginning with the Maastricht Treaty. First, its powers in general were improved and this led to the Parliament acquiring full legislative powers in the areas of foreign relations that were covered by the *ERTA* doctrine and fell under the (normal) legislative procedure after the Maastricht/Amsterdam Treaties. Before the entry into force of the Lisbon Treaty, the common commercial policy remained an exception, because it was allegedly too technical a subject for members of parliament to occupy themselves with in detail. Then, it became clear many matters that had become subjects of commercial policy (the so-called "behind-the–borders measures") actually had great impact on policies that hitherto had been regarded as being typically internal, such as taxes on domestic products, animal and plant health rules, and product safety measures.[13] Thus, a power of parliamentary approval of trade agreements found its way into the TFEU.

---

13 Covered respectively by Article III:2 General Agreement on Tariffs and Trade (GATT), the Agreement on Sanitary and Phytosanitary Measures and the Agreement on Technical Barriers on Trade.

III. The Post-Lisbon Institutional Balance on Paper

The Lisbon Treaty has obviously influenced the balance between the institutions in what is now called external action, that is to say a combined foreign policy of the "high" (Common Foreign and Security Policy, laid down in the TEU) as well as of the "low" character (laid down in the TFEU). First, the diplomatic service (the EEAS) that, together with the Member States in the Council, conceives and runs this external action has received the status of quasi-institution in the Lisbon Treaty. Led by the HR/VP, it is the new kid on the block in EU external relations and has clearly executive tasks, as we will see in more detail below. It has no officially recognised exclusive conceptual power, as the Commission has in the TFEU; the HR/VP and the EEAS may make proposals, but in the TEU the weight of the conceptual power is with the European Council and the Council of Ministers, with input from the Member States. Another new kid is the President of the European Council, which at his level, i.e. the presidential/heads of State level is supposed to maintain international relations with his counterparts and act as emissary of the European Council in the international sphere. This is where the Treaty of Lisbon continues the trend of "presidentialisation".

The Lisbon Treaty has made of the European Parliament almost a normal parliament, that is to say with full budgetary powers, with nearly full legislative powers (together with the Council of Ministers), including the right to approve or reject international agreements, as most national Parliaments have, agreements under the common commercial policy no longer excepted. The EP only lacks this power in the field of the CFSP, a continuing abnormality compared to national Parliaments.

Lisbon has clearly made the Commission, in general, more "executive", in particular through the better and clearer regulation on the delegation of legislative powers and of implementing powers in the TFEU and "low" foreign policy (Articles 290 and 291 TFEU). The latter article, moreover, makes it perfectly clear that the Council can only reserve executive powers for itself in specific and well-reasoned instances. Thus, the Council has become more legislative, while the Commission has become a more executive organ in the field of TFEU external policy. The Treaty text now says explicitly what was previously only implicit, namely that normally the Commission is the representative of the Union in the wider world (Article 17, paragraph 1, TEU) except in the field of the CFSP, where this is the role of the HR/VP (Article 18, paragraph 2, TEU). It is obvious that this new situation potentially sharpens the rivalry between these two executives on the international scene, which in theory should be reconciled by the coordinating powers of the HR/VP.

A somewhat similar trend is visible in the Treaty text concerning the CFSP. The provisions on the CFSP (Article 24, paragraph 1, second subparagraph, TEU) now stress that legislation is not permitted in this area. The legislative activity of the Foreign Affairs Council takes place only in the domain of the TFEU external relations, but "high" foreign policy has become purely decisional after Lisbon.[14] Moreover, the Council, or rather its Secretariat, has lost all executive powers in the field of CFSP after the creation of the EEAS. According to the Treaty text (Articles 26 and 27 TEU), the Council of Ministers develops the guidelines given by the European Council[15] into a detailed Common Foreign and Security Policy. Although the HR/VP may contribute through proposals to this development of the CFSP, in the end the HR/VP and the EEAS have the task of carrying out the CFSP as developed by the European Council and the Council of Ministers of Foreign Affairs. In doing so the EEAS, through the EU delegations (formerly the Commission's delegations) is the voice of the Union

---

14 Terms that were deemed to have a "legislative flavour", such as "common action" and "common position" were banned from the "new" TEU, especially at UK insistence. "Legislative acts" are not possible (Article 31, paragraph 1, TEU). Hence every CFSP act is now a decision, but such decisions will define certain actions or positions of the Union (Article 25 TEU). Van Middelaar has made an interesting distinction between "events policy" (European Monetary Union crisis and refugee crisis) and "legislative policy", and argues that the EU institutions have been built for the latter and are therefore bad at the former and must urgently adjust in order to show the citizens that they can also master the former. It might be possible to characterise "high foreign policy" (which includes defence policy) as events policy and "low foreign policy" as legislative policy. See L. van Middelaar, *De Nieuwe Politiek van Europa* (Amsterdam: Historische UItgeverij, 2017), in particular Part III "Regeren of niet. Emancipatie van de uitvoerende macht" (To Govern or not to Govern. Emancipation of the Executive).

15 In reality, the European Council could do no more than agree on a very broad European Security Strategy under the Amsterdam Treaty (2003), updated in 2008. A new European Security Strategy under the Lisbon Treaty was completed in the summer of 2016 under the title *Shared Vision, Common Action: A Stronger Europe*. European Council Conclusions of 28 June 2016, point 20, and Council Conclusions on the Global Strategy on the European Union's Foreign and Security Policy, 17 October 2016, Council doc. 13202/16. The work of developing more concrete security strategies was largely left in the hands of the Council of Ministers for Foreign Affairs.

in international organisations and at international conferences. In the CFSP as in the TFEU domain there is therefore a parallel trend of making the distinction between the Council as legislator (or policy-maker in the CFSP) and the Commission and the EEAS as executives sharper and clearer. At the same time the official recognition of the Commission as external representative in the TFEU, has been accompanied by the loss of its delegations in third countries to the EU and the EEAS. The Commission's civil servants are part of the EU's delegations, but perform the role of representatives of specialised ministries in the embassies of the Member States.

The position of the Court of Justice of the European Union (CJEU) in all of this has not changed much; the description of its jurisdiction and its principal task – ensuring that the rule of law is upheld – is not fundamentally different from what it was before. This does entail, however, much more activity in the field of foreign relations law and in interpretation of treaties than most of the highest courts in the Member States have on their plate, for the simple reason that foreign relations law is a question of the interpretation of the founding treaties of the Union much more often than it is a question of constitutional law in the Member States. It is perhaps also for this reason that the Member States as constitutional law makers were wary of the Court taking on its normal tasks in the field of the CFSP, fearing it might get more say in "high" foreign policy than national supreme courts normally have (Articles 24, paragraph 1, and 40 TEU and Article 275, first sentence, TFEU). It remains a pity that the Court of Justice thus has been prevented from showing that it could find its own way of practicing judicial restraint in political foreign policy cases, as the highest courts of many Member States have done. On the other hand, it may try to find a way to do so, by using its power of "border police" at the TFEU-CFSP border laid down in the Treaty (Article 275, second sentence, TFEU).[16]

After the entry into force of the Lisbon Treaty, on paper, certain things became clearer: the distinction between legislative or policy-making institutions (Council and Parliament, or Council alone) and executive institutions (Commission and EEAS), even though the Commission maintained

---

16 C. Hillion, "A Powerless Court? The European Court of Justice and the Common Foreign and Security Policy", in M. Cremona and A Thies (eds), *The European Court of Justice and External Relations Law – Constitutional Challenges* (Oxford: Hart, 2014) 47-72.

its right of initiative in the TFEU foreign relations. The recognition of Parliament as having the power to approve all international agreements (except in CFSP) is the most important in this overall picture. Other things became more complicated: the recognition in the Treaty of several external actors of the EU: Commission, HR/VP and EEAS, and President of the Council. Still others did not change very much: the power of the CJEU, leaving it a small opportunity to exercise marginal review of the scope of the CFSP and to protect the rights of individuals targeted by CFSP restrictive measures.

After the Lisbon Treaty, what happened in reality in respect of the balance between the institutions? In order to have a better idea, there will first follow a short section on general developments, which sets the scene for a more detailed discussion of the evolution of the balance between the institutions as it developed after Lisbon – largely through intensive litigation in the CJEU.

IV. The Post-Lisbon Institutional Balance in Action

A. Some Preliminary Observations

First of all, it is important to recall once again that we are not primarily concerned here with the vertical balance of powers between the Union and the Member States; we are concentrating on the horizontal balance between the institutions. The vertical balance is a subject that can never be entirely avoided in the field of EU foreign relations, if only because it is linked to the possibility of certain agreements becoming mixed or not. This has immediate repercussions on the position of the Commission as negotiator in relation to the Council, as well on the relation between the Parliament and the Council, for the simple reason that the Council is the institution in which the Member States are represented. In this way, the confirmation of the broad interpretation of what falls under the common commercial policy, combined with a liberal interpretation of Article 3, paragraph 2, TFEU on implied external relations powers will reduce the need for making what are in essence trade agreements into mixed agreements and thereby enhance the powers of the Commission and the Parliament in their relations with the Council.[17]

Secondly, the new powers of treaty approval of the European Parliament have had immediate political consequences for the Commission-Council-Parliament triangle in the field of external relations. It becomes more difficult for the Council to let a Commission proposal rot in the Council archives simply by doing nothing, when a considerable majority in the EP has a strong interest in a legislative proposal. This was palpable in the case of the Commission proposals in respect of two Regulations on the Union's new powers in the field of direct foreign investment, where a considerable number of Member States were extremely sceptical in the Council and might normally perhaps have succeeded in shelving the proposals. However, the (positive) interest in these proposals on the part of important segments of the EP helped to bring about a compromise text that was also broadly acceptable to the Commission.[18] It is clear in a different way during the negotiation of treaties where Parliament can also exercise its influence for the simple reason that it can say no to the final result, if its wishes are not sufficiently expressed in the directives for negotiation or, even at a later stage, in the draft text.[19]

Thirdly, it is important to realise, though this may sound trite, that the horizontal balance between the institutions in the field of foreign affairs under the Lisbon Treaty is in part directly influenced by where the frontier between the CFSP and the TFEU lies. This determines in particular how much power the Commission, the HR/VP and the EEAS, the Parliament and the Council have in relation to each other. This question is ultimately

17 See Opinion 2/15, *supra* note 12.

18 Parliament and Council Regulation 1219/2012/EU establishing transitional arrangements for bilateral investment agreements between Member States and third countries, OJ 2012 L 351, p. 40, and Parliament and Council Regulation 912/2014/EU establishing a framework for managing financial responsibility linked to investor-to-state dispute settlement tribunals established by international agreements to which the European Union is party, OJ 2014 L 257, p. 121.

19 This is still a relatively unexplored possibility for the Parliament, but the CETA and TTIP negotiations show that there are gains to be made by the Parliament here. This may lead to delicate cases before the Court about the balance between the institutions, as Parliament's assertiveness on this point is political and the Council's right to authorize, and to give directives for, negotiations is formally protected by Article 218, paragraphs 3 and 4, TFEU.

in the hands of the Court, which itself has to be careful not to cross certain lines laid down in Article 275 TFEU when deciding this issue.

Fourthly, a helicopter view of the application of the new rules on delegation and implementation of Union law under Articles 290 and 291 TFEU in the field of trade policy, in particular trade defence, shows that the rules on the implementation of these Treaty articles, as laid down in Regulation 812/2011,[20] have been included into the relevant basic regulations on anti-dumping, countervailing duties and safeguards[21] and are routinely applied. Thus, the Commission has been shifted more clearly into the executive role that thus far was still occupied in the last instance by the Council.

Finally, the ambitions laid down in the Lisbon Treaty with respect to a more unified and stronger external representation – which hailed back to the work of the Constitutional Convention and the Treaty for a Constitution of Europe – were quickly bypassed by the political mood in most of the Member States by the time of the entry into force of the Treaty in late 2009. This led to the strange spectacle of the Member States in the Council wanting to turn back the clock in the field of external relations, pretending that the Treaty of Lisbon limited the powers of the EU in this domain. This was in flagrant contradiction with the openly avowed message from the Member States accompanying the external relations provisions of the Constitution and the Treaty of Lisbon. It led to an almost total paralysis on the question of who ought to be the representative of the Union in international meetings and organisations and who had the right to say what in such meetings and organisations – a paralysis which was only lifted in late 2011 by an extremely complicated compromise.[22] It also led to a re-

20 Parliament and Council Regulation 2011/182/EU laying down the rules and general principles concerning mechanisms for control by Member States of the Commission's exercise of implementing powers, OJ 2011 L 55, p. 13.

21 E.g. for anti-dumping, the latest codification is Parliament and Council Regulation 2016/1036/EU on protection against dumped imports from countries not members of the European Union, OJ 2016, L 176, p. 21, Article 15. For recent examples of implementing regulations of the Commission based on Article 15 see Commission Implementing Regulations 2016/387 and 2016/388 imposing anti-dumping and countervailing duties on pipes and tubes of ductile cast iron originating in India, OJ 2016 L73, p. 1.

22 See "General Arrangements for EU Statements in Multilateral Organizations", in P. J. Kuijper, J. Wouters et al. (eds), *The Law of EU External Relations,* 2nd ed. (Oxford: OUP 2015), 38.

vival of very old questions of general scope, such as the question whether or not the Commission could retract a proposal that it had made, but had been totally perverted or "*dénaturé*" in the legislative stage by the Council so that the Council (and the Parliament) could no longer validly legislate. In short, the Member States no longer wanted the Treaty they had written and approved themselves.[23]

This led to a long series of external relations cases, many of which will play a role in the following overview of the development of the separation of powers and the balance between the institutions after the entry into force of the Lisbon Treaty.

B. The Border between CFSP and TFEU and the Balance Between the Institutions

As was already suggested above, any shift in the boundary line between CFSP and TFEU external relations modifies the balance between the political institutions involved in external action generally. An increase in the domain of CFSP means an increase in power for the Council and the HR/VP relative to a diminution of power for the Commission and the Parliament. It will also imply a limitation of the scope of competence of the CJEU, which itself may be called upon to sit in judgment on the question where the boundary line runs precisely.

This is well illustrated by the two so-called *Pirates cases,*[24] i.e. the two cases concerning the nature of the agreements by which the Union could deliver any Somali pirates who were captured in the framework of Operation Atalanta, the CFSP contribution to the UN action against the Somali

---

23 See P. J. Kuijper, "From the Board, Litigation on External Relations Powers after Lisbon: The Member States Reject Their Own Treaty", *Legal Issues of Economic Integration* 43, no. 1 (2015), 1-16. This rejection was particularly clear in all cases that related to foreign affairs powers, such as the interpretation of Article 3, paragraph 2, TFEU on implied powers, Article 207 on the scope of the common commercial policy, and Article 209 on the scope of the development policy.

24 See Judgment of 24 June 2014, *European Parliament* v *Council (Agreement with Mauritius),* C-658/11, EU:C:2014:2025 and Judgment of 14 June 2016, *European Parliament* v *Council (Agreement with Tanzania),* C-263/14, EU:C:2016:435. See further on these judgments the chapters by Marise Cremona and by Mauro Gatti in this volume.

pirate and robber groups.[25] These agreements organised the delivery of the captured pirates to neighbouring countries such as Mauritius and Tanzania with a view to being tried for piracy.[26] This was deemed necessary, since bringing the pirates back to the Member States whose warships had arrested them would interrupt the operations and/or lead to a prolonged period of pre-trial detention on board naval vessels ill equipped for such detention. Moreover, the pirates thus could not be formally charged with their alleged misdeeds within a reasonable period of time, which could easily lead to mistrials after arrival on European soil. These agreements had been concluded as CFSP agreements by the Council, on the basis that they were concluded in the framework of the Atalanta operation and were indispensable to the success of that operation and, therefore, had to be regarded as an integral part thereof. The Parliament and the Commission, however, were of the view that the substance of the agreements fell under the external aspects of judicial and police cooperation in the field of criminal law (Articles 82 and 87 TFEU) and was also part and parcel of development cooperation, insofar as they sought to assist these countries in developing their police and judicial resources.

The Court decided in favour of the Council, thus denying any decision-making role to the Parliament in respect of CFSP agreements. It, however, accepted that Parliament had at least a right to be informed at all stages of the treaty-making procedure of Article 218 TFEU, which laid down an integrated procedure for the preparation, negotiation, and conclusion of all agreements whether in the CFSP or TFEU domains, since paragraph 10 of that article made no distinction between these two types of agreements of

---

25 For Operation Atalanta, see Council Joint Action 2008/851/CFSP on a European Union military operation to contribute to the deterrence, prevention and repression of acts of piracy and armed robbery off the Somali coast, OJ 2008 L 301, p. 33, last updated by Council Decision 2016/713/CFSP amending Joint Action 2008/851/CFSP, OJ 2016 L 125, p. 12.

26 These agreements were approved by: Council Decision 2011/640/CFSP on the signing and conclusion of the Agreement between the European Union and the Republic of Mauritius on the conditions of transfer of suspected pirates and associated seized property from the European Union-led naval force to the Republic of Mauritius and on the conditions of suspected pirates after transfer, OJ 2011 L 254, p. 1 and Council Decision 2014/198/CFSP on the signing and conclusion of the Agreement between the European Union and the United Republic of Tanzania on the conditions of transfer of suspected pirates and associated seized property from the European Union-led naval force to the United Republic of Tanzania, OJ 2014 L 108, p. 1.

the Union. The Court did not restrict itself to textual arguments, but also invoked the fundamental principle that the people should participate in the exercise through the intermediary of a representative assembly, of which Article 218, paragraph 10, TFEU is the expression at the European level. This is the case even if the Parliament is restricted to exercising general scrutiny on the basis of the information received pursuant to that provision.[27]

Finally, it is important to point out that the Court saw no reason to regard the HR/VP (and the EEAS) as the responsible authority in respect of the lack of information during the treaty-making process under the CFSP. It took the view that, since the Council had broad responsibility during all the different phases of that process,[28] especially in the CFSP, the Council was responsible for fulfilling the obligation of keeping the Parliament informed during all the different stages, including the negotiation itself (even if in these cases that was principally carried out by the HR/VP).[29]

There is no doubt that these judgments reinforced the Council's powers in the different phases of CFSP treaty-making relative to those of the Commission and of the HR/VP, while leaving powers of general scrutiny of CFSP treaty-making to the European Parliament through forceful recognition of its right of being fully informed by the Council at all stages of the treaty-making process, in particular the preparatory phase. This recognition was achieved primarily by giving great weight, not so much to the subject-matter of the CFSP agreement, which arguably fell in the police and judicial cooperation provisions of the TFEU, but by seeing this subject-matter through the prism of its object and purpose.[30]

---

27 Judgment of 14 June 2016, *European Parliament* v *Council (Agreement with Tanzania), supra* note 24, paras 70-71.

28 These phases are: authorisation for opening negotiation to the HR or the Commission, issuing of directives for negotiation, the actual negotiation itself, the designation of a special committee, the acceptance of the result of the negotiations as finalised by the negotiator, signature, possibly provisional application, and conclusion. This is a weak point in the Court's reasoning; the Council only hears about the progress of the actual negotiations through reports of the Commission or, in this case, of the HR/VP. It is difficult to make the Council responsible for this part of keeping the Parliament informed of all stages of the negotiation.

29 Judgment of 14 June 2016, *European Parliament* v *Council (Agreement with Tanzania), supra* note 24, paras 73-74.

30 This is in line with the pre-Lisbon Judgment of 30 May 2006, *Commission* v *Council (ECOWAS),* C-459/03, EU:C:2006:345. This case ruled that an EU grant for capacity-building in relation to the elimination of small-arms and light

Nevertheless in a different constellation, concerning the treatment of EU personnel and personnel of the Member States seconded to civil or military missions created by the Union as part of UN missions or autonomous CFSP actions, the broad object and purpose test may not be decisive for the Court. Since it concerns the treatment of individual members of EU personnel (from Commission, EEAS or Council Secretariat), the application of the Statute of EU personnel and the access to the CJEU under that Statute prevails over the lack of competence of the Court in CFSP matters.[31] The principle of equal treatment of persons in the same situation is then seen by the Court as decisive for the treatment of Member State personnel in the service of an EU mission set up under the CFSP, including their right of access to the CJEU.[32] The decisions of the head of mission are and remain acts of staff management, even if they take place in the context of a CFSP mission. Hence the General Court and, on appeal, the Court of Justice have jurisdiction to review such acts for their legality under actions for annulment and for non-contractual liability.[33] In short,

---

weapons in the ECOWAS countries ought to have been based on the EC Article on development assistance and not on the CFSP articles. This case made clear that the criteria of content, object and purpose of an act in order to determine its proper legal basis also operated across the CFSP/Community law boundary. Together with the post-Lisbon Judgment of 28 April 2015, *Commission* v *Council (Hybrid Act),* C-28/12, EU:C:2015:282, which determined that a hybrid act, i.e. an act simultaneously containing a TFEU legal basis and an intergovernmental legal basis (decision of the governments of the Member States meeting within the Council) was not possible, if the TFEU basis required approval or consent of the Parliament and a qualified majority in the Council, which was nullified by the unanimity required by the intergovernmental aspect of the act. Under the present Treaty provisions only an international agreement of the EU including CFSP provisions as well as TFEU-based provisions can be concluded as a single Union agreement without arguably raising incompatibilities in decision-making, if it can be presented as an association agreement under Article 217 TFEU, requiring unanimity in the Council and approval by Parliament. An early example is the accession of the European Union to one of the basic treaties of the ASEAN, which contains both development and political aspects: Council Decision 2012/308/CFSP on the accession of the European Union to the Treaty of Amity and Cooperation in Southeast Asia OJ 2012 L 154, p. 1.

31 This is laid down, by the way, in the relevant CFSP decisions. See Judgment of 18 July 2016, *H.* v *Council, Commission and EUPM in Bosnia/Herzegovina,* C-455/14 P, EU:C:2016:569, paras 54 ff.

32 *Id.*, para 57.

33 *Id.*, para 58.

the exclusion of the jurisdiction of the CJEU over the CFSP is not absolute if there are good reasons to assume otherwise.[34]

C. The Powers of the Commission as Negotiator and Litigator in International Relations Relative to those of the Council

The powers of the Commission as negotiator on behalf of the Union and more generally as external representative of the Union in TFEU external relations, including in international litigation, have not changed much under the Lisbon Treaty, except that the EEAS has taken over some of its representative functions from it and from the rotating presidency (heading up delegations to third countries and (most) international organisations and being *porte-parole* there). In respect of litigation on behalf of the Union, the Commission's power had already been recognised by the Court in 2006, in a case concerning possible implication of US tobacco companies in large scale cigarette smuggling which deprived the EU of large sums of excise revenue.[35] This judgment of the Court was reinforced by the provision of Article 17, paragraph 1, TEU to the effect that the Commission was the external representative of the Union, except in respect of the CFSP.

In respect of the Commission's role as negotiator there has always been some tension between two approaches. Firstly, the "mandate approach", often propagated by the Council, which saw the Commission as the mandatory of the Council with no margin of manoeuvre of its own. Secondly, the "directives" approach, adhered to by the Commission, and broadly shared in the doctrine, which latched on to the "directives" or "guidelines" that the Commission received from the Council according to the Treaty language and which gave it a certain measure of autonomy.[36]

If one goes a step beyond negotiation and also a step beyond classic international agreements and one enters the world of non-binding agreements, memoranda of understanding (MoUs), common declarations, polit-

34 In the case in question the good reasons were the rights of the individuals carrying out those missions, whether from the Commission or from the Member States.

35 Judgment of 12 September 2006, *Reynolds Tobacco et al.* v *Commission*, C-131/03 P, EU:C:2006:541, para 94.

36 Opinion of Advocate General Wathelet of 17 March 2015, *Commission* v *Council (Negotiating Directives)*, C-425/13, EU:C:2015:174, paras 84 and 91.

ical commitments – and the Commission, like national ministries of foreign affairs, has not feared to tread on these shifting sands – the reaction of the Court has been very reluctant. It had another view of what was binding or not and felt that the strict doctrine of attribution did not leave any room for the Commission to underwrite an administrative agreement with the US anti-trust authorities about exchange of information and cooperation in competition cases.[37] At best, the Commission, within the framework of the Transatlantic Dialogue with the US, could agree, in the Court's view, to an arrangement called "Guidelines on Regulatory Cooperation and Transparency". But the Commission should satisfy the condition that it had followed the usual procedures prescribed in the Treaty in the field of the common commercial policy – which indeed happened to be the case.[38] In the post-Lisbon situation these precedents were to be tested once again.

As far as the Commission's role of negotiator is concerned, the classic position followed broadly in the academic literature, namely that the Commission has a certain margin for manoeuver within the framework of the directives for negotiation that the Council has issued to it, was wholeheartedly embraced by the Court. Directives cannot, in the view of the Court, become so detailed that no margin of discretion for the Commission as negotiator remains. What is possible, according to the Court, is that the Council lay down clear timetables and reporting requirements that should be followed by the Commission. These are procedural matters, but on substance the Commission should always be granted some room to find a deal.[39]

Where the Commission as litigator before international and foreign courts is concerned, the Court followed the line that was to be expected, given its judgment in the *Reynolds* case.[40] As in that case and in an intervention as *amicus curiae* before the US Supreme Court in a case concerning extra-territorial jurisdiction under the US *Alien Tort Claims Act*,[41] the Commission had extensively consulted with the relevant Council Working Groups about the line to be followed in the written submission of the

---

37 Judgment of 9 August 1994, *France* v *Commission,* C-327/91, EU:C:1994:305.

38 Judgment of 23 March 2004, *France* v *Commission,* C-233/02, EU:C:2004:173.

39 Judgment of 16 July 2015, *Commission* v *Council (Negotiating Directives),* C-425/13, EU:C:2015:483.

40 See Judgment of 18 July 2016, *H.* v *Council, supra* note 31.

41 See *Kiobel* v *Royal Dutch Petroleum Co.*, 133 S.Ct. 1659 (2013).

Commission on behalf of the Union, before sending it off to the International Tribunal of the Law of the Sea (ITLOS).[42] The Council argued that the Commission needed its permission before it could do so. The Court did not agree; the Commission was the external representative of the Union in such cases and as long as the Commission had obviously fulfilled the duty of loyal cooperation between the Union institutions among themselves and with the Member States, it was free to communicate its observations to ITLOS.[43]

However, in the case concerning the negotiation and the adoption of a non-binding agreement with Switzerland on increasing its financial contribution to the functioning of the internal market after its expansion with a new Member State, Croatia, the Commission seemed to believe that it had received sufficiently broad guidelines from the Council, not only to conduct and finalise the negotiations, and agree on the sum to be paid, but also to sign the non-binding commitment with Switzerland. Given that the Council's guidelines did not say anything about signing and concluding an agreement, even if it was non-binding, the Court reacted to the case brought by the Council against the Commission by limiting even further than it had already done in the earlier cases the conditions under which the Commission could bring about non-binding international legal acts. Again, the strict attribution of powers in the Union system of government was at the basis of this. Even in the case of a non-binding agreement, and even if the result of the negotiations of the non-binding agreement was in conformity with the directives for negotiation, the Commission cannot presume that the assessment of the agreement by the treaty-making institution(s) would be positive. Conditions might have changed (and presumably the composition of the treaty-making institution(s) also) during the relatively long period between the issuing of the directives by the Council and the completion of the negotiations by the Commission.[44] Hence, the Commission needed the Council's prior approval.

---

42 The ITLOS had been asked four preliminary questions about matters of jurisdiction in cases concerning so-called IUU fisheries by fishing vessels, not flying the flag of any of the Member States to a Regional Fisheries Agreement. See ITLOS Case no. 21, *Request for an advisory opinion submitted by the Subregional Fisheries Commission (SRFC)*, https://www.itlos.org/en/cases/list-of-cases/case-no-21.

43 *Council* v *Commission, supra* note 1, paras 84-87.

44 Judgment of 28 July 2016, *Council* v *Commission (Swiss contribution)*, C-660/13, EU:C:2016:616, paras 39-43.

Post-Lisbon, therefore, the balance of power between the Council and the Commission relating to negotiating agreements and litigating international disputes or disputes in the Courts of third countries has not been fundamentally changed. The Commission has retained a certain independence and margin of discretion in negotiation (subject to the Council's directives) and also in litigation (subject to loyal cooperation with the Council, and with the Member States, in cases which fall in the mixed domain). The Commission's position is somewhat more secure than before, having been bolstered by the Court's two recent decisions.

It is important to mention also the strengthening of the Commission's position in the legislative procedure generally by the Court's decision broadly to accept the Commission's long-standing position on its right to withdraw its proposal, even when the legislative process is in the final stage approaching an agreed text between Council and Parliament, when that text will have the effect of totally distorting (*dénaturer*) the original proposal, to the point of depriving it of its original rationale (*raison d'être*).[45] This was an enormously important protection of the Commission's right of proposal, especially of the spirit underlying its proposals. It is not without significance that the proposal at issue in the Court case was a piece of legislation on the method of disbursing balance of payments support to third countries. In the external relations sector this safeguarding of the Commission's power of proposal is of particular importance.

However, the Court has reinforced the discipline of the Council over the Commission in the case of the negotiation and conclusion of non-binding instruments. Both institutions (and presumably also the Parliament) have to follow the normal treaty-making procedure by analogy, which implies that the Commission cannot act on its own, as national executives very often can, when agreeing non-binding instruments.[46]

---

45 Judgment of 14 April 2015, *Council* v *Commission (Commission's right of withdrawing its proposals),* C-409/13, EU:C:2015:217. This was clearly so in the case submitted to the Court where the Council and the Parliament sought to replace the provision of a proposed framework regulation on the awarding of Macro-Financial Assistance (MFA) to third countries in short-term balance of payments difficulties, which aimed to enact implementing powers, subject to strict conditions, to be used by the Commission under the examination procedure (the most stringent procedure) by an *ad-hoc* procedure operated by the Council and the Parliament.

46 Judgment of 28 July 2016, *Council* v *Commission,* C-660/13, EU:C:2016:616. Such actions by the executive alone are, of course, always subject in most demo-

All this stands apart from the improvement of the Commission's and Parliament's position in the field of trade, where the need for mixed agreements has been reduced by the changes in the Treaty and by the Court's Opinion 2/15.[47]

D. Current Challenges for Separation of Powers in the EU

After having sketched, in the preceding paragraphs, how the CJEU has reacted to the new balance between the institutions in the field of foreign relations brought about by the Lisbon Treaty, there is still room for informed speculation about additional questions.

For instance, it is well known that the balance between the institutions, not to say the separation of powers, has played a certain role in the apparently unshakeable view of the CJEU that the WTO agreement cannot have direct effect. As it appears from such older cases as *Portugal* v *Council* and *Van Parys*[48], one of the important reasons why the Court was reticent to grant direct effect to provisions of the WTO agreements was that the Court, in doing so, would basically put itself in the Commission's position as negotiator or in the Council's position of legislator by declaring certain offending provisions of Union law as being set aside as contrary to self-executing provisions of GATT or other WTO agreements. This clearly was a bridge too far for the Court. What will the effect of the new powers of the European Parliament in treaty-making in the field of trade be on this separation of powers approach to (the lack of) direct effect of trade agreements, in particular the WTO agreements? This may well depend on the factual situation. Parliament's approval of a trade agreement brings important additional (democratic) legitimation to such an agreement. If Union law remains unchanged after the conclusion of such an agreement, but appears to be in conflict with the agreement (possibly after a decision of an international dispute settlement organ), this added democratic legitimation may serve as an argument to grant direct effect to the relevant provision of

---

cratic states to the general political oversight by parliament and that would not be different for the Commission.

47 See notes 12 and 17 and accompanying text.

48 Judgment of 23 November 1999, *Portugal* v *Council*, C-149/96, EU:C:199:574 and Judgment of 1 March 2005, *Van Parys*, C-377/02, EU:C:2005:121, para 53. See further the chapter by Miro Prek and Silvère Lefèvre in this volume.

the trade agreement. It might be different if the agreement included a recital or an article denying direct effect to the trade agreement, or if the EU legislature (Council and Parliament together) enacted implementing legislation that later turned out to be at odds with the agreement.

It is clear that there are different possible approaches to this new element that has been introduced into the Court's underpinning of its "no direct effect policy" to certain trade agreements because of the Parliament's new powers in this domain. The result of the pressures going either way will be eagerly awaited.

Another point on which the Parliament's new powers of approval of trade agreements may be brought to bear is the recourse to the procedure of Article 218, paragraph 9, TFEU relative to "establishing the positions to be adopted on the Union's behalf in a body set up by an agreement, when that body is called upon to adopt acts having legal effects". It has already been mentioned how the EP is seeking to exert at least some political influence on the execution by the Commission of the directives for negotiation that the Council issues to the Commission to guide it in its negotiations, given that the legal powers in this respect are reserved to the Council. The same goes for the exercise of the power of Article 218, paragraph 9, TFEU, which is after all about the management of an international delegation of legislative power to a treaty body or an organ of an international organisation and, without doubt, should be deserving of considerable attention from the European Parliament. Presumably, there were good reasons to provide for such a delegation of powers and it is an important and often used instrument in international organisations and treaty bodies. [49]Nonetheless, there are equally good reasons for Parliament to demand some political power of scrutiny (for instance by a special standing parliamentary committee that could react quickly) over deciding the Union's position in a treaty body or organ of an international organisation, when it will take a decision that will be binding on the Union, even if Article 218, paragraph 9, TFEU gives no legal power to the European Parliament to exercise such scrutiny.

49 A well-known example is the power of the World Health Organization to adopt binding International Health Regulations. Similarly, the ICAO is authorized to adopt so-called SARPS (standards and recognized practices). Multilateral Environmental Agreements very often give the power to modify lists of dangerous substances, e.g. of endangered species, with binding effect.

This is a point where the strength of the legal concept of institutional balance can be tested and where it may exist separately from the shifting EU constitutional texts. Would the Court accept such parliamentary scrutiny on the basis that the balance between the institutions requires it, as it would be anomalous for the Parliament to be able to exercise a right of consent over international agreements (including trade agreements), but not over the position of the Union when binding decisions are taken based on delegation to a treaty body based on such an agreement approved by Parliament? Or would it reject such scrutiny, as it was not provided for in the TFEU and the right to fix the position of the Union in such cases was limited to the Council alone?

The Parliament's power to approve trade agreements may also have consequences for the adoption of mixed agreements. If a mixed agreement is to a very large extent a trade agreement and its being mixed is a compromise between the Commission and the Member States in the Council,[50] normally there will be no specification about what part of the agreement is exclusive EU competence, what part is shared competence, and what is exclusive competence of the Member States. That is precisely the point of the compromise. However, even in most modern, so-called "deep and comprehensive" trade agreements commercial policy within the meaning of Article 207 TFEU in reality easily covers more than 90-95% of the agreement. In the past this meant, that such a "false mixity compromise" was an arrangement in which the Council delegated its exclusive power to conclude trade agreements back to the Member States and their Parliaments. Such distortion, if not to say breach, of the Treaty at that time was essentially victimless, as the Member States in the Council simply gave themselves a second bite at the cherry, even though it was probably already then contrary to *Donckerwolcke's* requirement that re-delegation of trade policy power to the Member States is only possible if done explicitly.[51] It can be argued that at the time such approval by national parliaments added an aspect of necessary democratic legitimacy, as the EP had no formal powers in the field of trade at all. In the new situation, such a

50 For the reduced risk of such mixed trade agreements being necessary, see Opinion 2/15, *supra* notes 12 and 17. See also the contribution by Chamon in this volume.

51 Judgment of 15 December 1976, *Donckerwolcke,* 41/76, EU:C:1976:182, para 32. It is to be noted that this case deals with a limited and discrete re-delegation, while giving back the power to stop a Union act that is for 90-95% exclusive power to one national Parliament is an entirely different matter.

compromise of "false mixity" is in essence at the expense of the Parliament's right to decide on its own about trade policy matters and not to have to share this power with national parliaments. The latter are not empowered to, and probably are not capable of, weighing up the different elements going into such an agreement at the European level. It is obvious that mixed agreements have an unsettling effect on the balance between the institutions in Union treaty-making now that the Parliament also weighs on the scales. Even if Parliament implicitly accepts the "false mixity", again the prohibition of implicit re-delegation kicks in.

The CETA episode has been a first tragic example of the problems set out here; it will be interesting to see what lessons the institutions will draw from it.[52] For the moment the Commission, after Opinion 2/15, has taken the road of henceforth proposing trade agreements that adhere strictly to the criteria laid down in this Opinion of the Court and thus would follow only the Union procedure for concluding such agreements. It remains to be seen what the reactions of the Member States and the Council would be. And if they are negative and Member States in the Council continue their long-standing practice to add elements to the Commission's proposed directives for negotiations assuring that the agreement becomes mixed, what would be the reaction of the other institutions in the legislative triangle? How strongly would the Commission defend its position by withdrawing its recommendation containing those directives, thus confronting the Council with the choice with no agreement or a Union-only-agreement?[53] Would the European Parliament support the Commission by announcing that it will not accept a mixed agreement? What alternative routes may be devised so that Member State Parliaments may contribute to the treaty-making process through their Member States in the Council without impinging on the exclusive powers of the Union? The questions of a politico-legal character determining the future shape of the Union's common commercial policy are myriad.

The new powers of the European Parliament in the field of trade and external relations are also likely to have external repercussions. As the Union's institutions in this field know only too well, the legislative powers

---

52 For more details, see P. J. Kuijper, "Post-CETA: How we Got There and How To Go On", *Revue trimestrielle de droit européen* 53, no. 3 (2017), 181-187.

53 In analogy to the case *Commission* v *Council*, *supra* note 45. See also P. J. Kuijper, "Post-CETA", *supra* note 52.

of the US Congress in the field of "Commerce with foreign Nations"[54] can cause considerable problems to other states. Legislation in direct conflict with the rights of the US's treaty partners in the WTO Agreements occurs with some regularity and the necessary litigation in the WTO is time consuming and requires a relentless effort to push the US toward conformity. It is to be expected that the European Parliament may be subject to the same temptation – to put it charitably – of testing the limits imposed by the WTO Agreements and their interpretation by WTO panels and the Appellate Body, with the likely result of being rebuffed by these WTO bodies, when other WTO Members bring cases to the dispute settlement system. Obviously the Council and the Commission have more constitutional possibilities than the US executive to restrain the Parliament from giving in to such temptations in trilogues, but sometimes compromises that none of the three can refuse may still carry considerable risks.[55]

Finally, the question may be asked whether the EEAS does not itself constitute an institution that is the embodiment of the notion of balance between the institutions.[56] There is indeed no doubt that the creation of the EEAS was an act of balance between the Council and the Commission, insofar as the EEAS was destined to float in a kind of vacuum between the Commission and the Council Secretariat, with the Member States as a collective third party also involved in this new, *sui generis* institution. However, this view of the EEAS was correct only at the moment of its creation. Once that moment had passed, the EEAS had to find its own place in the new balance between the institutions in external relations, which had been created by the Lisbon Treaty. That place is a kind of amalgam between the position of the Secretariat of the Council in the old CFSP and the position of the half-yearly presidency of the Council during the pre-Lisbon period, while it also functions as negotiator in the field of CFSP/CSDP under

54 See Article I, Section 8, of the US Constitution.

55 This may be the case with the compromise reached in September 2017 between the Council, the Parliament and the Commission on the inclusion of environmental elements and labour rights in the calculation of anti-dumping and countervailing duties by the Commission, when applying trade defence measures. See European Commission, "Commission welcomes agreement on new anti-dumping methodology", Strasbourg, 3 October 2017, http://trade.ec.europa.eu/doclib/press/index.cfm?id=1735.

56 See S. Blockmans, "Setting Up the European External Action Service: An Act of Institutional Balance", *European Constitutional Law Review,* no. 2 (2012), 246-279.

guidance of the Council in a way comparable to the Commission in the TFEU external relations.

It is obvious from a short passage in the *Pirates* cases that the Court also has some difficulty placing the EEAS in this new context and actually charges only the Council with informing the Parliament regularly on the progress of negotiations in CFSP agreements, while it was the EEAS that actually negotiated the agreement.[57] One might have expected that Court would give the same room for manoeuvre to the EAAS, as negotiator, as it gave to the Commission in the *Negotiating Directives* case,[58] but in that case the Court might have been accused of meddling in the institutional balance of the CFSP in too direct a fashion and without obvious need for deciding the case. Further developments have to be awaited before there are further indications about what exactly the position of the EEAS in the balance between the institutions may be. Serious arguments may also be made that the double-hatted character of the HR/VP and, consequently, of her service, the EEAS, has upset a functioning balance between the institutions. In this connection, the widespread negative reaction to the fusion between the functions of President of the Commission and President of the European Council, as suggested by Jean-Claude Juncker in his State of the Union speech of September 2017 is telling.

The title of this contribution announced that it was intended as an essay – an attempt to sketch the separation of powers (in Union language, institutional balance) in the field of external relations from the perspective of the evolution of foreign relations powers in national States with a democratic tradition. This perspective was then used for an appreciation of the changes brought to this balance between the institutions by the Lisbon Treaty and the Court's interpretation of these changes. It is hoped that this perspective has contributed to assuage the fears in the Member States that these changes are not as revolutionary as they may seem, while alerting observers of the process to the many issues and questions that are in need of an answer in the months and years to come.

---

57 See Judgment of 14 June 2016, *European Parliament* v *Council (Agreement with Tanzania), supra* note 24; see also *supra* note 27 to note 29 and accompanying text.

58 See Judgment of 16 July 2015, *Commission* v *Council (Negotiating Directives), supra* note 39.

La dimension « subjective » de l'invocabilité des accords internationaux / The Subjective Dimension of the Invocability of International Agreements

Miro Prek and Silvère Lefèvre[*]

Abstract

Even though international law forms an integral part of European Union law, it is not afforded the same legal status as other sources of European Union Law. An illustration of such differences in legal status lies in the existence of additional requirements that need to be fulfilled in order for the EU Courts to verify whether EU legislation complies with an international agreement. This article focuses on such extra conditions which are of a "subjective nature" in the sense that they imply the demonstration of the intention either of (a) the joint parties to the agreement or (b) the sole European Union to allow or refuse Courts to assess to validity of legislation by reference to such an agreement. A cross-cutting issue is whether the approaches favoured in relation to WTO rules can be extended to other types of international agreements.

The first part focuses on how the joint intention of the parties to an international agreement is relevant when the validity of EU legislation is challenged by reference to such an agreement. A distinction must be drawn according to the type of applicant that raises the issue of a potential incompatibility between EU legislation and an international agreement. Legal or natural persons must demonstrate that the intention of the parties to the agreement they invoke is to confer rights upon them. While such a requirement is not applicable when the applicant is a Member State, the intention of the parties might still be relevant when they raise arguments based on violations of WTO agreements. The settled case law according to which such agreements, given their nature and purpose, are not in principle among the rules in the light of which the Court is to review the legality of EU legislation can be linked with the idea that the intention of the parties was to search for a strict reciprocity in the implementation of such

---

* Les opinions exprimées le sont à titre personnel.

agreements. Allowing the review of validity of EU legislation would go against such quest for reciprocity since other parties to the agreement do not allow for an equivalent legal challenge against their own internal legislation.

The second part of the article examines whether the sole intention of the EU (rather than the joint intention of the parties) to allow the validity of its legislation to be assessed by reference to international agreements can also be relevant. The settled case law since the *Nakajima* and *Fediol* judgements seems to provide a positive answer to this question at least in relation to WTO agreements. Such case law accepts that in situations in which the Union intended to implement a particular obligation assumed in the context of the WTO, or where the Union measure refers expressly to the precise provisions of the WTO agreements, it belongs to the Court to review the legality of the Union measure in question in the light of such agreements. Yet such a possibility remains, so far, limited to WTO agreements, since attempts by the General Court to extend its scope to the review of EU legislation by reference to the Aarhus convention were not followed by the Court of Justice.

***

La lecture du Traité sur l'Union européenne (TUE) et du Traité sur le fonctionnement de l'Union européenne (TFUE) souligne l'ouverture de l'ordre juridique de l'Union au droit international. L'article 3, paragraphe 5, TUE se réfère, ainsi, à la contribution de l'Union au « strict respect et au développement du droit international ». Dans le même sens l'article 216, paragraphe 2, TFUE stipule que « les accords conclus par l'Union lient les institutions de l'Union et les États membres ». Cet esprit d'ouverture se retrouve dans la formule classique utilisée depuis l'arrêt *Haegeman*[1] selon laquelle les accords internationaux « forment une partie intégrante » de l'ordre juridique de l'Union.

Cette ouverture au droit international ne revêt cependant pas un caractère absolu et doit se concilier avec la préservation de l'autonomie et des spécificités de l'ordre juridique de l'Union. Sous l'angle de l'application du principe de primauté, cela se matérialise par une insertion, certes élevée du droit international dans la hiérarchie des normes, en ce qu'elle est

1 Arrêt de la Cour du 30 avril 1974, *Haegeman*, 181/73, EU:C:1974:41, point 5.

supérieure au droit dérivé, mais cependant inférieure au droit primaire[2]. S'agissant des accords internationaux cette soumission au droit primaire est révélée par la procédure de l'article 218, paragraphe 11, TFUE ainsi que par la jurisprudence acceptant le contrôle indirect de la « constitutionnalité » d'un accord international au travers de son acte de conclusion[3]. En ce qui concerne les autres normes de droit international, une approche équivalente a été appliquée à l'égard des résolutions du Conseil de sécurité adoptées sur le fondement du chapitre VII de la Charte des Nations unies, suivant les affaires *Kadi* et *Al Barakaat*[4].

Surtout, ce mélange d'ouverture et de prudence à l'égard du droit international se matérialise par l'existence d'obstacles à l'invocabilité des engagements internationaux conclus par l'Union.

Un premier obstacle concerne les particuliers (personnes physiques ou morales). Ceux-ci, aux fins d'écarter une norme interne contraire (ce qui est parfois qualifié en doctrine d' « invocabilité d'exclusion[5] ») sont tenus à la démonstration préalable de ce que l'engagement international est d'effet direct, c'est-à-dire « apte à créer par lui-même des droits ou des obliga-

---

2 Sur cette question v. P.-Y. Monjal, *Recherches sur la hiérarchie des normes communautaires*, Paris, LGDJ, 2000, p. 133.

3 V. par ex. arrêt de la Cour du 27 septembre 1988, *Commission/Conseil*, 165/87, EU:C:1988:458; arrêt de la Cour du 30 mai 2006, *Parlement/Conseil et Commission*, C-317/04 et C-318/04, EU:C:2006:346. Sur cette question v. notamment E. Neframi, « Accords internationaux. – Statut des accords internationaux dans l'ordre juridique de l'Union européenne », *JurisClasseur Europe Traité,* Fasc. 192-2, point 69 et s.

4 Arrêt de la Cour du 3 septembre 2008, *Kadi et Al Barakaat*, C-402/05 P et C-415/05 P, EU:C:2008:461.

5 L'invocabilité d'exclusion implique la mise à l'écart de la norme interne contraire. Elle se distingue, notamment, de l'invocabilité d'interprétation conforme qui implique seulement, autant que possible une interprétation de la norme interne à la lumière de l'engagement international, et de l'invocabilité de substitution, laquelle permet l'application de l'engagement international en lieu et place de la norme interne. Sur cette typologie v. D. Simon, *Le système juridique communautaire*, Paris, PUF, 2001, p. 438. Sur son application à l'invocabilité des engagements internationaux, v. notamment, J. F. Delile, « L'invocabilité des accords internationaux devant le juge de la légalité des actes de l'Union européenne. État des lieux à l'occasion des arrêts *Vereniging Milieudefensie* et *Stichting Natuur* », *Cahiers de droit européen*, vol. 51, n° 1/2015, p. 153.

tions au bénéficie ou à la charge des personnes privées »[6], alors qu'il est discutable que cela soit nécessaire à l'égard des normes internes de droit de l'Union.[7]

Cette condition est d'autant plus restrictive que la démonstration de l'effet direct d'un engagement international implique une condition additionnelle par rapport à celle des normes internes du droit de l'Union. Il appartient, certes, au particulier souhaitant invoquer la contrariété d'un acte de l'Union par rapport à un engagement international de démontrer que les dispositions invoquées « apparaissent, du point de vue de leur contenu, inconditionnelles et suffisamment précises[8] », ce qui correspond aux conditions classiques de l'effet direct appliquées aux normes internes de l'Union. De telles conditions peuvent être qualifiées d'objectives en ce qu'elles concernent les qualités de la norme devant servir de base de contrôle. Toutefois, outre ces conditions objectives, doit également être remplie une condition « subjective » de l'effet direct tenant dans l'intention des parties à l'accord de conférer des droits aux particuliers. La prise en compte d'une telle intention est loin d'être un phénomène nouveau; on en trouve une illustration dès le 15ème avis de la Cour permanente de justice

---

6 Selon la définition de R. Mehdi « Ordre juridique de l'Union européenne – Effet direct », *Jurisclasseur Europe Traité*, Fasc. 195, point 12. Une définition équivalente et plus fonctionnelle est donnée par K. Lenaerts et T. Corthaut : « it is the technique which allows individuals to enforce a subjective right, which is only available in the internal legal order in an instrument that comes from outside that order, against another (state or private) actor». V. K. Lenaerts, T. Corthaut « Of Birds and Hedges: the Role of Primacy in Invoking Norms of EU Law », *European Law Review,* vol. 31, n° 3/2006, p. 310.

7 V. en ce qui concerne l'invocabilité d'exclusion de normes de droit interne des États membres contraires à des directives dépourvues d'effet direct, les conclusions de l'Avocat général Saggio dans les affaires jointes *Océano Grupo Editorial* et *Salvat Editores*, C-240/98 à C-244/98, EU:C:1999:620, points 37 à 39, ainsi que les conclusions de l'Avocat général Léger dans l'affaire *Linster*, C-287/98, EU:C:2000:3, points 55 à 77. V. également en ce qui concerne le contrôle du respect d'une décision-cadre dépourvue d'effet direct les conclusions de l'Avocat général Bot dans l'affaire *Popławski*, C-579/15, EU:C:2017:116 points 79 à 90.

8 Arrêt de la Cour du 13 janvier 2015, *Vereniging Milieudefensie*, C-401/12 P à C-403/12 P, EU:C:2015:4, point 54; arrêt de la Cour du 3 juin 2008, *Intertanko*, C-308/06, EU:C:2008:312, point 45; arrêt de la Cour du 9 septembre 2008, *FIAMM,* C-120/06 P et C-121/06 P, EU:C:2008:476, points 110 et 120; arrêt de la Cour du 21 décembre 2011, *Air Transport Association of America*, C-366/10, EU:C:2011:864, point 54.

internationale portant sur la *compétence des Tribunaux de Dantzig*[9]. Dans la jurisprudence de la Cour de Justice cette intention est recherchée sous l'angle particulier du point de savoir si la nature et l'économie de l'accord ne s'opposent pas à son invocabilité.

La mise en exergue de cette condition supplémentaire est révélatrice de la différence de nature fondamentale entre une norme adoptée dans le cadre interne de l'Union pour laquelle l'intention de conférer des droits peut être présumée – sous réserve de l'examen de la qualité de la norme en question – et une norme juridique extérieure à l'ordre juridique de l'Union, à l'égard de laquelle cette intention doit être vérifiée.

Ainsi, comparée aux normes internes de l'Union, l'invocabilité des engagements internationaux par les particuliers à des fins de contrôle de légalité apparaît doublement restrictive. D'une part, elle est conditionnée par la démonstration de ce que la norme invoquée est d'effet direct, ce qui n'est pas le cas s'agissant des normes internes pour lesquelles ce type d'invocabilité peut s'apprécier en la seule conséquence du principe de primauté[10]. D'autre part, la démonstration de l'effet direct ne suppose pas seulement l'examen des qualités de la norme conventionnelle alléguée mais également de l'intention des parties à l'accord international.

À l'inverse des particuliers, un État membre n'est pas tenu de démontrer l'effet direct d'une disposition d'un accord international aux fins de contester la non-conformité d'un acte de l'Union[11]. Il en va différemment d'un second obstacle à l'invocabilité des engagements internationaux, lequel dispose d'une portée plus générale en ce qu'il empêche l'invocabilité de l'accord également par les États membres. Il tient dans la nécessaire satisfaction d'une condition de réciprocité dans la mise en œuvre de l'accord international[12]. Il se présente dans la situation où la Cour déduit

---

9 CPJI, avis n°15, 3 mars 1918, Série B, p. 17 et s.

10 Sur l'importance du principe de primauté comme fondement de l'invocabilité à des fins de contrôle de légalité v. K. Lenaerts et T. Corthaut, *supra* note 6, p. 297-310.

11 Arrêt de la Cour du 9 octobre 2001, *Pays-Bas/Parlement et Conseil* « Biotech », C-377/98, EU:C:2001:523, points 52-54.

12 L'existence autonome d'une condition tirée de la réciprocité de l'application d'un engagement international est parfois contestée en doctrine. V. J. Rideau « Accords internationaux », *Répertoire droit de l'Union européenne*, Paris, Dalloz, 2011, point 540. Est alors privilégiée une vision globale de l'effet direct des engagements internationaux dans laquelle la spécificité de l'invocabilité des accords de l'OMC est minorée. *Id.* point 514.

de la nature et de l'économie de l'accord la volonté des parties de le fonder sur des principes de réciprocité et d'avantages mutuels. L'invocabilité de l'accord dans l'ordre juridique de l'Union n'est, alors, possible que si les partenaires de l'Union permettent une invocabilité équivalente dans leur propre ordre juridique.

Cet obstacle présente deux particularités. D'une part, il ne vaut – tout au moins en l'état actuel de la jurisprudence – qu'à l'égard des accords conclus dans le cadre de l'Organisation mondiale du commerce (OMC). D'autre part, il a été soutenu de manière, à notre avis, convaincante en doctrine[13] que ce motif de refus d'invocabilité ne repose pas sur une absence d'effet direct de l'engagement international; il réside dans une condition autonome de réciprocité se situant en amont de l'examen du point de savoir si la norme alléguée est destinée à conférer des droits aux particuliers. Milite, en effet, en faveur de l'autonomie de cette condition de réciprocité, la circonstance qu'elle aboutit à une absence d'invocabilité non seulement au détriment des personnes physiques ou morales mais également des États membres, requérants privilégiés.

Ces deux limites à l'invocabilité des engagements internationaux sont la conséquence de la liberté dont jouissent les institutions de l'Union, qui sont compétentes pour négocier et conclure un accord avec des pays tiers, de convenir avec ceux-ci des effets que les dispositions de l'accord doivent produire dans l'ordre interne des parties contractantes. Une telle liberté implique nécessairement que les juridictions de l'Union ne peuvent jouer qu'un rôle supplétif dans la détermination de l'étendue des effets d'un engagement dans l'ordre juridique de l'Union[14]. En d'autres termes, soit la convention internationale explicite l'étendue de ses effets dans les ordres internes des parties contractantes et les juridictions de l'Union doivent en prendre acte[15]; soit elle est silencieuse et c'est alors au juge de rechercher cette intention et d'en tirer les conséquences quant à l'étendue des effets

---

13 J. F. Delile, *L'invocabilité des accords internationaux dans la CJUE et le Conseil d'État français*, Bruxelles, Bruylant, 2016, p. 160.

14 S'agissant de l'OMC, arrêt de la Cour du 23 novembre 1999, *Portugal/Conseil*, C-149/96, EU:C:1999:574, point 34. S'agissant des accords internationaux de droit commun, v. l'arrêt de la Cour du 13 janvier 2015, *Vereniging Milieudefensie*, *supra* note 8, point 53.

15 Par exemple l'accord de libre-échange entre l'Union européenne et ses États membres, d'une part, et la République de Corée, d'autre part, (*JO* L127 du 14 mai 2011, p. 1) contient plusieurs références explicites excluant l'invocabilité par les particuliers de certaines dispositions d'annexes à l'accord. Il en est ainsi de l'an-

que l'accord produit[16]. La recherche de cette « dimension subjective » de l'invocabilité d'un accord international implique, selon le cas, d'examiner si l'intention des parties a été de soumettre son invocabilité à une condition de réciprocité ou de conférer des droits au profit des particuliers (I).

Une forme particulière d'invocabilité, développée dans le cadre de la jurisprudence propre aux accords de l'OMC – et qui, au stade actuel de son développement, reste confinée à ces seuls accords – permet, en principe, de tempérer la rigueur de ces obstacles. Elle admet le contrôle de conformité d'un acte du droit de l'Union quand il a pour objet de mettre en œuvre une obligation internationale de l'Union. L'adoption d'une législation opérant un renvoi suffisamment explicite à une norme de l'OMC ou d'une législation destinée à mettre en œuvre une obligation particulière de l'Union au titre d'une norme de l'OMC est alors considérée comme justifiant que la disposition mise en œuvre, ou à laquelle il est fait une référence explicite, puisse être invoquée à des fins de contrôle de conformité de la législation de l'Union. Cette invocabilité de mise en œuvre s'apparente également en une illustration de la condition subjective de l'invocabilité des engagements internationaux en ce qu'elle manifeste l'intention unilatérale de l'Union de permettre à un engagement international de produire ses effets dans l'ordre juridique de l'Union. Analysée sous cet angle, la question de son extension en dehors du champ d'application des accords de l'OMC ne pouvait que se poser. Question à laquelle la jurisprudence de la Cour a donné une réponse négative, même si la portée exacte de ce refus demeure encore, à notre sens, floue (II).

---

nexe 7-A-2 relative à la liste des engagements de l'Union européenne relatives aux activités économiques libéralisées, laquelle précise de manière liminaire que «les droits et obligations résultant de la liste ci-après n'ont pas d'effet automatique et ne confèrent donc aucun droit directement à des personnes physiques ou morales ». Sur cette question v. M. Maresceau, « The Court of Justice and Bilateral Agreements », in Y. Bot, E. Levits, A. Rosas (dir.), *La Cour de justice et la construction de l'Europe : Analyses et perspectives de soixante ans de jurisprudence*, La Haye, Asser Press, 2013, p. 716.

16 Arrêt de la Cour du 26 octobre 1982, *Kupferberg*, 104/81, EU:C:1982:362, point 17; arrêt de la Cour du 9 septembre 2008, *FIAMM*, *supra* note 8, point 108.

I. L'intention des parties, critère d'identification des effets d'un engagement international dans l'ordre juridique de l'Union

Tout engagement international conclu par l'Union produit un degré minimal d'effet dans l'ordre juridique de l'Union en ce qu'il est pertinent aux fins de l'interprétation de la législation de l'Union. Il résulte, en effet, d'une jurisprudence constante que les textes de droit de l'Union doivent être interprétés, dans la mesure du possible, à la lumière du droit international, en particulier lorsque de tels textes visent précisément à mettre en œuvre un accord international conclu par l'Union[17]. Si l'interprétation conforme de l'acte de l'Union avec le droit international n'est pas possible au motif, notamment, que le sens de l'acte de l'Union est clair et dépourvu d'ambiguïté[18], la question se pose, alors, de la possibilité d'invoquer l'engagement en question au titre du contrôle de la conformité de l'acte de l'Union avec l'engagement international. Quand le requérant est une personne physique ou morale, la question essentielle consiste à vérifier si l'intention des parties a été de conférer des droits à son profit (B). Toutefois, de manière préalable, et y compris quand le requérant est un État membre, doit être prise en compte l'éventuelle intention des parties de conclure un accord sur une base strictement réciproque (A).

A. L'intention des parties de conclure un accord fondé sur les principes de réciprocité et d'avantages mutuels

Il s'agit là d'une condition qui, au stade actuel de développement de la jurisprudence – laquelle demeure fondée sur la position de la Cour dans son arrêt *Portugal/Conseil*[19] – est propre à l'invocabilité des accords de l'OMC. Derrière le refus de reconnaître une invocabilité à ces accords, y compris au profit des États membres, figurent deux lignes de raisonnement successives.

---

17 Voir, par exemple, arrêt de la Cour du 15 mars 2012, *SCF Consorzio Fonografici*, C-135/10, EU:C:2012:140, point 51.

18 Pour un exemple de l'impossibilité de recourir à une interprétation conforme, en raison du caractère clair de la législation de l'Union v. arrêt du Tribunal du 10 octobre 2012, *Gem-Year et Jinn-Well Auto-Parts (Zhejiang)*, T-172/09, EU:T:2012:532, points 131 et 132.

19 Arrêt de la Cour du 23 novembre 1999, *Portugal/Conseil*, *supra* note 14.

La première concerne la nécessité pour la Cour de rechercher ce qu'a été l'intention de l'Union quant à la manière dont elle entendait conférer des effets aux accords de l'OMC dans son ordre juridique et quant à l'étendue de ces effets, dès lors que le texte desdits accords est silencieux sur cette question[20]. Elle part de l'observation que le droit international, au-delà de l'obligation d'exécuter de bonne foi un accord international, laisse à chacune des parties contractantes la liberté de déterminer les moyens de droit propres à atteindre cette fin dans son ordre juridique, à moins que l'accord, interprété à la lumière de son objet et de son but, ne détermine, lui-même, ces moyens[21].

La seconde consiste dans l'examen de cette intention. Elle part de la mise en exergue du préambule de l'accord instituant l'OMC visant des négociations entreprises sur une base de réciprocité et d'avantages mutuels. Il y a là un facteur de différenciation important avec les accords dont il est explicitement prévu qu'ils instaurent une certaine asymétrie des obligations ou qui créent des relations spéciales d'intégration avec l'Union[22]. Dans cette logique de stricte réciprocité recherchée, il est alors constaté que certaines des parties contractantes, « qui sont, du point de vue commercial, parmi les partenaires les plus importants de la Communauté, ont tiré à la lumière de l'objet et du but des accords OMC la conséquence que ceux-ci ne figurent pas parmi les normes au regard desquelles leurs organes juridictionnels contrôlent la légalité de leurs règles de droit internes »[23]. Il en est déduit que « l'absence de réciprocité [...] de la part des partenaires commerciaux de la Communauté, par rapport aux accords OMC qui sont fondés sur 'le principe de réciprocité des avantages mutuels' [...], risque d'aboutir à un déséquilibre dans l'application des règles de l'OMC »[24]. À cela est associé le constat que le mécanisme de règlement des différends de l'OMC laisse une place importante à la négociation entre les parties[25] et que, partant, « imposer aux organes juridictionnels l'obligation d'écarter l'application des règles de droit internes qui seraient incompatibles avec les accords OMC aurait pour conséquence de priver les organes législatifs ou exécutifs des parties contractantes de la

20 *Id.*, point 40.
21 *Id.*, point 35.
22 *Id.*, point 42.
23 *Id.*, point 43.
24 *Id.*, point 45.
25 *Id.*, points 36 à 40.

possibilité [...], de trouver, fût-ce à titre temporaire, des solutions négociées »[26].

La logique de ce raisonnement semble impliquer que le défaut d'invocabilité a une base plus large que celle de la seule absence d'effet direct. Dans l'arrêt *Portugal/Conseil*, le débat n'a pas été posé sous l'angle de l'intention de conférer des droits aux particuliers, angle qui serait, en toute hypothèse, sans incidence dans le cadre d'un recours introduit par un requérant privilégié. Ce qui a été déterminant consiste plutôt dans le constat de l'importance attachée par les parties à l'équilibre de leurs prestations et la prise en compte du risque de déséquilibre impliquée par une invocabilité unilatérale des accords de l'OMC dans l'ordre juridique de l'Union, notamment en raison de la diminution de la marge de manœuvre des institutions lors du règlement des différends. Ainsi que le soulignent Koen Lenaerts et Tim Corthaut « the problem is not that the provisions are not intended to confer rights on individuals; it rather is that the Community as well as its major trade partners have indicated that they wanted to remain at liberty to negotiate a political solution for violations of the norms of WTO law »[27]. Par contre, dans les circonstances où l'invocabilité de l'accord international est alléguée par un requérant non privilégié, les arrêts de la Cour se placent plus facilement sous l'angle de l'absence d'effet direct de la disposition invoquée[28].

La question demeure cependant ouverte quant au champ exact de cette jurisprudence. À l'heure actuelle, elle est cantonnée aux seuls accords conclus dans le cadre de l'OMC[29]. Doit-on, cependant, en déduire que le défaut de réciprocité ne sera avancé à l'égard d'aucun autre accord international?

La justification de son application aux seuls accords de l'OMC apparaît résider dans la manière dont la Cour perçoit l'intention des parties quant à

26 *Id.*, point 40.

27 K. Lenaerts, T. Corthaut, *supra* note 6, p. 299, cité par J. F. Delile, *L'invocabilité des accords internationaux dans la CJUE et le Conseil d'État français, supra* note 13, p. 180.

28 V. par exemple l'arrêt de la Cour du 14 décembre 2000, *Dior*, C-300/98 et C-392/98, EU:C:2000:688, points 42-45.

29 Cela vaut à l'égard de l'ensemble des normes adoptées dans le cadre de l'OMC : l'Accord ADPIC (*Dior, supra* note 28), l'accord sur les sauvegardes (arrêt de la Cour du 22 novembre 2001, *Pays-Bas/Conseil*, C-301/97, EU:C:2001:621), décisions de l'ORD (arrêt de la Cour du 1er mars 2005, *Van Parys*, C-377/02, EU:C:2005:121).

la manière dont leurs obligations doivent être satisfaites. En ce que les accords de l'OMC sont fondés sur les principes de réciprocité et d'avantages mutuels, ils auraient été adoptés avec, en perspective, une stricte réciprocité d'application, se rapprochant de l'idée d'équivalence des prestations. À l'égard des autres accords existerait une obligation plus diffuse d'exécution de bonne foi, ne faisant pas naître de condition de réciprocité. Pour ceux-ci, ainsi que le souligne Panos Koutrakos « what is significant is that obligations contained in the agreement are fulfilled, in accordance with the general rules of international law, bona fide: whilst under a duty to comply fully with their contractual obligations, the parties are free, in the absence of express provision in the agreement, to determine how to do so »[30].

Les mêmes causes ayant tendance à produire les mêmes effets, il ne saurait, à notre avis, d'emblée être exclu qu'une convention, non négociée sous l'égide de l'OMC, mais fondée sur un strict respect du principe de réciprocité et dans laquelle ne figure pas de mécanisme de règlement des différends entre les parties, ou seulement un mécanisme marqué par sa souplesse, se voie refuser son invocabilité dans l'ordre juridique de l'Union. Dans cette optique, a été souligné en doctrine le développement de mécanisme souple de règlement des différends dans plusieurs accords bilatéraux conclus par l'Union et le potentiel risque d'une « contagion » de la mise en exergue de la condition de réciprocité à leur égard[31].

B. L'intention des parties de conférer des droits aux particuliers

La prise en compte de l'intention des parties à un engagement international de conférer ou non des droits aux particuliers ainsi que, de manière plus générale, de l'effet direct de l'engagement, comme condition de son invocabilité est, ainsi que l'a observé l'Avocat général Jääskinen dans ses conclusions sous l'affaire *Vereniging Milieudefensie*[32] révélatrice du tronc commun moniste de l'ordre juridique de l'Union. Il est bien connu que

30 P. Koutrakos, *EU International Relations Law*, Oxford, Hart Publising, 2015, p. 225; J. F. Delile, *L'invocabilité des accords internationaux dans la CJUE et le Conseil d'État français, supra* note 13, p. 177.

31 M. Bronckers, « The Relationship of the EC Courts with Other International Tribunals: Non-committal, Respectful or Submissive? », *Common Market Law Review,* vol. 44, n° 3/2007, p. 601, spéc. p. 613 et 617.

32 Conclusions de l'Avocat général Jääskinen, du 8 mai 2014, sous *Vereniging Milieudefensie*, C-401/12 P à C-403/12 P, EU:C:2014:310.

dans les ordres juridiques de ce type, l'absence de reconnaissance d'effet direct peut servir de bouclier contre l'application d'un engagement international[33]. Il sert alors une fonction de protection équivalente à celle de l'absence d'adoption de mesure de transposition dans un ordre juridique de type dualiste.

L'importance et la spécificité de la prise en compte de l'intention des parties dans l'examen de l'effet direct d'un engagement international au travers de la référence à sa nature et son économie générale ont été systématisés dans des termes clairs par l'Avocat général Darmon dans ses conclusions sous l'affaire *Demirel* : « il résulte de votre jurisprudence que, pour reconnaître à un accord externe un effet direct, vous recherchez, comme pour l'application des normes communautaires stricto sensu, les caractéristiques de la disposition à appliquer. Mais, alors qu'en droit communautaire la volonté des parties contractantes d'attribuer par les Traités des droits subjectifs est maintenant considérée comme toujours acquise, [...] pareille intention ne peut être présumée pour l'application d'un accord international. Ainsi, en pareille matière, vous commencez par vérifier si la nature et l'économie de l'accord font obstacle à l'invocabilité directe d'une de ses stipulations. Pour répondre ensuite à la question de savoir si une telle stipulation est inconditionnelle et suffisamment précise pour produire un effet direct, vous considérez qu'il faut d'abord l'analyser à la lumière tant de l'objet et du but de cet accord que de son contexte »[34].

C'est donc plutôt au travers de l'examen de la nature et de l'économie de l'accord que l'intention de conférer des droits est recherchée; la référence explicite à des droits subjectifs (ou à leur absence) crées au profit des particuliers demeurait relativement absente des arrêts de la Cour jusqu'à récemment, tout au moins s'agissant des conventions multilatérales. L'arrêt *Intertanko* a constitué, à cet égard, une certaine rupture dès lors qu'il y est explicitement fait référence à l'absence de mise « en place des règles destinées à s'appliquer directement et immédiatement aux particuliers et à conférer à ces derniers des droits ou des libertés susceptibles d'être invoqués à l'encontre des États[35] » pour refuser l'invocabilité

33 V. par ex. A. Nollkaemper, « The Duality of Direct Effect of International Law », *European Journal of International Law*, vol. 25, n° 1/2014, p. 105, spéc. p. 111 et s.

34 Conclusions de l'Avocat général Darmon du 19 mai 1987, sous *Demirel*, 12/86, EU:C:1987:232, point 18.

35 Arrêt de la Cour du 3 juin 2008, *Intertanko, supra* note 8, point 64.

de la troisième convention des Nations unies sur le droit de la mer. En doctrine, certains auteurs ont vu dans cette référence explicite aux particuliers le reflet d'une évolution du droit international faisant de plus en plus de l'individu un sujet de ce droit[36]. Il pourrait également être considéré que la terminologie utilisée s'explique par les spécificités de l'affaire, la Cour ayant voulu souligner que la convention sur le droit de la mer visait uniquement à conférer des droits et obligations aux États de pavillon des navires et qu'il n'existait pas d'automaticité avec la reconnaissance de droits ou d'obligations aux personnes physiques ou morales liées auxdits navires.

Il demeure qu'une formulation équivalente a été utilisée dans l'arrêt *Air Transport Association of America* s'agissant de l'accord « ciel ouvert » mais avec un résultat opposé en ce qu'il a été conclu qu'il « met en place certaines règles destinées à s'appliquer directement et immédiatement aux transporteurs aériens et à leur conférer ainsi des droits ou des libertés »[37]. Cet arrêt a également précisé les conditions dans lesquelles des particuliers peuvent soulever la contrariété d'un acte de l'Union avec des normes de droit international coutumier. Bien qu'adaptées aux spécificités des normes coutumières, il est remarquable qu'elles incluent un élément ayant trait à la situation des particuliers et se rapprochant de la « condition subjective » d'invocabilité des engagements internationaux. Non seulement les principes de droit coutumier allégués doivent mettre en cause la compétence de l'Union pour adopter l'acte dont la légalité est contestée, mais également est-il nécessaire que celui-ci soit susceptible d'affecter les droits que les justiciables tirent du droit de l'Union ou de leur imposer des obligations[38].

L'importance attachée à la dimension subjective de l'invocabilité des accords internationaux ne doit, cependant, pas être surestimée. Dans la

---

36 Piet Eeckhout effectue un parallèle, à cet égard, avec la prise de position de la Cour Internationale de Justice au point 77 de l'arrêt *LaGrand (Allemagne/Etats-Unis),* 27 juin 2001, Rapport, p. 446. V. P. Eeckhout, Commentaire de l'arrêt *Intertanko, Common Market Law Review*, vol. 46, n° 6/2009, p. 2054. Dans le même sens v. J. Dutheil de la Rochère (dir.), « L'effet direct des accords internationaux », in Y. Bot, E. Levits, A. Rosas, *supra* note 15, p. 651.

37 Arrêt de la Cour du 21 décembre 2011, *Air Transport Association of America, supra* note 8, point 84. Sur cet arrêt v. D. Simon, « Droit international conventionnel et coutumier : l'invocabilité au cœur de la lecture juridictionnelle des rapports de systèmes. – (à propos de l'arrêt Air Transport) », *Europe*, n° 3/2012, p. 6.

38 *Id.,* point. 107.

plupart des circonstances où elle a été saisie de la question, la Cour a conclu à l'invocabilité de l'accord international, les refus constituant clairement l'exception.

Au-delà des fondements juridiques mis en exergue pour justifier le refus d'invocabilité d'un engagement international par les particuliers, voire par les États membres, l'examen des accords pour lesquels la condition subjective a été, selon le cas, réputée ou non remplie démontre l'importance du caractère plus ou moins ouvert ou fermé de l'accord en question. En effet, il ressort de la jurisprudence qu'à l'égard de conventions bilatérales, ou tout au moins à participation réduite, l'intention des parties de conférer des droits à des particuliers est fréquemment relevée[39]. Il en a été ainsi à l'égard des accords d'association qu'ils soient conclus dans la perspective d'une adhésion[40] ou dans le cadre de la politique d'aide au développement[41], de l'accord sur l'EEE[42] et de plusieurs accords de

---

39 J. Rideau note s'agissant des conventions bilatérales que dans les cas traités par la Cour « la référence à l'objet et au but des accords est pour l'essentiel purement formelle et n'a donc pas servi de justification à des refus d'invocabilité ». J. Rideau, « L'invocabilité des accords internationaux : condition de l'application des accords internationaux dans l'ordre juridique de l'Union européenne », in B. Bertrand, F. Picod, S. Roland (dir.), *L'identité du droit de l'Union européenne – mélanges en l'honneur de Claude Blumann*, Bruxelles, Bruylant, 2015, p. 482.

40 Par ex. accord d'association avec la Grèce : arrêt de la Cour du 29 avril 1982, *Pabst & Richarz*, 17/81, EU:C:1982:129; avec Chypre: arrêt de la Cour du 5 juillet 1994, *Anastasiou*, C-432/92, EU:C:1994:277; avec la Pologne : arrêt de la Cour du 29 janvier 2002, *Pokrzeptowicz-Meyer*, C-162/00, EU:C:2002:57. L'exception concerne l'accord d'association avec la Turquie : arrêt de la Cour du 30 septembre 1987, *Demirel,* 12/86, EU:C:1987:400. Toutefois, l'étendue de cette exception est elle-même circonscrite dès lors qu'un effet direct a été reconnu aux articles de l'accord d'association dès lors qu'ils ont été précisés par des décisions du Conseil d'association. V. arrêt de la Cour du 20 septembre 1990, *Sevince*, C-192/89, EU:C:1990:322. Sur l'ensemble de cette question v. B. Tornay, « L'effet direct des traités internationaux dans l'ordre juridique de l'Union européenne» *Revue du droit de l'Union européenne*, vol. 16, n° 2/2006, p. 325, spéc. p. 342 et s.

41 Arrêt de la Cour du 5 février 1976, *Conceria Bresciani*, 87/75, EU:C:1976:18; arrêt de la Cour du 12 décembre 1995, *Chiquita Italia*, C-469/93, EU:C:1995:435. Dans le sens inverse, arrêt de la Cour du 24 novembre 1977, *Razanatsimba*, 65/77, EU:C:1977:193. V. B. Tornay, *supra* note 40, p. 346.

42 Arrêt du Tribunal du 22 janvier 1997, *Opel Austria/Conseil*, T-115/94, EU:T:1997:3. V. B. Tornay, *supra* note 40, p. 346.

coopération[43]. Un autre exemple est celui de l'accord « ciel ouvert » conclu entre l'Union européenne et les États-Unis[44].

Au contraire, la recherche de l'intention des parties de conférer des droits devient plus problématique à l'égard de conventions multilatérales ouvertes à de multiples partenaires économiques ou de type évolutif. Dans cette configuration, la jurisprudence de la Cour apparaît moins ouverte. Il serait ainsi tentant de créer un lien entre le rôle limité joué par l'Union dans la détermination de ses cocontractants et une plus grande prudence dans la reconnaissance d'effets dans son ordre juridique interne à l'accord en question. Il y aurait là la manifestation d'une certaine forme d'*intuitu personae* se matérialisant par une extension ou une restriction des effets d'un engagement dans l'ordre juridique de l'Union. Certes l'arrêt *International Air Transport Association*, relatif à la convention de Montréal pour l'unification de certaines règles relatives au transport aérien international, souligne que l'intention des parties de conférer des droits peut être décelée au sein d'une convention à participation large.[45] Mais cet exemple constitue plutôt une exception si on le compare à la jurisprudence relative aux accords de l'OMC ou concernant la convention des Nations unies sur le droit de la mer.

---

43 S'agissant de l'accord de coopération avec le Maroc : arrêt de la Cour du 31 janvier 1991, *Kziber*, C-18/90, EU:C:1991:36; de l'accord de coopération avec l'Algérie : arrêt de la Cour du 5 avril 1995, *Krid*, C-103/94, EU:C:1995:97; avec la Russie : arrêt de la Cour du 12 avril 2005, *Simutenkov*, C-265/03, EU:C:2005:213.

44 Arrêt de la Cour du 21 décembre 2011, *Air Transport Association of America*, *supra* note 8, points 79-85.

45 Arrêt de la Cour du 10 janvier 2006, *IATA et ELFAA*, C-344/04, EU:C:2006:10, points 36 et s. On notera, en outre, qu'il s'agit d'une convention portant sur un sujet précis, disposant d'une portée relativement étroite. Pour un autre exemple de reconnaissance de l'invocabilité d'une convention multilatérale ayant un champ d'application restreint v. arrêt de la Cour du 15 juillet 2004, *Pêcheurs de l'étang de Berre*, C-213/03, EU:C:2004:464, points 39 et s., reconnaissant l'effet direct de l'article 6, paragraphe 3, du protocole relatif à la protection de la mer Méditerranée contre la pollution d'origine tellurique, dans sa version modifiée (*JO* L 322 du 14 décembre 1999, p. 18).

II. La prise en compte de l'intention unilatérale et postérieure de l'Union de mettre en œuvre un engagement international

Dans le cadre spécifique du contentieux lié aux accords du GATT puis de l'OMC, ont été développées deux hypothèses particulières d'invocabilité de ces accords. Il s'agissait initialement de la jurisprudence *Fediol*[46], rendue dans le contexte du contentieux de la protection contre les pratiques illicites en provenance des pays tiers, concernant l'hypothèse d'une référence opérée par un acte communautaire aux accords du GATT. Elle permettait de contrôler l'acte de l'Union par rapport à l'obligation internationale à laquelle il renvoie. Ensuite est venue la jurisprudence *Nakajima*[47], rendue dans le contexte analogue de la protection contre le dumping en provenance des pays tiers, laquelle visait initialement la possibilité d'invoquer la non-conformité d'un acte législatif de la Communauté par rapport au code antidumping du GATT, au motif que ledit acte a été adopté aux fins de « satisfaire aux obligations internationales de la Communauté »[48].

Depuis lors, ces deux possibilités ont été envisagées conjointement dans une formule unique, laquelle leur attribue un sens plus restrictif. S'agissant de l'exception *Fediol*, elle a été réduite par la Cour à la seule hypothèse d'un renvoi explicite à des dispositions précises d'un accord[49]. Il a été souligné en doctrine que cette obligation tenant au caractère explicite du renvoi tend à la priver d'utilité, en ce qu'elle implique une condition de formalisation dans l'acte de l'Union de l'intention du législateur d'appliquer une disposition particulière. Celui-ci pouvant, dès lors, « se dispenser d'indiquer qu'il met en œuvre une norme internationale pour éviter d'activer [l'invocabilité Fediol][50] ». Quant à la jurisprudence *Nakajima*, à la notion large de satisfaction des obligations internationales de la Communauté a été préférée celle plus restrictive « d'obligation particulière assumée » dans le cadre du GATT et de l'OMC. D'où l'utilisation de la for-

---

46 Arrêt de la Cour du 22 juin 1989, *Fediol/Commission*, 70/87, EU:C:1989:254, points 19 et s.

47 Arrêt de la Cour du 7 mai 1991, *Nakajima/Conseil*, C-69/89, EU:C:1991:186.

48 *Id.*, point 31.

49 Arrêt de la Cour du 23 novembre 1999, *Portugal/Conseil*, *supra* note 14 point 49.

50 F. Schmied, *Les effets des accords de l'OMC dans l'ordre juridique de l'Union – L'invocabilité au service de l'influence de l'Union sur la mondialisation du droit*, Paris, Institut Universitaire Varenne, 2013, p. 387.

mulation suivante en jurisprudence, laquelle a été qualifiée en doctrine d'invocabilité de mise en œuvre[51]: ce n'est que « dans l'hypothèse où l'Union a entendu donner exécution à une obligation particulière assumée dans ce cadre ou dans l'occurrence où l'acte de l'Union renvoie expressément à des dispositions précises de ces accords, il appartient à la Cour de contrôler la légalité de l'acte de l'Union en cause au regard de ces accords[52] ».

En dépit du caractère restrictif de cette invocabilité et de la circonstance qu'elle est née et a exclusivement été appliquée dans le seul contexte des accords du GATT puis de l'OMC, il est possible de la percevoir comme une modalité particulière de la prise en compte de la condition subjective d'invocabilité des engagements internationaux. L'existence d'un renvoi explicite à une norme d'un accord de l'OMC ou l'adoption d'une législation destinée à mettre en œuvre une obligation particulière au titre de ces accords constitue la manifestation – unilatérale et postérieure à la conclusion de ces accords – de l'intention de l'Union de leur permettre de produire des effets dans son ordre juridique. Cette dimension subjective de l'invocabilité de mise en œuvre se reflète dans la jurisprudence la plus récente de la Cour, laquelle se réfère à son égard à « la volonté du législateur de l'Union de limiter lui-même sa marge de manœuvre dans l'application des règles de l'OMC» [53]. En cela, dans l'appréciation du point de savoir si la violation d'une norme de l'OMC peut être alléguée à des fins de contrôle de légalité, l'invocabilité de mise en oeuvre semble remplir une fonction équivalente à celle dévolue à la recherche de l'intention des parties au travers de l'examen de la nature et de l'économie générale d'un engagement international.

Admettre que la jurisprudence *Fediol* et *Nakajima* permet de satisfaire la condition subjective d'invocabilité des accords de l'OMC, ne peut manquer de soulever l'interrogation portant sur la possibilité qu'elle remplisse la même fonction à l'égard de l'ensemble des engagements internationaux. Cela d'autant plus qu'existe un précédent en ce sens. En effet, c'est en se

---

51 J. F. Delile, *L'invocabilité des accords internationaux dans la CJUE et le Conseil d'État français, supra* note 13, p. 459.

52 Formule constante depuis l'arrêt du 23 novembre 1999, *Portugal/Conseil*, *supra* note 14, point 49.

53 Arrêt de la Cour du 16 juillet 2015, *Rusal Armenal*, C-21/14 P, EU:C:2015:494, point 40.

référant explicitement à *Nakajima* que la Cour a, dans son arrêt *Racke*[54], justifié la possibilité pour un requérant d'invoquer à son profit des règles du droit coutumier international à l'encontre d'un règlement « pris en application de ces règles[55] ». Un tel raisonnement pourrait, cependant, ne sembler plus de mise au regard de l'annulation par la Cour des deux arrêts par lequel le Tribunal avait étendu cette approche à l'invocabilité de la convention d'Aarhus (A). Néanmoins, s'il se déduit logiquement des arrêts de la Cour qu'à l'heure actuelle l'invocabilité de mise en œuvre est cantonnée aux seuls accords de l'OMC – voire au seul accord antidumping – il serait peut-être exagérée de conclure que l'hypothèse d'une extension de l'invocabilité de mise en œuvre à d'autres accords que ceux de l'OMC est définitivement écartée (B).

A. La tentative de généralisation de l'invocabilité de mise en œuvre à d'autres domaines que le droit de l'OMC

Dans ses arrêts *Stichting Natuur en Milieu*[56] et *Vereniging Milieudefensie*[57] le Tribunal avait conclu que l'article 10 du règlement n°1367/2006[58] mettait en œuvre l'article 9, paragraphe 3, de la convention d'Aarhus et en avait déduit par référence aux arrêts *Nakajima* et *Fediol*, que les requérantes étaient en droit de soulever l'absence de conformité de l'article 10 du règlement avec l'article 9, paragraphe 3, de la convention d'Aarhus. Considérant qu'il existait une contrariété entre ces deux normes, il a fait droit aux exceptions d'illégalité présentées à l'encontre dudit article 10.

Le Tribunal a suivi, essentiellement, un raisonnement en deux étapes.

D'une part, il a généralisé l'invocabilité de mise en œuvre à la convention d'Aarhus en présentant son application dans le cadre du droit de l'OMC comme une simple illustration de cette forme particulière d'invo-

---

54 Arrêt de la Cour du 16 juin 1998, *Racke*, C-162/96, EU:C:1998:293.

55 *Id.*, point 48.

56 Arrêt du Tribunal du 14 juin 2012, *Stichting Natuur*, T-338/08, EU:T:2012:300.

57 Arrêt du Tribunal du 14 juin 2012, *Vereniging Milieudefensie*, T-396/09, EU:T:2012:301.

58 Règlement n° 1367/2006/CE du Parlement européen et du Conseil, du 6 septembre 2006, concernant l'application aux institutions et organes de la Communauté européenne des dispositions de la convention d'Aarhus sur l'accès à l'information, la participation du public au processus décisionnel et l'accès à la justice en matière d'environnement, *JO* L 264 du 25 septembre 2006, p. 13.

cabilité. À cet égard, il a mis en exergue un faisceau d'indices relevant l'intention du législateur de satisfaire aux obligations internationales de l'Union qui découlent de l'article 9, paragraphe 3, de la convention d'Aarhus en adoptant le règlement n° 1367/2006. Il ressort, ainsi, de l'article 1er, paragraphe 1, sous d), du règlement nº 1367/2006 qu'il a pour objet de contribuer à l'exécution des obligations découlant de la convention d'Aarhus en garantissant notamment l'accès à la justice en matière d'environnement au niveau de l'Union, dans les conditions prévues par le présent règlement. De même, le considérant 18 du règlement n° 1367/2006 se réfère expressément à l'article 9, paragraphe 3, de la convention d'Aarhus. Enfin, la Cour elle-même avait observé dans son arrêt *Lesoochranárske zoskupenie* que le règlement nº 1367/2006 a pour objet de mettre en œuvre les stipulations de l'article 9, paragraphe 3, de la convention d'Aarhus en ce qui concerne les institutions de l'Union[59].

D'autre part, il en a tiré la conclusion que le juge de l'Union devait pouvoir procéder au contrôle de la conformité de l'article 10, paragraphe 1, du règlement nº 1367/2006 avec l'article 9, paragraphe 3, de la convention d'Aarhus, sans vérifier au préalable si la nature et l'économie de la convention ne s'y opposent pas, et sans qu'il soit nécessaire d'examiner si la disposition alléguée apparaît, du point de vue de son contenu, inconditionnelle et suffisamment précise[60]. Cette seconde étape du raisonnement est intéressante en ce que l'invocabilité de mise en œuvre est interprétée par le Tribunal non seulement comme autorisant le contrôle de légalité de l'acte de l'Union, mais également comme suffisante, c'est-à-dire sans qu'il soit nécessaire d'examiner si les conditions objectives d'invocabilité – tenant à la nature de la norme dont la violation est alléguée – sont remplies.

Ces deux arrêts ont été censurés par la Cour au titre d'une erreur de droit dans l'examen de l'invocabilité de l'article 9, paragraphe 3, de la convention d'Aarhus. Suivant en cela les conclusions de son Avocat général et l'argumentation développée tant par le Parlement européen, le Conseil que la Commission, la Cour a retenu dans ses arrêts *Conseil e.a./*

---

59 Arrêt de la Cour du 8 mars 2011, *Lesoochranárske zoskupenie*, C-240/09, EU:C:2011:125, points 39 et 41.

60 Arrêt du Tribunal du 14 juin 2012, *Stichting Natuur*, *supra* note 56, points 53 et 54; arrêt du Tribunal du 14 juin 2012, *Vereniging Milieudefensie*, *supra* note 57, points 53 et 54.

Vereniging Milieudefensie et Stichting Stop Luchtverontreiniging[61] et *Conseil et Commission/Stichting Natuur en Milieu et Pesticide Action Network Europe*[62] (ci-après les arrêts du 13 janvier 2015) que « ces deux exceptions [Fediol et Nakajima] n'ont été justifiées que par les particularités des accords ayant donné lieu à leur application, à savoir le GATT et l'accord antidumping conclu en application de ce même GATT» [63].

B. Une invocabilité de mise en œuvre applicable aux seuls accords de l'OMC?

Doit-on cependant en conclure que le débat sur l'étendue du champ d'application de l'invocabilité de mise en œuvre est clos? Une réponse entièrement affirmative ne nous apparaît pas certaine. Deux éléments militent en faveur du maintien d'une certaine circonspection à cet égard.

Le premier élément tient dans le soin apporté par la Cour à l'explicitation, non seulement des particularités du droit de l'OMC, mais également des raisons pour lesquelles lesdites particularités ne se retrouvent pas à l'égard de la convention d'Aarhus. Plutôt que d'exclure par principe la possibilité de se prévaloir de ces exceptions en dehors du champ des règles de l'OMC, ce raisonnement pourrait être considéré comme posant des conditions, certes strictes, mais disposant d'une portée générale, pour que l'invocabilité de mise en œuvre trouve à s'appliquer.

S'agissant plus particulièrement de la jurisprudence *Nakajima*, au nombre des spécificités de l'accord antidumping soulignées par la Cour figurent, d'une part, la mise en exergue du caractère très dense du système antidumping de l'OMC « dans sa conception et son application, dans le sens qu'il prévoit des mesures à l'égard des entreprises accusées de recourir à des pratiques de dumping»[64] et, d'autre part, la circonstance que, au titre de l'article 9, paragraphe 3, de la convention d'Aarhus, les parties

61 *Supra* note 8.

62 Arrêt de la Cour du 13 janvier 2015, *Stichting Natuur*, C-404/12 P et C-405/12 P, EU:C:2015:5.

63 Arrêt de la Cour du 13 janvier 2015, *Vereniging Milieudefensie, supra* note 8, point 57; Arrêt de la Cour du 13 janvier 2015, *Stichting Natuur*, *supra* note 62, point 49.

64 Arrêt de la Cour du 13 janvier 2015, *Vereniging Milieudefensie, supra* note 8, point 59; Arrêt de la Cour du 13 janvier 2015, *Stichting Natuur*, *supra* note 62, point 51.

contractantes disposent d'une large marge d'appréciation quant à la définition des modalités de mise en œuvre des procédures administratives ou judiciaires[65].

Derrière cette explicitation pourraient apparaître deux critères de l'invocabilité d'exclusion, lesquels ne se retrouvaient pas à l'égard de la convention d'Aarhus[66].

Le premier critère n'apparaît pas clairement dans le raisonnement de la Cour et son existence est incertaine. On pourrait néanmoins considérer qu'une distinction est réalisée entre la mise en œuvre d'un accord privant les particuliers d'un droit et ayant ainsi une incidence négative avérée sur leur patrimoine juridique (tel l'imposition de droits antidumping) et une convention seulement susceptible de leur conférer un potentiel droit (celui d'engager des procédures judiciaires ou d'autres procédures de recours pour contester les actes ou omissions de particuliers ou d'autorités publiques allant à l'encontre du droit de l'environnement en application de l'article 9, paragraphe 3, de la convention d'Aarhus). Si l'intention de la Cour était de mettre en avant un tel critère, celui-di apparaîtrait, effectivement, pertinent dans la mesure où la teneur des effets sur les particuliers n'est pas la même dans les deux hypothèses, ce qui peut justifier des modalités d'invocabilité différentes.

Le second critère transparaît de manière plus évidente. Il repose dans une conception stricte de la notion de mise en œuvre, laquelle ne se retrouve pas à l'égard de l'article 9, paragraphe 3, de la convention d'Aarhus dès lors que les parties contractantes disposent d'une large marge d'appréciation quant à la définition des modalités de mise en œuvre des procédures administratives ou judiciaires. En d'autres termes, il n'est pas suffisant que le règlement n° 1367/2006 ait été adopté au visa de la convention d'Aarhus ou même qu'un lien indéniable existe entre son article 10, paragraphe 1, et l'article 9, paragraphe 3, de cette convention pour qu'il y ait

---

65 *Ibidem.*

66 Il convient de souligner qu'au point 52 de l'arrêt de la Cour du 13 janvier 2015, *Stichting Natuur*, *supra* note 62, et au point 60 de l'arrêt de la Cour du 13 janvier 2015, *Vereniging Milieudefensie, supra* note 8, la Cour met en exergue une autre condition, propre à l'invocabilité des accords mixtes et sortant du cadre de cette étude, portant sur la nécessaire mise en œuvre de l'engagement international dans un domaine de compétence de l'Union. Pour une analyse de cette condition v. J. F. Delile, « L'invocabilité des accords internationaux devant le juge de la légalité des actes de l'Union européenne », *supra* note 5, p. 175 et s.

mise en œuvre. Encore faut-il que cette mise en œuvre constitue l'exercice de ce qui s'apparenterait à une compétence liée.

Ce second critère se rapproche, dès lors, des conditions objectives de l'invocabilité d'une norme d'un engagement international impliquant son caractère précis et inconditionnel. La mise en exergue de ce critère apparaît assez conforme à l'idée selon laquelle l'invocabilité de mise en œuvre, en ce qu'elle manifeste l'intention de légiférer conformément à un engagement international, est seulement susceptible de démontrer que la condition subjective de l'invocabilité est satisfaite. Toutefois, ledit critère ne préjuge pas du point de savoir si les conditions objectives de ladite invocabilité sont remplies.

Or s'agissant de la convention d'Aarhus, la Cour avait déjà relevé dans son arrêt *Lesoochranárske zoskupenie*[67] que l'article 9, paragraphe 3, de la convention d'Aarhus était dépourvu d'effet direct au motif qu'il ne contenait aucune obligation inconditionnelle et suffisamment précise de nature à régir directement la situation juridique des particuliers. Il est, à cet égard, assez révélateur que si le Tribunal a considéré cette absence d'effet direct comme étant non pertinente, la Cour l'a rappelée de manière liminaire dans ses arrêts du 13 janvier 2015[68].

La portée générale de ce second critère, tenant dans une conception stricte du lien devant exister entre l'acte de l'Union et la norme internationale semble également ressortir de son application au détriment de l'invocabilité d'autre règles de l'OMC, voire dans le domaine d'élection de la jurisprudence *Nakajima*, à savoir le contentieux des mesures antidumping. En d'autres termes, il ne semble pas y avoir deux appréciations différentes de ce lien, l'une plus généreuse à l'égard des normes de l'OMC, l'autre moins favorable à l'égard des autres engagements internationaux.

D'une part, dans son arrêt *Van Parys II*[69], rendu seulement un mois avant les arrêts du 13 janvier 2015, la Cour avait déjà qualifié d'exceptionnelle l'invocabilité de mise en œuvre et avait refusé son application aux circonstances de l'espèce relevant, pourtant, du contexte du droit de l'OMC. En l'espèce, était invoquée la non-conformité des règles régissant

67 Arrêt de la Cour du 8 mars 2011, *Lesoochranárske zoskupenie, supra* note 59, points 41 à 47.

68 Arrêt de la Cour du 13 janvier 2015, *Vereniging Milieudefensie, supra* note 8, point 47; Arrêt de la Cour du 13 janvier 2015, *Stichting Natuur*, *supra* note 62, point 55.

69 Arrêt de la Cour du 18 décembre 2014, *LVP*, C-306/13, EU:C:2014:2465.

l'organisation commune de marché de la banane avec les règles de l'OMC, au motif que « l'Union n'a pas entendu assurer l'exécution dans l'ordre juridique de l'Union d'une obligation particulière assumée dans le cadre de l'OMC, susceptible de justifier une exception à l'impossibilité d'invoquer des règles de l'OMC devant le juge de l'Union et de permettre l'exercice par ce dernier du contrôle de la légalité des dispositions de l'Union en cause au regard de ces règles» [70].

D'autre part, la Cour, dans le domaine d'élection de la jurisprudence *Nakajima,* a, par son arrêt *Comission/Rusal Armenal,*[71] annulé l'arrêt du Tribunal ayant fait application de l'invocabilité de mise en œuvre pour faire droit à une exception d'illégalité avancée à l'encontre de l'article 2, paragraphe 7, du règlement n°384/96. Cette disposition serait contraire à l'accord antidumping de l'OMC, en ce qu'il maintenait l'Arménie parmi les pays ne disposant pas d'une économie de marché. La Cour a souligné qu'il ne suffisait pas que les considérants de l'acte de l'Union en cause fassent ressortir de manière générale que l'adoption de celui-ci est intervenue en tenant compte d'obligations internationales de l'Union, mais que l'on puisse déduire de la disposition spécifique du droit de l'Union contestée que celle-ci vise à mettre en œuvre en droit de l'Union une obligation particulière résultant des accords OMC. Or, pour la Cour, l'article 2, paragraphe 7, du règlement n°384/96, introduit un régime spécial établissant des règles détaillées en ce qui concerne le calcul de la valeur normale à l'égard des importations en provenance de pays de l'OMC n'ayant pas une économie de marché, dont l'Arménie, et constitue l'expression de la volonté du législateur de l'Union d'adopter, dans ce domaine, une approche propre à l'ordre juridique de l'Union[72]. Partant, dans la mesure où l'accord antidumping ne contient pas de règles spécifiques relatives aux importations en provenance des pays membres de l'OMC dépourvus d'une économie de marché, il ne pouvait être établi de correspondance entre les règles qui figurent à l'article 2, paragraphe 7, du règlement n°384/96 visant les importations en provenance des pays membres de l'OMC dépourvus d'une économie de marché et les règles définies à l'article 2 de l'accord antidumping. La Cour en a déduit que ladite disposition du règlement de base ne saurait être considérée comme une mesure destinée à as-

---

70 *Id.,* point 50.

71 Arrêt de la Cour du 16 juillet 2015, *Commission/Rusal Armenal*, C-21/14 P, EU:C:2015:494.

72 *Id.,* points 47 et 48.

surer dans l'ordre juridique de l'Union l'exécution d'une obligation particulière assumée dans le cadre de l'OMC[73].

Cela démontre une appréciation d'autant plus stricte du lien d'exécution devant exister entre l'acte de l'Union et l'obligation internationale mise en oeuvre, que dans l'arrêt annulé, le Tribunal ne s'était pas contenté de considérer que le règlement n°384/96 avait été adopté en vue de mettre en œuvre les obligations de l'Union au titre du droit de l'OMC. Il avait également relevé que ledit règlement comportait «un ensemble de règles claires, précises et détaillées établissant les modalités de calcul de la valeur normale du produit similaire [...] sans les assortir de conditions laissant leur application à la discrétion des membres de l'OMC » et que « la possibilité de déroger à ces règles sur le fondement de la deuxième disposition additionnelle au paragraphe 1 de l'article VI du GATT, à laquelle renvoie l'article 2.7 de l'accord antidumping, [était] circonscrite avec précision» [74].

Le second élément justifiant le maintien d'une certaine prudence quant à la portée exacte des arrêts du 13 janvier 2015, tient dans le raisonnement suivi par la Cour dans son arrêt *ClientEarth/Commission*[75] qui leur est postérieur. Dans le cadre de leur pourvoi, les requérantes reprochaient au Tribunal de ne pas avoir fait application de la jurisprudence *Nakajima* et *Fediol* aux fins de contrôler la conformité de l'article 4, paragraphe 2, troisième tiret, du règlement n° 1049/2001 avec l'article 4, paragraphes 1 et 4, de la convention d'Aarhus. Plutôt que de simplement souligner que ces arrêts n'étaient pas applicables en dehors du champ d'application du droit de l'OMC, la Cour a préféré privilégier la motivation suivante : « sans qu'il soit besoin de se prononcer sur la question de savoir si la jurisprudence [Fediol et Nakajima] est applicable en l'espèce, il suffit de constater que le règlement n° 1049/2001, en particulier son article 4, paragraphe 2, troisième tiret, n'opère aucun renvoi exprès à la convention d'Aarhus ni ne donne exécution à une obligation particulière découlant de celle-ci. Par conséquent, ladite jurisprudence n'est, en tout état de cause, pas pertinente pour la présente affaire »[76].

---

73 *Id.*, points 49 à 53.

74 Arrêt du Tribunal du 5 novembre 2013, *Rusal Armenal/Conseil*, T-512/09, EU:T:2013:571, point 50.

75 Arrêt de la Cour du 16 juillet 2015, *ClientEarth/Commission*, C-612/13 P, EU:C:2015:486.

76 *Id.*, point 37.

Cette motivation est un exemple topique de la technique rédactionnelle qualifiée « d'économie des motifs » ou de « motivation économique », en ce qu'elle consiste à rejeter un argument, non pas en se fondant sur l'examen de la condition d'application qui doit être examiné en premier dans l'ordre logique d'application d'une disposition, mais au regard de la condition dont le défaut est le plus apparent. Il s'agit, d'une certaine manière, d'une stratégie d'évitement d'une question juridique.

Or, il apparait évident que, dans l'éventualité où les arrêts du 13 janvier 2015 auraient dû être considérés comme clôturant définitivement la question du champ d'application de l'invocabilité de mise en œuvre, la logique eut voulu que l'argument des requérants soit rejeté au motif que les arrêts *Nakajima* et *Fediol* ne valent qu'à l'égard des accords conclus dans le cadre de l'OMC. Toutefois la Cour a préféré se fonder sur la circonstance que les conditions de cette jurisprudence ne sont pas remplies en l'espèce, tout en utilisant des précautions d'écriture pour éviter que son arrêt soit interprété *a contrario* comme impliquant une acceptation de l'extension du champ d'application de ladite jurisprudence. Il y a là, à notre sens, la manifestation d'une volonté d'éviter d'avoir à se prononcer sur cette question.

La conjonction de la mise en exergue de conditions de manière abstraite dans les arrêts du 13 janvier 2015 et d'un certain flou entretenu par la Cour sur la question du champ d'application de l'invocabilité de mise en œuvre, nous semble ainsi justifier le maintien d'une certaine prudence à l'égard de toute conclusion définitive quant à l'impossibilité d'en faire usage en dehors du champ d'application des accords de l'OMC, prudence équivalente à celle qu'il convient d'avoir s'agissant du point de savoir si la condition de réciprocité ne vaut que pour ces accords. C'est, certes, le reflet de l'état actuel de la jurisprudence. Néanmoins, il demeure que les conditions avancées par la Cour conservent un caractère général les rendant susceptibles de s'appliquer, éventuellement, à d'autres engagements internationaux, soit au détriment de la production d'effets dans l'ordre juridique de l'Union (condition de réciprocité), soit en sa faveur (invocabilité de mise en œuvre).

Réflexions sur la démocratisation des relations extérieures à l'aune du contentieux de l'accès aux documents / Reflections on the Democratisation of External Relations in the Light of the Case Law on Access to Documents

Hugo Flavier

Abstract

The limited transparency of public authorities' actions in the field of foreign policy has long been anchored in political and legal practice. The reasons for the hostility to transparency can be found both in political philosophy and in the requirements of protecting the secrecy of international relations. This tradition of secrecy, however, today constitutes an obstacle for democracy, an ideal closely linked to the principle of transparency. These difficulties of articulation of secrecy and transparency are particularly significant for the European Union. On the one hand, the strengthening of transparency has been conceived as a means for compensating for the EU's lack of legitimacy. On the other hand, the fact that the EU was built on law rather than on the idea of power probably contributed to the development of this requirement of transparency. A European Union that wishes – or claims – to be to a certain extent exemplary cannot ignore the demands of transparency.

This ambition of transparency, which carries with it quite laudable objectives, meets with some obstacles. In the specific field of external relations, secrecy is an attribute of power. In the relations between subjects of international law, secrecy and the possession of information constitute fundamental strategic weapons. It is clear that in recent years the European Union no longer hesitates to consider itself – and act – as a power. The logics of power, transparency and democracy can collide, and this conciliation of opposites is apparent in the context of litigation of access to documents in the field of external relations.

The purpose of this article is to assess the degree of democratization of external relations, through a systematic analysis of the jurisprudence of the Court of Justice on access to documents, in order to examine to what extent this access is desirable and possible. This study suggests that the judicialisation of external relations has made it possible to strengthen the democratization of the Union, from an institutional perspective, by favouring Parliament's access to information. In so doing, the Court has indirectly enriched the Union's "political law". This democratization, determined by the case–law, has also been perceptible in a dimension of the rule of law that directly affects individuals: the jurisdictional guarantees offered during litigation on restrictive measures. Despite some progress in these two dimensions of litigation over access to documents, the reflections on the democratization of external relations lead to rather pessimistic conclusions, since mistrust seems to remain the keyword in the field of access to documents.

***

La transparence de l'action publique et à travers elle, de l'action des gouvernants, est un élément indissociable de la conquête démocratique. Cette transparence a ainsi innervé l'ensemble des pouvoirs d'État, particulièrement s'agissant du législatif et de l'exécutif. Certes, l'ouverture de ces pouvoirs aux citoyens ne s'est pas généralisée *ab initio*. Elle s'est faite de manière incrémentale en commençant par le pouvoir législatif, lieu des débats par excellence, de la controverse et de la discussion politiques[1]. Elle s'est également diffusée grâce au renforcement de l'obligation de transparence de l'exécutif même si, force est de reconnaître que cet acquis ne fut obtenu qu'à la suite d'une lente transformation (inachevée) de son action, de son rapport aux citoyens et de sa soumission au droit[2]. En particulier, il est des domaines pour lesquelles cette quête de transparence – et l'on pourrait parfois parler de dogme de la transparence[3] – ne s'est développée que partiellement. À cet égard, le domaine des relations extérieures fait figure d'archétype.

L'idée selon laquelle les relations extérieures seraient un domaine qui devrait par nature échapper au contrôle et à la vigilance des citoyens est une idée ancienne. Dès le XVIIe et le XVIIIe siècle, la philosophie politique européenne construisit un cadre théorique justifiant et expliquant cet

1 S. Milacic, *De l'âge idéologique à l'âge politique. L'Europe postcommuniste vers la démocratie pluraliste*, Bruxelles, Bruylant, 2010.

2 J. Chevallier, *L'Etat post-moderne*, Tome 35, 4e éd., Paris, LGDJ-Lextenso, 2014.

3 G. Carcassonne, « Le trouble de la transparence », *Pouvoirs,* vol. 97, n° 2/2001, p. 17.

encadrement de la démocratie. On se limitera ici à citer J. J. Rousseau qui estimait ainsi que « l'exercice extérieur de la puissance ne convient point au peuple; les grandes maximes d'État ne sont pas à sa portée; il doit s'en rapporter là-dessus à ses chefs, qui, toujours plus éclairés que lui sur ce point, n'ont guère intérêt à faire au dehors des traités désavantageux à la patrie »[4]. Outre l'argument relatif à l'incompétence naturelle des citoyens, celui tenant à la nécessité de préserver un certain secret autour des relations extérieures est généralement invoqué. Cette exigence du secret trouve de nombreuses justifications : la protection des sources d'informations obtenues potentiellement par les services de renseignement nationaux, la tactique de négociation choisie ou l'exigence d'unité pour consolider la position nationale, etc. Ces contraintes, unanimement partagées, vont directement à l'encontre des nécessités démocratiques et se retrouvent au sein de l'Union européenne.

La demande de transparence n'a cependant cessé de croître et, dans l'Union européenne, celle-ci a été particulièrement significative, peut-être plus que dans certains États comme la France. D'une part, le renforcement de la transparence a été conçu comme un moyen de compenser le déficit de légitimité de l'Union. La légitimité de l'Union ne pouvant venir de l'histoire (la construction européenne étant trop récente), et les élections au Parlement européen n'étant pas perçues (à tort ou à raison) comme conférant une véritable légitimité, la transparence a constitué l'un des leviers d'action. D'autre part, le fait que l'Union européenne se soit construite sur le droit plus que sur l'idée de puissance a probablement contribué au développement de cette exigence de transparence. Il faudra pourtant attendre le traité de Maastricht et sa Déclaration n°17, pour que les États membres reconnaissent « que la transparence du processus décisionnel renforce le caractère démocratique des institutions, ainsi que la confi-

4 J.-J. Rousseau, *Du Contrat social*, Paris, Félix Alcan, 1896, p. 50. Cette spécificité des relations extérieures, de ce qui relève des « affaires du dehors » est tout à fait classique. Tel est cas de Hobbes, *Le Léviathan*, notes de F. Tricaud, Paris, Sirey, 1983, spécialement chap. XIII, « De la condition naturelle des hommes en ce qui concerne leur félicité et leur misère », et notamment p. 124; Spinoza, *Traité politique*, Paris, Librairie philosophique J. Vrin, coll. Bibliothèque des textes philosophiques, 1968, chap. III, § XI; Kant, *Projet de paix perpétuelle*, Paris, Librairie philosophique J. Vrin, coll. Bibliothèque des textes philosophiques, édition bilingue, 2002, deuxième section; Hegel, *Principes de la philosophie du droit*, Paris, Gallimard, coll. Tel, 1989, n° 333; R. Aron, *Paix et guerre entre les nations*, Paris, Calmann-Lévy, 1984, p. 19.

ance du public envers l'administration »[5]. Cette affirmation, qui prolonge des réflexions engagées au sein du Conseil de l'Europe[6], insiste sur l'une des caractéristiques fondamentales de la transparence de l'action publique : faire en sorte que l'action des pouvoirs publics, quel qu'en soit l'objet, quelle qu'en soit l'administration, agisse de manière ouverte et publique. Il s'agit en quelque sorte d'un principe de bienveillance administrative qui ne trouve pas sa finalité en lui-même, mais en-dehors, et vise à rehausser la qualité démocratique d'une société politique. Ce principe, ou plutôt cette exigence de transparence, se concrétise pour l'essentiel par deux droits, indissociables : l'accès aux documents administratifs et la motivation des décisions administratives. Ces deux droits, que la Charte des droits fondamentaux rattache au principe – plus large – de bonne administration[7], donnent ainsi une substance à l'exigence générale de transparence, exigence à laquelle le traité de Lisbonne se réfère à de nombreuses reprises, et en particulier en son article 15 du Traité sur le Fonctionnement de l'Union européenne (TFUE) et indirectement par l'article 298 TFUE[8].

Outre ces références conventionnelles à la transparence[9], de nombreux actes se sont employés à la renforcer au cours de ces dernières années dans le domaine des relations extérieures, suite à une pression continue du Parlement européen. De nombreux accords interinstitutionnels ont ainsi été conclus. Il s'agit par exemple de l'accord-cadre du 4 octobre 2010 dans lequel le Parlement européen a obtenu que la Commission l'informe, en continu, du déroulement et des négociations, en sachant que ces informa-

---

5 Exigence réaffirmée par la Déclaration n°41 annexée au traité d'Amsterdam.

6 V. la recommandation n° R (81) 19 du Comité des Ministres du Conseil de l'Europe sur l'accès à l'information détenue par les autorités publiques adoptée le 25 novembre 1981. Celle-ci a été enrichie par Recommandation Rec (2002)2 du Comité des Ministres sur l'accès aux documents publics, adoptée le 21 février 2002.

7 A ce sujet, v. E. Chevalier, *Bonne administration et Union européenne. Contribution à l'étude de l'espace administratif européen*, Thèse, Université de Limoges, 2010.

8 De même, v. l'article 11, paragraphe 2, TUE : « les institutions entretiennent un dialogue ouvert, transparent et régulier avec les associations représentatives et la société civile ». Et le paragraphe 3 d'ajouter : « en vue d'assurer la cohérence et la transparence des actions de l'Union, la Commission européenne procède à de larges consultations des parties concernées ».

9 Auxquelles on peut ajouter l'article 218, paragraphe 10, TFUE selon lequel « le Parlement européen est immédiatement et pleinement informé à toutes les étapes de la procédure » de conclusion des accords internationaux.

tions devaient couvrir « le projet de directives de négociation, les directives de négociation adoptées ainsi que le déroulement et la conclusion des négociations ». De même, a-t-il conclu avec le Conseil, le 12 mars 2014, un accord « relatif à la transmission au Parlement européen et au traitement par celui-ci des informations classifiées détenues par le Conseil concernant des questions autres que celles relevant de la politique étrangère et de sécurité commune ». Ce dernier organise de façon minutieuse les conditions dans lesquelles les députés auront accès aux informations classifiées, y compris les directives de négociation (art. 1er). Cet accord, concrétisant le devoir de coopération loyale, affermit, si besoin en était, l'importance que le Parlement attache à la transparence des relations extérieures, en tant qu'elle constitue le « fondement de la démocratie et une condition indispensable à son exercice »[10]. Enfin, le Parlement a conclu, le 20 novembre 2002, un accord avec le Conseil relatif à l'accès du Parlement européen à des informations sensibles du Conseil dans le domaine de la politique de sécurité et de défense. Le Parlement mettait d'ailleurs en avant l'argument du droit comparé selon lequel « dans la plupart des États membres, il existe des mécanismes spécifiques pour la transmission et le traitement d'informations classifiées entre les gouvernements et les parlements nationaux » et que l'accord en question « devrait assurer au Parlement européen un traitement s'inspirant des meilleures pratiques en vigueur dans les États membres ». Cette demande se retrouve également dans le Règlement du Parlement de 2004[11] et dans l'accord-cadre conclu avec la Commission en 2010[12].

---

10 Décision du Parlement du 13 sept. 2012 sur la conclusion de cet accord interinstitutionnel, P7_TA(2012)0339. Sur le principe de coopération loyale, v. E. Neframi, « The Duty of Loyalty: Rethinking its Scope through its Application in the Field of EU External Relations », *Common Market Law Review,* vol. 47 n°2/2010, p. 323.

11 Article 89.

12 Il prévoit, au point 9, que « dans les domaines de la politique étrangère et de sécurité commune, de la coopération policière et de la coopération judiciaire en matière pénale, la Commission prend des mesures propres à améliorer la participation du Parlement, de manière à tenir compte des vues de celui-ci dans la mesure du possible ». À propos de cet accord-cadre, v. C. Rapoport, « Aménager les procédures ou s'arranger avec les procédures? À propos du nouvel accord-cadre Parlement européen-Commission », *Revue du marché commun et de l'Union Européenne*, n° 550/2011, p. 461.

La référence principale en matière d'accès aux documents des institutions demeure toutefois le règlement n° 1049/2001 relatif à l'accès du public aux documents du Parlement européen, du Conseil et de la Commission[13]. Son importance tient non seulement au fait qu'il contient des obligations générales à l'égard de l'ensemble des institutions, mais aussi qu'il est régulièrement invoqué devant la Cour de justice et fait l'objet d'une pratique contentieuse suffisamment abondante pour donner un aperçu des enjeux de la transparence en matière de relations extérieures. Son importance tient aussi au fait qu'il est le témoignage d'une époque, celle de la juridictionnalisation grandissante des relations extérieures. Le temps où ce qui relevait de la *high politics* ne pouvait qu'être réglé dans les couloirs des chancelleries ou sur une décision du Prince a bel et bien disparu. Désormais, la justice est mise au concours du fonctionnement des relations extérieures et les acteurs n'hésitent pas à s'en servir pour défendre judiciairement soit des positions politiques, soit tout simplement la défense de droits qu'ils estiment bafoués. Cette montée en puissance du contentieux de l'accès aux documents en matière de relations extérieures est le résultat d'une augmentation des recours dans deux catégories de contentieux bien distinctes. En premier lieu, une partie des recours a pour origine des demandes du Parlement européen ou de ses membres qui, n'ayant pu obtenir politiquement satisfaction à ses demandes d'accès, tentent de faire défendre judiciairement certaines positions politiques[14]. Le Parlement européen part du principe, et on peut le comprendre, qu'une démocratie vivante est une démocratie informée et en mesure de prendre des décisions, y compris lorsque les relations internationales de l'Union sont en cause. Ainsi, le Parlement considère qu'il ne peut utilement exercer ses missions de contrôle qu'à la seule condition qu'il soit correctement informé, ce qui implique mécaniquement un accès aux informations.

---

13 Règlement du Parlement et du Conseil n° 1049/2001/CE du 30 mai 2001 relatif à l'accès du public aux documents du Parlement européen, du Conseil et de la Commission, *JO* L 145 du 31 mai 2001, p. 43. À ce sujet, v. M. Maes, « L'accès du public aux documents des Institutions de la Communauté européenne : vers une révision du règlement (CE) 1049/2001 », *Revue du droit de l'Union Européenne,* n° 2/2007, p. 411; P.-A. Feral, « L'accès du public aux documents des institutions communautaires : la consécration d'un droit fondamental de l'Union européenne », *Europe,* n° 7 /2001, p. 5.

14 A ce sujet, v. H. Flavier, « Parlement européen et relations extérieures : une révolution démocratique en marche? », *Revue trimestrielle de droit europeen*, volume 52, n° 2/2016, p. 293.

En ce sens, les batailles juridiques qui ont lieu entre le Parlement d'un côté, et la Commission et le Conseil de l'autre, sont le signe d'une construction et d'une consolidation d'un droit politique de l'Union, entendu comme « le droit de l'organisation et de l'institutionnalisation des processus politiques »[15]. Si l'on considère que l'accès à l'information des parlementaires est une condition essentielle à l'épanouissement d'une démocratie vivante, alors il faut considérer que le contentieux de l'accès aux documents vise non seulement à démocratiser les relations extérieures mais aussi à renforcer la place du Parlement dans ce domaine si particulier d'où il a longtemps été écarté.

Mais ce contentieux de l'accès aux documents ne se résume pas à cette lutte constitutionnelle entre le Parlement et les deux autres branches du triangle institutionnel et à la communication aux citoyens de certains documents. Il se prolonge donc, en second lieu, dans le cadre plus subjectif de la défense des droits fondamentaux et, plus précisément, dans celui du contentieux des mesures restrictives. L'accès aux documents est devenu l'un des principaux enjeux contentieux depuis que l'Union européenne a systématisé le recours aux sanctions et a fait des contre-mesures une véritable arme diplomatique. Ce contentieux est certes d'une nature différente de celui relatif à l'accès aux documents mais l'on remarque de forts points de convergence. Premièrement, les motifs invoqués pour refuser une communication de documents ou pour ne pas motiver la non-communication sont assez similaires : considérations diplomatiques, stratégiques, tradition du secret dans le domaine des relations internationales, etc. Deuxièmement, les actes invoqués peuvent être les mêmes. On remarque en effet, ces derniers temps, une tendance à l'invocation plus régulière du règlement n°1049/2001 dans le contentieux des mesures restrictives[16]. Troisièmement, dans les deux types de contentieux le lien entre l'accès aux documents et l'exigence – et la nécessité – de motivation est tout à fait similaire. Enfin, dans un cas comme dans l'autre, le développement du contentieux a permis de renforcer la nature démocratique de l'Union européenne en préservant les exigences d'un *due process* indissolublement lié à l'état de droit.

15 C. Gusy « Considérations sur le droit politique », *Jus Politicum*, n°1/2008, http://juspoliticum.com /article/Considerations-sur-le-droit-politique-26.html.

16 En dernier lieu, v. arrêt de la Cour du 28 mars 2017, *Rosneft Oil Company*, C-72/15, EU:C:2017:236.

Dit autrement, la juridictionnalisation des relations extérieures dont le contentieux de l'accès aux documents en est l'une des manifestations, a relevé le degré de démocratisation des relations extérieures dans sa dimension institutionnelle, en enrichissant indirectement le droit politique de l'Union européenne (I), et dans sa dimension subjective à travers les garanties juridictionnelles offertes à l'occasion de l'examen contentieux de mesures restrictives (II).

I. La dimension institutionnelle : un contentieux générateur d'un droit politique

Le contentieux de l'accès aux documents est un contentieux étroitement lié à la réalisation juridictionnelle de principes démocratiques. Qui plus est, il s'inscrit dans une stratégie politique de renforcement des prérogatives du Parlement, lui-même institution fondamentalement démocratique. Dès lors, le développement de ce contentieux doit être compris comme une pierre portée à l'édifice de la démocratisation des relations extérieures (A). On ne saurait cependant se cantonner à cette seule approche positive. Il est difficile en effet de ne pas s'interroger, aujourd'hui, sur le seuil optimal d'articulation entre cette exigence de transparence et l'ambition déterminée de l'Union à faire valoir son statut de puissance internationale (B).

A. L'accès aux documents, ferment d'une démocratisation des relations extérieures

Le contentieux de l'accès aux documents en matière de relations extérieures s'est concentré sur les documents afférents aux négociations internationales menées par la Commission et le Conseil. L'exclusion du pouvoir parlementaire en ce domaine est un grand classique[17]. Il aura fallu au Parlement européen une persévérance certaine et une action contentieuse fournie, fondée pour l'essentiel sur le règlement n° 1049/2001, pour que celui-ci obtienne, en partie seulement, satisfaction. Rappelons que ce règlement prévoit deux exceptions à la communication des docu-

17 V. H. Flavier, *La contribution des relations extérieures à la construction de l'ordre constitutionnel de l'Union européenne*, Bruxelles, Bruylant, collection droit de l'Union européenne, 2012.

ments qui peuvent se rapporter aux relations extérieures. D'une part, une série d'exceptions prévues à l'article 4, paragraphe 1, selon lequel « les institutions refusent l'accès à un document dans le cas où la divulgation porterait atteinte à la protection de l'intérêt public, en ce qui concerne [...] la sécurité publique, la défense et les affaires militaires, les relations internationale ». D'autre part, une exception tenant aux « avis juridiques » a également pu indirectement concerner les relations extérieures. Un refus de communication fondé sur l'appartenance des documents requis à la catégorie d'avis juridique, à la différence des précédentes, doit faire l'objet d'une justification plus rigoureuse de la part de l'institution sollicitée, puisqu'il ne vaut qu'à la seule condition « qu'un intérêt public supérieur ne justifie la divulgation du document visé » (article 4, paragraphe 2). On remarque ainsi que le règlement a laissé une liberté importante aux institutions dès lors que celles-ci considèrent que la divulgation du document pourrait porter atteintes aux relations extérieures. En toute logique, le juge de l'Union en a déduit qu'en ce domaine, les institutions disposaient d'une « large marge d'appréciation aux fins de déterminer si la divulgation de documents relevant des domaines couverts par lesdites exceptions est susceptible de porter atteinte à l'intérêt public »[18]. Partant, le contrôle du juge doit se limiter à l'erreur manifeste d'appréciation.

Le contentieux de l'accès aux documents a été en partie lancé, dans le domaine des relations extérieures, suite à l'activisme de la parlementaire Sophie In't Veld[19]. Dans une première affaire, il s'agissait d'un recours en annulation de la parlementaire contre une décision du Conseil n'autorisant

18 Arrêt de la Cour du 1er février 2007, *Sison*, C-266/05 P, EU:C:2007:75, point 34; Arrêt de la Cour du 3 juillet 2014, *Sophie In't Veld*, C-350/12 P, EU:C:2014:2039, point 63. En revanche, une fois qu'il est admis que le document demandé relève de l'exception considérée, l'institution en cause est dans l'obligation de refuser la communication dudit document (arrêt du Tribunal du 17 juin 1998, *Svenska Journalistförbundet*, T-174/95, EU:T:1998:127, point 111).

19 Ce n'est pas la première fois qu'un parlementaire européen saisit la Cour de justice : v. arrêt de la Cour du 6 décembre 2001, *Heidi Hautala,* C-353/99 P, EU:C:2001:392, à propos de la décision du Conseil refusant l'accès au rapport du groupe de travail « Exportations d'armes conventionnelles ». De façon générale, un certain nombre d'arrêts ont déjà abordé, au moins partiellement, cette question. On se rapportera notamment, aux arrêts suivants : arrêt de la Cour du 22 janvier 2004, *Olli Mattila,* C-353/01 P, EU:C:2004:42, à propos de l'accès à une série de documents relatifs aux relations UE/Russie mais ne concernant pas une négociation d'accord spécifique; arrêt du Tribunal du 25 avril 2007, *WWF European Policy Programme*, T-264/04, EU:T:2007:114, au sujet d'une demande d'accès aux

qu'un accès partiel à un avis du service juridique rédigé en vue de l'ouverture des négociations de l'accord SWIFT (Society for Worldwide Interbank Financial Telecommunication)[20]. Conscient des impératifs de la politique étrangère, le juge a estimé que ce domaine nécessitait « un degré de prudence tout particulier, eu égard notamment à la nature singulièrement sensible et essentielle de l'intérêt protégé »[21]. Il a ajouté toutefois que, dans une Union de droit, une certaine transparence était nécessaire afin « d'assurer une meilleure participation des citoyens au processus décisionnel, ainsi que de garantir une plus grande légitimité, efficacité et responsabilité de l'administration à l'égard des citoyens dans un système démocratique »[22]. La réponse de la Cour se devait de trouver un équilibre entre ces exigences contradictoires. En substance, confirmant la décision du Tribunal, elle a estimé que les particuliers pouvaient avoir accès aux bases juridiques envisagées pour la conclusion d'un accord, sur le fondement du règlement n°1049/2001, mais que cet accès ne leur permettait pas de prendre connaissance des directives de négociation ou du contenu spécifique de l'accord envisagé. La position de la Cour est constante, puisqu'elle confirme la position prise dans une autre affaire *In't Veld*, celle du 19 mars 2013 et tranchée par le Tribunal[23] où était en cause le traité ACTA (Accord commercial anti-contrefaçon/ Anti-Counterfeiting Trade Agreement) et pour lequel la Commission n'avait accédé qu'à certaines demandes de la requérante. Le Tribunal a donc conservé son hostilité de principe quant à la possibilité d'ouvrir l'accès au public aux directives de négociations. En particulier, le Tribunal a reconnu que la « divulgation des positions de l'Union dans les négociations [pouvait] permettre de connaître, indirectement, celles des autres parties aux négociations ». Or, « toute forme de négociation implique nécessairement un certain nombre de considérations tactiques de la part des négociateurs, et l'indispensable

---

documents traitant de la réunion du comité de l'article 133 consacrée aux suites de la conférence de Cancún; arrêt du Tribunal du 14 février 2012, *Allemagne / Commission*, T-59/09, EU:T:2012:75, à propos de l'opposition de l'Allemagne à la divulgation de ses propres documents par la Commission.

20 Arrêt du Tribunal du 4 mai 2012, *Sophie In't Veld*, T-529/09, EU:T:2012:215; arrêt de la Cour du 3 juillet 2014, *Sophie In't Veld*, *supra* note 18. V. également la résolution du Parlement européen du 17 septembre 2009 sur l'accord SWIFT (P7_TA(2009)0016), qui faisait état de ce refus au considérant D.

21 Arrêt du Tribunal du 4 mai 2012, *Sophie In't Veld*, *supra* note 20, point 24.

22 Considérant n°2 du règlement n° 1049/2001, *supra* note 13.

23 Arrêt du Tribunal du 19 mars 2013, *Sophie In't Veld*, T-301/10, EU:T:2013:135.

coopération entre les parties dépend, dans une large mesure, de l'existence d'un climat de confiance mutuelle ». C'est précisément au nom de cette confiance mutuelle entre partenaires de négociation, que le Tribunal a confirmé la légalité du refus d'accès aux documents dans lesquels transparaissait la position de l'Union.

En somme, les citoyens européens[24] – et donc les parlementaires – ne peuvent avoir accès qu'aux bases juridiques envisagées pour la conclusion d'un accord uniquement dans la mesure où cette communication ne leur permettrait pas de prendre connaissance des directives de négociation ou du contenu spécifique de l'accord envisagé[25]. Ce n'est donc que dans l'hypothèse où les directives de négociations ont déjà fait l'objet d'une communication aux partenaires que la divulgation des documents revient dans l'ordre du possible. En effet, il n'est plus possible, dans cette situation, de « justifier le risque d'atteinte à l'intérêt public en matière de relations internationales par le fait que la divulgation de cette directive affaiblirait la position de négociation de l'Union »[26].

Un refus d'accès qui serait fondé sur la protection des « relations internationales » de l'Union doit cependant être motivé. Pour chaque catégorie de document, les institutions, et tout particulièrement la Commission et le Conseil doivent préciser « les raisons spécifiques pour lesquelles [elles considèrent] que la divulgation des documents demandés tombe sous le coup d'une des exceptions »[27] et que le risque d'atteinte aux relations internationales doit être « raisonnablement prévisible et non purement hypothétique »[28] et de vérifier cela *in concreto*[29]. Enfin, les institutions doivent systématiquement vérifier si un accès partiel aux documents n'est pas envisageable. Cet accès partiel est d'ailleurs obligatoire « dans l'hypothèse où cette institution se limiterait à occulter les passages qui peuvent

---

24 Les bénéficiaires du droit d'accès sont, selon le règlement, constitués par « tout citoyen de l'Union et toute personne physique ou morale résidant ou ayant son siège dans un État membre » (article 2).

25 Arrêt de la Cour du 3 juillet 2014, *Sophie In't Veld*, *supra* note 20.

26 Arrêt du Tribunal du 12 septembre 2013, *Leonard Besselink*, T-331/11, EU:T:2013:419, point 58.

27 Arrêt du Tribunal du 17 juin 1998, *Svenska Journalistförbundet*, *supra* note 18, point 117.

28 Arrêt du Tribunal du 25 avril 2007, *WWF European Policy Programme*, *supra* note 19, point 41; arrêt du Tribunal du 12 septembre 2013, *Leonard Besselink*, *supra* note 26, point 103.

29 Arrêt de la Cour du 12 juin 2012, *IFAW*, C-135/11 P, EU:C:2012:376, point 73.

porter atteinte à l'intérêt public protégé »[30]. Et le juge contrôle, dans la limite de l'erreur manifeste d'appréciation, si les institutions lui fournissent les éléments de nature à apprécier si la divulgation des documents serait de nature à affecter l'intérêt public protégé, *i.e.* les relations internationales de l'Union, « ce qui permet d'exclure toute présomption qu'un débat rendu public concernant la base juridique correcte d'une telle décision puisse porter systématiquement une atteinte concrète et effective à l'intérêt public en ce qui concerne les relations internationales »[31].

Le contentieux de l'accès aux documents dans le domaine des relations extérieures, généré majoritairement par le Parlement européen ou ses membres, s'inscrit dans une stratégie classique du Parlement qui vise à faire valider par le juge une stratégie politique de conquête du pouvoir[32]. Cette démarche ne peut que susciter l'adhésion : comment ne pas laisser plus de place aux seules personnes dépositaires d'un mandat électif direct? Comment ne pas informer davantage ceux qui représentent la seule légitimité démocratique directe pour des questions qui engagent l'Union dans son ensemble à l'égard des tiers? Qui plus est, si l'on souhaite que le Parlement exerce effectivement la fonction de contrôle qui lui est échue par les traités, comment ne pas lui donner un accès véritable aux documents, et donc à l'information? En renforçant la position institutionnelle du Parlement dans le domaine des relations extérieures, la Cour a ainsi contribué à rééquilibrer le droit politique de l'Union au profit des représentants des peuples européens. Cette démarche du Parlement européen répond également à une aspiration populaire d'un meilleur contrôle des accords négociés et conclus par l'Union européenne. Cette aspiration n'est pas seulement le résultat d'une volonté de démocratiser les relations extérieures, mais elle est aussi la conséquence de ce que les accords internationaux d'aujourd'hui tendent à être de plus en plus des traités-lois et non des traités-contrats[33]. Dès lors, et eu égard à l'ambition renouvelée de

---

30 Arrêt du Tribunal du 25 avril 2007, *WWF European Policy Programme*, *supra* note 19, point 50.

31 Arrêt de la Cour du 3 juillet 2014, *Sophie In't Veld*, *supra* note 20, point 59.

32 A ce sujet, v., J.-C. Gautron, « Remarques sur une continuité. Le développement constitutionnel du Parlement européen », in *La Constitution et les valeurs : mélanges en l'honneur de Dmitri Georges Lavroff*, Paris: Dalloz, 2005, p. 171, spéc. p. 182 et s.

33 Si l'on considère que le Conseil agit en qualité de quasi-législateur dans le cas de traités-lois, l'accès aux documents apparaît ainsi d'autant plus impérieux. V. no-

ces accords[34], l'attente des citoyens en termes d'accès aux documents et à travers eux du Parlement justifient que ce dernier devienne également un colégislateur des accords internationaux, et qu'il ait donc accès aux informations nécessaires pour exercer cette mission.

Pourtant, malgré ces bons arguments et une avancée certaine dans l'ouverture et la démocratisation des relations extérieures, il est des forces qui restreignent encore cet accès. L'intérêt supérieur d'une puissance dans ses rapports stratégiques avec les tiers, ne commande-t-il pas de mettre un frein à un accès aux documents qui, en ce domaine, ne pourra jamais être entièrement débridé? Il est donc temps de se demander si une plus grande ouverture de l'accès aux documents ne risque pas de menacer la stratégie de puissance de l'Union européenne.

B. L'accès aux documents, une menace à la stratégie de puissance de l'Union européenne?

Poser une telle question au XXIe siècle pourrait paraître saugrenu. D'une part, les États européens ont globalement accepté le fait qu'aujourd'hui, la puissance publique devait être transparente ou du moins, s'efforcer de l'être. On sait désormais qu'il n'y a pas d'incompatibilité entre la transparence et l'action publique mais qu'au contraire, une logique d'*accountability* ne peut que renforcer l'efficacité de l'action administrative. D'autre part, à l'heure où en France l'on ne parle plus d'administrés ou d'usagers mais de citoyens administratifs, les canons démocratiques se sont étendus au cœur de l'activité administrative de l'État. Cette tendance est conforme à une logique démocratique et libérale pour des populations en demande

---

tamment, arrêt de la Cour du 13 octobre 2013, *Access Info Europe*, C-280/11 P, EU:C:2013:671 : « la Cour a également jugé que ces considérations sont, à l'évidence, d'une pertinence toute particulière lorsque le Conseil agit en sa qualité de législateur, ainsi qu'il résulte du considérant 6 du règlement n° 1049/2001, selon lequel un accès plus large aux documents doit être autorisé précisément dans un tel cas. La transparence à cet égard contribue à renforcer la démocratie en permettant aux citoyens de contrôler l'ensemble des informations qui ont constitué le fondement d'un acte législatif. En effet, la possibilité, pour les citoyens, de connaître les fondements des actions législatives est une condition de l'exercice effectif, par ces derniers, de leurs droits démocratiques » (point 33).

34 On pense notamment aux accords de libre-échange conclu par l'Union avec la Corée du Sud, le Canada ou Singapour.

d'horizontalité plus que de verticalité. Dès lors, évoquer l'accès aux documents comme une menace à la stratégie de puissance de l'Union devrait être considéré comme une remarque d'un autre temps.

Pourtant, dans le domaine des relations extérieures, l'accès aux documents demeure l'exception et le secret, le principe[35]. Ces exclusions ont reçu diverses justifications. La tendance « monarchique »[36] des relations extérieures, bien entendu. L'indispensable protection du renseignement national dont on ne dira jamais assez combien il se défie des institutions européennes considérées, à tort ou à raison, comme de véritables « passoires » et partant, des lieux qu'il est préférable d'éviter ou dont il faut se méfier. Dans un autre ordre d'idées, l'une des raisons à cette hostilité réside en l'idée selon laquelle les relations extérieures ont toujours eu un rapport, plus ou moins marqué, avec la *high politics* et donc au *hard power*. Ce *hard power* étant par lui-même lié au pouvoir de contrainte étatique et à la violence d'État, il porte en lui un certain tabou, quelque chose qui ne peut être revendiqué ni assumé. Quelque chose qui doit être tu. Enfin, et il s'agit sans doute du principal facteur explicatif aux réticences européennes à l'accès aux documents en matière de relations extérieures, la crédibilité internationale de l'Union dépend aussi de sa capacité à préserver certains secrets. Tel est le sens de la jurisprudence qui y voit le principal motif à la non-divulgation des directives de négociation. Communiquer certaines directives de négociation ou certains rapports sur les négociations, non seulement mettrait en péril la stratégie de l'Union à l'égard des tiers en en dévoilant les cartes, mais risquerait de dévoiler les positions des tiers eux-mêmes[37].

---

35 Sur ce constat, v., la résolution du Parlement européen du 11 mars 2014 sur l'accès du public aux documents, [P7_TA(2014)0203], point H. Dans cette même résolution, le Parlement européen s'inquiétait également « du recours fréquent à l'exception pour la protection des relations internationales comme motif de confidentialité des documents » (point 35).

36 E. Zoller, *Droit des relations extérieures*, Paris, PUF, Coll. Droit fondamental, 1992, p. 29.

37 Pour un cas typique, v. arrêt du Tribunal du 12 juillet 2001, *Olli Mattila*, T-204/99, EU:T:2001:190, point 63 : « il n'est pas contesté que les documents litigieux contiennent des informations sur la position de l'Union européenne dans le cadre de ses relations avec la Russie et l'Ukraine ainsi que dans les négociations à mener avec les États-Unis au sujet de l'Ukraine. Il convient dès lors de souligner que les documents auxquels un accès est demandé ont été établis dans un contexte de négociations internationales, dans lequel l'intérêt de l'Union européenne, envisagé sous

Cette crainte est, semble-t-il, en partie partagée par le juge, n'en déplaise et quoi qu'en dise le Parlement européen. La Cour de justice a effet réalisé un équilibre subtil où, tout en ouvrant un peu plus l'accès aux documents, il avalise globalement la position du Conseil et de la Commission. Certes, le juge de l'Union met en avant les principes démocratiques afin d'interpréter le règlement n°1049/2001[38]. De même, et conformément à une interprétation classique, les exceptions au titre des « relations internationales » du règlement n°1049/2001 doivent être d'interprétation stricte[39]. Pour autant, malgré ces garanties apportée à l'exigence de transparence, le juge semble en pratique donner plus de crédit aux positions défendues par la Commission et le Conseil en estimant par exemple que, « comme le relève la Commission, toute forme de négociation implique nécessairement un certain nombre de considérations tactiques de la part des négociateurs, et l'indispensable coopération entre les parties dépend, dans une large mesure, de l'existence d'un climat de confiance mutuelle » [40]. Dans cette même affaire, elle rappelle « à titre tout à fait incident » que « la conduite des négociations en vue de la conclusion d'un accord international est, en principe, du domaine de l'exécutif [...] et que ces négociations ne préjugent nullement du débat public susceptible de se développer, une fois l'accord international signé, dans le contexte de la procédure de ratification »[41]. À ce contexte particulier des relations extérieures s'ajoute celui du droit commun de la motivation du refus de communication où, en substance, le juge accepte des motivations brèves si les circonstances le permettent. Ainsi dans une affaire relative aux sanctions, la Cour a estimé que la brièveté d'une motivation pouvait tout à fait être justifiée afin de ne pas porter atteinte aux intérêts sensibles en cause, *i.e.* dans l'affaire en question, des informations provenant sans doute des services de renseignement[42]. Le Tribunal va plus loin, sans que sa position n'ait été ni confirmée ni infirmée par la Cour. Ainsi a-t-il estimé que « la brièveté et le caractère stéréotypé de la motivation fournie à cet égard par

---

l'aspect des relations de celle-ci avec des pays tiers, notamment, la Russie, l'Ukraine et les États-Unis, est en jeu ».

38 Arrêt de la Cour du 21 juillet 2011, *MyTravel Group*, C-506/08 P, EU:C:2011:496, point 72; arrêt de la Cour du 6 décembre 2001, *Heidi Hautala, supra* note 19, point 82; Arrêt *Access Info Europe*, *supra* note 33, point 33.

39 Arrêt de la Cour du 1er février 2007, *Sison*, *supra* note 18, point 63.

40 Arrêt du Tribunal du 19 mars 2013, *Sophie In't Veld*, *supra* note 23, point 119.

41 *Id.*, point 181.

42 Arrêt de la Cour du 1er février 2007, *Sison*, *supra* note 18, point 82.

la première décision de refus ne sauraient constituer un indice de défaut d'examen concret »[43]. De même, la Cour dans son ensemble, dans des affaires ne portant pas toujours sur les relations extérieures mais relatives au règlement n° 1049/2001, admet que, selon le type de documents, il peut exister une présomption de non-communication des documents. Dans une affaire portant sur l'accès aux documents à propos d'accès à des études relatives à la conformité de la législation de différents États membres au droit de l'environnement de l'Union, la Cour a ainsi jugé qu'« il est toutefois loisible à l'institution de l'Union concernée de se fonder [...] sur des présomptions générales s'appliquant à certaines catégories de documents, des considérations d'ordre général similaires étant susceptibles de s'appliquer à des demandes de divulgation portant sur des documents de même nature »[44].

La Commission et le Conseil ont donc à leur disposition tous les outils nécessaires à une limitation de l'accès aux documents et ne se privent pas pour en faire usage, au grand dam du Parlement[45]. Cette limite portée à l'accès aux documents doit être saluée. D'une part, elle préserve le secret indispensable aux relations internationales, secret qui a parfois été menacé par le comportement de certains particuliers[46]. Et l'on comprend mieux les réticences du Conseil et de la Commission à vouloir réviser le règlement

43 Arrêt du Tribunal du 26 avril 2005, *Sison*, T-110/03, EU:T:2005:143, point 88.

44 Arrêt de la Cour du 16 juillet 2015, *ClientEarth*, C-612/13 P, EU:C:2015:486, point 69; de même, v. arrêt de la Cour du 13 octobre 2013, *Access Info Europe*, *supra* note 33, point 72. Dans le cadre de l'accès à des documents en matière de contrôle des concentrations, v., arrêt de la Cour du 28 juin 2012, *Agrofert Holding*, C-477/10 P, EU:C:2012:394, point 57. Pour la question des avis juridiques auxquels la Cour applique là aussi cette présomption : arrêt de la Cour du 1er juillet 2008, *Suède et Turco*, C-39/05 P et C-52/05 P, EU:C:2008:374, point 50.

45 Résolution du 25 septembre 2003 sur l'accès aux documents du Parlement européen, du Conseil et de la Commission [P5_TA(2003)0413]. Il « estime que la situation laisse encore à désirer en ce qui concerne (…) le Conseil, qui semble rejeter systématiquement toutes les demandes concernant les mesures antiterroristes en invoquant l'article 4, paragraphe 1, du règlement; ceci pourrait être contraire à l'esprit et à la lettre du règlement ». La Commission était également visée puisque, « dans 38% des cas, a justifié son refus en invoquant "exceptions diverses et exceptions non spécifiées", ce qui est inacceptable ».

46 Arrêt de la Cour du 22 janvier 2004, *Olli Mattila*, *supra* note 19, où le requérant avait tout de même été condamné par la Cour suprême de Finlande pour avoir communiqué à la Russie des documents « au contenu recouvrant pratiquement celui des documents auxquels l'accès lui a été refusé par les institutions défenderesses » (point 72).

n°1049/2001, malgré les injonctions répétées du Parlement en ce sens[47]. D'autre part, et de façon plus générale, on pourrait se demander s'il revient bien au Parlement européen d'avoir accès à plus de documents encore. On a le sentiment que le Parlement, bien plus que de contrôler les relations extérieures de l'Union, souhaite en assurer l'administration[48]. Or du point de vue de la logique institutionnelle comme de la séparation des pouvoirs, la chose paraît difficile. Il est des moments où, sous couvert de démocratie et de défense de l'intérêt des peuples européens, le Parlement semble souhaiter un nouvel équilibre institutionnel qui ferait de lui-même le centre névralgique de l'intégralité des décisions politiques et stratégiques de l'Union européenne.

Entre un secret qui attire mécaniquement la suspicion et une ouverture trop importante de l'accès aux documents dans le cadre du règlement n° 1049/2001, dont on rappelle qu'il peut être invoqué par n'importe quel citoyen européen, une voie étroite peut toutefois être trouvée. Celle de privilégier l'accès aux parlementaires, lorsqu'ils interviennent en commission et notamment dans le cadre de la commission Affaires étrangères. Certes, des dispositions du règlement du Parlement européen abordent déjà la question de l'accès à des informations sensibles et de l'enclenchement d'une procédure confidentielle[49]. Les mesures paraissent strictes : outre les membres de la commission, seuls les fonctionnaires et les experts dont la présence est strictement nécessaire peuvent assister au débat. De même, « les documents, numérotés, sont distribués au début de la réunion et recueillis à la fin de celle-ci » et « aucune note, a fortiori aucune photocopie, ne peut être prise ». Mais en réalité, et du point de vue de l'indispensable protection du secret, ces mesures sont particulièrement laxistes. D'abord, la procédure confidentielle peut ne pas s'appliquer systématiquement puisqu'en cas de doute sur la confidentialité, la question est soumise à la commission interinstitutionnelle. Ensuite, la préservation du secret se heurte principalement à deux difficultés. D'une part, celle du nombre. Avec environ 144 membres, la commission Affaires étrangères ne peut pas sérieusement s'assurer qu'il n'y aura pas de fuites d'information. D'autre part, celle de la sanction. En cas de violation du secret, ce sont les articles

47 Résolution du Parlement européen du 11 mars 2014 sur l'accès du public aux documents, *supra* note 35.

48 V. H. Flavier, « Parlement européen et relations extérieures : une révolution démocratique en marche? », *supra,* note 14.

49 V. son annexe VII.

165, 166 et 167 du Règlement du Parlement européen qui ont vocation à s'appliquer. Les sanctions prévues en cas de violation du secret vont du blâme (sic) jusqu'au retrait du mandat. Cette dernière sanction n'a, à notre connaissance, jamais été appliquée. Dit autrement, et afin d'instaurer un climat de confiance entre institutions, d'assurer et de promouvoir le principe de coopération loyale entre institutions, deux réformes devraient être engagées. Premièrement, la réduction significative du nombre de parlementaires ayant accès à des documents retraçant les négociations internationales menées par la Commission et le Conseil. En en réduisant le nombre, peut-être réduira-t-on le risque d'utilisation d'informations confidentielles à des fins politiques? Deuxièmement, si les exigences de sécurité le commandent, les parlementaires pourraient avoir, dans certains cas, à se soumettre à une procédure d'habilitation comme il en existe dans tous les services de renseignement nationaux et qui permettrait d'écarter des députés qui sont parfois indélicats ou très proches d'État étrangers[50].

Ces mesures proposées, si elles peuvent paraître rigides, strictes, ou même suspicieuses à l'égard de l'attitude des représentants des peuples européens, auraient toutefois un double mérite : d'un côté, elles établiraient une confiance qui n'existe pas toujours entre les membres du Parlement et les fonctionnaires de la Commission ou du Conseil et qui n'existe parfois guère avec certains services nationaux. D'un autre côté, elles permettraient au Parlement européen, à travers une partie de ses membres, de prendre peut-être une part plus active dans les relations extérieures de l'Union sans considérer systématiquement que la Commission ou de Conseil agissent contre l'intérêt des peuples européens. En somme, ces règles mettraient en œuvre le principe de coopération loyale entre institutions dans un domaine particulier qui échappait traditionnellement à la vigilance des parlementaires et des particuliers faute d'un accès suffisant aux documents.

Le contentieux de l'accès aux documents, qu'il ait été généré sur initiative de particuliers ou de parlementaires européens aura eu pour effet de

---

50 Cela n'est pas de l'ordre de la fiction. Signalons à cet égard, le cas de la « diplomatie du caviar » de l'Azerbaïdjan à l'égard d'un certain nombre de députés de l'Assemblée parlementaire du Conseil de l'Europe (B. Vitkine, « "Diplomatie du caviar" : comment l'Azerbaïdjan s'offre l'amitié de responsables politiques européens », *Le Monde*, 4 septembre 2017; ainsi que l'enquête menée par l'ONG Organized Crime and Corruption Reporting Project : https://www.occrp.org/en/azerbaijanilaundromat/#all-stories).

densifier le droit politique de l'Union en améliorant l'accès à l'information de cette politique publique si particulière. Démocratiser les relations extérieures en renforçant les moyens de contrôle du peuple ou de ses représentants sur ceux qui sont en charge de les mener à bien est un pas important dans l'amélioration de ce droit politique et de la politisation de l'Union européenne. Mais l'intérêt général ne saurait se satisfaire d'une plus grande ouverture de l'accès aux documents à l'intégralité des citoyens[51]. Une véritable politique défendant l'intérêt public est une politique qui sait taire, lorsque nécessaire, des informations dont la divulgation serait contreproductive. Le secret, qui n'est pas nécessairement synonyme de confiscation oligarchique du pouvoir[52], est également une autre façon d'assurer l'intérêt général. Dès lors, si la divulgation et la protection du secret représentent deux façons d'assurer l'intérêt général, alors la seule issue possible si l'on souhaite améliorer la démocratisation des relations extérieures ne peut se trouver dans une révision du règlement n° 1049/2001 dont les bénéficiaires sont trop nombreux. Il s'agirait plutôt de modifier le Règlement du Parlement européen et d'en tirer les conséquences au plan national afin de renforcer sérieusement le contrôle et les sanctions de la procédure confidentielle en Commission parlementaire. On combinerait ainsi plus aisément – et plus démocratiquement – un meilleur accès aux documents, une meilleure sécurité sans que cela n'entrave la construction d'une Europe-puissance.

L'équilibre entre l'intérêt supérieur d'une Europe-puissance et le contentieux de l'accès aux documents ne se cantonne toutefois pas à l'approfondissement d'un droit politique de l'Union. Il touche également ce qui fait le cœur d'une société libérale : la protection des droits fondamentaux.

II. La dimension subjective : un contentieux protecteur des droits fondamentaux

L'accès aux documents dans le contentieux des mesures restrictives est *a priori* de nature fort différente de celui relatif à l'accès aux documents ad-

51 Le champ d'application du règlement n° 1049/2001, *supra* note 13, s'étend à l'ensemble des citoyens européens.

52 V. D. Soulez-Larivière, « La transparence et la vertu », *L'architecture du droit – Mélanges en l'honneur du Professeur Michel Troper*, Paris, Economica, 2006, p. 933; G. Carcassonne, « Le trouble de la transparence », *supra* note 3.

ministratifs. On se situe en effet dans une situation plus pathologique - car le contentieux s'est cristallisé - où une personne physique ou morale souhaite faire invalider une mesure restrictive adoptée par l'Union européenne à son encontre. Dans les années 2000 toutefois, la question de l'accès aux motifs et aux informations justifiant le recours aux mesures restrictives est devenue un enjeu crucial de ce contentieux. Contentieux, dont on peut dire à présent qu'il est devenu récurrent et au cours duquel le juge de l'Union a protégé le droit des requérants d'accéder aux motifs de ces décisions européennes. Ce droit d'accès aux motifs est inséparable du droit d'accéder aux documents fondant la motivation, même s'il s'en distingue juridiquement[53]. Cela étant, si l'accès aux motifs doit être maximal (A), l'accès aux documents, et donc aux preuves fondant les décisions, ne peut être total eu égard aux intérêts stratégiques qui sous-tendent ce type de mesures (B).

A. L'indispensable accès aux motifs

Qu'elle paraît loin la comparaison entre l'accès au dossier dans le cadre d'une procédure juridictionnelle et l'accès aux documents administratifs auprès d'institutions publiques. Pourtant, non seulement ce lien est parfois avancé par les requérants[54], mais il constitue également une manifestation plus large de l'exigence de transparence. Celle-ci doit irriguer l'action administrative mais aussi, et peut-être bien plus encore, le contentieux lui-même puisqu'elle est consubstantielle à l'idée de justice. Dès lors, dans un État de droit, relèverait de la pure évidence qu'un requérant ait accès à la décision faisant grief et partant aux motifs de la décision.

Pourtant, pendant de longues années, cette question ne s'est pas vraiment posée devant la Cour de justice dans le cadre du contentieux des mesures restrictives. Il faudra attendre les années 2000 pour que ce contentieux puisse véritablement s'épanouir et que la Cour de justice forge une jurisprudence concrétisant le droit à un recours juridictionnel effectif. Cette montée en puissance du contentieux des mesures restrictives va de pair avec la multiplication du recours aux sanctions, multiplication telle que l'on peut parfois se demander si les sanctions ne deviennent pas en

---

53 Arrêt de la Cour du 16 novembre 2011, *Bank Melli Iran*, C-548/09 P, EU:C:2011:735, point 88.

54 V. arrêt de la Cour du 28 mars 2017, *Rosneft Oil Company*, *supra* note 16.

elles-mêmes une politique étrangère alors que celles-ci devraient au contraire intervenir au soutien d'une politique étrangère. Quoi qu'il en soit, le contentieux des mesures restrictives a permis d'introduire la protection des droits fondamentaux dans des thématiques relevant directement des relations extérieures et notamment l'accès aux motifs de ces mesures. À cet égard, la Cour s'est appuyée sur une jurisprudence classique en la matière selon laquelle, en application de l'article 296 TFUE, la motivation « doit être adaptée à la nature de l'acte en cause et doit faire apparaître de façon claire et non équivoque le raisonnement de l'institution, auteur de l'acte, de manière à permettre aux intéressés de connaître les justifications de la mesure prise et à la juridiction compétente d'exercer son contrôle »[55]. Selon la Cour, il n'est pas nécessaire de spécifier l'ensemble des éléments de fait et de droit, il suffit que ceux-ci soient suffisants pour permettre au destinataire de l'acte d'en comprendre la portée[56]. Outre la situation où le Conseil ne donne que des motifs excessivement vagues[57], il faut que le destinataire sache donc concrètement et précisément les faits qui lui sont reprochés[58]. L'arrêt *Rosneft* a bien exposé ces exigences. Dans cette affaire la Cour a considéré que, si la motivation devait faire apparaître de manière non équivoque le raisonnement de l'institution [59], sachant que la mesure attaquée avait pour objet « d'accroître le coût des actions de la Fédération de Russie visant à compromettre l'intégrité territoriale, la souveraineté et l'indépendance de l'Ukraine »[60], alors, un opérateur majeur du secteur pétrolier comme Rosneft, « ne pouvait raisonnablement ignorer les raisons pour lesquelles le Conseil a adopté des mesures ciblées à son égard ». En somme, et on ne peut que souscrire – sur ce point précis de l'arrêt *Rosneft*

55 Arrêt de la Cour du 1er février 2007, *Sison*, *supra* note 18, point 80; arrêt de la Cour du 18 février 2016, *Bank Mellat*, C-176/13 P, EU:C:2016:96, point 74 et s.

56 Arrêt de la Cour du 18 février 2016, *Bank Mellat*, *supra* note 55, point 75.

57 V., l'affaire *Bank Mellat* et l'arrêt rendu par le Tribunal le 29 janvier 2013 (T-496/10, EU:T:2013:39) où ce dernier a considéré, notamment que le motifs suivants étaient trop vagues : la banque a eu « un comportement qui soutient et facilite les programmes nucléaires et de missiles balistiques de l'Iran »; elle « fournit des services bancaires à des entités figurant sur les listes des Nations unies et de l'UE, à des entités agissant pour le compte ou sur les instructions de celles-ci ou à des entités détenues ou contrôlées par elles »; elle « gère les comptes des hauts responsables de l'Organisation des industries aérospatiales et d'un responsable des achats iranien ».

58 Arrêt de la Cour du 18 février 2016, *Bank Mellat*, *supra* note 55, point 81.

59 Arrêt de la Cour du 28 mars 2017, *Rosneft Oil Company*, *supra* note 16, point 122.

60 *Id.*, point 123.

– à l'argumentation de la Cour, les destinataires des mesures restrictives, et particulièrement lorsqu'il s'agit d'entreprises aussi importantes que celles-ci, ne sont pas dans la même situation que le chaland[61]. La transparence, le respect des droits de la défense ou l'obligation de motivation ne doivent pas couvrir une naïveté feinte de la part du requérant.

La portée de l'obligation de motivation n'est toutefois pas la même selon le type d'acte en cause. Il s'agit de l'une des précisions apportées de nouveau par l'arrêt *Rosneft*, puisque, selon la Cour, lorsque sont visés uniquement des actes à portée générale, « la motivation peut se borner à indiquer, d'une part, la situation d'ensemble qui a conduit à son adoption et, d'autre part, les objectifs généraux qu'il se propose d'atteindre »[62]. En revanche, lorsqu'il s'agit de mesures restrictives à portée individuelle, « le respect des droits de la défense et du droit à une protection juridictionnelle effective exige, notamment, que l'autorité compétente de l'Union communique à la personne concernée les éléments dont dispose cette autorité à l'encontre de ladite personne pour fonder sa décision »[63]. Cette distinction, clarifiée et bienvenue, s'explique de deux façons. D'une part, lorsqu'un acte est de portée générale, outre qu'il rappelle immanquablement une loi, il ne peut en tant que tel saisir l'ensemble des situations concrètes auxquels il va s'appliquer. D'autre part, les mesures restrictives générales, et notamment de nombreuses décisions PESC, ne sont rien d'autres qu'une formalisation juridique d'une décision de politique étrangère dont la motivation ne peut consister qu'en des motifs généraux.

Toutefois, malgré cette constance dans l'exigence d'une motivation, une part d'aléa demeure. En effet, si le caractère précis et concret de la motivation constitue bien le fil rouge de cette jurisprudence, trois situations méritent d'être relevées. En premier lieu, l'arrêt *Kadi I* reconnaissait déjà que, lorsqu'un acte communautaire visait à mettre en œuvre une résolution du Conseil de sécurité, « des considérations impérieuses touchant à la sûreté ou à la conduite des relations internationales de la Communauté et de ses États membres peuvent s'opposer à la communication de certains éléments aux intéressés »[64]. De même, dans l'arrêt *Bank Melli Iran*, le Tri-

61 La Cour précise que Rosneft dispose d'actifs évalués à 1000 milliards de roubles russes, soit environ 14 milliards d'euros.

62 *Id.*, point 120.

63 *Id.*, point 121.

64 Arrêt de la Cour du 3 septembre 2008, *Kadi I*, C-402/05 P et C-415/05 P, EU:C:2008:461, point 342.

bunal a jugé que si le Conseil devait communiquer au destinataire de la mesure les éléments de fait et de droit, cela ne vaut pas si « des considérations impérieuses touchant à la sûreté de la Communauté ou de ses États membres ou à la conduite de leurs relations internationales [...] s'opposent à la communication de certains éléments »[65]. Cette exception qui, appliquée en matière de motivation recoupe celle de la preuve[66], révèle la proximité des enjeux du contentieux des sanctions et de l'accès aux documents des institutions lorsque sont en cause les spécificités des relations internationales et de la sécurité[67].

En deuxième lieu, si le Conseil doit motiver sa décision sur la situation individuelle du destinataire, il peut paraître logique que le seul lien familial ne constitue pas une motivation suffisante. La preuve du lien avec le gouvernement nécessite des éléments plus étoffés, sauf dans la situation où « le lien de rattachement au pays tiers en cause s'impose de toute évidence, c'est-à-dire aux dirigeants des pays tiers et aux individus qui sont associés à ces dirigeants »[68]. Pourtant, les méandres de cette position ne sont pas toujours des plus simples à saisir et offrent une latitude fort commode au juge lorsqu'il souhaite valider ou invalider une mesure restrictive. L'heureuse souplesse de ce critère fut perceptible lors de l'affaire *Al Assad*[69]. Dans cette affaire en effet, le Tribunal a jugé que « le seul fait que la requérante est la sœur de M. Bashar Al Assad suffit pour que le Conseil puisse considérer qu'elle est liée aux dirigeants de la Syrie [...], d'autant plus que l'existence dans ce pays d'une tradition de gestion familiale du pouvoir est un fait notoire dont le Conseil pouvait tenir compte »[70]. Le Tribunal estime donc que, dans le cas spécifique de la Syrie, la « tradition de gestion familiale du pouvoir » constitue une présomption de lien suffisant avec le régime pour justifier l'adoption de sanctions à l'égard de la sœur de Bachar El Assad. On veut comprendre l'évidence de l'argumentaire, mais il n'en demeure pas moins qu'une analyse plus poussée de la nature du régime syrien n'aurait pas été superflue afin de rendre l'argu-

---

65 Arrêt du Tribunal du 14 octobre 2009, *Bank Melli Iran*, T-390/08, EU:T:2009:401, point 81. V., de même, arrêt du Tribunal du 12 décembre 2006, *Organisation des Modjahedines du peuple d'Iran*, T-228/02, EU:T:2006:384, point 137; arrêt du Tribunal du 10 mai 2010, *Tay Za*, T-181/08, EU:T:2010:209, point 96.

66 V. *infra*.

67 V. *supra*.

68 Arrêt de la Cour du 13 mars 2012, *Tay Za*, C-376/10 P, EU:C:2012:138, point 68.

69 Arrêt du Tribunal du 12 mars 2014, *Al Assad*, T-202/12, EU:T:2014:113.

70 *Id.*, point 96.

ment plus persuasif. Se contenter de l'évidence dans des affaires aussi importantes tant symboliquement que diplomatiquement, n'apparaît jamais comme satisfaisant.

En troisième et dernier lieu, c'est également au nom de cette exigence de précision que le juge a rejeté les motifs qui ne reposaient que sur des informations « vraisemblables ». Si la motivation doit reposer sur des éléments précis et concrets, alors la seule vraisemblance ne saurait suffire. Dans l'affaire *Fulmen*, la Cour, confirmant la position du Tribunal, a jugé que « l'effectivité du contrôle juridictionnel garanti par l'article 47 de la Charte exige notamment que le juge de l'Union s'assure que la décision [...] repose sur une base factuelle suffisamment solide ». Ce qui implique que « le contrôle juridictionnel ne soit pas limité à l'appréciation de la vraisemblance abstraite des motifs invoqués, mais porte sur le point de savoir si ces motifs, ou, à tout le moins, l'un d'eux considéré comme suffisant en soi pour soutenir cette même décision, sont étayés »[71]. Elle reprend en ce sens la position choisie dans l'affaire *Kadi II* selon lequel « le juge de l'Union s'assure que cette décision, qui revêt une portée individuelle pour cette personne [...] repose sur une base factuelle suffisamment solide ». Ce qui implique « une vérification des faits allégués dans l'exposé des motifs qui sous-tend ladite décision [...], de sorte que le contrôle juridictionnel ne soit pas limité à l'appréciation de la vraisemblance abstraite des motifs invoqués »[72]. Mais aborder cette question, c'est déjà aborder celle de l'accès aux preuves avancées dans les motifs.

B. Le nécessaire accès raisonné aux preuves

L'accès aux preuves fondant les motifs avancés et justifiant des mesures restrictives constitue probablement l'étape la plus délicate du point de vue de l'équilibre entre le respect des droits de la défense et la protection des relations internationales de l'Union européenne et de ses États membres. La révision opérée par le traité de Lisbonne, rendue nécessaire par l'arrêt *Kadi I*[73], avait pour ambition d'inclure certaines garanties consub-

71 Arrêt de la Cour du 28 novembre 2013, *Fulmen*, C-280/12 P, EU:C:2013:775, point 63.

72 Arrêt de la Cour du 18 juillet 2013, *Kadi II*, C-584/10 P, EU:C:2013:518, point 119.

73 Arrêt de la Cour du 3 septembre 2008, *Kadi I*, *supra* note 64.

stantielles à l'État de droit dans la technique juridique des contremesures. Il en est notamment résulté la refonte de l'article 215 TFUE qui, en son paragraphe 3, prévoit dorénavant que les mesures restrictives « contiennent les dispositions nécessaires en matière de garanties juridiques ». Ces garanties juridiques visent notamment la motivation des décisions de sanction mais se rattachent plus largement à l'exigence d'un procès équitable. C'est donc en toute logique que, devant le juge, les requérants visés par des mesures restrictives ont demandé l'accès aux documents justifiant l'adoption de sanctions.

En ce domaine, l'accès aux informations est d'autant plus indispensable qu'il se rattache à l'accès aux preuves invoquées par le Conseil. Or, il est assez fréquent qu'en matière de lutte contre le terrorisme ou de décisions motivées par une stratégie de politique étrangère, ces informations soient classifiées. L'équilibre entre l'État de droit et la protection du secret des relations internationales n'a pas été un donné mais un construit et à ce titre, le juge de l'Union a joué un rôle considérable. Il a d'abord pu considérer que la communication de ces documents était obligatoire « à moins que des considérations impérieuses touchant à la sûreté de la Communauté ou de ses États membres ou à la conduite de leurs relations internationales » ne s'y opposent[74]. Lorsque l'accès aux documents contenant des informations est donné, le juge n'acceptera ces informations comme justifiant les sanctions que si elles sont précises, *i.e.* s'il existe des « preuves ou [des] indices sérieux et crédibles de l'implication de la personne concernée dans des activités terroristes, considérés comme fiables par les autorités nationales »[75].

La principale difficulté réside en ce que les autorités nationales ou les institutions européennes risquent de recourir abusivement à l'argument tiré du secret et de rejeter systématiquement toute demande d'accès aux documents. Afin de s'en prémunir, la Cour a jeté les bases des conditions

---

74 Arrêt *Bank Melli Iran*, *supra* note 65, point 81. C'est la raison pour laquelle le juge n'exige la communication de ces informations que dans l'hypothèse où elles ne sont pas classifiées : arrêt de la Cour du 28 juillet 2016, *Tomana*, C-330/15 P, EU:C:2016:601. Le juge précise, dans cette dernière affaire, que le « principe du respect des droits de la défense n'implique pas l'obligation pour [le Conseil] de donner spontanément accès aux documents contenus dans son dossier » (point 66). Cela ne peut donc se faire que sur demande de la partie intéressée.

75 Arrêt de la Cour du 15 novembre 2012, *Al-Aqsa*, C-539/10 P et C-550/10 P, EU:C:2012:711, point 104.

d'accès aux documents dans un arrêt *ZZ*[76]. En substance, le juge de l'Union a estimé que, s'il incombait aux autorités nationales de vérifier qu'il existe des raisons s'opposant à la communication des éléments de preuves, c'était à elles d'apporter la preuve « que la sûreté de l'État serait effectivement compromise par une communication à l'intéressé des motifs précis et complets qui constituent le fondement d'une décision prise »[77]. Dans cette affaire, le juge national avait donc l'obligation européenne d'évaluer si la communication des informations pertinentes ne remettrait pas en cause les intérêts publics défendus par l'autorité nationale compétente, c'est-à-dire en pratique, de près ou de loin, par les services de renseignements nationaux. S'il advenait que l'autorité nationale ne lui confiait pas les documents pertinents, alors « le juge procèd[erait] à l'examen de la légalité d'une telle décision sur la base des seuls motifs et éléments de preuve qui ont été communiqués »[78]. En revanche, si le refus des autorités nationales paraît justifié, alors, le juge contrôlera la légalité de la décision attaquée en vérifiant dans le cadre d'une procédure spécifique mettant en balance les exigences tirées de l'intérêt public protégé et du droit à une procédure juridictionnelle effective. Ainsi, et pour ce qui concerne les éléments de preuves qui seraient reconnues comme étant confidentielle, c'est au juge compétent « d'apprécier si et dans quelle mesure les restrictions aux droits de la défense du requérant découlant notamment d'une non-divulgation des éléments de preuve et des motifs précis et complets sur lesquels est fondée la décision [...] sont de nature à influer sur la force probante des éléments de preuve confidentiels »[79].

Cette position, qui concernait avant tout la question de la lutte contre le terrorisme, a été étendue et précisée dans l'affaire *Kadi II*[80]. La Cour de justice a en effet assoupli et renforcé les obligations pesant sur les autorités nationales. D'un côté, il n'est pas exigé de ces dernières qu'elles communiquent l'ensemble des informations, documents et éléments de preuve. Il suffit que « les informations ou les éléments produits étayent les

76 Arrêt de la Cour du 4 juin 2013, *ZZ*, C-300/11, EU:C:2013:363.
77 *Id.,* point 61.
78 Arrêt du Tribunal du 21 mars 2012, *Fulmen*, T-439/10 et T-440/10, EU:T:2012:142, point 63.
79 Arrêt de la Cour du 4 juin 2013, *ZZ*, *supra* note 76, point 67.
80 Arrêt de la Cour du 18 juillet 2013, *Kadi* II, *supra* note 72.

motifs retenus à l'encontre de la personne concernée »[81]. D'un autre côté, si des informations sont fournies, le juge de l'Union « doit vérifier l'exactitude matérielle des faits allégués au regard de ces informations ou éléments et apprécier la force probante de ces derniers en fonction des circonstances de l'espèce »[82].

La position endossée par le juge de l'Union, si elle peut parfaitement se comprendre eu égard à sa nécessité fonctionnelle de garantir le droit à un recours juridictionnel effectif et donc, s'agissant du contentieux des mesures restrictives, d'assurer un accès aux documents versés dans le dossier, n'est pourtant pas à l'abri de la critique. D'une part, il est demandé au juge de l'Union de vérifier l'exactitude matérielle des faits allégués. Ce qui suppose que le juge ait accès à un niveau d'information supérieur à celui se limitant à la seule révélation des faits qui peuvent être eux-mêmes d'ores et déjà classifiés. Il est fort probable que des résistances nationales se soient déjà manifestées à ce sujet et que l'on soit tenté de considérer que la seule divulgation des éléments de faits aurait pu être jugée comme suffisante. D'ailleurs, il n'est pas exclu que les services d'un État aient parfois préféré ne pas communiquer davantage d'informations à la Cour et risquer de voir la mesure restrictive annulée, plutôt que de sacrifier (car une telle divulgation est vécue ainsi) certains renseignements ayant justement permis de découvrir des faits qui ne sont généralement pas accessibles au grand public. D'autre part, comment être certain que les conditions sécuritaires d'accès auxdites informations soient d'un niveau suffisant au sein de la Cour pour que les autorités nationales concèdent plus facilement à transmettre de telles informations, qu'il s'agisse des bâtiments (ouverts au public) et des personnels de nationalités et de parcours divers?

C'est en partie pour répondre à ces questions que l'article 105 du règlement de procédure du Tribunal a été modifié[83]. Cette nouvelle disposition, entrée en vigueur le 1er juillet 2015, établit une procédure de divulgation des documents en essayant de combiner la préservation du secret et l'accès aux informations inséparable du respect des droits de la défense et du droit à une procédure juridictionnelle effective. En substance, il organise l'accès du juge à des documents sensibles fondant la décision portant mesures restrictives. Dès lors que le juge a eu accès aux documents, il peut décider si

81 *Id.*, point 122.
82 *Id.*, point 124.
83 V. la contribution d'Allan Rosas dans cet ouvrage.

le secret avancé est justifié. S'il ne l'est pas, il en ouvrira l'accès au requérant. Dans le cas contraire, il appréciera lui-même si les informations avancées sont suffisantes pour justifier une sanction, sans véritable contradictoire. Dans cette dernière hypothèse, il est manifeste que les droits de la défense ont été limités. Mais cette restriction est justifiée par la protection des intérêts en cause où la divulgation de renseignement directement aux destinataires des sanctions – dont on ne rappellera jamais assez qu'ils sont souvent bien connus des services ou des chancelleries, voire des structures commerciales ou financières internationales – risquerait de perturber fortement le fonctionnement des services concernés. Sans que nous ayons les moyens d'avancer des chiffres clairs, cette exception de confidentialité a été sans doute appliquée à plusieurs reprises[84]. Elle s'est d'ailleurs prolongée, en tout logique, par une révision du règlement de procédure de la Cour de justice le 19 juillet 2016 qui introduit un article 190 bis reprenant la logique de l'article 105 du règlement du Tribunal et s'appliquant lorsque la Cour de justice est saisie sur pourvoi « contre une décision du Tribunal adoptée dans le cadre d'une procédure au cours de laquelle des renseignements ou des pièces ont été produits par une partie principale au titre de l'article 105 du règlement de procédure du Tribunal et n'ont pas été communiqués à l'autre partie principale ».

Une dernière question se pose au sujet de l'accès aux documents dans l'état du droit postérieur à la révision de l'article 105 : ces changements ont-ils consolidé le lien de confiance entre les autorités nationales et les juges européens? Dit autrement, les autorités nationales sont-elles devenues plus enclines à laisser le juge européen accéder à des informations confidentielles et donc à prendre le risque d'invoquer l'article 105 du règlement de procédure du Tribunal? Rappelons à cet égard qu'il existe une défiance assez générale de ces services nationaux à l'égard de l'institution judiciaire, défiance plus grande encore lorsqu'il s'agit d'institutions judiciaires internationales. En ce sens, on doit reconnaître que la défiance est encore bien présente et que la révision de l'article 105 n'aura changé que peu de choses. D'un côté, les autorités nationales concernées considéreront toujours que le juge, fût-il européen, n'a ni la compétence ni l'expérience pour apprécier la valeur d'un renseignement. Elles n'apprécient d'ailleurs guère que la décision de transmettre ou non les docu-

---

84 V., ordonnance du Tribunal du 10 juin 2016, *Klymenko*, T-494/14, EU:T:2016:360; arrêt du Tribunal du 7 juillet 2017, *Azarov*, T-215/15. EU:T:2017:479.

ments au demandeur ne repose que sur la décision du seul juge européen. D'un autre côté, pour le juge, il est évident qu'il a déjà traité des dossiers fortement confidentiels impliquant des enjeux financiers colossaux sans qu'aucun problème n'ait été signalé du point de vue de la protection du secret. D'ailleurs, c'est bien au juge, dans une démocratie, d'apprécier à son niveau ce qui peut relever de l'intérêt général et il ne voit sans doute pas pour quelle raison il en serait privé s'agissant d'affaires impliquant des intérêts importants en termes de sécurité nationale ou internationale. En matière de relations extérieures, il semblerait donc que nous en soyons encore au stade d'une défiance mutuelle.

***

La défiance semble être ce qui unit le contentieux de l'accès aux documents relevant des relations extérieures, qu'il s'agisse du contentieux des documents administratifs ou des mesures restrictives. Dans un cas comme dans l'autre, nous assistons à une défiance généralisée à l'égard de l'exécutif. Cette défiance naturelle est heureuse dans une société démocratique. Si l'essentiel des pouvoirs est détenu par le pouvoir exécutif ou, dans le cas de l'Union européenne, par des institutions qui en ont endossé les responsabilités et les fonctions, il est bienvenu que celles-ci rendent des comptes. Et l'accès aux documents constitue justement l'un des procédés contraignant l'exécutif à rendre des comptes. Cependant, il faudrait se garder d'en arriver à l'excès inverse en présupposant que l'intérêt général ne saurait être défendu que par les citoyens, les parlementaires voire les requérants, c'est-à-dire tous ceux qui n'appartiendraient pas à la sphère de l'exécutif. Peut-être le temps est-il venu de dire que l'intérêt général, qu'il soit européen ou national, n'est défendu ni par la Commission, ni par le Conseil, ni par le Parlement, ni par la Cour de justice, ni par les États membres, ni par les citoyens mais par la conjonction, les fonctions et les missions de chacun d'entre eux, dans le respect des attributions et des fonctions des autres. Une telle prise de conscience combinée peut-être à un peu plus d'humilité de la part des acteurs et, pourquoi pas, à une certaine forme de bienveillance à l'égard de l'autre, pourrait être un prélude à la restauration d'une certaine confiance mutuelle. L'honnêteté intellectuelle commande cependant de constater que la route sera longue.

Effective Judicial Protection and Its Limits in the Case Law Concerning Individual Restrictive Measures in the European Union

Sara Poli

I. Introduction

Restrictive measures are enacted to counter terrorism or exercise pressure on third countries that breach international law (or, more broadly, values of the European Union) in order to end these violations.[1] Individual sanctions, rather than global sanctions (against third countries, as a whole), have become the norm in sanction policies at both the United Nations (UN) and the European Union level. The practice of subjecting natural and legal persons to autonomous restrictive measures for purposes connected to the Common Foreign and Security Policy (CFSP) has evolved throughout the years in the EU.[2] New designation criteria appeared in the Council decisions instituting restrictive measures after 2010: abuses of human rights were at the basis of sanctions as stand-alone criteria or in connection with others (such as the promotion of democracy). Furthermore, measures regarding misappropriation of State funds by former members of third countries' governments were enacted with respect to the EU South-

1 Monographs on the topic of restrictive measures are numerous. Amongst others, see C. Beaucillon, *Les mesures restrictives de l'Union européenne* (Brussels: Bruylant, 2014); C. Portela, *European Union Sanctions and Foreign Policy* (London: Routledge, 2011). See also edited collections: N. Ronzitti (ed), *Coercitive Diplomacy, Sanctions and International Law* (Leiden: Brill | Nijhoff, 2016); I. Cameron (ed), *EU Sanctions: Law and Policy Issues Concerning Restrictive Measures* (Cambridge: Intersentia 2013); A. Z. Marossi and M. R. Basset (eds), *Economic Sanctions under International Law* (The Hague: Springer, 2015).

2 The EU was provided with a competence to adopt measures restricting the economic relations with third countries with the Maastricht Treaty (see Articles 60 and 301 of the Treaty of the European Community -TEC). Sanctions freezing the assets of individuals were based on the mentioned provisions and on Article 308 of the TEC given the lack of an explicit competence to adopt this kind of measures vis-a-vis individuals.

ern and Eastern neighbours. The EU has also enlarged the circle of non-State actors who could be targeted to include not only third countries' leaders and members of the State apparatus, but also those who are associated with these leaders (such as family members), or persons providing political, logistical, and material support to these leaders. Natural and legal persons benefiting from links with the political leadership (such as businessmen or compagnies), or simply helping them in supporting the regime's propaganda (as in the case of journalists) are also included in the circle. As a result, the chances of being targeted by restrictive measures for non-State actors in third countries, as well as former members of third countries' governments, have multiplied in the last ten years.

It is necessary to examine to what extent natural and legal persons enjoy a right to judicial protection within the EU. This right is protected under the general principles of EU law or/and under Article 47 of the Charter of Fundamental Rights of the EU, which applies to all areas of EU law, including the CFSP. This principle requires on the one hand, that private parties be able to contest restrictive measures before a judge and, on the other hand, that the remedies at their disposal be effective. The Court of Justice has strengthened the right to an effective protection to the benefit of those who are included in the list of sanctions, as will be shown below. However, the right to effective judicial protection bears limits within the CFSP.

II. Access to Justice for Non-State Actors Targeted by Restrictive Measures in the Case Law of the Court of Justice

Although neither the Treaty on European Union (TEU), nor the Treaty of the European Community (TEC) provided for the EU's competence to enact restrictive measures against non-state actors, the latter were targeted by EU sanctions, even before the United Nations started the practice.[3] The EU's explicit competence to adopt decisions instituting restrictive measures *vis-a-vis* natural and legal persons was provided for the first time by Article 215, paragraph 2, of the Treaty on the Functioning of the European Union (TFEU). Yet, the Court of Justice played a significant role in turn-

3 S. Poli, "The Turning of Non-State Entities from Objects to Subjects of EU Restrictive Measures", in E. Fahey, S. Bardutzky (eds), *Framing the Subjects and Objects of EU Law* (Cheltenham: Edward Elgar, 2017), 158-181.

ing these targets from mere "objects of restrictive measures" to "subjects", even before the mentioned provision was included in EU primary law.[4] Indeed, the EU judiciary has made it possible for non-state actors to challenge regulations imposing economic sanctions in the context of annulment actions, despite the fact that, under former Article 46 TEC, the Court had virtually no competence over foreign and security policy matters.[5] In the *Organisation des Modjahedines du peuple d'Iran* (*OMPI*) case, the General Court established its jurisdiction to hear an action for annulment directed against a common position adopted on the basis of former Articles 15 and 34 TEU (third pillar), although only strictly to the extent that, in support of such an action, the applicant alleged an infringement of the Community's competences.[6] In *Segi,*[7] the Court of Justice interpreted Article 35, paragraph 1, TEU as allowing for preliminary rulings on the validity or interpretation of common positions[8] which intend to produce legal effects *vis-a-vis* third parties.[9] The competence to review the legality of these acts in actions brought by Member States and or the Commission was also recognised, under Article 35, paragraph 6, TEU.[10] The wide in-

---

4 For example, in the Judgment of 17 January 2007, *Osman Ocalan, on behalf of the Kurdistan Workers' Party (PKK)*, C-229/05 P, EU:C:2007:32, para 112, the Court held that: "Since, by Decision 2002/460, the Community legislature took the view that the PKK retains an existence sufficient for it to be subject to the restrictive measures laid down by regulation 2580/2001/EC, it must be accepted, on grounds of consistency and justice, that that entity continues to have an existence sufficient to contest this measure. The effect of any other conclusion would be that an organisation could be included in the disputed list without being able to bring an action challenging its inclusion".

5 M-G. Garbagnati Ketvel, "The Jurisdiction of the European Court of Justice in Respect of the Common Foreign and Security Policy", *International & Comparative Law Quarterly* 55, no. 1 (2006), 79.

6 See Judgment of 12 December 2006, *OMPI,* T-228/02, EU:T:2006:384. For an insightful examination of the early case- law on the right of access to a court, see C. Eckes, "Sanctions against Individuals. Fighting Terrorism within the European Legal Order", *European Constitutional Law Review* 4, no. 2 (2008), 205.

7 Judgment of 27 February 2007, *Segi and others*, C-355/04 P, EU:C:2007:116.

8 At the time of the Segi ruling, common positions to combat terrorism were adopted under the legal basis provisions of the CFSP (former Article 15 TEU) and the third pillar (former Article 34 TEU).

9 Judgment of 27 February 2007, *Segi, supra* note 7, paras 54-55.

10 In contrast, the EU judiciary excluded that an action in damages could be brought by the applicant against common positions, given that this would have been against the principle of conferral.

terpretation of the scope of the Court's competence in this ruling is consistent with the principle that the EU is based on the rule of law: if natural and legal persons can be hit by restrictive measures, these subjects should also be able to seek the annulment of their inclusion in the backlist and question the validity of the EU act in a preliminary ruling procedure. Therefore, the Court strengthened the position of non-State actors as subjects of restrictive measures even before the Treaty of Lisbon did so.

With the Treaty changes of 2009, the Court of Justice's lack of competence with respect to provisions within the scope of Chapter 2 of title V of the TEU – as provided for in Article 24, paragraph 1, TEU and Article 275, paragraph 1, TFEU – contemplated an important exception. Under Article 275, paragraph 2, TFEU,[11] the EU judicature may "rule in proceedings, brought in accordance with the conditions laid down in the fourth paragraph of Article 263 of this Treaty, reviewing the legality of decisions providing for restrictive measures against natural or legal persons adopted by the Council on the basis of Chapter 2 of Title V of the Treaty on European Union". This provision shows that the masters of the Treaties were willing to recognise a limited form of judicial oversight in this area. The rationale was "to offer legal safeguards to natural and legal persons, as opposed to countries".[12] Individuals affected by sanctions can not only impugn the regulation adopted on the basis of Article 215 TFEU, but they may also dispute CFSP decisions instituting restrictive measures.

Article 275, paragraph 2, TFEU did not specify whether the judicial oversight over the sanctions could be carried out only in the context of an annulment action or if this oversight could also be carried out in a preliminary ruling procedure on the validity of these measures. This issue was not

11 The Court of Justice of the European Union shall not have jurisdiction with respect to the provisions relating to the Common Foreign and Security Policy nor with respect to acts adopted on the basis of those provisions. However, the Court shall have jurisdiction to monitor compliance with Article 40 of the Treaty on European Union and to rule on proceedings, brought in accordance with the conditions laid down in the fourth paragraph of Article 263 of this Treaty, reviewing the legality of decisions providing for restrictive measures against natural or legal persons adopted by the Council on the basis of Chapter 2 of Title V of the Treaty on European Union.

12 C. Eckes, "EU Restrictive Measures against Natural and Legal Persons: From Counterterrorist to Third Country Sanctions", *Common Market Law Review* 51, no. 3 (2013), 869, at 882.

clarified until 2017 with the *Rosneft* ruling,[13] which concerns a number of prohibitions or restrictions adopted by the EU against the Russian Federation in the context of the conflict with Ukraine.[14] In this ruling, the scope of the exceptions laid down by Article 275, paragraph 2, TFEU to the EU Court of Justice's lack of jurisdiction, with respect to the provisions of the CFSP, is defined for the first time. The mentioned judgment was delivered shortly after those in the *Elitaliana*[15] and *H*[16] cases, and it fills an important gap in the case law of the Court of Justice.[17] As result of the three rulings, the exceptions to the Court of Justice's lack of jurisdiction, as far as the CFSP is concerned, should be interpreted in a restrictive manner. In particular, in *Rosneft,* such an interpretation is anchored to the respect of the general principle of the right to effective judicial protection and Article 47 of the Charter of Fundamental Rights.

In addition, the position is taken that, to the extent to which the Court of Justice has competence to rule on the legality of restrictive measures, it is necessary that the control on the validity of the sanctions is carried out by the EU judicature, and not by national courts, for the same reasons mentioned in *Foto-Frost.*[18] The EU judiciary provides private parties with the right to question the validity of a CFSP decision in the framework of a preliminary ruling, thus providing an additional window of opportunity for them to contest these measures beyond the annulment action.[19] Certainly,

---

13 Judgment of 28 March 2017, *Rosneft Oil Company*, C-72/15, EU:C:2017:236.

14 R. J. Neuwirth, A. Svetlicinii, "The Economic Sanctions over the Ukraine Conflict and the WTO: 'Catch-XXI' and the Revival of the Debate on Security Exceptions", *Journal of World Trade* 49, no. 5 (2015), 891.

15 Judgment of 12 November 2015, *Elitaliana* v *Eulex Kosovo*, C-439/13 P, EU:C:2015:753.

16 Judgment of 19 July 2016, *H.* v *Council of the European Union,* C-455/14 P, EU:C:2016:569.

17 As noted in Opinion 2/13, until 2015 the Court had not had the opportunity to "define the extent to which its jurisdiction was limited in CFSP matters", see Opinion of 18 December 2014, 2/13, *Accession of the European Union to the European Convention for the Protection of Human Rights and Fundamental Freedoms*, EU:C:2014:2454, para 251.

18 Judgment of 22 October 1987, *Foto-Frost* v *Hauptzollamt Lübeck-Ost*, 314/85, EU:C:1987:452.

19 For positions favourable to this interpretation of Article 275, paragraph 2, TFEU, see C. Hillion, "A Powerless Court? The European Court of Justice and the Common Foreign and Security Policy", in M. Cremona and A. Thies (eds), *The European Court of Justice and External Relations Law Constitutional Challenges* (Oxford: Hart, 2014), 47.

as a result of the *TWD* ruling,[20] natural and legal persons, whose legal standing to challenge CFSP decisions is uncontested, should first challenge these measures in an annulment action (as Rosneft did), within the time limit laid down by Article 263 TFEU; otherwise, the action could be declared inadmissible. However, apart from this procedural rule that could exceptionally lead to the inadmissibility of the preliminary ruling procedure,[21] private parties' right of access to justice is strengthened as a result of *Rosneft*.

An ambiguity remains as to whether judicial oversight stretches to include the competence to interpret a CFSP decision and hear an action in damages, under Article 340 TFUE. It is submitted that, as the primary law currently stands, it is possible to argue that the competence to interpret the provisions of a CFSP decision is included in terms of ruling on its validity; in contrast, it is more difficult to argue that extra-contractual responsibility is embedded in Article 275, paragraph 2, TFEU.

The question may be raised as to whether or not natural and legal persons could have access to justice before the European Court of Human Rights (ECtHR) in case the validity of a restrictive measure is not questioned by a national court in the framework of a preliminary ruling procedure. The answer is positive, as may be inferred from the *Al-Dulimi* ruling of 2016.[22] In this judgment of the Grand Chamber of the ECtHR, Switzer-

20 Judgment of 9 March 1994, *TWD Textilwerke Deggendorf*, C-188/92, EU:C:1994:90.

21 However, in a recent case, Judgment of 14 March 2017, *A and others*, C-158/14, EU:C:2017:202, the Court recognised that: "A request for a preliminary ruling concerning the validity of an act of the European Union can be dismissed only in the event that, although the action for annulment of an act of the European Union would unquestionably have been admissible, the natural or legal person capable of bringing such an action abstained from doing so within the prescribed period and is pleading the unlawfulness of that act in national proceedings in order to encourage the national court to submit a request for a preliminary ruling to the Court of Justice concerning the validity of that act, thereby circumventing the fact that that act is final as against him once the time limit for his bringing an action has expired" (para 70).

22 ECtHR, *Al-Dulimi and Montana Management Inc.* v *Switzerland*, Appl. N. 5809/08, Judgment of 21 June 2016. For insightful comments on Al-Dulimi and also on the inconsistencies on the ECtHR's case law on access to justice, see A. Peters, The New Arbitrariness and Competing Constitutionalisms: Remarks on ECtHR Grand Chamber Al-Dulimi, *EJIL:Talk!,* 30 June 2016, www.ejiltalk.org/the-new-arbitrariness-and-competing-constitutionalisms-remarks-on-ecthr-grand-chamber-al-dulimi.

land was held to violate the right of access to a court since its judicial authorities had refused to review the merit of the national measure confiscating Mr Al Dulimi's property, done in order to comply with a UN Security Council (UNSC) resolution of 2003. The view of the ECtHR was that the domestic court should have carried out judicial review for the purpose of avoiding arbitrary designations by the UNSC.[23] It is submitted that the legal avenues offered to individuals wishing to challenge restrictive measures are therefore strengthened as a result of the two rulings, and that the roles of the Court of Justice and the ECtHR are complementary in providing human rights scrutiny. Indeed, in case an EU domestic court does not question the validity of a CFSP decision and implements the UNSC resolution at the origin of the sanction, the victim of a possible breach of a right protected by the ECHR may turn to the ECtHR. It should be noted that, from the perspective of an individual affected by a CFSP decision setting up restrictive measures, implementing a UNSC resolution, in an EU Member State, it is preferable that a national court raises a preliminary ruling procedure. Indeed, the rule on the previous exhaustion of domestic

23 In this ruling, Switzerland was found to breach Article 6, paragraph 1, of the ECHR since, in 2008, the Swiss Federal court refused to examine the merit of the action brought by a number of former officials of the Iraq government against the confiscation of their properties, enacted by Switzerland to implement a UNSC Resolution of 2003. The reason leading the domestic court to take such a decision was that, under Art. 103 of the UN Charter, the obligations deriving from the latter Treaty prevail over those stemming from other sources of international law, except for the *jus cogens*. In addition, the UNSC resolution at stake did not leave any degree of flexibility to national authorities. The ECtHR excluded that there was a conflict of obligations between the UN Charter and the ECHR. There was no need to apply the equivalent protection test. The examination of the text of the UNSC resolution leads to conclusion that: '[...] where a [UNSC] resolution [...], does not contain any clear or explicit wording excluding the possibility of judicial supervision of the measures taken for its implementation, it must always be understood as authorising the courts of the respondent State to exercise sufficient scrutiny so that any arbitrariness can be avoided' (para 146). The Court went on to state that: 'Any State Party whose authorities give legal effect to the addition of a person – whether an individual or a legal entity – to a sanctions list, without first ensuring – or being able to ensure – that the listing is not arbitrary will engage its responsibility under Article 6 of the Convention.' See, for a comment, V. P. Tzevelekos, "The Al-Dulimi Case before the Grand Chamber of the European Court of Human Rights: Business as Usual? Test of Equivalent Protection, (Constitutional) Hierarchy and Systemic Integration", *Questions of International Law* (2017), 5.

remedies, applicable in context of the ECHR,[24] will inevitably delay the judgment of the ECtHR, whereas, in the EU, as a result of the *Rosneft* ruling, all national courts may raise a question on the validity of CFSP decisions instituting restrictive measures, and they are likely to receive a relatively speedy answer.[25]

Finally, it may be wondered whether or not the interpretation of Article 275, paragraph 2, TFEU provides for the widest form of access to justice for natural/legal persons and other non-state entities targeted by sanctions. The answer is negative as far as non-state entities blacklisted by a third country sanction regime are concerned.[26] Indeed, leaving aside that the notion of "restrictive measures" was interpreted narrowly to include only the sanction policy,[27] in the *Rosneft* ruling, the Court of Justice has substantially confirmed that natural and legal persons may challenge the listing decision resulting from the CFSP decision instituting restrictive measures against natural and legal persons.

However, the provisions of the same act that impose, in a general and abstract manner, on the EU operators to comply with a certain behaviour (prohibition to sell goods/services to the natural and legal persons subject-

---

24 Article 35, paragraph 1, ECHR.

25 The High Court of Justice of England and Wales referred its questions to the Court of Justice on 9 February 2015, and the Rosneft ruling was released on 28 March 2017. The notion of effective judicial protection entails also the notion of reasonably speedy protection. For this point, see E. Spaventa, "Annotation to Case T-256/07, People's Mojahedin Organization of Iran v. Council", *Common Market Law Review* 46, no. 4 (2009), 1239, at 1258.

26 In contrast, suspected terrorists or terrorist groups face fewer legal obstacles in challenging restrictive measures since they are interested in contesting the listing decision, only. And the interpretation of the legal standing requirements of Article 263, paragraph 4, TFEU has never been an obstacle for these addresses of sanctions. Before the Lisbon Treaty entered into force, the Court considered annulment actions against regulations laying down freezing orders admissible to the extent that the applicants were 'individually and directly concerned' by these acts, within the meaning of Article 230 paragraph 4, TEC. This implied that the name of the applicant had merely to be included in the list of addresses.

27 See Opinion of 16 May 2017, 2/13, *supra* note 17, para 252 and the comments made by S. O. Johansen, "Accountability Mechanisms for Human Rights Violations by CSDP Missions: Available and Sufficient?", *International & Comparative Law Quarterly* 66, no. 1 (2017), 181, at 200. See also the restrictive interpretation provided by the Court of Justice in the judgement of 19 July 2016, *H*, *supra* note 16, para 36.

ed to the sanctions) fall outside the Court of Justice's competence.[28] Indeed, Article 275, paragraph 2, TFEU empowers the Court to assess the legality of restrictive measures *vis-a-vis* natural and legal persons.[29] Only the listing decision qualifies as a restrictive measure. As a result, in the case in which an economic operator, like Rosneft, falls within the scope *ratione personae* of a third country sanction regime, he will not be able to contest provisions prohibiting or restricting the selling of a certain technology,[30] even if such an operator is one out of three listed in the annexes of the CFSP decision.

This interpretation, that is to say, that the mentioned provisions are of general nature, is frequently used in the case law of the Court of Justice[31] and General Court,[32] and may be criticised. Is Rosneft not a legal person targeted by a CFSP decision, which instituted a restrictive measure *vis-a-vis* natural and legal persons, as provided for by Article 275, paragraph 2, TFEU? Surely this is the case, and the Court has broadly construed "the notion of natural and legal persons" incorporated in Article 275, paragraph 2, TFUE to include emanations of the state;[33] it is not even excluded that third countries could rely on Article 263, paragraph 4, TFUE to contest re-

28 Both AG Whatelet and the Court of Justice excluded the so-called "oil sector provisions" (Article 4 and 4a) of the CFSP decision contested in *Rosneft*. See the *Rosneft, supra* note 13, paras 95-99 and opinion of AG Wathelet of 31 May 2016, *Rosneft,* EU:C:2016:381, paras 81-85.

29 Judgment of 28 March 2017, *Rosneft, supra* note 13, para 98.

30 Such as Articles 4 and 4a of the CFSP decision at stake in the *Rosneft* case.

31 The Court of Justice holds that it is the individual nature of the restrictive measures that permits access to the Courts of the European Union in its Judgement of 23 April 2013, *Gbagbo and Others* v *Council*, C-478/11P to C-482/11P, EU:C:2013:258, para 57.

32 Judgment of 17 February 2017, *Islamic Republic of Iran Shipping Lines*, T-14/14 and T 87/14, EU:T:2017:102, paras 37-39; Judgement of 4 June 2014, *Sina Bank*, T-67/12, EU:T:2014:348, para 38; and Judgement of 4 June 2014, *Hemmati*, T-68/12, EU:T:2014:349, para 31.

33 For an interpretation that "emanations of third states" qualify as natural and legal persons within the meaning of Article 275, paragraph 2, TFUE, see Judgement of 4 September 2015, *National Iranian Oil Company PTE Ltd (NIOC)*, T-577/12, EU:T:2015:596. This position contrasts with the practice of the ECtHR. Under Article 34 of ECHR, these applicants would not have legal standing to submit an individual application to the ECHR since this right is reserved for persons, non-governmental organizations, or group of individuals, the *ratio legis* being that a state cannot enjoy fundamental rights. However, the Court has not found similar limitations either in the Charter of Fundamental Rights of the European Union or in the

strictive measures. It is a choice of the Court to interpret the notion of "restrictive measures instituted *vis-a-vis* legal and natural persons" as excluding that natural and legal persons may challenge provisions of general nature included in the sanctions. Article 275, paragraph 2, TFEU could be interpreted, in the light of the right to an effective protection, as extending the Court's jurisdiction to all the provisions of the contested restrictive measures, and not only those including Rosneft in the list of addresses of the restrictive measures. The distinction between provisions of a general nature and those of an "individual nature" (the listing decision) within the CFSP decision that instituted restrictive measures is artificial and not anchored to the text of Article 275, paragraph 2, TFEU. Therefore, it should be abandoned.

The Court's interpretation does not sit comfortably alongside another preliminary ruling, released approximately 14 days before *Rosneft*, which made it possible for individuals to challenge the validity of the provisions of a CFSP decision instituting restrictive measures against a designated terrorist group, despite the fact that the appellants in the proceedings were not listed by that act.[34] If third parties can contest the legality of restrictive measures, why, then, can Rosneft, which is listed in the contested decision, not impugn an export prohibition that directly affects its activity?

III. *The Court of Justice's Contribution to an Effective Judicial Protection through the Scrutiny of Restrictive Measures*

Having clarified that the EU judicature provides a meaningful access to justice to non-state actors whose interests are affected by restrictive measures, let us now turn to the substance of the actions contesting the legality of these measures. In the years that followed the entry into force of the Lisbon Treaty, the *contentieux* on restrictive measures has grown constantly.[35]

Treaties. See Judgment of 28 November 2013, *Council/Manufacturing Support & Procurement Kala Naft*, C-348/12 P, EU:C:2013:776. See also Judgment of 29 January 2013, *Bank Mellat* v *Council*, T-496/10, EU:T:2013:39, paras 35-46, and Judgment of 5 February 2013, *Bank Saderat Iran* v *Council*, T-494/10, EU:T:2013:59.

34 Judgment of 14 March 2017, *A and others*, *supra* note 21.

35 The number of new cases concerning restrictive measures increased from 21 (in 2010) to 62 (in 2014). See EU Court of Justice, *Annual Report-Judicial Activity*,

It should be emphasised that the Council enjoys a wide margin of discretion in the CFSP; the Court of Justice cannot interfere with the power to decide the scope *ratione personae* of restrictive measures or choose their designation criteria. Yet, the EU judiciary exercises full judicial control over the CFSP acts, whose legality may be questioned before it for breach of the rights enjoyed by individuals in the EU and for a manifest error of assessment by the Council. The Court has greatly enhanced the procedural rights of the targets of restrictive measures, both with respect to sanctions of UN-origin, a context in which the absence of due process rights is conspicuous,[36] and autonomous EU sanctions. Since the Council should respect the right to an effective judicial protection and the right to a defence, it is bound to duly motivate the inclusion in the list of a natural and legal person by providing a summary of the reasons leading to their inclusion in the list, even if the sanction is of UN-origin;[37] this will enable the targets of these measures to make their observations known to the EU institutions and prepare their defence in a possible action for annulment of those measures before the EU Courts. The reasons justifying the decision to list[38] (or re-list) a natural or a legal person or a group of individuals should also not be too vague. The Council must have a set of indicia sufficiently specific, precise, and consistent[39] to establish that there is a sufficient link between the person subject to a measure freezing his funds and the regime being combated; the factual evidence at the basis of listing de-

2014, 183. See, for comments, V. B. Bertrand, "La particularité du contrôle juridictionnel des mesures restrictives: les considérations impérieuses touchant à la sûreté ou à la conduite des relations internationales de l'Union et de ses Etats membres", *Révue Trimestrielle de Droit Européen* 51, no. 3 (2015), 555.

36 For a recent in-depth study, see D. Hovell, "Due process in the EU United Nations", *American Journal of International Law* 110, no. 1 (2016), 1.

37 In adopting restrictive measures, the Council must respect the same principles, regardless of whether such measures are autonomously by the EU or they are of UN-origin.

38 Judgment of 30 November 2016, *Rotenberg*, T-720/14, EU:T:2016:689.

39 Judgment of 21 April 2015, *Anbouba*, C-605/13 P, EU:C:2015:248, para 53. In *Kadi II*, concerning counter- terrorism measures, the Court of Justice held that the effectiveness of judicial review requires that the listing decision is taken on sufficiently solid factual basis. See Judgment of 12 July 2013, *Commission* v *Kadi*, EU:C:2013:518, C-584/10 P, C-593/10 P, and C-595/10 P, para 119 (hereinafter: *Kadi II*).

cision must not be drawn from internet-based sources.[40] Failure to comply with these principles will lead the Court to annul the contested measures.

It should also be noted that actions in damages are available as a remedy to non-State parties in case they incur a damage as a result of a serious breach of a rule of law intended to confer rights on individuals and there is a causal link between the breach and damage. The addresses of the sanctions are empowered to claim for damages resulting from the adoption of a regulation made necessary by the enactment of a CFSP decision.[41] The Court has also afforded individuals the right to protect their reputation, by laying down the principle that the interest of the applicant in bringing proceedings may continue to exist despite the removal of his name from the list at issue. This case law applies both in relation to restrictive measures designed to counter terrorism[42] and in relation to third-country regimes.[43]

If one looks at the outcome of the *contentieux*, in some cases the annulment of a listing decision by the Court led the Council to de-list the successful applicant;[44] but there are also situations in which the General

40 Judgment of 17 December 2014, *Hamas*, T-400/10, EU:T:2014:1095, para 110. However, the Court has been ready to accept press articles as evidence of the use of Russian weapons by the Eastern Ukrainian separatists. See Judgment of 25 January 2017, *Almaz-Antey*, T-255/15, EU:T:2017:25, paras 147-148.

41 However, as far as action in damages *vis-à-vis* a CFSP decision instituting a restrictive measure are concerned, these are inadmissible. See Judgment of 28 January 2016, *Jannatian*, T-328/14, EU:T:2016:36, para 31, concerning a restriction on admission. This form of restrictive measures are decided through CFSP decisions and can only be challenged at national level.

42 Judgment of 28 May 2013, *Abdulrahim*, C-239/12 P, EU:C:2013:331, paras 71 and 82. See E. Cimiotta, "Rimozione dall'elenco di sospetti terroristi e interesse a proseguire l'azione di annullamento del provvedimento di listing: il caso Abdulrahim davanti alla Corte di giustizia dell'Unione europea", *Diritti umani e diritto internazionale* 8, no. 2 (2014), 451.

43 See, amongst others, Judgment of 4 June 2014, *Ali Sedghi*, T-66/12, EU:T:2014:347, and Judgment of 26 October 2015, *Portnov*, T-290/14, EU:T:2015:806.

44 See, e.g., Council Decision 2014/776/CFSP of 7 November 2014, OJ 2014 L 325/19; Council Implementing Decision 2014/730/CFSP of 20 October 2014, OJ 2014 L 301/36; Council Decision 2015/837/CFSP of 28 May 2015, OJ 2015 L 132; Council Implementing Decision 2016/2000/CFSP of 15 November 2016 implementing Decision 2013/255/CFSP, OJ 2016 L 308/20; Council Decision 2017/83/CFSP of 16 January 2017, OJ 2017 L 12/92.

Court annulled the re-listing of a person.[45] In addition, individuals won an action for failure to act against the Commission[46], and, in one case, the EU was also found responsible for the non-material damage caused to a company in the context of the nuclear proliferation sanction regime against Iran (in *Safa Nicu Sepaham*).[47] Therefore, effective judicial protection is guaranteed to the addresses of sanctions in the EU legal order.

Having this positive picture in mind, we should acknowledge that only in a minority of cases were applicants de-listed as a result of the Court's annulment of their inclusion in the list. Restrictive measures have never been considered to be incompatible with the right to property or to carry out an economic activity since the restrictions of these rights were justified by the primary importance of maintaining international peace and security.[48] Recently, an action for annulment, introduced by a Russian journalist, claiming that his inclusion in the blacklist breached the right to freedom of expression, was rejected.[49] In addition, most of the cases concerning actions in damages failed.[50]

It is true that a substantial number of actions challenging the legality of restrictive measures were fully (or partially) upheld by the Court if one looks only at those considered admissible, especially in 2014 and 2015.[51] However, in many cases, the Council better motivated inscription in the list[52] or provided additional evidence rather than de-listing the applicant; in others, it has reacted by extending the scope *ratione personae* of the

---

45 See, e.g., judgement of 24 May 2016, *Good Luck Shipping*, EU:T:2016:308; Judgement of 18 October 2016, *Sina Bank,* T-418/14, EU:T:2016:619.

46 Judgment of 21 March 2014, *Yusef,* T-306/10, EU:T:2014:141.

47 Judgment of 25 November 2014, *Safa Nicu Sepahan Co.*, T-384/11, EU:T:2014:986.

48 Judgment of 24 October 2009, *Bank Melli Iran*, T-390/08, EU:T:2009:401, para 71.

49 Judgment of 15 June 2017, *Kiselev*, T-262/15, EU:T:2017:392.

50 M. Messina, "Il controllo giurisdizionale delle misure restrittive antiterrorismo e il risarcimento del danno da "listing" nel diritto dell'Unione europea", *Diritto dell'Unione europea*, no. 3 (2016), 605, at 631.

51 S. Poli, *supra* note 3, 174-175.

52 For example, in 2017, Mr Rotenberg, a businessman in Mr Putin's close circle, was re-listed after his first listing decision had been partially annulled by the General Court. See Judgment of 30 November 2016, *Rotenberg*, *supra* note 38.

CFSP decision,[53] so as to make possible the listing of the person/entity who had won the annulment action. Indeed, "the restrictive measures adopted both by the [UN] Security Council and by the EU are progressive and justified by the lack of success of the measures adopted previously.[54]" The decision to re-list has been challenged in subsequent actions, but it has often been rejected by the General Court[55] or on appeal.[56]

The outcome of the case law can be explained by acknowledging that the Court of Justice must ensure that the law is respected, but, at the same time, it is also bound to interpret the Treaty without jeopardising the Council's power to act effectively in the sphere of the CFSP. The latter obligation derives from Article 13, paragraph 2, TEU, which imposes on all institutions to loyally cooperate with each other. The Court has also interpreted the provisions of CFSP decisions contested by individuals in such a way as to preserve the effectiveness[57] of the sanction and underlined that the importance of the objectives pursued by restrictive measures is such as to justify that operators, who are not responsible for the breach-

---

53 This is Decision 2014/512/CFSP concerning restrictive measures in view of Russia's actions, as amended by Council Decision 2014/659/CFSP of 8 September 2014, OJ 2014 L 271/54.

54 Judgment of 28 November 2013, *Council/Manufacturing Support & Procurement Kala Naft*, *supra* note 33, para 126; Judgment of 5 April 2017, *Sharif University of Technology*, C-385/16 P, EU:C:2017, 258, para 56.

55 See Judgment of 14 March 2017, *Bank Tejerat*, T-346/15, EU:T:2017:164; Judgment of 17 February 2017, *Islamic Republic of Iran Shipping Lines*, joined cases T-14/14 and T-87/14, EU:T:2017:102; Judgment of 30 November 2016, *Export development bank of Iran*, T-89/14, EU:T:2016:693; Judgment of 30 November 2016, *Bank Refah Kargaran*, T-65/14, EU:T:2016:692; Judgment of 26 October 2016, *Hamcho and Hamcho International*, T-153/15, EU:T:2016:630; Judgment of 26 October 2016, *Jaber*, T-154/15, EU:T:2016:629; Judgment of 26 October 2016, *Kaddour*, T-155/15, EU:T:2016:628.

56 Judgment of 7 April 2016, *Central Bank of Iran*, C-266/15 P, EU:C:2016:208; Judgment of 1 March 2016, *National Iranian Oil Company*, C-440/14 P, EU:C:2016:128. See also appeals brought by the Council against the General Court's decision annulling the listing decision in Judgment of 26 July 2016, *Council* v. *Hamas*, C-79/15 P, EU:C:2017:584; Judgment of 26 July 2016, *Council* v. *LTTE*, C-599/14 P, EU:C:2017:583.

57 Judgment of 14 April 2016, *Mehdi Ben Ali*, T-200/14, EU:T:2016:216, para 133; Judgment of 27 February 2014, *Ezz*, T-256/11, EU:T:2014:93, para 66.

es of their countries, may suffer negative consequences as a result of the application of these measures.[58]

However, an assessment of the Court of Justice's case law in the area of restrictive measures cannot be strictly based on the number of de-listing decisions resulting from successful annulment actions. The EU judiciary cannot do more than impose on the Council to respect procedural standards. When assessing the merit of an action against a restrictive measure, the Court's task is merely to check that the Council has not acted in an arbitrary manner.[59]

IV. Recent Developments in the Court of Justice's Case Law: A Decline in the Level of Judicial Protection?

Having highlighted the strengths and weaknesses of the case law on restrictive measures by taking the perspective of natural and legal persons subject to them, it is necessary to dwell on two recent developments,

---

58 Judgment of 18 February 2016, *Council* v *Bank Mellat*, C-176/13, EU:C:2016:96, para 204.

59 A similar standard of review was recognised by the European Court of Human Rights as the one prescribed by Article 6, paragraph 1, of the ECHR on national authorities of State parties to the ECHR. In the *Al Dulimi* ruling, Switzerland was found to breach the mention provision of the ECHR since, in 2008, the Swiss Federal court refused to examine the merit of the action brought by a number of former officials of the Iraq government against the confiscation of their properties, enacted by Switzerland to implement a UNSC Resolution of 2003. The view of the Court was that the domestic court should have carried out judicial review for the purpose of avoiding arbitrary designations by the UNSC. The reasons leading the domestic court to take such a decision was that, under Article 103 of the UN Charter, the obligations deriving from the latter Treaty prevail over other those stemming from sources of international law, except for the *jus cogens*. In addition, the UNSC resolution at stake did not leave any degree of flexibility to national authorities. The ECtHR excluded that there was a conflict of obligations between the UN Charter and the ECHR. The position was taken that: "[...] where a [UNSC] resolution [...], does not contain any clear or explicit wording excluding the possibility of judicial supervision of the measures taken for its implementation, it must always be understood as authorising the courts of the respondent State to exercise sufficient scrutiny so that any arbitrariness can be avoided". (para 146). The Court went on to state that: "Any State Party whose authorities give legal effect to the addition of a person – whether an individual or a legal entity – to a sanctions list, without first ensuring – or being able to ensure – that the listing is not arbitrary will engage its responsibility under Article 6 of the Convention".

which could decrease the robustness of judicial protection afforded to natural and legal persons targeted by restrictive measures.

The first development concerns the standard of proof for including a natural or legal person on a blacklist. It is not clear whether or not the General Court has lowered the standard of proof required to list a person involved in terrorist activities with respect to that applicable in *Kadi* imposing on the Council to have a sufficiently solid factual basis from which to insert the name of a natural/legal person in the Council decisions instituting restrictive measures.[60] In *Al Gabra*,[61] the General Court admitted that a person could be listed when there are "reasonable grounds for suspicion", provided that those grounds are supported by sufficient information or evidence.[62] This is the test that was used in the *Youssef*[63] case by the UK.[64] Yet, in a Union founded on the rule of law, the need to effectively fight terrorism must be balanced with respect for fundamental rights, consistently with the well-established jurisprudence of the Court of Justice.

A second development is the approval of new Rules of Procedure governing proceedings before the Courts of the EU, which entered into force in 2016[65]. Articles 105 and 190bis of, respectively, the General Court and the Court of Justice's Rules of Procedure, introduce the so-called "closed material procedure".[66] The latter makes it possible to derogate to the adversarial principles which characterise the proceedings before the Courts in order to preserve the confidentiality of certain information.[67] Article

60 The test that is applied in the case of listing decisions of businessmen associated with third country regimes is different and was clarified in the *Anbouba* (Judgment of 21 April 2015, *supra* note 39). In para 53, the Court of Justice held that "the Council discharges the burden of proof borne by it when it presents to the Courts of the European Union a set of indicia sufficiently specific, precise and consistent to establish that there is a sufficient link between the person subject to a measure freezing his funds and the regime being combated".

61 Judgment of 13 December 2016, *Al-Gabra*, T-248/13, EU:T:2016:721.

62 *Id.*, para 117.

63 *Youssef* (appellant) v *Secretary of State for Foreign and Commonwealth Affairs* (respondent) [2016] UKSC 3.

64 House of Lords, EU Committee, *The legality of EU sanctions*, 2017 11.

65 See the chapter by Allan Rosas in this volume.

66 This expression is used for the first time by AG Sharpston in her opinion of 14 July 2011, *France* v *People's Mojahedin Organization of Iran*, C-27/09, EU:C:2011:853, para 193. See further on the new security rules of EU Courts the Chapter by Allan Rosas in this volume.

67 Recital n. 9 of the General Court's Rules of Procedure, OJ 2015, L 105/1.

105 of the General Court Rules of Procedure and Article 190 bis of the Court of Justice Rules of Procedure do not specifically apply to the proceedings concerning restrictive measures; however, the Council has invoked EU security or the need to protect its international relations in proceedings concerning the legality of restrictive measures in order to not disclose to the other party the evidence at the basis of some restrictive measures. The new rules imply that the main party (the Council) may provide the information and material[68] supporting the inclusion in the list of natural and legal persons to the Courts without disclosing it to the other party (a natural/legal person included in the list and wishing to challenge it) – in consideration of the need to protect overriding interests related to Member States and EU's security and international relations – and the Courts may use this information in making their decisions.[69] That the Courts need not to disclose certain information to the person who challenges the listing decision was also admitted by the Court of Justice in *Kadi I*[70] and *Kadi II* rulings;[71] the Courts of the EU were given the task of using techniques which accommodate on the one hand, security concerns, and, on the other, the need to guarantee respect of procedural rights. However, under the rules of procedures in force at the time of this judgment, it was not possible for the Court to take material undisclosed to the other party into consideration when assessing the legality of these measures. As a result, in the absence of non-confidential evidence to support restrictive measures, the Council could not prove that these measures were based on solid factual evidence, and its decisions instituting sanctions were annulled.[72]

Under Article 105 of the General Court Rules of Procedure, when the main party in proceedings before the Court intends to base his claims on certain information or material but submits that its communication would

---

68 Such evidence may come from the Member States or from other sources.

69 See Article 105 of the General Court's Rules of Procedure and Article 190 bis of the Rules of Procedure of the Court of Justice, OJ 2016 L 217/71. The two provisions entered into force on December 2016. For a comment on Article 190 bis, see S. Poli, "Comment to article 190 bis of the Rules of Procedure of the Court of Justice", in C. Amalfitano, M. Condinanzi, P. Iannuccelli (eds), *Le regole del processo dinanzi al giudice dell'Unione europea* (Giuffré: Milano 2017), 901.

70 Judgment of 3 September 2008, *Kadi and Al Barakaat International Foundation*, C-402/05 P and 415/05P, EU:C:2008:461, para 342.

71 Judgment of 12 July 2013, *Kadi II*, *supra* note 39, para 125.

72 See, for example, Judgment of 21 April 2016, *Council* v *Fulmen*, C- 280/12 P, EU:C:2013:775, paras 100-103.

harm the security of the Union or that of one or more of its Member States or the conduct of their international relations, it may apply for confidential treatment of this information. The General Court will examine such information and may decide that it is not confidential (and, as such, can be communicated to the other party)[73] or that such material cannot be disclosed to the concerned party for the overriding reasons mentioned above. In the latter case, the General Court "shall [...] weigh the requirements linked to the right to effective judicial protection, particularly observance of the adversarial principle, against the requirements flowing from the security of the Union or of one or more of its Member States or the conduct of their international relations".[74] The Court may also issue a reasoned order imposing on the party that applied for the confidential treatment to provide "a non-confidential version or a non-confidential summary of the information or material, containing the essential content thereof and enabling the other main party, to the greatest extent possible, to make its views known". However, what is important is that the Court may consider that the information and material at its disposal is essential in order for it to rule in the case, and, as a result, the EU judges may, by way of derogation from Article 64 and confining themselves to what is strictly necessary, base their judicial decision on such information or material.[75] The new procedural rules, which also apply in proceedings before the Court of Justice,[76] will enable the Council to gain an advantage in the proceedings concerning restrictive measures. In addition, the confidentiality of the information transferred from the Council or the EU Member States to the EU Courts is now guaranteed by new internal rules adopted by the latter in order to ensure a high level of protection for this material.[77]

---

73 The sensitive material and information can be withdrawn by the party that produced it and applied for confidential treatment, under Article 105, paragraph 7. In this case, this material will not be taken into account in the determination of the case. However, the material cannot be withdrawn at any time.

74 Article 105, paragraph 5, of the General Court Rules of Procedure.

75 Article 105, paragraph 8, of the General Court Rules of Procedure.

76 See Article 190 bis of the Court of Justice Rules of Procedure.

77 Decision 2016/2386/EU of the Court of Justice of 20 September 2016 concerning the security rules applicable to information or material produced before the General Court in accordance with Article 105 of its Rules of Procedure, OJ 2016 L 355/5, and Decision 2016/2387/EU of the General Court of 14 September 2016 concerning the security rules applicable to information or material produced in ac-

At the moment, the impact on litigation concerning restrictive measures of the new legal framework is uncertain. Allan Rosas wishes that it will encourage the Council and EU Member States to submit information to the Court[78] so as to give evidence that the listing decision was well founded; however, consideration should be given to the fact that the UK abstained on the adoption of the General Court's Rules of Procedure; in addition, doubts were expressed on whether some Member States would consider the safeguards provided by the new security rules adopted by the Courts as strong enough to protect this information; in other words, would Member States be willing to provide certain confidential information and material to the Court?[79] In the case of a positive answer, it is to be hoped that the latter will be strict in assessing whether or not reliance on the information and material referred to in Article 105 of the Rules of Procedures is relevant for the adjudication of a given case. The application for confidential treatment of this material should be accepted only in exceptional cases, and, wherever possible, the Council should use non-confidential evidence to defend its measures. Indeed, there is nothing similar to the "special advocate procedure" in the EU in order to protect the rights of the targets of restrictive measures, and, therefore, doubts may be raised as to the compatibility of the new rules with the right to a fair hearing.[80] The EU Courts have the difficult task of guaranteeing the full respect of this right.

---

cordance with Article 105, paragraph 1 or 2 of the Rules of Procedure, OJ 2016 L 355/18.

78 See A. Rosas, "EU Restrictive Measures against Third States: Value Imperialism, Future Gesture Politics of Judicial Extravaganza", *Diritto dell'Unione europea*, no. 4 (2016), 630, at 650; see also the chapter by Allan Rosas in this volume.

79 House of Lords, *supra* note 64, 19.

80 *Id.*, p. 20.

EU Sanctions, Security Concerns and Judicial Control

Allan Rosas

I. Introduction

While the European Court of Justice has in the past been faced with certain situations relating to security concerns,[1] the problem of security has become more tangible in connection with EU sanctions policies. It should be recalled that especially since the 1990s, the development of an EU external relations policy has been matched by a gradual movement from sanctions undertaken by individual Member States towards a veritable EU sanctions policy.[2] Sanctions against third States and other parties are normally taken by the EU, acting, as it were, on behalf of the Union and its Member States. There is a range of instruments and mechanisms that can be used in this respect, such as suspending the operation of an autonomous regulation relating to financial assistance, suspending the operation of an international agreement (notably on the basis of a human rights clause inserted in a number of bilateral trade and cooperation agreements)[3] and, last but not least, adopting restrictive measures affecting economic and financial relations with third States. Such restrictive measures may imply,

---

1 Just to mention a few examples, see Judgement of 17 October 1995, *Werner,* C-70/94, EU:C:1995:328; Judgement of 17 October 1995, *Leifer,* C-83/94, EU:C:1995:329; Judgement of 14 January 1997, *Centro-Com,* C-124/95, EU:C:1997:8.

2 P. J. Kuijper, "Trade Sanctions, Security and Human Rights and Commercial Policy", in M. Maresceau (ed), *The European Community's Commercial Policy after 1992: The Legal Dimension* (Dordrecht: Martinus Nijhoff, 1993), 387; E. Paasivirta, A. Rosas, "Sanctions, Countermeasures and Related Actions in the External Relations of the EU: A Search for Legal Frameworks", in E. Cannizzaro (eds), *The European Union as an Actor in International Relations* (Alphen aan den Rijn: Kluwer Law International, 2002), 207.

3 See, e.g. A. Rosas, "The European Union and Fundamental Rights/Human Rights", in C. Krause, N. Scheinin (eds), *International Protection of Human Rights: A Textbook* (Turku: Åbo Akademi University Institute for Human Rights, 2012), 481, at 507-512.

inter alia, the freezing of funds, prohibitions or restrictions on conducting a business or restrictions on free movement.

It is above all in the context of restrictive measures that security concerns may become acute. Under Article 215 of the Treaty on the Functioning of the European Union (TFEU), such measures may be adopted on the basis of a decision adopted under the Common Foreign and Security Policy (CFSP). This possibility, which was, in a somewhat more restricted form, envisaged already in the Treaty of Maastricht (1992),[4] implies, according to Article 215, paragraph 1, TFEU,a Council CFSP decision providing for "the interruption or reduction, in part or completely, of economic and financial relations with one or more third countries", followed by the adoption, also by the Council, of a legally binding act, normally in the form of a regulation. The CFSP decision is as a rule adopted unanimously whilst the regulation adopted under Article 215, paragraph 1, TFEU only requires a qualified majority in the Council. Article 215, paragraph 2, TFEU, unlike the provisions preceding the Treaty of Lisbon, makes it clear that such restrictive measures may also be taken against "natural or legal persons and groups or non-State entities".[5]

The adoption of restrictive measures addressed to natural or legal persons engenders tension in the EU's legal order: while sanctions may be necessary to pursue a legitimate policy objective of the EU, they might also severely affect individuals' rights. The next section discusses the balancing of these concerns in the judicial practice.[6] To contribute to an appropriate balance between judicial protection and security concerns, the General Court and the Court of Justice recently introduced new procedures, which are presented in section III.

---

4 See Articles 73g and 228a of the Treaty establishing the European Community (TEC), based on Article G of the Treaty on European Union (TEU) of 1992, amending the Treaty establishing the European Economic Community.

5 As the provisions preceding Article 215 TFEU did not contain a similar clause on non-State entities, including private persons, the first sanctions against Al Qaida were also grounded in the then Article 308 TEC (now Article 352 TFEU).

6 Further on this issue, see the chapters by Sara Poli and by Hugo Flavier in this volume.

II. The Balancing of Judicial Protection and Security Concerns in the Case Law of the European Court of Justice

As is well known, in *Kadi I*, which concerned a case of alleged terrorist activities, the Court of Justice affirmed with emphasis its duty to "ensure the review, in principle the full review, of the lawfulness of all [Union] acts in the light of fundamental rights …., including review of [Union] measures which... are designed to give effect to the resolutions adopted by the Security Council under Chapter VII of the Charter of the United Nations".[7]

Whilst fundamental rights such as the right to effective judicial protection ride high in this judgment, the Court did acknowledge that in the fight against terrorism, security concerns are relevant when dealing with the right to be heard. Not only must restrictive measures, when adopted for the first time, take advantage of a surprise effect and thus apply with immediate effect, but "overriding considerations to do with safety or the conduct of the international relations of the [Union] and of its Member States may militate against the communication of certain matters to the persons concerned and, therefore, against their being heard on those matters".[8] In such a scenario, it is the task of the Union judicature to apply "techniques which accommodate, on the one hand, legitimate security concerns about the nature and sources of information taken into account in the adoption of the act concerned and, on the other, the need to accord the individual a sufficient measure of procedural justice".[9]

It is in this context interesting to note that the Court of Justice has more recently underlined that the fight against terrorism and against serious crime constitute objectives of general interest and that Article 6 of the EU Charter of Fundamental Rights states that everyone has the right "not only to liberty but also to security".[10] In this context, the Court has added that "the protection of national security and public order also contributes to the

---

7 Judgement of 3 September 2008, *Kadi and Al Barakaat* ("*Kadi I*"), C-402/05 P & C-415/05 P, EU:C:2008:461, para 326. See also A. Rosas, "Counter-Terrorism and the Rule of Law: Issues of Judicial Control", in A. M. Salinas de Frías a.o. (eds), *Counter-Terrorism: International Law and Practice* (Oxford: Oxford University Press, 2012), 83.

8 *Id.*, para 342.

9 *Id.* para 344.

10 Judgement of 8 April 2014, *Digital Rights Ireland*, C-293/12 & C-594/12, EU:C:2014:238, para 42.

protection of the rights and freedoms of others".[11] It is in other words not only a question of public security in the abstract but of ensuring that the right to security of each and everyone be respected.[12]

Especially in *ZZ* and *Kadi II*, [13] the Court of Justice had the opportunity to develop its reasoning on how to balance the requirements of security and effective judicial protection and on what techniques could be used in this respect. In *ZZ*, the Court, in the context of a request for a preliminary ruling and thus with a national court as addressee, affirmed that it may prove necessary, both in administrative proceedings and in judicial proceedings, not to disclose certain information to the person concerned, in particular in the light of overriding considerations connected with State security.[14] On the other hand, the fundamental right to an effective legal remedy would in principle be infringed "if a judicial decision were founded on facts and documents which the parties themselves, or one of them, have not had an opportunity to examine and on which they have therefore been unable to state their views".[15] The adversarial principle could on the other hand be derogated from in exceptional circumstances, and under strict conditions:

> "However, if, in exceptional cases, a national authority opposes precise and full disclosure to the person concerned of the grounds which constitute the basis of a decision taken under Article 27 of Directive 2004/38, by invoking reasons of State security, the court with jurisdiction in the Member State concerned must have at its disposal and apply techniques and rules of procedural law which accommodate, on the one hand, legitimate State security considerations regarding the nature and sources of the information taken into account in the adoption of such a decision and, on the other hand, the need to ensure sufficient compliance with the person's procedural rights, such as the right to be heard and the adversarial principle (see, by analogy, *Kadi and Al Barakaat International Foundation* v *Council and Commission*, paragraph 344)".[16]

---

11 Judgement of 15 February 2016, *J.N.*, C-601/15 PPU, EU:C:2016:84, para. 53.

12 A similar approach has been adopted by the Human Rights Committee, acting under the International Covenant on Civil and Political Rights, with respect to Article 9 (liberty and security of person) of the Covenant, see, eg M. Nowak, *U.N. Covenant on Civil and Political Rights: CCPR Commentary* (Kehl am Rhein: N.P. Engel, 2005), 213.

13 Judgement of 4 June 2013, *ZZ*, C-300/11, EU:C:2013:363; Judgement of 17 July 2013, *Commission and Others* v *Kadi* ("*Kadi II*"), C-584/10 P, C-593/10 P & C-595/10 P, EU:C:2013:518.

14 Judgement of 4 June 2013, *ZZ*, *supra* note 13, para. 54.

15 *Id.*, para 56.

16 *Id.*, para 57.

> "In this connection, first, in the light of the need to comply with Article 47 of the Charter, that procedure must ensure, to the greatest possible extent, that the adversarial principle is complied with, in order to enable the person concerned to contest the grounds on which the decision in question is based and to make submissions on the evidence relating to the decision and, therefore, to put forward an effective defence. In particular, the person concerned must be informed, in any event, of the essence of the grounds on which a decision refusing entry taken under Article 27 of Directive 2004/38 is based, as the necessary protection of State security cannot have the effect of denying the person concerned his right to be heard and, therefore, of rendering his right of redress as provided for in Article 31 of that directive ineffective".[17]
> "Accordingly, it is incumbent upon the national court with jurisdiction, first, to ensure that the person concerned is informed of the essence of the grounds which constitute the basis of the decision in question in a manner which takes due account of the necessary confidentiality of the evidence and, second, to draw, pursuant to national law, the appropriate conclusions from any failure to comply with that obligation to inform him".[18]

In *Kadi II*, the Court of Justice applied the approach taken in *ZZ* at the level of the Union judicature.[19] In this context, the Court specified that when striking an "appropriate balance" between the right to effective judicial protection and the security of the EU and its Member States or the conduct of their international relations, "it is legitimate to consider possibilities such as the disclosure of a summary outlining the information's content or that of the evidence in question".[20] It should be noted that the Court does not here mention the use of "special advocates" as an example of techniques to be used, in other words advocates or other lawyers appointed by the Court of Justice to assist it in assessing confidential material submitted by intelligence services (but who are not allowed to divulge such material to the other party such as an alleged terrorist).[21] In *ZZ,* again, the Court of Justice did not refer to examples at all but more generally to "techniques and rules of procedural law" (which, perhaps, at the national level could include the use of "special advocates").

17 *Id.*, para 65.

18 *Id.,* para 68.

19 Judgment of 17 July 2013, *Commission and Others* v *Kadi* ("*Kadi II*"), *supra* note 13, paras 125-129.

20 *Id.*, para 129.

21 The system of "special advocates" is in use in the United Kingdom in particular, see, eg House of Commons, Constitutional Affairs Committee, Seventh Report, Session 2004-05, Chapter IV.

The Court of Justice, in *Kadi II*, also made it clear that if the competent Union authority finds itself unable to provide the information and evidence required, "it is then the duty of the [Union Courts] to base their decision solely on the material which has been disclosed to them" and if the material provided is insufficient to allow a finding that a reason is well founded, the Union Courts shall disregard that reason as a possible basis for the contested decision to list or maintain a listing of a person.[22] So under exceptional circumstances, all material need not necessarily be disclosed to the person concerned (such as the alleged terrorist) but the material which is not disclosed must at any rate be submitted to the judge for evaluation.

Especially since the judgment in *Kadi I*, the case law of the Union Courts relating to restrictive measures has become both rich and extensive. Without going into this case law in any greater detail, the following statistics may be mentioned. Whilst in 2006 five actions of annulment were brought before the General Court, the more recent figures are as follows: 93 new cases in 2011, 59 in 2012, 41 in 2013, 69 in 2014, 55 in 2015 and 28 in 2016.[23] Clearly a less number of cases were brought on appeal before the Court of Justice. In 2015, for instance, the Court decided seven such cases. These figures do not cover cases brought under the preliminary ruling procedure (Article 267 TFEU) but they are quite few as compared to actions for annulment (Article 263 TFEU).[24]

Many of the direct actions have led to the annulment of the sanctions decision in whole or in part. In the *Kadi II* judgment, in particular, the Court of Justice, partly drawing upon earlier case law,[25] had occasion to specify, *inter alia*, the obligation to state reasons, holding that a decision to maintain the name of an individual on a sanctions list requires in all circumstances that the statement of reasons "identifies the individual, specif-

22 Judgement of 17 July 2013, *Commission and Others* v *Kadi* ("*Kadi II*"), *supra* note 13, para 123.

23 Court of Justice of the European Union, *Annual Report 2016: Judicial Activity* (Luxembourg, 2017), 208.

24 One example of a request for a preliminary ruling is Judgement of 4 June 2013, *ZZ, supra* note 13. Another example is Judgement of 28 March 2017, *Rosneft,* C-72/15, EU:C:2017:236.

25 See, e.g. Judgement of 16 November 2011, *Bank Melli Iran* v *Council,* C-548/09 P, EU:C:2011:735; Judgement of 15 November 2012, *Al-Aqsa,* C-593/10 P & C-550/10 P, EU:C:2012:711; Judgement of 15 November 2012, *Council* v *Bamba,* C-471/11 P, EU:C:2012:718.

ic and concrete reasons why the competent authorities consider that the individual concern must be subject to restrictive measures".[26] The Court further stated that the Council is under an obligation to examine, "carefully and impartially", whether the alleged reasons are well-founded and the decision is taken "on a sufficiently solid factual basis".[27] Whilst the Council has a "broad discretion" with respect to the defining of the general criteria which should be adopted for the purpose of applying restrictive measures,[28] the reasons and proof provided to demonstrate that a person or entity fall under the general criteria is subject to a more intense judicial scrutiny.

If the Council (which is normally the defendant in these cases) has not been able to satisfy those requirements, the sanctions decisions have been annulled. And, in line with what was said in *Kadi II*, as quoted above, the Council cannot rely on a claim that the evidence concerned comes from confidential sources and cannot, consequently, be communicated to the General Court. For instance, in *Fulmen*, the Court of Justice stated that "since the competent European Union authority refused to produce evidence to the Courts of the European Union, it is for those Courts … to base their decision solely on the material which has been disclosed to them".[29] And since the only information available to the Courts was the claim made in the statement of reasons, which was not substantiated by the production of any other information or evidence, both the General Court and the Court of Justice concluded that the persons concerned were not in a position to defend themselves against the allegations and that the Union Courts were not in a position to determine whether the acts at issue were well founded. The appeal was consequently dismissed and the General Court's judgment to annul the decisions and regulations imposing restrictive measures was upheld.

It may be instructive to compare this outcome with that of the *Kala Naft* ruling. Both cases concerned undertakings which were part of sanctions against Iran designed to prevent nuclear proliferation; the judgments were

26 Judgement of 17 July 2013, *Commission and Others* v *Kadi* ("*Kadi II*"), *supra* note 13 para 116.

27 *Id.*, paras 114 and 119.

28 See, e.g. Judgement of 21 April 2015, *Anbouba* v *Council,* C-630/13 P, EU:C:2015:247, para 42 and case law cited.

29 Judgement of 28 November 2013, *Council* v *Fulmen and Mahmoudian*, C-280/12 P, EU:C:2013:775, para 78.

given on the same day (28 November 2013).[30] In the latter case, the Court of Justice set aside the General Court's judgment and dismissed the action for annulment brought by *Kala Naft*, as the information and evidence communicated by the Council was considered sufficient to back up the listing. As demonstrated by this case, the fact that sanctions decisions are, in principle, subject to a "full" judicial control does not imply that the targeted persons or entities always, or even in most cases, succeed in obtaining the annulment of the restrictive measures. In fact, in 2015 most actions for annulment of Council decisions brought before the General Court were declared inadmissible or dismissed and this may be due to the fact that there seems to have been a gradual improvement in the formulation of sanctions decisions, including the reasons presented for the listings of persons or entities.

III. The New Security Rules of the Court of Justice of the European Union: Towards a Better Balancing of Security and the Rule of Law?

One of the main problems raised by the practice relating to restrictive measures is that the Council has not so far been able to communicate to the Union Courts any information which has been classified as secret or confidential – normally because the Member State providing or invoking such information has blocked its submission to the Union Courts. As this has been perceived as a major problem, the General Court and the Court of Justice undertook in 2014 to prepare procedural rules with a view to remedying the situation. The preparatory work was carried out in a joint working group of the two Courts,[31] which took as a point of departure the approach taken in the cases of *ZZ* and *Kadi II* referred to above.[32]

It was decided to start with the Rules of Procedure of the General Court, which were more generally subject to the preparation of a complete recast. With the agreement of the Court of Justice, and approval by the Council, the General Court established its new Rules of Procedure on 4

30 Judgement of 28 November 2013, *Council* v *Kala Naft,* C-348/12P, EU:C:2013:776.

31 The working group consisted of representatives of the two Rules of Procedure Committees. It was chaired by the present author, who at the time was also chairman of the Rules of Procedure Committee of the Court of Justice.

32 See *supra* note 13.

March 2015. This included the adoption of Article 105 of the Rules of Procedure of the General Court,[33] which governs that Court's "treatment of information or material pertaining to the security of the Union or to that of one or more of its Member States or to the conduct of their international relations". Whilst the new Rules of Procedure entered into force on 1 July 2015, the application of the provisions of Article 105 was made dependent on the publication and entry into force of a decision of the General Court relating to internal security rules for protecting the information or material produced in accordance with Article 105 from any outside access.[34] As these internal security rules were published on 24 December 2016, they entered into force the following day and Article 105 thus became applicable as of 25 December 2016.

It was from the outset obvious that Article 105 of the Rules of Procedure, and the internal security rules of the General Court, had to be matched by corresponding rules for the Court of Justice. In the preparation of such rules for the Court of Justice, it was decided to limit, at least at this stage, the exercise to cases of appeal from decisions of the General Court. At the same time, it was realized that a provision would have to be added to Article 105 of the Rules of Procedure of the General Court, guaranteeing that confidential information or material in the hands of the General Court would remain subject to the security rules of the General Court until the deadline for an appeal has expired, and in case of an appeal, be made available to the Court of Justice on the conditions laid down in the security rules. On 15 March 2016, the General Court submitted for the approval of the Council draft amendments to Article 105, paragraph 10, of its Rules of Procedure and the Court of Justice submitted corresponding amendments for the insertion of an Article 190a relating to the treatment, in the context of the appeals procedure, of information or material produced before the General Court in accordance with Article 105 of its Rules.[35] In parallel, the General Court and the Court of Justice adopted their respective internal security rules, which in fact had been prepared jointly and are practically identical in content. These rules, however, could not enter into force before the two Courts were in a position to establish definitively the afore-

33 OJ 2015 L 105/1.

34 See Article 105, paragraph 11, and Article 227, paragraph 3, of the new Rules of Procedure of the General Court; Decision of the General Court 2016/2387/EU of 14 September 2016, OJ 2016 L 355/18.

35 Council documents 7212/16 of 17 March 2016 and 7507/16 of 1 April 2016.

mentioned amendments to Article 105 of the Rules of Procedure of the General Court, and the new Article 190a of the Rules of Procedure of the Court of Justice respectively.[36]

The new regime is characterized by eight main features.

In the first place, the security regime covers in principle all situations where a main party wishes to base his claims on information or material the communication of which to the other main party would in his view "harm the security of the Union or that of one or more of its Member States or the conduct of their international relations" and is thus not limited to cases of restrictive measures (Article 105, paragraph 1 of the Rules of Procedure of the General Court);[37] the limitation to actions for annulment, however, will imply that the new provisions will normally concern actions against restrictive measures.

Secondly, even where the General Court has decided that the information or material produced before it, while relevant for the case at hand, is not to be regarded as confidential, that information or material must be returned to the party concerned if the latter objects to its communication to the other party; it can then not be taken into account in the determination of the case (Article 105, paragraph 4, of the Rules of Procedure of the General Court).

Thirdly, if the General Court has decided that the information or material is not only relevant but is also to be considered confidential vis-à-vis the other main party, it shall "weigh the requirements linked to the right to effective judicial protection, particularly observance of the adversarial principle, against the requirements flowing from the security of the Union or of one or more of its Member States or the conduct of their international relations" (Article 105, paragraph 5). To accommodate these requirements, the General Court shall specify the procedures to be adopted, "such as the production ... of a non-confidential version or a non-confidential summary of the information or material, containing the essential content thereof and enabling the other party, to the greatest extent possible, to make its

36 The establishment of these amendments, as the Rules of Procedure in general, requires the approval of the Council, see Article 253, paragraph 6, and Article 254, paragraph 5, TFEU.

37 The production of such information or material may also be requested by the General Court in the form of a measure of inquiry, see Article 105, paragraph 2, of the Rules of Procedure of the General Court.

views known" (Article 105, paragraph 6, of the Rules of Procedure of the General Court).

Fourthly, the possibility to communicate confidential information to "special advocates",[38] or to specially appointed members of the General Court, whilst being considered in the context of the preparatory work, is not mentioned as an example. It was considered that this technique could be difficult to apply at the Union level (how, for instance, would the "special advocates" be appointed?); some doubts were also expressed as to whether this technique offers a satisfactory solution for ensuring the defence of the party subject to restrictive measures.

Fifthly, the party which has produced the information or material is entitled to withdraw it within two weeks after service of the decision of the General Court pursuant to paragraph 5 and in that case it shall not be taken into account in the determination of the case (Article 105, paragraph 7 of the Rules of Procedure of the General Court).

Sixthly, where the confidential information or material which has not been withdrawn in accordance with the above rules is deemed by the General Court to be "essential" in order for it to rule in the case, it may, by way of derogation from the adversarial principle and "confining itself to what is strictly necessary, base its judgment on such information or material, but taking into account the fact that a main party has not been able to make his views on it known" (Article 105, paragraph 8, of the Rules of Procedure of the General Court).

In the seventh place, in case of an appeal, such confidential information or material which has not been communicated to the other main party should be made available by the General Court to the Court of Justice, on the conditions laid down in the internal security decisions and should not in this case be communicated to the parties before the Court of Justice. The information should be returned to the party that produced it before the General Court as soon as the decision closing the proceedings before the Court of Justice has been served, unless the case is referred back to the General Court (Article 190a of the Rules of Procedure of the Court of Justice).

Finally, the internal security regime provided for in the two decisions of the General Court and the Court of Justice, respectively, will be particularly rigid, based on the approach followed by the political EU institutions

---

38 See *supra,* note 21.

with regard to secret (rather than confidential) information. The information or material which has been classified as confidential and which has not been returned to the party concerned would stay in a closed "tunnel" and only be consulted, without using electronic means, in the premises specifically provided for and regulated in detail in the security rules.

As the new regime for treating confidential information only entered into force at the end of the year 2016, it is too early to foresee to what extent it will be used in actual practice. The two Union Courts are determined to make it work, at least as far as they are concerned, and they will be able to guarantee that information classified as confidential and held by them will be kept secret. It is to be hoped that the Council, the Commission and the Member States will trust the new procedures and that the new system will contribute to an appropriate balance being struck between quite legitimate security concerns and the requirements of the rule of law.

Droits fondamentaux des Etats tiers versus droits fondamentaux des personnes dans le cadre de la crise russe-ukranienne / Fundamental Rights of Third States versus Fundamental Rights of Individuals in the Framework of the Russia-Ukraine Crisis

Francette Fines

Abstract

This contribution investigates the confrontation between the fundamental rights of individuals and those of third States, evidenced by the disputes over the restrictive measures adopted by the EU in the context of Russian-Ukrainian crisis. The EU's response was triggered by the intervention of Russia in Ukraine in early 2014, and was meant to put pressure on the Russian decision-makers who were responsible for the infringement of human rights in Ukraine.

In the case law on the EU's restrictive measures, the Court of Justice acknowledged the conflict between rights of States and individuals, by holding that the importance of the objectives pursued by the EU's restrictive measures, namely the protection of Ukraine's territorial integrity, sovereignty and independence, may justify negative consequences for economic operators. This is the case, in particular, of the entities that are major players in sectors of the Russian economy, be they involved in the destabilization of Ukraine or not.

The disputes stemming from the Russian-Ukrainian crisis thus suggest that the balancing between the foreign policy objectives of the EU and individuals' rights may be performed at the expense of the latter.

***

Bien avant d'être instituée comme Union européenne, la Communauté européenne s'était reconnue compétente pour réagir face à des situations internationales qu'elle considérait comme illicites[1]. Au fondement à l'origine fragile[2], ces réactions vont peu à peu être affermies et consolidées dans les traités européens successifs. Ces mesures restrictives[3] sont désormais prévues par un chapitre spécifique composé d'un article unique, l'article 215 du Traité sur le fonctionnement de l'Union européenne (TFUE), article qui renvoie au titre sur la Politique étrangère et de sécurité commune (PESC) dans le traité sur l'Union européenne (TUE). En pratique, elles sont adoptées dans deux types de situations : soit en application de résolutions du Conseil de sécurité de l'Organisation des Nations Unies (ONU)[4], soit de façon autonome; de plus, elles peuvent viser soit des Etats tiers (alinéa 1er de l'article 215 TFUE), soit des personnes physiques ou morales, des groupes ou entités non étatiques (alinéa 2 de l'article 215 TFUE).

Exprimant le volontarisme politique de l'Union européenne, ces mesures restrictives vont voir leur régime juridique progressivement encadré par la Cour de justice de l'Union. Cette dernière va en effet développer une jurisprudence très novatrice sur les droits fondamentaux auxquels ces mesures restrictives portent atteinte, comme l'illustre le grand arrêt de principe *Kadi*[5]; commentant l'apport fondamental de cet arrêt, J.-P. Jacqué avait très judicieusement intitulé son article « Primauté du droit international *versus* protection des droits fondamentaux »[6]. Ainsi, en construisant

1 T. De Wilde d'Estmael, « L'élaboration du droit des sanctions économiques communautaires : enjeux et normativité politiques du processus », *Droit et société* 49, n° 2 (2001), p. 729-767; E. Cujo, *Les réactions décentralisées de l'Union européenne à l'illicite*, Thèse de doctorat, Université de Paris X-Nanterre, 2002 (dactyl.).

2 A. Pellet, « Les sanctions de l'Union européenne », in M. Benlolo-Carabot, U. Candas, E. Cujo (dir.), *Union européenne et droit international. Mélanges en l'honneur de Patrick Dailler,* Paris, Pedone, 2012, p. 431.

3 C. Beaucillon, *Les mesures restrictives de l'Union européenne*, Bruxelles, Bruylant, 2013.

4 Notamment en vue de lutter contre le terrorisme : N. Catelan, S. Cimamonti, J.-B. Perrier (dir.), *La lutte contre le terrorisme dans le droit et la jurisprudence de l'Union européenne*, Aix-Marseille, PUAM, 2014; V. le chapitre IV, « La jurisprudence de la Cour de justice relative aux mesures restrictives antiterroristes de gel de fonds », p. 157.

5 Arrêt de la Cour du 3 septembre 2008, *Yassin Abdullah Kadi et Al Barakaat International Foundation/Conseil et Commission*, C-402/05 P & C-415/05 P, EU:C:2008:461.

6 J-P. Jacqué, « Primauté du droit international *versus* protection des droits fondamentaux », *Revue trimestrielle de droit européen,* n°1/2009, p. 161.

le régime des mesures restrictives, la Cour de justice va souligner la nécessité de protéger les droits fondamentaux des personnes visées, dans l'ordre interne de l'Union; elle se présente ainsi en protectrice de ces droits, en raison de « la garantie constitutionnelle qu'incarne, dans une Union de droit… le contrôle juridictionnel de la légalité de tout acte de l'Union », selon l'arrêt *Kadi II*[7].

La Cour de justice, dans l'arrêt *Kadi II*, poursuit en affirmant qu'il revient au juge de « garantir un juste équilibre entre la préservation de la paix et de la sécurité internationales et la protection des libertés et des droits fondamentaux »[8]. L'établissement de cet équilibre peut être obtenu grâce à l'opération qui consiste à « mettre en balance […] les exigences liées au droit à une protection juridictionnelle effective, […] et celles découlant de la sûreté de l'Union ou de ses États membres ou de la conduite de leurs relations internationales »[9]. Ainsi, il est nécessaire que le juge effectue une mise en balance, ou une pondération[10] entre les droits des particuliers et ceux des Etats membres de l'Union. Mais qu'en est-il lorsque sont en cause les droits d'Etats tiers? Cette interrogation est au cœur de la jurisprudence rendue par la Cour de justice de l'Union européenne dans les affaires russo-ukrainiennes.

Cette contribution entend, en effet, montrer comment il peut y avoir confrontation, voire rivalité[11], entre les droits fondamentaux des personnes et ceux d'Etats tiers, comme en atteste le contentieux des mesures restrictives adoptées dans le cadre de la crise russo-ukrainienne. L'arrêt de grande chambre *Rosneft* paraît particulièrement révélateur de cette collision : « l'importance des objectifs poursuivis […] à savoir la protection de

---

7 Arrêt de la Cour du 1er juillet 2013, *Commission européenne e.a./Yassin Abdullah Kadi*, C-584/10 P, C-593/10 P & C-595/10 P, EU:C:2013:518, point 66.

8 *Id.*, point 131.

9 *Id.*, point 128.

10 Dans une affaire concernant l'accès au territoire d'un Etat membre, la Cour, dans son arrêt de grande chambre *ZZ/Secretary of State for the Home Department*, a aussi été amenée à mettre en exergue « la pondération du droit à une protection juridictionnelle effective avec la nécessité d'assurer la protection de la sûreté de l'État membre » (arrêt de la Cour du 4 juin 2013, C-300/11, EU:C:2013:363, point 66).

11 V. aussi, l'analyse des « figures de la rivalité » par N. Scandamis, « L'intérêt de sécurité à l'œuvre dans l'Union européenne : l'ordre des compétences pris en défaut », in E. Neframi (dir.), *Objectifs et compétences dans l'Union européenne*, Bruxelles, Bruylant, 2012, p. 123.

l'intégrité territoriale, de la souveraineté et de l'indépendance de l'Ukraine [...] est de nature à justifier des conséquences négatives, même considérables, pour certains opérateurs » [12]. Ce type de raisonnement, conduisant à souligner les conséquences négatives pour les particuliers, rappelle celui déjà suivi par la Cour de Luxembourg, dans ses arrêts antérieurs, tel l'arrêt *Bosphorus*[13], ou l'arrêt *Kadi*[14].

Pour saisir la portée de ce contentieux, il convient de rappeler le contexte russo-ukrainien. Le conflit s'est déclenché à partir du début de l'année 2014, en Crimée, puis s'est étendu à l'Est de l'Ukraine. Alors que le Conseil de sécurité est paralysé, l'Union européenne va réagir (comme aussi les Etats-Unis), inaugurant une nouvelle ère de sa politique russe[15]. Elle va prendre des mesures restrictives, d'un caractère tout à fait exceptionnel. Au début, sont d'abord concernés certains anciens dirigeants ukrainiens[16]; puis, l'Union européenne va progressivement viser la Russie[17], pour son rôle actif dans la crise en Ukraine; sont ciblés des dirigeants russes, ainsi que des entreprises russes, ou des individus de nationalité russe, dont certains vont contester les mesures prises à leur encontre. Signalons que d'autres juridictions internationales ont également

12 Arrêt de la Cour du 28 mars 2017, *PJSC Rosneft Oil Company/Her Majesty's Treasury e.a.,* C-72/15, EU:C:2017:236, point 150. V. aussi l'affaire en cours, devant le Tribunal de l'Union, *NK Rosneft a.o./Conseil,* T-715/14.

13 Arrêt de la Cour du 30 juillet 1996, *Bosphorus Hava Yollari Turizm ve Ticaret AS/ Minister for Transport, Energy and Communications e.a.*, C-84/95, EU:C:1996:312, point 23.

14 Arrêt de la Cour du 3 septembre 2008, *Yassin Abdullah Kadi et Al Barakaat International Foundation/Conseil et Commission*, *supra* note 5, point 361.

15 F. Fines, « Les soubresauts de la politique russe de l'Union européenne », in F. Fines, H. Flavier, L. Lankarani, L. Royer (dir.), *La Puissance russe, entre émergence et renaissance,* Paris, Pedone, à paraître.

16 Décision 2014/119/PESC et Règlement (UE) n° 208/2014 du Conseil, du 5 mars 2014, concernant des mesures restrictives à l'encontre de certaines personnes, de certaines entités et de certains organismes eu regard à la situation en Ukraine, *JO,* L 66 du 6 mars 2014, p. 1.

17 C. Beaucillon, « Crise ukrainienne et mesures restrictives de l'Union européenne : quelle contribution aux sanctions internationales à l'égard de la Russie? », *Journal du droit international,* n°3/2014, p. 787-807.

été saisies du conflit en Ukraine : la Cour européenne des droits de l'homme[18], et même la Cour internationale de justice[19].

Dans l'arrêt qui concerne l'entreprise russe *Rosneft*[20], la grande Chambre de la Cour de justice a dû statuer sur l'étendue de l'immunité juridictionnelle des décisions adoptées au titre de la PESC, en réaction à la crise russo-ukrainienne. Le Tribunal de l'Union a aussi rendu plus d'une quinzaine d'arrêts et ordonnances sur des mesures restrictives également adoptées, eu égard à la situation en Ukraine. Certains concernent, par exemple, d'anciens dirigeants ukrainiens, tel l'ancien président de l'Ukraine, M. Yanukovych ainsi que son fils[21], ou les anciens premiers ministres M. Azarov[22] et M. Arbuzov[23]. D'autres affaires russo-ukrainiennes, jugées par le Tribunal, sont relatives à des personnes de nationalité russe : soit un

---

18 Outre quelques affaires interétatiques opposant l'Ukraine à la Russie, la Cour européenne des droits de l'homme a été saisie de milliers de requêtes individuelles.

19 Ordonnance de la CIJ du 19 avril 2017, application de la Convention internationale pour la répression du financement du terrorisme et de la Convention internationale sur l'élimination de toutes les formes de discrimination raciale (*Ukraine c. Fédération de Russie*); P. Laval, *Revue générale de droit internationale public,* vol. 121, n°2/2017, p. 916.

20 Arrêt de la Cour du 28 mars 2017, *PJSC Rosneft Oil Company/Her Majesty's Treasury e.a., supra,* note 12. Les activités de l'entreprise Rosneft comprennent l'exploration, la production, le raffinage d'hydrocarbures ainsi que la commercialisation de pétrole brut et de gaz en Russie et à l'étranger. V. les commentaires de cet arrêt : I. Bosse Platière, « Le juge de l'Union, artisan de la cohérence du système de contrôle juridictionnel au sein de l'Union européenne, y compris en matière de PESC », *Revue trimestrielle de droit européen,* n° 3/2017, p. 555; L. Coutron, « Chronique Contentieux de l'Union européenne -Consécration de la compétence préjudicielle de la Cour de justice dans le contentieux des mesures restrictives », *Revue trimestrielle de droit européen,* n°2/2017, p. 418; E. Broussy, H. Cassagnabere, C. Gänser, P. Bonneville, « Chronique Compétence de la Cour-Renvoi préjudiciel-Politique étrangère et de sécurité commune », *Actualité juridique, Droit administratif,* 2017, p. 1106.

21 Deux arrêts du Tribunal du 15 septembre 2016, dans les affaires T-346/14 et T-348/14, ont fait l'objet de pourvois déjà tranchés par la Cour de justice : arrêt de la Cour du 19 octobre 2017, *Viktor Fedorovych Yanukovych/Conseil,* C-598/16 P, EU:C:2017:786; arrêt de la Cour du 19 octobre 2017, *Oleksandr Viktorovych Yanukovych/Conseil,* C-599/16 P, EU:C:2017:785.

22 Arrêt du Tribunal du 7 juillet 2017, *Mykola Yanovych Azarov/Conseil*, T-215/15, EU:T:2017:479.

23 Arrêt du Tribunal du 7 juillet 2017, *Sergej Arbuzov/Conseil*, T-221/15, EU:T:2017:478.

citoyen, entrepreneur tel M. Rotenberg[24], ou journaliste tel M. Kiselev[25], soit une entreprise, "Almaz-Antey" Air and Space Defence[26].

Nous allons exposer comment la Cour de justice de l'Union, saisie d'un recours en annulation ou sur renvoi préjudiciel à propos des sanctions adoptées, appréhende la réaction européenne à la crise russo-ukrainienne, en mettant l'accent sur la question de la confrontation entre les droits des personnes physiques et morales, d'un côté, et ceux de l'Etat ukrainien, de l'autre. Car le juge de l'Union a aussi été amené à définir et protéger les prérogatives de l'Etat ukrainien, au fondement desquelles il a été porté atteinte. Ainsi, dans notre étude, nous entendons principalement mettre en perspective l'arrêt de grande chambre *Rosneft* avec la jurisprudence principalement « russo-ukrainienne » du Tribunal, en ce que sont en cause des droits étatiques. Au plan doctrinal, nous les qualifions de droits, en nous appuyant, par exemple, sur le premier point du décalogue de l'Acte final d'Helsinki, consacré précisément au « respect des droits inhérents à la souveraineté » des Etats. Et quoi de plus fondamental[27], pour un Etat, que la jouissance paisible de tels droits? Bien sûr, et pour dissiper tout malentendu, nous devons d'emblée préciser que les droits fondamentaux étatiques (au sens où nous l'entendons) n'ont absolument pas le même contenu et la même portée que les droits fondamentaux subjectifs que possèdent les personnes physiques et morales.

---

24 M. Rotenberg est notamment propriétaire d'une entreprise qui s'est vue attribuer un marché public pour la construction d'un pont reliant la Russie à la Crimée. Il est également président du conseil d'administration de Prosvescheniye, qui a mis en œuvre une campagne de relations publiques destinée à persuader les enfants de Crimée qu'ils sont maintenant des citoyens russes vivant en Russie. Arrêt du Tribunal du 30 novembre 2016, *Arkady Romanovich Rotenberg/Conseil*, T-720/14, EU:T:2016:689.

25 M. Kiselev a été nommé, par décret du président Poutine, en tant que directeur de l'agence de presse nationale de la Fédération de Russie Rossiya Segodnya (RS), qui est une « entreprise unitaire » de l'État russe. Arrêt du Tribunal du 15 juin 2017, *Dmitrii Konstantinovich Kiselev/Conseil*, T-262/15, EU:T:2017:392.

26 La société Joint-Stock Company "Almaz-Antey" Air and Space Defence opère notamment dans le secteur de la défense et fabrique, notamment, des armements antiaériens tels que des missiles sol-air. Arrêt du Tribunal du 25 janvier 2017, *Joint-Stock Company "Almaz-Antey" Air and Space Defence Corp., anciennement OAO Concern PVO Almaz-Antey/Conseil*, T-255/15, EU:T:2017:25.

27 A. Pillet, *Recherches sur les droits fondamentaux des Etats, dans l'ordre des rapports internationaux et sur la solution des conflits qu'ils font naître*, Paris, Pedone, 1899.

Pour comprendre les principes qui sous-tendent la mise en balance exercée par le juge entre les droits des uns et des autres, il convient de ne pas perdre de vue que ces mesures restrictives doivent répondre aux objectifs de la PESC. Ainsi, nous entendons d'abord montrer que la Cour de justice de l'Union va admettre que la protection des droits de l'Etat ukrainien, recherchée par l'Union qui entend s'affirmer sur la scène internationale comme puissance, est de nature à justifier l'adoption des mesures restrictives (I). Ensuite, nous analyserons comment le contrôle qu'exerce la Cour de justice de l'Union sur les mesures restrictives, expression de l'Union de droit, va la conduire à accepter les préjudices causés aux personnes et opérateurs économiques ciblés, en particulier ceux qui ont un rôle majeur ou actif dans l'économie russe, même s'ils ne sont pas impliqués dans la déstabilisation de l'Ukraine (II).

I. L'Union européenne, puissance internationale dans le domaine de la politique étrangère : la réaction à l'égard de la Russie justifiée par la violation des droits de l'Etat ukrainien

Selon la Cour de justice de l'Union européenne, l'importance des objectifs poursuivis est de nature à justifier l'action menée dans le cadre de la PESC; en conséquence, le juge va confirmer l'Union européenne, dans ses missions de protection des droits d'un Etat tiers, en l'espèce l'Ukraine (A); et cela, face aux atteintes commises par un autre Etat tiers, aussi puissant soit-il, en l'occurrence, la Russie (B).

A. La PESC comme cadre de la protection de l'Etat ukrainien

Bénéficiant d'une marge importante, puisque la Cour n'exerce qu'un contrôle restreint à cet égard (1), le Conseil était fondé à réagir pour protéger les droits de l'Etat ukrainien (2), en intervenant au titre de la PESC.

1. Le contrôle juridictionnel restreint de la réaction européenne

Il paraît essentiel de souligner que, selon la Cour de justice, « le Conseil dispose d'une grande latitude » lorsqu'il définit l'objet de mesures restrictives, eu égard à « la vaste portée des buts et des objectifs de la PESC, tels qu'exprimés à l'article 3, paragraphe 5, TUE et à l'article 21 TUE ainsi qu'aux dispositions spécifiques relatives à la PESC, notamment aux articles 23 et 24 TUE »[28]. Ce large pouvoir d'appréciation va ainsi porter sur « les critères généraux à prendre en considération » en vue de l'adoption de ces mesures[29].

En conséquence, reprenant les éléments d'une jurisprudence déjà posée antérieurement[30], le juge n'exerce qu'un contrôle restreint en la matière[31], comme il est réaffirmé expressément : « Ce contrôle restreint s'applique, en particulier, à l'appréciation des considérations d'opportunité sur lesquelles de telles mesures sont fondées ». En effet, le juge de l'Union ne peut « substituer son appréciation des preuves, des faits et des circonstances justifiant l'adoption de telles mesures à celle du Conseil». Concrètement, le contrôle exercé par le juge« doit se limiter à la vérification du respect des règles de procédure et de motivation, de l'exactitude matérielle des faits ainsi que de l'absence d'erreur manifeste dans l'appréciation des faits et de détournement de pouvoir»[32].

A propos du contrôle de l'obligation de motivation, laquelle doit être suffisante, ce qui doit être distingué de l'appréciation du bien-fondé des

---

28 Arrêt de la Cour du 28 mars 2017, *Rosneft, supra* note 12, points 88 et 132.

29 Arrêt du Tribunal du 30 novembre 2016, *Arkady Romanovich Rotenberg, supra* note 24, point 71; arrêt du Tribunal du 15 juin 2017, *Dmitrii Konstantinovich Kiselev, supra* note 25, points 62 et 64; arrêt du Tribunal du 25 janvier 2017, *Joint-Stock Company "Almaz-Antey" Air and Space Defence, supra* note 26, points 99 et 127.

30 V. l'arrêt du Tribunal du 14 octobre 2009, *Bank Melli Iran/Conseil*, T-390/08, EU:T:2009:401, point 36, ou l'arrêt du Tribunal du 12 décembre 2006, *Organisation des Modjahedines du peuple d'Iran/Conseil (OMPI),* T-228/02, EU:T:2006:384, point 159.

31 Pour une étude générale du contrôle juridictionnel en matière de PESC, v. E. Daniel, *La politique opérationnelle de l'Union européenne dans le cadre de la PESC*, Université de Paris I Panthéon Sorbonne, Thèse de doctorat, Paris, 2016 (dactyl.).

32 Arrêt du Tribunal du 30 novembre 2016, *Arkady Romanovich Rotenberg, supra* note 24, point 70; arrêt du Tribunal du 15 juin 2017, *Dmitrii Konstantinovich Kiselev, supra* note 25, point 61; arrêt du Tribunal du 25 janvier 2017, *Joint-Stock Company "Almaz-Antey" Air and Space Defence, supra* note 26, point 95.

motifs[33], le juge de l'Union rappelle[34] que « le Conseil est tenu de porter à la connaissance d'une personne ou entité visée par des mesures restrictives les raisons spécifiques et concrètes pour lesquelles il considère qu'elles devaient être adoptées »[35]. Par exemple, le Tribunal relève que ce dernier « tirait avantage de ses relations personnelles avec le président Poutine, dans la mesure où, pendant la présidence de ce dernier, il a pu obtenir d'importants contrats par l'État russe »[36].

Toujours à propos de la motivation, la Cour de justice accepte que soit pris en compte des éléments tirés du contexte[37]. Se fondant sur une jurisprudence déjà établie[38], elle rappelle qu'un « acte faisant grief est suffisamment motivé dès lors qu'il est intervenu dans un contexte connu de l'intéressé, qui lui permet de comprendre la portée de la mesure prise à son égard »[39]. Alors que l'entreprise Rosneft invoquait un défaut de motivation, la Cour va déclarer que « le contexte politique à la date de l'adoption desdites mesures et l'importance que revêt le secteur pétrolier pour l'économie russe »[40] sont « notoires »; en conséquence, « le choix [...] d'adopter des mesures restrictives contre des acteurs de cette industrie peut être compris aisément »[41]; la motivation est donc considérée comme suffisante par la Cour de justice. Il en est de même, dans l'affaire *Kiselev,* dans laquelle le Tribunal relève que le directeur de l'agence russe de presse nationale avait compris qu'il était visé en raison de son rôle et de sa

---

33 Arrêt du Tribunal du 30 novembre 2016, *Arkady Romanovich Rotenberg, supra* note 24, point 58; arrêt du Tribunal du 15 juin 2017, *Dmitrii Konstantinovich Kiselev, supra* note 25, point 52; arrêt du Tribunal du 25 janvier 2017, *Joint-Stock Company "Almaz-Antey" Air and Space Defence, supra* note 26, point 61. Sur le contrôle complet du bien-fondé des motifs justifiant l'inscription sur les listes, v. *infra*.

34 Arrêt du Tribunal du 5 novembre 2014, *Mayaleh/Conseil*, T-307/12 & T-408/13, EU:T:2014:926.

35 Arrêt du Tribunal du 30 novembre 2016, *Arkady Romanovich Rotenberg, supra* note 24, point 48.

36 *Id.,* point 55.

37 F. Clausen, « Présomptions et contrôle des motifs dans le contentieux des mesures restrictives : développements et (in)certitudes jurisprudentiels. CJUE, 21 avril 2015, *Anbouba/Conseil,* C-605/13 P et C-630/13 P », *Revue des affaires européennes,* n°2/2015, p. 409.

38 V., en ce sens, l'arrêt de la Cour de justice du 15 novembre 2012, *Conseil/Nadiany Bamba*, C-417/11 P, EU:C:2012:718, point 54.

39 Arrêt de la Cour du 28 mars 2017, *Rosneft, supra* note 12, point 122.

40 V. *infra*, les développements liés au choix de ce secteur de l'économie russe.

41 Arrêt de la Cour du 28 mars 2017, *Rosneft, supra* note 12, point 124.

conduite professionnelle, en cela qu'il « était une figure centrale de la propagande gouvernementale russe au soutien du déploiement des forces armées russes en Ukraine »[42].

2. *Les fondements juridiques de la réaction européenne*

La réaction européenne a été déclenchée par l'atteinte aux droits de l'Etat ukrainien. Comme l'expose la Cour de justice, sont en cause « la protection de l'intégrité territoriale, la souveraineté et l'indépendance » de l'Ukraine. Les faits, qui ont conduit à la réaction européenne, dans l'affaire *Rosneft*, et comme le souligne la Cour de justice, visaient à les compromettre, toutes les trois. On est au cœur de la « crise ». Intégrité, souveraineté et indépendance se situent au fondement de l'existence même des Etats. Ce sont bien les droits inhérents à l'Etat ukrainien[43] qui sont menacés, et au soutien desquels l'Union européenne intervient.

Outre la protection des droits de l'Etat tiers, l'Union vise aussi, à travers ses actes, à « promouvoir un règlement pacifique de la crise en Ukraine »[44].

Ceci correspond bien aux objectifs généraux, poursuivis par les décisions et règlements adoptés par le Conseil, comme le relève la Cour de justice; cette dernière considère ainsi que cette réaction s'inscrit « dans l'objectif plus large du maintien de la paix et de la sécurité interna-

---

42 Arrêt du Tribunal du 15 juin 2017, *Dmitrii Konstantinovich Kiselev, supra* note 25, points 41, 44, 46. V. aussi, Arrêt du Tribunal du 30 novembre 2016, *Arkady Romanovich Rotenberg, supra* note 24, point 49 et arrêt du Tribunal du 25 janvier 2017, *Joint-Stock Company "Almaz-Antey" Air and Space Defence, supra* note 26, point 56.

43 A ce propos, il est intéressant de comparer les affaires strictement ukrainiennes avec celles russo-ukrainiennes. La formulation, retenue notamment dans les deux arrêts précités *Yanukovych (supra* note 21), est notable : dans ces deux arrêts, le Tribunal vise l'atteinte aux « fondements institutionnels et juridiques » de l'Ukraine. En l'espèce, il a posé qu'un détournement de fonds, ou d'avoirs publics, pouvait être considéré comme susceptible de porter atteinte à ces fondements. Le Tribunal ajoute que l'UE a pu agir « en vue de renforcer et de soutenir l'État de droit […] en Ukraine ».

44 Arrêt de la Cour du 28 mars 2017, *Rosneft, supra* note 12, points 29, 115, 123, 134, et 150; arrêt du Tribunal du 25 janvier 2017, *Joint-Stock Company "Almaz-Antey" Air and Space Defence, supra* note 26, point 105.

tionale »[45]. La Cour estime donc que l'Union a réagi « conformément aux objectifs de l'action extérieure [...] énoncés à l'article 21 TUE »[46], c'est-à-dire que la réaction se situe dans le cadre de la PESC. Les institutions de l'Union ont donc agi dans le cadre de leurs compétences, telles qu'établies par les traités européens.

Toutefois, il n'existe pas de base internationale servant de fondement plus précis à ces sanctions. En effet, la difficulté tient à ce qu'elles n'ont pas été prises en application de résolutions du Conseil de sécurité, lequel était paralysé par le veto russe. Cela signifie donc que l'action européenne, à l'encontre de la Russie, est autonome par rapport au Conseil de sécurité de l'ONU. Comment, d'ailleurs, pourrait-il en être autrement, compte tenu de l'implication de ce membre permanent du Conseil de sécurité dans cette crise? La validité de ces mesures européennes ne provient donc que du seul ordre juridique qui les a produites, en l'occurrence l'ordre juridique européen[47].

En même temps, le juge fait aussi remarquer, en citant l'article 21, paragraphe 1, premier alinéa, et paragraphe 2, sous c), TUE, que l'Union doit agir dans « le respect des principes et des buts de la charte des Nations unies »[48]; ainsi, l'action de l'Union doit être conforme au droit international général, ce qui avait été également précisé par les actes contestés du Conseil. A cet égard, le Tribunal prend soin de citer la résolution 68/262, intitulée « Intégrité territoriale de l'Ukraine », adoptée le 27 mars 2014 par l'Assemblée générale des Nations Unies[49].

---

45 Arrêt de la Cour du 28 mars 2017, *Rosneft, supra* note 12, point 150; arrêt du Tribunal du 25 janvier 2017, *Joint-Stock Company "Almaz-Antey" Air and Space Defence, supra* note 26, point 102.

46 Arrêt de la Cour du 28 mars 2017, *Rosneft, supra* note 12, points 115 et 150.

47 R. Bismuth, « Odyssée dans le *conundrum* des réactions décentralisées à l'illicite », *Journal de droit international,* n°3/2014, p. 719-732.

48 Arrêt de la Cour du 28 mars 2017, *Rosneft, supra* note 12, point 112.

49 Arrêt du Tribunal du 30 novembre 2016, *Arkady Romanovich Rotenberg/Conseil, supra* note 24, point 177; arrêt du Tribunal du 15 juin 2017, *Dmitrii Konstantinovich Kiselev/Conseil, supra* note 25, point 82; arrêt du Tribunal du 25 janvier 2017, *Joint-Stock Company "Almaz-Antey" Air and Space Defence Corp., supra* note 26, point 102.

B. Les mesures restrictives à l'égard de la Russie et l'atteinte aux intérêts russes

Le juge va lister les différentes violations qui ont été commises, notamment par la Russie (1), et qui justifient les mesures adoptées à l'encontre des intérêts russes (2).

1. La désignation de la Russie comme « responsable » des atteintes

Le juge de l'Union va reprendre les indications contenues dans les actes du Conseil, qui ciblent clairement la Russie dans plusieurs des faits dénoncés. La situation constatée « corrobore l'existence d'une implication russe dans le conflit ukrainien »[50]. Le Tribunal affirme encore plus nettement, que revient à l'Etat russe « la responsabilité ultime des actions et des politiques que le Conseil condamne »[51].

Les multiples atteintes matérielles, aux fondements de l'Etat ukrainien, sont répertoriées par le juge. Le Tribunal a considéré que l'évolution politique et militaire, dans la région, a été marquée par « les actions de la Russie ayant conduit à la tenue d'un prétendu référendum sur le statut de la Crimée, puis […] à l'annexion illégale de la Crimée »[52]. Il est affirmé que « les documents fournis par le Conseil démontrent suffisamment que la Fédération de Russie a effectivement fourni des armes aux séparatistes à l'est de l'Ukraine »[53]. Dans l'arrêt *Rosneft*, la Cour fait référence aux « actions de la Fédération de Russie visant à compromettre l'intégrité territoriale, la souveraineté et l'indépendance de l'Ukraine »[54]. Le raisonnement du Tribunal est largement fondé sur la prise en compte des actions et politiques du gouvernement russe déstabilisant l'Ukraine.

---

50 Arrêt du Tribunal du 25 janvier 2017, *Joint-Stock Company "Almaz-Antey" Air and Space Defence Corp., supra* note 26, point 148.

51 Arrêt du Tribunal du 15 juin 2017, *Dmitrii Konstantinovich Kiselev/Conseil, supra* note 25, point 115.

52 Arrêt du Tribunal du 30 novembre 2016, *Arkady Romanovich Rotenberg/Conseil, supra* note 24, point 121.

53 Arrêt du Tribunal du 25 janvier 2017, *Joint-Stock Company "Almaz-Antey" Air and Space Defence Corp., supra* note 26, point 138.

54 Arrêt de la Cour du 28 mars 2017, *Rosneft, supra* note 12, points 124 et 147.

Confrontée à ces éléments démontrant que la nouvelle situation internationale, à l'Est de l'Europe, a été établie par la force[55], l'Union pouvait s'en prendre aux intérêts russes.

2. *Les finalités légitimes des mesures ciblant les intérêts russes*

Les finalités légitimes des mesures ciblant les intérêts russes apparaissent dans l'arrêt *"Almaz-Antey" Air and Space Defence*, en ces termes : « le Conseil pouvait légitimement espérer que de telles actions cessent ou qu'elles deviennent plus coûteuses pour ceux qui les entreprennent »[56]. L'arrêt *Rosneft* insiste sur ce but d'accroître le coût des actions de la Fédération de Russie[57]. L'arrêt *Kiselev* est aussi intéressant par l'acceptation explicite et réitérée de « l'exercice d'une pression sur les décideurs russes responsables de la situation en Ukraine »[58]; cette « pression » est présentée comme un objectif d'intérêt général[59], afin que les autorités russes mettent fin à leurs actions et à leurs politiques déstabilisant l'Ukraine.

Pour aboutir à ces résultats, le moyen est de « cibler » certains opérateurs économiques[60]. Mais quels entités ou opérateurs l'Union peut-elle précisément cibler? Selon quels critères? La Cour de justice de l'Union retient une approche plurielle, en acceptant de prendre en compte la pluralité

---

55 Pour une approche doctrinale, en ce sens : T. Christakis, « Les conflits de sécession en Crimée et dans l'est de l'Ukraine et le droit international », *Journal du droit international,* n°3/2014, p. 733; A. Tancredi, « The Russian Annexation of the Crimea : Questions Relating to the Use of Force », *Questions of International Law*, vol. 1, 2014, p. 5. http://www.qil-qdi.org/the-russian-annexation-of-the-crimea-questions-relating-to-the-use-of-force/.

56 Arrêt du Tribunal du 25 janvier 2017, *Joint-Stock Company "Almaz-Antey" Air and Space Defence Corp., supra* note 26, point 105.

57 Arrêt de la Cour du 28 mars 2017, *Rosneft, supra* note 12, points 124 et 147.

58 Arrêt du Tribunal du 15 juin 2017, *Dmitrii Konstantinovich Kiselev/Conseil, supra* note 25, point 85. V aussi : arrêt du Tribunal du 30 novembre 2016, *Arkady Romanovich Rotenberg/Conseil, supra* note 24, point 176; Conclusions de l'Avocat général Wathelet, présentées le 31 mai 2016, sous l'affaire *Rosneft*, C- 72/15, EU:C:2016:381, point 147.

59 Il s'agit alors de l'une des conditions permettant d'apporter une limitation à l'exercice d'un droit fondamental; V. *infra.*

60 Arrêt de la Cour du 28 mars 2017, *Rosneft, supra* note 12, point 147.

des critères retenus par le Conseil pour fonder les inscriptions sur la liste des personnes visées.

Il en est ainsi de la notion, examinée par le Tribunal, de soutien actif ou matériel à des actions portant atteinte à l'Ukraine. L'arrêt *Kiselev* donne au Tribunal l'occasion de préciser la notion de « soutien actif », que l'on trouve dans les actes du Conseil, et qui diffère de celle de responsable direct ou même d'exécutant : le soutien actif vise « les formes d'appui qui, par leur importance quantitative ou qualitative, contribuent à la poursuite des actions et des politiques du gouvernement russe qui déstabilisent l'Ukraine »[61]. En se référant à la jurisprudence de la Cour européenne des droits de l'homme, le Tribunal rappelle « l'importance du rôle que les médias, surtout ceux qui relèvent de l'audiovisuel, jouent dans la société contemporaine »; en conséquence, « il était prévisible qu'un soutien médiatique d'envergure », comme l'a apporté M. Kiselev, entraîne une sanction de la part de l'Union[62]. L'arrêt *"Almaz-Antey" Air and Space Defence* permet au Tribunal de faire une distinction entre soutien matériel et participation directe. Il fait remarquer qu'une participation directe à la déstabilisation de l'Ukraine, ou un lien direct avec les séparatistes en Ukraine n'est pas nécessaire[63]; l'entreprise n'a pas forcément « personnellement menacé ou compromis » les droits de l'Ukraine[64]; peu importe que ce ne soit pas elle qui ait directement livré des armes aux séparatistes[65]. En revanche, il apparaît bien que cette entreprise russe "Almaz-Antey" Air and Space Defence fabrique des armements lourds « qu'elle fournit à la Fédération de Russie, laquelle fournit à son tour des armes aux séparatistes »[66]. « L'élément déterminant », selon le Tribunal, est celui selon lequel, en fournissant à la Russie des armes qu'elle fabrique, cette entreprise « soutient matériellement des actions qui compromettent ou menacent » l'Ukraine[67]. En conséquence, « le Conseil pouvait à bon droit conclure que la requérante contribuait à la déstabilisation de l'Ukraine »[68].

61 Arrêt du Tribunal du 15 juin 2017, *Dmitrii Konstantinovich Kiselev/Conseil*, *supra* note 25, points 73, 74, 114.

62 *Id.*, point 76.

63 Arrêt du Tribunal du 25 janvier 2017, *Joint-Stock Company "Almaz-Antey" Air and Space Defence Corp.*, *supra* note 26, points 141 et 149.

64 *Id.*, point 98.

65 *Id.*, point 137.

66 *Id.*, point 141.

67 *Id.*, point 135.

68 *Id.*, point 158.

En revanche, alors même que l'entreprise Rosneft n'apportait aucun soutien de ce type, la Cour de justice estime que « cibler un opérateur majeur du secteur pétrolier, par ailleurs détenu majoritairement par l'État russe, répond de manière cohérente » à l'objectif recherché, à savoir accroître le coût pour la Russie[69]; si la société Rosneft présente la double caractéristique d'être à la fois un opérateur économique majeur et liée à l'Etat russe, l'emploi de la locution « par ailleurs » conduit à considérer que les deux éléments peuvent être dissociés. Le critère économique paraît particulièrement déterminant; la Cour reconnaît qu'« il est notamment loisible au Conseil d'imposer, s'il le juge approprié, des restrictions qui visent des entreprises actives dans des secteurs spécifiques de l'économie russe dans lesquels les produits, les technologies ou les services provenant de l'Union occupent une place particulièrement importante »[70]. Il s'agit, par ce moyen de « garantir l'efficacité des mesures restrictives » et d' « éviter que l'effet de ces mesures soit neutralisé par l'importation, vers la Russie, des produits, des technologies ou des services substituables en provenance de pays tiers »[71]. Selon la Cour de justice, il existe « un rapport raisonnable » entre le contenu des actes litigieux et l'objectif poursuivi; elle en tire la conclusion qu'une telle approche n'est manifestement pas inappropriée[72], ce qui renvoie au principe de proportionnalité (V. *infra*).

Il convient de s'interroger davantage sur le lien entre le comportement de la Russie et le choix des opérateurs russes ciblés, ainsi que sur les effets des mesures restrictives.

II. Les contraintes de l'inscription des mesures restrictives dans une « Union de droit » : Une ingérence acceptée dans les droits fondamentaux des personnes ciblées

Du fait de l'origine des mesures examinées, qui se rattachent à la PESC, le contrôle juridictionnel exercé sur les mesures restrictives présente cer-

69 Arrêt de la Cour du 28 mars 2017, *Rosneft, supra* note 12, point 147.
70 *Id.*, point 132.
71 *Ibid.*
72 *Id.*, point 147.

taines particularités[73]. Certes, ce contrôle paraît étendu à plusieurs égards (A). Néanmoins, l'atteinte aux prérogatives de l'Etat ukrainien est de nature à entraîner, en réaction, un impact négatif sur la protection juridictionnelle des personnes ciblées (B).

A. L'étendue du contrôle juridictionnel sur les mesures individuelles restrictives

Dans l'affaire *Rosneft*, la réponse au renvoi préjudiciel impliquait que la Cour se reconnaisse compétente, à partir d'une interprétation extensive des traités (1), à propos d'un contentieux, qu'elle connaît habituellement par le biais de recours directs en annulation. Se prononçant sur les griefs invoqués, dans l'ensemble des affaires russo-ukrainiennes, la Cour va mettre en œuvre un contrôle de type dual : en effet, le contrôle restreint, sur la décision d'adopter de telles mesures est complété par un contrôle complet portant sur la légalité des mesures restrictives au regard des droits fondamentaux (2).

1. La conception extensive de la compétence préjudicielle de la Cour de justice

Dans l'affaire *Rosneft*, la Cour de justice, saisie par la Haute Cour de justice (Angleterre et Pays de Galle), va devoir répondre aux arguments, visant à contester ou réduire sa compétence préjudicielle dans le domaine de la PESC. La Cour de justice est confrontée au silence des traités. D'un côté, l'article 275, alinéa 2, TFUE a établi une exception à l'immunité juridictionnelle des décisions PESC; cet article prévoit la compétence explicite de la Cour de justice, pour exercer un contrôle direct (c'est-à-dire selon les conditions prévues à l'article 263, quatrième alinéa, TFUE) de la légalité des décisions restrictives à l'encontre de personnes physiques ou morales. Mais de l'autre côté, rien n'est prévu expressément pour le con-

73 B. Bertrand, « La particularité du contrôle juridictionnel des mesures restrictives : les 'considérations impérieuses touchant à la sûreté ou à la conduite des relations internationales de l'Union et de ses Etats membres' », *Revue trimestrielle de droit européen,* n°3/2015, p. 555.

trôle indirect, exercé à l'occasion d'un renvoi préjudiciel en appréciation de validité.

Or, la Cour de justice fait remarquer que la mise en œuvre d'une décision restrictive « relève pour partie de la responsabilité des États membres »[74]. N'est-il pas alors nécessaire de consacrer la possibilité, pour les juridictions étatiques, d'interroger la Cour de justice de l'Union sur la validité des décisions du Conseil servant de base à l'adoption de telles mesures nationales de mise en œuvre? La Cour de justice va l'admettre, en affirmant sa compétence préjudicielle, et combler ainsi une lacune du Traité[75].

La « protection juridictionnelle effective »[76] et la « cohérence du système de protection juridictionnelle »[77] ainsi que la notion « d'Etat de droit »[78] vont se situer au cœur de son raisonnement, en vue d'établir sa compétence, dans l'arrêt *Rosneft*. Cette approche correspond à la conception d'un ordre juridique intégré aux systèmes juridiques des Etats membre, telle que développée dans la jurisprudence fondatrice du 15 juillet 1964, *Costa/ ENEL*[79].

Mais cette compétence préjudicielle n'est pas absolue. Elle est circonscrite à deux hypothèses. Soit, le contrôle ne peut porter que sur le respect de l'article 40 TUE. Soit, il ne peut concerner que les décisions restrictives à l'encontre de personnes physiques ou morales, comme le rappelle la Cour : « en ce qui concerne les actes adoptés sur le fondement des disposi-

---

74 Arrêt de la Cour du 28 mars 2017, *Rosneft, supra* note 12, point 71.

75 L'Avocat général Kokott avait exprimé une position contraire, dans sa prise de position relative à l'avis 2/13 : « nous doutons fort que l'interprétation des deux possibilités offertes à l'article 275, deuxième alinéa, TFUE [...] soit un moyen juridiquement praticable de garantir à toute personne une protection juridictionnelle effective »; selon l'Avocat général, cela « heurte de front le libellé sans équivoque de la deuxième possibilité offerte à l'article 275, deuxième alinéa, TFUE, qui ne prévoit la compétence de la Cour qu'en matière de recours en annulation formés par des particuliers conformément à l'article 263, paragraphe 4, TFUE contre des mesures restrictives, [...] et certainement pas en matière de demandes préjudicielles formées par des juridictions nationales en application de l'article 267 TFUE ». Prise de position présentée le 13 juin 2014, Avis 2/13, *Adhésion de l'Union à la Convention européenne de sauvegarde des droits de l'homme et des libertés fondamentales,* EU:C:2014:2475, points 88 et 89.

76 Arrêt de la Cour du 28 mars 2017, *Rosneft, supra* note 12, points 71 à 81.

77 *Id*, point 78.

78 *Id.,* points 72 et 73.

79 Arrêt de la Cour du 15 juillet 1964, *Flaminio Costa/E.N.E.L.*, 6/64, EU:C:1964:66.

tions relatives à la PESC, c'est la nature individuelle de ces actes qui ouvre, conformément aux termes de l'article 275, second alinéa, TFUE, l'accès aux juridictions de l'Union »[80]. Pour le reste, la PESC bénéficie d'une large immunité juridictionnelle, conformément à l'article 24 TUE.

2. Le contrôle complet des mesures restrictives à portée individuelle

La Cour de justice de l'Union européenne va souligner qu'elle exerce un contrôle complet sur les mesures qui revêtent une portée individuelle[81]; il en va ainsi d'un contrôle juridictionnel effectif, notamment garanti par l'article 47 de la Charte des droits fondamentaux. Selon l'arrêt *Rosneft*, portant sur un règlement adopté sur le fondement de l'article 215 TFUE, qui donne effet aux positions de l'Union arrêtées dans le contexte de la PESC, « la compétence de la Cour ne se trouve aucunement limitée [...]. En effet, de tels règlements constituent des actes de l'Union, [...] à l'égard desquels les juridictions de l'Union doivent, conformément aux compétences dont elles sont investies en vertu des traités, assurer un contrôle, en principe complet, de légalité »[82]. La Cour de justice avait déjà affirmé la nature complète du contrôle exercé, dans le cadre de l'arrêt *Kadi*[83].

S'agissant du contrôle juridictionnel du bien-fondé des motifs sur lesquels s'appuie la décision d'inscrire ou de maintenir le nom d'une personne déterminée sur une liste de personnes faisant l'objet de mesures restrictives[84], il sera précisé que « le juge de l'Union s'assure que cette décision [...] repose sur une base factuelle suffisamment solide »[85], ce qui,

---

80 Arrêt de la Cour du 28 mars 2017, *Rosneft, supra* note 12, point 103. V., en ce sens, l'arrêt de la Cour du du 23 avril 2013, *Gbagbo e.a./Conseil*, C-478/11 P à C-482/11 P, EU:C:2013:258, point 57.

81 H. Labayle, R. Mehdi, « Le contrôle juridictionnel de la lutte contre le terrorisme : les 'blacks lists' de l'Union dans le prétoire de la Cour de justice », *Revue trimestrielle de droit européen,* vol. 45, n°2/2009, p. 231.

82 Arrêt de la Cour du 28 mars 2017, *Rosneft, supra* note 12, point 106.

83 Arrêt de la Cour du 3 septembre 2008, *Yassin Abdullah Kadi et Al Barakaat International Foundation/Conseil et Commission*, *supra* note 5, point 326.

84 Rappelons qu'il s'agit d'une question différente du contrôle du caractère suffisant de la motivation : V. *supra* sous IA.

85 Arrêt du Tribunal du 30 novembre 2016, *Arkady Romanovich Rotenberg, supra* note 24, point 71; point 56.

pour le Tribunal, « implique une vérification des faits allégués dans l'exposé des motifs qui sous-tend ladite décision »; en conséquence, cela signifie que le contrôle juridictionnel n'est « pas limité à l'appréciation de la vraisemblance abstraite des motifs invoqués, mais porte sur la question de savoir si ces motifs[...] sont étayés de façon suffisamment précise et concrète »[86]. Il s'agit de l'application des modalités déjà définies, notamment dans l'arrêt précité *Kadi II*[87]. Dans l'affaire *Rotenberg*[88], cette approche rigoureuse a conduit à annuler la première inscription de M. Rotenberg sur les listes, en juillet 2014, parce que le juge a pu établir que le Conseil ne disposait pas, à ce moment, des preuves suffisantes du fait que le requérant contrôlait la société qui avait été chargée de la réalisation d'une étude de faisabilité sur la construction d'un pont entre la Russie et la Crimée; en revanche, le Tribunal a accepté la décision de maintenir M. Rotenberg sur les listes, parce que le Conseil, qui avait pris soin de modifier, en 2015, la motivation des sanctions visant M. Rotenberg, était, antérieurement à l'adoption de ses actes de 2015, en possession des preuves que ce dernier était propriétaire d'une autre société chargée, elle, de construire le pont.

B. La conciliation avec les objectifs de la PESC au détriment de la protection juridictionnelle des personnes

Ces affaires conduisent également à s'interroger sur la teneur de la protection juridictionnelle offerte, alors que la Cour de justice va souligner les conséquences négatives que la crise ukrainienne peut entraîner sur les droits fondamentaux des personnes russes ciblées (1), et alors même que ces dernières ne sont pas toujours impliquées dans le conflit ukrainien (2).

---

86 Arrêt du Tribunal du 25 janvier 2017, *Joint-Stock Company "Almaz-Antey" Air and Space Defence, supra* note 26, points 84 et 127.

87 Arrêt de la Cour du 1er juillet 2013, *Commission européenne e.a./Yassin Abdullah Kadi, supra* note 7, point 119. V. aussi l'arrêt de la Cour du 3 septembre 2008, *Yassin Abdullah Kadi et Al Barakaat International Foundation/Conseil et Commission, supra* note 5, point 336.

88 Arrêt du Tribunal du 30 novembre 2016, *Arkady Romanovich Rotenberg, supra* note 24.

1. Des droits fondamentaux susceptibles de restrictions ou limitations[89]

La Cour de justice va examiner l'ingérence dans les droits fondamentaux des personnes ciblées.

Parmi les arguments soulevés par les entreprises visées[90], prenons d'abord l'exemple de l'ingérence dans la liberté d'entreprise et le droit de propriété, tels que consacrés, respectivement, aux articles 16 et 17 de la Charte des droits fondamentaux de l'Union européenne. Conformément à sa jurisprudence très classique[91], la Cour de justice va souligner que de tels droits et libertés ne constituent pas des prérogatives absolues, et que leur exercice peut faire l'objet de restrictions justifiées par des objectifs d'intérêt général poursuivis par l'Union. Ainsi la Cour entend « reconnaître un large pouvoir d'appréciation au législateur de l'Union dans des domaines qui impliquent de la part de ce dernier des choix de nature politique, économique et sociale, et dans lesquels celui-ci est appelé à effectuer des appréciations complexes »[92]. Néanmoins certaines conditions doivent être réunies, ce qui implique notamment de rechercher si l'ingérence est démesurée ou disproportionnée. La Cour fait état de « l'évolution progressive de l'intensité des mesures restrictives » adoptées[93]; une telle formulation est explicitée dans l'arrêt "*Almaz-Antey" Air and Space Defence*, en ces termes : « C'est donc en raison de la persistance, voire de l'aggravation, de la situation en Ukraine à la suite des pre-

---

89 V., par exemple, dans l'affaire Rosneft, la remarque de l'Avocat général Wathelet selon laquelle « les dispositions en cause visent précisément à limiter l'approvisionnement en équipements et en financement du secteur pétrolier russe ». Conclusions présentées le 31 mai 2016, supra note 58, point 203.

90 La société Rosneft soulève aussi l'imprécision de plusieurs des dispositions du texte européen qui impose aux Etats d'adopter des sanctions pénales, et invoque donc la violation du principe *nulla poena sine lege certa*. Pour Rosneft, tant que la Cour ne s'est pas prononcée sur ces notions pour les préciser, des sanctions pénales ne sauraient être imposées en cas d'infraction au règlement européen. Mais la Cour de justice ne partage pas ce point de vue, considérant que le libellé des actes législatifs concernés « ne peut présenter une précision absolue ». Arrêt de la Cour du 28 mars 2017, *Rosneft, supra* note 12, point 164.

91 La Cour prend soin de citer son arrêt de principe du 14 mai 1974, *Nold/Commission,* 4/73, EU:C:1974:51.

92 Arrêt de la Cour du 28 mars 2017, *Rosneft, supra* note 12, point 146. V. aussi, Arrêt du Tribunal du 30 novembre 2016, *Arkady Romanovich Rotenberg, supra* note 24, point 179.

93 Arrêt de la Cour du 28 mars 2017, *Rosneft, supra* note 12, point 150.

mières mesures restrictives adoptées que le Conseil a estimé devoir élargir le cercle des personnes et des entités visées par ces mesures, afin d'atteindre les objectifs poursuivis »[94]. Le constat « d'une telle démarche fondée sur la progressivité de l'atteinte aux droits en fonction de l'effectivité des mesures »[95] permet alors au juge d'affirmer le caractère proportionné de l'ingérence dans les droits de la société "Almaz-Antey" Air and Space Defence; ce raisonnement conduit aussi à considérer qu'il en est de même dans l'arrêt *Rosneft*.

Dans l'affaire *Kiselev,* M. Kiselev, en tant que journaliste, soutenait que les mesures restrictives (gel des fonds et ressources économiques) le visant constituaient une atteinte à sa liberté d'expression. Mais le juge va accepter de telles mesures, en soulignant à plusieurs reprises que le requérant se livrait en fait à des activités de « propagande » en faveur des actions et des politiques du gouvernement russe déstabilisant l'Ukraine, « en utilisant les moyens et le pouvoir qui sont propres à la charge de directeur » de l'agence de presse russe RS Il en conclut que l'atteinte était possible : l'adoption par le Conseil de telles mesures restrictives « ne peut pas être considérée comme étant une restriction disproportionnée à son droit à la liberté d'expression » [96].

2. *Des préjudices causés à des personnes russes très inégalement impliquées dans la crise*

La comparaison des affaires montre le rôle très différencié des entreprises et ressortissants russes visés, quant à leur implication dans l'atteinte aux droits de l'Etat ukrainien. Deux types de situations, selon qu'il y a soutien ou non, peuvent être identifiés, à la lumière de la réaction européenne à la crise russo-ukrainienne. Nous avons vu que certaines des entreprises ciblées avaient apporté un soutien actif ou matériel à la déstabilisation de l'Ukraine.

94 Arrêt du Tribunal du 25 janvier 2017, *supra* note 26, point 104.

95 *Ibid.* V. aussi le point 126 de l'arrêt de la Cour du 28 novembre 2013, *Conseil/ Manufacturing Support & Procurement Kala Naft Co., Tehran*, C-348/12 P, EU:C:2013:776.

96 Arrêt du Tribunal du 15 juin 2017, *Dmitrii Konstantinovich Kiselev/Conseil*, *supra* note 25, points 97, 99, 107, 111, 112 et 117.

Mais le juge de l'Union accepte des mesures restrictives qui peuvent aussi viser des entreprises, actives ou importantes dans l'économie russe, tel Rosneft, qui n'ont pas contribué, même indirectement, à la crise en Ukraine : et en effet, la Cour de justice reconnaît que ces parties n'ont « aucune responsabilité quant à la situation ayant conduit à l'adoption des sanctions »[97]. Une telle approche n'est pas nouvelle, puisque la Cour l'avait déjà consacrée, en des termes exactement similaires, dès l'arrêt *Bosphorus*[98]. A cet égard, il convient aussi de citer l'arrêt de la Grande chambre *National Iranian Oil Company,* relatif aux sanctions adoptées contre l'industrie du pétrole et du gaz de l'Iran, à cause des activités nucléaires iraniennes : dans cette affaire, le juge identifie des activités « qui, même si elles n'ont, en tant que telles, aucun lien direct ou indirect avec la prolifération nucléaire, sont cependant susceptibles de favoriser celle-ci, en fournissant au gouvernement iranien des ressources ou des facilités d'ordre matériel, financier ou logistique lui permettant de poursuivre les activités de prolifération »[99].

Ainsi, même sans qu'une entreprise ait pris part à la déstabilisation de l'Ukraine, une atteinte aux droits de cette entreprise peut être légale[100]. Une telle ingérence résulte de mesures qui « comportent, par définition, des effets qui affectent les droits » fondamentaux des personnes[101]; la Cour ajoute qu'il en résulte « des préjudices » causés aux parties[102]. Causer des préjudices aux intérêts des entreprises russes, quel que soit leur degré de responsabilité, est un moyen accepté par le juge de l'Union, pour faire pression sur la Russie, et essayer de l'amener à changer d'attitude, et à se rallier à un règlement pacifique du différend. Dans l'affaire *Rosneft*, la balance paraît ainsi pencher en faveur de la réalisation de la PESC et au détriment des droits d'une entreprise, dont la Cour reconnaît pourtant qu'elle n'est pour rien dans la situation de crise.

---

97 Arrêt de la Cour du 28 mars 2017, *Rosneft, supra* note 12, point 149.

98 Arrêt de la Cour du 30 juillet 1996, *Bosphorus Hava Yollari Turizm ve Ticaret AS/Minister for Transport, Energy and Communications e.a., supra* note 13, point 22.

99 Arrêt de la Cour du 1er mars 2016, *National Iranian Oil Company/Conseil*, C-440/14 P, EU:C:2016:128, point 80.

100 Nous avons déjà vu (V. *supra*, Partie I) qu'étaient pris en compte notamment l'importance majeure de l'opérateur économique ou le rôle actif de ce dernier dans des secteurs spécifiques de l'économie russe.

101 Arrêt de la Cour du 28 mars 2017, *Rosneft, supra* note 12, point 149.

102 V. aussi l'arrêt de la Cour du 30 juillet 1996, *Bosphorus, supra* note 13, point 22.

Ainsi, malgré la projection externe de l'Etat de droit à travers la protection juridictionnelle des personnes, la crise russo-ukrainienne montre que la conciliation avec les objectifs de la PESC peut se faire au préjudice des droits fondamentaux d'entités dont certaines sont pourtant non impliquées dans la crise. En réalité, de tels choix, qui résultent de la mise en balance de l'effectivité de la PESC et des droits fondamentaux, sont au cœur du contentieux des mesures restrictives.

Objectif de sécurité et protection des données personnelles: projection dans l'ordre international d'un système constitutionnel propre à l'Union européenne / Security Objective and Personal Data Protection: Constitutional Advances of a European Union-Specific System in the International Order

Laurence Potvin-Solis

Abstract

Personal data protection continuously presents key topical issues for the Union's legal order in terms of its external action and which stand out as a constitutional matter for its internal order. These issues show the extent to which the Union's external objectives must be related to its internal objectives and to the twofold dimension of the Union's external action, which develops itself both in the context of its sectorial policies and as a means for the Union to assert itself as a global and credible player on the international stage. Thus, the European Union's compliance with personal data protection is characterised by close links between the internal and external dimensions of this protection. The European Union is progressively defining its own independent approach to personal data protection, which has become progressively extended and refined within EU law. This protection is defined in Article 16 of the Treaty on the Functioning of the European Union (TFEU) and Article 8 of the EU Charter of Fundamental Rights (EUCFR). In this regard, personal data protection, as well as the normative developments surrounding it, should be considered as a component of the Union's "constitutional framework", as pointed out by the Court of Justice Opinion 2/13 of 18 December 2014, which pertains to the draft agreement providing for the accession of the European Union to the Convention for the Protection of Human Rights (ECHR) and which is essential both to the Union's secondary legislation but also for negotiations aimed at concluding agreements with third countries. Recently, the Court of Justice has firmly stressed this point in Opinion 1/15 of the Grand Chamber of 26 July 2017, declaring the Canada-EU draft agreement on the transfer of Passenger Name Record (PNR) incompatible with the EU-CFR.

The close link between the internal and external dimensions of personal data protection, both inside and by the European Union, is another characteristic feature of pursuing the goal of security, which must be reconciled with personal data protection requirements and can give rise to great tensions between the legal systems, as demonstrated by Opinion 1/15 of 26 July 2017. The development of tools and agreements to ensure security, particularly in the context of the fight against terrorism and serious transnational crime, calls upon the EU to define a concept of personal data protection which can be clearly identifiable in both its domestic law and its external relations. In parallel, reconciling the objective of security and the protection of personal data takes on a strong constitutional dimension in the Union's legal order, once this objective is treated, like the Union's policies and actions as a whole, in accordance with the European Union's values and fundamental rights of its respective field. Personal data protection was confirmed as a constitutional requirement by the Lisbon Treaty. Indeed, this issue is expressly governed by Article 39 TEU and Article 16 TFEU. The latter states in its first paragraph that "everyone has the right to the protection of personal data concerning them", and its second paragraph provides for the European Council and Parliament's competence to lay down, in accordance with the ordinary legislative procedure "rules relating to the protection of individuals with regard to the processing of personal data by Union institutions, bodies, offices and agencies, and by the Member States when carrying out activities which fall within the scope of Union law, and the rules relating to the free movement of such data". This paragraph specifies that "the rules adopted on the basis of this article shall be without prejudice to the specific rules laid down in Article 39 of the TEU". According to the latter, "in accordance with Article 16 of the TFEU and by way of derogation from paragraph 2 thereof, the Council shall adopt a decision laying down the rules relating to the protection of individuals with regard to the processing of personal data by the Member States when carrying out activities which fall within the scope of this Chapter, and the rules relating to the free movement of such data". Both Article 16 TFEU and Article 39 TEU state that the "compliance with these rules shall be subject to the control of independent authorities".

Personal data protection falls within the scope of European Union law and is also associated with the scope of the EUCFR. It must be related not only to the free movement of data within the internal market of the area of freedom, security and justice (AFSJ), but also to the objectives of security and the fight against crime which, just like personal data protection, can impact this freedom of movement and establish themselves both internally and in terms of the Union's external action. It benefits from the Lisbon Treaty's recognition of the EUCFR's legal status. Unlike the European Convention on Human Rights, in which personal data protection is covered as a fundamental right falling within the scope of Article 8 (related to the right to respect for private and family life), the Charter includes an Article that expressly applies to this type of protection. Indeed, after setting out the right to liberty and security in Article 6, and the respect for private and family life in Article 7, Article 8 of the Charter makes a provision for the protection of personal data, by stating: "1. Everyone has the right to the protection of personal data concerning him or her. 2. Such data must be processed fairly for specified purposes and on the basis of the consent of the person concerned or some other legitimate basis laid down by law. Everyone has the right of access to data which has been collected concerning him or her, and the right to have it rectified". Like Article 16 TFEU and Article 39 TEU, this Article sets out in its third paragraph that "compliance with these rules shall be subject to control by an independent authority".

The progress achieved in terms of a legal framework of personal data protection peculiar to the European Union and to its sectoral development goes hand in hand with the increase in personal data control, collection, conservation, and transfer instruments that aim to meet the objective of security for both the domestic order and the foreign relations of the European Union. This progress is driven by the closer ties and tensions between the European Union, its Member States, and third countries. It must meet the increasing requirements of the case law of the Court of Justice of the European Union. It presents a challenge of coherence for the Union's legal system (as laid out by Article 13 TEU), since it affects not only the values on which it is founded (in particular as stated in Article 2 TEU), such as the respect for freedom, democracy, the rule of law, and human rights, but also applies to all of the Union's actions, internal or external. Promoting these values is the first of the objectives set out in Article 3 TEU. To handle the divergent views between Member States and the international arena, the autonomy of the European Union, its law and its Court of Justice are put forward, especially when it comes to reconciling personal data protection and the objectives of security with the scope of international order, so as to be consistent with its constitutional internal framework. The international terms under which the promotion of these values is laid out cannot be disassociated from the necessary assertion of a system of protection peculiar to the European Union to ensure the respect for fundamental rights related to personal data processing, access, retention, alteration, and transfer, as well as the right to be forgotten.

This contribution brings to light the identification details and constitutional nature of such a system of protection peculiar to the European Union, with regard to requirements of the Court of Justice's jurisprudence and to developments of the Union's regulatory framework and of their external repercussions. It includes the challenges of negotiating the international agreements and ongoing reforms as well as the input of Opinion 1/15 of the Grand Chamber of 26 July 2017 regarding the agreement envisaged between Canada and the European Union on the transfer and processing of Passenger Name Record data. It highlights the imperative of a global approach to the relationship between personal data protection and the pursuit of the objective of security, an approach that can be defined and carried out by the European Union in its foreign relations and as an expression of its identity in the international arena.

The paper firstly analyses the European Union's appropriation of the constitutional terms for reconciling data protection with the pursuit of these objectives. In this context, it considers the necessity for the European Union to provide consistency: (*a*) In its pursuit of a high level of personal data protection in its general and sectoral regulations and their external aspects; (*b*) In its control of the interdependence of internal and external challenges of reconciling the European Union's general and sectoral objectives; and (*c*) In the autonomy of assessment set in the European Union's constitutional framework relating to the interpretation of the fundamental rights and concepts governing personal data protection and the increasing control of the objectives which justifies interferences.

Secondly, the contribution analyses the advances of a European constitutional identity as a consequence of the assertion of a system of protection peculiar to the European Union. To this effect, it considers: (*a*) The internal and external scope of constitutional advances achieved by the Court of Justice's jurisprudence that act in favour of personal data protection; (*b*) The broad implications of constitutional requirements regarding the independence of supervisory authorities within the European Union, its Member States and towards third-countries; And (*c*) The increasingly unique characteristics of the European Union's system of protection as a result of the relationship between the objectives and the legal bases and the necessity to ensure a continuity in personal data protection that is equivalent and suited to the high level of protection within the European Union.

***

La protection des données personnelles présente des enjeux de constante actualité pour l'ordre juridique de l'Union européenne sous l'angle de son action extérieure et qui s'imposent comme une question constitutionnelle pour son ordre interne. Ces enjeux montrent combien les objectifs externes de l'Union doivent être rapportés à ses objectifs internes et à la double dimension de l'action extérieure de l'Union qui se développe tant dans le cadre de ses politiques sectorielles que comme moyen d'affirmation de l'Union en tant qu'acteur global identifiable et crédible sur la scène internationale. Ainsi, le respect par l'Union européenne de la protection des données personnelles est caractérisé par une très forte imbrication entre les dimensions interne et externe de cette protection. L'Union européenne définit progressivement une conception autonome de la protection des données personnelles qui lui est propre et qui s'est trouvée progressivement élargie et affinée en droit de l'Union. Cette protection fait aujourd'hui l'objet de l'article 16 du Traité sur le fonctionnement de l'Union européenne (TFUE) et de l'article 8 de la Charte des droits fondamentaux de l'Union européenne (CDFUE). Elle doit en cela et dans les développements normatifs dont elle fait l'objet, être perçue comme une composante du « cadre constitutionnel » de l'Union mis en avant par la Cour dans l'avis 2/13[1], qui s'impose tant au droit dérivé de l'Union que dans le cadre des négociations en vue de la conclusion d'accords avec les États tiers, comme l'a rappelé fermement la Cour de justice dans son avis 1/15, constatant l'incompatibilité avec la CDFUE du projet d'accord entre le Canada et l'Union européenne sur le transfert des données des dossiers passagers aériens depuis l'Union vers le Canada[2].

La forte imbrication entre les dimensions interne et externe de la protection des données personnelles dans et par l'Union caractérise également

1 Avis de la Cour du 18 décembre 2014, 2/13, *Projet d'accord d'adhésion de l'Union européenne à la Convention européenne des droits de l'homme*, EU:C:2014:2454, points 155 à 177.

2 Avis de la Cour du 26 juillet 2017, 1/15, *Transfert des données des dossiers passagers aériens depuis l'Union vers le Canada*, EU:C:2017:592. V. nos développements *infra.*

la poursuite de l'objectif de sécurité qui doit être concilié avec les exigences de cette protection et qui est source de vives tensions entre les ordres juridiques, comme le montre l'avis 1/15. Le développement des instruments et des accords au service de la sécurité, tout particulièrement dans le cadre de la lutte contre le terrorisme et contre la criminalité transnationale grave, invite l'Union à définir une conception de la protection des données à caractère personnel qui puisse être clairement identifiable dans son ordre interne comme dans ses relations extérieures. La conciliation entre l'objectif de sécurité et la protection des données personnelles revêt en même temps une forte dimension constitutionnelle dans l'ordre juridique de l'Union dès lors que cet objectif est rapporté, comme l'ensemble des politiques et actions de l'Union, au respect des valeurs de l'Union et des droits fondamentaux dans son champ[3]. La protection des données personnelles a été confortée comme exigence constitutionnelle par le traité de Lisbonne. Elle est en effet expressément régie par l'article 39 du Traité sur l'Union européenne (TUE) et par l'article 16 TFUE. Ce dernier énonce, dans son premier paragraphe, que « toute personne a droit à la protection des données à caractère personnel la concernant » et son deuxième paragraphe prévoit la compétence pour adopter, sur la base de la procédure législative ordinaire, « les règles relatives à la protection des personnes physiques à l'égard du traitement des données à caractère personnel par les institutions, organes et organismes de l'Union, ainsi que par les États membres dans l'exercice d'activités qui relèvent du champ d'application du droit de l'Union, et à la libre circulation de ces données ». Ce paragraphe précise que « les règles adoptées sur la base du présent article sont sans préjudice des règles spécifiques prévues à l'article 39 TUE ». Selon ce dernier, « conformément à l'article 16 TFUE et par dérogation à son paragraphe 2, le Conseil adopte une décision fixant les règles relatives à la protection des personnes physiques à l'égard du traitement des données à caractère personnel par les États membres dans l'exercice d'activités qui relèvent du champ d'application du présent chapitre, et à la libre

3 R. Tinière, C. Vial (dir.), *La protection des droits fondamentaux dans l'Union européenne. Entre évolution et permanence*, Bruylant, Bruxelles, Coll. Droit de l'Union européenne, 2015; L. Potvin-Solis (dir.), *Les valeurs communes dans l'Union européenne, Onzièmes Journées Jean Monnet,* Bruylant, Bruxelles, Colloques Jean Monnet, 2014; L. Potvin-Solis (dir.), *Politiques de l'Union européenne et droits fondamentaux, Treizièmes Journées Jean Monnet,* Bruylant, Bruxelles, Colloques Jean Monnet, 2016.

circulation de ces données ». Les articles 16 TFUE et 39 TUE précisent tous deux que « le respect de ces règles est soumis au contrôle d'autorités indépendantes ».

La protection des données personnelles est donc source d'obligations pour l'Union et pour ses États membres et donne lieu à un titre de compétence expressément affirmé au bénéfice de l'Union et à l'égard des États membres. Son champ se conjugue au champ d'application du droit de l'Union et implique celui de la Charte des droits fondamentaux de l'Union. Elle doit être rapportée tant à la libre circulation des données au sein du marché intérieur et de l'espace de liberté, de sécurité et de justice qu'aux objectifs de sécurité et de lutte contre la criminalité qui peuvent, comme elle, agir sur cette liberté de circulation. Qui plus est, elle bénéficie de la reconnaissance par le traité de Lisbonne de la valeur juridique de la Charte qui, à la différence de la Convention européenne des droits de l'homme[4] comporte un article qui lui est expressément consacré. La Charte prévoit en effet, après le droit à la liberté et à la sûreté énoncés dans son article 6, et le respect de la vie privée et familiale garanti par son article 7, la protection des données à caractère personnel, dans son article 8, selon lequel :

«1. Toute personne a droit à la protection des données à caractère personnel la concernant.

2. Ces données doivent être traitées loyalement, à des fins déterminées et sur la base du consentement de la personne concernée ou en vertu d'un autre fondement légitime prévu par la loi. Toute personne a le droit d'accéder aux données collectées la concernant et d'en obtenir la rectification [...]».

Comme les articles 16 TFUE et 39 TUE, cet article pose dans son troisième paragraphe que « le respect de ces règles est soumis au contrôle d'une autorité indépendante ».

Les progrès d'un cadre légal de protection des données personnelles propre à l'Union s'imposent de façon corrélative à l'accroissement des instruments de contrôle, de collecte, de conservation et de transfert des données personnelles visant à répondre à l'objectif de sécurité dans l'ordre interne et dans l'action extérieure de l'Union. Ils se nourrissent des rapprochements et des tensions entre l'Union, ses États membres et les États

4 La Convention couvre la protection des données personnelles comme droit fondamental compris dans le champ d'application de son article 8 sur le droit au respect de la vie privée et familiale.

tiers et doivent répondre aux exigences grandissantes de la jurisprudence de la Cour de justice. Ils représentent un enjeu de cohérence pour l'ordre juridique de l'Union d'autant plus qu'ils touchent aux valeurs qui sont placées à ses fondements, telles que le respect de l'État de droit et des droits de l'homme, et qui s'imposent à toutes ses actions, internes et externes. Ils conduisent l'Union à définir une protection autonome et « son » identité par les développements progressifs d'une harmonisation des législations nationales au sein du marché intérieur, de ses politiques et de l'espace de liberté, de sécurité et de justice et d'exigences qui lui sont propres dans le cadre de son action extérieure et de ses négociations pour la conclusion d'accords internationaux avec les États tiers. La protection des données personnelles suscite un intérêt croissant et de vifs débats dans un contexte international marqué par les contestations qui se sont élevées face à des pratiques de surveillance et de collecte de données de masse, telles que les écoutes de la *National Security Agency (NSA)*. Face aux divergences de conception en présence, l'autonomie de l'Union, de son droit et de son juge est mise en avant, tout particulièrement lorsqu'il s'agit de concilier la protection des données personnelles aux objectifs de sécurité dans l'ordre international en cohérence avec son ordre interne. La protection des données personnelles obéit alors à un raisonnement similaire à celui mené dans l'arrêt *Kadi* marquant l'autonomie du contrôle juridictionnel de la garantie des droits fondamentaux dans l'Union européenne[5]. Les termes internationaux dans lesquels elle se pose à l'Union ne peuvent être dissociés de l'affirmation nécessaire d'un système de protection propre à l'Union pour le respect des droits fondamentaux en matière d'accès, de conservation (et d'oubli) et de transfert.

C'est donc à partir d'une mise en relief des éléments d'identification de ce système et de la mise en exergue de sa nature « constitutionnelle » pour l'Union que sera ici analysée la protection des données personnelles rapportée aux objectifs de sécurité de l'Union. Les enjeux constitutionnels des termes de la conciliation des intérêts s'imposent à chaque étape des progrès du droit dérivé et sont mis en relief devant la Cour de justice. Par sa jurisprudence, au sein de laquelle tous les intérêts convergent, la Cour encadre la marge d'appréciation des autorités publiques des États membres et de l'Union en prenant en considération les aspects généraux et sec-

5 Arrêt de la Cour du 3 septembre 2008, *Kadi et Al Barakaat International Foundation/Conseil et Commission,* C-402/05 P, EU:C:2008:461.

toriels ainsi que les dimensions internes et externes. C'est sous l'impulsion du développement d'un cadre juridique spécifique à l'Union qu'ont été progressivement révélés les traits d'un système constitutionnel propre à l'Union et identifiable comme tel dans l'ordre international. Les apports de la jurisprudence toujours plus étoffée de la Cour de justice occupent une place centrale dans cette évolution qui traduit les prolongements externes des finalités internes de l'Union. Les enjeux généraux et transversaux des réformes en cours dans l'Union et des négociations par l'Union d'accords internationaux portant sur les données personnelles montrent la nécessité d'une appropriation par l'Union des termes constitutionnels de la conciliation des objectifs (I) qui puisse trouver un fondement solide par l'affirmation d'un système constitutionnel propre à l'Union et à même d'exprimer son identité sur la scène internationale (II).

I. L'appropriation par l'Union des termes constitutionnels de la conciliation des objectifs

La jurisprudence de la Cour de justice permet d'affiner les termes de cette conciliation. Les progrès d'un cadre général de protection des données personnelles dans l'Union se combinent avec les développements sectoriels de cette protection. Ils sont par ailleurs marqués, d'un point de vue général comme sur le plan sectoriel, par la forte imbrication entre les dimensions internes et externes de la conciliation entre les objectifs et entre les intérêts en présence. Ils forment donc un enjeu de taille pour la cohérence du cadre normatif de l'Union et pour l'autonomie de la garantie et de l'interprétation des droits fondamentaux par l'Union. Cette interprétation doit être menée par référence au cadre constitutionnel de l'Union au sens de l'avis 2/13 sur le projet d'accord d'adhésion de l'Union à la Convention européenne des droits de l'homme[6]. Elle doit permettre d'assurer la cohérence dans la poursuite d'un niveau élevé de protection des données personnelles (A) et la maîtrise par l'Union de l'interdépendance des enjeux internes et externes de la conciliation entre la protection des données personnelles et les objectifs de sécurité (B). Elle exprime toujours davantage une autonomie d'appréciation ancrée dans le cadre constitutionnel de l'Union (C).

6 Avis de la Cour du 18 décembre 2014, 2/13, *supra* note 1.

A. La cohérence dans la poursuite d'un niveau élevé de protection des données personnelles

Les exigences de cohérence sont multiples et invitent l'Union à mener une approche globale de la protection des données personnelles et à en développer une conception autonome y compris lorsqu'elle est rapportée aux objectifs de sécurité. Telle qu'elle est posée dans l'article 13 TUE, cette cohérence doit être rapprochée de la promotion par l'Union de ses valeurs, de la poursuite de ses objectifs et de la réalisation de « ses intérêts, ceux de ses citoyens, et ceux des États membres ». Elle est affirmée en lien avec la nécessité pour l'Union d'assurer « l'efficacité et la continuité de ses politiques et de ses actions ». Elle s'impose à l'action extérieure de l'Union mais ne peut être conçue qu'en partant de son ordre interne. Elle s'est trouvée progressivement affirmée, tant dans les rapports entre la règlementation applicable aux États membres et celle applicable à l'Union (1) que dans l'articulation entre la règlementation générale et les règlementations sectorielles de l'Union (2).

1. La cohérence entre la règlementation applicable aux États membres et celle applicable à l'Union

Concernant les États, la directive 95/46/CE relative à la protection des personnes physiques à l'égard du traitement des données à caractère personnel et à la libre circulation de ces données a constitué le texte de base[7]. Selon la Cour de justice, cette directive a abouti « à une harmonisation qui est, en principe, complète » et ne se limite pas à une harmonisation minimale même si elle comporte « des règles caractérisées par une certaine souplesse laissant dans de nombreux cas aux États membres le soin d'arrêter les détails ou de choisir parmi des options » et préserve donc une certaine marge d'appréciation nationale[8]. Elle a imposé cette protection au sein des échanges entre les États membres, face aux progrès des technolo-

7 Directive 95/46/CE du Parlement européen et du Conseil, *JO* L 281, du 23 novembre 1995, p. 31.

8 V. not. : Arrêt de la Cour du 6 novembre 2003, *Lindqvist,* C-101/01, EU:C:2003:596, points 95 et 96; Arrêt de la Cour du 16 décembre 2008, *Huber,* C-524/06, EU:C:2008:724, points 50 et 51; Arrêt de la Cour du 7 mai 2009, *Rijkeboer,* C-553/07, EU:C:2009:293, point 56.

gies de la communication et comme corollaire de la garantie des droits fondamentaux dans les États. Elle a contribué à l'objectif de cohérence dès lors qu'elle a cherché à assurer « un niveau de protection des droits et libertés des personnes à l'égard du traitement de ces données » qui soit « équivalent dans tous les États membres »[9] en visant l'objectif d'un niveau de protection élevé à partir duquel la Cour de justice exerce son contrôle[10]. La directive 95/46/CE a été abrogée et remplacée par le règlement général sur la protection des données personnelles n° 2016/679/UE (RGPD),[11] entré en application le 25 mai 2018. Ce règlement poursuit le mouvement d'unification du cadre juridique de l'Union et contribue à renforcer les droits des personnes[12] et les obligations qui pèsent sur les responsables du traitement des données et sur les sous-traitants ainsi que les conditions tenant à l'indépendance des autorités de contrôles[13], la coopération et la cohérence[14]. Il procède à une modernisation de la directive qui a donné lieu à une importante jurisprudence dont il reprend certaines avancées et s'inscrit dans un mouvement de réforme plus large[15].

Vis-à-vis de l'Union, le règlement n° 45/2001/CE relatif à la protection des personnes physiques à l'égard du traitement des données à caractère personnel par les institutions et organes communautaires et à la libre circulation de ces données a également posé l'objectif d'un niveau de protection élevé des données à caractère personnel[16]. Il vise à « assurer dans l'ensemble de la Communauté une application cohérente et homogène des

---

9 Cons. 8 de la directive.

10 Arrêt de la Cour du 13 mai 2014, *Google Spain et Google,* C-131/12, EU:C:2014:317, point 66.

11 Règlement n° 2016/679/UE du Parlement européen et du Conseil du 27 avril 2016 relatif à la protection des personnes physiques à l'égard du traitement des données à caractère personnel (règlement général sur la protection des données), *JO* L 119, du 4 mai 2016, p. 1.

12 En matière de droit d'accès, de rectification, de suppression (avec le droit à l'oubli ou le droit à l'effacement), d'opposition, de droit de limitation du traitement des données, de droit à la portabilité des données personnelles ou encore les droits en matière de profilage.

13 V. le chap. VI du règlement.

14 V. le chap. VII du règlement.

15 V. not. la directive 2016/680/UE du Parlement européen et du Conseil du 27 avril 2016, *JO* L 119, du 4 mai 2016, p. 89 et la directive 2016/681/UE du Parlement européen et du Conseil du 27 avril 2016, *JO* L 119, du 4 mai 2016, p. 132.

16 Règlement n° 45/2001/UE du Parlement européen et du Conseil du 18 décembre 2000, *JO* L 8, du 12 janvier 2001, p. 1.

règles de protection des libertés et droits fondamentaux des personnes à l'égard du traitement des données à caractère personnel »[17]. Il reste applicable au traitement des données à caractère personnel par les institutions, organes et organismes de l'Union après l'intervention du règlement n° 2016/679/UE. Mais ce dernier prévoit que, comme les autres actes juridiques de l'Union régissant le traitement des données à caractère personnel, il doit être adapté « aux principes et aux règles »[18] qu'il fixe et il exige leur réexamen « afin d'assurer une protection uniforme et cohérente des personnes physiques à l'égard du traitement » en précisant que « cela concerne en particulier les règles relatives à la protection des personnes physiques à l'égard du traitement par des institutions, organes et organismes de l'Union et à la libre circulation de ces données »[19].

2. *La cohérence entre la réglementation générale et les règlementations sectorielles de l'Union*

Certaines règlementations sectorielles ont pour objet même la protection des données personnelles dans un champ spécifique tandis que d'autres poursuivent des objectifs d'ordre sécuritaire mais intègrent la protection des données personnelles dans les dispositifs de contrôle qu'elles mettent en place. Dans le domaine des communications électroniques, la protection des données personnelles a été prévue par la directive 97/66/CE[20] à laquelle renvoie la directive sur le commerce électronique 2000/31/CE[21], puis par la directive 2002/58/CE[22], qui comporte notamment des dispositions relatives à la conservation des données de connexion par les États membres à des fins de surveillance policière. Ces directives peuvent susciter des questions d'interprétation liées à celle de la règlementation

---

17 *Id.*, considérant 12.

18 Article 2, paragraphe 3 du règlement n° 2016/679, *supra* note 11.

19 *Id.*, article 98.

20 Directive 97/66/CE du Parlement européen et du Conseil du 15 décembre 1997 concernant le traitement des données à caractère personnel et la protection de la vie privée dans le secteur des télécommunications, *JO* L 24, du 30 janvier 1998, p. 1.

21 Directive 2000/31/CE du Parlement européen et du Conseil du 8 juin 2000, *JO* L 178, du 17 juillet 2001, p. 1, cons. 14 et s.

22 Directive 2002/58/CE du Parlement européen et du Conseil du 12 juillet 2002, *JO* L 201, du 31 juillet 2002, p. 37.

générale des données personnelles dans l'Union[23] et au respect de la Charte des droits fondamentaux de l'Union. La Cour de justice a notamment jugé dans l'arrêt *Tele2 Sverige* que l'article 15 paragraphe 1 de la directive 2002/58/CE s'oppose à « une réglementation nationale prévoyant, à des fins de lutte contre la criminalité, une conservation généralisée et indifférenciée de l'ensemble des données relatives au trafic et des données de localisation de tous les abonnés et utilisateurs inscrits concernant tous les moyens de communication électronique »[24]. Cette directive fait l'objet d'une réforme en cours qui marque les imbrications entre les objectifs généraux et les objectifs sectoriels. Elle doit en effet être abrogée par un réglement *ePrivacy* qui vise à développer l'harmonisation des législations nationales en matière de confidentialité des communications électroniques et à garantir un niveau élevé de protection des données issues de ces communications afin de ne pas réduire celui garanti par le RGPD. Cette proposition de règlement « vie privée et communications électroniques » constitue donc un pas supplémentaire dans le processus d'harmonisation dans ce secteur et est orientée vers les objectifs de la stratégie pour le marché unique numérique. Le retard pris dans son adoption témoigne de la force des résistances qu'elle suscite de la part des milieux professionnels concernés. Elle vise à actualiser les dispositions de la directive 2002/58/CE et à en étendre le champ à l'ensemble des fournisseurs de services de communications électroniques. Les questions de cohérence ont notamment été soulevées par le contrôleur européen de la protection des données (CEPD) dans son avis rendu sur la proposition de règlement *ePrivacy*. Il les a notamment relevées en ce qui concerne la détermination du sens même des notions sur lesquelles cette proposition repose dans la mesure où leurs définitions devront être posées dans « le code des communications électroniques européen » et seront donc « centrées sur la concurrence et le marché », et, dès lors, selon le CEPD, mal « adaptées au contexte des

23 V. not. le renvoi préjudiciel introduit par le Bundesgerichtshof le 30 novembre 2017, *Planet49 GmbH.*, C-673/17.

24 Arrêt de la Cour du 21 décembre 2016, C-203/15 et C-698/15, EU:C:2016:970. Sur cette jurisprudence et les questions d'interprétation de la directive 2002/58/CE au regard des droits fondamentaux et de la CEDH, v. not. le renvoi préjudiciel introduit par le Investigatory Powers Tribunal-London le 31 octobre 2017, *Privacy International*, C-623/17.

droits fondamentaux »[25]. Les questions de cohérence entre la réglementation générale et les règlementations sectorielles de l'Union se mesurent à l'aune du nombre d'avis rendus par le CEPD des données, comme en témoignent par exemple, l'avis sur la proposition d'un cadre commun pour des statistiques européennes relatives aux personnes et aux ménages[26] ou, de façon toute particulière, l'avis sur une application cohérente des droits fondamentaux à l'ère des données massives (*Big Data*) qui en souligne les enjeux en termes de légalité, de responsabilité et de valeurs[27].

Les règlementations sectorielles de l'Union qui visent des objectifs de sécurité peuvent concerner des secteurs aussi variés que le secteur bancaire, le secteur financier et fiscal (et pour la protection des données fiscales, l'assistance administrative internationale), le secteur du E-commerce, celui de la santé et de la E-santé, le cyberespace et internet, la lutte contre la fraude, ou encore la propriété intellectuelle[28]. La question de la protection des données personnelles fait aussi l'objet de dispositions particulières en matière pénale, dans des textes généraux[29] et dans des actes spécifiques comme la décision cadre 2008/977/JAI relative à la protection des données traitées dans le cadre de la coopération judiciaire et policière en matière pénale[30]. Cette décision-cadre a été abrogée et remplacée par la directive 2016/680/UE relative à la protection des personnes physiques à l'égard du traitement des données à caractère personnel par les autorités compétentes à des fins de prévention et de détection des infractions pénales, d'enquêtes et de poursuites en la matière ou d'exécution de sanc-

---

25 Avis du Contrôleur européen de la protection des données du 24 avril 2017 sur la proposition de règlement relatif à la vie privée et aux communications électroniques (2017/C 234/03), *JO* C 234, du 20 juillet 2017, p. 3.

26 Avis du Contrôleur européen de la protection des données du 1er mars 2017 (2017/C87/01), *JO* C 87, du 21 mars 2017, p. 1.

27 Avis 8/2016 du 23 septembre 2016. V. aussi le *Rapport annuel du contrôleur européen de la protection des données*, Luxembourg, Office des publications de l'Union européenne, 2017.

28 V. le séminaire qui s'est tenu à la Cour de justice de l'Union, les 18-20 septembre 2014 sur « les enjeux européens et mondiaux de la protection des données personnelles ».

29 V. not. l'article 10 du règlement général sur la protection des données personnelles 2016/679, *supra* note 11.

30 Décision cadre 2008/977/JAI du Conseil du 27 novembre 2008, *JO* L 350, du 30 décembre 2008, p. 60.

tions pénales[31]. La protection des données personnelles est également directement concernée par les instruments normatifs qui se sont développés dans le domaine de la prévention de l'utilisation du système financier aux fins du blanchiment de capitaux ou du financement du terrorisme[32]. Par exemple, la quatrième directive intervenue dans ce domaine, la directive 2015/849/UE, prévoit une évaluation des risques qui repose sur une coopération et des échanges de données avec les États membres qui doivent être respectueux des droits fondamentaux et de la protection des données personnelles[33]. Cette directive pose des exceptions et restrictions au droit d'accès justifiées par l'objectif d'efficacité dans la poursuite de ses objectifs. Elle a fait l'objet d'une proposition de directive modificative[34] qui étend la prise en compte des risques à ceux provenant de l'utilisation de nouvelles technologies dans les transactions financières, qui permet un renforcement et une harmonisation des contrôles exercés sur les flux financiers provenant de pays tiers à haut risque, et qui accroît les exigences de transparence et les compétences des cellules de renseignement financier des États membres. Dans son avis du 2 février 2017 sur cette proposition de directive, le CEPD a rappelé les exigences du principe de proportionnalité et du « principe de limitation de la finalité ». Il a souligné notamment que « le traitement de données à caractère personnel recueillies à certaines fins pour d'autres fins, sans aucun lien avec les premières, constitue une infraction au principe de protection des données de limitation de la finalité et menace l'application du principe de proportionnalité ». Selon cet avis, les modifications prévues « soulèvent en particulier la question de savoir pourquoi certaines formes de traitement invasif des données à caractère personnel, acceptables quand il est question de lutte contre le blanchiment de capitaux et contre le terrorisme, sont néces-

31 Cette directive (*supra* note 15) est entrée en vigueur le 5 mai 2016 et doit être transposée au plus tard le 6 mai 2018.

32 V. not. L. Potvin-Solis, « La lutte contre le terrorisme et son financement : la nécessité d'un cadre constitutionnel renforcé », *Revue du droit de l'Union européenne,* n°3/2017, p. 11.

33 Cons. 65 et 66 de la directive.

34 Proposition de directive du Parlement européen et du Conseil modifiant la directive 2015/849 et la directive 2009/101/ CE, COM(2016) 450 final du 5 juillet 2016. V. not. Avis du Parlement européen du 30 janvier 2018 sur la base juridique de cette proposition de directive, PE 616.787 v 01-00-C8-0265/2016.

saires en-dehors de ces contextes et si elles sont proportionnées »[35]. La protection des données personnelles se pose dans les mêmes termes au sein du dispositif de l'Union visant à assurer la traçabilité des virements de fonds et des mouvements de liquidités. Le règlement n° 1889/2005/CE vise à renforcer les contrôles de l'argent liquide entrant ou sortant de l'Union.[36] Le règlement n° 2015/847/UE détermine les conditions relatives à l'obtention et à la conservation des données et leur protection en ce qui concerne les informations accompagnant les transferts de fonds. Il prévoit que ces conditions doivent respecter la directive 95/46/CE et le règlement n° 45/2001/CE. Une proposition a été adoptée par la Commission en décembre 2016 pour un nouveau règlement relatif aux contrôles d'argent liquide entrant dans l'Union ou sortant de l'Union[37]. Les exigences de cohérence sont d'autant plus prégnantes que la matière est mouvante et en cours de réforme d'ensemble.

La jurisprudence de la Cour de justice peut préciser l'articulation entre la protection générale des données personnelles et les instruments juridiques catégoriels ou sectoriels. Elle contribue à la cohérence d'ensemble notamment quand elle procède par des rapprochements entre les interprétations jurisprudentielles entre elles. Par exemple, dans l'arrêt *Institut professionnel des agents immobiliers*[38], la Cour de justice interprète l'article 13, paragraphe 1, de la directive 95/46/CE qui prévoit des exceptions à l'obligation d'informer les personnes concernées du traitement de leurs données à caractère personnel, par référence à l'interprétation donnée dans son arrêt *Promusicae* de l'article 15, paragraphe 1, de la directive « vie privée et communications électroniques ».[39]. Elle juge que cette disposition ne contient pas une obligation mais une faculté pour les États de transposer dans leur droit national une ou plusieurs des exceptions qu'elle

35 Avis 1/2017 du Contrôleur européen de la protection des données du 2 février 2017, *JO* C 162, du 23 mai 2017, p. 9.

36 Règlement n° 1889/2005/CE du Parlement européen et du Conseil du 26 octobre 2005, *JO* L 309, du 25 novembre 2005, p. 9. V. not. Potvin-Solis, « La lutte contre le terrorisme et son financement », *supra* note 30, p. 41 et s.

37 Proposition de règlement abrogeant le règlement n° 1889/2005/CE, COM (2016) 825 final; v. les commentaires du Contrôleur européen de la protection des données du 21 février 2017.

38 Arrêt de la Cour du 7 novembre 2013, *Institut professionnel des agents immobiliers* (*IPI*), C-473/12, EU:C:2013:715.

39 Arrêt de la Cour du 29 janvier 2008, *Promusicae*, C-275/06, EU:C:2008:54.

mentionne[40] et que l'activité de détective privé dont il était question entre dans son champ[41].

B. *La maîtrise de l'interdépendance des enjeux internes et externes de la conciliation*

Nombreux sont les secteurs impliqués dans leurs dimensions interne et externe par la protection des données personnelles et les avancées de la règlementation de l'Union. Les développements du droit dérivé et de la jurisprudence fixent l'étendue des obligations qui pèsent sur les États et sur l'Union et permettent d'affiner toujours davantage les modalités de la protection des données personnelles et le cadre légal des ingérences dans les droits fondamentaux justifiées par des objectifs de sécurité. Les progrès du cadre normatif de l'Union en matière de transfert des données personnelles illustrent parfaitement cette évolution vers une appropriation par l'Union des termes constitutionnels de la conciliation des intérêts et des droits en présence et des conditions de la rencontre entre les enjeux internes et externes de cette conciliation. Les avancées de la règlementation générale à l'égard des États membres et de l'Union (1) présentent en effet des enjeux similaires à ceux qui dominent la poursuite par l'Union de ces objectifs dans ses relations extérieures et dans la négociation et la conclusion d'accords internationaux, comme en témoigne l'avis 1/15 rendu par la Cour de justice sur le projet d'accord entre le Canada et l'Union européenne sur le transfert des données des dossiers passagers aériens depuis l'Union vers le Canada (2).

1. *L'interdépendance dans la règlementation générale à l'égard des États membres et de l'Union*

La directive 95/46/CE marquait déjà l'imbrication entre les dimensions internes/externes de la protection des données personnelles par la notion même d'établissement permettant de couvrir l'établissement dans un pays tiers du responsable du traitement de données. Selon son considérant 20,

---

40 Arrêt de la Cour du 7 novembre 2013, *Institut professionnel des agents immobiliers (IPI)*, *supra* note 38, point 37.

41 *Id.*, point 34.

cet établissement ne doit pas contrarier la protection qu'elle met en place, et que les traitements de données personnelles doivent alors être soumis à la loi de l'État membre où sont localisés les moyens utilisés pour ces traitements et respecter « des garanties » pour que les droits et obligations posés par cette directive « soient effectivement respectés ». Cette même imbrication apparaît aussi dans les dispositions de la directive relatives aux transferts de données à caractère personnel d'un État membre de l'Union vers un État tiers qui imposent que les transferts ne soient autorisés que si « ce dernier assure un niveau de protection adéquate ». Si tel n'est pas le cas, de tels transferts ne peuvent en principe être opérés sauf dérogations limitativement énumérées. Cette condition se retrouve dans les décisions relatives aux clauses contractuelles types pour le transfert des données vers des pays tiers en vertu de la directive 95/46/CE[42], dès lors que ces clauses visent à assurer des garanties adéquates lors du transfert des données à caractère personnel de l'Union européenne vers des États tiers.

La directive PNR 2016/681/UE complète la directive 2004/82/CE relative à l'obligation pour les transporteurs de communiquer les données relatives aux passagers dans le cadre de l'amélioration des contrôles aux frontières et de la lutte contre l'immigration illégale. Elle vise à « créer un cadre juridique pour la protection des données PNR en ce qui concerne leur traitement par les autorités compétentes ». Elle rappelle le respect du principe de proportionnalité entre la protection des données personnelles et les objectifs spécifiques de sécurité qu'elle vise ainsi que le respect des droits fondamentaux, par référence à la Charte, en particulier ses articles 8, 7 et 21, du droit à la protection des données à caractère personnel, du droit au respect de la vie privée et du droit à la non-discrimination. Elle précise son articulation avec la directive 2004/82/CE, avec le droit de l'Union et le droit national concernant le principe de l'accès du public aux documents officiels ou encore avec la décision-cadre 2008/977/JAI. Elle précise qu'elle peut exiger, pour le respect du principe de proportionnalité et « pour des points spécifiques, des règles de protection des données plus strictes ». Lorsqu'il s'est prononcé sur la proposition de directive adoptée

---

42 Décision 2001/497/CE de la Commission du 15 juin 2001, *JO* L 181, du 4 juillet 2001, p. 19, et décision 2004/915/CE du 27 décembre 2004 la modifiant, *JO* L 385, du 29 décembre 2004, p. 74.

par la Commission[43], le contrôleur européen de la protection des données personnelles a souligné les risques présentés par une utilisation qui serait « systématique et sans discernement pour tous les passagers », et a mis en évidence la nécessité d'en limiter le champ d'application, de définir davantage la nature des différentes menaces autorisant l'échange de données et d'introduire un niveau de protection élevé par référence à la directive 95/46/CE. Il a invité à limiter la durée de conservation des données à 30 jours « sous une forme identifiable, sauf dans les cas nécessitant une enquête plus approfondie » et à réduire la liste des données PNR à traiter. Il a également appelé à un renforcement des conditions relatives à l'évaluation de la directive. Concernant l'imbrication entre les enjeux internes et externes de la protection des données personnelles, il a recommandé que les développements relatifs à un système PNR au niveau de l'Union soient évalués « dans une perspective plus large, incluant l'évaluation générale actuelle de l'ensemble des instruments européens dans le domaine de la gestion de l'échange de l'information mise en œuvre par la Commission »[44]. Le lien entre les enjeux internes et externes s'observe dans la jurisprudence lorsque la Cour de justice exerce son contrôle, sur la base de la directive PNR 2016/681/UE, du respect par les institutions de l'Union du droit à la protection des données personnelles. Il s'observe également dans le règlement général sur la protection des données 2016/679/UE[45] et dans la directive 2016/680/UE relative à la protection des données à caractère personnel dans le cadre de la coopération en matière pénale qui consacrent tous deux dans des termes identiques leur chapitre V aux transferts de données à caractère personnel vers des pays tiers ou à des organisations internationales[46].

---

43 Proposition de la Commission du 2 février 2011 de directive du Parlement européen et du Conseil relative à l'utilisation des données des dossiers des passagers, COM(2011) 32 final.

44 Avis du Contrôleur européen de la protection des données du 25 mars 2011 (2011/C/ 181/02), *JO* C 181, du 22 juin 2011, p. 24.

45 *Supra* note 11.

46 *Supra* note 15.

2. L'interdépendance dans le cadre des accords internationaux de l'Union européenne

Les accords internationaux conclus par l'Union tendent à se multiplier dans le cadre d'une stratégie extérieure de l'Union reposant sur une « démarche globale en matière de transfert des données des dossiers passagers (PNR) aux pays tiers »[47]. Cette stratégie a donné l'occasion au CEPD de mettre en avant la nécessité « d'assurer une cohérence entre les différentes initiatives directement ou indirectement liées au traitement des données PNR », de prévoir de façon plus précise les garanties minimales applicables aux accords internationaux et d'imposer que ces derniers comportent des droits directement applicables[48]. Le CEPD est amené à se prononcer sur de tels accords[49]. La Cour de justice peut être saisie pour statuer sur leur compatibilité avec le droit de l'Union et le bien-fondé de la base juridique retenue pour leur conclusion. Ainsi, l'arrêt *Parlement/Conseil*[50] a annulé la décision 2004/496/CE du Conseil, concernant la conclusion d'un accord entre la Communauté européenne et les États-Unis sur le traitement et le transfert de données PNR par des transporteurs aériens au bureau des douanes et de la protection des frontières du ministère américain de la sécurité intérieure ainsi que la décision 2004/535/CE de la Commission, qui constatait le niveau de protection adéquat des données à caractère personnel contenues dans les dossiers des passagers aériens transférés au Bureau des douanes et de la protection des frontières des États-Unis d'Amérique.

Plus récemment, la Cour de justice a été saisie d'une demande d'avis introduite par le Parlement européen[51] sur la compatibilité avec le droit de

47 Communication de la Commission du 21 septembre 2010, COM(2010)492 final.

48 Avis du contrôleur européen de la protection des données du 19 octobre 2010, *JO* C 357, du 30 décembre 2010, p. 7.

49 V. not. les avis du Contrôleur européen de la protection des données : du 15 juillet 2011, sur la proposition de décision du Conseil relative à la conclusion de l'accord *PNR* entre l'UE et l'Australie, *JO* C 322 du 5 novembre 2011, p. 1; du 9 décembre 2011, sur la proposition de décision du Conseil relative à la conclusion de l'accord PNR entre les États Unis d'Amérique et l'UE, *JO* C 35, du 9 février 2012, p. 16; du 30 septembre 2013, sur la proposition de décision du Conseil relative à la conclusion et à la signature de l'accord entre le Canada et l'UE sur le transfert et le traitement des données des dossiers passagers, *JO* C 51, du 22 février 2014, p. 12.

50 Arrêt de la Cour du 30 mai 2006, *Parlement/Conseil et Commission,* C-317/04 et C-318/04, EU:C:2006:346, v. nos développements *infra*.

51 En vertu de l'article 218, paragraphe 11, TFUE.

l'Union de la décision relative à l'accord entre l'Union et le Canada pour le transfert et le traitement des données de dossiers passagers dans le cadre de la lutte contre le terrorisme et la criminalité transnationale grave. La Cour devait se prononcer sur la compatibilité de cet accord avec l'article 16 TFUE et les articles 7, 8 et 52 paragraphe 1, CDFUE et sur le bien-fondé de la base juridique retenue et l'articulation entre l'article 82, paragraphe 1, d) et l'article 87, paragraphe 2, a) TFUE d'une part, et l'article 16 TFUE qui porte spécifiquement sur le droit à la protection des données personnelles, d'autre part. L'Avocat général Paolo Mengozzi proposait à la Cour de poursuivre dans le sens des progrès de son contrôle juridictionnel réalisés par ses arrêts *Digital Rights Ireland et Seitlinger e.a.*[52] et *Schrems*[53] en appliquant un contrôle strict du respect des articles de la Charte invoqués et de n'admettre que des restrictions strictement nécessaires à la réalisation de l'objectif sécuritaire poursuivi par l'accord[54]. Dans son avis 1/15 la Cour constate l'incompatibilité de cet accord avec les articles 7, 8, 21 et 52, paragraphe 1, de la Charte. Cette incompatibilité tient en premier lieu à ce qu'il peut concerner des données sensibles dont le transfert est pourtant interdit par le droit de l'Union. L'exclusion de ces données sensibles du champ du transfert conditionne la compatibilité de l'accord avec le droit de l'Union qui doit par ailleurs respecter les droits fondamentaux et le principe de proportionnalité. Après avoir relevé que cet accord constitue une ingérence dans les articles 7 et 8 de la Charte, la Cour rappelle que l'article 52, paragraphe 1 de la Charte exige que toute limitation aux droits et libertés qu'elle protège soit prévue par la loi et respecte leur contenu essentiel et le principe de proportionnalité, strictement contrôlé. La Cour précise alors de façon détaillée les conditions de compatibilité de cet accord avec les articles 7, 8 et 52 paragraphe 1 de la Charte. Le même type de problématique soulevant des questions de cohérence dans la garantie des droits fondamentaux et de la protection des données personnelles se pose au regard des progrès déjà envisagés des instruments normatifs de l'Union pour lutter contre le blanchiment et le financement du terrorisme et pour assurer la traçabilité des virements de fonds et des mouvements de liquidités. Ces objectifs peuvent donner lieu à

---

52 Arrêt de la Cour du 8 avril 2014, *Digital Rights Ireland et Seitlinger e.a.,* C-293/12 et C-594/12, EU:C:2014:238.

53 Arrêt de la Cour du 6 octobre 2015, *Schrems,* C-362/14, EU:C:2015:650.

54 Conclusions de l'Avocat général Mengozzi sur l'avis 1/15, présentées le 8 septembre 2015, EU:C:2016:656.

des accords avec des États tiers portant sur le contrôle des données financières, comme le montre l'accord conclu avec les États-Unis sur l'accès aux données financières dans le cadre du programme de surveillance du financement du terrorisme développé par les États-Unis (Terrorism Finance Tracking Program, TFTP)[55].

C. L'autonomie d'appréciation ancrée dans le cadre constitutionnel de l'Union

Cette autonomie d'appréciation tient aux progrès du droit dérivé et aux apports de la jurisprudence de la Cour de justice. Elle doit être rattachée au cadre constitutionnel de l'Union. Comme l'a souligné l'avis 2/13 c'est « dans le respect de ce cadre constitutionnel (...) que les droits fondamentaux, tels que reconnus en particulier par la Charte, doivent être interprétés et appliqués au sein de l'Union »[56]. Cette autonomie d'interprétation s'impose pour l'appréciation des objectifs poursuivis par l'action normative de l'Union ainsi que pour l'appréciation de la proportionnalité et de la nécessité des traitements des données personnelles. L'autonomie d'interprétation de la Cour participe à la définition positive des droits fondamentaux, des concepts et du champ matériel de la protection des données personnelles (1) et à l'interprétation stricte des exceptions tenant aux objectifs de sécurité et à l'encadrement croissant de l'appréciation de ces objectifs (2).

1. L'interprétation autonome des concepts et du champ matériel de la protection des données personnelles

La Cour de justice contrôle le respect par le droit dérivé des droits fondamentaux garantis par l'Union européenne, comme principes généraux du droit et sur le fondement de la Charte des droits fondamentaux. Elle veille au respect de l'obligation d'interprétation du droit dérivé conforme au respect des droits fondamentaux. Le contrôle à la lumière de la Charte porte tant sur la protection des données personnelles protégée comme droit fon-

55 V. Potvin-Solis, « La lutte contre le terrorisme et son financement », *supra* note 32.

56 Avis 2/13, *supra* note 1, point 177.

damental que sur celle des droits fondamentaux qui lui sont liés, tout particulièrement celui du respect de la vie privée qui recouvre un champ et des bénéficiaires différents. Le principe de soumission aux traités et à leurs principes constitutionnels s'impose au droit dérivé de l'Union et aux accords internationaux avec des États tiers. La directive 95/46/CE a posé des principes de protection qui valent à l'égard de « tout traitement de données à caractère personnel dès lors que les activités du responsable du traitement relèvent du champ d'application du droit communautaire »[57]. Elle s'est appliquée aux données qui font l'objet de fichiers autonomisés ou non automatisés et a défini les notions de « données personnelles »[58] et de « traitement » de telles données[59] ainsi que les principales notions sur lesquelles la protection qu'elle a établie repose[60]. Elle a exclu notamment de son champ « le traitement de données à caractère personnel effectué par une personne physique pour l'exercice d'activités exclusivement personnelles ou domestiques »[61]. Le règlement général sur la protection des données personnelles n° 2016/679/UE qui la remplace depuis le 25 mai 2018[62] précise aussi dans ses premiers articles son objet et ses objectifs, son champ d'application matériel et territorial, les définitions de ses principales notions[63] et il en est de même des directives adoptées le même jour[64].

La Cour de justice fournit une interprétation large de la notion de données personnelles, de celle de traitement[65] et du principe de non-discrimination et d'égalité de traitement[66]. Sa jurisprudence permet de préciser le champ du droit dérivé qui couvre celui de la conciliation entre les ob-

---

57 Cons. 12 de la directive 95/46/CE, *supra* note 7.

58 *Id.,* article 2, a).

59 *Ibid.*

60 *Id.,* article 2, b).

61 Cons. 12 et article 3 de la directive.

62 Règlement n° 2016/679/UE (règlement général sur la protection des données), *supra* note 11.

63 *Id.,* article 1 à 4.

64 Directive 2016/681 et directive 2016/680, *supra* note 15.

65 Pour des questions d'interprétation de ces notions, v. par ex., les renvois préjudiciels introduits par l'Augstākā tiesa le 12 juin 2017, *Buivids,* C-345/17 et par l'Oberlandesgericht Düsseldorf le 26 janvier 2017, *Fashion ID,* C-40/17.

66 Dans son avis 1/15, *supra* note 2, la Cour considère que la compatibilité de l'accord entre le Canada et l'Union sur le transfert et le traitement de données PNR avec les articles 7, 8 et l'article 52, paragraphe 1, de la Charte des droits fondamentaux exige notamment que cet accord prévoie « que les modèles et les critères

jectifs de sécurité nationale d'une part, et la garantie des droits fondamentaux et de la protection des données personnelles, d'autre part. La Cour a notamment interprété la directive 95/46/CE par référence à la Charte des droits fondamentaux de l'Union[67] en soulignant la mention expresse dans ses dispositions du respect des droits fondamentaux et la définition même de son objet dans son article 1er[68]. Elle relève de façon constante que « la protection des données à caractère personnel, résultant de l'obligation explicite prévue à l'article 8, paragraphe 1, de la Charte, revêt une importance particulière pour le droit au respect de la vie privée consacré à l'article 7 de celle-ci »[69]. Elle interprète de façon large l'objectif de la directive 95/46/CE[70] et son champ d'application territorial[71].

2. *L'encadrement croissant des objectifs sécuritaires justifiant le traitement des données personnelles*

La directive 95/46/CE prenait en compte les objectifs de sécurité dans les limites posées à son champ d'application et dans la portée des droits garantis. Son article 3 excluait de son champ d'application les traitements de données à caractère personnel « mis en œuvre pour l'exercice d'activ-

---

utilisés dans le cadre du traitement automatisé des données des dossiers passagers seront spécifiques et fiables ainsi que non discriminatoires ».

67 V. not. : Arrêt de la Cour du 6 mars 2001, *Connolly/Commission,* C-274/99 P, EU:C:2001:127, point 37; arrêt de la Cour du 20 mai 2003, *Österreichischer Rundfunk e.a.,* C-465/00, EU:C:2003:294, point 68; arrêt de la Cour du 13 mai 2014, *Google Spain et Google, supra* note 10, point 68; arrêt de la Cour du 11 décembre 2014, *Ryneš,* C-212/13, ECLI :EU:C:2014:2428, point 29; arrêt de la Cour du 6 octobre 2015, *Schrems, supra* note 53, point 38.

68 V. arrêt de la Cour du 7 mai 2009, *Rijkeboer, supra* note 8, points 46-47; arrêt de la Cour du 20 mai 2003, *Österreichischer Rundfunk e.a., supra* note 67, point 70; arrêt de la Cour du 6 novembre 2003, *Lindqvist, supra* note 8, points 97 et 99; arrêt de la Cour du 29 janvier 2008, *Promusicae, supra* note 39, point 63; arrêt de la Cour du 16 décembre 2008, *Satakunnan Markkinapörssi et Satamedia,* C-73/07, EU:C:2008:727, point 52.

69 Arrêt de la Cour du 8 avril 2014, *Digital Rights Ireland et Seitlinger e.a., supra* note 52, point 53.

70 V. arrêt de la Cour du 13 mai 2014, *Google Spain et Google, supra* note 10, point 53, citant par analogie, l'arrêt de la Cour du 12 juillet 2011, *L'Oréal e.a.,* C-324/09, EU:C:2011:474, points 62 et 63.

71 V. arrêt de la Cour du 13 mai 2014, *Google Spain et Google, supra* note 10, point 54.

ités qui ne relèvent pas du champ d'application du droit communautaire, telles que celles prévues aux titres V et VI du traité sur l'Union européenne », et, « en tout état de cause », les traitements « ayant pour objet la sécurité publique, la défense, la sûreté de l'État (y compris le bien-être économique de l'État lorsque ces traitements sont liés à des questions de sûreté de l'État) et les activités de l'État relatives à des domaines du droit pénal »[72]. Elle ajoutait qu'elle ne préjugeait pas « des règles de territorialité applicables en matière de droit pénal »[73]. Elle précisait les motifs légitimes de limitation par les États, dans le respect du principe de légalité et de proportionnalité, des droits et obligations qu'elle posait [74] et fixait, dans son article 7, les principes relatifs à la légitimation des traitements de données. La Cour de justice a interprété cet article comme permettant le traitement de données à caractère personnel « lorsqu'il est nécessaire à la réalisation de l'intérêt légitime poursuivi par le responsable du traitement ou par le ou les tiers auxquels les données sont communiquées, à condition que ne prévalent pas l'intérêt ou les libertés et les droits fondamentaux de la personne concernée, notamment son droit au respect de sa vie privée à l'égard du traitement des données à caractère personnel, qui appellent une protection au titre de l'article 1er, paragraphe 1, de cette directive ». Selon la Cour de justice, l'application de cette disposition « nécessite ainsi une pondération des droits et des intérêts opposés en cause dans le cadre de laquelle il doit être tenu compte de l'importance des droits de la personne concernée résultant des articles 7 et 8 de la Charte »[75]. De même, la Cour de justice encadre de façon stricte les limitations à la protection des données personnelles et le champ des exceptions prévues par la directive

---

72 V. aussi les considérant 13 et 16 de la directive 95/46/CE, *supra* note 7.

73 *Id.,* considérant 21.

74 Article 13 de la directive qui vise : « a) la sûreté de l'État; b) la défense; c) la sécurité publique; d) la prévention, la recherche, la détection et la poursuite d'infractions pénales ou de manquements à la déontologie dans le cas des professions réglementées; e) un intérêt économique ou financier important d'un État membre ou de l'Union européenne, y compris dans les domaines monétaire, budgétaire et fiscal; f) une mission de contrôle, d'inspection ou de réglementation relevant, même à titre occasionnel, de l'exercice de l'autorité publique, dans les cas visés aux points c), d) et e); g) la protection de la personne concernée ou des droits et libertés d'autrui ».

75 Arrêt de la Cour du 13 mai 2014, *Google Spain et Google, supra* note 10, point 74, qui renvoie à l'arrêt de la Cour du 24 novembre 2011, *ASNEF et FECEMD,* C-468/10 et C-469/10, ECLI/EU:C:2011:777, points 38 et 40.

95/46/CE. Dans l'arrêt *Institut professionnel des agents immobiliers* elle rappelle sa jurisprudence constante, selon laquelle « la protection du droit fondamental à la vie privée exige que les dérogations à la protection des données à caractère personnel et les limitations de celles-ci doivent s'opérer dans les limites du strict nécessaire »[76].

Le règlement général sur la protection des données personnelles qui remplace la directive 95/46/CE fixe le même ordre de restrictions à son champ d'application et de motifs légitimes pouvant limiter les droits et obligations qu'il pose. Son article 2, paragraphe 2, exclut de son champ d'application les traitements effectués : « a) dans le cadre d'une activité qui ne relève pas du champ d'application du droit de l'Union; b) par les États membres dans le cadre d'activités qui relèvent du champ d'application du chapitre 2 du titre V du traité sur l'Union européenne; c) par une personne physique dans le cadre d'une activité strictement personnelle ou domestique; d) par les autorités compétentes à des fins de prévention et de détection des infractions pénales, d'enquêtes et de poursuites en la matière ou d'exécution de sanctions pénales, y compris la protection contre des menaces pour la sécurité publique et la prévention de telles menaces ». Il reprend, dans son article 23, en les complétant, les motifs légitimes pouvant justifier des limitations aux droits et obligations qu'il pose[77].

---

76 Arrêt de la Cour du 7 novembre 2013, *Institut professionnel des agents immobiliers* (*IPI*), *supra* note 38, point 39, se référant aux arrêts du 16 décembre 2008, *Satakunnan Markkinapörssi et Satamedia*, *supra* note 68, point 56, et arrêt de la Cour du 9 novembre 2010, *Volker und Markus Schecke et Eifert,* C-92/09 et C-93/09, EU:C:2010:662, points 77 et 86.

77 « a) la sécurité nationale; b) la défense nationale; c) la sécurité publique; d) la prévention et la détection d'infractions pénales, ainsi que les enquêtes et les poursuites en la matière ou l'exécution de sanctions pénales, y compris la protection contre les menaces pour la sécurité publique et la prévention de telles menaces; e) d'autres objectifs importants d'intérêt public général de l'Union ou d'un État membre, notamment un intérêt économique ou financier important de l'Union ou d'un État membre, y compris dans les domaines monétaire, budgétaire et fiscal, de la santé publique et de la sécurité sociale; f) la protection de l'indépendance de la justice et des procédures judiciaires; g) la prévention et la détection de manquements à la déontologie des professions réglementées, ainsi que les enquêtes et les poursuites en la matière; h) une mission de contrôle, d'inspection ou de réglementation liée, même occasionnellement, à l'exercice de l'autorité publique, dans les cas visés aux points a) à e) et g); i) la protection de la personne concernée ou des droits et libertés d'autrui; j) l'exécution des demandes de droit civil ».

II. Les progrès de l'identité européenne par l'affirmation d'un système constitutionnel de protection propre à l'Union

C'est par l'autonomie d'un tel système, de nature constitutionnelle, que peut être assurée la maîtrise par l'Union de la conciliation des intérêts. Cette autonomie s'observe dans la jurisprudence de la Cour de justice qui fait apparaître tant les jeux d'influences avec la jurisprudence de la Cour européenne des droits de l'homme que le progrès de l'autonomie du droit de l'Union dans la garantie des droits fondamentaux et les avancées spécifiques à la protection des données personnelles. L'impératif d'un tel système, d'ordre constitutionnel et qui appartienne en propre à l'Union, s'impose à bien des égards : pour fonder sur des bases solides l'articulation entre les dimensions interne et externe de la protection des données personnelles par l'Union; pour déterminer, dans le respect des principes de cohérence et de proportionnalité, la conciliation entre la protection des données personnelles, la libre circulation de ces données et les objectifs de sécurité poursuivis tant par les États membres que par l'Union; pour identifier la base juridique fondant l'activité normative et décisionnelle de l'Union en fonction des politiques en présence et des objectifs poursuivis. Les traits d'un tel système se trouvent progressivement affinés par la double portée interne et externe des progrès du contrôle juridictionnel (A) et par la portée transversale de l'exigence d'indépendance des autorités de contrôle (B) qui participent à la singularité croissante du système de protection de l'Union (C).

A. La double portée interne et externe des progrès du contrôle juridictionnel

La jurisprudence de la Cour de justice précise les conditions d'appréciation de la proportionnalité qu'elle lie au cadre constitutionnel de l'Union et qui exigent, on l'a vu, un rapport de stricte proportionnalité. Elle contribue à l'identification de l'essentiel des droits fondamentaux garanti par la Charte tant au regard de leur substance matérielle que du point de vue de leur garantie procédurale. Elle permet une interprétation évolutive de la protection des données personnelles et des droits qui entrent dans ce champ tout en montrant qu'ils ne constituent pas des prérogatives absolues. Il s'agit d'une jurisprudence dynamique qui contribue aux avancées matérielles de la substance des droits fondamentaux et des éléments essentiels de la protection des données personnelles (1) et qui rapporte le contrôle de stricte proportionnalité à l'exigence de clarté et de précision qui s'impose à l'encadrement légal des ingérences (2).

1. Les avancées matérielles de la substance des droits fondamentaux et des éléments essentiels de la protection des données personnelles

Les progrès du droit dérivé peuvent amener ces avancées matérielles et font alors l'objet d'une interprétation extensive de la part de la Cour de justice. Ainsi, la directive 95/46/CE a énoncé les garanties des personnes concernées par le traitement des données personnelles en termes de qualité et d'exactitude des données, qui doivent être traitées loyalement et licitement, et être collectées pour des finalités déterminées, explicites et légitimes. Elle a exigé le consentement de la personne[78] en prévoyant les hypothèses dans lesquelles celui-ci peut être limité lorsque le traitement des données est nécessaire pour la poursuite d'intérêts légitimes définis. Elle a précisé les catégories de traitements interdits, en particulier ceux qui portent sur des données sensibles « qui révèlent l'origine raciale ou ethnique, les opinions politiques, les convictions religieuses ou philosophiques, l'appartenance syndicale, ainsi que le traitement des données relatives à la santé et à la vie sexuelle »[79]. Elle a énoncé les droits des personnes concernées en matière d'information[80], d'accès[81], d'opposition[82], de confidentialité et de sécurité des traitements[83], de notification, de contrôle préalable et de publicité des traitements[84] et de recours, de responsabilité et de sanctions en cas de non-respect des dispositions prises pour son application[85]. La jurisprudence a fixé l'étendue des bénéficiaires de la protection des données personnelles qui vaut à l'égard des personnes physiques mais non à l'égard des personnes morales[86] ainsi que l'articula-

78 Articles 6 et 7 de la directive 95/46/CE, *supra* note 7.
79 *Id.,* Article 8-1.
80 *Id.,* Articles 10 et 11.
81 *Id.,* Article 12.
82 *Id.,* Articles 14 et 15.
83 *Id.,* Articles 16 et 17.
84 *Id.,* Articles 18 à 21.
85 *Id.,* Articles 22 à 24.
86 Arrêt de la Cour du 17 décembre 2015, *WebMindLicenses,* C-419/14, EU:C:2015:832, point 79.

tion entre l'article 8 CDFUE et l'article 7 CDFUE qui est quant à lui applicable à ces dernières[87].

Dans l'arrêt *Google Spain*[88], la Cour de justice se prononce sur la responsabilité de l'exploitant d'un moteur de recherches sur internet pour le traitement qu'il effectue des données à caractère personnel apparaissant sur des pages web publiées par des tiers. La Cour souligne la facilité d'accéder à une multitude d'aspects de la vie privée par des moteurs de recherches et la possibilité d'établir un profil plus ou moins détaillé de la personne recherchée ainsi que l'ingérence qui en résulte dans les droits de la personne recherchée. Elle met en avant l'intérêt légitime des internautes à avoir accès à des informations concernant une personne déterminée. Mais elle recherche, en même temps, le juste équilibre entre cet intérêt des utilisateurs des réseaux internet et les droits fondamentaux des personnes concernées. De plus, elle relève que le traitement licite de données exactes « peut se transformer dans le temps et devenir incompatible avec la directive 95/46/CE si au regard des circonstances elles apparaissent inadéquates, pas ou plus pertinentes, ou excessives au regard des finalités pour lesquelles elles ont été traitées et du temps qui s'est écoulé ». La Cour pose ainsi une jurisprudence créatrice en reconnaissant le droit à l'effacement et à la suppression des liens vers les pages web contenant des informations sur des données d'une personne[89] avec une exception tenant à la prise en compte du rôle de la personne concernée dans la vie publique justifiant un intérêt prépondérant du public à accéder à ces informations.

Les apports matériels de la jurisprudence de la Cour de justice tiennent aussi à ce qu'elle permet de préciser les contours des éléments essentiels de la protection des données personnelles et des droits fondamentaux œuvrant dans ce champ. Ont par exemple été considérées comme portant atteinte à ces éléments essentiels : la possibilité laissée aux autorités publiques d'accéder de manière généralisée au contenu de communications électroniques (portant atteinte aux éléments essentiels du droit fondamental au respect de la vie privée, tel que garanti par l'article 7 de la

---

87 *Id.*, point 80.

88 Arrêt de la Cour du 13 mai 2014, *Google Spain et Google*, *supra* note 10.

89 V. la demande de décision préjudicielle présentée par le Conseil d'État français le 21 août 2017, *Google Inc. / Commission nationale de l'informatique et des libertés (CNIL),* C-507/17, qui vise à ce que la Cour de justice précise la portée du « droit au déréférencement » consacré par l'arrêt *Google Spain* et l'étendue des obligations qu'il engendre pour l'exploitant d'un moteur de recherche.

Charte)[90]; l'absence de voie de droit ouverte au justiciable permettant d'avoir accès à des données à caractère personnel le concernant, ou d'obtenir la rectification ou la suppression de celles-ci (portant atteinte aux éléments essentiels du droit à une protection juridictionnelle effective garanti par l'article 47 de la Charte)[91]. Le droit à un contrôle par des autorités indépendantes est aussi considéré comme « un élément essentiel du respect de la protection des personnes à l'égard du traitement des données à caractère personnel »[92].

2. *Le contrôle strict de proportionnalité et l'exigence de clarté et de précision de l'encadrement légal des ingérences*

La Cour de justice applique un contrôle strict du respect des conditions de proportionnalité des ingérences dans le droit à la protection des données personnelles. Elle encadre la marge d'appréciation du législateur de l'Union et exige que la base légale définisse elle-même la portée des limitations qu'elle prévoit à la protection des données personnelles. En se référant notamment à la jurisprudence de la Cour européenne des droits de l'homme, elle relève que « l'exigence que toute limitation de l'exercice de ce droit doit être prévue par la loi implique que la base légale (…) doit être suffisamment claire et précise et que, en définissant elle-même la portée de la limitation de l'exercice du droit garanti par l'article 7 de la Charte, elle offre une certaine protection contre d'éventuelles atteintes arbitraires de cette administration »[93]. Pour reprendre les termes de ses arrêts, « en ce qui concerne le contrôle juridictionnel du respect de ces conditions, dès lors que des ingérences dans des droits fondamentaux sont en cause, l'étendue du pouvoir d'appréciation du législateur de l'Union peut s'avérer limitée en fonction d'un certain nombre d'éléments, parmi

---

90 Arrêt de la Cour du 8 avril 2014, *Digital Rights Ireland et Seitlinger e.a., supra* note 52, point 39 et arrêt de la Cour du 6 octobre 2015, *Schrems, supra* note 53, point 94.

91 Arrêt de la Cour du 6 octobre 2015, *Schrems, supra* note 53, point 95.

92 *Id.*, point 41 et point 68 renvoyant notamment à l'arrêt de la Cour du 16 octobre 2012, *Commission/Autriche*, C-614/10, EU:C:2012:631.

93 Arrêt de la Cour du 17 décembre 2015, *WebMindLicenses, supra* note 86, point 81, qui renvoie aux arrêts de la Cour EDH, du 2 août 1984, *Malone/Royaume-Uni,* paragraphe 67, et du 12 janvier 2010, *Gillan et Quinton/Royaume-Uni,* paragraphe 77.

lesquels figurent, notamment, le domaine concerné, la nature du droit en cause garanti par la Charte, la nature et la gravité de l'ingérence ainsi que la finalité de celle-ci»[94]. Le CEPD rappelle régulièrement les exigences du principe de proportionnalité dans la jurisprudence de la Cour de justice. Cette jurisprudence impose un encadrement par des règles claires et précises des ingérences dans le droit à la protection des données personnelles tant à l'égard du droit dérivé de l'Union que des accords internationaux avec des États tiers. Dans l'arrêt *Digital Rights Irelands*[95], la Cour de justice déclare invalide la directive 2006/24/CE[96]. Elle constate « une ingérence d'une vaste ampleur et d'une gravité particulière dans les droits fondamentaux au respect de la vie privée et à la protection des données à caractère personnel » qui n'est pas limitée au strict nécessaire. Elle rappelle que « la réglementation de l'Union en cause doit prévoir des règles claires et précises régissant la portée et l'application de la mesure en cause et imposant un minimum d'exigences de sorte que les personnes dont les données ont été conservées disposent de garanties suffisantes permettant de protéger efficacement leurs données à caractère personnel contre les risques d'abus ainsi que contre tout accès et toute utilisation illicites de ces données »[97]. Tel n'était pas le cas des dispositions de la directive 2006/24/CE qui est par conséquent jugée invalide[98].

La Cour de justice encadre également le renvoi au droit des États membres pour la définition des infractions graves justifiant le traitement de données personnelles. Les mêmes exigences s'imposent dans les relations avec les États tiers[99] et les accords internationaux relatifs aux transferts de données personnelles doivent prévoir des ingérences limitées au strict nécessaire et comporter des règles claires et précises au regard tant des données à transférer que de l'encadrement de la portée de l'ingérence dans

---

94 Arrêt de la Cour du 8 avril 2014, *Digital Rights Ireland et Seitlinger e.a., supra* note 52.

95 *Ibid.*

96 Directive 2006/24/CE du Parlement européen et du Conseil du 15 mars 2006 sur la conservation de données générées ou traitées dans le cadre de la fourniture de services de communications électroniques accessibles au public ou de réseaux publics de communications, *JO* L 105, du 13 avril 2016, p. 54.

97 Arrêt de la Cour du 8 avril 2014, *Digital Rights Ireland et Seitlinger e.a., supra* note 52, point 54. La Cour applique ici une interprétation par analogie de la jurisprudence de la Cour EDH relative à l'article 8 de la CEDH.

98 *Id.*, point 65.

99 Arrêt de la Cour du 6 octobre 2015, *Schrems, supra* note 53, points 91 et s.

les droits fondamentaux[100]. De tels accords sont ainsi appréciés à l'aune de l'exigence de clarté et de précision telle qu'elle est entendue et appliquée par la Cour de justice.

B. La portée transversale de l'exigence d'indépendance des autorités de contrôle

Le paragraphe 2 de l'article 16 TFUE vise tant « les institutions, organes et organismes de l'Union » que « les États membres dans l'exercice d'activités qui relèvent du champ d'application du droit de l'Union ». Les termes de cette obligation d'indépendance sont définis par le droit de l'Union européenne dans son champ de protection et tiennent à la liaison et à l'interdépendance entre les ordres juridiques. Il en est ainsi tout particulièrement de l'exigence d'indépendance des autorités de contrôle du respect des règles relatives à la protection des données personnelles qui est expressément posée aux articles 16 TFUE, 39 TUE et 8 CDFUE. Il s'agit d'une obligation opposable tant aux États qu'à l'Union (1) et qui fait l'objet d'une interprétation large par l'autonomie du concept d'indépendance et ses prolongements externes (2).

1. Une obligation opposable aux États membres et à l'Union aux plans interne et externe

L'indépendance est imposée à toute autorité, européenne et nationale, de contrôle du respect du droit à la protection des données personnelles, par le paragraphe 3 de l'article 8 de la Charte des droits fondamentaux de l'Union. À l'égard des États membres, le considérant 62 de la directive 95/46/CE soulignait que « l'institution, dans les États membres, d'autorités de contrôle exerçant en toute indépendance leurs fonctions est un élément essentiel de la protection des personnes à l'égard du traitement des données à caractère personnel ». Cette exigence faisait l'objet de l'article 28 de la directive 95/46/CE[101]. Elle est confortée par le règlement général sur la protection des données personnelles n° 2016/679/UE et est

---

100 Avis de la Cour du 26 juillet 2017, 1/15, *supra* note 2.

101 Selon les paragraphes 1 et 2 de cet article : « 1. Chaque État membre prévoit qu'une ou plusieurs autorités publiques sont chargées de surveiller l'application,

également posée par le règlement n° 45/2001/CE qui prévoit notamment l'établissement d'une instance de surveillance indépendante chargée de contrôler l'application de ses dispositions. La Cour de justice peut être amenée à statuer sur le respect de cette exigence. Dans l'arrêt *Commission/Allemagne,* elle juge que l'Allemagne n'a pas respecté les exigences du paragraphe 1 de l'article 28 de la directive 95/46/CE, « en soumettant à la tutelle de l'État les autorités de contrôle compétentes pour la surveillance du traitement des données à caractère personnel par le secteur non public dans les différents Länder » [102]. Dans l'arrêt *Commission/ Autriche*[103], elle se prononce dans le même sens en jugeant que l'Autriche n'a pas pris « toutes les dispositions nécessaires » pour satisfaire au critère d'indépendance concernant la Datenschutzkommission (commission de protection des données, ci-après la «DSK»), instituée en tant qu'autorité de contrôle de la protection des données à caractère personnel »[104]. Puis, dans l'arrêt *Commission/Hongrie*[105], la Cour condamne la décision du gouvernement hongrois de mettre fin brutalement aux fonctions du Commissaire hongrois à la protection des données. Elle insiste sur la nécessaire indépendance des autorités qui dans les États sont chargées de veiller au respect de la directive 95/46/CE. Elle souligne que « l'exigence de contrôle par une autorité indépendante du respect des règles de l'Union relatives à la protection des personnes physiques à l'égard du traitement des données à caractère personnel résulte également du droit primaire de l'Union, notamment de l'article 8, paragraphe 3, de la Charte des droits fondamentaux de l'Union européenne et de l'article 16, paragraphe 2,

---

sur son territoire, des dispositions adoptées par les États membres en application de la présente directive. Ces autorités exercent en toute indépendance les missions dont elles sont investies. 2. Chaque État membre prévoit que les autorités de contrôle sont consultées lors de l'élaboration des mesures réglementaires ou administratives relatives à la protection des droits et libertés des personnes à l'égard du traitement de données à caractère personnel ».

102 Arrêt de la Cour du 9 mars 2010, *Commission/Allemagne,* C-518/07, EU:C:2010:125, point 56.

103 Arrêt de la Cour du 16 octobre 2012, *Commission/Autriche, supra* note 92.

104 *Id.,* point 66, précisant que, selon le cadre réglementaire autrichien : « – le membre administrateur de la DSK est un fonctionnaire fédéral assujetti à une tutelle de service; -le bureau de la DSK est intégré aux services de la chancellerie fédérale, et – le chancelier fédéral dispose d'un droit inconditionnel à l'information sur tous les aspects de la gestion de la DSK ».

105 Arrêt de la Cour du 8 avril 2014, *Commission/Hongrie,* C-288/12, EU:C:2014:237.

TFUE »[106]. Elle rappelle à cette occasion sa jurisprudence selon laquelle « l'institution, dans les États membres, d'autorités de contrôle indépendantes constitue ainsi un élément essentiel du respect de la protection des personnes à l'égard du traitement des données à caractère personnel »[107], « comme cela est d'ailleurs relevé au considérant 62 de la directive 95/46 ». Elle juge qu' « en mettant fin de manière anticipée au mandat de l'autorité de contrôle de la protection des données à caractère personnel, la Hongrie a manqué aux obligations qui lui incombent en vertu de la directive 95/46/CE relative à la protection des personnes physiques à l'égard du traitement des données à caractère personnel et à la libre circulation de ces données ».

La directive 95/46/CE prévoyait l'institution d'un groupe de protection des personnes à l'égard du traitement des données à caractère personnel composé de représentants des autorités de contrôle national, de représentants des autorités de contrôle des institutions et organismes de l'Union et d'un représentant de la Commission européenne. Le règlement n° 45/2001/CE relatif à la protection des personnes physiques à l'égard du traitement des données à caractère personnel par les institutions et organes de la Communauté et à la libre circulation des données prévoit l'établissement d'une instance de surveillance indépendante chargée de contrôler l'application de ses dispositions. Selon son considérant 2, « un système à part entière de protection des données à caractère personnel impose non seulement de conférer des droits aux personnes concernées et des obligations à celles qui traitent des données à caractère personnel, mais aussi de prévoir des sanctions appropriées pour les contrevenants ainsi qu'une autorité de contrôle indépendante »[108]. Ce règlement institue, pour le contrôle de l'application de ses dispositions « à tous les traitements effectués par une institution ou un organe communautaire », une « autorité de contrôle indépendante », le « contrôleur européen de la protection des données »[109]. Enfin, le règlement général sur la protection des données

106 *Id.,* point 48.

107 Point 48 citant l'arrêt de la Cour du 9 mars 2010, *Commission/Allemagne, supra* note 102, point 23, et l'arrêt de la Cour du 16 octobre 2012, *Commission/Autriche, supra* note 92, point 37.

108 Règlement n° 45/2001/CE, *supra* note 16.

109 *Id.,* article 1, paragraphe 2.

personnelles 2016/679/UE, qui remplace la directive 95/46/CE,[110] prévoit l'institution dans les États membres d'un délégué à la protection des données[111] et consacre son chapitre VI aux autorités de contrôle indépendantes. Les mêmes dispositions sont reprises dans la directive 2016/680/UE dans le domaine de la coopération en matière pénale[112].

2. *L'autonomie du concept d'indépendance dans la jurisprudence et ses prolongements externes*

La Cour de justice a adopté une conception large de la notion d'indépendance en précisant qu'elle respecte, ce faisant, la répartition des compétences entre l'Union et ses États membres. Selon la Cour de justice : « La garantie d'indépendance des autorités nationales de contrôle vise à assurer l'efficacité et la fiabilité du contrôle du respect des dispositions en matière de protection des personnes physiques à l'égard du traitement des données à caractère personnel et doit être interprétée à la lumière de cet objectif. Elle a été établie en vue de renforcer la protection des personnes et des organismes qui sont concernés par les décisions de ces autorités »[113]. La notion d'indépendance est définie comme une notion autonome et largement entendue par l'arrêt *Commission/Allemagne*[114]. Cet arrêt situe l'exigence d'indépendance dans le contexte plus large de la protection des droits fondamentaux, de la protection de la vie privée et du principe de démocratie. Il se réfère à la jurisprudence de la Cour européenne des droits de l'homme pour dégager une vision systémique de cette indépendance telle qu'elle s'impose dans l'ordre juridique de l'Union. Il écarte l'argumentation selon laquelle l'interprétation large de la notion d'indépendance dépasse les limites de la compétence de l'Union. Selon les arrêts *Commission/Allemagne*, *Commission/Autriche* et *Commission/Hongrie*, la notion d'indépendance « exclut notamment toute injonction et toute autre influence extérieure sous quelque forme que ce soit,

110 Règlement n° 2016/679/UE (règlement général sur la protection des données), *supra* note 11.

111 Articles 37 à 39 du règlement.

112 Directive 2016/680/UE, *supra* note 15; v. les articles 32 à 34 de la directive relatifs à l'institution dans les États membres d'un délégué à la protection des données et son chapitre VI relatif aux autorités de contrôle indépendantes.

113 Arrêt de la Cour du 6 octobre 2015, *Schrems, supra* note 53, point 41.

114 Arrêt de la Cour du 9 mars 2010, *Commission/Allemagne, supra* note 102.

qu'elle soit directe ou indirecte, qui seraient susceptibles d'orienter leurs décisions et qui pourraient ainsi remettre en cause l'accomplissement, par lesdites autorités, de leur tâche consistant à établir un juste équilibre entre la protection du droit à la vie privée et la libre circulation des données à caractère personnel »[115]. La Cour impose une indépendance fonctionnelle et exige que l'autorité puisse être « considérée comme pouvant opérer, en toute circonstance, au-dessus de tout soupçon de partialité »[116]. Cette lecture rejoint la conception de l'indépendance et de l'impartialité développée par la jurisprudence de Strasbourg qui fait intervenir un double critère objectif et subjectif. La Cour de justice a également été amenée à opérer un raisonnement par analogie dans l'interprétation des exigences d'indépendance au sens du règlement n° 45/2001/CE[117].

Dans l'arrêt *Digital Rights Ireland*, la Cour de justice a relevé que la directive 2006/24/CE sur la conservation de données générées ou traitées dans le cadre de la fourniture de services de communications électroniques accessibles au public ou de réseaux publics de communications, « n'impose pas que les données en cause soient conservées sur le territoire de l'Union, de sorte qu'il ne saurait être considéré qu'est pleinement garanti le contrôle par une autorité indépendante, explicitement exigé par l'article 8, paragraphe 3, de la Charte, du respect des exigences de protection et de sécurité »[118]. De même, la Cour a exercé son contrôle, dans l'arrêt *Schrems,* sur la décision de la Commission constatant l'adéquation de la protection des données personnelles dans un État tiers, en soulignant que cette dernière n'a pas compétence pour « restreindre les pouvoirs des autorités nationales de contrôle »[119]. Dans l'arrêt, *Tele2 Sverige*, elle a inter-

---

115 V. l'arrêt de la Cour du 9 mars 2010, *Commission/Allemagne, supra* note 102, point 30, l'arrêt de la Cour du 16 octobre 2012, *Commission/Autriche, supra* note 92, points 41 et 43 et l'arrêt de la Cour du 8 avril 2014, *Commission/Hongrie, supra* note 105, point 51.

116 V. l'arrêt de la Cour du 8 avril 2014, *Commission/Hongrie, supra* note 105, point 55 qui en conclut notamment que « l'exigence d'indépendance figurant à l'article 28, paragraphe 1, second alinéa, de la directive 95/46 doit, dès lors, nécessairement être interprétée comme incluant l'obligation de respecter la durée du mandat des autorités de contrôle jusqu'à son échéance et de n'y mettre fin de manière anticipée que dans le respect des règles et des garanties de la législation applicable ».

117 *Id.,* points 56 et s.

118 Point 68 renvoyant notamment à l'arrêt de la Cour du 16 octobre 2012, *Commission/Autriche, supra* note 92, point 37.

119 Arrêt de la Cour du 6 octobre 2015, *Schrems, supra* note 53, points 99 à 104.

prété l'article 15, paragraphe 1, de la directive 2002/58, par référence aux articles 7, 8, 11 et 52, paragraphe 1, de la Charte des droits fondamentaux, pour juger que cette disposition « s'oppose à une réglementation nationale régissant la protection et la sécurité des données relatives au trafic et des données de localisation, en particulier l'accès des autorités nationales compétentes aux données conservées, sans limiter, dans le cadre de la lutte contre la criminalité, cet accès aux seules fins de lutte contre la criminalité grave, sans soumettre ledit accès à un contrôle préalable par une juridiction ou une autorité administrative indépendante, et sans exiger que les données en cause soient conservées sur le territoire de l'Union »[120]. Ainsi, dans l'avis 1/15, la Cour de justice a exigé que l'accord entre le Canada et l'Union européenne sur le transfert et le traitement de données des dossiers passagers garantisse que « la surveillance des règles » qu'il prévoit pour la protection des passagers aériens à l'égard du traitement des données des dossiers passagers les concernant, soit « assurée par une autorité de contrôle indépendante »[121].

C. La singularité croissante du système de protection des données personnelles par l'Union

La conciliation entre l'objectif de protection des données personnelles et l'objectif de sécurité implique des précisions sur la répartition des compétences entre l'Union et ses États membres et sur le choix de la base juridique des actes de l'Union. Il en est ainsi même dans le contexte des relations externes avec des États tiers. L'imbrication entre les objectifs internes et externes agit sur l'articulation des bases juridiques et des compétences en fonction des objectifs poursuivis (1). Elle invite à l'affirmation d'une identité de l'Union qui progresse notamment par la continuité imposée entre la protection substantiellement équivalente établie par référence à un niveau élevé de protection dans l'Union et la protection adéquate exigée des État tiers (2).

120 Arrêt de la Cour du 21 décembre 2016, *supra* note 24.

121 Avis de la Cour du 26 juillet 2017, 1/15, *supra* note 2.

1. L'imbrication entre les objectifs internes et externes et l'articulation des bases juridiques et des compétences

La conciliation entre la protection des données personnelles et les autres objectifs du droit de l'Union se pose en termes d'articulation des bases juridiques. La Cour de justice rappelle de façon constante que le choix de la base juridique d'un acte de l'Union doit reposer « sur des éléments objectifs susceptibles de contrôle juridictionnel, parmi lesquels figurent la finalité et le contenu de cet acte »[122]. Il peut conduire à déterminer la finalité prépondérante de l'acte ou de l'accord international en présence ou à retenir une double base juridique en cas de finalités indissociables de l'une de l'autre et d'absence d'incompatibilité entre les procédures auxquelles elles renvoient respectivement. Les termes de la conciliation entre les objectifs de protection des données personnelles et de sécurité peuvent donc impliquer de rechercher quel est l'objectif dominant pour déterminer la base juridique. De plus, la délimitation du domaine des exceptions prévues par les actes du droit dérivé à leur champ d'application, notamment pour la préservation d'objectifs de sécurité, agit sur la détermination des bases juridiques. Ainsi, dans l'arrêt *Parlement/Conseil et Commission*, la Cour relève que la décision 2004/535/CE de la Commission, qui était en cause dans cette affaire avait trait au transfert des données des passagers provenant des systèmes de réservation des transporteurs aériens situés sur le territoire des États membres au Bureau des douanes et de la protection des frontières du ministère de la Sécurité intérieure des États-Unis. Elle souligne que ce traitement de données « n'était pas nécessaire à la réalisation d'une prestation de services par les transporteurs aériens », mais était considéré comme tel « pour sauvegarder la sécurité publique et à des fins répressives ». Ce traitement relevait donc de l'article 3, paragraphe 2, de la directive 95/46/CE[123]. Elle en conclut que la décision de conclusion de l'accord ne relevait pas du champ d'application de la direc-

122 V. notamment l'avis de la Cour du 26 juillet 2017, 1/15, *supra* note 2, points 76 et s.

123 Excluant de son champ « les traitements de données personnelles ayant pour objet la sécurité publique et les activités de l'État relatives à des domaines du droit pénal » (v. nos développements *supra*), arrêt de la Cour du 30 mai 2006, *Parlement/Conseil et Commission*, *supra* note 50, points 57 à 59.

tive 95/46/CE et ne pouvait donc pas être fondée sur l'article 95 CE[124]. Dans l'arrêt *Irlande/Parlement et Conseil,* la Cour refuse de transposer ce raisonnement à la directive 2006/24/CE (communications électroniques)[125]. Elle souligne qu' « à la différence de la décision 2004/496/UE, qui concernait un transfert de données personnelles s'insérant dans un cadre institué par les pouvoirs publics en vue d'assurer la sécurité publique, la directive 2006/24/CE vise les activités des fournisseurs de services dans le marché intérieur et ne comporte aucune réglementation des activités des pouvoirs publics à des fins répressives ». Elle en conclut que l'adoption de la directive 2006/24/CE sur la base de l'article 95 CE s'imposait.

Dans son avis 1/15, la Cour rappelle la méthode de détermination des bases juridiques en soulignant que cette question revêt une « importance de nature constitutionnelle »[126] et que « le recours à une base juridique erronée est susceptible d'invalider l'acte de conclusion lui-même et, partant, de vicier le consentement de l'Union à être liée par l'accord auquel cette dernière a souscrit »[127]. La Cour se prononce en faveur du double fondement car le projet d'accord PNR possède « une double composante, l'une concernant la nécessité d'assurer la sécurité publique et l'autre concernant la protection des données PNR » et car ses deux composantes « sont liées de façon indissociable » et « doivent donc être considérées toutes les deux comme présentant un caractère essentiel »[128]. La Cour en conclut que la décision de conclusion de l'accord PNR projeté entre l'Union et le Canada doit être fondée conjointement sur l'article 16, paragraphe 2, et sur l'article 87, paragraphe 2, sous a), TFUE, après avoir statué dans le sens de la compatibilité entre leurs procédures respectives[129].

---

124 L'arrêt en conclut que « l'article 95 CE, lu en combinaison avec l'article 25 de la directive, n'est pas susceptible de fonder la compétence de la Communauté pour conclure l'accord ». Arrêt de la Cour du 30 mai 2006, *Parlement/Conseil et Commission, supra* note 50, points 68 et 69.

125 Arrêt du 10 février 2009, C-301/06, *Parlement/Conseil et Commission,* EU:C:2009:68.

126 Point 71 de l'avis 1/15, *supra* note 2, renvoyant à l'arrêt de la Cour du 1er octobre 2009, *Commission/Conseil*, C-370/07, EU:C:2009:590, point 47.

127 Point 72 de l'avis 1/15, *supra* note 2.

128 *Id.,* points 90 et 94.

129 *Id.,* point 105 et s. Dans ses conclusions sur l'avis 1/15 (*supra* note 54) l'Avocat général Paolo Mengozzi proposait à la Cour de juger que l'accord devait être

2. L'identité de l'Union par la continuité entre la protection substantiellement équivalente visant un niveau élevé de protection et la protection adéquate exigée des États tiers

L'exigence d'une protection adéquate s'impose dans les rapports avec les États tiers et est appréciée dans ce contexte externe par référence aux exigences internes à l'Union. Si la protection adéquate ne renvoie pas à une protection identique, elle tend à être alignée par la Cour de justice sur le niveau élevé de protection recherché dans l'Union. Le niveau de protection adéquate rejoint ainsi le niveau de protection élevé par référence à celui applicable en interne à l'Union. La Cour de justice peut ainsi être amenée à contrôler le caractère adéquat du niveau de protection assuré par les États tiers avec lesquels l'Union entend procéder à des transferts de données personnelles. Elle a ainsi jugé dans l'arrêt *Schrems* que l'intervention d'une décision de la Commission européenne constatant le caractère adéquat du niveau de protection dans un pays tiers « ne fait pas obstacle à ce qu'une autorité de contrôle d'un État membre, au sens de l'article 28 de cette directive, telle que modifiée, examine la demande d'une personne relative à la protection de ses droits et libertés à l'égard du traitement de données à caractère personnel la concernant qui ont été transférées depuis un État membre vers ce pays tiers, lorsque cette personne fait valoir que le droit et les pratiques en vigueur dans celui-ci n'assurent pas un niveau de protection adéquat »[130]. Comme le montre cet arrêt, le contrôle exercé à l'égard de l'État tiers n'est que le pendant du niveau de protection défini en interne à l'Union. Il s'agit d'éviter que l'État membre puisse contourner le niveau de protection exigé dans l'Union en procédant par des transferts de données personnelles vers des États tiers pour leur traitement dans ces États[131].

Le niveau de protection adéquate est interprété par la Cour de justice par référence au droit dérivé « lu à la lumière de la Charte ». Il exige que le pays tiers « assure effectivement, en raison de sa législation interne ou de ses engagements internationaux, un niveau de protection des libertés et droits fondamentaux substantiellement équivalent à celui garanti au sein de l'Union en vertu de la directive 95/46/CE, lue à la lumière de la

---

basé tant sur l'article 16 paragraphe 2, alinéa 1, TFUE que sur l'article 87 paragraphe 2, a) TFUE.

130 Arrêt de la Cour du 6 octobre 2015, *Schrems, supra* note 53, point 38.

131 *Id.*, point 73.

Charte » avec des moyens qui « doivent néanmoins s'avérer, en pratique, effectifs afin d'assurer une protection substantiellement équivalente à celle garantie au sein de l'Union »[132]. La Cour applique ce raisonnement dans l'avis 1/15, dans lequel elle rappelle fermement les conditions d'appréciation et les exigences constitutionnelles qui gouvernement l'étendue de son contrôle juridictionnel. En premier lieu, « l'exigence selon laquelle toute limitation de l'exercice des droits fondamentaux doit être prévue par la loi implique que la base légale qui permet l'ingérence dans ces droits doit définir elle-même la portée de la limitation de l'exercice du droit concerné ». En second lieu, le respect du principe de proportionnalité implique que « les dérogations à la protection des données à caractère personnel et les limitations de celle-ci s'opèrent dans les limites du strict nécessaire » et « pour satisfaire à cette exigence, la réglementation en cause comportant l'ingérence doit prévoir des règles claires et précises régissant la portée et l'application de la mesure en cause et imposant des exigences minimales, de telle sorte que les personnes dont les données ont été transférées disposent de garanties suffisantes permettant de protéger efficacement leurs données à caractère personnel contre les risques d'abus »[133].

L'appréciation de la protection adéquate comporte donc celle de l'encadrement légal par des règles claires et précises des ingérences dans les droits fondamentaux justifiées par des raisons de sécurité dans l'État tiers[134]. Elle s'impose à la Commission lorsqu'elle se prononce sur le niveau d'adéquation de la protection assurée dans un État tiers. Ainsi, dans l'arrêt *Schrems,* la Cour relève que la décision de la Commission constatant que les États-Unis assurent un niveau de protection adéquat, « ne comporte aucune constatation quant à l'existence, aux États-Unis, de règles à caractère étatique destinées à limiter les éventuelles ingérences dans les droits fondamentaux des personnes dont les données sont transférées depuis l'Union vers les États-Unis, ingérences que des entités étatiques de ce pays seraient autorisées à pratiquer lorsqu'elles poursuivent des buts légitimes, tels que la sécurité nationale » et qu'elle « ne fait pas état de l'existence d'une protection juridique efficace contre des

---

132 *Id.*, points 73 et 74.

133 Avis de la Cour du 26 juillet 2017, 1/15, *supra* note 2; v. Potvin-Solis « La lutte contre le terrorisme et son financement », *supra* note 30.

134 Arrêt de la Cour du 6 octobre 2015, *Schrems, supra* note 53,point 87.

ingérences de cette nature »[135]. L'avis 1/15 rappelle fermement le contrôle strict qu'entend opérer la Cour de justice pour assurer la garantie des droits fondamentaux et du droit à la protection des données personnelles par les accords internationaux conclus par l'Union pour le traitement et le transfert des telles données. Il poursuit ainsi dans la voie d'une affirmation grandissante de l'autonomie du système de protection et de l'identité constitutionnelle de l'Union européenne dans cette garantie face aux objectifs de sécurité.

135 *Id.*, points 88 et 89.

Loyalty in External Relations Law: The Fabric of Competence, Autonomy and Institutional Balance

Andrés Delgado Casteleiro

I. Introduction

The multiple ways in which the principle of loyalty has been described[1] show not only how multifaceted this principle is but also its significance. Loyalty underpins the most basic principles of the legal order of the European Union (EU), and to a certain extent it is the main basic principle holding EU law together. It could be seen as an elastic fabric from which EU law is woven allowing it to extend in all sorts of directions without breaking apart.

The principle of loyalty is one of the main unifying principles of the EU legal order.[2] Even in the realm of EU external relations law where a certain duality between the Common Foreign and Security Policy (CFSP) and other external policies continues to exist after de-pillarisation, the principle of loyalty plays a crucial role in giving a certain sense of unity to the post-Lisbon constitutional architecture.[3] Moreover, the Court of Justice of the European Union (CJEU)'s interpretation of the principle of loyalty has played a crucial role in bringing together the CFSP and the rest of EU ex-

1 E.g. C. Hillion, "Mixity and Coherence in EU External Relations: The Significance of the 'Duty of Cooperation'", in C. Hillion, P. Koutrakos (eds), *Mixed Agreements Revisited* (Oxford: Hart Publishing, 2010), 87; A. Delgado Casteleiro, J. Larik, "The Duty to Remain Silent: Limitless Loyalty in EU External Relations?", *European Law Review* 36, no. 4 (2011), 524; E. Neframi, "The Duty of Loyalty: Rethinking its Scope through its Application in the Field of EU External Relations", *Common Market Law Review* 47, no. 2 (2010), 323.

2 F. Casolari, "The Principle of Loyal Co-Operation: A "Master Key" for EU External Representation?", in S. Blockmans, R. Wessel (eds), *Principles and Practices of EU External Representation* (CLEER Working Paper no. 5, 2012).

3 C. Hillion, *supra* note 1, 88.

ternal relations law, even when the pillars were still standing.[4] The Court's approach has added coherence and unity to the EU's external representation, and clarified the scope of application of the EU´s constitutional principles as regards EU external policies.

This chapter analyses the role that the principle of loyalty plays in the development of the EU external relations law. More specifically, to what extent does it contribute to the conceptualization of the EU legal order as a single legal order? To put it another way, can the EU legal order be viewed as a single legal order from the perspective of the specific features which make it a distinct legal order from the international legal order, but also especially, as a single legal order from the perspective of internal unity? How has the principle of loyalty contributed to this unitary understanding? The chapter also shows how, as the principle of loyalty gains more relevance as an autonomous constitutional principle, its potential for encroachment on other constitutional principles increases, raising questions as to what role the principle of loyalty should play in the EU constitutional order.

Through the analysis of how the principle of loyalty underpins three of the most relevant principles of EU external relations law -the autonomy of the EU legal order, institutional balance, and the principle of conferral- this chapter highlights the fundamental place that that principle has as a unifying principle, as well as some of the constitutional questions that might be raised by its current application. The analysis is divided into three main parts. After a reminder of how the EU Treaties envision loyalty (II), the chapter moves to examining the ways in which loyalty has informed the autonomy of the EU legal order (III). It then turns to the impact of the principle of loyalty on the principle of institutional balance (IV). The final part of the paper analyses how loyalty underpins the development of the principle of conferral (V). The chapter also gives some conclusions at the end.

4 R. Wessel, "The Dynamics of the European Union Legal Order: An Increasingly Coherent Framework of Action and Interpretation" *European Constitutional Law Review* 5, no. 1 (2009), 117.

II. I Have a Name, Not a Number: Loyalty in the EU Treaties

The obvious starting point for an analysis of the principle of loyalty is its constitutional embedment in Article 4, paragraph 3, of the Treaty on European Union (TEU):

> "Pursuant to the principle of sincere cooperation, the Union and the Member States shall, in full mutual respect, assist each other in carrying out tasks which flow from the Treaties.
> The Member States shall take any appropriate measure, general or particular, to ensure fulfilment of the obligations arising out of the Treaties or resulting from the acts of the institutions of the Union.
> The Member States shall facilitate the achievement of the Union's tasks and refrain from any measure which could jeopardise the attainment of the Union's objectives".

The multifaceted nature of the principle of loyalty is present even in its name. While the Treaties remained silent for many years as to the name of the principle first enshrined in Article 5 of the Treaty establishing the European Community (TEC) -and later Article 10 TEC- it was often referred to as the principle of loyalty.[5] Nowadays, this principle has finally been given a name: the principle of sincere cooperation.[6]

Given this new name, at first sight it would appear that the drafters of the Treaty of Lisbon have decided to drop the term "loyal" in favour of the term "sincere". The Oxford English Dictionary defines "loyal" as: "Faithful in allegiance to the sovereign or constituted government", whilst it defines "sincere" as: "characterised by the absence of all dissimulation or pretence; honest, straightforward". [7] Thus, since loyalty and sincerity are not synonyms, could it be argued that the content of the provision favours a more flexible approach to the obligations enshrined in this provision than before? The flexibility would stem from the fact that, before the entry into force of the Lisbon Treaty, Member States had an obligation of faithful allegiance to the EU, wheras after the Lisbon Treaty that allegiance no longer had to be faithful but merely honest.

However, when the English version of Article 4, paragraph 3, TEU is compared to other versions of the Treaties, the newfound flexibility of the

---

5 M. Klamert, *The Principle of Loyalty in EU Law* (Oxford: Oxford University Press, 2013), 33.
6 E. Neframi, *supra* note 1, 324.
7 Oxford English Dictionary: http://www.oed.com/.

principle is nowhere to be seen.[8] On the contrary, in the other language versions, the term "loyalty" continues to play an important role. The French version speaks of "le principe de coopération loyale", the Spanish one refers to "el principio de cooperación leal", the Italian one speaks of the "principio di leale cooperazione", the Portuguese mentions the "princípio da cooperação leal", and the German version speaks, *inter alia*, of "Grundsatz der loyalen Zusammenarbeit".

Furthermore, the language confusion leading to different conceptions has played a role in the literature on the principle of loyalty. In the (English) EU external relations literature, this language confusion led to discussions on the nature of the principle. Hyett argued that, since the case law of the Court of justice referred to a duty of cooperation and not to the principle of loyalty, the two should be distinguished.[9] The autonomous nature of the duty of cooperation posited by Hyett was contested by other authors, who saw the duty of cooperation as a specific manifestation of the principle of loyalty enshrined in ex Articles 10 TEC and 5 TEC.[10]

Both lines of reasoning are based on the premise that Member States have a duty to cooperate, instead of having to abide by a principle of loyalty. From a theoretical standpoint, this distinction makes the nature of the obligation envisaged in Article 4, paragraph 3, TEU vary depending on whether we consider it a duty or a principle. As Heliskoski argues, a duty does not entail legal obligations but obligations of a moral nature.[11] Therefore, if the obligation in Article 4, paragraph 3, TEU were to be regarded as a duty and not a principle, it would only entail an obligation of best ef-

8 P. J. Kuijper, "Re-reading External Relations Cases in the Field of Transport: The Function of Community Loyalty", in M. Bulterman a.o. (eds), *View of European Law from the Mountain, Liber Amicorum Piet Jan Slot* (Alpen aan den Rijn: Wolters Kluwer, 2009), 293.

9 S. Hyett, "The Duty of Cooperation: a Flexible Concept", in A. Dashwood, C. Hillion (eds), *The General Law od EC External Relations* (London: Sweet & Maxwell, 2000), 248.

10 M. Klamert, *supra* note 5, 33; E. Neframi, *supra* note 1, 325. Cf. M. Cremona, "Defending the Community Interest: the Duties of Cooperation and Compliance", in M. Cremona, B. De Witte (eds), *EU Foreign Relations Law Constitutional Fundamentals* (Oxford: Hart Publishing, 2008), 126.

11 J. Heliskoski, *Mixed Agreements as a Technique for Organizing the International Relations of the European Community and its Member States* (Alpen aan den Rijn: Kluwer Law International, 2001), 123.

forts or good faith.[12] By contrast, were it to be viewed as a principle, it would give rise to legal obligations, and would thus entail an obligation of result.[13]

This distinction between duties and principles is somehow absent from the Court's reasoning. When read in their original language (French), the cases only speak of obligations without further qualification. For instance, in Opinion 1/94, the Court speaks of "l'obligation de coopération entre États membres et institutions communautaires",[14] whereas the English version mentions "the duty of cooperation between the Member States and the Community institutions".[15] Since obligations can be both legal and moral, it could be argued that the Court *prima facie* has not made a clear choice in favour of one or the other. Moreover, even in those cases where the Court refers to a "devoir de coopération",[16] the nature of the obligation is one of result and not one of best endeavours. For instance, in *PFOS*, the Court held that such a duty ultimately meant that:

> "Member States are subject to special duties of action and abstention in a situation in which the Commission has submitted to the Council proposals which, although they have not been adopted by the Council, represent the point of departure for concerted Community action"[17]

The most recent case law shows how the discussions regarding the role of the principle of loyalty in EU external relations law are based on this mischaracterisation of the principle of loyalty as a duty.[18] If we understand Article 4, paragraph 3, TEU as a principle providing the foundation for the

---

12 G. De Baere, T. Roes, "EU Loyalty as Good Faith", *International & Comparative Law Quarterly* 64, no. 4 (2015), 829.

13 Hugo Flavier considers that the principle of loyalty "devient le fondement spécifique d'une obligation à la charge des États membres dont la finalité est d'assurer l'unité de représentation externe de l'Union". H. Flavier, *La contribution des relations extérieures à la construction de l'ordre constitutionnel de l'Union européenne* (Bruxelles : Bruylant, 2012), 409.

14 Opinion of 15 November 1994, 1/94, *Competence of the Community to conclude international agreements concerning services and the protection of intellectual property,* EU:C:1994:384 para 106.

15 Judgment of 20 April 2010, *Commission* v *Sweden (PFOS),* C-246/07 EU:C:2010:203.

16 *Id.*, para 72.

17 *Id.*, para 74.

18 *Contra*: G. De Baere, T. Roes, *supra* note 12.

development of legal obligations and other principles, it will be easier to understand its place within the EU legal order.

III. Loyalty and the Principle of Autonomy of the EU Legal Order

It is common knowledge that the principle of loyalty is at the centre of the development of the basic constitutional principles of the EU.[19] References to Article 4, paragraph 3, TEU in its previous wording and numbering can be found in such seminal cases as *Costa* v *Enel,*[20] *Van Colson,*[21] and *Brasserie de Pecheur*.[22] The principle of loyalty has been inextricably linked to the idea of the unity of the EU legal order, both internally (supremacy, consistent interpretation) and externally (unity of external representation, exclusivity).

Moreover, the unity of the EU legal order and its autonomous character go hand in hand. There is no doubt that the unity of the EU legal order and uniform application of its rules operate by that legal order asserting its independence from international law. [23] In other words, autonomy from international law is co-extensive with autonomy from domestic law.[24]

In Opinion 1/09,[25] the principle of loyalty was described as one of the elements that inform the autonomy of the EU legal order. That opinion highlighted it as one of the defining factors of the unity of the EU legal order. Thus, the Court held that the establishment of a Patent Court, that would deprive national courts of their functions as European courts of the

---

19 M. Klamert, *supra* note 5, 71; J. Temple Lang, "Development by the Court of Justice of the Duties of Cooperation of National Authorities and Community Institution under Article 10 EC", *Fordham International Law Journal* 31, no. 5 (2007), 1483; B. Van Vooren, R. Wessel, *EU External Relations Law. Text, Cases and Materials* (Cambridge: Cambridge University Press, 2014), 189.

20 Judgment of 15 July 1964, *Costa* v *ENEL*, 6/64, EU:C:1964:66.

21 Judgment of 10 April 1984, *Van Colson*, 14/83, EU:C:1984:153, para 26.

22 Judgment of 31 March 1971, *Commission* v *Council (ERTA)*, 22/70, EU:C:1971:32.

23 J. W. Van Rossem, "The Autonomy of EU Law: More is Less?", in R. Wessel, S. Blockmans (eds), *Between Autonomy and Dependence: The EU Legal Order Under the Influence of International Organisations* (The Hague: T.M.C. Asser Press/ Springer, 2013), 19.

24 P. Eeckhout, "Human Rights and the Autonomy of EU Law: Pluralism or Integration?", *Current Legal Problems* 66, no. 1 (2013), 169, at 171.

25 Opinion of 8 March 2011, 1/09, *European Patent Court,* EU:C:2011:123.

EU legal order, would be contrary to the principle of autonomy of EU law, inasmuch as the obligation on national courts to fully apply EU Law would be undermined:[26]

> "It is for the Court to ensure respect for the autonomy of the European Union legal order thus created by the Treaties [...]
> It should also be observed that the Member States are obliged, by reason, inter alia, of the principle of sincere cooperation, set out in the first subparagraph of Article 4(3) TEU, to ensure, in their respective territories, the application of and respect for European Union law (...). Further, pursuant to the second subparagraph of Article 4(3) TEU, the Member States are to take any appropriate measure, general or particular, to ensure fulfilment of the obligations arising out of the Treaties or resulting from the acts of the institutions of the European Union. In that context, it is for the national courts and tribunals and for the Court of Justice to ensure the full application of European Union law in all Member States and to ensure judicial protection of an individual's rights under that law...
> The national court, in collaboration with the Court of Justice, fulfils a duty entrusted to them both of ensuring that in the interpretation and application of the Treaties the law is observed (...)".[27]

According to the Court, the uniform interpretation of EU law by national courts as guaranteed by the principle of loyalty is part of the essential character of the powers that the Treaties confer on the institutions of the European Union and on the Member States and which are indispensable to the preservation of the very nature of EU law.[28] The principle of loyalty is an essential instrument in preserving the very foundations of EU law. Consequently, given the prominent role that the principle of loyalty seems to have in the EU legal order, to what extent has the principle of loyalty in fact protected the foundations of the EU legal order while applied in EU external relations?[29]

The principle of loyalty has served the principle of autonomy in two ways. On the one hand, loyalty has been used by the Court as a means of guaranteeing the principle of autonomy through the uniform interpretation

26 B. De Witte, "A Selfish Court? The Court of Justice and the Design of International Dispute Settlement beyon the European Union", in M. Cremona, A. Thies (eds), *The European Court of Justice and External Relations Law* (Oxford: Hart Publishing, 2014), 40.

27 Opinion of 8 March 2011, 1/09, *supra* note 25, paras 67-69.

28 *Id.*, para 89.

29 Opinion of 14 December 1991, 1/91, *European Economic Area Agreement,* EU:C:1991:490, para 46.

of international law. On the other hand, the principle of loyalty preserves the autonomy of the EU legal order from actions taken by Member States outside the EU framework.

Concerning the first way in which loyalty preserves autonomy, in *Dior*[30] the Court was faced with the question of procedural provisions such as Article 50 of the TRIPs Agreement, an agreement that at the time fell within the sphere of shared competence.[31] Procedural provisions enshrined in mixed agreements constitute a challenge to the division of competences of the European Union. Since such provisions not only establish an obligation to adapt internal procedures to the safeguards and requirements of those provisions, but also fall within the scope of both EU and national law, the European Union, inasmuch as it has not laid down common rules on the issue only has competence to adapt its own procedures.[32] Therefore, the Member States would not be under a EU law obligation to adapt their national procedures, and the national courts would have jurisdiction under their national rules to examine the compatibility of those procedures with the obligations laid down in the international agreement. Therefore, as would be the case with any other international agreement falling within the Member States's competence, national courts could give contradicting interpretations. It is in this situation that the principle of loyalty would apply. According to the Court:

> "Where a provision such as Article 50 of TRIPs can apply both to situations falling within the scope of national law and to situations falling within that of Community law, as is the case in the field of trade marks, the Court has jurisdiction to interpret it in order to forestall future differences of interpretation (see *Hermes*, paragraphs 32 and 33).
> In that regard, the Member States and the Community institutions have an obligation of close cooperation in fulfilling the commitments undertaken by them under joint competence when they concluded the WTO Agreement, including TRIPs (see, to that effect, Opinion 1/94, cited above, paragraph 108).

30 Judgment of 14 December 2000, *Parfums Christian Dior and Others*, C-300/98 & C-392/98 EU:C:2000:688.

31 Opinion 1/94, *supra* note 14, para 105.

32 Other examples of the Court dealing with procedural provisions contained in mixed agreements: Judgment of 16 June 1998, *Hermès International* v *FHT Marketing Choice BV*, C-53/96, EU:C:1998:292; Judgment of 8 March 2011, *Lesoochranárske zoskupenie VLK* v *Ministerstvo zivotného prostredia Slovenskej republiky,* C-240/09, EU:C:2011:125. For a discussion: P. Koutrakos, "Intepretation of Mixed Agreements", in C. Hillion, P. Koutrakos (eds), *Mixed Agreements Revisited* (Oxford: Hart Publishing, 2010), 116.

> Since Article 50 of TRIPs constitutes a procedural provision which should be applied in the same way in every situation falling within its scope and is capable of applying both to situations covered by national law and to situations covered by Community law, that obligation requires the judicial bodies of the Member States and the Community, for practical and legal reasons, to give it a uniform interpretation.
> Only the Court of Justice acting in cooperation with the courts and tribunals of the Member States pursuant to Article 177 of the Treaty is in a position to ensure such uniform interpretation".[33]

The Court's use of the principle of loyalty allows it to extend its exclusive jurisdiction and consequently avoid possible conflicting interpretations of a provision that binds both the EU and its Member States. Hillion has described this use of Article 4, paragraph 3, TEU as having the effect of granting the Court pre-emptive jurisdiction.[34] In *Dior,* the Court used loyalty as a mechanism to expand its reach to places outside the scope of EU law. To put it differently, loyalty can extend the exclusive jurisdiction of the CJEU beyond the realm of EU competences. By virtue of the principle of loyalty, national courts now have an obligation even when acting outside the scope of EU law to interpret national rules in line with EU law. While procedural provisions like Article 50 of TRIPS are a special case and should be treated as such,[35] *Dior* shows how the principle of loyalty can be used to protect the autonomy of the EU legal order and the EU's international commitments. The principle of loyalty seems to safeguard the autonomy of the EU legal order by ensuring the uniform interpretation of its rules regardless of the competences involved.

Moving to the second way in which loyalty informs the autonomy of EU law, in *Kadi*, the Court was clear when establishing that Member States' international agreements may in no circumstances permit any challenge to the principles that form the very foundations of the EU legal order.[36] Given what was established by the Court in Opinion 1/09, it is clear

---

33 Judgment of 14 December 2000, *Parfums Christian Dior and Others*, *supra* note 29, paras 35-38.

34 C. Hillion, *supra* note 1.

35 P. Koutrakos, *EU International Relations Law* (Oxford: Hart Publishing, 2015), 255; E. Neframi, "Mixed Agreements as a Source of European Union Law", in E. Cannizzaro, P. Palchetti, R. Wessel (eds), *International Law as Law of the European Union* (Leiden: Martinus Nijhoff, 2012), 288.

36 Judgment of 3 September 2008, *Yassin Abdullah Kadi, Al Barakaat International Foundation* v *Council of the European Union and Commission of the European Communities*, C- 402/05 P & C-415/05 P EU:C:2008:461, para 304.

that, when conducting their international relations, Member Sates must not affect the very foundations of EU law. Whilst the issue of the autonomy of the EU legal order has become a hotly-debated issue after Opinion 2/13, it should nevertheless be noted that the link between the autonomy of EU law and loyalty remains underexplored. In Opinion 2/13, the Court drew a clear line between the principle of loyalty, the autonomy of the EU legal order and the exclusive jurisdiction of the European Union:

> "the obligation of Member States to have recourse to the procedures for settling disputes established by EU law — and, in particular, to respect the jurisdiction of the Court of Justice, which is a fundamental feature of the EU system — must be understood as a specific expression of Member States' more general duty of loyalty resulting from Article 4 (3) TEU, it being understood that, under that provision, the obligation is equally applicable to relations between Member States and the EU".[37]

As in *Dior,* where the Court used the principle of loyalty to extend its exclusive jurisdiction vis-à-vis national courts and reinforce the autonomous nature of the EU legal order, in Opinion 2/13 the Court referred to the principle of loyalty to further anchor its reading of the scope of its exclusive jurisdiction. Whereas in *MOX Plant*, loyalty was not fully deployed as Article 344 of the Treaty on the functioning of the European Union (TFEU)[38] was regarded as a specific manifestation of the principle of loyalty,[39] in Opinion 2/13, the Court used loyalty to expand the scope of Article 344 TFEU. Thus, its exclusive jurisdiction would cover not only disputes between Member States but also claims between the EU and its Member States.

Opinion 2/13 shows that loyalty is not only a fundamental feature of the autonomy of the EU legal order, it is also a fundamental means of safeguarding that autonomy. The Court's application of the principle of loyalty reinforces the autonomous nature of the EU legal order by expanding and clarifying the scope of the EU's exclusive jurisdiction.

---

37 Opinion of 18 December 2014, 2/13, *Accession of the European Union to the ECHR* EU:C:2014:2454, para 202.

38 Article 344 TFEU: "Member States undertake not to submit a dispute concerning the interpretation or application of the Treaties to any method of settlement other than those provided for therein".

39 Judgment of 30 May 2006, *Commission* v *Ireland (MOX Plant)*, C-459/03, EU:C:2006:345, para 169.

IV. Institutional Balance as a Specific Manifestation of the Principle of Loyalty

Although Article 4, paragraph 3, TEU lays down obligations of a vertical nature (that is between the Member States and the EU), the Court has not hesitated in extending it to horizontal situations. More interestingly, the principle of loyalty when applied to issues of institutional balance seems to further advance a unified vision of the EU legal order.

The starting point would be Article 13, paragraph 2, TEU. This provision provides that:

> "Each institution shall act within the limits of the powers conferred on it in the Treaties, and in conformity with the procedures, conditions and objectives set out in them. The institutions shall practice mutual sincere cooperation".

The reference to sincere cooperation in Article 13, paragraph 2, TEU characterises this provision as an expression of the principle of loyalty that applies to the horizontal division of powers. The principle of institutional balance means that the practice of one institution cannot deprive the other institutions of a prerogative granted to them by the Treaties.[40] Given that the principle of institutional balance is a specific manifestation of the principle of loyalty, what is the relationship between this provision and Article 4, paragraph 3, TEU?

In principle it could be argued that the relation between these two provisions is one of *lex specialis derogat lex generalis*. Thus, the principle of loyalty would apply whenever the principle of institutional balance does not. However, the special nature of the principle of institutional balance should not be understood as establishing a hierarchical relation. The CJEU has, rightly, been quite clear in establishing that the principle of loyalty does not trump the principle of institutional balance and the procedural implications that the latter entails. In *EU-US Air Transport Agreement,* the Council put forward the argument that the necessity to ensure close cooperation between the Member States and the EU institutions, both in the process of negotiation and conclusion and in the fulfilment of the commitments entered into within mixed agreements allowed for a greater flexibility when considering the scope of the principle of institutional balance.[41]

40 Judgment of 10 July 1985, *Wybot*, 149/85, EU:C:1986:310, para 23.

41 Judgment of 28 April 2015, *Commission* v *Council (Hybrid decisions)*, C-28/12, EU:C:2015:282, para 54.

Nevertheless, the Court understood that the principle of loyalty can not justify a flexible reading of the principle of institutional balance.[42] In other words, inasmuch as the principle of loyalty is an underpinning structural principle informing the principle of institutional balance, the latter cannot be derogated from so as to comply with the former. The Court has also expressed this view in relation to the voting arrangements within the Council. In *Portugal* v *Council*,[43] the Portuguese Government put forward the argument that the principle of loyalty would allow a derogation from the qualified majority voting required by Article 207 TFEU (then Article 113, paragraph 4, TEC). The Court was quite clear in that regard and held that:

> "the principle of cooperation in good faith between the Community institutions and the Member States has no effect on [...]the legislative procedure to be followed".[44]

Moreover, in *Pupino*, the absence of a specific manifestation of the principle of loyalty triggered the application of the general rule. The Court understood that "it would be difficult for the Union to carry out its tasks effectively if the principle of loyal cooperation", which requires in particular that Member States take all appropriate measures, did not apply outside the realm of what used to be the first pillar.[45] With *Pupino*, the CJEU showed the trans-pillar nature of the principle of loyalty. More importantly, *Pupino* showed that the principle of loyalty would be accompanied by all its constitutional baggage.[46] The principle of loyalty brought the different pillars of the EU together.

Even after the de-pillarisation of EU law, some of the divisions between the pillars have remained within the EU legal order. [47] On the institutional side, the role of the European Parliament in forming the Common Foreign

---

42 *Id.*, para 55.

43 Judgment of 23 November 1999, *Portugal* v *Council*, C-149/96, EU:C:1999:574, para 62.

44 *Id.*, para 67.

45 Judgment of 16 June 2005, *Maria Pupino*, C-105/03, EU:C:2005:386, para 42.

46 *Id.*, para 43. The Court applied the principle of consistent interpretation to the former third pillar in the same way it had applied in the first pillar. See E. Spaventa, "Opening Pandora's Box: Some Reflections on the Constitutional Effects of the Decision in *Pupino*", *European Constitutional Law Review* 3, no. 1 (2007), 5, at 14.

47 On the de-pillarization of EU Law see: A. Cebada Romero, "Análisis Reciente de la Práctica Convencional de la UE: Cambios Introducidos en el Procedimiento Convencional por el Proyecto de Tratado Constitución de la UE", *Revista General*

and Security Policy (CFSP) continues to be minimal when compared with its role in the areas previously covered by the first pillar.[48] However, the principle of loyalty has allowed it to further increase its role, albeit to a limited extent, within the realm of the CFSP. The *Pirates* cases point in this direction. In the first of those cases, the issue of the extent to which the same degree of cooperation was owed to the Parliament during the negotiation and conclusion of international agreements within the CFSP was interpreted differently by the Advocate General and the Court. For Advocate General Bot, the obligations laid down in Article 218, paragraph 10, TFEU allowed for a graduation in the degree of cooperation owed to the Parliament. Inasmuch as the prerogatives of the Parliament in the field of the CFSP were not the same as in other fields of EU external relations, a reading allowing for relaxation of the obligation laid down in Article 218, paragraph 10, TFEU to fully and immediately inform the Parliament would make sense.[49] For Advocate General Bot the specific nature of the CFSP might also entail a different reading of the same obligation of cooperation and institutional balance.

The Court disagreed with the Advocate General and understood that the same obligation of cooperation applied independently of the nature of the agreement:

---

de Derecho Europeo 4, no. 7 (2004), 23; M. Cremona, "Defining Competence in EU External Relations: Lessons from the Treaty Reform Process", in A. Dashwood, M. Maresceau (eds), *Law and Practice of EU External Relations Salient Features of a Changing Landscape* (Cambridge: Cambridge University Press, 2011), 34; P. Van Elsuwege, "EU External Action after the Collapse of the Pillar Structure: In search of a New Balance between Delimitation and Consistency", *Common Market Law Review* 47, no. 4 (2010), 987; R. Gosalbo Bono, "Some Reflections on the CFSP Legal Order", *Common Market Law Review* 43, no. 2 (2006), 337; C. Herrmann, "Much Ado About Pluto? The 'Unity of the Legal Order of the European Union", in M. Cremona, B. De Witte (eds), *EU Foreign Relations Law Constitutional Fundamentals* (Oxford: Hart 2008) 19; R. Wessel, *supra* note 4.

48 D. Thym, "Beyond Parliament's Reach? The Role of the European Parliament in the CFSP", *European Foreign Affairs Review* 11, no. 1 (2006), 109; E. Wisniewski, "The Influence of the European Parliament on the European External Action Service", *European Foreign Affairs Review* 18, no. 1 (2013), 81.

49 Judgment of 14 June 2016, *Parliament* v *Council (Tanzania Agreement),* C-263/14, EU:C: 2016:435, para 156.

> "It cannot be inferred from that fact that despite its exclusion from the procedure for negotiating and concluding an agreement relating exclusively to the CFSP, the Parliament has no right of scrutiny in respect of that EU policy.
> On the contrary, it is precisely for that purpose that the information requirement laid down in Article 218(10) TFEU applies to any procedure for concluding an international agreement, including agreements relating exclusively to the CFSP".[50]

Inasmuch as there is no specific manifestation of the principle of horizontal loyalty in the field of CFSP, the same kind of obligations of loyalty applicable outside the CFSP should apply within the CFSP as well.[51]

What does the Court's interpretation of the principle of loyalty in the CFSP tell us about the internal unity of the EU legal order? Loyalty can be seen as a *passerelle* provision like Article 215 TFEU. In the absence of a specific manifestation it will apply, bringing together most its substance regardless of the specific nature of the policy area. As Article 215 TFEU provides for a bridge between the CFSP and the rest of EU law,[52] the principle of loyalty would also be another bridge connecting different legal regimes within the EU legal order. Loyalty would bring further internal cohesion and coherence to the EU legal order through the principle of institutional balance.

---

50 Judgment of 24 June 2014, *Parliament* v *Council (Mauritius Agreement),* C-658/11, EU:C:2014:2025, para 84. For a more in-depth commentary of the case see: A. Delgado Casteleiro, "Los últimos restos del dodo. La elección de bases jurídicas y su influencia en el papel del Parlamento Europeo en la nueva PESC a la luz del asunto Acuerdo sobre piratería con Mauricio (C-658/2011)", *Revista Española de Derecho Europeo* 53, no. 1 (2015), 177.

51 Judgment of 14 June 2016, *Parliament* v *Council (Tanzania Agreement), supra* note 49, para 68. See also the chapters by Cremona, Kuijper and Gatti in this volume.

52 P. Koutrakos, *EU International Relations Law, supra* note 35, 431. See as the leading example: Judgment of 3 September 2008, *Kadi, supra* note 36. Cf. P. Van Elsuwege, *supra* note 47, 1000.

V. The Principle of Loyalty and ERTA

A. Loyalty as the Constitutional Foundation of the ERTA *Principle*

In the *ERTA* judgment the Court understood that:

> "Under Article 3 (e), the adoption of a common policy in the sphere of transport is specially mentioned amongst the objectives of the Community.
> Under Article 5, the Member States are required on the one hand to take all appropriate measures to ensure fulfilment of the obligations arising out of the Treaty or resulting from action taken by the institutions and, on the other hand, to abstain from any measure which might jeopardize the attainment of the objectives of the Treaty".[53]

The Court's recourse to the principle of loyalty in *ERTA* continues to be hotly debated.[54] In addition, the confusion in that judgment between the existence and the nature of a competence does not help to shed light on the role that loyalty plays in developing the principle of conferral. For Klamert, "the Principle of Loyalty in *ERTA* should be seen as the central legal basis for pre-empting the Member States because of the passing of common rules".[55] By contrast, for Kuijper, the principle of loyalty was not indispensable for the inception of the implied powers doctrine, or for the establishment of exclusivity in that matter. [56] Instead, he considers that the EU's international legal personality is the main element of the judgment informing the formulation of the implied powers doctrine, and regards the primacy of the internal common rules as the crucial factor determining the exclusivity of the external competence. [57] However, he seems to disregard the fact that the principle of loyalty is also at the heart of the principle of primacy.[58]

---

53 Judgment of 31 March 1971, *Commission* v *Council (ERTA)*, *supra* note 22, paras 20-21.

54 These are just an example of three recent publications in which the topic plays a central role: R. Schütze, *Foreign Affairs and the EU Constitution* (Cambridge: Cambridge University Press, 2014); B. Van Vooren, R. Wessel, *supra* note 19; P. J. Kuijper a.o., *The Law of EU External Relations. Case, Materials and Commnetary on the EU as an International Legal Actor* (Oxford: Oxford University Press, 2013).

55 M. Klamert, *supra* note 5, 75.

56 P.J. Kuijper, *supra* note 8, 294.

57 *Ibidem.*

58 B. Van Vooren, R. Wessel, *supra* note 19, 130. See R. Schütze, *supra* note 54, 258.

Unlike Kuijper, Koutrakos understands that the principle of loyalty clearly relates to the nature of the competence and not its implied existence.[59] However, he finds the reference puzzling insofar as it "puts forwards a construction of exclusivity which differs from that already laid down in paragraph 17".[60] This reference to the principle of loyalty can only be understood as a way of cementing the constitutional foundation of principle of exclusivity.[61] Thus, the principle of loyalty seems to transfer its constitutional gravitas to the principle of pre-emption. In other words, this reference to now Article 4, paragraph 3, TEU emphasizes the constitutional place that this new principle has in the EU legal order.[62]

B. *The Two Thin Lines Dividing Loyalty and Exclusivity*

That loyalty is the constitutional anchor of the doctrine of pre-emption can be seen as the logical consequence of the absence of specific provisions on the nature and effects of the EU competences pre-Lisbon. However, the case law especially after Lisbon has blurred the lines dividing, first, the effects of loyalty and *ERTA*, and, second, albeit to a lesser degree the methodology used to establish a breach of loyalty and whether pre-emption has taken place. This is especially clear in the light of a series of decisions, starting with the *Open Skies* saga,[63] passing through the *International-*

59 See P. Eeckhout, *EU External Relations Law* (Oxford: Oxford University Press, 2011) 74.

60 "In particular, each time the Community, with a view to implementing a common policy envisaged by the Treaty, adopts provisions laying down common rules, whatever form these may take, the Member States no longer have the right, acting individually or even collectively, to undertake obligations with third countries which affect those rules". Judgment of 31 March 1971, *Commission v Council (ERTA)*, *supra* note 22, para 17; P. Koutrakos, *EU International Relations Law* (Oxford : Hart Publishing, 2006), 82.

61 *Ibidem.*

62 J. Temple Lang, *supra* note 19, 1515.

63 Judgments of 5 November 2002, *(Open Skies): Commission* v *United Kingdom*, C-466/98 EU:C:2002:624; *Commission* v *Luxembourg,* C-472/98, EU:C:2002:629*; Commission* v *Denmark,* C-467/98 EU:C:2002:625; *Commission* v *Germany,* C-476/98 EU:C:2002:631; *Commission* v *Austria,* C-475/98 EU:C:2002:630. For an overview of the broader constitutional implications see: C. Hillion, "A Look Back at the Open Skies Judgments", in M. Bulterman a.o. (eds),

al Organization of Vine and Wine (OIV) [64] judgment and finishing (for now) with Opinions 2/15 and 3/15. These cases show how nowadays there is a challenge in drawing the lines separating conferral and cooperation.[65]

1. What Difference does it Make? ERTA *and Loyalty from the Perspective of their Effects*

As Klamert's analysis shows,[66] the current conceptualisation of the principle of conferral based on the principle of loyalty also works in the opposite direction. The Court's recourse to the principle of loyalty to the detriment of the principle of conferral has had the consequence of transferring the effects of the latter (pre-emption, supremacy) to the former.

In the *Open Skies* cases, the Court recalled that the principle of loyalty was at the heart of the *ERTA* principle. After a long and detailed analysis of the relevant internal rules to determine whether the EU Member States' Open Skies Agreements could affect them, the Court concluded that :

> "Article 5 of the Treaty requires Member States to facilitate the achievement of the Community's tasks and to abstain from any measure which could jeopardise the attainment of the objectives of the Treaty.
> In the area of external relations, the Court has held that the Community's tasks and the objectives of the Treaty would be compromised if Member States were able to enter into international commitments containing rules capable of affecting rules adopted by the Community or of altering their scope".[67]

From this extract, it is perhaps difficult to grasp the dividing line between the principle of loyalty and the *ERTA* principle in these cases. Was it really necessary to establish a breach of what is now Article 4, paragraph 3, TEU? Does this mean that any breach of the *ERTA* principle logically entails a breach of the principle of loyalty?[68]

Views of European Law from the Mountain Liber Amicorum Piet Jan Slot (Alpen aan den Rijn: Wolters Kluwer 2009), 257.

64 Judgment of 7 October 2014, *Germany* v *Council (OIV)*, C-399/12, EU:C:2014:2258.

65 B. Van Vooren, *EU External Relations Law and the European Neighbourhood Policy. A Paradigm for Coherence* (Oxford: Routledge 2012), 77.

66 M. Klamert, *supra* note 5, 75.

67 Judgments of 5 November 2002, *(Open Skies), supra* note 63, paras 135-136.

68 P. J. Kuijper, *supra* note 8, 298.

In Opinion 1/03, the Court followed the line of reasoning established in Open Skies and reaffirmed that the principle of loyalty informed the *ERTA* principle:

> "The Court noted in that regard that, in all the areas corresponding to the objectives of the Treaty, Article 10 EC requires Member States to facilitate the achievement of the Community's tasks and to abstain from any measure which could jeopardise the attainment of the objectives of the Treaty".[69]

For some authors like Van Vooren, the Courts pronouncement in Opinion 1/03 shows how the principle of loyalty can operate as *de facto* pre-emption.[70] Following this reasoning, judgments such as *IMO*,[71] or those in the *Inland Waterways* cases[72], further blur the application of the principle of loyalty as it would establish specific duties of abstention for those Member States daring to act in the international sphere alone because otherwise the EU´s (internal) action would be put at risk.[73] In other words, the obligations and effects enshrined in the principle of loyalty would be the same as those stemming from the exercise of an EU competence: the primacy of EU law, and an obligation for the EU Member States to refrain from acting insofar as their actions conflict with EU law.[74]

This argument would also be supported by the *OIV* judgment. The Court had to decide on whether the Council could adopt a decision establishing the position to be adopted on behalf of the European Union with regard to certain recommendations to be adopted in the framework of the OIV by virtue of Article 218, paragraph 9, TFEU. According to the Court:

---

69 Opinion of 14 October 2014, 1/13, *Hague Convention of 25 October 1980 on the Civil Aspects of International Child Abduction,* EU:C:2014:2303, para 119.

70 B. Van Vooren, *supra* note 65, 87.

71 Judgment of 12 February 2009, *Commission* v *Greece (IMO)*, C-45/07 EU:C:2009:81.

72 Judgment of 2 June 2005, *Commission* v *Luxembourg (Inland Waterways)*, C-266/03, EU:C:2005:341; Judgment of 14 July 2005, *Commission* v *Germany (Inland Waterways)*, C-433/03, EU:C:2005:462.

73 On how in any case, especially the IMO judgement entails a considerable extension of the *ERTA* Principle: A. Delgado Casteleiro, B. Larik, *supra* note 1; M. Cremona, "Extending the Reach of the *AETR* Principle: Comment on Commission v Greece (C-45/07)", *European Law Review* 34, no. 5 (2009) 754.

74 R. Schütze, "Supremacy Without Pre-Emption? The Very Slowly Emergent Doctrine Of Community Pre-Emption", *Common Market Law Review* 43, no. 4 (2006) 1023.

> "Where an area of law falls within a competence of the European Union, such as the one mentioned in the preceding paragraph, the fact that the European Union did not take part in the international agreement in question does not prevent it from exercising that competence by establishing, through its institutions, a position to be adopted on its behalf in the body set up by that agreement, in particular through the Member States which are party to that agreement acting jointly in its interest".[75]

Pre-emption and primacy entail an obligation for the EU Member States not to act externally inasmuch as their actions may potentially externally influence the EU decision-making process. In this regard, Wessel and Van Vooren have tried to draw a dividing line between pre-emption and the principle of loyalty: "pre-emption is connected with protecting the principle of conferral from encroachment, whereas cooperation exists to ensure that the objectives laid down in Union Law are attained". [76] Thus the difference will reside in the type of obligation where the principle of loyalty triggers an obligation of best efforts whereas pre-emption entails an obligation of result.

However, in this picture in which the principle of loyalty does not entail the same kind of obligations as the *ERTA* principle, how does the *PFOS* judgment fit in? The Court seem to support the view, at least when conducting an analysis in relation to unilateral proposals to include certain environmentally harmful substances, more precisely *perfluoroctane sulfonate* (PFOS), in the Annex to the Stockholm Convention on Persistent Organic Pollutants,[77] that the principle of loyalty would establish the same de-facto obligations as the *ERTA* principle.[78] The EU Member States would be barred from acting even when the EU has no exercised its competence on a certain subject. The Court is quite clear in explaining that the distinction between shared and exclusive competence does not operate in relation to the application of the principle of loyalty and consequently that

---

75 Judgment of 7 October 2014, *Germany* v *Council (OIV), supra* note 63, para 52.

76 B. Van Vooren, R. Wessel, *supra* note 19, 191.

77 Both Cremona and De Baere contextualize the decision: M. Cremona, "Case C-246/07, *Commission v. Sweden (PFOS)*, Judgment of the Court of Justice (Grand Chamber) of 20 of April 2010", *Common Market Law Review* 48, no. 5 (2011), 1639; G. De Baere, " 'O, Where is Faith? O, Where is Loyalty?' Some Thoughts on the Duty of Loyal Co-operation and the Union's External Environmental Competences in the Light of the PFOS Case", *European Law Review* 36, no. 3 (2011), 405.

78 B. Van Vooren, R. Wessel, *supra* note 19, 206.

obligations of result and abstention might also apply in those areas in which no primacy or pre-emption would apply. [79]

> "[...] the duty of genuine cooperation is of general application and does not depend either on whether the Community competence concerned is exclusive or on any right of the Member States to enter into obligations towards non-member countries".[80]

Consequently, if the principle of loyalty is of general application, its scope must be the same regardless of the competence involved and the specific legal duties for the Member States will remain the same: an obligation to refrain from acting. As it has been argued elsewhere, "even if the ECJ uses different words, at the end it seems that it continues to speak the language of exclusive competence with regard to the duty of co-operation".[81]

Interestingly, Opinion 2/15 seems to give some kind of clarification as regards the blurring of the principle of loyalty and the *ERTA* principle in terms of effects. As mentioned before, in the *BITs* cases the Court gave a broad reading of paragraph 2 of Article 351 TFEU, arguing that, even in the absence of an actual incompatibility, Member States were under an obligation to terminate their *BITs* inasmuch as the free capital transfer clauses contained therein were incompatible with an unexercised shared competence: the free movement of capitals. A joint reading of the *BITs* cases and Opinion 2/15 gives an interesting result: the transfers of capitals contained in the Singapore agreement inasmuch as they relate to free movement of capitals fall under shared competence, yet by virtue of the *BITs* judgment it is unclear to what extent Member States could really conclude an agreement on the free transfer of capitals without it being incompatible with the free movement of capitals. The only solution to this conundrum would be to accept that, contrary to common understanding, a mixed agreement would be legally compulsory not only when both an EU competence and a Member States exclusive competence are needed for the conclusion of the agreement but also whenever there is a shared competence. Thus, inasmuch as an EU external shared competence would always

---

79 Contra: E. Neframi, "The Duty of Loyalty: Rethinking its Scope through its Application in the Field of EU External Relations", *supra* note 1, 350; C. Hillion, *supra* note 1; S. Hyett, *supra* note 9.

80 Judgment of 20 April 2010, *Commission* v *Sweden (PFOS), supra* note 15, para 71.

81 A. Delgado Casteleiro, J. Larik, *supra* note 1, 539.

entail a certain degree of EU exclusivity a certain type of pre-emption will always be triggered through the principle of loyalty.

2. *The Court's Methodology as the Only Line Separating Loyalty and ERTA*

The alignment in terms of effects between *ERTA* and loyalty does not necessarily mean that pre-emption and implied powers have no role to play in the case law of the Court of Justice[82], but merely opens the door to a further blurring of the effects of EU competences. Since the principle of loyalty entails an obligation of result, which means that in certain situations the EU Member States must refrain from acting regardless of the competence involved, does it make any sense to continue to speak about areas of external shared competences in EU external relations law?

It could be argued that the difference between loyalty and *ERTA* is to be found in the methodology deployed by the Court in ascertaining whether pre-emption has taken place and a competence has become exclusive. For instance in the *Open Skies* cases, the application of the *ERTA* principle to the specific circumstances of those cases was a narrow one, based on the existence of an identical overlap between the international and the European rule (rule of pre-emption).[83] The *Open Skies* cases showed that it was not enough to have common rules on a certain area, it was necessary either to have achieved complete harmonization or "in the absence of complete harmonisation, the Court seemed to be searching for some substantive conflict between the … agreements and the European legislation before it would admit that the former 'affected' the latter".[84] The narrow application of the *ERTA* principle in *Open Skies* seemed to support the idea that the principle of loyalty continued to be the constitutional basis of the principle of pre-emption inasmuch as the methodology deployed by the Court

82 Judgment of 24 November 2013, *Green Network*, C-66/13, EU:C:2014:2399; Judgment of 4 September 2014, *Commission* v *Council (Broadcasting Rights Convention),* C-114/12 EU:C:2014:2151; Judgment of 22 October 2013, *Commission* v *Council (Conditional Access Convention)*, C-137/12 EU:C:2013:675; Opinion of 14 October 2014, 1/13, *supra* note 69; Opinion of 16 May 2017, 2/15, *EU- Singapore Free Trade Agreement* EU:C:2017.

83 R. Schütze, *supra* note 54, 288.

84 *Id.*, 293.

was based on the existence of an actual normative conflict and not just the mere jeopardising of the EU´s external action.

However, the Court has slightly retreated from its previous narrow application of the principle of pre-emption and has raised the possibility that in the absence of complete harmonisation or a substantive conflict, an implied exclusive power would nevertheless arise. In Opinion 1/03, instead of overruling its previous precedent the Court contextualised its previous pronouncements on the *ERTA* effect. It first clarified that the requirement to have achieved complete harmonisation was just an example, and was not a prerequisite for the *ERTA* effect to be triggered. Second and more importantly, it began to distance itself from the idea that the "affectation" part of the test entailed the presence of some sort of substantive conflict between the international obligations and the EU common rules.

Opinion 1/13 concerning the Hague Convention on Child Abduction continued to build on the shift of the logic of the "affectation" test rendering the idea of risk or jeopardy more prominent in the Court´s analysis. The idea that complete harmonisation was needed was completely dropped. Now it was enough for the international agreement to be covered to a large extent by the common rules. Moreover, there was no need for a substantial conflict to take place, only a risk that the common rules might be affected. In the Court`s view, EU rules may be affected by international commitments even if there is no possible contradiction between those commitments and the EU rules.[85] Opinion 3/15 on the Marrakesh Agreement continued to automatise the "affectation" test. That opinion drew a comparison between the agreement and Directive 2001/29/EC of the European Parliament and of the Council of 22 May 2001 on the harmonisation of certain aspects of copyright and related rights in the information society[86]. The Court observed that even though there was not complete harmonisation there was an overlap between the two legal rules:

> "Accordingly, the body of obligations laid down by the Marrakesh Treaty falls within an area that is already covered to a large extent by common EU

---

85 Opinion of 14 October 2014, 1/13 *supra* note 69, para 86. See: A. Delgado Casteleiro, "Opinion 1/13: on the Scope of the EU's Exclusive Competence after the Lisbon Treaty", *Revista de Derecho Comunitario Europeo* 51 (2015), 669.

86 OJ L 167, 22.6.2001, p. 10.

> rules and the conclusion of that treaty may thus affect those rules or alter their scope".[87]

Moving to the most recent example, Opinion 2/15, when addressing the question of implied powers, the way the Court approaches the question whether transport services are covered by an implied exclusive power, focuses first and foremost on the comparison and overlap between the common rules and the EU-Singapore free trade agreement. The affectation test is applied in a rather automatic way:

> "where an agreement between the European Union and a third State provides for the application, to the international relations covered by that agreement, of rules that will overlap to a large extent with the common EU rules applicable to intra-Community situations, that agreement must be regarded as capable of affecting or altering the scope of those common rules".[88]

It should be noted that the Court changed the modal verbs in the description of the *ERTA* effect. From a possibility ("may" in Opinion 3/15) the affectation has now become an inevitable consequence ("must") stemming from the existence of an overlap. The mere overlap between internal European rules and Member States' external competence seems to jeopardise the former, and therefore pre-emption seems the logical means of protecting the EU *acquis*.

How to evaluate this broad interpretation of the *ERTA* effect based on field pre-emption and automatic affectation? The methodology employed by the Court is becoming much clearer adding legal certainty to its case law. However, it also further blurs the line, methodologically speaking, between loyalty and exclusivity.

VI. Conclusions

This chapter shows that regardless of the original aim of the loyalty principle,[89] its development further entrenches the idea that, in EU external relations law, the duty of sincere cooperation should be better regarded as a

87 Opinion of 14 February 2017, 3/15, *Marrakesh Treaty to Facilitate Access to Published Works for Persons who are Blind, Visually Impaired or Otherwise Print Disabled,* EU:C:2017, para 129.

88 Opinion of 16 May 2017, 2/15, *supra* note 79, para 201.

89 G. De Baere, T. Roes, *supra* note 12.

principle of loyal cooperation, which entails legal obligations, and not merely moral obligations leading to an obligation of best efforts.

The principle of loyalty can be seen as a major driving factor in the development of the EU legal order because of its versatility. This chapter has shown not only that the principle of loyalty underpins some of the basic structural principles informing the external aspect of the EU legal order but also how it gears its development towards a more cohesive, coherent and unified legal order. This is the logical consequence of its conceptualisation as a principle entailing an obligation of result. The obligation of result that loyalty gives rise to means that Member States are precluded from concluding agreements that would jeopardise the autonomy of the EU legal order. Likewise, even in those situations where it is unclear whether the other EU constitutional principles would apply (such as the CFSP), the Court has recognised that loyalty would apply nevertheless and that the special nature of the CFSP does not affect the scope and effects of the principle. Lastly, the normative pull of loyalty also unifies the understanding of the different external competences, fostering the unity not only of the EU´s external representation but also the unity of the external effects of those competences.

Division of Competences, EU Autonomy and the Determination of the Respondent Party: Proceduralisation as a Possible Way-Out?

Cristina Contartese and Luca Pantaleo

I. Introduction

The academic debate concerning the international responsibility of the European Union (EU) has flourished in recent years.[1] Much ink has been

The present contribution reflects the shared opinion of its authors. Nevertheless, Sections II and III should be attributed to Cristina Contartese, and Section IV to Luca Pantaleo. As for Cristina Contartese, the present project was supported by the National Research Fund – Luxembourg, and co-funded under the Marie Curie Actions of the European Commission (FP7-COFUND). The authors wish to thank Simone Vezzani for his useful comments. The usual disclaimer applies.

1 It would probably be impossible, and certainly unnecessary, to provide an exhaustive list of the scholarly writings devoted to this issue. See, in particular, F. Hoffemeister, "Litigating Against the European Union and Its Member States – Who Responds under the ILC's Draft Articles on International Responsibility of International Organizations?", *European Journal of International Law* 21, no. 3 (2010), 723-747; L. Gasbarri, "Responsabilità di un"organizzazione internazionale in materia di competenza esclusiva: imputazione e obbligo di risultato secondo il Tribunale internazionale del diritto del mare", *Rivista di diritto internazionale*, 2015, 911; A. Nollkaemper, "Joint Responsibility between the EU and Member States for non-performance of obligations under multilateral environmental agreements", in E. Morgera (ed), *The External Environmental Policy of the European Union: EU and International Law Perspectives* (Cambridge: Cambridge University Press, 2012), 304; P.J. Kuijper, E. Paasivirta, "EU International Responsibility and its Attribution: From the Inside Looking Out", in M. Evans, P. Koutrakos (eds), *The International Responsibility of the European Union: European and International Perspectives* (Oxford: Hart Publishing, 2013), 35; J. Heliskoski, *Mixed Agreements as a Technique for Organizing the International Relations of the European Community and its Member States* (Deventer: Kluwer Law International, 2001); J. D"Aspremont, "A European Law of International Responsibility?", in V. Kosta et al. (eds), *The EU Accession to the ECHR* (Oxford: Hart Publishing, 2014), 75; A. Dimopoulos, "The Involvement of the EU in Investor-State Dispute Settlement: A Question of Reponsibilities", *Common Market Law Review* 51, no. 6 (2014), 1671; P. Palchetti, "The Allocation of International Responsibility in the Context of In-

spilled on how well-suited the rules on the responsibility of international organisations as codified by the International Law Commission (ILC) are to the EU.[2] In particular, as is well known, the fact that the EU has traditionally advocated that the allocation of responsibility between a regional economic international organisation (REIO) and its Member States should follow the internal rules of the organisation, while the ILC has embraced this doctrine only to a limited extent, is at the heart of that debate. Less attention, however, has been devoted to the techniques for identifying the respondent in a dispute involving the EU and its Member States, notwithstanding that the determination of the respondent party is deeply intertwined with the question as to how to allocate responsibility. For instance, filing a claim against the wrong respondent, inevitably, entails consequences for the outcome of the proceedings, as the risk of a responsibility gap is not excluded should the wrong respondent be brought before an international court or tribunal. Furthermore, under certain circumstances, enabling the EU and its Member States to determine the respondent party would amount to an implicit recognition of their (alleged) responsibility. The relationship between the identification of the respondent and the allocation of responsibility is the issue that the present work aims to tackle.

In the course of the analysis, attention will be devoted to the principle of the autonomy of the EU legal order as well as to the requirements for legal certainty of the third parties involved in the dispute. The interests of both parties to a dispute, in fact, need to be secured while determining whether the Union and/or one or more of its Member State is the respondent. From a third party's perspective, the Union cannot underestimate their requests for predictability. From an EU perspective, the decision of an international court or tribunal regarding the determination of the respondent may potentially affect the division of competences between the Union and its Member States, resulting in an infringement of the autonomy of the EU legal order as defined by the case law of the Court of Justice of the European Union ("the CJEU", "the ECJ" or "the Court of Luxem-

vestor-State Dispute Settlement Mechanism Established by EU International Agreements", in L. Pantaleo, M. Andenas (eds.), C. Reul (ass. ed.), *The European Union as a Global Model for Trade and Investment,* University of Oslo Faculty of Law Legal Studies Research Paper Series no. 2 (2016), 77.

2 See Draft Articles on Responsibility of International Organisations (DARIO), UN Doc A/Res/66/100, 27 February 2012.

bourg") over the years.[3] As is well known, although the Court of Justice has constantly emphasised that "The Community's competence in the field of international relations and its capacity to conclude international agreements necessarily entails the power to submit to the decisions of a court which is created or designated by such an agreement as regards the interpretation and application of its provisions",[4] it has also stated that "an international agreement may affect its own powers only if the indispensable conditions for safeguarding the essential character of those powers are satisfied and, consequently, there is no adverse effect on the autonomy of the EU legal order".[5] In particular, regarding the need to protect the division of competences during the determination of the respondent by an international jurisdiction, the CJEU, in Opinion 1/91, observed that the fact that a court "may be called upon to interpret the expression 'Contracting Party', within the meaning of ... the agreement, in order to determine whether, for the purposes of the provision at issue, [such an] expression ... means the Community, the Community and the Member States, or simply the Member States [implies that such a court] will have to rule on the respective competences of the Community and the Member States as regards the matters governed by the provisions of the agreement".[6] In the more recent Opinion 2/13, the CJEU ruled that the European Court of Human Rights (ECtHR or "the Court of Strasbourg"), in reviewing whether the condi-

3 See C. Contartese, "The Autonomy of the EU Legal Order in the CJEU"s External Relations Case-Law: From the "Essential" to the "Specific Characteristics" of the Union and Back Again", *Common Market Law Review* 54 (2017), 1627-1672.

4 Opinion of 14 December 1991, 1/91, *Draft agreement between the Community, on the one hand, and the countries of the European Free Trade Association, on the other, relating to the creation of the European Economic Area*, EU:C:1991:490, paras 40 and 70. Later recalled in Opinion of 8 March 2011, 1/09, *Creation of a unified patent litigation system*, EU:C:2011:123, para 74; and Opinion of 18 December 2014, 2/13, *Accession of the European Union to the European Convention for the Protection of Human Rights and Fundamental Freedoms*, EU:C:2014:2454, para 182.

5 Opinion of 18 December 2014, 2/13, *supra* note 4, para 183. See also Opinion of 18 April 2002, 1/00, *Proposed agreement between the European Community and non-Member States on the establishment of a European Common Aviation Area*, EU:C:2002:231, paras 21, 23 and 26, and Opinion of 8 March 2011, 1/09, *supra* note 4, para 76; and, to that effect, Judgment of 3 September 2008, *Yassin Abdullah Kadi and Al Barakaat International Foundation* v *Council and Commission*, C-402/05 P & C-415/05 P EU:C:2008:461, para 282.

6 Opinion of 14 December 1991, 1/91, *supra* note 4, para 34.

tions to allow both the Union and its Member State to be parties to the proceedings are met, "would be required to assess the rules of EU law governing the division of powers between the EU and its Member States as well as the criteria for the attribution of their acts or omissions, in order to adopt a final decision in that regard which would be binding both on the Member States and on the EU".[7] The Court of Luxembourg concluded that "such a review would be liable to interfere with the division of powers between the EU and its Member States".[8]

A succinct overview of the techniques to which an applicant and an international court or tribunal may refer in order to identify the respondent will be provided in Section II. These techniques, namely declarations of competence, rules providing for the automatic allocation of joint responsibility to both the EU and the Member State(s) concerned, and "proceduralisation", will be briefly presented from a comparative perspective aiming at identifying which is best suited to accommodate the interests of both third parties and the Union. After demonstrating that declarations of competence and rules on joint responsibility are not sufficient to safeguard the EU's *sui generis* characteristics, and that the former is unable to secure legal certainty and transparency for third parties, it will be suggested that a (procedural) rule that allows the EU and its Member States to coordinate their position on the matter is the most suitable solution, from an EU law perspective as well as from the point of view of the third party involved, in so far as it enables the latter to correctly address the respondent. The chapter will then focus on two recent case-studies concerning the codification of procedural rules. Section III will analyse the co-respondent mechanism as proposed under the Draft agreement on the accession of the European Union to the Convention for the Protection of Human Rights and Fundamental Freedoms ("the Draft EU Accession Agreement"). Section IV will examine the mechanism laid down in the EU investment agreements (such as CETA and TTIP) for the settlement of Investor-State disputes. Some conclusions will be presented in Section V.

7 Opinion of 18 December 2014, 2/13, *supra* note 4, para 224.
8 *Id.*, para 225.

II. Techniques for Identifying the Respondent: Declaration of Competences, Joint Responsibility and Rules of Proceduralisation

In order to identify the respondent, a party to a dispute as well as an international court or tribunal may rely on various techniques as set out under certain mixed agreements.[9] The first one is the declaration of competences, whereby the EU and its Member States attempt to inform the contracting parties of the division of competences in relation to provisions regulated in the agreement. The second technique is the "joint responsibility" rule, which implies an automatic allocation of responsibility to both the EU and its Member States in the case of mixed agreements without questioning the respective division of competences or any other relevant rule for that purpose. The third mechanism is "proceduralisation", which establishes a procedural framework for deciding the matter at stake. [10] In the context of the present chapter, attention will be given to those rules of proceduralisation that allow the Union and its Member States to determine, internally, the proper respondent. This section will provide an overview of the three mentioned techniques and will conclude, while highlighting differences and limits, that the mechanism that allows the EU and its Member States to manage the issue as an internal matter appears to be

---

9 For the purpose of the present work, only techniques expressly laid down in the agreements are taken into consideration. Consequently, treaties that are silent on the matter under consideration, such as the World Trade Organisation agreement (WTO), will not be part of the analysis. For the arrangements of the Union and its Member States before the WTO dispute settlement bodies that are the result of a pragmatic approach leading to an active role of the European Commission, see J. Heliskoski, "Joint Competence of the European Community and its Member States and the Dispute Settlement Practice of the WTO", *Cambridge Yearbook of European Legal Studies* (1999-2000), 61-85.

10 For the definition of "proceduralisation", see J. Heliskoski J., *Mixed Agreements as a Technique for Organizing the International Relations of the European Community and its Member States*, *supra* note 1, 158, who refers to the strategy of proceduralisation explaining that, as for mixed agreements, "in actual practice, the problems of whether the other parties are entitled to address at will anyone on the Community side or whether the latter should rather be given the right to object and decide the matter for themselves are capable of being subjected to a procedure which defers material solutions to the problems, in a sense that none of the interests relating to the conduct of the settlement will have to be overridden". See also A. Delgado Casteleiro Casteleiro, "The International Responsibility of the European Union— The EU Perspective: Between Pragmatism and Proceduralisation", *Cambridge Yearbook of European legal studies* 15 (2012), 575-577.

the most appropriate solution from an EU perspective, as it safeguards the autonomy of the EU legal order, as well as from a third party's side, as it ensures the correct respondent is addressed.

A. Declarations of Competence

Declarations of competence are instruments inserted into mixed multilateral agreements, and are usually adopted as an annex to the ratifying decision of the Council and filed with the agreement at the ratification or accession stage.[11] This practice is the result of a request from one or more third parties, who are concerned about the allocation of obligations and responsibility between the EU and its Member States for the purpose of the agreement at stake. However, despite being a widespread practice,[12] declarations of competence display several limits that undermine the purpose of their adoption. Amongst their criticisms of such declarations, legal scholars rightly point out that these are not accurately drafted because of the inherent difficulty in doing so, do not reflect the dynamic nature of the division of competences, and are not usually updated.[13]

Moreover, their (limited) application, at EU and international level, does not allow further light to be shed on the relevance of these instruments. As for their application by the CJEU,[14] it has been rightly stated

---

11 On declarations of competence, see, in particular, L. Lijnzaad, "Declarations of Competence in the Law of the Sea, a Very European Affair", in M. W. Lodge, M. H. Nordquist (eds), *Peaceful Order in the World"s Oceans. Essays in Honor of Satya N. Nandan* (Leiden: Brill, 2014), 186-207; J. Heliskoski, "EU Declarations of Competence and International Responsibility", in M. Evans, P. Koutrakos (eds), *The International Responsibility of the European Union: European and International Perspectives*, *supra* note 1, 189-212; A. Delgado Casteleiro Casteleiro, "EU Declarations of Competence to Multilateral Agreements: A Useful Reference Base?", *European Foreign Affairs Review* 17, no. 4 (2012), 491.

12 For a list of agreements with a declaration of competence, see the EU Treaties Office Database, available at http://ec.europa.eu/world/agreements/viewCollection.do?fileID=76198.

13 A. Delgado Casteleiro Casteleiro, "EU Declarations of Competence to Multilateral Agreements: A Useful Reference Base?", *supra* note 11, 498; J. Heliskoski, "EU Declarations of Competence and International Responsibility", *supra* note 11, 200.

14 For the Court of Justice"s case law where declarations of competence played a role, see Judgment of 8 March 2011, *Lesoochranárske zoskupenie VLK* v *Ministerstvo zivotného prostredia Slovenskej republiky (LZ)*, C-240/09, EU:C:2011:125;

that the Court's case law is not consistent.[15] This emerges, in particular, from the comparison of the two most recent cases dealing with declarations of competence. While in the *MOX Plant* case the declaration of competence played an important role in the Court's concluding that "there has been a transfer to the Community of areas of shared competence" [16] and was deemed "a useful reference base",[17] in the "*Brown bear"* case it was dismissed by the Court, which did not provide any interpretation thereof for the purpose of defining its jurisdiction.[18]

At the international level, some cases seem to suggest that it was the existence of a declaration of competence that played a key role in identifying the proper respondent or the responsible entity in a dispute. In the *Chile* v *European Communities* case,[19] as regards the choice to bring the case against the EU rather than one of its Member States, the declaration of competence, laying down an EU exclusive competence on the subject in question, was probably decisive.[20] The recent *Advisory Opinion* of the International Tribunal for the Law of the Sea (ITLOS)[21] has in common with

---

Judgment of 20 April 2010, *Commission* v *Sweden, (PFOS),* C-246/07, EU:C:2010:203; Judgment of 10 January 2006, *Commission* v *Council (Rotterdam Convention),* C-94/03, EU:C:2006:2; Judgment of 30 May 2006, *Commission* v *Ireland (MOX Plant),* C-459/03, EU:C:2006:345; Opinion of 6 December 2001, 2/00, *Cartagena Protocol*, EU:C:2001:664.

15 See, in particular, A. Delgado Casteleiro Casteleiro, "EU Declarations of Competence to Multilateral Agreements: A Useful Reference Base?", *supra* note 11, 491-510.

16 Judgment of 30 May 2006, *Commission* v *Ireland (MOX Plant), supra* note 14, paras 99-108.

17 *Id.*, para 109.

18 Judgment of 8 March 2011, *Lesoochranárske zoskupenie VLK* v *Ministerstvo zivotného prostredia Slovenskej republiky (LZ), supra* note 14, paras 39-40.

19 ITLOS, Case No. 7, *Case concerning the Conservation and Sustainable Exploitation of Swordfish Stocks in the South-Eastern Pacific Ocean (Chile/European Union),* so-called "Swordfish" case.

20 See T. Treves, "The European Community and the Law of the Sea Convention: New Developments", in E. Cannizzaro (ed), *The European Union as an Actor in International Relations* (The Hague: Kluwer, 2002), 294.

21 ITLOS, "Request for an Advisory Opinion submitted by the Sub-Regional Fisheries Commission", Case n. 21, 2 April 2015. See C. Contartese, "Competence-Based Approach, Normative Control and the International Responsibility of the EU and its Member States: What does the Recent Practice Add to the Debate?", *International Organizations Law Review* (forthcoming); L. Gasbarri, *supra* note 1, 911.

the aforementioned case the fact that it relates to matters falling under the exclusive competence of the Union as expressed in the declaration of competence. However, the ITLOS did not rely solely on the declaration of competence, as another legal element was also decisive. The Tribunal, as a preliminary point, recalled that, under the 1982 United Nations Convention on the Law of the Sea (UNCLOS), the liability of an international organisation for an internationally wrongful act is linked to its competence and that the declaration of competence lays down the exclusive competence of the EU for the subject matter in question. It relied, moreover, on the fact that the EU was the only contracting party to the agreement with the third party concerned, as the Union declared in its written statement, to conclude that "only the international organization may be held liable for any breach of its obligations arising from the fisheries access agreement, and not its member states".[22] The case in point, therefore, is one falling under the debate on the obligations and responsibility for pure EU agreements, that is, agreements concluded by the EU only, as opposed to mixed agreements.[23] What can be inferred from this (limited) practice is that the role of the declarations of competence cannot be ruled out, or that, at the very least, competences have a role to play together with other internal rules of the organisation concerned.

A further argument against adopting declarations of competence comes from the perspective of the international responsibility regime. Heliskoski, in particular, has questioned the direct relationship between the possession of a competence and the allocation of responsibility. The author observes that "if there had been a declaration of competence, however meticulously drafted, the relationship between the concepts of competence and responsibility is a much more nuanced one, so that, within the system of general international law of international responsibility, the incidence of competence should not be conceived of as providing an appropriate criterion for determining the incidence of responsibility".[24] He further explains that

---

22 ITLOS, Case n. 21, para 173.

23 On the responsibility under pure EU agreements, see A. Rosas, "International Responsibility of the EU and the European Court of Justice", in M. Evans, P. Koutrakos (eds.), *supra* note 1, p. 139, at 151; P. Palchetti, "The Allocation of International Responsibility in the Context of Investor-State Dispute Settlement Mechanisms Established by EU International Agreements", *supra* note 1, 82-83.

24 Heliskoski, "EU Declarations of Competence and International Responsibility", *supra* note 11, 192.

"the essential criterion for the purposes of establishing responsibility is rather the impact or influence that a measure undertaken by the organization (decision, authorization, recommendation) is deemed to have upon the Member States. The mere possession of certain "competence" by the organization is not sufficient for that organization to incur responsibility for an act attributable to its Member State".[25]

For the purposes of the present work, additional observations can be drawn from EU and third party perspectives. As far as the autonomy of the EU legal order is concerned, the declarations of competence do not seem able to preserve this principle, as the international court or tribunal that is required to give a ruling on the international responsibility of the Union and/or its Member States could potentially deal with the division of competences while interpreting these declarations. Moreover, in light of their "imprecise, incomplete and open-ended"[26] nature, much room for interpretation would be left to the international court or tribunal charged with applying them. Once again, because of their nature, they are not able to guarantee certainty to third parties. Against this background, it comes as no surprise that legal scholars are particularly critical of declarations of competence as a technique for informing third parties as to the division of competence between the EU and its Member States.[27]

---

25 *Id.*, 194.

26 *Id.*, 202.

27 See, in particular, A. Delgado Casteleiro, "EU Declarations of Competence to Multilateral agreements: A useful reference base?", *supra* note 11, 502-503, who concludes that "These declarations externalize not only the internal division of competences, but also the problems and questions attached to the vertical division of powers in the EU"; J. Heliskoski, ("EU Declarations of Competence and International Responsibility", *supra* note 11, 205), observes that "some of the objectives behind the requirement of such declarations, including the achievement of legal certainty and predictability in regard to the question of international responsibility, are, if not shattered, at least seriously compromised"; I. Govaere, ("Beware of the Trojan horse: Dispute Settlement in (Mixed) Agreements and the Autonomy of the EU Legal Order", in C. Hillion, P. Koutrakos (eds.), *Mixed Agreements Revisited. The EU and its Member States in the World* (Oxford: Hart Publishing, 2010), 204), states that the "practice of inserting a 'declaration of competence" ... exports EU problems to the international level". For the perspective of third states, see P. Olson, ("Mixity from the Outside: the Perspective of a Treaty Partner", in Hillion, Koutrakos (eds.), 335-337, spec. 336), who argues that "Such a declaration is not a particularly useful document from the point of view of the EU"s treaty partners". See also A. Rosas, "Exclusive, Shared and National Competence in the Context of EU External Relations: Do Such Distinctions Matter?", in I. Govaere et

B. Joint Responsibility

Under mixed agreements, a further technique that may appear appropriate for "easily" identifying the respondent is the rule on joint responsibility. As is well known, the principle of joint responsibility means that, "when the EU and one or more Member States commit an internationally wrongful act that results in a single injury, both are responsible for the injury caused, not individually, or for separable parts of the injury, but jointly, for the same, undivided injury".[28] For the purpose of the present work, the existence of a rule of joint responsibility in an international agreement would suggest to an applicant party that the correct respondents are both the EU and its Member States, while an international court or tribunal would be able to allocate responsibility to both respondents without investigating EU law.

Amongst the agreements to which the EU and its Member States are parties, the ones that expressly foresee joint responsibility as the rule are rare.[29] Nevertheless, in academic debate, the relevance of joint responsi-

---

al. (eds.), *The European Union in the World. Essays in Honour of Marc Maresceau* (The Hague: Martinus Nijhoff Publishers, 2014), 30, at 37; P.J. Kuijper, E. Paasivirta, "EU International Responsibility and its Attribution: From the Inside Looking Out", *supra* note 1, 55-57. A more nuanced position is expressed by F. Hoffmeister, ("Curse or Blessing? Mixed Agreements in the Recent Practice of the European Union and its Member States", in C. Hillion, P. Koutrakos (eds), *supra* 260), who, while recalling the vague nature of the declarations of competence, recognise some merits in them.

28 A. Nollkaemper, "Joint Responsibility between the EU and Member States for Non-Performance of Obligations under Multilateral Environmental Agreements", *supra* note 1, 310.

29 See United Nations Convention on the Law of the Sea (Montego Bay, 10 December 1982, in force 16 November 1994) UNTS 1833, Article 139 "Responsibility to ensure compliance and liability for damage"; Kyoto Protocol to the United Nations Framework Convention on Climate Change (Kyoto, 11 December 1997, in force 16 February 2005), Article 4, para 6. Under other agreements, joint responsibility is a subsidiary rule should the European Union and its Member States be unable to provide the necessary information on their respective competence. See UNCLOS, footnote n. 48; and Galileo/GPS Agreement – Agreement on the promotion, provision, and use of Galileo and GPS Satellite-based Navigation Systems and related applications, done at Dromoland Castle, Co. Clare (Ireland), 26 June 2004, Article 19 "Responsibility and Liability". For a comment on this latter, see P. Olson, "Mixity from the Outside: the Perspective of a Treaty Partner", in C. Hillion, P. Koutrakos (eds), *Mixed Agreements Revised, supra* note 27, 343-344,

bility arises from its having been supported, more broadly, in the case of mixed agreements.[30] This was so especially in light of the reading of the *European Parliament* v *Council* judgment, which seemed to suggest that the Union and the Member States are collectively responsible for their obligations under international mixed agreements unless a declaration of competence is provided.[31] In reality, this case specifically refers to a mixed bilateral agreement where the then EC and its Member States were one, undivided contracting party to the treaty.

Moreover, further arguments militate against the automatic application of joint responsibility to any mixed agreement. It has been pointed out, in fact, that in some circumstances, joint responsibility would lead to unacceptable results, such as where wrongful acts are committed *ultra vires,*[32] and where the phenomenon of "false mixed agreements", that is, agree-

---

332. P. Olson also stated that "the United States and EU were able in Galileo/GPS to agree that uncertain cases would result in joint and several liability unless the European side provided a timely statement definitively assigning responsibility. Despite initial reservations, the EU eventually accepted this provision. Neither side was happy with this result, however, nor is it clear that either would be prepared to accept a similar solution in other cases". On joint responsibility and multilateral environmental agreements, see A. Nollkaemper, "Joint Responsibility Between the EU and Member States for Non-Performance of Obligations under Multilateral Environmental Agreements", *supra* note 1, 304.

30 For the early debate on mixed agreements and international responsibility, see, *inter alia*, G. Gaja, "The European Community"s Rights and Obligations under Mixed Agreements", in D. O"Keeffe, H. Schermers, (eds.), *Mixed Agreements* (Deventer: Kluwer, 1983), 133; C. Tomuschat, "Liability for Mixed Agreements", *id.,* 125; for the more recent debate, see E. Neframi, "International Responsibility of the European Community and its Member States under Mixed Agreements", in E. Cannizzaro (ed), *The European Union as an Actor in international relations*, *supra* note 20, 193; M. Cremona, "External Relations of the EU and the Member States: Competence, Mixed Agreements, International Responsibility, and Effects of International Law", *EUI Working Papers*, no. 22/2006, 20; P-J. Kuijper, "International Responsibility for EU Mixed Agreements", in C. Hillion, P. Koutrakos (eds), *supra* note 27, 208.

31 Judgment of 2 March 1994, *European Parliament* v *Council*, C-316/91, EU:C:1994:76, paras 24-35; Judgment of 7 October 2004, *Commission* v *French Republic ("Etang de Berre")*, Case C-239/03, EU:C:2004:598, paras 26-30.

32 M. Björklund, "Responsibility in the EC for Mixed Agreements – Should non-member Parties Care?", *Nordic Journal of International Law* 70 (2001), 373, who argues that "if applied strictly, in what would have to be conceived as its fullest extent, joint liability in the context of mixed agreements might apparently lead to certain unacceptable results" (at 387).

ments where mixity is not necessary or is a mere possibility, takes place.[33] Most importantly, the main argument against joint responsibility under mixed agreements is based on the fact that it is not disputed that identifying who bears responsibility under international law goes beyond the (exclusive or shared) nature of the competences leading to mixity. As is well known, the attribution of responsibility may depend on different models, such as the organic model, the competence model or the consensus model,[34] suggesting that their application should be assessed on a case-by-case basis or, at least, within the framework of each individual international treaty regime.

To summarise, although there may be cases where joint responsibility is correctly attributed, what is challenged here is its automatic application under any mixed agreement. This technique could appear as an "easy solution" for accommodating the specific characteristics of the EU legal order, given that neither the applicant party nor the international jurisdiction is required to investigate the relevant EU norms at stake. However, the joint responsibility rule is "reductive" in relation to the complexities of the regime of international responsibility of international organisations.[35]

C. Proceduralisation

The third technique for identifying the respondent is "proceduralisation".[36] Historically, the first international agreement laying down a procedure in order to allow the Union and its Member States to identify the correct re-

---

33 P-J. Kuijper, E. Paasivirta, "EU International Responsibility and its Attribution: From the Inside Looking Out", in M. Evans, P. Koutrakos (eds), *supra* note 1, 44-45.

34 *Id.,* 48-67.

35 A. Nollkaemper (*supra* note 1, 346) referring to non-compliance institutions, concludes that joint responsibility is "not a very efficient approach" given that "eventually, responsibility needs to follow power [to undo the situations and ensure performance of the obligation] … – though it may be a means of last resort when even non-compliance proceedings cannot determine which party has the power to do what".

36 On the rules of proceduralisation under international agreements concluded by the EU, see J. Heliskoski, *Mixed Agreements as a Technique for Organizing the International Relations of the European Community and its Member States*, *supra* note 1, 157-208; A. Rosas, "International Dispute Settlement – EU Practices and Procedures", *German Yearbook of International Law*, 46 (2004), 299-303.

spondent was the Convention for the Protection of the Rhine against Chemical Pollution (Bonn Convention), adopted on 3 December 1976.[37] Under this Convention, the applicant party to the dispute is required to transmit its request to the Member State as well as to the Union, which will have to jointly notify the party of the correct respondent/s within two months. Should that time limit not be observed, both the Union and its Member State will be regarded as constituting "one and the same party to the dispute". The same applies should the Union and its Member States jointly be a party to the dispute. The provision at issue was added later, in the Convention on the Protection of the Rhine.[38] An identical article is also foreseen under some of the Council of Europe's treaties, namely, the Additional Protocol of 10 May 1979 to the European Convention for the Protection of Animals during International Transport,[39] the Convention on the Conservation of the European Wildlife and Natural Habitats,[40] and the Convention on Transfrontier Television of 5 May 1989.[41]

The 1982 United Nations Convention on the Law of the Sea (UNCLOS)[42] laid down a procedural rule as well,[43] which nevertheless displays

37 OJ 1977 L 240/37.

38 OJ 2000 L 289/31. Annex – paragraph 7 of the Convention on the Protection of the Rhine: "In the case of a dispute between two Contracting Parties, only one of which is a Member State of the European Community, which is itself a Contracting Party, the other Party shall simultaneously transmit its request to that Member State and to the Community, which shall jointly notify the party within two months following receipt of the request whether the Member State, the Community or the Member State and the Community together are parties to the dispute. If such notification is not given within the appointed time, both the Member State and the Community shall be regarded as constituting one and the same party to the dispute for the purposes of applying this Annex. The same shall obtain when the Member State and the Community are jointly a party to the dispute".

39 OJ 2004 L 241/22, Article 47, paragraph 2 of the Convention (ETS n. 65) as amended by the additional protocol (ETS n. 103).

40 OJ 1982 L 38/3, Chapter VIII, Article 18, paragraph 3 of the Convention on the Conservation of the European Wildlife and Natural Habitats (1979).

41 Annex on arbitration, paragraph 2 of the Convention on Transfrontier Television of 5 May 1989 (ETS N. 132). The EU is not a Contracting Party.

42 OJ 1998 L 179/3.

43 Article 6, paragraph 2 of Annex IX, on "participation by international organizations": "Any State Party may request an international organization or its member States which are States Parties for information as to who has responsibility in respect of any specific matter. The organization and the member States concerned

important differences in relation to the aforementioned provisions.[44] First of all, under the UNCLOS, the State Party is not under an obligation to request information from an international organisation or its Member States, the provision under consideration rather leaves it as an option for the applicant State. The expression "in the case of a dispute between two Contracting Parties …, the other Party shall simultaneously transmit its request to that Member State and to the Community" is, in fact, replaced, under the UNCLOS, with "any State Party may request an international organization or its member States which are States Parties for information". Second, the UNCLOS states that this information has to be provided "within a reasonable time", failing to specify a time limit, which is, under the other aforementioned provisions, "within two months following receipt of the request". There is no difference between the UNCLOS and the other provisions with regard to the consequence of the Union and/or its Member States failing to provide the requested information, where the rule of joint responsibility would apply.

With regard to investor-State disputes under the Energy Charter Treaty ("the ECT"),[45] the procedural rule was inserted in the Union's declaration to a treaty provision, rather than in the text of the agreement.[46] The wording of such a declaration appears weaker than the provisions mentioned

shall provide this information. Failure to provide this information within a reasonable time or the provision of contradictory information shall result in joint and several liability". Although the rationale of UNCLOS" provision is to pursue the same result as the other procedural rules, it needs to be read in the broader context of the Convention. Article 6, paragraph 2 of Annex IX to the UNCLOS lays down a procedural rule, while Article 4, paragraph 2 and Article 5, paragraphs 1-2 recall the role of declarations of competence. The relationship between competence and responsibility is expressly set out under Article 6, paragraph 1, establishing that "Parties which have *competence* under article 5 of this Annex shall have responsibility for failure to comply with obligations or for any other violation of this Convention".

44 J. Heliskoski, *Mixed Agreements as a Technique for Organizing the International Relations of the European Community and its Member States, supra* note 1, 168-169.

45 OJ 1994 L 380/24.

46 Statement submitted by the European Communities to the Secretariat of the Energy Charter Treaty pursuant to Article 26, paragraph 3, b, ii, of the Energy Charter Treaty (OJ 1994 L 336/115): "The Communities and the Member States will, if necessary, determine among them who is the respondent party to arbitration proceedings initiated by an Investor of another Contracting Party. In such case, upon the request of the Investor, the Communities and the Member States concerned

above as the determination of the respondent by the Union and its Member States is not compulsory, but takes place, at the request of the investor, "if [deemed] necessary". Most importantly, the footnote to the declaration seems to frustrate the purpose of the statement as it specifies that such determination is "without prejudice to the right of the investor to initiate proceedings against both the Communities and their member states". As for bilateral agreements, third parties are not generally allowed to inquire into the division of competences between the EU and its Member States.[47] What can be regarded as an exception is the agreement concluded between the EU and US on the promotion, provision and use of Galileo and GPS based satellite systems and related applications,[48] which has succinctly established that, "if it is unclear whether an obligation under this Agreement is within the competence of either the [EU] or its Member States, at the request of the United States, the [EU] and its Member States shall provide the necessary information".[49]

It is worth emphasising that a rule of proceduralisation, in order to be effective, should foresee some specific legal features. The most appropriate solution is certainly to lay down a provision that is binding – and not a simple entitlement – on the applicant party. The binding nature of the provision would then avoid a scenario where bringing the case against the wrong respondent may be contested by the respondent party before the in-

will make such determination within a period of 30 days". The footnote to the declaration specifies that the determination made by the EU and its Member States "is without prejudice to the right of the investor to initiate proceedings against both the Communities and their member states". See T. Roe, M. Happold, *Settlement of Investment Disputes under the Energy Charter Treaty* (Cambridge: Cambridge University Press, 2011), 89-103, 171.

47 The recent mixed bilateral agreements usually refer to the EU and its Member States as an undivided contracting party, using the expression "the EU and its Member States, of the one part", and the third Party, "of the other part". See, for example, Association Agreements between the European Union and its Member States, and Ukraine (OJ 2014 L 161/3), Moldova (OJ 2014 L 260/4), and Georgia (OJ 2014 L 261/4). It not uncommon, however, that under some bilateral agreements, the wording of specific articles determines who is responsible for the implementation of those obligations. See, for instance, the Agreement on Trade, Development and Cooperation between the European Community and its Member States, on one side, and the Republic of South Africa, on the other part (OJ 1999 L 311).

48 OJ 2011 L 348/3.

49 Article 19.

ternational court or tribunal, and the claim rejected as inadmissible. A specific time limit should be established for the respondent party to provide the necessary information. Lastly, should the latter fail to do so, specific consequences are to be set out.

From this succinct overview on the different techniques for identifying the respondent, what can be inferred is that proceduralisation is an appropriate means of protecting the autonomy of the EU legal order, while enabling the applicant party to correctly address the respondent. Such a mechanism has to be preferred, therefore, to the other possible approaches for dealing with the division of competences and/or the allocation of responsibility mentioned above.[50] Currently, what is the trend in this area, and what can be expected in the future? Historically, the first of the three techniques to be put in place was the rule of proceduralisation under the Bonn Convention, in 1976. Nevertheless, from a quantitative point of view, what prevailed in subsequent treaties was declarations of competence, which to date have been added to about 30 agreements.[51] The agreements foreseeing a procedure which allows the Union and its Member States to identify the correct respondent are less frequent than the ones laying down declarations of competence, but less rare than the ones estab-

50 "Proceduralisation" is also to be preferred to treaties that are silent as to how to identify the correct respondent. The fact that a procedural rule is absent under the WTO agreement led the Panel, in the *Airbus* case (European Communities and Certain Member States – Measures Affecting Trade in Large Civil Aircraft, WT/DS316/R, 30 June 2010) to state that "whatever responsibility the European Communities bears for the actions of its member States does not diminish their rights and obligations as WTO Members, but is rather an internal matter concerning the relations between the European Communities and its member States" (para 7.175). Accordingly, although the Union declared that it "takes full responsibility in these proceedings for the actions of its member States [and requested] that the term 'and certain member states' be dropped from the name of the case" (para 7.171), the Member States were parties to the proceedings together with the EU (see P-J. Kujper, E. Paasivirta, "EU International Responsibility and its Attribution: From the Inside Looking Out", *supra* note 1, 62-63). This suggests that, before the WTO DS bodies, the EU and its Member States are entitled to affirm their view as far as the proper respondent is concerned: nevertheless, their statement is not binding in the dispute proceedings.

51 The list of agreements requiring declarations of competence is available on the European Union Treaty Office Database, available at http://ec.europa.eu/world/agreements/viewCollection.do?fileID=76198 (last access in February 2016), as well as in J. Heliskoski, "EU Declarations of Competence and International Responsibility", *supra* note 11, 210-212.

lishing a joint responsibility rule. This trend does not seem to have altered in recent years, where declarations of competence have been inserted into recent international agreements.[52] As a consequence, there is not sufficient evidence to indicate which approach will prevail in the future. Interestingly, in the recent Draft EU Accession Agreement, whose negotiation led to the co-respondent mechanism, and in the EU Investment Agreements, which took inspiration from the ECT, what prevails is the choice of a procedural rule. However, the provisions of these agreements, while drafted in detail, are far from unambiguous, as will be discussed in the following sections.

III. The Case of the Draft EU Accession Agreement to the European Convention of Human Rights: the Co-Respondent Mechanism

As is well known, under the Draft EU Accession Agreement to the European Convention of Human Rights (ECHR), two innovative mechanisms were introduced in order to accommodate the specific characteristics of the EU legal order, that is, the co-respondent mechanism and the prior involvement of the Court of Luxembourg in proceedings before the Court of Strasbourg. Under the first procedure, the European Union and its Member States are allowed, under certain circumstances, to both become parties to proceedings instituted against only one of them,[53] while the prior involvement procedure enables the CJEU to assess the compatibility with the rights enshrined in the Convention of the provision of EU law concerned, if it has not yet done so.[54] The two mechanisms are intertwined, as the prior involvement procedure is triggered when the Union has the status of co-respondent.[55]

The rationale behind the co-respondent mechanism is twofold. From a human rights protection perspective, it helps "to avoid gaps in participation, accountability and enforceability in the Convention system",[56] in the light of the specific nature of the EU as a non-State entity which implies that "there could arise the unique situation in the Convention system in

52 *Supra* note 12.
53 See Article 3 of the Draft EU Accession Agreement.
54 See Article 3, para 6, of the Draft EU Accession Agreement.
55 *Idem.*
56 Draft Explanatory Report, para 39.

which a legal act is enacted by one High Contracting Party and implemented by another".[57] From an EU law perspective, it provides "the mechanisms necessary to ensure that proceedings by non-Member States and individual applications are correctly addressed to Member States and/or the Union as appropriate", in accordance with the requirements of Article 1(b) of Protocol No 8 to the EU Treaties. As for applicant parties, this mechanism does not affect their rights as they are allowed to make submissions to the Court before a decision on adding a co-respondent is taken, and the admissibility of their applications "shall be assessed without regard to the participation of the co-respondent in the proceedings".[58]

The co-respondent mechanism is certainly a more sophisticated technique than the rules of proceduralisation.[59] Article 3, paragraphs 2 to 4, of the Draft EU Accession Agreement in fact, lays down the conditions for triggering that mechanism. The Union may obtain such a status to the proceedings if it appears that an alleged infringement by one or more Member States calls into question the compatibility between the ECHR and a provision of (primary or secondary) EU law.[60] It is also possible for one or more Member States to become a co-respondent. This is the case if the application is directed against the European Union and "it appears that [the alleged infringement] calls into question the compatibility with the rights at issue defined in the Convention or in the protocols to which the European Union has acceded of a provision of [primary law] or any other provision having the same legal value pursuant to those instruments, notably where that [infringement] could have been avoided only by disregarding an obligation under those instruments".[61] Should both the Union and its Member States be respondents in the case, the status of either may be changed to that of a co-respondent.[62] The rationale behind these triggering criteria, as indicated in the Draft Explanatory Report, is to bring the correct Party or Parties before the ECtHR. This means that the respondent is the Party to which the impugned act, measure or omission is to be attributed, while the co-respondent is the Party that has the power to bring about an amendment of the provisions of EU law relating to that act, measure or

57 *Id.*, para 38.
58 Draft explanatory report, para 40.
59 *Supra* Section II.
60 Article 3, paragraph 2, Draft EU Accession Agreement.
61 Article 3, paragraph 3, Draft EU Accession Agreement.
62 Article 3, paragraph 4, Draft EU Accession Agreement.

omission. In the case of EU secondary law, this would be the EU itself, while in the case of EU primary law, it would be one or more of its Member States.[63] The Draft EU Accession Agreement assigns jurisdiction to decide on the status of co-respondent to the Court of Strasbourg. The latter can either invite a high contracting party to become a co-respondent or accept a party's request to that effect. In both circumstances, the Court of Strasbourg is under an obligation to seek the views of all parties to the proceedings in order to assess whether the conditions for triggering the co-respondent mechanism are met.[64] The mechanism obviously only works to the extent that the potential co-respondent does not refuse to play such a role. This is why the Union has added a declaration stating that "it will request to become a co-respondent to the proceedings before the European Court of Human Rights or accept an invitation by the Court to that effect, where the conditions set out in Article 3, paragraph 2, of the Accession Agreement are met".[65] In reality, any model of proceduralisation requires that both the Union and its Member States apply the principle of loyal cooperation in their reciprocal relationship.[66]

Although it is not disputed that the co-respondent mechanism is useful for safeguarding the principle of autonomy as well as for avoiding gaps under the system laid down by the ECHR, it displays limits and ambiguities from an EU as well as an ECHR system perspective. In particular, this section, especially in the light of Opinion 2/13 of the CJEU, will closer investigate three different – albeit interconnected – issues, which are: Who has to decide on the triggering of the co-respondent mechanism? What is the effect of the co-respondent mechanism on the allocation of responsibility? Who has the competence to review the correct application of the rules on responsibility?

---

63 Draft Explanatory Report, para 56. For a critique of the capability of the EU and its Member States to amend the EU law at the origin of the ECHR violation, see A. Delgado Casteleiro, "United We Stand: The EU and its Member States in the Strasbourg Court", in V. Kosta et al. (eds), *The EU Accession to the ECHR*, *supra* note 1, 111-115.

64 Article 3, paragraph 5, of the Draft EU Accession Agreement.

65 Appendix II – Draft declaration by the European Union to be made at the time of signature of the Accession Agreement.

66 On the principle of loyal cooperation and the Draft EU Accession Agreement, see A. Delgado Casteleiro "United We Stand: The EU and its Member States in the Strasbourg Court", *supra* note 63, 117-119.

As for the triggering of the co-respondent mechanism, as recalled above, the Draft EU Accession Agreement lays down two options: invitation of the co-respondent by the ECtHR; or a request for involvement by the co-respondent. As regards observing the principle of autonomy, the Court of Luxembourg, in its Opinion 2/13, did not consider the Court of Strasbourg's competence to invite the Union or its Member States to become a co-respondent problematic. The CJEU explains that the fact that the invitation of the ECtHR is not binding[67] allows the Union and its Member States to "remain free to assess whether the material conditions for applying the co-respondent mechanism are met".[68] By contrast, a request by a contracting party to become co-respondent does not guarantee that the autonomy of the EU legal order will be protected. As the Court of Strasbourg is called to decide on the plausibility of the reasons provided by the Union or its Member States to that end, the CJEU has ruled that, given that "[the material conditions for applying the co-respondent mechanism] result, in essence, from the rules of EU law concerning the division of powers between the EU and its Member States and the criteria governing the attributability of an act or omission that may constitute a [breach] of the ECHR, the decision as to whether those conditions are met in a particular case necessarily presupposes an assessment of EU law".[69] The CJEU, therefore, concluded that "such review would be liable to interfere with the division of powers between the EU and its Member States".[70] As a consequence, as suggested in the academic debate on the subject, the most appropriate means of accommodating the co-respondent mechanism with Opinion 2/13 would be to remove the Court of Strasbourg's power to review it.[71]

While the aforementioned models of proceduralisation remain silent on the allocation of responsibility, or at the most, establish a joint responsibility rule in an alternative approach,[72] the draft article on the co-respondent mechanism expressly regulates this issue. Article 3, paragraph 7, of the

67 Draft Explanatory Report, para 53.

68 Opinion of 18 December 2014, 2/13, *supra* note 4, para 220.

69 *Id.*, para 221.

70 *Id.*, para 225.

71 See T. Lock, "The Future of the European Union"s Accession to the European Convention on Human Rights after Opinion 2/13: is it Still Possible and is it Still Desirable?", *European Constitutional Law Review* 11 (2015), 248.

72 *Supra* Section II.

Draft EU Accession Agreement, which is worth recalling in its entirety, lays down a rule on joint responsibility, albeit nuanced by a possible exception:

> "If the violation in respect of which a High Contracting Party is a co-respondent to the proceedings is established, the respondent and the co-respondent shall be jointly responsible for that violation, unless the Court, on the basis of the reasons given by the respondent and the co-respondent, and having sought the views of the applicant, decides that only one of them be held responsible".

As emphasised in the academic debate, the rationale behind joint responsibility as the general rule is to prevent the ECtHR from giving a ruling on the allocation of responsibility between the Union and its Member States and, hence, deciding on the relevant EU rules.[73] Nevertheless, the Court of Justice, in Opinion 2/13, is not satisfied with the text of the provision and criticises the rule on allocating responsibility as set out under Article 3, paragraph 7[74] for two reasons. First of all, the provision on joint responsibility may have the effect of holding a Member State responsible together

---

73 See, in particular, J-P. Jacqué, "The Accession of the European Union to the European Convention on Human Rights and Fundamental Freedoms", *Common Market Law Review* 48, no. 4 (2011), 995; O. De Schutter, "L'adhésion de l'Union européenne à la Convention européenne des droits de l'homme : feuille de route de négotiation", *Revue trimestrielle des droits de l'homme* 83 (2010), 535, 555; P.J. Kuijper, E. Paasivirta, "EU International Responsibility and its Attribution: From the Inside Looking Out", *supra* note 1, 65.

74 For a critique of the text of Article 3, paragraph 7, see in particular, G. Gaja, ("The "Co-Respondent Mechanisms" According to the Draft Agreement for the Accession of the EU to the ECHR", in V. Kosta *et al.* (eds), *The EU Accession to the ECHR*, *supra* note 1, 346), who rightly observes that "letting the ECtHR decide when the EU is responsible would be more consistent with what is required by Protocol No 8 to the Treaties than what is suggested in Article 3(7) of the Draft [EU] Accession Agreement. The relevant text of the Protocol, which I quote again, requires the Agreement to provide for 'the mechanisms necessary to ensure that... individual applications are correctly addressed to Member States and/or the Union, as appropriate'. This requirement does not imply, but rather seems to exclude, that a mechanism be established according to which the EU be considered as a rule jointly responsible when, as in the example of a breach committed through the implementation of a directive, the application has been correctly addressed against a Member State which breached its obligations under the ECHR in the exercise of its discretion in the implementation of the directive. This would also correspond to the position that the EU may have taken as co-respondent in the case". See also T. Lock, "Accession of the EU to the ECHR: Who Would be Responsible in Strasbourg?", in D. Ashiagbor, N. Countouris, I. Lianos (eds), *The European Union after the Treaty of Lisbon* (Cambridge: Cambridge University Press, 2012), 129-34.

with the EU for an infringement of a provision of the ECHR in respect of which the Member State may have made a reservation under Article 57 ECHR. Such a possibility, which is in contrast with Article 2 of Protocol No 8 EU, providing that the accession agreement cannot affect the situation of Member States in relation to the ECHR, applies to reservations as well.[75] Second, the Court of Luxembourg has ruled, once again, on the Court of Strasbourg's jurisdiction to decide whether only one of them is to be held responsible for that infringement. The ECtHR is allowed to do so only on the basis of the reasons given by the respondent and the co-respondent, and after having sought the views of the applicant. The Court of Luxembourg recalled that "a decision on the apportionment as between the EU and its Member States of responsibility for an act or omission constituting a violation of the ECHR established by the ECtHR is also one that is based on an assessment of the rules of EU law governing the division of powers between the EU and its Member States and the attributability of that act or omission".[76] The CJEU concludes that, "accordingly, to permit the ECtHR to adopt such a decision would also risk adversely affecting the division of powers between the EU and its Member States".[77] As for the question of allocation of responsibility, the Court of Justice clarifies that, "even [if] it is assumed that a request for the apportionment of responsibility is based on an agreement between the co-re-

75 Opinion of 18 December 2014, 2/13, *supra* note 4, paras 226-228. For a comment on this issue, see T. Lock, "The Future of the European Union's Accession to the European Convention on Human Rights after Opinion 2/13: is it Still Possible and is it Still Desirable?", *supra* note 71, 249-250. See, in particular, S. Vezzani, "Addio My Darling, Goodbye My Love? Unione Europea e sistema CEDU dopo il parere 2/13", in L. Cassetti (ed), *Diritti, garanzie ed evoluzioni dei sistemi di protezione* (Perugia: Università degli Studi di Perugia, 2016), 478. After recalling that EU Member States cannot be responsible for breaches of norms where there is a reservation, and that the rationale of the co-respondent mechanism relies on avoiding a situation where the Court of Strasbourg would be required to apportion responsibility between the EU and its Member States. Vezzani suggests revising Article 3, paragraph 7 of the Draft EU Accession Agreement as follows: "7. If the violation in respect of which a High Contracting Party is a co-respondent to the proceedings is established, the respondent and the co-respondent shall be jointly responsible for that violation. The European Union shall however bear exclusive responsibility where the violation concerns a provision of the ECHR in respect of which that Member State has made a reservation in accordance with Article 57 of the ECHR".

76 Opinion of 18 December 2014, 2/13, *supra* note 4, para 230.

77 *Id.*, para 231.

spondent and the respondent, that in itself would not be sufficient to rule out any adverse effect on the autonomy of EU law".[78] Recalling that the question of the apportionment of responsibility must be "resolved solely in accordance with the relevant rules of EU law",[79] the Court of Justice concludes that "to permit the ECtHR to confirm any agreement that may exist between the EU and its Member States on the sharing of responsibility would be tantamount to allowing it to take the place of the Court of Justice in order to settle a question that falls within the latter's exclusive jurisdiction".[80]

According to the Court of Justice of the Union, not only must the identification of the correct respondent remain an "internal" EU issue, so must the allocation of responsibility between the EU and its Member States. As for the possible revision of the co-respondent mechanism, it has been suggested that an amendment of the Draft EU Accession Agreement, to the effect that the ECtHR is unable to give a ruling on the allocation of responsibility, would be the appropriate solution.[81] This conclusion is consistent with the scenario, recalled above, where the provision on the co-respondent mechanism is to be revised so as to enable only the EU and its Member States to identify the correct respondent(s), while the Court of Strasbourg would have no discretion in reviewing the mechanism. Should this solution be foreseen in the new provision of the revised agreement, as a consequence, it will be for the Union and its Member States to acknowledge or indicate where the responsibility lies, as they have the right to do so. In this scenario, the joint responsibility rule would no longer appear as a "quick fix solution" laid down to prevent the Court of Strasbourg from deciding on the allocation of responsibility between the EU and its Member States. It will rather be allocated as deemed appropriate by the EU and its Member States, as the result of the application of the rules of EU law governing their relationship.

---

78 *Id.*, para 234.

79 *Ibid.*

80 *Ibid.*

81 On the role of the applicant "to give permission to a request by the respondent and co-respondent that responsibility should be allocated to only one of them", see T. Lock, "The Future of the European Union's Accession to the European Convention on Human Rights after Opinion 2/13: is it Still Possible and is it Still Desirable?", *supra* note 71, 248-249.

As recalled above, while ruling on the compatibility of the co-respondent mechanism with EU law, the Court of Justice reminded the EU institutions and the Member States of its role in reviewing, if necessary, agreements between co-respondents and respondents in accordance with the relevant rules of EU law. More specifically, the Court stated that "the question of the apportionment of responsibility must be resolved solely in accordance with the relevant rules of EU law and be subject to review, if necessary, by the Court of Justice, which has exclusive jurisdiction to ensure that any agreement between co-respondent and respondent respects those rules".[82] This statement in the Opinion deserves a close scrutiny in light of its potential impact on the co-respondent mechanism. The process of review, in fact, could be of particular relevance in the event of disagreement between the EU and the Member State as concerns their roles as respondent and co-respondent.[83] It is not disputed that loyal cooperation and the unity of external representation are the essential principles for ensuring the smooth implementation of the co-respondent mechanism as they imply a close level of coordination on the position to be submitted before the ECtHR.[84] Nevertheless, these principles do not rule out any potential disagreement between the EU institutions and the Member States.

In this situation, a key role could be played by the prior involvement of the Court of Justice of the Union.[85] This procedure, although it has been

82 Opinion of 18 December 2014, 2/13, *supra* note 4, para 234.

83 On disagreements between the Commission and the Member States as far as dispute settlement is concerned before the WTO DS bodies and investment-State disputes under the FRR, see, respectively, J. Heliskoski, "Joint competence of the European Community and its Member States and the Dispute Settlement Practice of the WTO", *supra* note 9, 83-84; A. Dimopoulos, "The Involvement of the EU in Investor-State Dispute Settlement: A Question of Reponsibilities", *supra* note 1, 1680.

84 On the role of the duty of cooperation and unity of external representation in the context of the co-respondent mechanism, see A. Delgado Casteleiro Casteleiro, "United We Stand: The EU and its Member States in the Strasbourg Court", in V. Kosta et al. (eds), *The EU Accession to the ECHR*, *supra* note 1, 117-119.

85 See T. Lock, "EU Accession to the ECHR: Implications for the Judicial Review in Strasbourg", *European Law Review* 35 (2010), 787. Lock suggests different solutions in order to solve potential disagreements between the EU and its Member States on the allocation of responsibility where compensation is awarded.

strongly criticised in the academic debate,[86] could in reality display some advantages at the EU internal level. Under the current Draft EU Accession Agreement, as recalled previously, that prior involvement is of limited application as this procedure can be triggered only when the EU is a co-respondent and provides the opportunity for the Court of Justice to rule on the "assessment of compatibility", that is, on the validity and interpretation of EU law. Nevertheless, the future text, adapting to Opinion 2/13, may be revised in order to allow the wider involvement of the Court of Justice.[87] The provision could be modified, for example, in order to enable the triggering of the procedure not only in the narrow circumstance where the EU is a co-respondent. Interestingly, Gaja has already observed that

86 See, *inter alia*, L. Halleskov Storgaad, "EU Law Autonomy versus European Fundamental Rights Protection – On *Opinion 2/13* on EU Accession to the ECHR", *Human Rights Law Review* (2015), 502; A. Torres Pérez, "Too Many Voices? The Prior Involvement of the Court of Justice of the European Union", in V. Kosta et al. (eds), *The EU Accession to the ECHR*, *supra* note 1, 29; S. Vezzani, "The EU and its Member States before the Strasbourg Court: A Critical Appraisal of the Co-respondent Mechanism", in G. Repetto (ed), *The Constitutional Relevance of the ECHR in Domestic and European Law. An Italian Perspective* (Cambridge/Antwerp/Portland: Intersentia, 2013), 232; G. Gaja, "Accession to the ECHR", in A. Biondi, P. Eeckout, S. Ripley (eds), *EU Law after Lisbon* (Oxford: Oxford University Press, 2012), 180-196; J. P. Jacqué, "The Accession of the European Union to the European Convention on Human Rights and Fundamental Freedoms", *supra* note 73, 1019.

87 Interestingly, A. Torres Pérez (*supra* note 86, 41-43), proposes broadening the range of actors that may trigger the prior involvement procedure so to include any of the parties, that is, the Commission – representing the EU, respondent States and individual applicants. Moreover, the author argues that, given that "enforcement could be further delayed if there were disagreements as to who should pay the compensation, or whether the violation was triggered by obligations under EU law. ... In general, the prior intervention of the CJEU could help to indicate the allocation of responsibilities between the EU and its Member States" (at 42). The appropriateness of the conditions for triggering the co-respondent mechanism has been criticised because of its strict test by S. Vezzani ("The EU and its Member States before the Strasbourg Court: A Critical Appraisal of the Co-respondent Mechanism", *supra* note 86, 221-235), who recalls that a better model was unfortunately dropped during the *travaux préparatoires*, according to which "in cases in which there seems to be a substantive link between the alleged violation and a provision of EU law, and in which the application is directed against one or more Member State(s) of the European Union, but not against the European Union itself (or vice versa), the co-respondent mechanism would allow a High Contracting party which is substantively implicated by the application to join proceedings as a full party" (CDDH-UE(2010)16,2).

"there is little reason why this procedure should not be applicable also when the EU is respondent. It would be even more logical to make it applicable in all the instances in which a question of compatibility of a provision of EU law with the European Convention arises".[88] Moreover, under the current provision, the Court of Justice is allowed to rule on the interpretation of primary EU law and validity of EU acts, whereas, should the suggested amendment be inserted, it would be possible for the Court to clearly decide on the division of competences or any other relevant EU rule so that its role as the "guardian" of the interpretation of the EU Treaties is safeguarded. One may challenge this "internal" use of a procedure, which was laid down to accommodate not only the specific characteristics of the EU legal order, but also the requirements of the ECHR. Nevertheless, in the prior involvement procedure as currently drafted, the CJEU would already have jurisdiction to rule on matters of EU law that are not directly relevant for the purpose of the proceedings before the ECtHR, that is, assessing the validity of the EU norms at issue. After all, the prior involvement procedure is nothing more than an internal review before the ECtHR carries out its external review. Therefore, further tasks may be assigned to the Court of Luxembourg within the framework of this procedure. The advantage of this solution is that it offers clarity and transparency on questions of allocation of international responsibility that have not yet been settled at EU level.[89]

Although a solution which bases the allocation of responsibility on an agreement between respondent and co-respondent seems to accommodate the need to safeguard the autonomy of the EU legal order, this may appear a questionable approach from the perspective of the system laid down by the ECHR. The co-respondent mechanism, as conceived in Opinion 2/13, in fact, prevents the development of the Court of Strasbourg's case law in the field of international responsibility when the Union is a party to the proceedings, and would limit its role to merely declaring infringements of the ECHR. One may ask whether the protection of the principle of autonomy of the EU legal order should be stretched to this point.

---

88 G. Gaja, "The "Co-Respondent Mechanisms" According to the Draft Agreement for the Accession of the EU to the ECHR", *supra* note 74, 347.

89 *Supra* Section II.

IV. The Case of EU Investment Agreements: Unilateral Designation of the Respondent Party

The Union is a party alongside its Member States to only one international investment agreement currently in force, namely the Energy Charter Treaty. However, at the time of writing, the Union is negotiating or about to conclude a number of investment agreements (IAs) or free trade agreements (FTAs) with an investment chapter, on the basis of the new competence concerning foreign direct investment conferred on the EU by the Lisbon Treaty.[90] All those agreements include or will supposedly include investment dispute settlement (IDS) provisions. More specifically, the EU-Singapore FTA and the EU-Vietnam FTA are currently awaiting ratification,[91] while the EU-Canada Agreement (CETA) is also awaiting ratification but is currently being provisionally applied. The provisions concerning the settlement of disputes are to be exempted from that provisional application under agreements between the Parties.[92] More agreements are still in the negotiation phase, the most famous of which is certainly the (currently dormant) Transatlantic Trade and Investment Partnership (TTIP). The analysis that follows will mostly concentrate on this new generation of IAs. In order to keep things simple, the rules of the CETA will

---

90 See the general overview provided at http://ec.europa.eu/trade/policy/accessing-markets/investment/. As a result of the CJEU's findings in Opinion 2/15 (see below, note 91), the EU has decided to split the trade and the investment components of the new FTAs, which will therefore be concluded as separate agreements. See Council, New approach on negotiating and concluding EU trade agreements adopted by Council, Press Release, available at http://www.consilium.europa.eu/en/press/press-releases/2018/05/22/new-approach-on-negotiating-and-concluding-eu-trade-agreements-adopted-by-council/.

91 As is well known, the EU-Singapore FTA has been the object of an Opinion issued by the CJEU on 16 May 2017. See Opinion of 16 May 2017, 2/15, *EU- Singapore Free Trade Agreement*, EU:C:2017:376. The Opinion is focused on the nature and scope of the EU external competence to conclude the agreement in question rather than on issues concerning the IDS. See, in this volume, the chapters by Merijn Chamon and by Eleftheria Neframi.

92 In particular, CETA"s provisional application has taken effect on 21 September 2017. See European Commission, Press Release, "EU-Canada trade agreement enters into force", available at http://europa.eu/rapid/press-release_IP-17-3121_en.htm.

be used as a model and a starting point.[93] In addition, the analysis of the provisions of the agreements will be complemented with that of Regulation (EU) n° 912/2014 "establishing a framework for managing financial responsibility linked to investor-to-state dispute settlement tribunals established by international agreements to which the European Union is party" approved on 23 July 2014 ("the FRR").[94]

A. The Dispute Settlement Provisions of the Investment Agreements

To begin with, the EU IAs do not contain any rule concerning the allocation of responsibility between the EU and its Member States. Any reference to responsibility is entirely absent from the text. However, one can infer indications concerning issues of responsibility by analysing the rules relating to the submission of a claim against the EU and its Member States by an investor of the other party to the agreement. In particular, all EU IAs contain a mechanism aimed at identifying the respondent in such disputes. The mechanism in question is exemplified by Article 8.21 CETA. It is meaningfully titled "Determination of the respondent for disputes". According to this provision, an investor of the other party must send a notice to the EU prior to the submission of the claim. The notice shall request the EU to determine who will act as respondent in the proceedings. The notice has to identify the treatment that allegedly breached the investor's rights. The EU has to inform the claimant within 50 days as to whether the EU itself or a Member State is to be the respondent in the dispute. The determination thus made cannot be objected to by the investor and the arbitral tribunal. However, Article 8.21 CETA does not specify the criteria on the basis of which the determination in question is made.

It is interesting to point out a discrepancy between the four IAs mentioned above. The TTIP and the EU-Vietnam agreements do not lay down any other rules concerning the determination of the respondent. Not only do they avoid elaborating on the criteria relied on by the EU to determine

93 In particular, reference will be made to the TTIP investment court proposal tabled by the EU Commission in November 2015. For an overview of the proposal see L. Pantaleo, "Lights and Shadows of the TTIP Investment Court System", in L. Pantaleo, W. Douma, T. Takacs (eds), *Tiptoeing to TTIP: What Kind of Agreement for What Kind of Partnership*, CLEER Paper 1/2016, 77.

94 See Regulation (EU) 912/2014, OJ 2014 L 257/121.

who is going to act as respondent, they also refrain from providing any guidance as to what rules the investor and the arbitral tribunal would have to apply to make such a determination if the EU fails to deliver a response within the prescribed period. By contrast, CETA and the EU-Singapore agreements do foresee such an instance. They each contain a similar clause, according to which, in the event that the investor has not been informed in due time:

a) if the measures identified in the notice are exclusively measures of a Member State of the EU, the Member State shall be the respondent;
b) if the measures identified in the notice include measures of the European Union, the European Union shall be the respondent.[95]

Although the language employed by this provision contains some degree of ambiguity, it seems safe to say that the Member State will be the respondent only when the claim challenges measures that were taken exclusively by that Member State. In other words, this provision seems to refer to acts adopted by the Member State not in order to fulfil its EU law obligations and most probably in areas falling completely outside the scope of EU law, such as direct taxation.[96] The EU would be the respondent in all other cases, including where the claim identifies (a) measures that are partly attributable to the EU and partly to the Member State, in other words, in cases of potential joint responsibility (which is ruled out by the EU IAs), or (b) measures taken by the Member State in order to fulfil EU law obligations.

All in all, the rationale behind the rules for determining the respondent analysed above seems to be to avoid both the investor and the arbitrators passing judgement on issues of EU law. An example will help to illustrate this concept. Suppose that an investor is confronted with a *Micula* scenario in which a Member State has repealed business incentives that the Union has found to be incompatible with its law on State aid.[97] If the choice as to the proper respondent were left to the investor, the latter

---

95 See, for example, Chapter 8, Article 21, paragraph 4, CETA.

96 For an analysis of the potential interaction between tax measures and investment protection see E. De Brabandere, "Complementarity or Conflict? Contrasting the Yukos Case before the European Court of Human Rights and Investment Tribunals", *ICSID Review* (2015), 345.

97 As is well known, in the *Micula* case Romania was ordered by an arbitral tribunal to pay compensation to a foreign investor for discontinuing business incentives

would have to apply the rules of general international law. According to the provisions of the Draft Articles on Responsibility of States (DASR) and the Draft Articles on Responsibility of International Organisations (DARIO),[98] the investor could sue the Member State as the entity to which, under the rules of DASR, the wrongful act – in our example, the repealing of business incentives – is attributable. On the other hand, it could also invoke the (shared) responsibility of the EU under Article 17 DARIO for adopting a binding decision – such as a Decision of the Commission or a ruling of the ECJ – that eventually led the Member State to breach the investor's rights. However, the rules of international law may not necessarily be in line with what is considered to be the best solution in order to protect the autonomy of the EU legal order. In addition, one has to bear in mind that the EU has no proper administration: its legislation is implemented and enforced by Member States" administrations. Hence, it is likely that the breach of an investor's right may be the result of an act taken by an organ of a Member State on the basis of EU law. Here again, if the investor (and the tribunal) were left free to choose in accordance with the rules of international law, both the Member State in question and the Union could be designated as respondents.[99] However, it is obvious that such a situation would run counter to positions traditionally advocated by the EU,[100] and would put into question its autonomy It is precisely in order to avoid a scenario of this type that the CETA and the like contain rules aimed at internalising the choice of the respondent to an investment dispute based on the EU IAs.

The aforementioned internalisation of the choice of the respondent creates a proceduralisation of the dispute and of the substantive issues relating to the attribution of responsibility between the EU and the Member

---

that were found incompatible with EU state aid law. For an analysis of the case and its implications see C. Tietje, C. Wackernagel, "Enforcement of Intra-EU ICSID Awards: Multilevel Governance, Investment Tribunals and the Lost Opportunity of the 'Micula' Arbitration", *The Journal of World Investment and Trade* 16 (2015), 205.

98 *Supra* note 2.

99 Although not necessarily at the same time. While it is true that DARIO establishes different forms of international responsibility, it does not seem to impose an obligation to invoke all of them in the context of the same dispute.

100 For a brief examination of such positions see *supra*, Section I.

States.[101] By depriving the investor of the right to choose the respondent, and the court or tribunal of the power to review such a choice, the EU IAs are intended to protect the autonomy of the EU legal order from external interference.[102] No doubt the mechanism in question reduces the risk of interference to a large extent. However, it does not eliminate the risk altogether. One has to consider that the EU may not determine the respondent party within the time limit prescribed by the agreements. In such a situation, while under CETA and the EU-Singapore FTA the investor would have to apply the alternative criteria set out in those agreements, under the TTIP and the EU-Vietnam FTA it would have no indications whatsoever. Therefore, it seems reasonable to expect that the investor would resort to general international law and designate the respondent accordingly. In both cases the arbitral tribunal would also have its say on the matter. Under CETA and the EU-Singapore FTA it would have to review whether the investor has correctly applied the alternative criteria laid down in Article 8.21, paragraph 4, CETA and referred to above. Under the TTIP and EU-Vietnam FTA it would review, apply and interpret the rules of international law in order to determine the proper respondent. From this perspective, the solution adopted by CETA and the EU-Singapore FTA seems to be more suitable to protect the autonomy of the EU legal order. As has been already pointed out above, the broad language employed by the clause included in such agreements seems to make sure that the Member States will be the respondent only when the claim relates to questions falling under their exclusive competence – that is, questions that are of no EU law relevance whatsoever. Whenever the dispute contains an EU law component, it is the Union that will have to act as respondent, no matter how little relevance the EU law component has with respect to the number and range of legal issues at stake in the dispute taken as a whole. By contrast, failure to determine the respondent on time may have massive conse-

---

101 See A. Dimopoulos, "The Involvement of the EU in Investor-State Dispute Settlement: A Question of Reponsibilities", *supra* note 1, 1702.

102 See N. Lavranos, "Is an International Investor-State Arbitration System under the Auspices of the ECJ Possible?", in N. Jansen Calamita, D.C. Earnest, M. Burgstaller (ed), *The Future of ICSID and the Place of Investment Treaties in International Law* (London: BIICL, 2013) 129; S. W. Schill, "Luxembourg Limits: Conditions for Investor-State Dispute Settlement under Future EU Investment Agreements", in M. Bungenberg, A. Reinisch, C. Tietje (eds), *EU and Investment Agreements: Open Questions and Remaining challenges* (Baden-Baden: Nomos/Hart, 2013), 37.

quences under the TTIP. Such a failure would trigger the application of the rules of general international law concerning international responsibility. It is therefore regrettable that the TTIP and the EU-Vietnam FTA do not replicate the safeguard clause contained in CETA.

Another relevant question is whether the investor and the arbitral tribunal would be able to make an independent assessment of questions relating to responsibility even when the determination of the respondent is duly delivered by the EU in good time. After all, as has been rightly pointed out, "arbitral tribunals must be satisfied that the respondent party bears international responsibility, in order to consider a claim admissible".[103] Hence, the question may be put in these terms. In order to ascertain that the claim is admissible, investment tribunals should not only make sure that the investor has sued the respondent designated in accordance with the rules set out in the IA, they should also verify – albeit *prima facie* – that the respondent so determined is the one that bears international responsibility. No doubt the tribunal concerned must reach that *prima facie* conclusion at the "preliminary objections" stage in order not to dismiss the claim as inadmissible. Given that the EU IAs contain no rule whatsoever on issues of responsibility, the question is therefore how, or on the basis of what rules, that *prima facie* assessment must be made. According to one observer, "the attribution of respondent status to either the EU or a Member State cannot have the effect of automatically attributing responsibility to the party thus identified".[104] As a consequence, the tribunal concerned, in assessing the admissibility of the claim, would have no choice but to carry out an "assessment of the attribution of responsibility under DARIO" and may declare the claim inadmissible *ratione personae* "where the conduct or responsibility is attributed to a party other than the respondent".[105]

However, it is not easy to see how an arbitral tribunal could disregard the text of a treaty in favour of the rules of general international law. The principle of *lex specialis* would seem sufficient to authorise the tribunal to do exactly the opposite. It could be objected that the rules concerning the identification of the respondent do not deal with responsibility issues and that, as a result, they are not special with respect to the general rules estab-

---

103 See A. Dimopoulos, *supra* note 1, 1683.

104 See H. Lenk, "Issues of Attribution: Responsibility of the EU in Investment Disputes under CETA", *Transnational Dispute Management* 13, no. 1 (2016), 21.

105 *Ibidem.*

lished by DASR and DARIO. After all, the principle in question only applies to rules governing the same subject matter. That objection is, however, not very convincing. First of all, it is highly unlikely that a claim would be declared inadmissible by the tribunal *proprio motu*, that is to say without an explicit objection being raised by the interested party.[106] In other words, in order for a claim to be found inadmissible *ratione personae* on this ground, the EU or the Member State would have to repudiate their own determination of the respondent made in accordance with the agreement. They would have to claim that the determination thus made is wrong. That would evidently be nonsensical and would suggest that the determination of the respondent was not made in good faith. However, the EU IAs include a provision that seems to have been devised precisely to avoid such an absurd scenario. Pursuant to Article 8.21 CETA,

> "neither the European Union nor the Member State concerned may assert the inadmissibility of the claim, lack of jurisdiction of the Tribunal or otherwise object to the claim or award on the ground that the respondent was not properly determined".

All the other EU IAs include a similar provision, which is part of the clause concerning the determination of the respondent. Therefore, it seems more sensible to concur with the view, expressed by a scholar, that the identification of the respondent made under the EU IAs should be taken as an implicit recognition of responsibility.[107] A different question is whether or not the determination of the respondent could also be understood as acknowledgment and adoption of conduct within the meaning of Article 11 DASR and Article 9 DARIO.[108] In other words, in the absence of any special rules on the allocation of responsibility, the identification of the respondent by the EU under the EU IAs amounts to an indirect acceptance of the responsibility that would arise from the claim. From this perspective, a distinction between rules on responsibility and rules on the determi-

---

106 See M. Waibel, *Investment Arbitration: Jurisdiction and Admissibility*, Legal Studies Research Paper Series, Paper no. 9 (2014), University of Cambridge, 67-68.

107 See P. Palchetti, "The Allocation of International Responsibility in the Context of Investor-State Dispute Settlement Mechanism Established by EU International Agreements", *supra* note 1, 84.

108 This question cannot be further analysed in this article. However, it is discussed, perhaps in a somewhat cursory way, by the ILC in its commentary to Article 9 DARIO. See *Report of the International Law Commission*, A/66/10, 97.

nation of the respondent party seems to be only ostensible: the one necessarily entails the other. In the merely hypothetical – and slightly farcical – event that the respondent party raises an objection concerning the inadmissibility of the claim on this ground, the arbitral tribunal could easily reject the objection in question in accordance with Article 8.21 CETA and the like.[109]

B. The Financial Responsibility Regulation

At the end of this brief overview of the rules contained in the EU IAs, it seems appropriate to succinctly analyse the internal rules laid down in the Financial Responsibility Regulation (FRR). From the outset, it is worth emphasising that the latter does not contain rules concerning the allocation of international responsibility for breaches of the EU IAs to the Union or its Member States. From an international law perspective, that regulation represents domestic legislation. As such, it cannot unilaterally impose rules on third countries. This circumstance is explicitly recognised by the FRR itself. According to Recital 5, that regulation aims to allocate (financial) responsibility "as a matter of Union law". However, its provisions are inextricably interconnected with questions relating to international responsibility. Recital 3 contains a declaration incorporating the traditional competence-based approach advocated by the Union in the field of international responsibility. According to this provision,

> "international responsibility for treatment subject to dispute settlement follows the division of competences between the Union and the Member States. As a consequence, the Union will in principle be responsible for defending any claims alleging a violation of rules included in an agreement which fall

---

109 As a matter of principle, an objection of inadmissibility could be raised also by the claimant itself. However, if such an objection is upheld by the tribunal concerned and the claim is therefore set aside, the investor would have no other option than to start the proceedings all over again and hope that the EU designates a different respondent – which seems a very unlikely contingency. Alternatively, the investor may also challenge the determination of the respondent before the EU courts as an EU act affecting it directly and individually. However, it does not seem that the EU courts could come to a different conclusion. For an in-depth analysis of these and other questions see L. Pantaleo, "Respondent Status and Allocation of International Responsibility under EU Investment Agreements", *European Papers* 3 (2016), 854.

within the Union's exclusive competence, irrespective of whether the treatment at issue is afforded by the Union itself or by a Member State".

In brief, according to the rules laid down by the FRR, the allocation of financial responsibility generally corresponds to the acquisition of the respondent status in a dispute – which, in turn, amounts to recognition of (international) responsibility for breach of the IA. With a few exceptions,[110] the general principle is that the EU is to bear financial responsibility and act as respondent where (a) the treatment challenged was afforded by the Union, or (b) it was afforded by a Member State in order to comply with EU law – unless the action taken by the Member State was necessary to remedy an inconsistency with Union law of a prior act.[111] The aim of this provision is clearly to avoid the EU (literally) paying the price of a *Micula* scenario.[112] The rationale behind the FRR is that financial responsibility and respondent status lie with the entity that has the competence to adopt the treatment in question, in accordance with the EU's longstanding competence-based approach to responsibility.[113] A general departure from this scheme would occur if the treatment that has allegedly breached the investor's right were the result of a Member State's incorrect implementation or enforcement of EU law. This instance would hardly be covered by the provision of the FRR stating that the EU would assume responsibility where the Member State's action was required by Union law. Thus, this would be the only scenario in which a Member State might find itself acting as respondent in a dispute concerning a field falling under an EU competence, including an exclusive competence. However, given that the Member State's action was not strictly speaking required by EU law, an arbitral decision rendered against that action would hardly encroach upon an EU competence. In addition, the FRR seems to offer some adequate instruments to this end. For example, Article 9, paragraph 1, b, of the FRR stipulates that a Member State can agree with the Commission not to appear as respondent in a dispute in which it would otherwise do so accord-

110 To name but one exception, according to Article 9, paragraph 3, FRR the general criteria do not apply "where similar treatment is being challenged in a related claim against the Union in the WTO". In such instance, the Commission may decide that the EU is to act as respondent also in the investment dispute irrespective of any other rule laid down in the FRR.

111 See Article 3 and Article 9 FRR.

112 *Supra* note 98.

113 See P. Palchetti, *supra* note 1, 78.

ing to the rules set out in regulation. Such a rule could be applied whenever the dispute concerns an area falling under EU exclusive competence. Furthermore, one has to bear in mind that the Member States can always be empowered by the EU to act in areas falling within the latter's exclusive competence, in accordance with Article 2, paragraph 1, TFEU. Acting as respondent in an investment dispute upon designation made by the EU could certainly be covered by such empowerment.

V. Conclusions

As Govaere has rightly stated, "it is hard to contest that if the EU wants to be a credible (and important) actor on the international scene then it should be able to play according to the international public law rules and obey international law principles too, if not especially so, in relation to dispute settlement".[114] The EU, certainly aware of the importance of dispute settlement, negotiates provisions that endeavor to accommodate third parties" request for legal certainty as well as to safeguard the autonomy of its legal order. The techniques that, under some mixed agreements, address the matter of the identification of the respondent have to be assessed in the light of the need to balance these two competing and partly-conflicting interests. The overview presented above has clearly demonstrated that both declarations of competence and the joint responsibility rule appear less appropriate for reaching those purposes and present more disadvantages than advantages.

Against this background, the establishment of mechanisms aimed at "proceduralising" substantive issues concerning international responsibility by conferring on the EU the power to determine the appropriate respondent seems to represent the most viable solution. Such mechanisms should ensure that the matter remains an "internal" one and that international courts or tribunals are prevented from interpreting and applying EU law. As has been pointed out above, the Draft EU Accession Agreement and the EU Investment Agreements provide two recent examples of rules of proceduralisation. The Draft EU Accession Agreement, however, did not create proceduralisation allowing the determination of the proper respon-

114 I. Govaere, "Beware of the Trojan Horse: Dispute Settlement in (Mixed) Agreements and the Autonomy of the EU Legal Order", *supra* note 27, 190.

dent to integrally remain an EU internal matter. This was because it gave the ECtHR the power to decide on the plausibility of the reasons provided by the Union and/or its Member States for appearing as the respondent(s) in a dispute. In other words, it conferred on the Court of Strasbourg quite a broad power to review the choice made by the EU and its Member States, and to scrutinise the reasons behind it. Should the future text of the accession agreement be modified in accordance with Opinion 2/13, the determination of the correct respondent would have to remain a purely EU internal issue, as is already the case under the more recent EU IAs. These seem to rule out the possibility of an investor questioning the determination of the respondent made by the EU, and of the investment tribunal reviewing that determination. From an EU-perspective, no doubt this is the most suitable solution to protect the autonomy of the Union's legal order.

However, one may wonder whether the mechanism devised under the EU IAs is also suitable under the regime created by the ECHR. An investment tribunal and the ECtHR are in fact only partly comparable. While the former is based on a (brand new) bilateral agreement, the ECtHR is a court established under a multilateral human rights convention that has already developed case law on issues of responsibility. From this perspective, it should not go unmentioned that the Draft EU Accession Agreement is, by and large, the result of a delicate balancing exercise aimed at reconciling the (well-established) rules and principles developed under the regime laid down by the ECHR on the one hand and the EU's *sui generis* nature on the other. One may legitimately wonder whether the overall systemic coherence of the regime created by the ECHR should be sacrificed on the altar of EU autonomy, to the point of reducing the Court of Strasbourg's rulings to mere declarations as to whether the ECHR has (or has not) been breached.

The need to accommodate the specific characteristics of each different regime to which the EU is – or may become – a party does not, however, invalidate the conclusion that the adoption of rules of proceduralisation is the best way forward from the perspective of both the Union and the applicant party as far as the determination of the proper respondent is concerned. It should probably become the EU's standard position when it comes to participating in international dispute settlement.

Remarques conclusives / Final Remarks

Antonio Tizzano

Les différentes contributions à cet ouvrage témoignent du développement extraordinaire de l'action extérieure de l'Union européenne et de la richesse et la complexité des questions qu'elle continue à poser. Les questions constitutionnelles « classiques », telle la répartition des compétences, l'équilibre institutionnel ou le respect des droits fondamentaux, acquièrent une dimension propre lorsque l'on se place dans le domaine de l'action extérieure de l'Union. Cela est dû, comme il est démontré par les différents auteurs et sous des angles différents, à l'interaction des objectifs et à la quête d'équilibre entre l'objectif de l'Union de s'affirmer comme un acteur international global et efficace et la nécessité de respecter les principes qui sont à la base de l'autonomie de l'ordre juridique de l'Union.

C'est d'ailleurs cette spécificité des objectifs qui justifie le développement de l'action extérieure de l'Union et qui s'est pour la première fois manifestée avec le prononcé de l'arrêt *AETR* en 1971. Alors que dans les premières années de la construction européenne la compétence externe de la Communauté était surtout perçue en tant que limitée dans le domaine de la politique commerciale, l'arrêt *AETR* bouleversa cette conviction et ses implications. En établissant pour la première fois le parallélisme entre les compétences internes et externes, il a démontré l'interaction entre les objectifs internes et externes, la différenciation entre la compétence par nature externe et l'aspect externe d'une compétence interne et a ouvert la voie à un développement potentiellement tous azimuts des relations extérieures de l'Union.

Les réactions que cet arrêt inattendu a provoquées ont été dans un premier temps fortement critiques. Il a fallu à la Cour de justice préciser et détailler, dans la jurisprudence qui s'en est suivie, les critères qui permettent de dégager une compétence externe exclusive de l'Union à partir des dispositions du traité consacrées aux compétences internes. Il est significatif que, malgré l'inscription de « l'effet *AETR* » dans l'article 3, paragraphe 2, du Traité sur le fonctionnement de l'Union européenne, depuis l'entrée en vigueur du Traité de Lisbonne, les critères qui permettent à l'Union d'agir sur le plan international à partir d'une compétence interne continuent à être précisés. L'interaction des objectifs internes et externes, sectoriels et généraux, détermine la portée de l'effet *AETR* dans des situations complexes, notamment en cas d'harmonisation partielle. Mais c'est cette interaction des objectifs qui confirme que l'arrêt *AETR* exprimait la perspective historique et politique sous-jacente à la méthode – que l'on qualifie de « téléologique » – qui a marqué l'orientation jurisprudentielle de la Cour depuis. Par une jurisprudence en évolution continue, mais fondée sur un raisonnement détaillé et rigoureux, exprimant l'attachement au principe d'attribution des compétences et le rapport entre objectifs et compétences, la Cour de justice a réussi à faire accepter l'arrêt *AETR* et ses suites par tous les acteurs de la construction européenne, et notamment les « Herren der Verträge », les Etats membres.

Si la dimension externe des objectifs internes donne une dynamique particulière à l'action extérieure de l'Union dans les domaines « communautaires », un autre domaine d'action – la politique étrangère – se développe progressivement et donne à l'Union un véritable potentiel pour être un acteur international. Il est bien connu que la politique étrangère entre tard dans l'orbite de la coopération entre les Etats membres, d'abord de manière informelle, avant de se formaliser progressivement. Et même sa première inscription dans le Traité se fait dans l'Acte unique européen, ce qui marque la spécificité de la nouvelle politique, mais aussi souligne la coexistence dans un seul texte (*Single Act*) de la coopération communautaire et la coopération politique. Toutefois, cela n'empêche pas le développement de cette dernière forme de coopération qui se fait parallèlement à la confirmation de sa spécificité, s'exprimant non seulement par son insertion dans un traité différent que celui qui concerne les autres politiques, mais également par la méthode qui la régit et la difficulté d'identification d'un objectif propre. D'ailleurs le Traité de Lisbonne a conservé le barrage dont la porte d'ouverture et de fermeture est représentée par l'article 40 du Traité sur l'Union européenne.

Il convient toutefois de souligner que cette spécificité de la PESC est atténuée, non seulement par l'interaction des objectifs de l'action extérieure exprimée dans l'article 21 TUE, mais également par le rôle horizontal de la Charte des droits fondamentaux, qui guide l'interprétation de la portée de la compétence de la Cour de justice dans ce domaine. La spécificité de l'action extérieure de l'Union ne se traduit ainsi pas uniquement dans la spécificité institutionnelle de la PESC. L'interaction entre objectifs et valeurs marque la spécificité de l'action extérieure comprenant la PESC par rapport à l'approche « interne » des principes constitutionnels.

Admettre le régime spécifique de l'action extérieure de l'Union permet de concilier la poursuite des objectifs externes, et notamment celui de confirmer l'Union en tant que véritable acteur international, avec l'importance constitutionnelle des principes structurels fondamentaux. En même temps, comme les différents chapitres de l'ouvrage le montrent, la poursuite des objectifs sur le plan international doit se faire dans le respect d'un autre principe transversal, celui de l'autonomie de l'ordre juridique de l'Union.

La complexité des nombreuses questions étudiées dans cet ouvrage se résume ainsi autour de l'exercice d'insertion de la spécificité de l'action externe de l'Union dans le cadre uni d'un ordre juridique autonome et intégré.

List of Contributors

Isabelle Bosse-Platière
Professor, University of Rennes 1
Jean Monnet Chair, Institut de l'Ouest : Droit et Europe (IODE, UMR CNRS 6262)

Merijn Chamon
Postdoctoral Researcher, Ghent University

Cristina Contartese
Lecturer, European Law and Governance School /
European Public Law Organization

Marise Cremona
Professor Emeritus, European University Institute

Andrés Delgado Casteleiro
Lecturer, Universidad Diego Portales, Santiago, Chile

Francette Fines
Professor, University of La Rochelle
Centre d'Etudes Juridiques et Politiques (CEJEP)

Hugo Flavier
Associate Professor, University of Bordeaux
Codirector of the France-Belarus Center of European Studies

Mauro Gatti
Postdoctoral Researcher, University of Luxembourg

Pieter Jan Kuijper
Professor Emeritus, University of Amsterdam

Silvère Lefèvre
Référendaire at the General Court of the European Union

Eleftheria Neframi
Professor, University of Luxembourg

Luca Pantaleo
Lecturer, The Hague University of Applied Sciences

Nicolas Pigeon
PhD, University Paris 1 – Panthéon-Sorbonne,
Postdoctoral Researcher, University of Rennes 1

Sara Poli
Associate Professor, University of Pisa

Laurence Potvin-Solis
Professor, University of Caen-Normandie
Jean Monnet Chair

Miro Prek
Judge at the General Court of the European Union

Allan Rosas
Judge at the European Court of Justice

Antonio Tizzano
Vice-President of the European Court of Justice